Hawaii For Dummies, 1st Edition

Waikiki

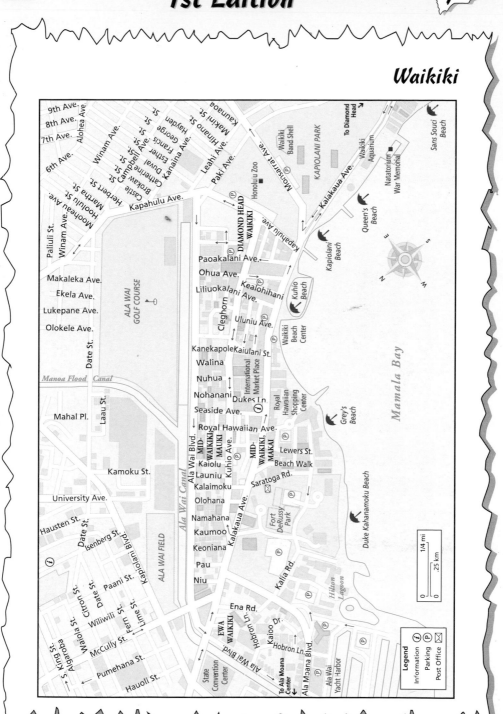

Waikiki Band Shell

KAPIOLANI PARK

To Diamond Head

Sans Souci Beach

Waikiki Aquarium

Natatorium War Memorial

Honolulu Zoo

Queen's Beach

Kapiolani Beach

Kuhio Beach

Waikiki Beach Center

Mamala Bay

Grey's Beach

Duke Kahanamoku Beach

Hilton Lagoon

Fort DeRussy Park

State Convention Center

To Ala Moana Center

Ala Wai Yacht Harbor

DIAMOND HEAD WAIKIKI

MID-WAIKIKI MAUKA

MID-WAIKIKI MAKAI

EWA WAIKIKI

9th Ave.
8th Ave.
7th Ave.
6th Ave.
Alohea Ave.
Winam Ave.
Castle St.
Brokaw St.
Campbell Ave.
Esther St.
Duval St.
Catherine Ave.
Francis St.
Kanaina Ave.
George St.
Hayden St.
Hinano St.
Makini St.
Kaunaoa
Leahi Ave.
Paki Ave.
Monsarrat Ave.
Kapahulu Ave.
Herbert St.
Martha St.
Moohua Ave.
Hoolulu St.
Winam Ave.
Paliuli St.
Makaleka Ave.
Ekela Ave.
Lukepane Ave.
Olokele Ave.
Date St.
ALA WAI GOLF COURSE
Manoa Flood Canal
Mahal Pl.
Laau St.
Kamoku St.
University Ave.
Hausten St.
Date St.
Isenberg St.
Paani St.
Kapiolani Blvd.
Walola St.
Algaroba St.
Citron St.
Date St.
Wiliwili St.
Fern St.
Lime St.
McCully St.
Pumehana St.
Hauoli St.
S. King St.
ALA WAI FIELD
Ala Wai Canal
Paoakalani Ave.
Ohua Ave.
Kealohihani
Liliuokalani Ave.
Cleghorn
Uluniu Ave.
Kanekapole
Kaiulani St.
Walina
Nuhua
Nohanani
Dukes Ln.
Seaside Ave.
Royal Hawaiian Ave.
International Market Place
Royal Hawaiian Shopping Center
Ala Wai Blvd.
Kaiolu Ave.
Kuhio Ave.
Launiu Ave.
Kalaimoku
Olohana
Namahana
Kaumoo
Keoniana
Pau
Niu
Kalakaua Ave.
Kapahulu Ave.
Kalakaua Ave.
Lewers St.
Beach Walk
Saratoga Rd.
Kalia Rd.
Ena Rd.
Hobron Ln.
Kaioo Dr.
Hobron Ln.
Ala Moana Blvd.
Ala Wai Blvd.

Legend
Information
Parking
Post Office

1/4 mi
.25 km

Hawaii For Dummies,
1st Edition

Honolulu

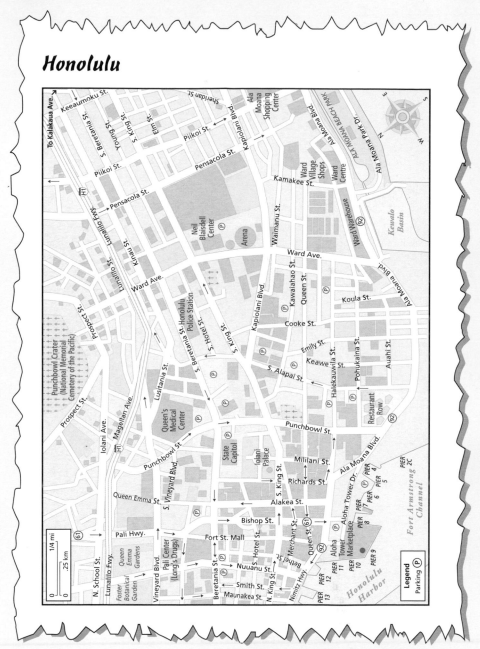

For Dummies™: Bestselling Book Series for Beginners

Hawaii

FOR

DUMMIES®

1ST EDITION

Hawaii
FOR
DUMMIES®
1ST EDITION

by Cheryl Farr Leas

IDG Books Worldwide, Inc.
An International Data Group Company

Foster City, CA ✦ Chicago, IL ✦ Indianapolis, IN ✦ New York, NY

Hawaii For Dummies? 1st Edition

Published by
IDG Books Worldwide, Inc.
An International Data Group Company
909 Third Avenue
New York, NY 10022
www.idgbooks.com (IDG Books Worldwide Web site)
www.dummies.com (Dummies Press Web site)

Library of Congress Control Number: 00-108215

ISBN: 0-7645-6200-2

ISSN: 1531-1597

Printed in the United States of America

10 9 8 7 6 5 4 3 2 1

1B/QY/RS/QQ/IN

Distributed in the United States by IDG Books Worldwide, Inc.

Distributed by CDG Books Canada Inc. for Canada; by Transworld Publishers Limited in the United Kingdom; by IDG Norge Books for Norway; by IDG Sweden Books for Sweden; by IDG Books Australia Publishing Corporation Pty. Ltd. for Australia and New Zealand; by TransQuest Publishers Pte Ltd. for Singapore, Malaysia, Thailand, Indonesia, and Hong Kong; by Gotop Information Inc. for Taiwan; by ICG Muse, Inc. for Japan; by Intersoft for South Africa; by Eyrolles for France; by International Thomson Publishing for Germany, Austria and Switzerland; by Distribuidora Cuspide for Argentina; by LR International for Brazil; by Galileo Libros for Chile; by Ediciones ZETA S.C.R. Ltda. for Peru; by WS Computer Publishing Corporation, Inc., for the Philippines; by Contemporanea de Ediciones for Venezuela; by Express Computer Distributors for the Caribbean and West Indies; by Micronesia Media Distributor, Inc. for Micronesia; by Chips Computadoras S.A. de C.V. for Mexico; by Editorial Norma de Panama S.A. for Panama; by American Bookshops for Finland.

For general information on IDG Books Worldwide's books in the U.S., please call our Consumer Customer Service department at 800-762-2974. For reseller information, including discounts and premium sales, please call our Reseller Customer Service department at 800-434-3422.

For information on where to purchase IDG Books Worldwide's books outside the U.S., please contact our International Sales department at 317-572-3993 or fax 317-572-4002.

For consumer information on foreign language translations, please contact our Customer Service department at 1-800-434-3422, fax 317-572-4002, or e-mail rights@idgbooks.com.

For information on licensing foreign or domestic rights, please phone +1-650-653-7098.

For sales inquiries and special prices for bulk quantities, please contact our Order Services department at 800-434-4322 or write to the address above.

For information on using IDG Books Worldwide's books in the classroom or for ordering examination copies, please contact our Educational Sales department at 800-434-2086 or fax 317-572-4005.

For press review copies, author interviews, or other publicity information, please contact our Public Relations department at 650-653-7000 or fax 650-653-7500.

For authorization to photocopy items for corporate, personal, or educational use, please contact Copyright Clearance Center, 222 Rosewood Drive, Danvers, MA 01923, or fax 978-750-4470.

About the Author

Cheryl Farr Leas may live on the mainland, but she's a Hawaii girl at heart. She fell in love with Diamond Head, aloha wear, and mai tais in 1994, and has had trouble staying away ever since. Whenever she's not in the islands — and until she can figure out a way to trade in her Brooklyn co-op for a Lanikai beach house — she and her husband, Rob, call New York City home.

Before embarking on a writing career, Cheryl served as senior editor at Macmillan Travel (now IDG Books), where she edited the *Frommer's Hawaii* travel guides for the better part of the '90s. Now happy to be a globetrotting freelancer, Cheryl also authors the *Frommer's New York City* travel guides and *California For Dummies,* and contributes to *Best Places Los Angeles* (Sasquatch Books) and *Frommer's USA.* She also adds her two cents to *Daily Variety, Continental* (Continental Airlines' in-flight magazine), Expedia Travels Online, and other media outlets on a regular basis.

ABOUT IDG BOOKS WORLDWIDE

Welcome to the world of IDG Books Worldwide.

IDG Books Worldwide, Inc., is a subsidiary of International Data Group, the world's largest publisher of computer-related information and the leading global provider of information services on information technology. IDG was founded more than 30 years ago by Patrick J. McGovern and now employs more than 9,000 people worldwide. IDG publishes more than 290 computer publications in over 75 countries. More than 90 million people read one or more IDG publications each month.

Launched in 1990, IDG Books Worldwide is today the #1 publisher of best-selling computer books in the United States. We are proud to have received eight awards from the Computer Press Association in recognition of editorial excellence and three from Computer Currents' First Annual Readers' Choice Awards. Our best-selling ...For Dummies® series has more than 50 million copies in print with translations in 31 languages. IDG Books Worldwide, through a joint venture with IDG's Hi-Tech Beijing, became the first U.S. publisher to publish a computer book in the People's Republic of China. In record time, IDG Books Worldwide has become the first choice for millions of readers around the world who want to learn how to better manage their businesses.

Our mission is simple: Every one of our books is designed to bring extra value and skill-building instructions to the reader. Our books are written by experts who understand and care about our readers. The knowledge base of our editorial staff comes from years of experience in publishing, education, and journalism — experience we use to produce books to carry us into the new millennium. In short, we care about books, so we attract the best people. We devote special attention to details such as audience, interior design, use of icons, and illustrations. And because we use an efficient process of authoring, editing, and desktop publishing our books electronically, we can spend more time ensuring superior content and less time on the technicalities of making books.

You can count on our commitment to deliver high-quality books at competitive prices on topics you want to read about. At IDG Books Worldwide, we continue in the IDG tradition of delivering quality for more than 30 years. You'll find no better book on a subject than one from IDG Books Worldwide.

John Kilcullen
Chairman and CEO
IDG Books Worldwide, Inc.

Eighth Annual Computer Press Awards ≥1992

Ninth Annual Computer Press Awards ≥1993

Tenth Annual Computer Press Awards ≥1994

Eleventh Annual Computer Press Awards ≥1995

IDG is the world's leading IT media, research and exposition company. Founded in 1964, IDG had 1997 revenues of $2.05 billion and has more than 9,000 employees worldwide. IDG offers the widest range of media options that reach IT buyers in 75 countries representing 95% of worldwide IT spending. IDG's diverse product and services portfolio spans six key areas including print publishing, online publishing, expositions and conferences, market research, education and training, and global marketing services. More than 90 million people read one or more of IDG's 290 magazines and newspapers, including IDG's leading global brands — Computerworld, PC World, Network World, Macworld and the Channel World family of publications. IDG Books Worldwide is one of the fastest-growing computer book publishers in the world, with more than 700 titles in 36 languages. The "...For Dummies®" series alone has more than 50 million copies in print. IDG offers online users the largest network of technology-specific Web sites around the world through IDG.net (http://www.idg.net), which comprises more than 225 targeted Web sites in 55 countries worldwide. International Data Corporation (IDC) is the world's largest provider of information technology data, analysis and consulting, with research centers in over 41 countries and more than 400 research analysts worldwide. IDG World Expo is a leading producer of more than 168 globally branded conferences and expositions in 35 countries including E3 (Electronic Entertainment Expo), Macworld Expo, ComNet, Windows World Expo, ICE (Internet Commerce Expo), Agenda, DEMO, and Spotlight. IDG's training subsidiary, ExecuTrain, is the world's largest computer training company, with more than 230 locations worldwide and 785 training courses. IDG Marketing Services helps industry-leading IT companies build international brand recognition by developing global integrated marketing programs via IDG's print, online and exposition products worldwide. Further information about the company can be found at www.idg.com. 1/26/00

Dedication

This book is for Rob, for loving Hawaii as much as I do.

Author's Acknowledgments

Much love and many heartfelt thanks to Jeanette Foster, for her expert contributions and true-blue friendship; Nathaniel R. Leas, for his unflagging support, keen eye while on the road, and readiness to hit the phones when time was of the essence; Jocelyn Fujii, for her warm heart and willingness to share Hawaii's hidden joys with me; and Stephanie Avnet Yates, for making me go in the first place. Without them, this book could not have come to pass.

Publisher's Acknowledgments

We're proud of this book; please send us your comments through our IDG Books Worldwide Online Registration Form located at www.dummies.com.

Some of the people who helped bring this book to market include the following:

Editorial

Project Editor: Mary Goodwin

Development Editor: Alexis Lipsitz

Cartographer: Roberta Stockwell

Senior Photo Editor: Richard Fox

Assistant Photo Editor: Michael Ross

Editorial Assistant: Michelle Hacker, Carol Strickland

Production

Project Coordinator: Maridee V. Ennis

Associate Project Coordinator: Nicole Doram

Layout and Graphics: Beth Brooks, LeAndra Johnson, Kristin Pickett, Brian Torwelle, Jeremey Unger

Proofreaders: Laura Albert, John Bitter, David Faust, Susan Moritz, Susan Sims

Indexer: Sharon Hilgenberg

General and Administrative

IDG Books Worldwide, Inc.: John Kilcullen, CEO; Bill Barry, President and COO

IDG Books Consumer Reference Group

> **Business:** Kathleen A. Welton, Vice President and Publisher; Kevin Thornton, Acquisitions Manager
>
> **Cooking/Gardening:** Jennifer Feldman, Associate Vice President and Publisher
>
> **Education/Reference:** Diane Graves Steele, Vice President and Publisher; Greg Tubach, Publishing Director
>
> **Lifestyles:** Kathleen Nebenhaus, Vice President and Publisher; Tracy Boggier, Managing Editor
>
> **Pets:** Dominique DeVito, Associate Vice President and Publisher; Tracy Boggier, Managing Editor
>
> **Travel:** Michael Spring, Vice President and Publisher; Suzanne Jannetta, Editorial Director; Brice Gosnell, Managing Editor

IDG Books Consumer Editorial Services: Kathleen Nebenhaus, Vice President and Publisher; Kristin A. Cocks, Editorial Director; Cindy Kitchel, Editorial Director

IDG Books Consumer Production: Debbie Stailey, Production Director

IDG Books Packaging: Marc J. Mikulich, Vice President, Brand Strategy and Research

◆

The publisher would like to give special thanks to Patrick J. McGovern, without whom this book would not have been possible.

◆

Contents at a Glance

Cartoons at a Glance

By Rich Tennant

page 7

page 59

page 383

page 87

page 461

page 293

page 183

Fax: 978-546-7747
E-mail: richtennant@the5thwave.com
World Wide Web: www.the5thwave.com

Maps at a Glance

Table of Contents

Introduction

● ●

I'm here to spread the good news: Hawaii really lives up to its heady promise. These islands of Aloha offer all the ingredients of a care-free beach vacation.

One of Hawaii's most magical and winning qualities is its ability to fulfill everyone's own island dream — whether you're six or 60, single or the head of a growing family, the *Survivor* type or a *Who Wants to Be a Millionaire* hopeful. It's just a matter of knowing what you want from your island vacation — and how to make it happen.

Planning a Hawaii vacation is easy — too easy, in fact. Far too many people head off to Hawaii blindly, without exerting the little bit of effort it takes to tailor a vacation to their own needs, tastes, and desires. So just knowing that you want to look before you leap puts you well ahead of the pack. And picking up this guidebook shows that you have the right instincts about your vacation planning.

About This Book

Hawaii For Dummies, 1st Edition, cuts the wheat from the chaff — or the husk from the pineapple, as it were. An island vacation, after all, is supposed to be easy and fun, and your Hawaii trip-planning should be easy and fun, too. I've done the legwork for you, and I want you to ben-efit accordingly. I'm not afraid to take a stand to help you decide what to include in your island vacation, and, even more important, what *not* to include. I understand that you work hard to set aside a few precious weeks of vacation time, and that money doesn't grow on trees — no matter how much you have, you don't want to waste it. After all, the time to figure out this stuff is now, in the planning stage, not when you get to Hawaii.

No one right answer exists for everyone, of course — that's why you're here. With *Hawaii For Dummies,* 1st Edition, I give you the tools you need — *just* what you need, not too much — so that you can make smart decisions about what works for you and what doesn't. I've tried to give you the clearest picture of what you need to know, what choices you have to make, and what your options are so that you can make informed decisions easily and efficiently. Because this book is a reference guide, you can start reading at any point and concentrate on finding out exactly what you want to know at any given time.

Think of building your Hawaii vacation less as a step-by-step process and more as a jigsaw puzzle. This book helps you assemble the right puzzle pieces so that they interlock smoothly and the finished product reflects the picture *you* want, not somebody else's image of what your island paradise should be.

Conventions Used in This Book

The structure of this book is non-linear: You can dig in anywhere to get information on a specific issue without any hassles. Hotels and restaurants are listed alphabetically with prices and frank evaluations. In addition, some abbreviations are used for credit cards:

AE – American Express

CB – Carte Blanche

DC – Diners Club

DISC – Discover

JCB – Japan Credit Bank

MC – MasterCard

V – Visa

I divided the hotels into two categories — my personal favorites and those that don't quite make my preferred list but still get a hearty seal of approval. Don't be shy about considering these "runners up" hotels if you're unable to get a room at one of my favorites or if your preferences differ from mine — the amenities that the runners up offer and the services that each provides make all these accommodations good choices to consider as you determine where to rest your head at night.

I also include some general pricing information to help you as you decide where to unpack your bags or dine on the local cuisine. I've used a system of dollar signs to show a range of costs for one night in a hotel or a meal at a restaurant (included in the cost of each meal is an appetizer, entree, dessert, one drink, taxes, and tip — per person). Check out the following table to decipher the dollar signs:

Cost	Hotel	Restaurant
$	Under $75	Under $15
$$	$75–$150	$15–$25
$$$	$150–$225	$25–$40
$$$$	$225–$300	$40–$70
$$$$$	$300 and up	Over $70

Foolish Assumptions

Standard guides often include everything but the kitchen sink in the misguided belief that quantity outweighs quality. Not so here.

Hawaii For Dummies, 1st Edition, is different from other guidebooks in that it was conceived as a comprehensive trip-planning tool for readers who, for any number of reasons, want expert assistance in an easy-to-use form: This could be your first trip to Hawaii, or maybe you haven't been in ages, or perhaps you haven't seen all you want to see of the islands. Or maybe you don't want to dedicate your life to trip planning or waste a vacation's worth of time wading through hundreds of dense pages of a conventional guidebook to figure out what's *really* worth your time and money, and what's not.

How This Book Is Organized

Hawaii For Dummies, 1st Edition, is divided into seven parts — among them, two are dedicated to deciding on and planning your vacation, one is dedicated to each of Hawaii's destination islands that you should consider including in this trip, and one neatly wraps things up. You can read each chapter or part without reading the one that came before it — no need to study up on Oahu or Kauai if you're only heading to Maui and the Big Island, after all — but, as you read, I may refer you to other chapters of the book for more information on certain subjects.

Part 1: Getting Started

This first part touches on everything you want to consider before actually getting down to the nuts and bolts of trip planning, including:

- An introduction to each of the Hawaiian islands, plus a fun quiz that helps you decide which islands suit your fancy and which ones you'd rather leave for the next trip

- Time-tested advice on how to divide your time between the islands you'd like to visit

- The details on when to go

- How much you can expect your trip to cost, and how to save if money is a concern

- Special considerations for families, seniors, travelers with disabilities, and gay and lesbian travelers

- A how-to guide for couples who'd like to tie the knot in the Aloha State

Part II: Ironing Out the Details

This is where I get down to the serious trip preparation, including:

- ✔ The pros and cons of planning your trip on your own, using a travel agent, and buying an all-inclusive package deal
- ✔ The ins and outs of flying to Hawaii, and how to travel between the islands once you're there
- ✔ Getting ready to go, from the pluses and minuses of buying travel insurance to renting cars to making advance luau reservations to *akamai* (smart) packing tips

Parts III through VI: Being There — The Islands

These parts form the bulk of the book and cover the destinations you may visit in hands-on detail. Each part is dedicated to one of the major Hawaiian islands — Oahu, Maui, the Big Island, and Kauai — and offers all of the specific details and recommendations you need while you're there, including:

- ✔ Where to stay
- ✔ Where to eat
- ✔ How to get your bearings and get around
- ✔ How to enjoy both sand and sea once you arrive

Part VII: The Part of Tens

Every *...For Dummies* book has a Part of Tens. If Parts III through VI are the meat of a travel sandwich, think of these fun top-ten-list chapters as dessert. Chapter 23 tells you how to ditch the tourist look and act like a local, with tips on everything from how to pronounce those tongue-twisting Hawaiian place names to getting to know a few points of island-style etiquette. Chapter 24 focuses on one of everybody's favorite topics — food! Use it to familiarize yourself with common island food terms and local-style dishes, so that once you arrive you'll know whether you want the *saimin,* the *poke,* or the *opakapaka* — and whether or not you'll want to save room for a little *haupia* for dessert.

Quick Concierge and Worksheets

The Quick Concierge puts facts about Hawaii at your fingertips, from the lowdown on taxes to Web sites where you can find accurate online weather forecasts and everything in between. You also get toll-free numbers and Web addresses for all of the major airlines, car-rental agencies, and hotel chains for easy reference. And, in case you want more information, I give you the contact numbers for all of the local visitor bureaus you may want to consult. At the back of the book I also include a bunch of worksheets to make your travel planning easier. You can use these worksheets to determine your vacation budget and to track the names of restaurants you may want to visit, among other things.

Icons Used in This Book

Think of the following icons as signposts. I've used them to highlight especially useful advice, to draw your attention to things you won't want to miss, and to introduce a variety of topics.

Useful advice on things to do, ways to schedule your time, and any other tips I'm sure you won't want to miss.

Tourist traps, ripoffs, time-wasters, and other things to beware.

Attractions, hotels, restaurants, or activities that are especially family-friendly.

Money-saving tips or particularly great values.

Bits of well-guarded *kamaaina* (local) advice that I let out of the bag so you can have the edge over *malihinis* (newcomers) who don't know better.

Any plans that you should make before you leave home.

Hotels, restaurants, beaches, and activities for lovebirds in search of the ultimate in island-style romance.

Where to Go from Here

As you read through this book and start to formulate your vacation, remember this: The planning really *is* half the fun. Don't think of choosing your island destinations and solidifying the details as a chore. Make the homebound part of the process a voyage of discovery, and you'll end up with an experience that's that much more rewarding, enriching, and relaxing — *really*. Have a blast with it. Happy planning!

Part I
Getting Started

The 5th Wave   By Rich Tennant

HAWAII'S ESCALATOR FALLS

In this part . . .

This part of the book will help you get your Hawaii vacation off the ground. I guide you through all the essential steps in preparing for your trip, including deciding which islands you wish to visit — and when — and mapping out your budget. This part also features a chapter full of savvy advice for travelers with special interests.

Chapter 1

Discovering Hawaii and Deciding Where to Go

· ·

· ·

*I*t's been a stressful day at the office. Or the kids have been driving you crazy, and you realize that everybody in the family needs a break. Or maybe you've just had it with gray skies and gloomy weather.

Then the idea comes, and it's a gem: Hawaii. Ah, Hawaii.

Just thinking about a Hawaii vacation warms the soul, doesn't it? Turquoise waves, white sand, toasty sun. Palm trees sway in the breeze as emerald-green cliffs rise up to meet a sweet blue sky. The fragrance of orchids fills the air as the music of a slack-key guitar carries you into tropical reverie. . . .

Vacation has long been the ultimate antidote to the stresses and strains of daily life — and no destination is more relaxing and restorative than the exquisite Hawaiian Islands. Don't just take it from me — take it from Mark Twain, who lauded Hawaii as "the loveliest fleet of islands that lies anchored in any ocean." Recovery calls for total escape to this idyllic tropical paradise, where days of soaking up the island sun are interwoven with easygoing adventuring and plenty of friendly aloha.

But don't get carried away in the fantasy just yet. You'll have plenty of time for that later, after you're actually parked on that perfect beach, frosty cocktail in hand. First, read a little bit about Hawaii so that you can best plan the ultimate escape.

The Hawaiian Islands

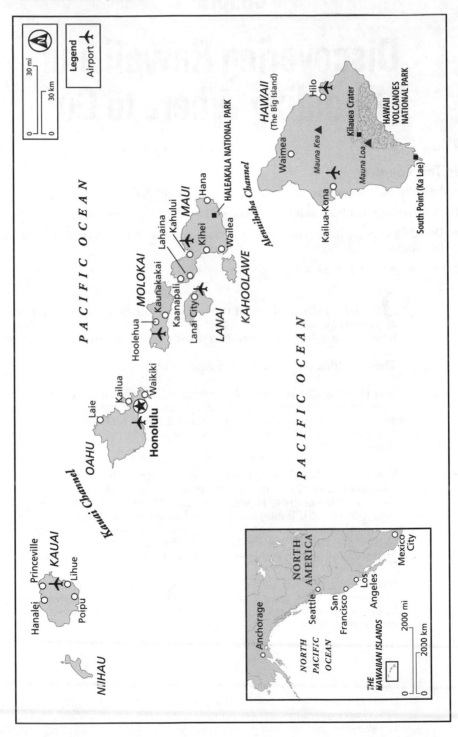

Taking a Quick Tour of Hawaii's Islands

Hawaii isn't just one place — it's an entire island chain comprising eight major islands and 124 islets. Together they form a 1,500-mile crescent that slices a lush, volcanic swath through the sparkling Pacific waters just above the equator (in the north Pacific Ocean, not the south Pacific, as many believe).

The Hawaiian Islands are just a hair's breadth larger, in total land mass, than the state of Connecticut — but oh, what glorious square miles they are. The islands are actually the summits of underwater volcanoes that have grown tall enough, in geologic time, to peek above the waves. (All of the volcanoes are dormant except for two on the Big Island, Mauna Loa and Kilauea, part of Hawaii Volcanoes National Park. See Chapter 18 for more information.) A volcanic core gives each island a breathtakingly rugged mountainous heart.

Most of the island development is at sea level, along the sunny coastal fringe of each island. Thanks to Hawaii's proximity to the equator, those coastal areas experience near-perfect weather year-round: high 70s, clear skies, and gentle tradewinds.

The eight main islands are Oahu (oh-WA-hoo), the hub of the Hawaii island chain, and the "neighbor" islands: Maui (MOW-ee); Hawaii, or the Big Island, as it's commonly called; Kauai (ka-WAH-ee); Molokai (mo-lo-k-EYE); Lanai (la-NAH-ee); Niihau (nee-EE-how); and Kahoolawe (ka-ho-ho-LA-vay). These islands make up more than 99 percent of the state's land mass. Of these, the first six are prime tourist destinations, each with its own personality, attractions, and tropical appeal. (Niihau is a privately owned island with a tiny population, and Kahoolawe is an unpopulated island that was formerly a U.S. military bombing target.) Of the six islands that are open to tourists, four are ideal choices for first-time visits to Hawaii: Oahu, Maui, the Big Island, and Kauai.

The Gathering Place: Oahu

Oahu is the most developed of the Hawaiian Islands and its greatest population center — about 80 percent of Hawaii's residents (about 870,000 people) live on this gateway island. About three-quarters of Oahuans reside in Honolulu, the 11th largest city in the U.S., and the only real incorporated city in the state. Hawaii's most famous district is the area of Honolulu called Waikiki, an urban beach resort that stretches along the south coast of the island to the landmark crater known as Diamond Head. A compact city of concrete and high-rises, Waikiki is the most densely built of Hawaii's beach resorts. This is where you find Hawaii's biggest crowds — nine out of every 10 visitors to the islands stop here.

Despite the crowds, Oahu is a wonderful destination. It's home to some of Hawaii's best sightseeing, including the USS *Arizona* Memorial in Pearl Harbor, the most moving tribute to World War II in existence; the best little museum in the Pacific, the Bishop Museum; the world's best cultural theme park, the Polynesian Cultural Center; and much more. Oahu also boasts the state's finest restaurants, shopping, and nightlife (yes, Don Ho still sings "Tiny Bubbles" nightly, folks). And Waikiki Beach really is fabulous, which is why travelers from around the world regularly converge on this sunny little haven. In the last few years, formerly kitschy Waikiki has been reinvented along more sophisticated lines, mainly as a result of its popularity with Japanese honeymooners, who love to shop the couture boutiques (hello, Prada!) along the main drag, Kalakaua Avenue. Still, Waikiki maintains some of Hawaii's best bargain hotels. In addition, a comprehensive, easy-to-use public transportation system makes Oahu the one-and-only choice for those who don't want to rent a car.

Leave Oahu off your itinerary entirely if your singular goal is to get away from it all. But if you're up for endless diversion and don't mind a few crowds with your aloha — if you're the type who revels in the glitz and energy of it all — justifiably world-famous Waikiki is the place for you. Still, many newcomers who visit only Waikiki leave with the wrong idea about Hawaii — that it's more crowded, overbuilt, and urbanized than a real tropical paradise should be. So if you'd like to go home without feeling like you missed out on the magic, pair a stay on Oahu with a visit to at least one of the neighbor islands. I also highly recommend that you dedicate a day to visiting Oahu's Windward Coast and north shore (ground zero for Hawaii's surf culture), which offer some of the most gorgeous territory in the state.

The Valley Isle: Maui

When people think Hawaiian paradise, they usually think Maui. Almost everyone who comes here falls in love with this island, and for good reason: It offers the ideal mix of unspoiled natural beauty and tropical sophistication, action-packed fun and laid-back island style. In fact, Maui has so much of that special something that the readers of *Condé Nast Traveler* have voted Maui "Best Island in the World" for six years running, and "World's Best Travel Destination" three years in a row.

The Valley Isle is more like the mainland than any other place in Hawaii (yes, even Honolulu). The highways and L.A.–style traffic jams and mini-malls will look comfortingly familiar, or annoyingly so — it all depends on your perspective. Despite the mainland-style development, Maui really is a tropical paradise, with golden beaches, misty tropical cliffs, and countless waterfalls along the Heavenly Road to Hana, one of America's most spectacular drives. Maui also happens to be the most exciting of Hawaii's islands, especially for those who like ocean and outdoor activities: Offshore are two of Hawaii's finest snorkel and dive spots; onshore, at the summit of one of the island's two great mountains (between which lie the valley for which the island is nicknamed), is Haleakala National Park, a wild, otherwordly place that's hugely popular with hikers, bicyclers, and sunrise-watchers. Hawaii's finest luau, a brand-new theater, and an energetic party vibe in Lahaina make Maui a great choice for those who like after-dark activities.

Everybody loves Maui — so expect to battle a few crowds and pay for the privilege of visiting. The beach resorts are quite built up   not the density of Waikiki yet, but a few come close — and I've heard an increasing number of complaints about crowds in the last couple of years. And thanks to the rules of supply and demand, Maui tends to be more expensive than other islands, and booked-to-capacity hotels are often less than willing to entertain negotiations on reduced rates; the high cost of all those available activities doesn't help matters. What's more, the tacky heart of Hawaii now beats in the old whaling town of Lahaina, which has superceded newly refined Waikiki as a cheesy tourist center, and Kihei's dominant architectural style is high strip mall. Still, nothing can dull the sheen on Maui, which sports enough excitement to keep even the most go-go-go travelers busy.

The Big Island: Hawaii

Salt-and-pepper beaches, primal rain forests, stark lava fields as far as the eye can see — this otherworldly island simply may not be your idea of a tropical paradise. But travelers with a taste for adventure or an eye for the unusual will think they've found heaven on earth.

The island that gave the entire island chain its name is the largest in the bunch — twice the size of all the others combined — and a real study in contradictions: The left (Kona-Kohala) side is hot, dry, and studded with expansive, ultra-deluxe beach resorts that add up to the finest collection of luxury resorts in all of Hawaii. The coast is one of the finest water-sports playgrounds there is for divers, snorkelers, and kayakers, while sun-worshippers will love white-sand Hapuna Beach, one of Hawaii's finest. The right (Hilo-Volcano) side is lush, wet, green, and fragrant with tropical flowers; Hilo is the prettiest city in the Pacific, and Volcano Village puts you right in the heart of tropical rain forest. In between are two of the tallest mountain peaks in the Pacific, Mauna Kea and Mauna Loa. Don't be surprised if you spot snow atop the nearly 14,000-foot peaks while you're deep-sea fishing off the legendary Kona Coast — considered the Sportfishing Capital of the World — or snorkeling in the some of the warmest waters in the Pacific. North of Mauna Kea is vast ranchland, complete with herds of beef cattle and its own *paniolo* (cowboy) culture.

At the heart of the island is Kilauea volcano, the world's largest active volcano, currently in the midst of recorded history's longest-ever uninterrupted volcanic eruption. Most people think of volcanic activity as solely destructive, but Kilauea's eruptions have actually been productive, adding more than 20,000 acres of new land (and counting) to the Big Island since January 1983. Needless to say, Hawaii Volcanoes National Park is one of the coolest — excuse me, hottest — places you'll ever have a chance to visit in your lifetime. If you like weird places, you won't want to miss it.

The Big Island can, however, dash expectations. It's jaw-droppingly spectacular — force me to choose and I'll name it as my favorite of the islands — but it falls short of some people's tropical-island fantasies. Chocolate-brown lava fields in every direction greet visitors flying into Kona Airport. Sure, you can experience a traditional tropical idyll on white-sand beaches as wide as a football field, or revel in the scent of wild orchids in flowering rain forests — but you may have to go out of your way to find them. Also, this is rural Hawaii, so nightlife is scarce.

Still, this island is so big that you're likely to have the place to yourself once you arrive. With lots of room to spread out, Hawaii makes for a more laid-back, quieter vibe than what you find on Oahu or Maui — and, much of the time, you'll also find lower prices. B&B lovers will discover the island's best collection of inns, most offering an excellent base for visitors looking for something other from the average beachfront resort or affordable condo experience. Just remember that the sheer size of this extra-large island makes for longer driving times; either plan on spending a week, or limit yourself to one coast.

The Garden Isle: Kauai

Of all the Hawaiian islands, Kauai is the one that comes closest to embodying the Hawaiian ideal — it's the ultimate in tropical romance and beauty. Even Hollywood thinks so, which is why Kauai has had starring roles as Paradise in movies ranging from *Blue Hawaii* and *South Pacific* to *Jurassic Park* and *Six Days/Seven Nights.* The island landscape doesn't get any finer than what you'll find on Kauai. Every time I visit, I'm newly wowed by how exquisite it all is. Kauai boasts the kind of natural beauty that cameras can't really capture, that even mere memory can't conjure up.

Kauai is the perfect place to leave the modern world behind. Garden-like Kauai is quieter and less developed than its sister islands; you can count the number of full-fledged resorts on one hand. (This lack of choice makes it important to book way in advance if you plan on staying at one of the resorts.) Don't come expecting Cancun-style nightlife or St. Thomas-worthy shopping. Discover instead the oldest of the Hawaiian islands, an unspoiled place boasting wind-carved cliffs, fertile valleys rich with taro, powder-fine white-sand beaches, and gorgeous vistas in every direction. It's an ideal setting for some well-deserved relaxation time: The north shore is the most tranquil and beautiful shoreline in all of Hawaii, while the south shore's Poipu (poy-EE-poo) Beach is a fabulous, family-friendly playground that's the ideal place to kick back and paddle around in the waves for days on end.

Kauai is great for adventurous souls, too. The island boasts two remote natural wonders: the jagged emerald cliffs of the Na Pali Coast, and Waimea Canyon, called the "Grand Canyon of the Pacific" for its remarkable resemblance to the multi-colored Arizona crater. The otherwise inaccessible Na Pali Coast, in particular, is a tropical dream-come-true for hikers, but you can also see these magical cliffs on a day cruise along the coastline.

It takes a lot of rain to keep Kauai so lush, fertile, and flower-fragrant; consequently, the weather on Kauai is a little less reliable than on the other islands. This is the one island where a week of rain can quash your fun-in-the-sun plans; this is most likely to happen in winter, but it's happened to me even in May. Kauai's Mt. Waialeale is actually the wettest spot on earth, commanding an average annual rainfall of 444 inches; luckily, the coasts stay substantially drier. Still, stick to the south shore if you have your heart set on a string of sunny days. The super-lush north shore is best for summer vacations, when the wild winter surf has calmed down and the days tend toward dry and sunny.

The Most Hawaiian Isle: Molokai

Sleepy Molokai is a rural island that's largely untouched by modern development (although, as residents like to boast, they do have KFC now). This lean, funky, scruffy little place is often called the most Hawaiian island because it's the birthplace of the hula, and has a larger native Hawaiian population than any other in the chain. While it offers some lovely, secluded beaches, the island's most famous site is Kalaupapa, a world-famous 19th-century leper colony that can only be reached by mule, prop plane, or helicopter.

I don't cover Molokai fully in this book, since I don't recommend making it part of your first visit to Hawaii. It's worth seeing eventually for its unsullied beauty and true Hawaiian spirit, but you should fully explore the other islands before you devote a significant amount of time to Molokai. The island has plenty of aloha, no question, and is working on its image as a tourist destination, but facilities for visitors are minimal: a few condos, a handful of B&Bs, one almost-desolate resort, and an overpriced, upscale camping-and-activities spread run by the Molokai Ranch, the most dominant presence on the island. Frankly, I hear way too many complaints about the ranch to recommend that you spend your time and money there.

If you're intrigued by the idea of Molokai and/or the fascinating Kalaupapa National Historical Park, a still-active leper colony that sits on a remote peninsula at the foot of the world's tallest sea cliffs, consider coming in for the day, or an overnighter, from nearby Maui. I tell you how to do that in Chapter 14.

If your heart is set on dedicating a larger chunk of your vacation to Molokai, check out *Frommer's Hawaii* or *Frommer's Hawaii from $60 a Day,* both of which include complete coverage of the island. Or contact the Molokai Visitors Association, the Molokai Ranch, or the Maui Visitors Bureau (Molokai is part of Maui County); see the Quick Concierge for Web sites and contact info.

The Private Island: Lanai

This tiny island (pop. 3,500) is featured on a few packages, but I don't recommend spending time here until you conquer the other islands. Staying on Lanai is less a Hawaiian experience and more a generic park-yourself-at-a-resort vacation, which you can do with more local flavor elsewhere in the islands. For this reason, I don't cover Lanai in detail in this book.

If you're committed to visiting Lanai, you don't need me or this book, anyway — this is where you come to *really* get away from it all. Formerly dedicated to pineapple production, Lanai is not particularly beautiful, nor does it offer much in the personality department. There's little or nothing to do here, which is the entire idea of this getaway island. Just about everything that *is* here is completely handled through the two mega-expensive resorts that have taken over this humble little place: the English manor-house-style Lodge at Koele, which sits on the cool, misty peak of the island, and the more what-you'd-expect-from-Hawaii beachfront Manele Bay Hotel.

If you visit, plan on eating every meal at the two sister resorts, and otherwise being entirely at their mercy. Still, Lanai has fans who love the total pampering and utter solitude (Bill Gates booked up the entire island so that he could get married here beyond the prying eyes of the media and public a few years back). Golfers also like its two world-class courses.

Make Lanai a day trip, rather than staying for a few days. I prefer visiting Lanai for a day of beachgoing, snorkeling, and sightseeing on one of Trilogy Excursions' day and overnight cruises from Maui; I tell you how to sign up in Chapter 14. Golfers might also consider flying over for the day to hit the links, which is what many locals do.

If you really want to make Lanai a more substantial part of your vacation, see *Frommer's Hawaii,* which includes complete coverage of the island. Or contact Destination Lanai, the Maui Visitors Bureau (Lanai is part of Maui County), or the resorts themselves; see the Quick Concierge for Web sites and contact info.

Deciding How Many Islands You Have Time to See

Most Hawaii vacationers visit more than one island, which I highly recommend you do. But don't try to see all of the islands, or even the four major ones, unless you have at least a month of vacation time to do it. About a week per island is a good rule of thumb — or else you'll end up spending what feels like your entire vacation in the airport, at the car-rental counter, and checking in and out of hotels. Trust me: Nonstop packing and unpacking can really put the kibosh on relaxation and the laidback pace that should be the crux of any Hawaii vacation.

In a two-week vacation, three islands is the most you should try to see, and that's only if you're the kind of traveler who can't take more than three days of bustling Waikiki.

Determining Which Islands Are Right for You

By awarding point values to each island based on your interests, needs, and expectations, the "quiz" in this section offers a foolproof and time-tested way to help you decide which islands most fit you and your vacation. Not only will you know which islands to start planning for, but you'll get to know the ones you're interested in a little better in the process.

Step #1: Using the scorecard

Your scorecard has a column for each island, and a row for each category on which the islands have been rated.

The "Rate the Islands" Scorecard

	Oahu	Maui	Big Island	Kauai	Molokai	Lanai
1) Beaches						
2) Resorts						
3) Bargain Rates						
4) Golf						
5) Sightseeing						
6) Water Sports						
7) Sportfishing						
8) Surfing						
9) Whale-Watching						
10) Kids						
11) Weddings						
12) Peace & Quiet						
13) Keeping Busy						
14) Eden-like Scenery						
15) Natural Wonders						
16) Theme Parks						
17) No Rental Car						
18) Restaurants						
19) Shopping						
20) Nightlife						
Total Score						

In the following section, I rate each island on each of the interests listed on the scorecard. Each island can receive from 1 to 5 points, based on how well suited it is to the interest or activity in that category. Five points is the highest rating; one is the lowest. If an island isn't listed, assume that it scores a zero in that particular category, and fill in the scorecard accordingly.

Step #2: Scoring the Islands

As you read the sections that interest you, record the score of each island in that category on your scorecard. For example, if you are coming to Hawaii to play golf, stop at the "Teeing off" section and insert each island's score — 5 points each for Maui, the Big Island, and Kauai; 4 points for Lanai; 0 each for Oahu and Molokai — into your scorecard.

Stop only at those categories that interest you. For example, if you're not traveling with kids, skip over the "Bringing the kids" category, and don't plug in any points for any of the islands into the "Kids" row in the scorecard. (For example, Maui shouldn't earn 5 points here, because its kid appeal isn't relevant to you.)

1) Hitting the beach

Rating	Island	Rationale
5 points	Kauai	Home to the powdery-white, palm-lined, postcard-perfect beaches you fantasize about — and you're likely to have them virtually all to yourself once you get here.
4 points	Oahu	One word: Waikiki. Yes, Waikiki is overbuilt and over-crowded — but it's still pure magic. If you want some alone time, idyllic Windward Coast beaches like Lanikai and Kailua are just a short drive away.
3 points	Maui	The Valley Isle scores for abundant, wide, breathtaking beaches.
2 points	Big Island	You find some unusual beaches here, including a number of striking black-sand ones. Even has some great beaches in the classical sense — like Hapuna Beach, one of my all-time favorites — but they're more scarce here.
1 point	Lanai	Hulopoe Bay deserves a point for its wonderful away-from-it-all vibe and dancing spinner dolphins.

2) Restoring at a resort

Rating	Island	Rationale
5 points	Big Island	The place to park yourself in style. You'll find a string of terrific megaresorts along the Kona-Kohala Coast, where all have plenty of room to spread out. Resort livin' doesn't get any better than the Four Seasons Hualalai.
4 points	Maui	Enjoy a wealth of wonderful resorts, particularly in Wailea.
3 points	Kauai	You only have two options here — the Hyatt Regency at Poipu and the north shore's Princeville Resort — but both will please the resort-minded vacationer.
2 points	Lanai	People love the island's two ultra-private luxury resorts dedicated to the easy life — but do you really want to stay in a faux English hunting lodge in the misty upcountry or at a beach resort that's not actually on the beach?
1 point	Oahu	Deserves a token point for the restful Kahala Mandarin, plus its string of fabulous Waikiki hotels — but if you just want to sit around and do nothing, why hassle with Honolulu? Head to a neighbor island instead.

3) Watching your budget while still staying on the beach

Rating	Island	Rationale
5 points	Kauai	Gorgeous Poipu boasts some of the best-value beachfront condos in the tropics. You won't feel like you're skimping one bit.
4 points	Maui	Despite its popularity and high resort rates, Maui has a decent number of beachfront bargains. If you don't want to go condo, try the Kaanapali Beach Hotel, one of my mid-priced faves.
1 point	Oahu	Don't expect cheap, but Waikiki does boast a surprising number of reasonably priced hotels right on — or a stone's throw from — the sand, including any number of centrally located Outrigger and Ohana hotels.

4) Teeing off

Rating	Island	Rationale
5 points	**Kauai**	Robert Trent Jones, Jr., called Kauai "the best island for golf there is." Need I say more?
5 points	**Maui**	Maui has enough world-class courses to keep club-wielders happy for a good, long time.
5 points	**Big Island**	Offers spectacular championship resort courses, each an oasis of manicured green surrounded by a sea of black lava. Simply wild.
4 points	**Lanai**	For quality and seclusion, Lanai's two championship courses can't be beat. Tee off in the morning at the Nicklaus-designed oceanfront course, then head to the cool upcountry to play among the pines.

5) Sightseeing

Rating	Island	Rationale
5 points	**Oahu**	Take in the only royal palace on U.S. soil, the heartrending USS *Arizona* Memorial at Pearl Harbor, or any other of the island's scores of attractions.
4 points	**Big Island**	The big kahuna is rich with one-of-a-kind sightseeing opportunities, including Hawaii Volcanoes National Park, a number of ancient petroglyph parks, and a Hawaiian village (now a National Historical Park) that tells the story of island life as it once was.
3 points	**Maui**	Haleakala National Park isn't much more than a giant hole in the ground — but boy, what a hole it is. You'll think you've landed on the moon. The gorgeous drive to "heavenly" Hana and the Maui Ocean Center, the best aquarium in the Pacific, also help Maui to score.
3 points	**Kauai**	The best island for catching up on relaxation time — but the spectacular scenery alone earns serious kudos in this category.
2 points	**Molokai**	Want to ride a mule down the world's highest sea cliffs to a leper colony? Here's your island. A spectacular, life-changing activity — but keep in mind that you can also do it as a day trip or overnighter from Maui.

6) Hitting the waves

Rating	Island	Rationale
5 points	Big Island	Kealakekua Bay is the best snorkeling and dolphin-watching spot in all of Hawaii, and the whole coast is tops for sea turtle spotting. Great offshore diving, too. And the icing on the cake? The Big Island's a sportfisher's mecca.
5 points	Maui	Again, a winner for the sheer variety of great snorkel and dive spots, including Molokini, a sunken crater where you can see everything from clouds of colorful fish to manta rays and reef sharks. Tops for humpback whale spotting in winter, too.
3 points	Kauai	Poipu Beach features great snorkeling. You also get a kaliedoscopic collection of marine life off the north shore beaches (not safe for snorkeling in winter).
1 point	Oahu	Home to Hawaii's most famous snorkel spot, Hanauma Bay. Sure, it gets crowded — but a whole new world awaits you underwater here.

7) Sportfishing

Rating	Island	Rationale
5 points	Big Island	If you're set on hooking a big one, the Sportfishing Capital of the World deserves an extra five points from you. Don't miss it.

8) Experiencing Hawaii's legendary surf culture

Rating	Island	Rationale
5 points	Oahu	The birthplace, and still the epitome, of surf culture. If you want to learn, you already know how, or you just like to watch, this is the island for you — no question. Waikiki's beach boys swear they can teach anyone to surf (or stand up, anyway). Come in winter and point your rental car to the north shore to see the big kahunas hang-ten in legendary style.
1 point	Maui	Oahu is where it's really at, but the windsurfers at Maui's Hookipa Beach are a blast to watch.

9) Spotting wintering humpback whales

Rating	Island	Rationale
5 points	Maui	The humpback's favorite place to hang offshore; if you show up during prime whale season (January through March) you're bound to see them, even if you don't head out to sea.
3 points	Big Island	Head to the Kona Coast if you want to spot the Neptunian behemoths.
3 points	Kauai	Another good vantage — a Na Pali cruise will definitely (fingers crossed) do the trick.

10) Bringing the kids

Rating	Island	Rationale
5 points	Maui	This action-packed island wins for its wealth of kid-friendly condos and beaches, plus activities galore, from snorkel cruises to hikes to family-fun luaus. Your kids will wonder why you haven't come here before.
4 points	Big Island	Scores big for its WOW! factor. From fantasy mega-resorts to that amazing volcano, the Big Island should keep your kids dazzled for awhile. You'll also find some affordable family condos here.
3 points	Oahu	The whole family will enjoy the multitude of kid-friendly sightseeing attractions and parks, plus Waikiki Beach, the perfect kiddie playland. However, Oahu loses points for costliness, though.
2 points	Kauai	While mostly for the relaxation-minded, Kauai does have lots of kid-friendly condos, and Poipu Beach is fun for kids.

11) Getting married

Rating	Island	Rationale
5 points	Kauai	No question — the undisputed winner in the romance category.
4 points	Big Island	The fabulous resorts make great wedding locations — and you're on the honeymoon as soon as you cut the cake. On the other side of the island, the lush rain forests and romantic B&Bs make great places to hide away from the rest of the world.
3 points	Maui	More great resorts for getting hitched — but this honeymoon favorite doesn't have enough of a romantic, get-away-from-it-all vibe to score higher.

| 1 point | **Oahu** | I'm not sure why, but Waikiki still has a magical attraction for newlyweds. But I suggest you head elsewhere if you want true romance. |
| 1 point | **Lanai** | Bill Gates got married here, so why not? The resorts are terrific ceremony spots — but expect big bills and few options. |

12) Enjoying some peace and quiet

Rating	*Island*	*Rationale*
5 points	**Kauai**	Hands down, the place to indulge your antisocial tendencies.
5 points	**Lanai**	Even quieter and more removed — but the totalitarian nature of the resorts here may undo some of the sense of on-your-own solitude.
4 points	**Big Island**	All that room to spread out means that it's easy to be alone on this big, empty, wonderful island.
3 points	**Molokai**	This scruffy, funky little island welcomes loners with open arms.

13) Keeping busy

Rating	*Island*	*Rationale*
5 points	**Oahu**	Keep on the run by visiting sights such as Pearl Harbor. You can also enjoy lots of people-watching, shopping, and nighttime fun.
5 points	**Maui**	Outdoor fun is the name of the game here. There's something new to do around every corner, from riding a bike down a volcano to taking a snorkel cruise.
3 points	**Big Island**	You'll find lots of activities here to keep you busy, including visiting the phenomenal Hawaii Volcanoes National Park — but plan on increased driving time getting around.
2 points	**Kauai**	The best island for kicking back — but you'll have lots to do if you want it, from movie tours to world-class golf to ocean activities galore.

14) Beholding natural wonders

Rating	Island	Rationale
5 points	**Kauai**	The Garden Isle is the closest you'll come to the realization of the tropical dream — it's simply stunning. Don't miss the north shore, even if you only drive up for a day.
4 points	**Maui**	If you have a yen to frolic among waterfalls, do not pass go, do not collect $200 — head straight to Maui. The drive to Hana is chock-full of fabulous falls, and at the end of the road is the grandaddy of 'em all, Oheo Gulch.
2 points	**Big Island**	Also known as the "Orchid Isle," it earns deserved points for beautiful rain-forest lushness around Hilo and Volcano Village — but the dry, arid Kona-Kohala Coast is the antithesis of some folks' island dreams.
1 point	**Oahu**	Honolulu may not fulfill your dreams of Eden, but the gorgeous Windward Coast may do the trick. Still, you'll have to go in search of it.

15) Discovering jaw-dropping natural wonders

Rating	Island	Rationale
5 points	**Big Island**	How many times in your life do you get to walk on a live volcano? Don't miss Hawaii Volcanoes National Park. In fact, the whole Big Island landscaping is astonishingly otherworldly, from Kona's vast black lava fields to Holstein-dotted ranchlands to Hilo's misty rain forest.
3 points	**Kauai**	Scenery hardly gets more spectacular than the remote Na Pali Coast; book a cruise before you leave home, or dedicate a day to the hike in. Waimea Canyon, the "Grand Canyon of the Pacific," is also impressive.
2 points	**Maui**	You'll think you've landed on the moon when you drive to the summit of the Haleakala crater. If you're willing to wake up before the birds, check it out at sunrise.

16) Enjoying tropical theme-park fun

Rating	Island	Rationale
5 points	**Oahu**	With Sea Life Park, the Honolulu Zoo, the Waikiki Aquarium, Hawaiian Waters Adventure Park, Hawaiian Ocean Thrills, the Polynesian Cultural Center, Waimea Valley Adventure Park, and more to choose from, you're certain to find a theme park or island-themed attraction to suit your fancy.

2 points	**Maui**	The Grand Wailea is the best theme-park-like resort without a doubt — fantasy pools don't get more fantastic. And the walk-through tank at the fabulous new Maui Ocean Center offers a once-in-a-lifetime experience — when was the last time you saw a great white swim directly over your head?
1 point	**Big Island**	The Hilton Waikoloa Village is the second-best theme-park-style mega-resort in Hawaii. It's downright Disneylike — except Disneyland doesn't have this many waterslides.

17) Avoiding renting a car

Rating	*Island*	*Rationale*
5 points	**Oahu**	Waikiki is eminently walkable, the bus system is easy to figure out, and the Waikiki Trolley takes you to many popular destinations.

18) Eating out

Rating	*Island*	*Rationale*
5 points	**Oahu**	The winner for sheer volume of world-class chefs and award-winning restaurants. Both Alan Wong's and Chef Mavro's should be musts on any visiting gourmand's lists.
5 points	**Maui**	The most innovative dining scene in the island these days, from casual to chic — and with a wealth of beautifully situated oceanfront restaurants to boot.
2 points	**Kauai**	Poipu is home to the Beach House, the most beautifully situated restaurant in Hawaii, and my favorite branch of Roy's, the temple of Hawaii Regional Cuisine.
1 point	**Big Island**	A respectable slate of restaurants in both the moderate and expensive price ranges, but the driving distance between them puts a strain on your nightly choices.

19) Shopping, Hawaiian style

Rating	Island	Rationale
4 points	Oahu	The destination for serious shoppers. The finest collection of alfresco malls in the country is home to everything from Prada and Versace boutiques to first-rate department stores to one-of-a-kind shops carrying top-quality aloha shirts, surf gear, island-accented homewares, and more.
3 points	Big Island	An abundance of natural resources makes this island tops for quality offerings of island art and crafts. Expect to go on the hunt for the best galleries, though.
2 points	Maui	The spending that's done here is more Mall of America than island special. Some good antiquing, though.
1 point	Kauai	Minimal in terms of quantity, but excellent for quality, especially if you like retro looks.

20) Partying the night away

Rating	Island	Rationale
5 points	Oahu	For drinks, dancing, and live entertainment, you can't do better anywhere else in the islands.
5 points	Maui	A party mood characterizes Lahaina town; the resorts offer lots of after-dark fun; and the Old Lahaina Luau is Hawaii's best.
1 point	Big Island	Much quieter than Oahu and Maui, with a low-key waterfront bar scene in Kailua-Kona and some chic cocktail spots at the resorts — but if Kilauea's spouting red-hot lava, there's no better after-dark show around.

Step #3: Tallying the scores

After totaling each island's score, you can declare a winner! The island with the highest total score should be your primary destination. If a second island scores high, consider splitting your time between the two high scorers. If a third island scores high and you have more than two weeks for vacation (lucky you!), think about visiting three islands. If your scores are really close, don't agonize. Flip a coin and vow to hit the losing island on your next vacation.

Chapter 2

Deciding When to Go

● ●

In This Chapter

▶ Understanding Hawaii's climate

▶ Decoding the secrets of the travel seasons

▶ Discovering special events you may want to catch

▶ Planning your trip quickly and easily

● ●

Situated in the north Pacific just 1,470 miles above the equator, the Hawaiian Islands enjoy fabulous weather all year round. Winter is virtually nonexistent. Severe storms are a rarity. Even what is considered the "off-season" — spring and fall — is gorgeous, which means that those of you on a budget can save a bundle if you choose the right dates.

Still, some times are better than others — especially for those travelers who prefer to avoid crowds. Read on to figure out when everybody else comes to Hawaii so that you can either join the party, or avoid it like the plague.

Understanding Hawaii's Climate

Hawaii lies at the edge of the tropics, so it really has only two seasons: warm (winter) and warmer (summer). Temperatures generally don't vary much more than 15°F or so from season to season, depending on where you are. The average daytime summer temperature at sea level is 85°F, while the average daytime winter temperature is 78°F.

Temperatures stay even steadier when you consider the coastal areas alone: At Waikiki, the average summer high is 87°F, while the average winter high is 82°F — not much difference. Nighttime temps drop about 10° to 15° — less in summer, a little more in winter. August is usually the warmest month of the year; February and March are the coolest months. Almost-constant tradewinds bring a cooling breeze even in the hottest weather.

Each of the islands has a leeward side (the west and south shores of the islands), which tends to be hot and dry, and a windward side (the east and north shores), which is generally cooler and wetter. For sun-baked, desert-like weather, visit the leeward side of an island. When you want lush, jungle-like weather, go windward.

Locals like to say that if you don't like the weather, just get in the car and drive — you're bound to find something different. That's because each island also has many microclimates, which are highly localized weather patterns based on a region's unique position and topography. On the Big Island, for example, Hilo gets 180 inches of rainfall annually, which makes it the wettest city in the nation — yet only 60 miles away is desert-like Puako, which gets less than 6 inches of rain per year.

Generally speaking, each island has a mountain (or mountains) at its center. The higher you go in elevation, the cooler it gets. Thus, if you travel inland and upward, the weather can change from summer to winter in a matter of hours. If you visit Maui's Haleakala National Park, for instance, you climb from sea level to 10,000 feet in just 37 miles — and it's not uncommon for the temperature to be 30 to 35 degrees cooler at the summit than it is at the beach.

In general, November to March marks Hawaii's rainy season. The weather can get gray during this season — but, fortunately, it seldom rains for more than three days in a row. Winter isn't a bad time to go to Hawaii; the sun's just a little less reliable, that's all.

The good news about Hawaii's rainy season is that it's almost never raining *everywhere* on an island, even in winter. So if it's raining on your parade, just get in the car and drive — you'll likely reach a sunny spot in no time. (The south and west coasts are usually your best bet.)

If you want guaranteed sunshine year-round — or, at least as close as you can get to a guarantee — base yourself in one or more of the following regions:

- ✔ Waikiki, on Oahu
- ✔ Maui's south coast (Kihei and Wailea)
- ✔ The Big Island's Kona-Kohala Coast
- ✔ The south and southwest coasts of Kauai (Poipu Beach and Waimea)

Sea Changes

Hawaii's ocean waters stay warm year-round. The average water temperature is a warm 74°F, and reaches a jump-right-in 80° or so in summer.

Wave action, though, varies greatly between winter and summer, and from coast to coast. All of Hawaii's beaches tend to be as placid as lakes in the summer months. In winter, the islands' north-facing beaches are hit with swells and the surf goes wild, especially in places like Oahu's north shore, where daredevil surfers with a death wish hang-ten on monster curls that can reach 50 feet. South-facing beaches, however, like Waikiki, generally remain calm and friendly to swimmers and snorkelers of all ages and abilities throughout winter.

If the waves are too powerful for you, seek calmer conditions by taking a short drive to another beach that's more sheltered. In the island sections later in this book (Parts III through VI), I recommended the best local beaches, including the safest for inexperienced swimmers. When in doubt on where to go, ask one of the staff at your hotel or call the local tourist office for recommendations — and watch for warning flags and posted beach conditions at the beach.

Never turn your back on the ocean when you're at the beach. A big wave can come out of nowhere before you can say aloha. Always watch the surf, even if you're just taking a casual stroll along the shoreline. Also, ocean conditions can change dramatically in a matter of hours — surf that was safe for swimming one day can develop a dangerous undertow the next. Get out of the water when the big swells come.

The Secret of the Seasons

Hawaii's high season is during the winter months, from mid-December through mid-April, when people flee the cold, snow, and gray skies of home for the warm sun and bathing-suit temperatures of Hawaii. During this winter high season, prices go up and resorts are booked to capacity. This is especially true in the last two weeks of December through the first weekend in January (the holiday season); book far in advance for a trip during this period, and expect to pay the highest prices. While not nearly as bad as Christmastime, Easter week can also be crowded, as West Coast families flock to the islands for a few days of sunshine over spring break.

Summer (mid-June through August) is a secondary high season in Hawaii. Since so many families travel over the summer break, you won't find the bargains of spring and fall — but you may still do better on accommodations, airfare, and packages than you will in the winter months.

Hawaii's off-seasons have traditionally been spring (from mid-April to mid-June) and fall (from September to mid-December) — which, paradoxically, also happen to be the best seasons in Hawaii in terms of reliably great weather. Herein lies the secret of the seasons: In spring and fall, hotel rates traditionally drop, package deals abound, airfares are often at their lowest rates of the year (sometimes as cheap as $400 round-trip from the West Coast), and you can expect constantly clear skies and 80° days once you arrive. Still, with a strong economy and so many travelers with money in their pockets these days, hotels no longer empty out so completely in the "off seasons," and deals may not be quite as good as they were a few years back.

Because the weather is relatively constant year round, the decision on when to visit Hawaii is ultimately up to you . It's a good bet that you can arrive at any time of year and enjoy prime island conditions. It really boils down to how much you want to spend, how willing you are to deal with crowds, and what's available.

Avoiding the Crowds

Yes, there are times when coming to Hawaii is simply a bad idea, especially if you're allergic to crowds. At the very least, you should know what you're getting into.

The entire nation of Japan basically shuts down over Golden Week, which falls annually in late April or early May and encompasses three Japanese holidays. During Golden Week, Japanese tourists flock to Hawaii — especially Waikiki. Be sure to book hotels, inter-island air reservations, and car rentals well in advance.

The Big Island's Kona-Kohala Coast fills up during Ironman week (which leads up to the Saturday closest to the full moon in October). Hotels book to capacity, rental cars sell out, and you'll pay top dollar for everything. People flock to Hilo during the Merrie Monarch Hula Festival, the week after Easter; plan well in advance if you're coming for these events.

On Maui, Halloween in Lahaina is a major event; up to 20,000 people come for the festivities, and you need to book a hotel room more than a year in advance. You shouldn't have a problem elsewhere on the island, though. Additionally, more than 30,000 runners descend on Oahu for the week before the Honolulu Marathon (usually the second Sunday in December).

And keep in mind that the islands are at maximum capacity during the Christmas holidays, and Easter week can also be crowded. Stay at home during these seasons if you don't want to fight crowds or pay over-the-top prices.

A Hawaii Calendar of Events

Here's a rundown of the top events that take place annually throughout the Hawaiian Islands. This brief list is merely a microdrop in the bucket, of course; for a complete rundown, as well as the latest events information, point your web browser to www.calendar.gohawaii.com. For details on the events on a given island, your best bet is to contact the local visitors bureau directly; see the Quick Concierge for contact information.

✔ **January through March:** This is Hawaii's prime whale-watching season, when humpback whales — the world's largest mammals — make their way from frigid Alaska to the balmy waters of Hawaii. Because whales prefer water depths of less than 600 feet, these endangered gentle giants come in relatively close to shore. You can see them regulary from the beach in prime season, spouting and spyhopping (peeking above the waterline to "spy" on what's going on). They often prefer the west, or leeward, sides of the islands. Maui is particularly terrific for whale watching, as the giants love to frolic in the channel separating the Valley Isle from Molokai and Lanai.

If you happen to be in the islands during whale season, you won't want to miss seeing these remarkable behemoths. For the best views, take any one of the variety of whale-watching cruises that are offered from each island; I recommend the best later in this book.

✔ **Mid-January:** The annual **Hula Bowl Football All-Star Classic** features America's top college teams competing at Maui's War Memorial Stadium. The all-star event is preceded by **Hula Fest,** a week full of football-oriented fun. Ticket orders start being processed on April 1 for next January's game, so be sure to call ☎ 888-716-4852 or 808-947-4141 well in advance of kick-off time.

✔ **Mid-January:** The **Senior PGA MasterCard Championship,** at the Big Island's Four Seasons Hualalai, is the season-opening competition for golfers who have won a Senior PGA Tour event. A million dollars go to the winner of this prestigous event. Call ☎ 800-417-2770 or 808-325-8000 for exact dates and tickets.

✔ **Mid- or Late January:** The all-day **Ala Wai Challenge** takes place on a Sunday in late January at Ala Wai Park in Waikiki (Oahu). Among the ancient Hawaiian competitions on display are a quarter-mile outrigger canoe race and a tug of war. This is a great place to get a taste of the local culture and hear traditional Hawaiian music. Call ☎ 808-923-1802 for more information and this year's exact date.

✔ **Late January:** The **Annual Senior Skins Game** showcases the big names in golf as they tee up for a chance at $500,000 in prize money. Come to the Mauna Lani Resort to watch; call ☎ 808-885-6655 for dates and tickets.

✔ **Late January through Early February:** Help ring in the **Chinese New Year** in Honolulu, on the island of Oahu. Additional New Year's events include a pageant, a coronation ball, lion dances through the streets of Chinatown, a narcissus and bonsai exhibition, cooking demonstrations, and a festival bazaar. Call ☎ 808-533-3181 for this year's schedule and dates. Additionally, Chinese New Year events usually take place throughout the islands; contact each island's visitors bureau (see the Quick Concierge) for specifics.

✔ **Late January through Early February:** The world's greatest female bodysurfers compete at the birthplace of bodyboarding, the legendary Banzai Pipeline on Oahu's north shore, in the **Extreme Bodyboard Series.** This wave-riding competition is just wild to watch. Call ☎ 808-638-1149 for exact dates.

✔ **First Sunday in February:** The National Football League's best pro players get it on in the **NFL Pro Bowl.** This annual all-star game takes place at Oahu's Aloha Stadium. Call ☎ 808-486-9300 well in advance for ticket information for next year's game. A week's worth of gridiron-oriented fun usually proceeds the big event; call ☎ 808-233-4NFL for a schedule.

✔ **Early February:** Honolulu's most prestigious private school hosts the **Punahou School Carnival,** and it's well worth seeking out. This huge two-day fun fair features everything from high-speed thrill rides to art shows by island artists to traditional Hawaiian food booths. Excellent island-style fun! Call ☎ 808-944-5711 for this year's schedule of events.

✔ **Mid-February:** The Pacific Whale Foundation honors the majestic humpback whale with **Whale Week on Maui,** a full and fun calendar of events that includes a parade, a regatta, and more, plus — in 2001 — the 21st annual Whale Day Celebration on Saturday, February 17th. Call the foundation at ☎ 808-879-8860, or go online to www.pacificwhale.org for all the details.

✔ **Early March:** The annual **Oahu Kite Festival** has been one of Honolulu's most colorful events for more than 40 years. The family fun takes place in Kapiolani Park over two days, usually the first weekend in March, and spectating is absolutely free. Call ☎ 808-735-9059 for this year's date.

✔ **March 17:** All of Honolulu becomes Irish for an evening when the annual **St. Patrick's Day Block Party** takes over downtown. The epicenter of the merriment is the corner of Merchant Street and Nuuanu Avenue. Start the day in Waikiki, where the **St. Patrick's Day Parade** sets the tone starting at noon. Call ☎ 808-734-6900 for this year's exact schedule. On Maui, Kaanapali features its hometown-style parade; call ☎ 808-661-3271 for details.

✔ **Mid-March:** The second humpback-themed celebration of the year rules Maui during **Whalefest,** Lahaina's own weeklong series of special events honoring the island's most high-profile visitors. Call ☎ 888-310-1117 or 808-667-9193 for this year's schedule.

✔ **Mid-March:** Running exactly 26.2 miles from Kahului to Kaanapali, the **Maui Marathon** is regularly named one of the 10 most scenic marathons in North America. The date for 2001 is Sunday, March 18; call ☎ 808-871-6441 or point your Web browser to www.mauimarathon.com for entry information.

✔ **Last week in March:** Events mark the birth of Jonah Kuhio Kalanianaole, born March 26, 1871, who might have been Hawaii's next king had the Hawaiian monarchy not been overthrown in January 1893 and Hawaii annexed to the U.S. (instead, he was elected to Congress in 1902). Kauai celebrates its favorite son with the annual **Prince Kuhio Festival,** which often includes lots of traditional Hawaiian entertainment, food, arts, and crafts. Call ☎ 808-822-5521 for this year's schedule of events.

✔ **Easter Sunday:** People from near and far have been gathering for the **Easter Morning Sunrise Services** at Honolulu's National Cemetery of the Pacific, in Punchbowl Crater, since 1902. Call ☎ **808-566-1430.**

✔ **Week following Easter:** Hawaii's biggest annual cultural event, above all others, is the **Merrie Monarch Hula Festival,** which sweeps the misty city of Hilo, on the Big Island, for a full week in spring, usually the week following Easter Sunday. The island's largest and most prestigious hula festival features four nights of modern and ancient dance in honor of King David Kalakaua, the "merrie monarch" who revived the dance, which had been all but forgotten with the coming of Western ways to the islands. Tickets sell out by late January, so reserve early; some events are free, however, and a limited number of returned tickets may be available at the last minute. Competitions wind down with a festive parade on the final Saturday of the event. Call ☎ **808-935-9168** for details — and plan to stay away from booked-solid Hilo during festival week if you don't plan to participate.

✔ **Mid-April:** The International Pro Windsurfing Meet, known as the **Da Kine Wave Sailing Hawaiian Pro Am,** attracts windsurfers from around the globe to the best windsurfing beach on the planet, Maui's Hookipa Beach. Come and watch, because these daredevils and their colorful sails are quite a sight to see as they pirouette over the wild winter waves. Call ☎ **808-575-9264** for this year's dates.

✔ **May 1:** May Day is **Lei Day** in Hawaii — and cause for big-time rejoicing. Hawaii's most colorful and fragrant holiday is celebrated with lei-making contests, art-and-crafts fairs, and pageants. The crowning event is a big concert by the Brothers Cazimero, kings of the Hawaiian music scene, at the Waikiki Band Shell in Oahu's Kapiolani Park; tickets usually go on sale in early April. Call ☎ **808-547-7393** for Oahu Lei Day events, and ☎ **808-597-1888** for concert information. Additionally, major Lei Day events take place on every island; contact the individual visitors bureaus (see the Quick Concierge) for specifics.

✔ **Mid-May:** Oahu's Polynesian Cultural Center hosts the **World Fire-Knife Dance Competition**, literally the world's hottest competition, in which fire dancers of all ages gather from around the globe to compete for the title of world champion fire-knife dancer. It's all part of the annual **We Are Samoa** festival, celebrated with authentic Samoan food and festivities. Contact the Polynesian Cultural Center at ☎ **800-367-7060** for this year's details, or go online to www.polynesia.com.

✔ **Memorial Day Weekend:** The Valley Isle hosts some of the biggest names in contemporary jazz at the annual star-studded Maui Music Festival, which dominates the Kaanapali resort for the three-day holiday weekend. Order your tickets as far in advance as possible; call ☎ **800-628-4767** or 808-667-2628, or go online to www.mauimusicfestival.com.

✔ **Memorial Day:** There's no better place to honor past war heroes than at the USS *Arizona* Memorial, in Honolulu's Pearl Harbor; call ☎ **808-422-2771** for the program of events.

✔ **Late May through Early June:** The **Hawaiian Airlines OceanFest** takes over Oahu from Waikiki to the north shore. You can watch the excitement as the world's top ocean athletes vie in various ocean competitions — kayaking, lifeguarding, surfskiing, outrigger canoeing, and much more — as part of the Hawaii International Ocean Challenge, with the results broadcast on ESPN. One of the biggest and most exciting events is the **Outrigger's King's Race**, the Ironman of ocean sports competitions, consisting of a one-mile beach run, a three-mile surfski, a one-mile ocean swim, and a one-mile paddleboard — all for a $6,500 cash purse. Opening and closing ceremonies include live entertainment and other festivities. Call ☎ **808-521-4322** for more information and dates, or visit `www.oceanfest.net`.

✔ **June 11 (or nearest weekend):** In honor of the great chief who united the Hawaiian Islands, **King Kamehameha Day** is celebrated as a statewide holiday, with massive floral parades, slack-key guitar concerts, Hawaiian crafts shows, and lots of partying. Contact the individual island visitors bureaus (see the Quick Concierge) for the full calendar of local celebrations.

✔ **Late June through Early July:** See demonstrations of traditional arts-and-craft-making, sample traditional foods, watch Hawaiian royal court living-history reenactments, and even learn to shake your hips to the hula at the **Puuhonua o Honaunau National Historical Park Annual Cultural Festival,** which takes place at Puuhonua o Honaunau — one of Hawaii's most well preserved and fascinating cultural landmarks — on the Big Island's South Kona Coast. Call ☎ **808-328-2288,** or point your Web browser to `www.nps.gov/puho`.

✔ **Late June through Early July:** World-famous winemakers and chefs gather, along with appreciative gourmands, on Maui for the highly acclaimed — and appropriately grand — **Kapalua Wine & Food Symposium,** a bounteous week-long series of wine tastings, cooking demonstrations, and gourmet meals prepared by celebrity chefs. Well worth attending if you fancy yourself a foodie. Call ☎ **808-669-0244,** or visit `www.kapaluamaui.com` and click on "Events" for details.

✔ **July 4:** Each island celebrates **Independence Day** with a variety of star-spangled accompaniments. But the best event of all is **Turtle Independence Day,** at the Big Island's Mauna Lani Bay Hotel, in which scores of three- and four-year-old endangered green sea turtles, all raised in the shelter of the resort's historic fishponds, are released from captivity. Watching their race to the sea is a sight to behold — an epic celebration of freedom. Call the Mauna Lani at ☎ **808-885-6622** or visit `www.maunalani.com` for this year's details.

✔ **Third Weekend in July:** The one-day **Prince Lot Hula Festival,** held annually at Honolulu's Moanalua Gardens, features authentic performances of ancient and modern hula, plus craft demonstrations, traditional island games, live music, and food vendors. This is a wonderful way to discover Hawaii's unique and fascinating culture — and it's absolutely free. Call ☎ **808-839-5334** or visit `www.mgf-hawaii.com` for the exact date and other details.

✔ **Mid- or Late July:** The annual **Hawaii International Jazz Festival** is held at the Hawaii Theater Center in Honolulu. This four-day affair includes evening concerts and daily jam sessions by jazz and blues artists of local, national, and international renown, plus performances by the USC Big Band. Call the theater's box office at ☎ **808-528-0506** for this year's dates and ticket info, or visit www.hawaiijazz.com.

✔ **Late July:** Koloa, the historic town just inland from Poipu Beach, on Kauai's southern coast, celebrates its plantation past with **Koloa Plantation Days,** a week of events that includes a rodeo, a craft fair and block party, luaus, historic walks, and much more. Call ☎ **808-822-0734** for this year's schedule of events.

✔ **Late July through Early August:** Chefs from all the world's sunny climes show off their skills at **Cuisines of the Sun,** a four-day eating and drinking extravaganza — billed as a "Summer Camp for Foodies" — at the Mauna Lani Bay Hotel on the Big Island. The guest-chef roster is always phenomenal. It's a favorite event among return gourmands, so plan well in advance. Call ☎ **888-424-1977** or go online to www.maunalani.com for exact dates and ticket information.

✔ **Late July through Mid-August:** The annual **International Festival of the Pacific** celebrates and showcases Hawaii's varied ethnic cultures. A monthlong slate of events centered in Hilo, on the Big Island, runs the gamut from martial arts and Japanese tea ceremony demonstrations to the A Taste of Hilo food festival. A real pancultural delight. Call ☎ **808-934-0177** for this year's calendar of events.

✔ **Late July through Mid-August:** Hawaii's most prestigious fishing tournament, the **Hawaiian International Billfish Tournament,** takes place in the sportfishing capital of the Pacific: Kailua-Kona, on the Big Island. Watching teams from around the globe show off their monster catches is thrilling. Call ☎ **808-329-6155** or visit www.konabillfish.com for this year's schedule.

✔ **Mid-September:** In the 36-mile race known as the **Haleakala Run to the Sun,** the world's top ultra-marathoners race from sea level to the summit of the 10,000-foot Haleakala crater. It's not for first-time marathoners, needless to say. Call the Valley Island Road Runners Club at ☎ **808-871-6441** for details.

✔ **Mid-September through October:** 'Tis the season in Hawaii for statewide **Aloha Festivals,** conceived to celebrate the venerable Hawaiian custom of *aloha.* Each week from mid-September through October is Aloha Week on a different island, with events running the gamut from parades and royal balls to ethnic days and street festivals. This is serious celebration time. My favorite is always Waikiki's street party, usually the first on the annual calendar. Call ☎ **800-852-7690** or 808-589-1771, or go online to www.alohafestivals.com for a complete schedule of events.

✔ **Early October:** The **Bankoh Hinano Molokai Hoe Outrigger Canoe Race** is the world championship of men's open-ocean outrigger canoe racing. Muscle-bound teams from around the globe start the 41-mile course on Molokai; the best action is at the finish line at Fort DeRussy Park in Waikiki. Call ☎ **808-337-2323** for this year's date and time.

✔ **October:** The world's finest athletes converge on the Big Island's Kona-Kohala Coast every October to run (26.2 miles), swim (2.4 miles), and bike (112 miles) in one of sportsdom's biggest events, the punishing **Ironman Triathlon World Championship.** I'm not suggesting you join in; participate instead by cheering on the contestants along the route. The best place to see the 7 a.m. start is along the seawall on Alii Drive in Kailua-Kona; get there before 5:30 a.m. for a prime spot. Alii Drive is also the best vantage for watching the bike and run portions; park on a side street and walk down to Alii since it's closed to traffic. To watch the finishers come in, line up along Alii Drive from Holualoa Street to the finish at Palani Road and Alii Drive; the winner can come as early as 2:30 p.m., and the course closes at midnight. The Ironman is usually held on the Saturday nearest the full moon; call ☎ 808-329-0063 for this year's date and details. If you're not interested, you may want to avoid the Kona-Kohala Coast while Ironman is in swing.

✔ **Late October through Early November:** The **Aloha Classic World Windsurfing Championships,** the final event in the Pro Boardsailing World Tour, is held at Maui's Hookipa Beach. Don't miss this spectacular event if you're on the island. Call ☎ 808-575-9151 for this year's dates.

✔ **October 31:** Some 20,000 to 30,000 people show up to celebrate **Halloween** in Lahaina, Maui. Front Street is closed off for the costumed revelers. Lahaina is so gung ho on Halloween, in fact, that the party starts the week prior to October 31 with myriad events and costume contests about town. Call ☎ 888-310-1117 or 808-667-9193, or visit www.visitlahaina.com, for this year's program of events.

✔ **Early November:** Hawaii's finest coffee-growing country, the Big Island's Kona Coasts, celebrates the mighty caffeinated bean with the **Kona Coffee Festival.** The weeklong series of events include a bean-picking contest, lei contests, music, a parade, the Miss Kona Coffee pageant, and more. Call ☎ 808-326-7820 for this year's schedule.

✔ **First two weeks in November:** The U.S.'s only statewide film festival, the prestigious **Hawaii International Film Festival** specializes in films from Asia, the Pacific Islands, and North America. The majority of screenings and other events take place on Oahu. Call ☎ 808-528-FILM, or point your browser to www.hiff.org.

✔ **November through December:** The **Vans G-Shock Triple Crown of Surfing Series** is the World Series of professional big-wave surfing. These daredevils will put on a thrill show to end all shows, guaranteed, so don't miss the opportunity to watch. Events are held on the north shores of Oahu and Maui; the wave action determines the schedules. Call ☎ 808-337-2323 for the latest information.

✔ **Early December:** More than 30,000 runners converge annually on Oahu for the **Honolulu Marathon,** one of the largest marathons in the world. Whether you're a potential participant or merely a spectator, call ☎ 808-734-7200 or go online to www.honolulumarathon.org for all the details. If you're not coming to Honolulu specifically to run in, or to watch, the marathon, it's a good idea to avoid Oahu entirely while it's on, because hotels get booked up to capacity and the island is overrun with out-of-towners.

✔ **December 25:** The winner of the PAC 10 plays the winner of the Big 12 in the collegiate football classic known as the **Aloha Bowl,** held at Oahu's Aloha Stadium. Seats are always filled to capacity, so plan well ahead if you wish to attend. Call ☎ **808-947-4141** or go to www.alohabowl.net.

Planning Your Itinerary

As you plan your itinerary, keep the following tips in mind:

✔ **Try to fly directly from the mainland to the island of your choice.** Doing so can save you a two-hour layover in Honolulu and another plane ride on an interisland carrier — a process that can add another four or five hours to your total travel time. Oahu, the Big Island, Maui, and Kauai all receive direct flights from the mainland. However, expect to pay for the privilege of flying direct: Mainland flights to the neighbor islands are often more expensive and less frequent than those that arrive in Honolulu.

✔ **Remember the one week, one island rule of thumb.** Don't try to see all of the islands — or even the four major ones — unless you have a month. About a week per island is the golden planning rule. Otherwise, you'll end up spending your whole vacation in the airport and at the car-rental counter, which would just be a crying shame. For a two-week vacation, three islands is max — and that's only if you're the kind of traveler who can't handle more than three days amid the hustle and bustle of Waikiki.

✔ **If you have two weeks and your heart is set on seeing three islands, consider the following:** Arrive in Honolulu and spend three days seeing the highlights. Then head to Kauai to kick back on the beach for four or five days and recover from the time you spent running around Honolulu. After that, head to the Big Island, which easily has a week's worth of activities to keep you busy.

✔ **Pass on seeing a third island if you're committed to visiting both Oahu and Maui in two weeks.** Believe me, there's more than enough to keep you busy on these two powerhouse islands for two months, much less two weeks.

✔ **Never budget fewer than five days on the Big Island.** The Big Island is the size of Connecticut, and just about everything is located on the island's coastline; therefore, you're going to be spending plenty of time in the car if you mean to see everything. If you book yourself fewer than five days, you'll spend most of your time in the car — which would be a major disappointment on this fabulous island.

✔ **Don't overplan your itinerary or try to do everything.** If relaxing is number one on your agenda, work plenty of do-nothing time into your travel plans. Keep your days loose and go with the flow; don't plan up your time the way you would on a sightseeing tour of Europe. A Hawaii vacation is less about seeing everything and more about letting go with the island flow — and a big part of the experience is just taking things as they come. Don't feel guilty that you're not doing or seeing enough — you do enough the other

50 weeks out of the year, don't you? Trust me — everything you missed the first time around will be waiting for you when you get back.

✔ **Leave at least one day per island to chance.** Don't book a big activity for every day of your vacation. Leave at least one day on each island for whatever strikes your fancy, whether it be sight-seeing or shopping or just sitting on your condo's oceanfront lanai, soaking up a beach read and the laid-back vibe. I can't say it enough: A Hawaii vacation is about leaving the conventions of regular life — including a hardcore commitment to time — behind. Make the most of these few carefree weeks in your life.

✔ **If you're dividing your day between land and sea activities, make mornings your ocean time.** Beaches tend to be less crowded, and the surf and winds tend to be calmer, in the morning hours — especially in winter. Always take the first snorkel and dive cruise of the day, when conditions are calmest and clearest; you'll under-stand why outfitters offer discounts on their afternoon sails.

✔ **Keep an eye on the weather, and plan accordingly.** Say you've planned to see the *Arizona* Memorial at Pearl Harbor on Friday. On Thursday night you're watching the late news before you hit the sack and the local weatherlady tells you that Friday will be a glorious beach day, but to expect rain showers on Saturday. Don't be a slave to your schedule — make the most of that great weather. Move your Pearl Harbor trip to Saturday — and hit the beach first thing Friday morning.

Chapter 3
Planning Your Budget

• •

In This Chapter

▶ Thinking about your major expenses

▶ Using AAA and American Express membership to your advantage

▶ Getting cost-cutting tips

• •

"So, how much is this trip going to cost me, anyway?"

It's a reasonable question, no matter where you fall on the income ladder. Vacation is a considerable endeavor no matter where you go, with costs that can add up before you know it — and, as destinations go, Hawaii is a relatively pricey one. So you'll want to plan ahead to keep your budget on track. I show you how in this chapter, plus I give you tips on ways to save money on major expenses.

Adding up the Costs

The good news is that it's easy to structure a Hawaii trip to suit any budget. Hotels will probably end up being your largest cash outlay; other things, like rental cars, are relatively cheap. Your choice of activities will also determine how much you spend: Relaxing on the beach or taking in Hawaii's natural beauty generally doesn't cost a dime; but guided tours and organized activities — like snorkel trips and helicopter rides during the day, luaus and dinner cruises after dark — can carry heavy price tags. The "Making Dollars and Sense of It" worksheet at the end of this book will help you figure out where your money's going to go and what exactly you can afford to do.

Transportation

The cost of your flight to Hawaii, which will be one of your top two expenses (right up there with hotels), will vary depending on your departure point, and when you travel. Of course, airfares at any time of year are almost impossible to predict and can change at the drop of a hat. Still, to give you an idea of the cost of flying to Hawaii, here's a sampling of potential fares from season to season: If you're going to Hawaii in the off season — say, May or maybe October — you may be able to snag a round-trip ticket for as little as $400 or $500 from San Francisco or Los Angeles, or anywhere from $600 to $900 from the east coast. If you're traveling in the high season (late December to April, or in summer), you'll pay more — probably in the $500 to $800 range from the West Coast, between $700 and $1,400 from back east. But you may still be able to get a decent deal, especially if you consider a package (see "The Ins & Outs of Travel Packages" in Chapter 5). If you're traveling to Hawaii over the Christmas holidays, expect to pay full fare. Also expect to pay more if you're departing from a city that's not a major airline hub.

Interisland flights

If you plan to visit more than one island at any time during your stay, you will need to take an interisland flight. Fares for trips between the islands, which are run through Aloha Airlines and Hawaiian Airlines, average about $96. However, both carriers offer multiflight discounts based on the number of days you're traveling and/or the number of flights you're booking; see "Flying Between the Islands" in Chapter 5 for details.

Car rentals

Rental cars are relatively cheap in the islands. You can often get a compact for as little as $30 to $38 a day, sometimes less if you hit on a bargain or can book a weekly rate. If you need a family-size car, expect to pay more on the order of $40 to $55 per day, depending on where you're staying and the time of year you're booking. Of course, everybody wants a convertible in the islands — so expect to pay upward of $75 a day in season for one (you can sometimes wheel and deal for one at the rental counter in the low season, when business is slower).

Do yourself a favor and book a rental car with unlimited mileage. You'll be doing plenty of driving no matter which island you're on, and you don't want to end up paying for your rental on a per-mile basis. Trust me — you will end up on the short end of this stick. Luckily, most of the major car-rental companies rent on an unlimited-miles basis. Be sure to confirm this policy when you book.

And because you'll probably cover a good deal of ground, don't forget to factor in gas, which at press time was hovering around $2 a gallon (on some islands, it actually crept perilously close to the $2.50 mark!). Also remember to account for any additional insurance costs. Parking, thankfully, is generally free.

You may not have to worry about shopping around or wrangling a lower rate. Often, rental cars and interisland flights are part-and-parcel of a package deal. In many hotel and airline packages, they're thrown in for a nominal fee or for free. See "The Ins and Outs of Travel Packages" in Chapter 5 for more details.

Lodging

Hawaii has a wealth of luxury hotels and resorts, but it also offers plenty of affordable choices — especially on the condo market. Still, while there are decent hotel rooms to be had for $100 or so a night, you really shouldn't expect to pay much less than that. Once you start adding on amenities — kitchenettes, room service, ocean views — expect room rates to climb from there.

 The good news is that you can score very reasonable rates on a per-person basis if you're traveling in a group or with your family. Hawaii boasts lots of apartment-style condos that sleep four or more at very reasonable prices — between $100 and $150 per night on the bottom end, and $200 or more for more luxurious digs. Of course, if you stay at a condo, you'll miss out on resort-style amenities and services — concierge, room service, kids' programs, and the like — but it may be worth it to you to keep your per-night costs down.

 Booking a package deal can be a huge moneysaver when it comes to hotels. For more information on packages, see Chapter 5, "The Pros and Cons of Package Tours."

I've taken care to recommend a range of choices in each of the destinations covered in this book to give you plenty to choose from, no matter what your needs or budget. In the chapters that follow, each hotel, resort, condo, or B&B name is followed by a number of dollar signs, ranging from one ($) to five ($$$$$). Each represents the median price range for a double room per night, as follows:

$	Super-cheap — less than $75 per night
$$	Still affordable — $75 to $150
$$$	Moderate — $150 to $225
$$$$	Expensive but not ridiculous — $225 to $300
$$$$$	Ultra-luxurious — more than $300 per night

 So that there are no unwanted surprises at payment time, be sure to account for the 11.41 percent in taxes that will be added to your final hotel bill when planning your budget.

Dining

Hawaii has become something of a culinary mecca in the last few years, with each island boasting its own slate of top-quality restaurants — often charging top-dollar prices. So think about your bottom line. Many of you, no doubt, look forward to indulging in the island's bounty and won't mind paying for the privilege. But if you'd rather spend your vacation dollars on other activities and attractions, the islands offer plenty of opportunities to dine on the cheap: You can spend as little as $5 to $7 for breakfast (a continental breakfast may even be included in your hotel deal), grab a quick-and-easy lunch for less than $10, and enjoy a casual dinner for $10 to $15 (of course, extra niceties like wine or cocktails will drive up dinner costs).

In the chapters that follow, each restaurant name is followed by a number of dollar signs, ranging from one ($) to five ($$$$$). The dollar signs are meant to give you an idea of what a complete dinner for one person — including appetizer, main course, one drink, tax, and tip — is likely to set you back. The price categories go like this:

$	Cheap eats — less than $15 per person
$$	Still inexpensive — $15 to $25
$$$	Moderate — $25 to $40
$$$$	Pricey — $40 to $70
$$$$$	Ultra-expensive — more than $70 per person

Of course, just about any menu has a range of prices, and the final tally depends on how you order. The wine or bar tab is more likely to raise the tab quicker than anything else.

Restaurant bills can add up fast, so if you'd like to save in this category, I strongly suggest booking a room or condo with kitchen facilities. By preparing a few daytime meals yourself (breakfast, in particular, can be a big money-saver), you'll be in a better position to splurge on a great dinner. Kitchen facilities are a virtual must if you're traveling with kids.

Sightseeing and activities

Here's where the bills can really start to pile up, especially if you're traveling with the family — but it ultimately depends on what you want to do. If you're coming to Hawaii to simply kick back at the beach and leave your mainland worries behind, you won't have to budget much in this category, since going to the beach is free. Even snorkel gear rentals are cheap.

But if you're planning to schedule some organized activities and tours — which I strongly suggest you do — plan ahead to see what your budget can handle, since they can get pricey. Expect to pay about $50 or $70 a head for your average snorkel cruise, and about the same for your average luau. Helicopter rides can easily run up to $100 a head. and you don't need to have the kids in tow to spend a pretty penny. Budget-minded golfers may want to think twice before they tee up — tee times at Hawaii's top courses don't come cheap.

I tell you how much you can expect to pay for activities, entertainment, tee times, admission fees, and the like in the chapters that follow so that you can budget your money realistically.

Shopping and nightlife

These two areas are the most flexible parts of your budget. Shopping is a huge temptation in Hawaii. But if money is an issue, do yourself a favor and bypass the souvenirs.

The islands aren't overloaded with nightlife options; Oahu and Maui are the liveliest in terms of after-dark diversions. It's easy to avoid racking up the bills in these categories if you just don't want to.

What things cost in Hawaii	
An average cup of coffee	$1.25
Compact rental car on Oahu (per day)	$28
Compact rental car on Maui (per day)	$38
All-day ticket aboard the Waikiki Trolley	$18
Admission to the Bishop Museum (Oahu)	$15
Admission to the Maui Ocean Center	$18
Fair Wind snorkel cruise to Kealakekua Bay (Big Island)	$48 to $83
A day at the beach	Free!
Luxury room for two at the Halekulani (Oahu)	$310 to $520
Moderate room for two at the Kaanapali Beach Hotel (Maui)	$170 to $265
Affordable room for two at Ohana/ Best Western Waikiki Tower (Oahu)	$98 to $159
Affordable one-bedroom condo for four at Kahana Sunset (Maui)	$100 to $190
Gourmet dinner for two at Alan Wong's (Oahu)	$150
Oceanfront dinner for two at Hula Grill (Maui)	$70
Casual dinner for two at Norberto's El Cafe (Kauai)	$30
Cheap dinner for two at Bubba Burgers (Maui/Kauai)	$10

Keeping a Lid on Expenses

I don't care how much money you have — nobody wants to spend more than they have to. In this section, I give you some tips on how to avoid spending more of your hard-earned cash than is necessary.

Getting the best airfares

Getting the best fares on both trans-Pacific and interisland air travel is such a huge topic that I've dedicated the better part of a chapter to it. Before you even start scanning for fares, see Chapter 5, "Getting to Hawaii — and Traveling Between the Islands."

How to avoid paying for full-price hotel rooms

Because Hawaii is an enormously popular place to visit these days, and hotel occupancy rates are correspondingly high, the gap between hotels' official "published" (full-price) rates and what you actually pay is narrowing. Still, there are ways for savvy travelers to widen the margin.

The best way to avoid paying the full rack rate when booking your hotel is stunningly simple: Just ask for a cheaper or discounted rate. You may be pleasantly surprised — I've been, many times. But you have to take the initiative and ask, because no one is going to volunteer to save you money.

Here are a few more potentially money-saving tips:

- ✔ **Rates are generally lower in the slower seasons.** The time of year you decide to visit may affect your bargaining power more than anything else. During the peak seasons — basically mid-December through mid-April and summer — when a hotel is booked up, management is less likely to extend discount rates or package deals. In the slower seasons — generally mid-April through mid-June and September through mid-December — when capacity is down, they're often willing to negotiate; in fact, many places drop rates by 10 to 30 percent automatically in the less-busy times of year. If you haven't decided when you want to visit Hawaii yet, see Chapter 2, "Deciding When to Go."

- ✔ **Membership in AAA, AARP, or frequent flyer/traveler programs often qualifies you for discounted rates.** (For details on joining AAA, see "The AAA Advantage" sidebar later in this chapter.) You may also qualify for corporate, student, or senior discounts even if you're not a AARP member (although I highly recommend joining; see "Advice for Seniors" in Chapter 4 for details). Members of the military or those with government jobs may also qualify for price breaks.

- ✔ **Ask about package deals.** Even if you're not traveling on an all-inclusive package (see "The Ins and Outs of Travel Packages" in Chapter 5), you may be able to take advantage of packages offered by hotels, resorts, and condos directly. They often include such value-added extras as a free rental car, champagne and in room breakfast for honeymooners, free spa treatments, discounted tee times, a room upgrade, an extra night thrown in for free (some-times the fifth, sometimes the seventh), or some other freebie. I've found that properties often list these deals on their Web sites, but not always; therefore, you should always ask about any specials the hotel may have.

✔ **Call the hotel direct in addition to going through central reservations.** See which one gives you the better deal. Sometimes the local reservationist knows about packages or special rates, but the hotel may neglect to tell the central booking line.

✔ **Surf the Web to save.** A surprising number of hotels advertise great packages via their Web site, and some even offer Internet-only special rates. In addition to surfing the hotel's individual sites (**Rooms.com** — www.rooms.com — offers one-stop-shopping connections to all of the hotel and resort chains that are represented in Hawaii), you might try using a travel booking site devoted primarily to lodging. Acting much like airline consolidators, these sites can sometimes offer big discounts on rooms. Many of the big players in this field don't offer Hawaii properties, but **Places to Stay** (www.placestostay.com) does. Some of the rates you'll find here aren't any better than what you can get through other channels, but some properties offer special deals (indicated with a cute little gift box) that offer you excellent savings. Another site worth surfing is **TravelWeb** (www.travelweb.com), which focuses on chains such as Hyatt, Hilton, and Best Western. If you'd like a condo, visit the Web site of the **Hawaii Condo Exchange** (wwte.com/condos), which acts as a consolidator for condo properties throughout the islands.

✔ **Ask innkeepers for a break.** Bed-and-breakfasts are generally nonnegotiable on price. Sometimes, however, you can negotiate a discount for longer stays, such as a week or more. You may also be able to score a price break if you're visiting off-season. And some do offer AAA and senior discounts. Remember — it never hurts to ask, politely.

✔ **Look for price breaks and value-added extras when booking condos.** Condos are usually pretty flexible on rates. They tend to offer discounts on multi-night stays, and many throw in a free rental car to sweeten the deal. Some condo properties have units handled by multiple management companies; if that's the case, price through both companies and see where you get the better deal.

✔ **Check the "Deals" section in the hotel listings in this book.** I've taken care to note what kind of discounts tend to be available at each resort, hotel, condo property, and B&B I've included in these pages. I can't guarantee what the rates will be when you reserve, of course, but these tips should give you a heads up on the kinds of special deals or discounted rates on offer.

Other tips for cutting costs

Here are a few more useful tips:

- ✔ **Consult a reliable travel agent.** A travel agent can often negotiate a better price with certain hotels and assemble a better-value complete travel package than you can get on your own. In fact, in a recent *Condé Nast Traveler* investigation, travel agents could always price out Hawaii resort vacations more cheaply than any other outlet (including airline packagers). Even if you book your own airfare, you may want to contact a travel agent to price out your hotel. On the other hand, hotels, condos, and even B&Bs are sometimes willing to discount your rate as much as 30 percent — the amount they'd otherwise pay an agent in commissions — if you book direct. For more advice on the pros and cons of using a professional go-between, see "Working with a Travel Agent" in Chapter 5.

- ✔ **If you're an American Express cardholder, sign up to receive AmEx-only special offers.** American Express offers cardholders a surprisingly good array of discounts at local and national vendors via its "Offer Zone" program (previously called "Online Extras"). You can receive discounts — often 20 percent — from airlines, hotel chains, rental-car companies, restaurants, and shops throughout the country (even in your hometown), as well as with a good number of online merchants, and participants change constantly. At press time, the number of local Hawaii merchants participating in the program was minimal, but the national offers — particularly those from car companies like Avis and hotel chains like Starwood — could be extremely beneficial to Hawaii visitors. Be sure to check the expiration dates as well as the terms and conditions carefully. Note that some offers require you to register your AmEx card with the Offer Zone program to qualify. Sign up at www.americanexpress.com; click on "Offer Zone" on the home page.

- ✔ **Book your rental car at weekly rates when possible.** Several major rental firms let you rent a car on one island, turn it in when you're done there, fly to another island, and pick up a new car under the same contract. This way, if you go to Oahu for four days and Kauai for three, you pay for one week at the cheaper weekly rate rather than four times the daily rate on Oahu and three times the daily rate on Maui. See "Arranging for Rental Cars" in Chapter 6 for details on this and other money-saving tips.

- ✔ **Reserve a hotel room with a kitchenette or a condo with a full kitchen and do your own cooking.** You may miss the pampering that room service provides, but you can save lots of money. Even if you only prepare breakfast and an occasional picnic lunch in the kitchen, you still save significantly in the long run. Plus, if the beach is right outside your door, you won't ever have to leave it to go on restaurant runs.

✔ **Skip the ocean views, or stay away from the ocean altogether.**
Being steps away from the surf is wonderful, but you'll pay through
the nose for the privilege: Ocean-view rooms are the most expensive rooms in any hotel, especially those on the upper floors.
Mountain or garden views are usually much cheaper — and you
probably don't plan on hanging out in your room much, anyway.
A stay in a hotel that is located a few blocks from the beach, especially in Waikiki, can be even cheaper.

✔ **Ask if the kids can stay in your room.** Or, better yet, book a
condo with a sleeper sofa in the living room or a separate bedroom. A room with two double beds usually doesn't cost any more
than one with a king-size bed, and most hotels don't charge an
extra-person rate if the additional person is a kid. If that's a bit too
much togetherness for you, book one of the many one-, two-, or
three-bedroom condos that are available throughout the islands.
These full apartments are often no more expensive than your standard hotel room — and they're always cheaper than having to
book two or more hotel rooms. What's more, they solve the expensive eating-out-at-every-meal problem, too.

✔ **Remember: It doesn't take much luxury to make Hawaii feel like
paradise.** To find true Hawaii happiness, the rule is always this:
The simpler, the better. You won't need 27-inch TVs, 24-hour butler
service, or a telephone in the bathroom to be happy here. So when
reserving your accommodations, don't overdo it by booking a
place that taxes your budget too much. Save that extra dough for
having fun!

✔ **Order a Hawaii Entertainment Book.** This jam-packed discount
book bursts with hundreds of coupons offering 20 to 50 percent
off at selected hotels, restaurants, tour and outdoor-activity operators, attractions, live performances, and more. It's especially
good if you're spending a good amount of time in Waikiki
(although discounts are available on all the major islands). You
can order the $30 book by calling ☎ **800-933-2605,** or by going
online to www.entertainment.com, where you can preview the
list of participating vendors before you buy.

✔ **Skip the souvenirs.** I've heard it more than once: "That whale
print that looked so right in the art gallery was all wrong back in
my living room in Cincinnati." Spend your money on memories,
not tchotckes.

✔ **Look out for the Bargain Alert icon as you read this book.** This
icon will alert you to money-saving opportunities and especially
good values as you travel throughout Hawaii.

The AAA Advantage

If you aren't already a member, consider taking a few minutes to join the American Automobile Association (AAA) before you launch your Hawaii vacation. In addition to providing you with a wealth of trip-planning services, membership can save you big bucks on hotel rates, car rentals, interisland airfares, and even admission to attractions in Hawaii. The AAA Travel Agency will help you book air, hotel, and car arrangements as well as all-inclusive tour packages to Hawaii. Membership in AAA can also give you a full 25 percent savings on interisland flights with Aloha Airlines and let you qualify for hotel discounts of 10 percent or more. Discounts and benefits at 3,000 attractions and restaurants and 44,000 retail locations nationwide are available through AAA's Show Your Card and Save program. And don't forget the free maps — they are comprehensive, indispensable, and absolutely free to members. I hate to sound like a shill, but you really can't go wrong with AAA. Whether it's a discount at an Outrigger hotel or a stress-relieving flat-tire fix, membership will pay itself back before you know it. Annual membership fees vary slightly from region to region, but you can expect to spend around $55 per individual (primary member) and $25 to $30 for each additional family member.

To find the AAA office nearest you, look in the phone book under "AAA" or log onto www.aaa.com, where you can link up to your regional club's home page once you enter your home zip code. You can even get instant membership by calling the national 24-hour emergency roadside service number (☎ 800-AAA-HELP), which can connect you to any regional membership department during expanded business hours (only roadside assistance operates 24 hours a day). If you're a resident of Canada, similar services (plus reciprocal benefits with AAA) are offered by the **Canadian Automobile Association** (www.caa.com).

Once you're in Hawaii, the local office is in Honolulu at 1270 Ala Moana Boulevard, between Piikoi Street and Ward Centre (☎ 800-736-2886 or 808-593-2221; Internet: www.aaa-hawaii.com). The office is open Monday through Wednesday and Friday from 9 a.m. to 5 p.m., Thursday from 9 a.m. to 7 p.m., and Saturday from 9 a.m. to 2 p.m.

Chapter 4

Planning Ahead for Special Travel Needs

*T*ravelers don't come in a standard package, of course — they come in all ages, sizes, and configurations. You may want to know: How welcoming will Hawaii be to me and . . . (pick one or more) a) my kids? b) my senior status? c) my disability? d) my same-sex partner? If so, you've come to the right place. This is also the chapter where I tell you the ins and outs of tying the knot in the romantic islands of Hawaii.

Traveling with Children

Hawaii is the perfect *ohana* (family) vacation destination. You and the *keikis* (kids) will love the beaches and the wealth of kid-friendly activities. Families are especially prevalent in the islands in the school-free summer months (although that pattern is changing a bit as more and more schools shift to year-round calendars with non-traditional breaks). Families with kids are also a major presence at holiday time and during the spring break season.

Most hotels and condo complexes, from luxury to budget, welcome the entire family. Virtually all of the larger hotels and resorts have great supervised programs for kids 12 and under — which means that you, mom and dad, can have plenty of relaxation time to yourselves as well as playtime with the kids. Most hotels can also refer you to reliable babysitters if you want a night on the town sans the youngsters.

By Hawaii state law, hotels can only accept children between the ages of 5 and 12 into their supervised activity programs.

Condos are particularly suitable for families who'd like lots of living space in which to spread out as well as cooking facilities for preparing meals. They won't have the kinds of facilities, like kids' activities programs, that the resorts will, however.

If you don't want to cart your own kid stuff across the ocean, **Baby's Away** (www.babysaway.com) rents car seats, cribs, strollers (including jogging strollers), high chairs, playpens, room monitors, and even toys on Maui (☎ **800-942-9030**), the Big Island (☎ **800-931-9030**), and Kauai (☎ **800-996-9030**). Give them a call and they'll deliver whatever you need to wherever you're staying and pick it up when you're done; I suggest arranging your rentals before you leave home to ensure availability. On Oahu, call **Dyans Rentals** (☎ **808-845-2080**).

The following are excellent resources for general advice on family travel:

- ✔ **BabyCenter** (www.babycenter.com/travel) has terrific recommendations for planning baby's first trip, and even on traveling while pregnant.

- ✔ **Family Travel Files** (www.familytravelfiles.com) is a comprehensive Web site dedicated to family travel. Not only will you find general advice and destination-specific recommendations, but you can also sign up to receive their regular free e-zine, which comes packed with ideas, tips, and current travel deals targeted to families.

- ✔ **Family.com** (www.family.com), part of the ABC/Disney Go network, features a great travel page with both general and destination-specific travel advice.

- ✔ **Family Travel Times** is an excellent bimonthly newsletter covering all aspects of family travel. Subscriptions are $39 a year; subscribe by calling ☎ **888-822-4388** or 212-477-5524. You can also peruse back issues and subscribe to an online version of the newsletter at www.familytraveltimes.com.

Here are a few tips for family travel-planning:

- ✔ **Don't try to do too much.** I can't say this too strongly. You'll all consider it the trip from hell if you spend too much time in the car or on interisland flights.

- ✔ **Take it slow at the start.** Give the entire family time to adjust to a new time zone, and just being on the road. The best way to do this is to budget a few days in your initial destination that don't require strict itineraries or lots of moving around.

- ✔ **Look for the Kid Friendly icon as you flip through this book.** I've used it to highlight hotels, restaurants, and attractions that are particularly welcoming to families traveling with kids. Zeroing in on these listings will help you plan your trip more efficiently.

✔ **Book some private time for mom and dad.** Most hotels are prepared to hook you up with a reliable babysitter that can entertain your kids while you enjoy a romantic dinner for two or another adults-only activity. To avoid disappointment, ask about babysitting when you reserve. Local visitors bureaus can also usually recommend licensed and bonded babysitting services in their area; see the Quick Concierge for contact info.

✔ **Bring along a few comforts from home.** Pack a few easy-to-carry books, games, and toys to occupy the kids on the occasional rainy day or during a few hours of travel or downtime. A well-loved stuffed animal will make an unfamiliar bed feel more like home. Tapes are great for entertaining the family in the room or car (many hotel rooms, condos, and even rental cars have CD players these days).

Advice for Seniors

One of the many benefits of getting older is that travel often costs less. Many airlines and package-tour operators give discounted rates to senior travelers. Discounts for seniors are also available at almost all of Hawaii's major attractions, and occasionally at hotels and restaurants. The statewide Outrigger and Ohana hotel chains, for example, offer all travelers over age 50 a 20 percent discount off regular published rates. So, when making reservations or buying tickets, always ask about senior discounts; keep in mind, though, that the minimum age requirement can vary between 50 and 65 (it's usually between 55 and 65). And always carry an ID card with you, especially if you've kept your youthful glow.

If you're not a member of **AARP (American Association of Retired Persons),** 601 E St. NW, Washington, DC 20049 (☎ **800-424-3410,** 800-303-4222, or 202-434-AARP; Internet: www.aarp.org), I recommend that you join. Members qualify for discounts of up to 25 percent on airfares, hotels, car rentals, Gray Line sightseeing tours, and vacation packages. Membership also includes *Modern Maturity* magazine, a monthly newsletter, special rates on insurance, mutual funds, prescriptions, vision care, and much, much more. For just $8 a year, with all the associated benefits, you can't afford *not* to sign up for membership.

Mature Outlook, P.O. Box 9390, Des Moines, IA 50322 (☎ **800-336-6330**), is an organization similar to AARP. It offers discounts on car rentals and hotel stays at many Holiday Inns, Howard Johnsons, and Best Westerns. The $19.95 annual membership fee also gets you $200 in Sears coupons and a magazine.

The Book of Deals offers over 1,000 senior discounts on airlines, lodging, tours, and attractions around the country; it's available for $9.95 by calling ☎ **800-460-6676**.

Another helpful publication is *101 Tips for the Mature Traveler,* available from **Grand Circle Travel,** 347 Congress St., Suite 3A, Boston, MA 02210 (☎ **800-221-2610;** Internet: www.gct.com). Grand Circle Travel is one of the hundreds of travel agencies that specialize in vacations for seniors, including trips to Hawaii. But beware: Many of these outfits are of the tour-bus variety, with free trips thrown in for those who organize groups of 20 or more. If you're more the independent type, a general business travel agent may be more for you.

Seniors 62 or older who want to visit Hawaii's national parks — including Hawaii Volcanoes National Park and Puuhonua o Honaunau National Historical Park on the Big Island, and Haleakala National Park on Maui — can save sightseeing dollars by picking up a Golden Age Passport from any national park, recreation area, or monument. This lifetime pass has a one-time fee of $10 and provides free admission to all of the parks in the National Park system, plus 50 percent savings on camping and recreation fees. You can get one at any park entrance as long as you have a proof-of-age ID on hand.

Advice for Travelers with Disabilities

These days, a disability shouldn't stop anyone from traveling. The Americans with Disabilities Act requires that all public buildings be wheelchair-accessible and have accessible rest rooms. Hawaii is very friendly to disabled travelers. The city of Honolulu alone has more than 2,000 ramped curbs, and most hotels throughout the islands are on the newer side and boast wheelchair ramps, extra-wide doorways and halls, and dedicated disabled-accessible rooms with extra-large bathrooms, low-set fixtures, and/or fire-alarm systems adapted for deaf travelers.

Your best bet is to contact the local visitors bureaus for the islands you're interested in visiting. They can provide you with all the specifics on accessibility in their locale; see the Quick Concierge for contact info.

The following are excellent resources for information on accessible travel:

✔ Both **Moss Rehab ResourceNet** (www.mossresourcenet.org) and **Access-Able Travel Source** (☎ 303-232-2979; Internet: www.access-able.com) are comprehensive resources for disabled travelers. Both sites feature links to travel agents who specialize in planning accessible trips to Hawaii. Access-Able's user-friendly site also features relay and voice numbers for hotels, airlines, and car-rental companies, plus links to accessible accommodations, attractions, transportation, tours, and local medical resources and equipment repairers throughout Hawaii, making this an invaluable resource.

✔ You can join the **Society for the Advancement of Travelers with Handicaps (SATH)**, 347 Fifth Avenue Suite 610, New York, NY 10016 (☎ 212-447-7284; Internet: www.sath.org), to gain access to their vast network of travel connections. They provide information sheets on destinations and referrals to tour operators that specialize in accessible travel. Their quarterly magazine, *Open World*, is full of good information and resources.

✔ An excellent source for trip-planning assistance is **Access Aloha Travel** (☎ **800-480-1143** or 808-545-1143; Internet: www.alohaaccesstravel.com). This Hawaii-based travel agency has been planning accessible trips for disabled travelers for more than 25 years — and donates half of its profits to the disabled community.

✔ The **Hawaii Services on Deafness** (☎ **808-926-4763** voice and TTY; Internet: www.hsod.org) can provide aid and advice to hearing-impaired travelers, including sign-language interpreters in emergency situations.

✔ Vision-impaired travelers who use a seeing-eye dog can usually bypass Hawaii's animal quarantine rules. For specifics, call **Animal Quarantine** at ☎ **808-483-7151**. Contact the **American Foundation for the Blind,** 11 Penn Plaza, Suite 300, New York, NY 10001; ☎ **800-232-5463;** Internet: www.afb.org), for further travel information.

I highly recommend procuring a copy of the *Aloha Guide to Accessibility.* Part one of three can be found online at www.state.hi.us/health/cpd/cpdalmnu.htm; the full set can be ordered online for $15. For further information or to order a copy by phone, contact the Disability and Communication Access Board at ☎ **808-586-8121,** or the Hawaii Centers for Independent Living at ☎ **808-522-5400.**

Before you book any hotel room, always ask lots of questions based on your needs. Once you arrive, call restaurants, attractions, and theaters to make sure they are fully accessible.

Consider the following sources for getting around, either on your own or with assistance:

✔ Many of the big car-rental companies — including **Avis** (☎ **800-230-4898;** Internet: www.avis.com), **Hertz** (☎ **800-654-3131;** Internet: www.hertz.com), and **National** (☎ **800-227-7368;** Internet: www.nationalcar.com) — rent hand-controlled cars for disabled drivers at Hawaii's major airports. At least 48 to 72 hours advance notice is a must, but do yourself a favor and book further in advance to guarantee availability.

✔ **Wheelchair Getaways of Hawaii** (☎ **800-638-1912;** Internet: www.wheelchairgetaways.com) rents full-size vans and minivans with wheelchair lifts, ramps, hand controls, and/or other features for disabled travelers; call well in advance for exact availability.

✔ **Handicabs of the Pacific** (☎ **808-524-3866**) offers taxi services and tours for wheelchair-bound travelers around Honolulu and the rest of Oahu. Their air-conditioned vehicles are specially equipped with ramps and wheelchair lock-downs.

✔ **Accessible Vans of Hawaii** (☎ **800-303-3750** or 808-871-7785; Internet: www.accessiblevanshawaii.com) has wheelchair-accessible vans for rent on Oahu, Maui, Kauai, and Kona. They can also help arrange accessible accommodations and recommend accessible activities, sightseeing, restaurants, medical equipment rentals, and personal care attendants at no additional charge to you.

Advice for Gay and Lesbian Travelers

Hawaii is extremely popular with same-sex couples due to its long-standing reputation for welcoming all groups.

If you want help planning your trip, **IGLTA,** the **International Gay & Lesbian Travel Association** (☎ 800-448-8550 or 954-776-2626; Internet: www.iglta.org), is your best source. IGLTA can link you up with the appropriate gay-friendly service organization or tour specialist; the organization also offers quarterly newsletters and a membership directory that's updated quarterly. Members are kept informed of gay and gay-friendly hoteliers, tour operators, and airline and cruise-line representatives. The IGLTA site will link you to other useful sites like **Gay Wired** (www.gaywired.com), **Gay.com** (www.gay.com), **Planet Out** (www.planetout.com), and other resources that can help you plan your Hawaii vacation.

If you want assistance in planning a gay-friendly Hawaiian holiday, **Pacific Ocean Holidays** (☎ 800-735-6600 or 808-923-2400; Internet: www.gayhawaii.com) is your best resource. They can help you arrange a good-value trip that features either gay-friendly hotels serving the general public or those that serve a predominately gay clientele (your choice); you can even book your entire vacation online. Even if you don't want help planning your trip, you'll find the Web site to be an invaluable resource. Their *Pocket Guide to Hawaii: A Guide for Gay Visitors & Kamaaina* (locals) is a terrific community resource directory and guide to gay-owned and gay-friendly businesses throughout Hawaii. You can find it on the Web site or order a hard copy of the most current issue for $5 via mail order; write P.O. Box 88245, Dept. PGO, Honolulu, HI 96830.

Rainbow Handbook Hawaii, by Big Island resident Matthew Link, is an excellent source for gay and lesbian travelers. To order a copy, call ☎ 800-260-5528 or point your Web browser to www.rainbowhandbook.com.

Out and About (☎ 800-929-2268 or 212-645-6922; Internet: www.outandabout.com) has been hailed for its "straight" reporting about gay travel. It offers a monthly newsletter packed with good information on the global gay and lesbian scene. Out and About's guidebooks are available at most major bookstores, but the Web site alone is a first-rate resource.

The **Gay and Lesbian Community Center**, 2424 S. Beretania Avenue, in Honolulu (☎ 808-951-7000), offers referrals for nearly every kind of service you might need. Another great helpline and referral resource for gay-friendly businesses is the Gay and Lesbian Education and Advocacy Foundation's **Gay Community Resource Directory;** call ☎ 808-532-9000 on Oahu, ☎ 808-244-4566 on Maui, ☎ 808-823-6248 on Kauai. You'll also find good information on GLEA's Web site at www.hawaiigaymarriage.com.

As you probably know, Vermont beat Hawaii to the altar in the same-sex marriage debate. As of December 1999, this issue was tabled by the Hawaii Supreme Court. For the latest information, visit GLEA's Web site (above) or point your browser to www.hawaiilawyer.com/same_sex/samesex.htm.

Advice for Foreign Visitors

The U.S. State Department has a **Visa Waiver Pilot Program** allowing citizens of about 30 countries — including Australia, New Zealand, and the United Kingdom — to enter the U.S. without a visa for stays of up to 90 days. Citizens of these countries need only a valid passport and a round-trip air ticket upon arrival.

If you're a citizen of a country not included in the Waiver Program, you must have both a valid passport that expires at least six months later than the scheduled end of your visit to the U.S.; and a tourist visa, which you can get without charge from any U.S. consulate.

For a quick and easy update on current passport and visa issues, plug in to the U.S. State Department's Internet site at www.state.gov. Further information is available from any U.S. embassy or consulate. Always check for the latest updates before you leave home.

You are not allowed to bring foodstuffs (particularly fruit, cooked meats, and canned goods) and plants into the U.S. You may bring in or take out up to $10,000 in U.S. or foreign currency with no formalities; larger sums must be declared to U.S. Customs on entering or leaving. For more information regarding U.S. Customs, call your nearest U.S. embassy or consulate, or contact **U.S. Customs** at ☎ **202-927-1770** or on the Net at www.customs.ustreas.gov.

Foreign driver's licenses are mostly recognized in the U.S., although you may want to get an international driver's license if your home license is not written in English.

1 Do! 1 Do! Planning a Hawaiian Wedding

Hawaii is the perfect place to get married — which is why so many couples from around the country, and the world, tie the knot here every year. What better place to do the official deed? The honeymoon begins even before the ceremony does, and your friends and family will need little prompting to attend.

For a rundown of the legalities, contact the **Honolulu Marriage License Office,** State Department of Health Building, 1250 Punchbowl Street, Honolulu, HI 96813 (☎ **808-586-4545** or 808-586-4544). Or visit the government Web site at www.hawaii.gov/doh and click on Vital Records, where you'll find all the details, including a downloadable license form.

A marriage license costs $50 and is good for 30 days from the date of issue. Both parties must be at least 18 years of age (16- and 17-year-olds must have written consent of both parents, legal guardian, or family court) and can't be more closely related than first cousins. You'll need a photo ID, such as a driver's license; a birth certificate is only necessary if you're 18 or under. No blood tests, citizenship, or residency minimum is required.

Using a wedding planner or coordinator

Wedding planning is a thriving industry in Hawaii, so you should have no problem finding assistance no matter what kind of wedding you desire, whether it be a huge formal affair at a luxury resort or an informal beachside ceremony.

Many wedding planners are marriage license agents themselves, so not only can they take care of the legalities for you with only minimal effort on your part, but they can arrange everything else too, from providing an officiant to ordering flowers. A wedding planner can cost from $500 and up, depending on how involved you want her to be and what kind of wedding you want.

Your best bet for finding a reputable wedding planner is to choose one endorsed by the **Hawaii Visitors and Convention Bureau**, which offers a complete list of wedding planners to suit any budget, with links, on their Web site; go to www.gohawaii.com and click on Weddings & Honeymoons. You can also call them for recommendations at ☎ **800-GO-HAWAII**, or — even better — contact the individual island bureaus for local recommendations; see the Quick Concierge for contact information.

In addition, virtually all of the big resorts I recommend in the hotel chapters in Parts III through VI employ full-time wedding coordinators. Arranging your nuptials directly through a resort may be pricey, but it's a relatively worry-free option — these women (they usually are) are experts, they'll take all the pesky little details off of your shoulders, and they'll usually offer the whole event to you as a pay-one-price wedding package, including accommodations. What's more, the hotels generally offer prime locations for both the ceremony and reception, whether it's for two or 200 guests.

Great choices include:

- ✔ The Halekulani, the Royal Hawaiian, the Sheraton Moana Surfrider, and the Kahala Mandarin Oriental on Oahu (see Chapter 7).
- ✔ The Four Seasons Maui, the Grand Wailea, the Kea Lani, and the Ritz-Carlton on Maui (see Chapter 11).

✔ The Four Seasons Hualalai, Kona Village, the Mauna Lani, and the Orchid at Mauna Lani on the Big Island (see Chapter 15).

✔ The Hyatt Regency Kauai and the Princeville Hotel on Kauai (see Chapter 19).

Keep in mind that more affordable hotels and condos, even some B&Bs, can often recommend wedding coordinators that have a proven track record with them. Maui's Kaanapali Beach Hotel, for example, makes a great affordable option (see Chapter 11). The setting is magical, the hotel works with a very reliable local planner, and the on-site food-and-beverage director can arrange a pleasing reception. On the Big Island, Horizon Guest House (see Chapter 15) makes a wonderful setting for a small wedding, and Clem Classen, Horizon's thoughtful and meticulous innkeeper, will go out of his way to work with you and make sure everything is perfect for your big day. These are just a few suggestions; don't hesitate to contact any property that strikes your fancy; most have wedding experience or can offer recommendations.

Do-it-yourself planning

Once you get to Hawaii, you and your intended must go together to the marriage license agent to get the license (bring cash). You can either go to the nearest Department of Health office (see www.hawaii.gov/doh for locations), or the main Honolulu office can direct you to a marriage license agent (basically, a local official who helps you wrap up the legalities) closest to where you'll be staying. These local agents can refer you to someone who's licensed by the state of Hawaii to perform the ceremony, whether you're looking for an officiant of a certain denomination or justice of the peace. They also usually know great places to have the ceremony for free or a nominal fee.

Some marriage licensing agents are state employees, and under law they can't recommend anyone with a religious affiliation — they can only give you phone numbers for local judges to perform the ceremony. Ask first what their limitations are if it matters to you.

For those of you interested in arranging a ceremony at a church, check the Yellow Pages or inquire with the visitors bureau to locate an appropriate venue.

You can have a ceremony at any state or county beach or park for free, but keep in mind that you'll be sharing the site with the general public. Here are some romantic spots you might consider:

✔ **Oahu:** Waikiki's **Kapiolani Park**, on Kalakaua Avenue, is ideal at sunset. You can take gorgeous wedding photos with Waikiki Beach in the background, then turn around and take another photo with Diamond Head as your backdrop. I also adore **Lanikai Beach,** on the lush and gorgeous windward side; tucked away in a residential neighborhood, it's usually quiet and crowd-free (weekdays will be best if you want the sand to yourself). See Chapter 10.

✔ **Maui:** For a genuine Hawaiian experience, get married at **Keawali Congregational Church** (☎ 808-879-5557), a vintage 1831 ocean-front coral-block church in picturesque Makena. The gorgeous grounds — with palm trees, ti leaves, and exotic tropical flowers — make a perfect backdrop for your wedding photo. Another great site is **D.T. Fleming Beach Park,** just north of Kapalua in West Maui; this crescent-shaped beach is generally empty on weekdays, so you can enjoy a quiet wedding on the beautiful beach as sailboats skim along offshore.

✔ **Big Island:** If you picture yourself getting married on a long, white-sand beach with gorgeous, emerald-green waves rolling in, **Hapuna Beach State Park** is the spot for you. On the mistier side of the island, along bayfront Banyan Drive in romantic Hilo, is **Liluokalani Gardens,** the largest formal Japanese garden this side of Tokyo. This postcard-pretty park has a dozen different areas that are ideal for a tropical ceremony, and the half-moon bridge is a great spot for wedding photos. See Chapter 18.

✔ **Kauai:** One of the most dramatic spots in all of Hawaii is the north shore's **Hanalei Beach,** with gorgeous, green Bali Hai-like cliffs in the background. (Remember *South Pacific?* Filmed here!) For those who don't mind spending a little money for a bit more privacy, the extraordinary **Allerton Gardens** (☎ 808-742-2623; Internet: www.ntbg.org), on the south shore, is home to some prime examples of formal landscape gardening that would have made William Randolph Hearst turn green with envy. Perfect for a wedding of any scope. See Chapter 22.

Part II
Ironing Out the Details

The 5th Wave   By Rich Tennant

HAWAIIAN RESORT ACTIVITY TO AVOID

SWIM WITH THE GIANT SQUID

SWIM WITH THE MORAY EELS

SWIM WITH THE JELLYFISH

SWIM WITH THE OCTOPUS

"SINCE WE LOST THE DOLPHINS, BUSINESS HASN'T BEEN QUITE THE SAME."

In this part . . .

The information you find in these two chapters will make the nitty-gritty details of planning your trip to Hawaii as painless as possible. I talk about the various ways to book a trip to and around the islands, and I help you gather all the loose ends together into one organized bunch.

Chapter 5

Getting to Hawaii and Traveling Between the Islands

• •

In This Chapter

▶ Making your own travel plans versus using a travel agent

▶ Taking advantage of all-inclusive package deals

▶ Getting the best airfares

▶ Traveling from island to island on interisland carriers

▶ Figuring out what kind of accommodations are right for you

• •

*G*etting there may not *really* be half the fun, but it's a necessary step — and a big part of the planning process. Should you use a travel agent, or go the independent route? Should you reserve a package deal, or book the elements of your vacation separately?

In this chapter, I give you all the information you need to make the decision that's right for you.

Working with a Travel Agent

Any travel agent can help you find a bargain airfare, hotel, or rental car; in fact, in a recent *Condé Nast Traveler* investigation, travel agents could invariably put together a complete travel package at a better price than anybody else. (*Condé Nast* did, however, research exclusively luxury vacations, which may have tainted the results, since travel agents often have the most favorable arrangements with luxury hotels.)

A good travel agent will save you money, yes, but a *really* good travel agent will go the extra mile and stop you from ruining your vacation by trying to save a few dollars. The best travel agent to use for booking your Hawaii vacation is one who is well versed in the islands. He or she can knowledgeably advise you on how you should budget and divide your time in Hawaii, find you affordable trans-pacific flights that don't require excessive plane changes, get you a better hotel room than you can find on your own for about the same price, arrange for competitively priced rental cars, and even give recommendations on activities and restaurants.

To really maximize your time with a travel agent, you need to do some research first:

- ✓ **Read up on your destination.** Peruse the pages that follow and decide which islands you'd like to visit. Pick out accommodations and attractions that you think you'll like.

- ✓ **Read some more.** If you want even more recommendations, check out *Frommer's Hawaii*. Also published by IDG Books Worldwide, Inc., *Frommer's Hawaii* is a comprehensive guidebook that goes beyond the best sites to include a wide variety of information on the islands.

- ✓ **Check prices on the Internet.** This will give you a ballpark sense of airline, car-rental, and hotel costs.

Once you've done a bit of research and familiarized yourself with what's out there, take your guidebook and Web information to a travel agent and ask him or her to make the arrangements for you. Because they can access more resources than even the most complete travel site, travel agents should be able to get you a better price than you can get yourself. They can also issue your tickets and vouchers right on the spot. If they can't get you into the hotel of your choice, they can recommend an alternative, and you can look for an objective review in your guidebook.

Travel agents usually work on commission. However, it is the responsibility of the airlines, accommodations, and tour companies to pay these commissions, not the consumer. Sounds great, right? Unfortunately, some unscrupulous travel agents will try to persuade you to book the vacations that reward them the most money in commissions. What's more, over the past few years, some airlines and resorts have begun limiting or even eliminating travel-agent commissions. Consequently, many agents don't bother booking certain services unless you specifically ask for them. Beware if you're led down a path that doesn't seem to suit you; simply move on to another agent whose first priority is to meet your needs and desires.

The best way to find a good travel agent is the same way you locate a good plumber or mechanic or doctor — through word of mouth. Your best bet is to use an agent that already has a proven track record with a friend or family member; ask around for referrals. Or, if you're pleased with the service that you get from the agency that books business travel in your workplace, ask them if they book personal travel as well; many do.

If you aren't already a member, consider joining the American Automobile Association (AAA), which will give you access to the AAA Travel Agency. It's a full-service agency, with experienced travel agents who can book air, hotel, and car arrangements as well as comprehensive packages. And they'll always tell you when a AAA member discount is available. For details, see "The AAA Advantage" in Chapter 3. American Express members have access to the American Express Travel Service; to locate the office (or official travel-agent representative) nearest you, call ☎ 800-297-3429, or go online to www.americanexpress.com and click on Find a Travel Service Location. You can also use the site's online locator to locate an agent that specializes in Hawaii travel.

Buying Your Vacation as a Pay-One-Price Package Deal

Comprehensive, pay-one-price travel packages are often the smart way to go when booking your Hawaii vacation.

Besides the convenience of having all of your travel needs taken care of at once, a package can often save you lots of money. In many cases, a package that includes trans-pacific and interisland airfares, hotel, and rental car will cost less than the hotel alone if you booked it yourself. Tour operators can sell these packages so cheaply because they buy them in bulk, and pass the savings on to you. Each destination, including Hawaii, usually has a few packagers (tour operators) that are better than the rest because they buy in even bigger bulk. The time you spend shopping around is likely to be well rewarded.

Travel packages come in a variety of forms. Some offer better hotels than others. Others offer the same hotels for lower prices. Some offer flights on scheduled airlines; others book charters. Some packages may limit your choice of accommodations and travel days. Some let you choose between escorted vacations and independent vacations; others allow you to add on just a few excursions or escorted day trips (also at discounted prices) without booking an entirely escorted tour.

The best places to start looking for a suitable package are at your travel agency — an agent may be able to do the comparison-shopping for you and get you the best overall package rates — or by checking the travel section of your local Sunday newspaper.

Or cut out the middleman and contact a reputable packager directly. **Liberty Travel** (☎ 888-271-1584; Internet: www.libertytravel.com) is one of the oldest and biggest packagers in the east and runs a full-page ad in many Sunday papers. At press time, Liberty was offering excellent-value packages, with or without air, to all of the Hawaiian islands — and their agents are willing to help you construct a multi-island trip.

Pleasant Hawaiian Holidays (☎ 800-7-HAWAII; Internet: www.pleasantholidays.com), the biggest and most comprehensive packager to Hawaii, has more than 40 years experience in the business and offers tons of package options: At press time, they were offering a high-quality collection of more than 100 condos and hotels to choose from, and they book air travel aboard multiple airlines (as well as on their own charters), which gives you lots of flexibility if you have an established frequent-flyer account with an airline. Pleasant can arrange just about any kind of vacation you want, including fly/drive packages and land-only deals. And because they buy airfares and hotel-room blocks in such bulk, their deals are often excellent (although they offer better deals on some properties than others). Another plus is their Service Desks on all the major islands, which can help you book activities and answer any questions you might have. These guys can even finance your vacation for you — just watch out for those interest rates.

SunTrips/Sunquest (☎ 800-SUNTRIPS or 800-357-2400; Internet: www.suntrips.com or www.sunquest.org) is committed to arranging affordable and comprehensive Hawaii vacations, and the majority of the 150 or so properties they can book you into are budget and moderately priced hotels and condos. If money is no object, head elsewhere — but if you're looking for a bargain, SunTrips may just be the packager for you.

Aloha Vacations (Internet: www.alohavacations.com) is an online packager that books trips that can include interisland air travel, hotels and condos, rental cars, and/or activities. You'll have to book your own trans-Pacific airfare, but you may be able to arrange a great-value multi-island trip by linking together various single-island packages via this site. Keep in mind, however, that Aloha Vacations only works with select vendors (they only book interisland air with Hawaiian Airlines, for example, not Aloha), so you won't get a full picture of what's available.

Many major airlines also offer travel packages to Hawaii. I always recommend comparison shopping, but you may want to choose the airline that has frequent service to your hometown or the one on which you accumulate frequent flyer miles; you may even be able to pay for your trip using miles. The following airlines offer travel packages as part of their services:

- **Air Canada Vacations** (☎ 800-662-3221; Internet: www.aircanadavacations.com).

- **American Airlines Vacations** (☎ 800-321-2121; Internet: www.aavacations.com), one of the best, after United, in terms of value and range of accommodations.

- **Continental Airlines Vacations** (☎ 800-634-5555; Internet: www.coolvacations.com).

- **Delta Vacations** (☎ 800-872-7786; Internet: www.deltavacations.com), which just came out as the price-comparison leader among airline packagers in an informal poll conducted by *Condé Nast Traveler.*

- **Northwest WorldVacations** (☎ 800-800-1504; Internet: www.nwaworldvacations.com).

- **United Vacations** (☎ 800-328-6877; Internet: www.unitedvacations.com), which is the most comprehensive airline packager to Hawaii.

Still want more information? Go online to www.vacationpackager.com, an excruciatingly extensive Web-search engine that can link you up with an exhausting list of package-tour operators that offer Hawaii vacations. It has a lot of excess to wade through, but it's the place to learn what *all* of your options are. Remember to look under both Hawaii and Hawaiian Islands.

Choosing between a travel agent and a packager isn't an either/or proposition; in fact, your travel agent can be your best source in sorting through the various deals that are available. If you're an Amex customer, you might consider going through American Express Travel Service, which can book travel packages through various vendors, including Continental Vacations and Delta Vacations. Ditto for members of the American Automobile Association, who have access to the AAA Travel Agency, which can also book excellent-value package deals. For contact information, see "Working with a Travel Agent" earlier in this chapter.

Hawaii is such a foolproof place to visit that I strongly recommend traveling on your own rather than signing on to an escorted tour. If you really prefer to be led around, however, or you're not able to drive yourself, you may want to consider one. The well-conceived escorted tours offered by **Tauck Tours** (☎ 800-788-7885; Internet: www.tauck.com) are far more luxurious and far less structured than your average escorted tour; pricey, but worth it if you'd rather put someone else in charge of the itinerary. If you're looking for more affordable options, try sister companies **Globus** and **Cosmos** (☎ 800-221-0090; Internet: www.globusandcosmos.com), whose Web site can direct you to a travel agent in your area that arranges Globus and Cosmos tours. **Perillo Tours** (☎ 800-431-1515; Internet: www.perillotours.com) also offers midpriced multi-island tours.

With the multitude of packages on the market, you may need some help sorting through their various merits. Follow these tips as you sift your way through the options:

- ✔ **Read up on Hawaii.** Read through the hotel listings in this book and select the places that sound interesting. Compare the rates that I list with the packagers' prices to best gauge which packagers are really offering a good deal and which have simply gussied up the rack rates to make their full-fare offer sound like a smart buy. Remember that the amount you save depends on both the property and the packager; most packagers can offer bigger savings on some properties than at others. For example, Liberty Travel may give you a much better rate on Waikiki's Royal Hawaiian, say, than Pleasant Holidays can, but Pleasant may offer you a substantial savings on the Maui condo you want.

- ✔ **Compare apples to apples.** When comparing packages, make sure you know *exactly* what's included in the quoted price, and what's not. Don't assume anything: Some packagers include everything — including value-added extras like lei greetings, free continental breakfast, and dining discounts — while others don't even include airfare. Additionally, when considering package prices, be sure to factor in add-in costs if you're flying from somewhere other than Los Angeles or San Francisco — some packagers price packages directly from your hometown, and some require additional premiums for airfares from your hometown to their Los Angeles or San Francisco gateway.

✔ **Before you commit to a package, make sure you know how much flexibility you have.** Some packagers require iron-clad commitments, while others only charge minimal fees for changes or cancellations. Consider the possibility that your travel plans could change, and select a packager with the degree of flexibility that suits your needs.

✔ **Don't believe in fairy tales.** Unfortunately, shady dealers and fly-by-night operations are out there. If a package appears too good to be true, it probably is. Any knowledgeable travel agent should be able to help you determine if a specific packager is on the level or not.

Booking Your Own Air Travel

Most trans-Pacific flights arrive at Oahu's Honolulu International Airport, but an increasing number land directly on the bigger neighbor islands — Maui, the Big Island, and Kauai.

The following major airlines fly between mainland North America and one or more of Hawaii's major airports:

✔ **Air Canada** (☎ 888-247-2262; Internet: www.aircanada.ca) flies direct from Toronto and Vancouver to Oahu's Honolulu International Airport, plus once a week from Vancouver to Maui's Kahului Airport.

✔ **Aloha Airlines** (☎ 877-TRY-ALOHA or 800-367-5250; Internet: www.alohaair.com), one of Hawaii's two major interisland carriers, now flies nonstop daily from Oakland International Airport, in the San Francisco Bay Area, to Honolulu and Maui.

✔ **American Airlines** (☎ 800-433-7300; Internet: www.americanair.com) flies direct from Chicago, Dallas, and Los Angeles to Honolulu and Maui.

✔ **Canadian Airlines** (☎ 800-426-7000; Internet: www.cdnair.ca) flies nonstop from Vancouver to Honolulu and Maui, and from Toronto to Honolulu.

✔ **Continental Airlines** (☎ 800-525-0280; Internet: www.continental.com) flies nonstop from New York, Houston, and Los Angeles to Honolulu.

✔ **Delta Airlines** (☎ 800-221-1212; Internet: www.delta-air.com) flies direct from Atlanta, Los Angeles, Dallas, and San Francisco to Honolulu, and from Los Angeles to Maui.

✔ **Hawaiian Airlines** (☎ 800-367-5320; Internet: www.hawaiianair.com) flies direct from Los Angeles, San Francisco, Portland, and Seattle to Honolulu; from Los Angeles and Seattle to Maui; and from Los Angeles to Kona International Airport on the Big Island.

✔ **Northwest Airlines** (☎ 800-225-2525; Internet: www.nwa.com) flies direct from Detroit, Los Angeles, San Francisco, and Seattle to Honolulu.

✔ **TWA** (☎ 800-221-2000; Internet: www.twa.com) flies nonstop from St. Louis to Honolulu, from St. Louis direct to Maui, and from Los Angeles to the Big Island's Kona Airport.

✔ **United Airlines** (☎ 800-241-6522; Internet: www.ual.com) flies direct from Chicago's O'Hare, Los Angeles, and San Francisco to Honolulu; from Los Angeles and San Francisco to Maui; from San Francisco and Los Angeles to Kona on the Big Island; and direct from Los Angeles and San Francisco to Kauai's Lihue Airport.

Getting the best airfare

Business travelers who need to purchase their tickets at the last minute, change their itinerary at a moment's notice, or want to get home before the weekend pay the premium rate, known as the full fare. Passengers whose travel agenda is more flexible — who can book their tickets far in advance, who don't mind staying over Saturday night, or who are willing to travel on a Tuesday, Wednesday, or Thursday — pay the least, usually a fraction of the full fare. On most flights to Hawaii, even the shortest hops, the full fare is more than $1,000, but a 7-day or 14-day advance-purchase ticket from the West Coast is often closer to $500. Obviously, I can't guarantee what fares will be when you book, but you can almost always save big by planning ahead.

The airlines also periodically offer sales, bringing down prices on their most popular routes. These fares carry advance-purchase requirements and date-of-travel restrictions, but the price is usually worth the restrictions: sometimes no more than $300 or $400 for trans-Pacific flight from the West Coast to Hawaii (even less on some discount airlines). Keep your eyes open for these sales, which are advertised in the newspapers, on the Internet, and sometimes on TV, as you plan your vacation. The sales tend to take place in seasons of low travel volume. You'll almost never see a sale around the peak summer vacation months or in the winter high season.

Consolidators, also known as bucket shops, are a good place to check for the lowest fares. Their prices are much better than the fares you can get yourself, and are often even lower than what your travel agent can get you. Check for their ads in the small boxes at the bottom of the page in your Sunday travel section. Some of the most reliable consolidators include:

✔ **Cheap Tickets** (☎ 800-377-1000; Internet: www.cheaptickets. com), which is based in Honolulu and often has the best trans-Pacific air deals, bar none.

✔ **Travac Tours & Charters** (☎ 800-TRAV-800; Internet: www. thetravelsite.com), which also books complete Hawaii travel packages.

✔ **Council Travel** (☎ 800-226-8624; Internet: www.counciltravel. com) caters to young travelers, but their bargain-basement prices are available to people of all ages.

Here are a few more tips that might help you save on airfares:

- **Travel on off days of the week.** Airfares vary depending on the day of the week. Everybody wants to travel on the weekend; if you can travel on a Tuesday, Wednesday, or Thursday, you may find cheaper flights to Hawaii. When you inquire about airfares, ask if you can get a cheaper rate by flying on a different day. Remember, too, that staying over on a Saturday night can cut your airfare.

- **Reserve your flight well in advance.** Take advantage of advance-purchase fares — or watch the last-minute "e" fares on-line for bargains. (See "Booking your tickets online" later in this chapter for a discussion of online strategies.)

- **Fly direct to the island of your choice to save on interisland airfares.** The Big Island, Maui, and Kauai all receive direct flights from the mainland. It's not always possible to fly to or from the neighbor island of your choice; it all depends on the trans-Pacific carrier you choose and your origination point. But look into it if your island-hopping itinerary dictates — because doing so can save you a one- or two-hour layover in Honolulu and the additional cost of an interisland flight (see "Flying between the Hawaiian Islands" later in this chapter).

As you make your flight plans, use the worksheet called "Fare Game: Choosing an Airline" to help keep your information organized.

Booking your tickets online

Another way to find the cheapest fare is to scour the Internet. Too many travel-booking sites exist to mention them all, but a few of the better-respected (and more comprehensive) ones are **Travelocity** (www.travelocity.com), **Microsoft Expedia** (www.expedia.com), and **Yahoo Travel** (http://travel.yahoo.com). Each has its own little quirks, but all provide variations on the same service. Just enter the dates you want to fly and the cities you want to visit, and the computer looks for the lowest fares. Several other features have become standard to these sites: the ability to check flights at different times or dates in hopes of finding a cheaper fare, e-mail alerts when fares drop on a route you have specified, and a database of last-minute deals that advertises super-cheap vacation packages or airfares for those who can get away at a moment's notice.

You can be notified of late-breaking airfare deals for all the major airlines at once by logging on to **Smarter Living** (www.smarterliving.com), or you can go to each individual airline's Web site and sign up. These sites offer schedules, flight booking, and often information on special deals or fare sales.

Flying between the Hawaiian Islands

The only way to travel from island to island is by airplane. Two major interisland carriers serve the islands: Aloha Airlines and Hawaiian Airlines. Both offer similar schedules — flights between the major islands every hour or so — at competitive prices. I prefer Aloha — I've found them to have shorter check-in lines, be more timely on average, and have friendlier service. But the differences between the two carriers are minor, so you should choose your carrier based on schedule, price, and in which account you prefer to earn frequent flyer miles.

Aloha Airlines (☎ **800-367-5250,** 877-879-2564, or 808-484-1111; Internet: www.alohaairlines.com) employs an all-jet fleet of Boeing 737 aircraft. Aloha's sibling company, **Island Air** (☎ **800-323-3345,** 800-652-6541, or 808-484-2222), operates deHavilland DASH-8 and DASH-6 aircraft and serves Hawaii's smaller interisland airports on Maui (Kapalua Airport), Molokai, and Lanai. Try Aloha first; if you need to take an Island Air flight because there's no accommodating Aloha flight, Aloha can book it for you.

Aloha Airlines is a mileage partner with United Airlines, so you can earn 500 miles in your Dividend Miles account for every Aloha Airlines interisland segment you fly.

Hawaiian Airlines (☎ **800-367-5320**, 800-882-8811, or 808-838-5300; Internet: www.hawaiianair.com) offers interisland jet service similar to Aloha's. Hawaiian is one of the world's safest airlines, never having had a fatal incident since it started flying in 1929.

Hawaiian is mileage partners with American, Continental, and Delta airlines; however, the rules and mileage awards change depending on the airline and flight class, so you should check on the current regulations before you book.

At press time, the full interisland fare was about $96 per one-way segment on both airlines, with fares dropping as low as $66 on occasion, depending on the dates and routes you wish to fly. But there are a few ways to save on interisland fares without being subject to the whims of the market. Note that all prices were current at press time and are subject to change at any time, but this should give you an idea of what's available.

Aloha Airlines has a few great deals for non-residents of Hawaii:

- ✔ If your island-hopping falls within the course of a week, consider purchasing a **Visitor 7-Day Island Pass.** For $321 per person (including tax) you get unlimited travel on Aloha and Island Air for seven consecutive days. This is a good option for those of you who plan to be doing lots of island-hopping in a short time. Keep in mind, though, that each traveler has to have his or her own Island Pass. The Island Pass can be ordered online.

- ✔ Much more practical for most visitors, who are usually island-hopping two or three times in the course of a two- or three-week stay, is the **Coupon Book:** For $354, you get six blank tickets that you can use — for yourself or any other traveler — anytime within one year of purchase. If two of you are coming to Hawaii for three weeks and visiting three islands in the course of your visit, a $354 coupon book will work perfectly for both of you — and that makes each segment just $59. Not bad. You can reserve your flights in advance, but you'll have to purchase the coupon book when you land in Hawaii.

✔ If all else fails, note that **AAA members qualify for a 20 percent discount.** This discount only applies to first-class and full fare tickets, however, not to previously discounted fares.

Hawaiian Airlines offers similar values:

✔ Their version of an unlimited travel pass, called the **Hawaiian Island Pass,** gets you all the interisland flights you want for $299 per person for five consecutive days, $315 for seven days (cheaper than Aloha's version at press time), $369 for ten days, and $409 for two weeks. These passes can be purchased from Hawaiian ticket desks in the islands, or from any travel agency on the mainland.

✔ Hawaiian's **Coupon Book** is similarly priced to Aloha's — $352.50 for six one-way tickets — but they're only good for six months from the date of purchase (Aloha's are good for a year), which limits your ability to pass on any leftovers to family or friends who might be visiting Hawaii after you. Again, you can reserve flights in advance, but you won't be able to actually purchase the coupon book itself until you arrive in Hawaii.

 Hawaii-based consolidator **Cheap Tickets** (☎ 800-377-1000; Internet: www.cheaptickets.com) can sometimes save you big bucks on individual interisland tickets.

 If you're traveling on a package, you probably don't have to worry about any of this — your interisland flights are most likely included in your package deal, on whichever interisland carrier the packager is affiliated with. For more on all-inclusive travel packages, see "Buying Your Vacation as a Pay-One-Price Package Deal" earlier in this chapter.

Looking Ahead to Accommodations

Accommodations in Hawaii are notoriously expensive. Hotels won't hesitate to charge $300 a night for a partial oceanview room with little more than a queen-size bed in it. So prepare yourself for the fact that accommodations may take up a larger portion of your total travel budget than you might expect.

That said, don't forsake Hawaii for the Jersey Shore just yet. The islands boast plenty of excellent values for every budget if you just know where to look — and I include the best of them in the chapters that follow. For general tips on how to save, check out "Keeping a Lid on Expenses" in Chapter 3.

Understanding your options

Before you book your accommodations, you need to figure out what kind of place you want. You find five types of accommodations in the islands: resorts, hotels, condos, bed-and-breakfasts, and vacation rentals.

Resorts

Most resorts (or resort hotels) are multi-acre, multi-building complexes located directly on the beach. Some are sophisticated (sometimes too sophisticated, for Hawaii), ultra-luxury affairs geared to monied adults; others are theme park-like spreads that cater largely to families with kids. More than a few fall somewhere in between.

A resort (or resort hotel) offers everything your average hotel offers — plus much more. Every resort hotel is different, of course, but you can expect such amenities as direct beach access, with beach cabanas and chairs, and often beach-toy rentals and ocean activities as well; pools (often more than one) and a Jacuzzi, often with poolside bar service; an activities desk; a fitness center and (more and more) a full-service spa; a variety of restaurants, bars, and lounges; a 24-hour front desk; concierge, valet, and bell services; room service; tennis and golf (some of the world's best courses are at Hawaii's resorts); a business center; extensive children's programs; and more.

Rooms may be in high-rise towers, but they're often scattered through-out the property in low-rise buildings or clustered cottages. They tend to be done in the same safe, mass-market style throughout the resort — generally, room 101 is going to look exactly like room 1901. As travelers' tastes increasingly demand more, however, many newer properties (and savvy new renovations) are reinventing the resort with smart, high-style concepts that are intended to heighten the resort's own unique setting, concept, or personality. The standards tend to be high, and rooms are usually outfitted with high-quality furnishings and linens. Many luxury resorts also boast an increasing slate of in-room extras, such as big TVs with Nintendo systems and VCRs.

Being the most well-outfitted, and usually the best located, of Hawaii's accommodations options, resorts are also the priciest choices on the market (although the islands do boast a few mid-range resorts). That said, you can score attractive rates, even at some of the islands' most luxurious resorts, especially if you book through a packager (see "Buying Your Vacation as a Pay-One-Price Package Deal" earlier in this chapter).

Hotels

Hotels tend to be smaller and have fewer facilities than resorts — you may get a swimming pool, but don't expect a golf course or tennis courts, more than one or two restaurants and/or bars, and everything else that comes with a full-fledged resort. You'll find the greatest number of non-resort hotels in Waikiki, where the shoulder-to-shoulder urban setting simply hasn't allowed for much full-fledged resort development.

Hotels are often a short walk from the beach rather than beachfront (although some, like the Sheraton Moana Surfrider in Waikiki, are right on the sand). Generally a hotel offers daily maid service and has a restaurant and/or coffee shop, a bar or lounge, on-site laundry facilities, a swimming pool, and a sundries or convenience-type shop (rather than the shopping arcades that many resorts have these days).

Top hotels also have activities desks, concierge and valet service, limited room service, and a business center.

Boutique hotels are smaller — maybe 40 or 50 rooms rather than 200 or more — and more intimate than your average Doubletree or Hilton. The rooms are often more stylish, less cookie-cutter, and usually have more amenities. They tend to cater to adults rather than families. Again, Hawaii's boutique-hotel boom is centered in Waikiki.

Hotels run the gamut from very expensive to downright cheap. But even the priciest ones (usually boutique hotels) tend to be less expensive than fully outfitted resorts.

Condos

Condominium apartments make up a large percentage of Hawaii's inventory of accommodations. They're a great option for everyone, because they're outfitted like a real, fully operational home and can accommodate anywhere from two to eight vacationers in one-, two-, or three bedrooms. There's no better way to go if you're traveling as a family or in a group, but even couples enjoy the extra space and home-style amenities.

Condos are usually apartments in either a single high-rise or a cluster of low-rise buildings, often on the beach, sometimes not. Since they're real apartments, condos almost always come complete with fully outfitted kitchen, a living room with pullout sofa (which usually means that one-bedrooms can easily accommodate four guests, two-bedrooms can accommodate six), a private phone line, and a washer/dryer (usually), as well as other homestyle amenities. Two-bedrooms often (but not always) have a second bath; in fact, a good number of one-bedroom condos in Hawaii also have a second bath. (Never assume; always ask when you book what the exact configuration will be.) On-site you'll usually find a swimming pool, laundry facilities (if units are not in the apartments themselves), tennis courts (sometimes), a front desk or property manager to deal with any questions you may have, and sometimes an activity desk to book snorkel cruises, luaus, and the like.

Don't expect the kind of service you'd get at a hotel. If you'd rather have room service over your own kitchen, or you want somebody else to schlep your bags or do your laundry, go with a hotel or resort instead.

Rental condos often share real estate with owned time-shares. Often, they're individually owned vacation apartments that the owners use maybe a month or two out of the year. When not owner-occupied (which is most of the time), the units are managed and cared for by a management company or agent, which also rents them out to folks like you and me. You might book a condo through any number of individuals: an on-site agent or manager, an off-site agent or manager, or an off-site individual owner. Often, at some condo complexes (but not all), more than one manager may be representing units at any one time. The units that I recommend in the accommodations chapters (later in this book) are all managed by reputable companies with good track records. (In the cases where more than one agent represents a property, I've listed the one I felt would give you the best deal and the best service.)

Since they are privately owned homes, condo apartments are almost always individually decorated. However, the management company will always require a certain standard of decor and certain amenities, so the rental agent you use should be able to tell you exactly what to expect.

Condos range in price from bargain-basement to ultra-luxury, with the majority falling on the affordable end of the continuum. I find that condos are the best values that Hawaii has going, bar none, no matter what your price range — you'll almost always get more for your money than you will at a comparable resort. Also, since competition between condo properties is so tight, many good properties offer such extras as a free rental car and the seventh night free to lure you in. Packagers are a great source for bargain rates on condos (see "Buying Your Vacation as a Pay-One-Price Package Deal" earlier in this chapter).

If you'd like more choices than those listed in these pages, contact **Hawaii Condo Exchange** (☎ 800-442-0404 or 323-436-0300; Internet: wwte.com/condos), a Southern California-based agency that acts as a consolidator for condo properties throughout the islands; they'll work to match you up with the place that's right for you and try to get you a good deal in the bargain.

Most condos offer some kind of maid service, from the kind of full daily service that you get in a hotel to nothing more than weekly linen change, depending on the property. However, I've found that minimal maid service is fine, even pleasant — I like not having the daily intrusion, and I don't mind rinsing my own breakfast dishes. But it can be an entirely different story if you're traveling with a big brood. Also, most properties that offer daily or midweek maid service include it in the rate, but a few charge extra for it. Make sure to ask for specifics when inquiring about a condo.

Bed-and-Breakfasts (or B&Bs)

Staying in a bed-and-breakfast is a great way to discover Hawaii's genuine aloha spirit. More often than not, B&Bs offer a more intimate setting than your average impersonal resort and a host who's more than happy to help you get to know Hawaii as it really is. If you'd like to experience a real slice of island life, B&Bs are the way to go.

B&Bs vary widely in size, style, and services. Generally speaking, they're usually comprised of several bedrooms in a home, or several cottages or suites scattered about a property, each of which may or may not have a private bathroom. (All the B&Bs that I recommend in the accommodations chapters that follow have units with private baths.)

Although they offer a few more services than vacation rentals (see the following section), B&Bs are most suited to independent travelers.

Staying in one is really like staying in someone's home, so extras in the form of services and facilities may be minimal. Breakfast may a full-cooked affair or simply fixings that you prepare on your own. And most B&Bs are situated inland, a short drive from the beach, usually not directly on the sand.

By and large, lodging in a bed-and-breakfast is more affordable than a resort stay, and rates tend to be fixed. Expect to pay anywhere from $100 to $200 in a nice B&B; a few extra-luxurious ones can go as high as $250 per night or more. The B&B may have a minimum-stay requirement, but not always. And, as elsewhere, B&Bs are usually more suitable for adults than families traveling with kids.

I list a number of excellent B&Bs in the accommodations chapters later in this book; however, Hawaii has more terrific B&Bs than I have room to discuss in these pages. Therefore, if you want further options, I recommend contacting one or more of the following options.

Tops in the state is **Hawaii's Best Bed & Breakfasts** (☎ **800-262-9912** or 808-885-4550; Internet: www.bestbnb.com). Barbara Campbell and her staff personally inspect (and regularly revisit) the B&Bs and inns that they represent, and they're not afraid to say "no" to any property that doesn't meet their exacting standards. You pay $15 on top of the rate (usually $20 if you book multiple reservations on different islands), but it's well worth it to know that you're getting a great B&B. They only represent accommodations with private baths, and all are nonsmoking. Some of their units are free-standing cottages that resemble vacation homes more than B&Bs; they even represent a few really nice condos.

Hawaii's Best B&Bs can also help you arrange discounted interisland flights and favorable car-rental rates.

You won't get the same personal service from the Web, but you will find lots of useful resources there. The **Hawaii Directory of Bed-and-Breakfasts, Country Inns, and Small Hotels** (www.virtualcities.com/ons/hi/hionsdex.htm) offers direct Web links to B&Bs and vacation rentals throughout the state. **InnSite** (www.innsite.com) features B&B listings in all 50 U.S. states, including Hawaii, and around the globe. Find an inn on the island of your choice, see pictures of the rooms, and check prices and availability; text is only included if the proprietor submitted it (it's free to get an inn listed). The descriptions are written by the innkeepers; and many listings link to the inn's own Web sites. Another site that's well worth surfing for Hawaii B&Bs is **BedandBreakfast.com** (www.bedandbreakfast.com).

Vacation rentals

"Vacation rental" usually means that you have a full cottage or house all to yourself. You may never even see an owner, agent, or manager after you pick up the keys. This is another great option for families, or anybody who likes their space — but if you prefer a full-service experience, this option may not be for you.

The rental may be a studio cottage in a residential neighborhood or a huge beachfront multi-bedroom house — or anything in between. Vacation rentals usually have some sort of kitchen facilities (ask when booking); laundry facilities; at least one TV; and at least one phone. Because vacation rentals are often privately owned homes, they also may come with such extras as TV, VCR, and stereo (never assume; always ask if it matters to you). Like condos, they usually come outfitted with the basics, such as sheets or towels.

Vacation rentals vary greatly in price depending on their size, location, and amenities. Still, like condos, they tend to be much better values than similarly priced resort or hotel accommodations, especially if you're trying to accommodate a group or you plan a long stay. Just make sure that you get a 24-hour contact person for those times when the toilet won't flush or you can't figure out how to turn on the air-conditioning.

Both **Hawaii's Best Bed & Breakfasts** and the **Hawaii Directory of Bed-and-Breakfasts, Country Inns, and Small Hotels** are useful sites for statewide vacation rentals. I also recommend island-specific reservation agencies and management companies in the accommodations chapters later in this book.

Hawaii how-to: Choosing rooms with a view

If you want to see the ocean from your room or condo, expect to pay for the privilege. Oceanview rooms usually cost substantially more than non- or partial-view rooms, to the tune of $100, $200, or even $250 higher per night than the rate for a similar room without the view.

Deciding whether or not to pay for a view isn't a clear-cut issue. In fact, what constitutes "oceanview" is far from an agreed-upon industry standard; witness these variations on the theme:

- ✔ **Oceanfront:** Only hotels or condo complexes that sit squarely on the beach can have oceanfront rooms or apartments. Positioned directly over the sand, a stone's throw from the waves, these units are the best in the house, and usually the most expensive. You may still have to walk through the lobby the get to the water, but you will have an unblocked view of the beach. Keep in mind, however, that you'll only be able to hear the waves from lower-floor rooms; these are often my favorites.

- ✔ **Oceanview:** Watch out here — some hotels and resorts don't distinguish between oceanfront rooms and oceanview rooms, which also have a full view of the ocean. "Oceanview" rooms, however, don't have to be directly over the sand. They may sit farther back — or even across the street — from the beach, or they might look over the rooftops of other buildings. These units are still fabulous, and still expensive.

✔ **Partial Oceanview:** "Partial oceanview" is subject to a whole host of interpretations, depending on who's doing the offering. It can be almost as good as full oceanview, or it may mean that you see a razor-thinslice of blue between two high-rise mountains of concrete. Ask lots of questions about any unit offered as "partial oceanview," and know exactly what you're paying for before you book.

✔ **City, Mountain, or Garden View:** "City view" is a term that you usually only hear regarding Waikiki hotels. On the neighbor islands, most non-oceanview rooms are called "mountain view," meaning they face the island's inland mountains, or "garden view," which means they face an inner courtyard or grounds. The view can be good or bad, depending on the location and the layout of the grounds; again, your best bet is to ask lots of questions when you reserve. These are usually the least expensive rooms in a hotel or condo complex. They're not usually of poorer quality — they just don't have the million-dollar views that those on the other side of the building or grounds have.

I highly recommend staying in an oceanfront, or oceanview, room if you can, because falling asleep to the rhythm of the waves and waking to gorgeous ocean views is an unforgettable experience. But don't blow your whole budget just to make it happen. First choose the hotel or condo you'd like based on your needs. Make sure the style of accommodation suits you, and that the property features all of the amenities and services you'll need to be comfortable. Once you've chosen your property, see if you can afford to book oceanfront. If you can, great! But if staying in an oceanfront room means you'll have to skip activities or skimp on meals or souvenirs, then go with a cheaper room with a lesser view. Having an oceanview room isn't worth compromising the rest of your trip.

Chapter 6

Tying Up the Loose Ends

● ●

In This Chapter

▶ Using credit cards, traveler's checks, and ATMs while you travel

▶ Dealing with losing your wallet and other money emergencies

▶ Arranging for car rentals in the islands

▶ Buying travel insurance

▶ Making reservations for meals, activities, and entertainment before you leave home

▶ Packing what you really need

● ●

This chapter will help you shore up the final details — from getting travel insurance to advance planning for activities to packing the appropriate gear.

Using Credit Cards, Traveler's Checks, or Cash

For most people traveling in Hawaii, carrying a combination of credit cards and cash works best.

All of the major Hawaiian islands have 24-hour ATMs linked to a national network that almost always includes your bank at home. **Cirrus** (☎ **800-424-7787**; Internet: www.mastercard.com/atm) and **Plus** (☎ **800-843-7587**; Internet: www.visa.com/atms) are the two most prevalent networks; check the back of your ATM card to see which network your bank belongs to. Most cards also have 800 numbers and Web sites listed on the back that you can access to find specific locations of ATMs. The easy accessibility of these ATMs means that you can withdraw cash as needed every day or so, which eliminates the insecurity (and the pickpocketing threat) of carrying around a wad of cash.

 Many banks charge from 50 cents to $3 whenever a non-account-holder uses their ATMs. Your own bank may also assess a fee for using an ATM that's not one of their branch locations. This means that in some cases you get charged twice just for using your bank card when you're on vacation. Make sure you understand your bank's policies before you leave for vacation.

If you're not arriving in Hawaii from another country, using an ATM card also lets you eliminate money-changing hassles. You can simply withdraw cash in U.S. dollars, at an extremely advantageous exchange rate. However, many banks charge a "foreign currency transaction fee" for this service, which may make reverting to traveler's checks cheaper (though certainly less convenient).

If you prefer the security of traveler's checks (you can report them missing if they are lost or stolen), you can get them at almost any bank. **American Express** offers checks in denominations of $20, $50, $100, $500, and $1,000. You pay a service charge ranging from 1 percent to 4 percent, though AAA members can obtain checks without a fee at most AAA offices. You can also order AmEx traveler's checks by calling ☎ 800-221-7282.

Visa (☎ 800-227-6811) also offers traveler's checks, which you can purchase at Citibank branches and other banks. The service charge ranges between 1½ percent to 2 percent; checks come in denominations of $50, $100, $500, and $1,000. **MasterCard** also offers traveler's checks; call ☎ 800-223-9920 for the details.

Credit cards provide a safe way to carry money and a convenient record of your travel expenses. You can also get a cash advance off your credit card at most ATMs if you know your PIN number. (If you need help locating your PIN, call the phone number on the back of the credit card for assistance.) Do this before you leave home, however: It generally takes five to seven business days to get your PIN sent to you through the mail, although some banks may give it to you over the phone if you provide some sort of security clearance (such as your mother's maiden name).

A cash advance can cost you: Interest rates for cash advances are often significantly higher than rates for purchases. Also, you start paying interest on the advance the moment you receive the cash. On an airline-affiliated credit card, a cash advance doesn't earn frequent-flyer miles.

Taking Action if Your Credit Cards Are Lost or Stolen

If your wallet disappears, you should take immediate steps to rectify the situation so that you can get on with enjoying your vacation.

For emergencies such as this, most credit card companies list an 800 number on the back of their cards. The company may be able to wire you a cash advance off your credit card immediately. In many places, they will send an emergency credit card to you within a couple of days.

Of course, if the card is lost or stolen, you won't be able to access the 800 number on the back. To be on the safe side, before you leave home write down the 800 number from the back of your card in a notebook and then keep the notebook in a safe place, such as the safe in your hotel room. Otherwise, just call the 800 directory-information line. Citicorp Visa's U.S. emergency number is ☎ **800-645-6556.** American Express cardholders and traveler's check holders should call ☎ **800-221-7282** for all money emergencies; MasterCard's number is ☎ **800-307-7309.**

If you choose to carry traveler's checks, be sure to keep a separate record of their serial numbers so you can handle just such an emergency.

Even though it's unlikely that the police will be able to recover your stolen or lost wallet or purse, you should still report the loss after you cancel your credit cards. You may need the police report number for credit card or insurance purposes later.

Taxing Matters

Hawaii's sales tax is 4 percent. Expect 11.42 percent in taxes to be added to every hotel bill.

Buying Travel and Medical Insurance

There are three primary kinds of travel insurance: trip cancellation insurance, medical insurance, and lost luggage insurance.

If you've paid a large portion of your vacation expenses up front, you should consider trip cancellation insurance to cover you in the unlikely event that you have to cancel your trip — due to illness, work commitments, or whatever — or if your travel provider doesn't meet its commitment to you for some reason (bankruptcy being the likeliest). Trip cancellation insurance usually costs approximately 6 to 8 percent of the total value of your vacation.

The other two types — medical insurance and lost luggage insurance — don't make sense for most travelers. Your existing health insurance should cover you if you get sick while you're traveling (if you belong to an HMO, be sure to check on the extent of your coverage when away from home). Homeowners' insurance should cover stolen luggage in the event of an off-premises theft. Check your existing policies before you buy any additional coverage. The airlines are responsible for $2,500 on domestic flights (and $9.07 per pound, up to $640, on international flights) for lost luggage. If you plan to bring valuables along, carry them with you onto the plane.

Some credit cards (American Express and certain gold and platinum Visa and MasterCards, for example) offer automatic flight insurance against death or dismemberment in case of an airplane crash.

If you still feel you need more insurance, try one of the following reputable companies:

✔ **Access America,** 6600 West Broad Street, Richmond, VA 23230
(☎ **800-284-8300;** Fax: 800-346-9265; Internet: www.accessamerica.com).

✔ **Travelex Insurance Services,** 11717 Burt Street, Suite 202, Omaha, NE 68154 (☎ **800-228-9792;** Internet: www.travelex-insurance.com).

✔ **Travel Guard International,** 1145 Clark Street, Stevens Point, WI 54481 (☎ **800-826-1300;** Internet: www.travel-guard.com).

✔ **Travel Insured International, Inc.,** P.O. Box 280568, 52-S Oakland Avenue, East Hartford, CT 06128-0568 (☎ **800-243-3174;** Internet: www.travelinsured.com).

When you buy travel insurance, be careful not to purchase more than you need. For example, if you only need trip cancellation insurance, don't purchase coverage for lost or stolen property. And if you're buying a complete travel package or an escorted tour, don't buy trip-cancellation insurance from your tour operator — which is the fiscal equivalent of giving a kid the candy jar. Buy it from an outside vendor instead.

In the unlikely event that you do get sick in Hawaii, keep the following in mind:

✔ By law, all employers in Hawaii must provide health insurance for their employees, and almost all islanders have insurance. As a result, many doctors simply won't see patients who aren't insured. If you don't have insurance (or you don't have insurance that travels with you) and you need to see a doctor while you're in Hawaii, be sure to inform him when you call to make an appointment. If the doctor won't see you, your other alternative is a trip to the hospital emergency room.

✔ Long's Drugs, which has branches throughout the islands, accepts most national prescription cards, such as PCS — so if you have one, bring it with you. If you get sick and need to fill a prescription during your trip, chances are good that you'll only have to pay a co-pay, just like back home, instead of the full price for prescribed medicines.

Arranging for Rental Cars

Hawaii has so many fabulous things to see and do that it would be a real shame for you to miss out. The more you want to see, however, the more you'll be moving around. In order to maximize your time on each of the islands, you need to rent a car. The only island that's navigable without a car is Oahu, but you'll be sorry — and stuck in Waikiki — if you have to rely on public transportation.

The following companies rent cars on all of the major Hawaiian islands:

- **Alamo:** ☎ **800-GO-ALAMO** (800-462-5266); Internet: `www. alamo.com`

- **Avis:** ☎ **800-230-4898**; Internet: `www.avis.com`

- **Budget:** ☎ **800-527-0700**; Internet: `www.budget.com`

- **Dollar:** ☎ **800-800-4000**; Internet: `www.dollar.com`

- **Enterprise:** ☎ **800-325-8007**; Internet: `www.enterprise.com`

- **Hertz:** ☎ **800-654-3131**; Internet: `www.hertz.com`

- **National:** ☎ **800-227-7368**; Internet: `www.nationalcar.com`

- **Thrifty:** ☎ **800-THRIFTY** (800-847-4389); Internet: `www. thrifty.com`

Be sure to book your rental cars well ahead. Rental cars are almost always at a premium on Kauai, Molokai, and Lanai, and may be sold out on all the neighbor islands on holiday weekends.

For tips on renting hand-controlled cars or vans equipped with wheel-chair lifts, see "Advice for Travelers with Disabilities" in Chapter 4.

Getting the best deal

Rental cars are quite affordable in Hawaii, although they do vary from island to island and from season to season. Of course, I can't guarantee what you'll pay when you book, but you can often get a compact car for between $100 to $200 a week. If you want something family-size — or a convertible — expect to pay anywhere from $225 to $400 a week, which is still reasonable.

The price you pay depends on the size of the car, the length the rental, your pickup and drop-off points, and several other factors. The following tips could save you a considerable amount of money on your car rental:

- **Book your rental car at weekly rates when possible.** Weekly rentals will almost always save you money. Several major rental firms, in fact — most notably Hertz and Avis — offer multi-island contracts. For example, if you plan to visit both Oahu and Kauai, you can pick up a car in Oahu, keep it for four days, return it, fly to Kauai, and then pick up another car for your three days there, all under the same contract. You end up paying for one week at the weekly rate rather than four times the daily rate on Oahu and three times the daily rate on Maui — which will always be much cheaper. Ask when you book.

- **Mention membership in AAA, AARP, and frequent-flyer programs when booking.** These memberships may qualify you for discounts ranging from 5 percent to 30 percent. Ask your travel agent to check any and all of these rates.

✔ **Ask the reservations agency that books your hotel or your interisland air travel if they book rental cars.** Many hotels, condo rental agents, and even B&B owners can book rental cars at seriously discounted rates; ditto for the interisland air carriers, Hawaiian and Aloha (see Chapter 5). Often, you can save as much as 30 percent off the rate.

✔ **If you see an advertised special, ask for that specific rate when booking.** The car rental company may not offer this information voluntarily. Make sure to remind them; otherwise, you may be charged the standard (higher) rate.

✔ **Consider booking your car as part of a complete travel package.** Package deals will not only save you dollars on airfare and accommodations but also on your rental cars, too. This one-stop shopping can help streamline the trip-planning process. For more on package deals, see Chapter 5.

✔ **Don't forget to ask about frequent-flyer mileage.** Most car rentals are worth at least 500 miles on your frequent-flyer account. Be sure to find out which airlines the rental-car company is affiliated with so that you can earn mileage. Bring your card with you, and make sure your account is credited at pick-up time.

✔ **Make sure you're getting free unlimited mileage.** Thankfully, most of the major car-rental companies rent on an unlimited-miles basis, but you should confirm this policy when you book. Even on an island, the miles you drive can really add up.

Some companies assess a drop-off charge of around $50 if you don't return the car to the location where you rented it; others, notably National, don't. This may be an issue on the Big Island, where you might want to fly into Kona Airport, on one side of the island, and leave Hilo, on the other side (or vice-versa), so ask when you book.

Using the Internet can make comparison shopping much easier. All the major booking sites — **Travelocity** (www.travelocity.com), **Expedia** (www.expedia.com), **Yahoo Travel** (http://travel.yahoo.com), and **Cheap Tickets** (www.cheaptickets.com), for example — feature search engines that can book car rentals for you.

In addition to the standard rental price, optional charges can apply to car rentals. You may opt to pay for a collision damage waiver, which covers damage in the case of an accident. Many credit card companies offer this coverage automatically, so check the terms of your credit card before you shell out money for this hefty charge (as much as $15 a day).

The car-rental companies also offer additional liability insurance (if you harm others in an accident), personal accident insurance (if you harm yourself or your passengers), and personal effects insurance (if someone steals your luggage from your car). If you have insurance on your car at home, that insurance probably covers you for most of these scenarios. If your own insurance doesn't cover you for rentals, or if you don't have auto insurance, consider signing on for additional coverage (as much as $20 per day combined). Also keep in mind that car-rental companies are liable for certain base amounts, depending on the state.

Most major car-rental companies obligate you to return your car with a full tank of gas. You can do it yourself, or you can buy a refueling package from the rental company, which allows you to pay for an entire tank of gas up front. The price is usually fairly competitive with local gas prices, but you don't get credit for any gas remaining in the tank. If you reject this option, you pay only for the gas you use, but you have to return it with a full tank or else you face charges of $3 to $4 a gallon for any shortfall. Make sure to allot enough time for refueling on the way to the airport if you decline the refueling package.

Hawaii How-To: Renting convertibles

Renting a convertible is a lot like booking an oceanview room; it's a must if you can afford it, not worth it if it's going to put a strain on your budget. The cost of going topless can be double or more what you'd pay for a regular car. Expect to pay between $50 and $80 a day for a convertible, compared with $30 or $40 a day for a better-equipped midsize car (with such extras as power windows and power locks that don't usually come with convertibles).

If you'd really like to rent a convertible for your island driving but you're worried about cost, consider the following:

- ✔ **Rent a convertible for just part of your trip.** If you're going to be visiting two or three islands, book a convertible on one of them. Consider renting one on Maui — cruising the road to Hana with the top down really is the ultimate Hawaii vacation dream.

- ✔ **Ask about upgrades when you pick up your rental car.** This may prove especially beneficial if you're visiting in the off-season. Sometimes, if a rental-car branch has a few idle convertibles sitting around, they'll offer you an on-the-spot upgrade for just $10 or $15 more a day. If you negotiated a decent compact or midsize rate when you booked, the total should come out to substantially less than the convertible rate offered over the phone.

Following the rules of the road

Know these driving rules and common practices before you get behind the wheel in Hawaii:

- ✔ **Hawaii is a no-fault insurance state.** If you drive without collision-damage insurance, you are required to pay for all damages before you leave the state, regardless of who is at fault. Your personal auto policy may provide rental-car coverage; read your policy or check with your insurer before you leave home, and be sure to bring your insurance ID card if you decline the rental-car company's optional insurance. Some credit card companies also provide collision damage insurance; check with yours.

- ✔ **Seatbelts are mandatory for everyone in the car, all the time.** The law is strictly enforced, so be sure to buckle up. All small children must be strapped into car seats.

✔ **You can turn right on red unless a posted sign specifies otherwise.** Make sure you make a full stop first — no rolling.

✔ **Pedestrians always have the right of way.** This is true even if they're not in a crosswalk.

✔ **Use your horn judiciously.** Honking your horn to express your anger at another driver is considered the height of rudeness in Hawaii. Don't do it. Horns are used to greet friends in Hawaii.

 Remember that your rental car is not a safe in which to store valuables. Don't leave anything you don't want to lose in the car or trunk, not even for a short time. Be especially careful when you park at beaches, where thieves know you're going to leave your car for awhile (and you're likely to leave goodies in the glove compartment).

The islands are very easy to negotiate, and all of the rental-car companies hand out very good map booklets on each island. If all you have is what National or Hertz gives you, you'll do just fine.

Making Reservations before You Leave Home

In addition to buying your airfare, booking your accommodations, and reserving a rental car, you may want to make a few advance plans before you leave home.

In general, you don't have to call ahead to reserve most activities until you arrive in Hawaii. Most snorkel cruises, guided tours, and the like can be reserved a day or two in advance. Even high-profile restaurants can usually get you in within a few days of the day you call.

Still, advance planning is always a good idea, even for those activities that don't require it. And it's an absolute necessity for certain special events and activities, including the following:

✔ **Luaus:** Maui's **Old Lahaina Luau** is the best luau in the islands — and it always sells out at least a week in advance, often more, as does its sister luau, **The Feast at Lele.** It's never too early to reserve your seats; see Chapter 13 for contact information. Second-best is the Big Island's **Kona Village Luau,** which is only offered on Friday nights; see Chapter 17.

✔ **Snorkel cruises:** Maui's finest snorkel-cruise operator is **Trilogy Excursions.** They're hugely popular, so you may want to book your trip to Molokai or Lanai, both red-hot snorkel spots, before you leave home (see Chapter 14).

✔ **Special events:** Certain special events require advance planning or arrangements, such as the **Merrie Monarch Hula Festival,** the **Maui Music Festival,** and the **Kapalua Wine & Food Symposium.** Check "A Hawaii Calendar of Events" in Chapter 2 to see what will be on while you're in town, and whether it requires advance planning or not. You also might want to check with the individual island visitors bureaus; see the Quick Concierge at the back of the book for contact information.

✔ **Special-occasion or holiday meals:** These should always be reserved in a advance to avoid disappointment. This is especially true on holidays, when the nicer restaurants are overrun with locals and visitors alike. Take it from me on this one — I couldn't get a same-day table at a decent restaurant on Mother's Day to save my life.

✔ **Scuba classes:** First-time scuba divers may want to look into the various resort courses that are available, as they differ from outfitter to outfitter; see the chapters called "Fun On and Off the Beach" in Parts III through VI for reputable local dive instructors.

Consider taking scuba certification classes before you leave home; that way, you don't waste time learning in some resort swimming pool and can dive right in once you get to Hawaii. A great way to find a local scuba instructor is via the Professional Association of Diving Instructors (PADI) Web site; go online to www.padi.com, click on Dive Centers and Resorts.

As you thumb through this book, look for this icon:

I use it to highlight these and other activities and attractions that require advance arrangements; otherwise, you might miss out. I also indicate reservations policies in all restaurant reviews. Be sure to peruse the restaurant listings for those islands where you'll want to book a special meal, and let your red flags be such phrases as "reservations highly recommended," "reservations required," and "reservations a must."

Planning your activities in advance is often the best way to guarantee that you won't miss out on an event or a restaurant you've been counting on — that way, if there's a sudden rush on tour spots or a restaurant is planning to close down for a few days to install a new stove in the kitchen, you have the opportunity to amend your plans accordingly. Advance planning will also start to give useful form to your itinerary, so you'll begin to have an idea of where your busy days and your free days fall. Besides, you don't want to spend your valuable Hawaii time on the phone in your hotel room, do you?

Packing Tips

To start your packing, set aside everything you think you need to take. Then get rid of half of it.

Even if the airlines will let you take it all (with some limits), carting loads of stuff around Hawaii is a big fat drag. Believe me, you really can do without that sixth pair of sandals. Besides, suitcase and duffel-bag straps can be particularly painful on sunburned shoulders — and you'll probably spend all day in your bathing suit, anyway. What's more, almost all hotel and condo complexes have on-site laundry facilities, lest you actually run out of clothes or spill a mai tai on your favorite sundress.

Here are the essentials that you should pack:

- ✔ **More than one swimsuit:** It's a real bummer to find out that yesterday's swimsuit isn't dry today. You'll use the extra, I swear.

- ✔ **Sunglasses, a sunhat, and high-SPF sunscreen:** Take SPF 15, at minimum (30 is better); the Hawaiian sun is very strong.

- ✔ **Beach sandals:** I don't want you to scorch your tootsies on the sand. Inexpensive flip-flops do the trick.

- ✔ **A sweater or light jacket:** The evenings can get breezy.

- ✔ **Good, comfortable walking shoes.** Bring hiking boots if you plan to hike, especially if you're going to visit the national parks on Maui and the Big Island.

- ✔ **A warm jacket and long pants:** You really need these if you plan to visit Haleakala or Hawaii Volcanoes National Park or some other upcountry location that gets cool even in summer. Basically, count on the temperature dropping 3½ degrees for every 1,000 feet you climb, which means that it's can be 35 degrees cooler atop Haleakala's peak than it is at the beach. And it's always cooler at Hawaii Volcanoes than anyone expects it to be, so come prepared.

- ✔ **Rain gear:** A waterproof jacket with a hood is always a good idea if you're visiting Hawaii between November and March.

- ✔ **Binoculars:** These come in handy during whale-watching season or to spot dolphins, birds, or other critters at any time of year.

- ✔ **Dramamine or nausea-prevention wristbands:** These can save the day on a snorkel or sunset cruise. (If you plan to rely on Dramamine to prevent car- or seasickness, be sure to take it *before* you set out — because it's too late once you're on the curving coastal road or rough open seas.)

- ✔ **A cellphone:** It can be an invaluable lifeline in the event that you get a flat or your rental car breaks down.

- ✔ **An extra pair of eyeglasses or contact lenses.** Always a good idea to prevent an inconvenient "Ack — I can't see!" emergency.

Hawaii is a very easygoing place — so leave the pantyhose and pumps and the jacket and tie at home. A casual dress or a polo shirt and khakis will get you by in most dining rooms in the islands — even the expensive ones. A few ultra-fancy resort restaurants require a jacket — but that's all wrong for Hawaii, so I don't recommend them.

Hawaiian-print aloha wear is acceptable universally throughout the islands; I'll tell you where to buy the best quality and most beautiful aloha clothes on each island later in this book. You say you'll never wear it again once you get home? You should — aloha wear looks great everywhere!

Bring all of your prescription meds, of course, but don't bother hauling a half-dozen bottles of saline solution or 16 rolls of film from home. Hawaii has a fine collection of drugstores throughout the islands. In fact, if you forget anything, don't panic. You can buy everything you need — and lots of stuff you don't — on any of the major islands.

Part III
Honolulu and the Rest of Oahu

The 5th Wave   By Rich Tennant

Doug shows the vacation video he shot diving among the pool toys

Watch how close I'm able to get to the noodles.

In this part . . .

Busier and more developed than the other islands, Oahu is often called "the Gathering Place." It's home to the gateway into Hawaii, Honolulu International Airport, so even if you plan to spend the length of your stay on another island, it's a good bet you'll come to Oahu first. The four chapters in this part will help you plan your trip to this beautiful island and offer a wide variety of accommodations, dining, and attractions to choose from.

Chapter 7

The Lowdown on Oahu's Hotel Scene

. . . .

In This Chapter

▶ Deciding where to base yourself in Honolulu

▶ Choosing among the island's top resorts, hotels, and condos

▶ Arranging for a vacation-home rental or a B&B beyond the confines of the city

. . . .

*T*here's only one place to stay when you come to Oahu: Honolulu's most famous district, Waikiki. Frankly, if you're planning a trip to the liveliest island in the Pacific, you'll want to revel in the energy of it. If staying in the heart of the action doesn't sound appealing to you, you might consider skipping Oahu entirely and heading to a neighbor island.

That said, if you do want peace and quiet, you can find it here, too. A number of the hotels listed in this chapter are located on the quieter fringe of Waikiki, in less densely developed or residential neighborhoods. And if you'd really prefer to stay beyond the city, on the residential Windward Coast or the island's funky north shore, I show you how to book the B&B or vacation rental of your dreams.

Choosing Your Location

Keep in mind that Waikiki is hardly Las Vegas — not by a long shot. Waikiki's version of raucous fun is pretty darn easygoing — more like a laid-back, high-rise beach party than anything else. Still, there are degrees. (See the maps in Chapter 8 for more information about the following areas.)

Mid-Waikiki

Mid-Waikiki is prime Waikiki territory — the heart of the action. This is Waikiki at its most densely built, but it's also Waikiki at its most convenient. Restaurants, shopping, and — most important — the city's most popular and celebrated stretch of sand are all within walking distance.

While it retains some vestiges of cheese, mid-Waikiki has become more sophisticated of late, with respectable restaurants and both midrange and couture boutiques replacing former T-shirt shops and tacky souvenir posts. Still, plenty of affordable hotels remain; the neighborhood has simply improved around them.

Ewa Waikiki

Ewa (EE-va) Waikiki is the western end of the neighborhood, on the way to downtown Honolulu. (Oahuans say "ewa" to indicated a westerly direction, meaning toward the town called Ewa on the west side of Oahu.) This western end of Waikiki, beyond Saratoga Road (on the other side of Fort DeRussy Park from mid-Waikiki), is a tad removed but plenty convenient. The beach is quieter at this more residential (mostly high-rise apartments), less dense end, but you may find yourself getting in the car (or hopping the Waikiki Trolley) to mid-Waikiki destinations.

Diamond Head Waikiki

For those who want both quiet and convenience, this easternmost section of Waikiki is the place to stay. Many call this their favorite section of town, thanks to its pretty setting, easygoing vibe, great beach, and prime panoramic views of the rest of Waikiki. A handful of small hotels and condo buildings sit at the foot of Diamond Head crater, separated from the rest of the neighborhood by well-manicured Kapiolani Park (Honolulu's answer to Central Park). The beach here, called Sans Souci Beach, is the locals' favorite stretch, thanks to its attractive disposition (Diamond Head makes a gorgeous backdrop) and intimate, low-key vibe.

Beyond Waikiki: Kahala

This exclusive residential neighborhood on the other side of Diamond Head, just a ten-minute drive east of prime Waikiki, is the perfect compromise for those who want an away-from-it-all vibe and a freeway-convenient location. Expect to dig deep, though — the only hotel in these parts is the Kahala Mandarin, Honolulu's finest full-fledged resort.

Waikiki's Best Hotels and Condos

As you peruse the options, keep in mind that Waikiki is a densely developed resort, so it contains more hotels and fewer full-fledged resort spreads and condos than what you'll find on the neighbor islands. Three hotel chains dominate, each offering top value for dollar: Starwood Hotels (Sheraton, Luxury Collection, and W) at the high end; and Hawaii-based-chains Aston and Outrigger/Ohana in the middle range and at the low end (Ohana is an umbrella for Outrigger's budget-oriented hotels).

In the listings that follow, each resort, hotel, or condo name is followed by a number of dollar signs, ranging from one ($) to five ($$$$$). Each represents the median price range for a double room per night, as follows:

$	Super-cheap — less than $75 per night
$$	Still affordable — $75 to $150
$$$	Moderate — $150 to $225
$$$$	Expensive but not ridiculous — $225 to $300
$$$$$	Ultra-luxurious — more than $300 per night

Also, don't forget that the state adds 11.42 percent in taxes to your hotel bill.

 A number of Waikiki's inexpensive and mid-priced hotels feature rooms whose bathrooms have showers only, no tubs. If you need a full tub, be sure to check that one will be available when booking to avoid disappointment.

Don't forget to use the "Sweet Dreams: Choosing Your Hotel" worksheet at the back of this book to help you organize your accommodations choices.

Aston Coconut Plaza

$–$$ Mid-Waikiki

This small hotel offers excellent value for those on a budget — and pretty good views, too, considering that it's blocks from the beach. The light and airy hotel establishes a tropical plantation vibe (quite an achievement in the heart of Waikiki) with lots of greenery, island-style rattan, and aloha-spirited service. Rooms have cool terra-cotta floors, fridge and coffeemaker (many have full kitchenettes with microwave, so request one when booking), and lanai (ask for one overlooking the pretty canal for maximum advantage, and a higher floor for maximum quiet). Extras include a nice pool and sundeck, plus a coin-op laundry. The free continental breakfast makes a good deal even better. The only down side? A ten-minute walk to the beach.

450 Lewers St. (at Ala Wai Blvd.). ☎ *800-922-7866 or 808-923-8828. Fax: 808-923-3473. Internet:* www.aston-hotels.com. *Valet parking: $9. Rack rates: $70–$115 double, $120–$140 junior suite. Rates include continental breakfast. Deals: Excellent opportunities for discounts. Internet-only ePriceBreaker rates as low as $65 at press time. Ask for AAA, senior (50-plus), and corporate discounts, and other special rate programs. Qualify for 25% discount if you stay at Aston properties for 7 or more nights with Aston's "Island Hopper" program. AE, CB, DC, DISC, JCB, MC, V.*

Waikiki Hotels and Condos

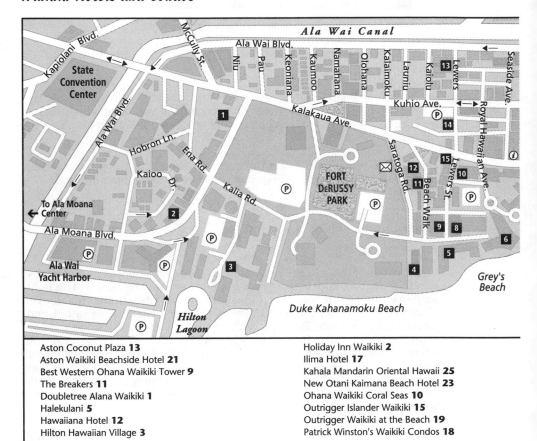

Aston Coconut Plaza **13**	Holiday Inn Waikiki **2**
Aston Waikiki Beachside Hotel **21**	Ilima Hotel **17**
Best Western Ohana Waikiki Tower **9**	Kahala Mandarin Oriental Hawaii **25**
The Breakers **11**	New Otani Kaimana Beach Hotel **23**
Doubletree Alana Waikiki **1**	Ohana Waikiki Coral Seas **10**
Halekulani **5**	Outrigger Islander Waikiki **15**
Hawaiiana Hotel **12**	Outrigger Waikiki at the Beach **19**
Hilton Hawaiian Village **3**	Patrick Winston's Waikiki Condos **18**

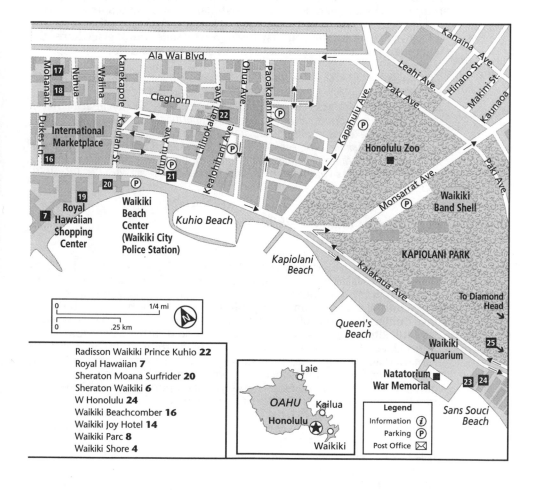

Ala Wai Blvd.

Kanaina Ave.

Leahi Ave.

Hinano St.

Makini St.

Paki Ave.

Kaunaoa

Mohanani

Nuhua

Walina

Kanekapole

Ohua Ave.

Paoakalani Ave.

17

18

Cleghorn

Kaiulani Ave.

Liliuokalani Ave.

22

Kapahulu Ave.

P

P

Honolulu Zoo

Dukes Ln.

International
Marketplace

16

Kealohilani Ave.

Uluniu Ave.

P

P

21

Paki Ave.

20

P

19

Royal
Hawaiian
Shopping
Center

7

Waikiki
Beach
Center
(Waikiki City
Police Station)

Kuhio Beach

Monsarrat Ave.

P

Waikiki
Band Shell

KAPIOLANI PARK

Kapiolani
Beach

Kalakaua Ave.

To Diamond
Head

0 ——— 1/4 mi
0 ——— .25 km

N

Queen's
Beach

Waikiki
Aquarium

25

Radisson Waikiki Prince Kuhio **22**
Royal Hawaiian **7**
Sheraton Moana Surfrider **20**
Sheraton Waikiki **6**
W Honolulu **24**
Waikiki Beachcomber **16**
Waikiki Joy Hotel **14**
Waikiki Parc **8**
Waikiki Shore **4**

Laie

OAHU
Honolulu

Kailua

Waikiki

Natatorium
War Memorial

23 24

Sans Souci
Beach

Legend
Information *(i)*
Parking *(P)*
Post Office ⊠

Aston Waikiki Beachside Hotel

$$$–$$$$ Mid-Waikiki

Situated directly across the street from a prime stretch of beach — with no buildings to interrupt ocean views or access — this boutique hotel is an oasis of unruffled elegance on Waikiki's main drag. It's intimate and attractive, with a gracious, attentive staff (and full-service concierge); lovely rooms with lots of extras, including VCR; twice-daily maid service (a blessing after a day on the sand); and a location that can't be beat. The rooms are miniscule, however — which won't matter much if you'd rather sacrifice square footage for a stellar location and a level of style and service you'd usually pay more to get. But if more than two are intending to share, or you just need your space, book elsewhere. Do whatever you can to book at a room level above standard.

2452 Kalakaua Ave. (between Uluniu and Liliuokalani aves.). ☎ *800-922-7866 or 808-931-2100. Fax: 808-922-2129. Internet:* www.aston-hotels.com. *Valet or self-parking: $9.50. Rack rates: $185–$329 double, $267–$379 junior suite. Rates include continental breakfast. Deals: Excellent opportunities for discounts. Internet-only ePriceBreaker rates can result in savings of up to 45% (doubles as low as $99 at press time). Ask for AAA, senior (50-plus), and corporate discounts, and other special rate programs. Qualify for 25% discount if you stay at Aston properties for 7 or more nights with Aston's "Island Hopper" program. AE, CB, DC, DISC, JCB, MC, V.*

Best Western Ohana Waikiki Tower

$$ Mid-Waikiki

This newly renovated gem is my favorite in the value-minded Ohana chain, and it's a mere half block from the beach. The rooms hardly burst with individual style, but the textiles and furnishings are on the quality side of motel-standard, and everything is fresh and attractive. All rooms have mini-fridges and coffeemakers, and all above the standard category have full kitchenettes — a boon for those who'd rather save a few bucks on breakfast. If you can snare a discount on a studio suite, book it; with a sofabed and dining area, these corner units are perfectly suitable for a small family, and most have ocean views. Amenities include a restaurant, shops, tour desk, and coin-op laundry, plus a pool if you don't want to crawl the few yards to the sand. An excellent value!

200 Lewers St. (between Kalia and Helumoa roads). ☎ *800-462-6262 or 808-922-6424. Fax: 808-923-7437. Internet:* www.ohanahotels.com. *Parking: $8. Rack rates: $139–$159 double; $209 studio suite. Deals: Almost nobody pays rack with Ohana. Better-than-average discounts for AAA and AARP members and seniors (50-plus), plus corporate, government, and military discounts. SimpleSaver rates as low as $99. Ask about first night free, bed-and-breakfast, room-and-car, and other package deals. Also check* www.bestwestern.com *for value rates. AE, DC, DISC, JCB, MC, V.*

The Breakers

$$ Mid-Waikiki

This low-rise charmer in the midst of high-rise Waikiki is a great option for budget-minded travelers who don't want to succumb to chain-hotel conformity simply to save a buck or two. This two-story '50s-style garden motel boasts a friendly staff, a loyal following, a fab location less than two blocks from the beach, and a warmly nostalgic Old Waikiki vibe. Units are set around an attractive pool and tropical garden blooming with brilliant hibiscus; wooden jalousies and Japanese-style shoji doors further the island ambience. The spacious rooms are older but very nicely maintained, and they boast electric-range kitchenettes and lanais overlooking the pool. The poolside cafe serves up killer burgers and great mai tais; it's very popular with the local gay crowd, but the hotel caters to visitors from all walks of life, including families. A coin-op laundry is on site.

250 Beach Walk (between Kalakaua Ave. and Helumoa Rd.). ☎ 800-426-0494 or 808-923-3181. Fax: 808-923-7174. Internet: www.breakers-hawaii.com. *Limited free parking; $6–$8 a day across the street. Rack rates: $94–$100 studio double, $125–$151 suite. AE, DC, MC, V.*

Halekulani

$$$$$ Mid-Waikiki

I adore the Halekulani — the finest hotel in Waikiki is the epitome of gracious and elegant aloha. This open, low-rise beachfront hotel exudes understated luxury (although some may consider it a tad formal for a beach hotel). The rooms are uniformly oversized and done in a supremely comfortable natural-on-white style. Each one features a sitting area, a large furnished lanai, a sumptuous bath, and all the extras you'd expect from a hotel of this caliber, including twice-daily maid service; most have some sort of ocean view. The service is among the best I've ever experienced, the restaurants are first-rate, the alfresco lounge is Oahu's most romantic spot for sunset cocktails and hula, and the pool is magnificent. Only one niggling complaint: The beach is small, and the hotel offers only pool service; if you want to sit in a chair rather than on a towel, you're stuck behind a hedge — and if you want to recline, forget about an ocean view.

2199 Kalia Rd. (at the beach end of Lewers St.). ☎ 800-367-2343, 800-323-7500, or 808-923-2311. Fax: 808-926-8004. Internet: www.halekulani.com. *Valet parking: $10. Rack rates: $320–$530 double, $700–$4,500 suite (most $700–$1,700). Deals: Numerous good-value packages usually on offer, including breakfast, spa services, dinner and champagne, or other extras. AE, CB, DC, JCB, MC, V.*

Hawaiiana Hotel

$$–$$$ Mid-Waikiki

Much like the neighboring Breakers (above), this low-rise garden motel is affordable, comfortable, well-located — less than a block from the beach — and full of old-time aloha spirit. I always get good reports from guests about this place, and I was very impressed on a recent inspection. Every spacious room features a full kitchenette; the concrete-block walls can be a bit of a downer, but the rooms are light and bright, most appliances are on the newer side, and maintenance is very impressive. The pricier Alii rooms boast better-quality furnishings, prime positions in the complex, bathtub-shower combos, and such extras as hair dryers and bathrobes, but the standard rooms are just fine for tight budgets. Free coffee and juice are served mornings in the courtyard, and the lush grounds feature two nice pools, barbecues, and a coin-op laundry.

260 Beach Walk (between Kalakaua Ave. and Helumoa Rd.). ☎ *800-367-5122, 800-628-3098, or 808-923-3811. Fax: 808-926-5728. Parking: $8. Rack rates: $85–$105 double, $165–$190 Alii studio, $135–$145 1-bedroom. AE, DC, DISC, JCB, MC, V.*

Hilton Hawaiian Village

$$$$ Ewa Waikiki

Spread out over 20 tropical acres featuring exotic wildlife — including flamingoes, peacocks, and even tropical penguins! — and fronting a gorgeous stretch of beach that feels private even though it's not, Waikiki's biggest resort is my favorite choice for families. It feels like a tropical theme park, with its own lagoon (with submarine rides), three pools, two minigolf courses, a wealth of restaurants (including the excellent Golden Dragon for Chinese and the ultra-romantic Bali by the Sea), a theatrical dome, enough shopping to stock a mid-size mall, a handful of bars and lounges, and more — even its own post office. Still, thanks to the size limitations of tightly packed Waikiki, this Hilton isn't so big that it's overwhelming. On the contrary — it's a blast to stay here. Rooms are housed in multiple towers and range from comfortable to first-class depending on what you want to spend, but all are large, well-outfitted, and laden with amenities. Among the other pleasing extras is one of Waikiki's best kids' programs.

2005 Kalia Rd. (at Ala Moana Blvd.). ☎ *800-HILTONS or 808-949-4321. Fax: 808-947-7898. Internet:* www.hawaiianvillage.hilton.com. *Valet parking: $12; self-parking: $9. Rack rates: $220–$445 double, suites from $415. Deals: A range of packages and special offers is almost always available, including romance packages, discounts on multi-night stays, free breakfast, free giveaways for kids, and much more. Also ask for AAA, AARP, corporate, frequent-flyer, and other discounts. AE, CB, DISC, ER, JCB, MC, V.*

Ilima Hotel

$$ Mid-Waikiki

This local-style condo hotel is a bargain for families, or anybody who wants accommodations that go above and beyond what an average hotel can offer. The roomy studios and one-, two-, and three-bedroom apartments are recently renovated and boast full modern kitchens with microwave and coffeemaker, nice new baths, sofabeds in the living room, and a lanai. Extras include daily maid service (not a given in condo units), free local calls (a nice plus), a heated pool with adjacent sauna, a rooftop sundeck, and laundry facilities. The service is friendly, and the heart-of-Waikiki location is central to shopping and dining. The beach is a ten-minute walk away — but at these prices, you can put on your walkin' shoes.

445 Nohonani St. (between Kuhio Ave. and Ala Wai Blvd.). ☎ *808-923-1877. Fax: 888-864-5462 or 808-924-2617. Internet:* www.ilima.com. *Limited free parking, or $8 across the street. Rack rates: $95–$137 studio, $140–$177 1-bedroom, $195–$207 2-bedroom, $295–$307 3-bedroom. Deals: Ask for heavily discounted senior (55 and older) and corporate rates. Ask about sixth night free, summer values, and other seasonal deals, and check for Internet specials. AE, CB, DC, DISC, JCB, MC, V.*

Kahala Mandarin Oriental Hawaii

$$$$$ Kahala

If you want easy access to Honolulu's sights but Waikiki sounds like a big fat drag, the Kahala Mandarin is the perfect compromise. It's just a ten-minute drive east of Waikiki, staked out on its own perfect crescent beach in one of Honolulu's most prestigious neighborhoods. In fact, the tranquil Mandarin is ideal for anybody who likes first-rate service, an ambience that blends T-shirts-and-flip-flops comfort with gracious elegance, and big, beautiful rooms with CD players and consistently high-quality everything — including the best bathrooms in the business, with soaking tub, separate shower, and his-and-her sinks and dressing areas. Hoku's, one of Honolulu's most celebrated restaurants, is named for the most charming of the three bottlenosed dolphins that live on premises; ask for a room with a lanai that overlooks the dolphin lagoon and sea, and the world is yours. Even if you end up in a mountain-view room, take heart: The vistas are almost as fine. The dolphin-encounter program and year-round kids' club make the Kahala great for families, too.

5000 Kahala Ave. (east of Diamond Head, next to the Waialae Country Club). ☎ *800-367-2525 or 808-739-8888. Fax: 808-739-8800. Internet:* www.mandarin-oriental.com. *Valet parking: $12. Rack rates: $295–$675 double, $590–$3,650 suite. Deals: Numerous package deals, including wedding and honeymoon packages, are almost always on offer, so ask. Also inquire about AAA discounts. AE, CB, DC, DISC, JCB, MC, V.*

New Otani Kaimana Beach Hotel

$$$ Diamond Head Waikiki

Located at the quiet, pretty foot of Diamond Head, this boutique hotel is Waikiki's best beachfront bargain. It sits right on the locals' favorite stretch of Waikiki Beach, with leafy Kapiolani Park at its back door — which means that the views are pleasing in almost any direction. An inviting open-air lobby leads to contemporary rooms that are more Holiday Inn than stylish, but perfectly comfortable. The most basic rooms are tiny, so spring for a superior one if you can. The junior suites are large enough for families, and corner rooms boast Waikiki's finest views. The airy lobby opens onto the Hau Tree Lanai, a wonderfully romantic restaurant that sits right on the sand; great breakfasts make it the right place to start the day even if you're not staying here. Amenities include VCRs, mini-fridges, and coin-op laundry. A formerly surly staff has seriously upped the friendly quotient, transforming this into one of my favorite midpriced hotels in the process. An excellent value on all fronts.

2863 Kalakaua Ave. (across the street from Kapiolani Park). ☎ *800-35-OTANI, 800-421-8795, or 808-923-1555. Fax: 808-922-9404. Internet:* www.kaimana.com. *Valet parking: $10. Rack rates: $130–$285 double, $200–$810 suite. Deals: Ask about package rates. AE, CB, DC, DISC, JCB, MC, V.*

Ohana Waikiki Coral Seas

$$ Mid-Waikiki

Give up any thought of views — the Coral Seas has none — but this budget hotel has a great location, just 1½ blocks from the beach, and value in spades. Management has taken the coral thing to heart, outfitting the rooms in a 1970s peach color scheme that's pleasant, nonetheless. Rooms are bigger than most in this price range, making the double/doubles suitable for budget-minded families (and your kids will love the Nintendo on the TV). Bathrooms have showers only, so book elsewhere if you need a tub. Two restaurants, a handful of shops, and a coin-op laundry are on site, and guests have use of the pool at the adjoining hotel.

250 Lewers St. (between Helumoa Rd. and Kalakaua Ave.). ☎ *800-462-6262 or 808-923-3881. Fax: 808-924-6361. Internet:* www.ohanahotels.com. *Parking: $8. Rack rates: $109 double; $119 double with kitchenette; $169 suite. Deals: Almost nobody pays rack with Ohana. Better-than-average discounts for AAA and AARP members and seniors (50-plus), plus corporate, government, and military discounts. SimpleSaver rates as low as $99. Ask about first night free, bed-and-breakfast, room-and-car, and other package deals. AE, DC, DISC, JCB, MC, V.*

In addition to the Ohana Waikiki Coral Seas, directly preceding, and the Best Western Ohana Waikiki Tower, earlier in this chapter, the Ohana family of hotels features 13 more value-minded hotels in Honolulu, all recommendable and most within walking distance of Waikiki Beach. If you're looking for cheap sleeps, it's hard to go wrong with Ohana. For further information, see "No Room at the Inn?" later in this chapter.

Outrigger Islander Waikiki

$$$ Mid-Waikiki

Waikiki's newest hotel is attractive and well located, across the street from the Royal Hawaiian and just 2½ blocks from the beach. A pleasant tropical-style lobby leads to guest rooms that are more sophisticated than most in the Outrigger chain, with such pleasant touches as Italian tile entryways and soft Berber carpets underfoot; a mini-fridge, coffeemaker, and hair dryer in every room; and a small furnished lanai. The furniture was bulk-purchased from the no-personality catalog, but everything is pleasant and fresh. Affordable connecting rooms are great for families who don't want *too* much togetherness. Amenities include a nice pool, a coin-op laundry, shops and casual restaurants (including an on-site Starbuck's, perfect for the morning joe), and room service.

270 Lewers St. (at Kalakaua Ave.). ☎ *800-688-7444 or 808-923-7711. Fax: 808-924-5755. Internet:* www.outrigger.com. *Parking: $8. Rack rates: $175–$195 double, $205 studio. Deals: Almost nobody pays rack with Outrigger, the king of package deals. Better-than-average discounts for AAA and AARP members and* seniors (50-plus), plus corporate, government, and military discounts. First night free, bed-and-breakfast, room-and-car, and other packages regularly on offer. AE, DC, DISC, JCB, MC, V.

Outrigger Waikiki at the Beach

$$$$ Mid-Waikiki

I'll make no bones about it — the rack rates here are just too high. Don't get me wrong — I *like* this 16-story oceanfront hotel, the flagship of the Outrigger chain, I really do. It sits in the center square, right in the heart of the party on Waikiki's absolute best stretch of beach. Even the standard rooms are large and comfortable, with big closets, roomy bathrooms, good amenities (fridge, hair dryer, and coffeemaker), and spacious lanais. Facilities include a fitness center, an oceanfront pool and spa, and plenty of shops and restaurants, including one of my Waikiki faves, Duke's Canoe Club. But this Outrigger still has the air of a budget hotel about it — so when I know you can stay at the Hilton Hawaiian Village for the same money, I'm gonna tell you to try there first. Do what you can to negotiate a better rate or land a package deal before you sign on.

2335 Kalakaua Ave. (on the ocean, between the Royal Hawaiian Shopping Center and the Sheraton Moana Surfrider). ☎ *800-688-7444 or 808-923-0711. Fax: 808-921-9749. Internet:* www.outrigger.com. *Valet or self-parking: $10. Rack rates: $230–$495 double, $600–$645 suite. Deals: Almost nobody pays rack with Outrigger, the king of package deals. Better-than-average discounts for AAA and AARP members and seniors (50-plus), plus corporate, government, and military discounts. First night free, bed-and-breakfast, room-and-car, and other packages regularly on offer. AE, DC, DISC, JCB, MC, V.*

Patrick Winston's Waikiki Condos

$–$$ Mid-Waikiki

Pat Winston deals in budget apartments, so don't show up expecting the condo equivalent of the Ritz — but you will find a high value-for-dollar ratio waiting for you. This friendly man manages 24 clean, comfortable suites in a well-kept five-story garden-apartment building located on a quiet, central-to-everything street two blocks from the beach. Each of the individually decorated units has a sofabed, a furnished lanai overlooking the tropical courtyard and pool, A/C *and* ceiling fans, and a full kitchen with microwave; most have a washer/dryer (coin-op facilities are also on site). Pat does all the renovation, maintenance, and cleaning himself, and he does a great job. His newest is the memorabilia-filled Hawaii Five-O suite — ideal for budgeteers with a taste for classic TV kitsch (nonsmokers only). Bursting with aloha spirit, Pat goes the extra mile to do what he can — book activities, make restaurant recommendations, and so on — to make sure you go home happy.

In the Hawaiian King, 417 Nohonani St. (between Kuhio Ave. and Ala Wai Blvd.). ☎ *800-545-1948, 808-924-3332, or 808-922-3894 (front desk). Fax: 808-924-3332. Internet:* www.winstonswaikikicondos.com. *Parking: $7. Rack rates: $75–$125 1-bedroom suite; $115–$135 2-bedroom suite. 4-night minimum; extra* person beyond two $10 each; $25 out-cleaning fee. Deals: Internet discounts and monthly rates available. Patrick can book money-saving air-room-car packages on the neighbor islands, too. AE, CB, DC, DISC, JCB, MC, V.

Royal Hawaiian

$$$$$ Mid-Waikiki

This shocking-pink oasis hidden among blooming gardens in the heart of Waikiki has been *the* symbol of Hawaiian luxury since 1927 — and it still exudes elegance from a time when travelers arrived by Matson Line rather than jumbo jet, with steamer trunks instead of nylon totes in tow. It sits right in the heart of the action on Waikiki's most exciting stretch of sand. Every guest room is lovely, and I have a real soft spot for the Historic wing; still, that Pepto Bismol pink gets old after awhile. Perks abound, including lei greetings, concierge service, an oceanfront patio restaurant that's an ideal place to start your day, poolside bar service, a grand Monday-night luau, and preferential tee times for golfers. All in all, I prefer the Moana (see the following listing), but the Royal is second in terms of nostalgic appeal.

2259 Kalakaua Ave. (at the end of Royal Hawaiian Ave.). ☎ 800-782-9488, 800-325-3589, or 808-923-7311. Fax: 808-924-7098. Internet: www.royal-hawaiian. com or www.luxurycollection.com. Valet parking: $13; self-parking $9. Rack rates: $325–$600 double, suites from $800. Deals: Numerous package deals are almost always available, so be sure to ask. Romance, wedding, and honeymoon packages are legendary — and, if you're lucky, may include airport transfers in the Royal's signature pink limousine. Also ask for AAA-member and senior discounts. AE, DC, DISC, JCB, MC, V.

Sheraton Moana Surfrider

$$$$–$$$$$ Mid-Waikiki

The Moana isn't quite as luxurious as the neighboring Royal Hawaiian, but I still prefer it on all counts. Even with a '60s extension and a modern tower, this elegant white-clapboard Victorian — Waikiki's first hotel, built in 1901 — overflows with beachy nostalgia. It's more understated and intimate, and less expensive, than the Royal, and the location is equally ideal. The original U-shaped building embraces a hundred-year-old banyan tree and the ocean beyond; it exudes a magical back-in-time vibe that all guests share in, even if your room has a stucco ceiling. I recommend the Banyan rooms, which are small but loaded with historical detail and charm. If space or ocean views win out over vibe for you, book in one of the newer wings, where you'll get more modern fixtures and a lanai. Both the service and the facilities are great. I love any excuse — breakfast, high tea, Sunday brunch — to snag a seat on the oceanfront veranda, where live music and cocktails are on tap every evening.

2365 Kalakaua Ave. (on the beach, across from Kaiulani St.). ☎ 800-782-9488 or 808-922-3111. Fax: 808-923-0308. Internet: www.moana-surfrider.com or www.sheraton.com. Valet parking: $15; $9 self-parking. Rack rates: $265–$520 double. Deals: Promotional rates and/or package deals are almost always available, so ask for these as well as AAA-member and senior discounts. AE, CB, DC, DISC, JCB, MC, V.

Sheraton Waikiki

$$$$–$$$$$ Mid-Waikiki

Being a sucker for the romantic history of the Sheraton's sister hotels, the Moana and the Royal (directly preceding), I never gave this neighboring monolith much thought — until I was invited in this year, and discovered a newly renovated and amenity-laden hotel brimming with modern comforts and glorious ocean views. The winged high-rise was built in such a way that about 60 percent of the nearly 1,900 rooms boast a full ocean view (80 percent have some kind of ocean view). The rooms are big, comfortable, and fresh-feeling. While a new sea-turtle theme adds charm, the entire place is a tad nondescript. Come instead for the stunning beach out front; one of the finest kids' programs on the islands (and free to boot!); numerous restaurants and bars, including Waikiki's only oceanfront dance club; two oceanside pools; a fitness center; extensive shops and services; and much more.

2255 Kalakaua Ave. (at the end of Royal Hawaiian Ave.). ☎ *800-782-9488 or 808-922-4422. Fax: 808-922-9567. Internet:* www.sheraton-waikiki.com *or* www.sheraton.com. *Rack rates: $260–$485 Waikiki double, suites from $675. Valet parking: $13; self-parking: $9. Deals: Multiple money-saving promotions and/or package deals are almost always on offer; also check for AAA-member and senior discounts. AE, CB, DC, DISC, JCB, MC, V.*

If you want access to the Sheraton Waikiki's extensive facilities but the rates quoted above are too rich for your blood, ask about the rooms in the adjacent Manor Hotel Annex ($$$), which usually go for a more affordable $160 per night.

W Honolulu

$$$$$ Diamond Head Waikiki

This super-stylish mid-rise boutique hotel boasts impeccable rooms, a tranquil location at the foot of Diamond Head, and an impressively attentive staff that could easily fit in at the standard-bearing Halekulani. The large, gorgeous Balinese-style rooms boast rich white-on-white textiles, elegantly rustic teak furnishings, heavenly beds, marble bathrooms with plush bathrobes, huge furnished lanais, and high-tech extras — cordless phones, CD players, VCR, Web TV, and video games. Luxury-level services include leis and juice upon arrival, twice-daily maid service, and excellent concierge, 24-hour room service, and valet services. The highly regarded Diamond Head Grill serves top-flight Hawaii Regional cuisine. Unfortunately, the building is saddled with a couple of permanent physical faults: a perpendicular orientation to the coastline, giving all rooms only mediocre views, and another building between it and the sand, requiring you to walk across a parking lot to reach the beach. Still, it's the ultimate outpost of 21st-century chic.

2885 Kalakaua Ave. (across the street from Kapiolani Park). ☎ *877-W-HOTELS or 808-922-1700. Fax 800-923-2249. Internet:* www.whotels.com. *Valet parking: $14. Rack rates: $325–$375 double, $500–$550 suite. Deals: Ask about golf packages and other available discounts. AE, DC, DISC, JCB, MC, V.*

Waikiki Beachcomber

$$$ Mid-Waikiki

First-rate package deals and online discounts make this attractive and well-located hotel — the home of the legendary Don "Tiny Bubbles" Ho show, it's worth noting — an excellent value. It lies in the heart of Waikiki's gentrified main drag, across the street from the Royal Hawaiian and just a block from the beach. Rooms boast Berber carpets, firm beds, attractive contemporary furniture, handheld showers, mini-fridges, coffeemakers, and private lanais. Also on-site are a nice pool, a cafe, a coin-op laundry, and Don Ho's domain, the showroom. Hawaiian cultural activities (hula, lei-making, and ukulele lessons) and a summer kids' program are offered (uncommon in this price range). All in all, a great midrange choice.

2300 Kalakaua Ave. (at Duke's Lane). ☎ *800-622-4646 or 808-922-4646. Fax: 808-923-4889. Internet:* www.waikikibeachcomber.com. *Parking: $9. Rack rates: $180–$225 double, $315–$515 suite. Deals: Room-and-car and room-and-breakfast packages from $125. Terrific Internet specials on regular offer, as low as $89. AE, JCB, MC, V.*

Waikiki Joy Hotel

$$–$$$ Mid-Waikiki

This stylishly contemporary hotel features a Jacuzzi tub and a Bose entertainment system in every room — otherwise unheard of for these prices. The lovely open-air lobby sets the scene for bright, clean-lined, comfortable guest rooms, each with a marble entryway, a fridge, a coffeemaker, a nice bathroom with that groovy tub, and a lanai that's wide enough for you to sit and enjoy the views while you listen to your stereo; some of the suites have wet bars, while others have full kitchens. A cafe, laundry, and a furnished deck with heated pool and sauna are on site, plus a karaoke studio if you're in the mood for a little warbling. In the negative column, the beach is a good four blocks away — but cheer up, the free breakfast makes a good deal even better.

320 Lewers St. (between Kalakaua and Kuhio aves.). ☎ *800-922-7866 or 808-923-2300. Fax: 808-924-4010. Internet:* www.aston-hotels.com. *Valet parking: $10. Rack rates: $125–$170 double, $180–$280 suite. Rates include continental breakfast. Deals: Excellent opportunities for discounts. Ask for AAA, senior (50-plus), and corporate discounts, and other special rate programs. Qualify for 25% discount if you stay at Aston properties for 7 or more nights with Aston's "Island Hopper" program. AE, CB, DC, DISC, JCB, MC, V.*

Waikiki Parc

$$$ Mid-Waikiki

This sister hotel to the ultra-deluxe Halekulani is the ideal choice for travelers looking for impeccable service and little luxuries at bargain rates, plus a terrific at-the-beach location. What's more, a phenomenal slate of packages improves an already good value. Boasting a cool cream-and-blue palette and an Asian-tinged island vibe, the stylish designer-done rooms feature chic rattan, tile floors, plush carpeting, sitting areas, lanais with louvered shutters (go for an ocean view if you can — they're fabulous), mini-fridges, and generous bathrooms. Amenities include a first-rate Japanese restaurant; the Parc Cafe, which will win over even avowed buffetphobes; concierge and room service; a coin-op laundry as well as valet service; and a staff that provides plenty of signature Halekulani service. There's an eighth-floor pool for those who can't rough the 100-yard walk to the beach via a beach-access walkway.

2233 Helumoa Rd. (at Lewers St., east of the Halekulani). ☎ *800-422-0450 or 808-921-7272. Fax: 808-923-1336. Internet:* www.waikikiparc.com. *Parking: $9. Rack rates: $175–$275 double. Deals: A bevy of excellent money-saving packages are always on offer, including the Parc Sunrise (two-night stay, plus parking and breakfast, from $246), the Parc Room & Car (two-night stay, compact car, breakfast, and parking, from $316), plus family plans (offering 50–60 percent off a second room), golf, sail, fly, romance, and additional options. AE, CB, DC, JCB, MC, V.*

Waikiki Shore

$$$ Mid-Waikiki

Waikiki's only beachfront condo is a wonderful choice for families looking for at-home comforts in an on-the-sand location. The individually decorated one-, two-, and three-bedroom condos feature full kitchens with microwaves (studios have kitchenettes), A/C *and* ceiling fans, washer/dryers, and big lanais. Daily maid service makes it feel like a real vacation. Since full-time residents live here, the complex tends to be quiet, and security is tight. Aston manages the front desk, so you get more on-site concierge-style service from them, but Outrigger guests have access to the concierge, pool, and fitness room at the adjacent Outrigger Reef. Reservations are hard to get — book way in advance.

2161 Kalia Rd. (on the ocean at Saratoga Rd.). **Aston at the Waikiki Shore:** ☎ *800-922-7866 or 808-926-4733. Fax: 808-922-2902. Internet:* www.aston-hotels.com. *Parking: $10. Rack rates: $190–$215 studio, $220–$290 1-bedroom, $365–$535 2-bedroom. Deals: Internet-only ePriceBreaker rates as low as $144 at press time. Ask for AAA, senior (50-plus), and corporate discounts, and other special rate programs. Qualify for 25% discount if you stay at Aston properties for 7 or more nights with Aston's "Island Hopper" program. AE, CB, DC, DISC, JCB, MC, V.* **Outrigger:** ☎ *800-688-7444 or 808-971-4520. Fax: 808-971-4580. Internet:* www.outrigger. com. *Rack rates: $205–$235 studio, $285–$315 1-bedroom, $400–$550 2-bedroom. Deals: Almost nobody pays rack with Outrigger; better-than-average discounts for AAA and AARP members and seniors (50-plus), plus corporate, government, and military discounts are available. First night free, bed-and-breakfast, room-and-car, and other packages regularly on offer. AE, DC, DISC, JCB, MC, V.*

No Room at the Inn?

A number of the top national and worldwide chains have reliable Waikiki branches that you might try if my favorites are full.

Holiday Inn Waikiki

$$ Ewa Waikiki   A pleasant and attractive choice, two blocks from the beach, two blocks from the best shopping mall in the Pacific, and home to my favorite Chinese restaurant, Hawaii Seafood Paradise (see Chapter 10). 1830 Ala Moana Blvd. ☎ **888-9WAIKIKI** or 808-955-1111. Internet: www.holiday-inn-waikiki.com.

Doubletree Alana Waikiki

$$$ Ewa Waikiki   More upscale and surprisingly pleasant, and home to a terrific restaurant, Padovani's (see Chapter 10). 1956 Ala Moana Blvd. ☎ **800-222-TREE** or 808-941-7275. Internet: www.doubletreehotels.com.

Radisson Waikiki Prince Kuhio

$$$ Mid-Waikiki   Has a great central location and comfortable, pleasantly appointed guest rooms. 2500 Kuhio Ave. ☎ **888-557-4422** or 808-922-0811. Internet: www.radisson.com.

In addition to the ones already recommended in this chapter, Aston Hotels & Resorts (☎ **800-922-7866** or 808-931-1400; Internet: www.aston-hotels.com) offers a number of additional options in the Waikiki area, from cheap-and-cheerful on up, which are worth checking into.

If you're looking for the most reliable bargain in town, there's nowhere to go but Ohana Hotels (☎ **800-462-6262** or 303-369-7777; Internet: www.ohanahotels.com). The value-minded arm of the Outrigger chain offers 13 hotels in the Waikiki area in addition to the Best Western Ohana Waikiki Tower and Ohana Waikiki Coral Seas (already recommended in this chapter), with rates starting at $109. You can pay even less if you snare one of the many available discounts, promotions, or package deals, including better-than-average discounts for AAA and AARP members and seniors (50-plus); corporate, government, and military discounts; and first-night-free, bed-and-breakfast, room-and-car, and other package deals.

If you're a B&B fan and you want more options, contact **Hawaii's Best Bed & Breakfasts** (☎ **800-262-9912** or 808-885-4550; Internet: www.bestbnb.com), which can book you a room in a wonderful Oahu inn that has been personally inspected and approved. Some of my favorites are Diamond Head B&B and the Manoa Valley Inn in the Honolulu area, Ingrid's Bed & Breakfast on the Windward Coast, and Santa's by the Sea, much more elegant than the name implies and situated on a gorgeous stretch of north shore sand.

Bed & Breakfast Honolulu (☎ **800-288-4666** or 808-595-7533; Internet: www.hawaiibnb.com) offers vacation rentals around the island of Oahu and throughout the state.

Arranging for a Windward Coast or North Shore Rental

If you'd really like to stay in the heart of the north shore's Surf City action, your best bet is to call **Team Real Estate** (☎ **800-982-8602** or 808-637-3507; Internet: www.teamrealestate.com). This Haliewa-based agency manages a fleet of fully furnished vacation homes in Surf City, from affordable cottages to multibedroom beachfront homes, at rates ranging from $90 to $300 per night. Most rates are based on a minimum stay of one week, but shorter stays are available, and you might be able to arrange a discount on longer stays.

Naish Hawaii (☎ **808-262-6068;** Internet: www.naish.com), which also happens to be Hawaii's premier windsurfing school, can help arrange for accommodations in and around Kailua, Oahu's premier windward coast community. Double rooms, cottages, and apartments for two run $50 to $100 nightly, while larger homes range from $150 to $300 nightly, depending on size and location.

Also contact **Hawaii's Best Bed & Breakfasts** and **Bed & Breakfast Honolulu** (see the preceding section for contact information) for additional windward and north shore options.

Chapter 8

Settling in on Oahu

● ●

In This Chapter

▶ Getting from Honolulu Airport to your hotel

▶ Finding your way around Waikiki, Honolulu, and the rest of Oahu

▶ Using Oahu's bus system

▶ Catching a ride on the Waikiki Trolley

▶ Getting reports on the weather, prescriptions filled, traveler's checks cashed, and more — an easy-reference list of important contacts

● ●

*O*ahu is the busiest and most complex island to get to know in the Hawaiian chain, but it's still a relatively simple place to learn your way around. It's the one island that doesn't require a rental car, since there's a reliable public transportation system. Still, you may want to book one for freedom of movement.

No matter where you're coming from, whether the mainland or a neighbor island, you'll arrive at Honolulu International Airport. That's where this chapter picks up. I tell you everything you need to know to get situated in this beautiful spot.

Arriving at Honolulu International Airport

Some transpacific flights fly directly to the neighbor islands. However, it's more than likely that you'll come to Oahu first, even if you plan to visit other islands during your stay. **Honolulu International Airport** (☎ 808-836-6413 or 808-836-6411) is located on the south shore of Oahu near Pearl Harbor, west of downtown Honolulu and Waikiki. It's nine miles, or about a 20- to 30-minute drive, into Waikiki.

Honolulu International is a large but easily navigable airport. All mainland flights arrive in the **Main Overseas Terminal;** the Baggage Claim area is on the ground level. After collecting your bags, exit to the palm-lined street, where you can pick up taxis, Waikiki shuttles, and rental-car vans. For more information on transportation options, see "Getting from the Airport to Your Hotel" later in this chapter.

Oahu Orientation

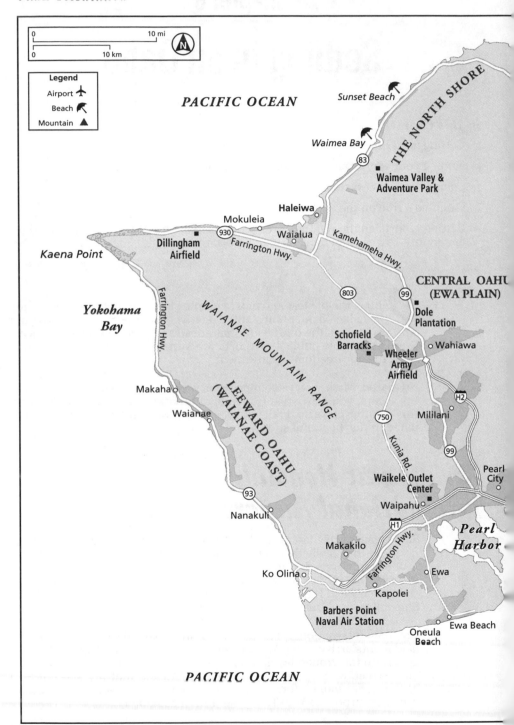

Legend
Airport ✈
Beach 🏄
Mountain ▲

PACIFIC OCEAN

0   10 mi
0   10 km

THE NORTH SHORE

Sunset Beach

Waimea Bay

83

Waimea Valley & Adventure Park

Haleiwa

Mokuleia

Waialua

Kamehameha Hwy.

Dillingham Airfield

Farrington Hwy.

930

Kaena Point

CENTRAL OAHU (EWA PLAIN)

803

99

Yokohama Bay

Farrington Hwy.

WAIANAE MOUNTAIN RANGE

Dole Plantation

Schofield Barracks

Wheeler Army Airfield

Wahiawa

Makaha

LEEWARD OAHU (WAIANAE COAST)

Waianae

750

Mililani

H2

99

Pearl City

Waikele Outlet Center

Kunia Rd.

93

Waipahu

Nanakuli

H1

Pearl Harbor

Makakilo

Ko Olina

Farrington Hwy.

Ewa

Kapolei

Barbers Point Naval Air Station

Oneula Beach

Ewa Beach

PACIFIC OCEAN

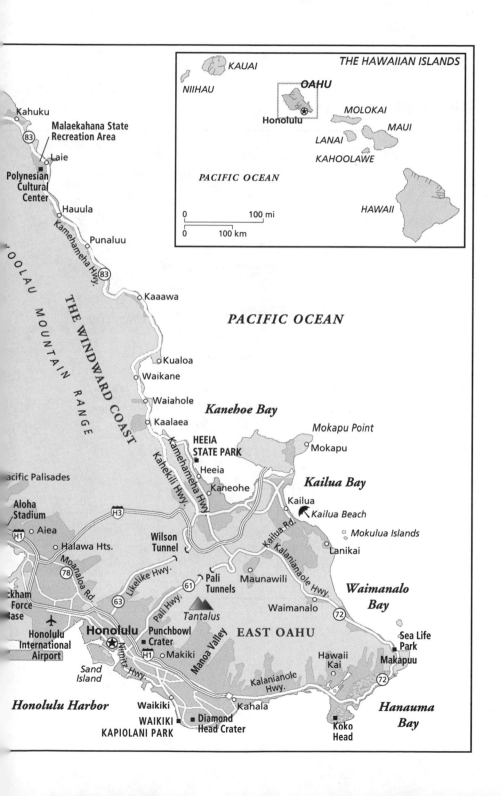

THE HAWAIIAN ISLANDS

KAUAI

NIIHAU

OAHU

Honolulu

MOLOKAI

MAUI

LANAI

KAHOOLAWE

PACIFIC OCEAN

HAWAII

0   100 mi
0   100 km

Kahuku

Malaekahana State
Recreation Area

83

Laie

Polynesian
Cultural
Center

Hauula

Punaluu

Kamehameha Hwy.

83

Kaaawa

PACIFIC OCEAN

Kualoa

Waikane

Waiahole

Kaalaea

Kanehoe Bay

Mokapu Point

Mokapu

HEEIA
STATE PARK

Heeia

Kailua Bay

Kaneohe

Kailua

Kailua Beach

Mokulua Islands

Lanikai

acific Palisades

Aloha
Stadium

H3

Aiea

Halawa Hts.

Wilson
Tunnel

Kahekili Hwy.

Kamehameha Hwy.

Kailua Rd.

Kalanianaole Hwy.

*Waimanalo
Bay*

H1

Moanaloa Rd.

78

Likelike Hwy.

61

*Pali
Tunnels*

Maunawili

Waimanalo

72

ckham
Force
ase

63

Pali Hwy.

Tantalus

EAST OAHU

Honolulu
International
Airport

Honolulu

Nimitz Hwy.

Punchbowl
Crater

H1

Makiki

Manoa Valley

Hawaii
Kai

Sea Life
Park

Makapuu

72

Sand
Island

*Kalanianaole
Hwy.*

Koko
Head

Honolulu Harbor

Waikiki

Kahala

WAIKIKI
KAPIOLANI PARK

Diamond
Head Crater

*Hanauma
Bay*

THE WINDWARD COAST

THE KOOLAU MOUNTAIN RANGE

Honolulu & Waikiki Orientation

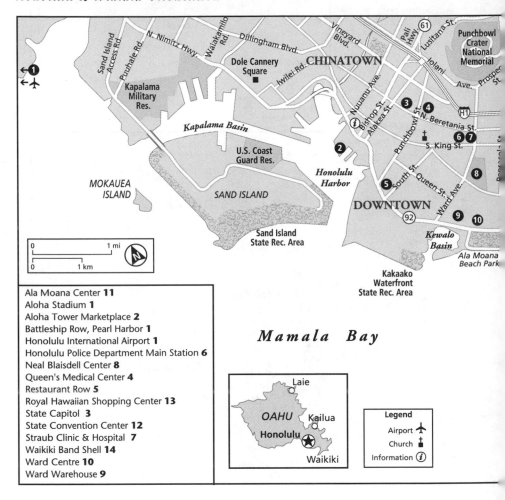

Ala Moana Center **11**
Aloha Stadium **1**
Aloha Tower Marketplace **2**
Battleship Row, Pearl Harbor **1**
Honolulu International Airport **1**
Honolulu Police Department Main Station **6**
Neal Blaisdell Center **8**
Queen's Medical Center **4**
Restaurant Row **5**
Royal Hawaiian Shopping Center **13**
State Capitol **3**
State Convention Center **12**
Straub Clinic & Hospital **7**
Waikiki Band Shell **14**
Ward Centre **10**
Ward Warehouse **9**

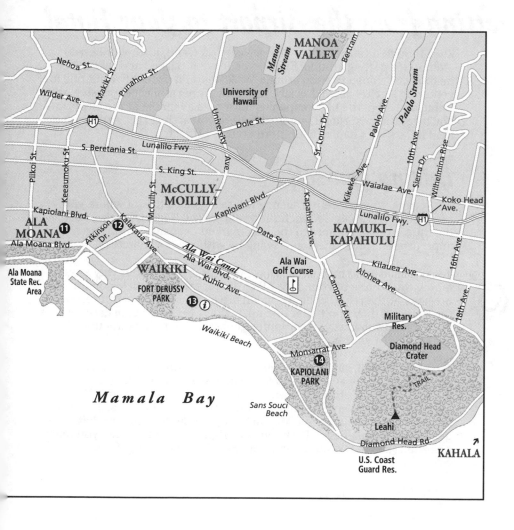

Nehoa St.

Wilder Ave.

Makiki St.

Punahou St.

University of Hawaii

MANOA VALLEY

Manoa Stream

Bertram

H1

S. Beretania St.

Lunalilo Fwy

Dole St.

Palolo Ave.

Palolo Stream

Piikoi St.

Keeaumoku St.

S. King St.

University Ave.

St. Louis Dr.

10th Ave.

Sierra Dr.

Wilhelmina Rise

McCULLY– MOILIILI

McCully St.

Kikene Ave.

Waialae Ave.

Koko Head Ave.

Kapiolani Blvd.

Kapiolani Blvd.

Lunalilo Fwy.

H1

ALA MOANA ⓫

Atkinson Dr.

⓬ Kalakaua Ave.

Kapahulu Ave.

KAIMUKI– KAPAHULU

16th Ave.

Ala Moana Blvd.

Date St.

Ala Moana State Rec. Area

WAIKIKI

Ala Wai Canal

Ala Wai Blvd.

Kuhio Ave.

Ala Wai Golf Course

Kilauea Ave.

Alohea Ave.

18th Ave.

FORT DERUSSY PARK

⓭ ⓘ

Campbell Ave.

Military Res.

Waikiki Beach

Monsarrat Ave.

Diamond Head Crater

Mamala Bay

Sans Souci Beach

KAPIOLANI PARK

⓮

TRAIL

Leahi

Diamond Head Rd.

U.S. Coast Guard Res.

KAHALA ↗

To catch a neighbor-island flight, walk to the large **Interisland Terminal** serving Aloha and Hawaiian Airlines, which takes 10 to 15 minutes, or hop on the **Wiki-Wiki Bus,** a free airport shuttle that links the terminals ("wiki wiki" means "quick" in Hawaiian). I usually prefer the walk after being parked in an airline seat for hours.

Getting from the Airport to Your Hotel

Even though a rental car isn't a necessity on Oahu, it's my preferred method for getting around. Even if you leave it parked and take other methods of transportation around Waikiki, you'll probably want one for venturing farther afield. Luckily, rental cars are rather inexpensive on Oahu, and all of the big companies have cars available at the airport. You'll get the best rate if you book before you arrive; see "Arranging for Rental Cars" in Chapter 6 for more on this subject.

Driving yourself

A van from your car-rental agency will take you to the lot where you can pick up your car. To catch the van from the Baggage Claim, head out the automated doors to the well-marked curbside waiting area. The appropriate rental van should swing by within a few minutes.

You'll need a good map to get your bearings and find your way around during the course of your stay. All of the rental-car agencies offer map booklets at the rental counter, which are invaluable for getting around the island. If they don't offer one up, just ask for one. Some car-rental agents can even give you computer-generated, detailed directions from the airport to your hotel.

To get to Waikiki, simply turn right out of the airport (signs are clear) onto Nimitz Highway (Highway 92), which will run directly under the H-1 (one of Oahu's three freeways) for a few minutes. In about 10 minutes, Nimitz Highway deposits you onto Ala Moana Boulevard, which takes you past the huge Ala Moana Shopping Center (on your left) and grassy Ala Moana Beach Park (on your right). Moments later, you reach Kalakaua (ka-la-COW-ah) Avenue, Waikiki's main thoroughfare.

Taking a taxi

The taxi stand is located just outside the automated doors in the Baggage Claim area. You should have no trouble getting a taxi, but if you need help, an attendant is on hand to assist you. Taxi fare to Waikiki is about $25, plus tip.

Star Taxi (☎ **808-942-7827;** Internet: www.hawaii-oahu.com/taxi. html) will take you from the airport to Waikiki for $15 (plus tip) if you arrange for airport pickup in advance. **City Taxi** (☎ **808-524-2121**) often runs a similar special, but not always. Be sure to have your airline, flight number, and arrival time on hand when you call either company.

Catching a shuttle ride

TransHawaiian (☎ **800-533-8765** or 808-566-7000; Internet: www.transhawaiian.com) operates shuttles between the airport and Waikiki around the clock, with passenger vans departing every 30 to 40 minutes, depending on traffic (waits may be slightly longer during off hours). The fare is $8 per person to Waikiki, $13 round-trip. No reservation is necessary. You can pick up the shuttle at street level outside Baggage Claim; look for red-shirted attendants and vans that say **Airport Waikiki Express Shuttle** on the side. You're allowed to board with two pieces of luggage and a carry-on at no extra charge; surfboards and bicycles are prohibited for safety reasons.

You find a $2-off coupon on round-trip airport shuttle service at www.transhawaiian.com. Print it out and present it to the driver upon boarding.

No reservation is necessary for your trip to the airport, but be sure to book a hotel pickup for your departing flight at least 48 hours in advance by calling TransHawaiian at ☎ **808-566-7000** daily between 8 a.m. and 5 p.m.

The island's descriptively named bus system, TheBus, does travel between the airport and Waikiki, and the one-way fare is just $1. Bus nos. 19 and 20 (Waikiki Beach and Hotels) run to downtown Honolulu and Waikiki. The hitch is that TheBus is a viable airport-transfer option only for the most freewheeling travelers, simply because you're not allowed to board with any substantive luggage. You can bring on a carryon or small suitcase as long as it fits under the seat and doesn't disrupt other passengers; otherwise, you have to take a shuttle or taxi. What's more, the ride to Waikiki will take more than an hour, as opposed to 20 minutes or a half-hour if you take a taxi or shuttle.

If you're not going to rent a car, I suggest taking a taxi or shuttle from the airport, then using TheBus to get around town after you've settled in. For more information on TheBus, read on.

Getting around Oahu

Waikiki and Honolulu are a tad complicated to get around, simply because so many streets are one-way. Still, this is no Los Angeles, by any means — and drivers are much more easygoing. Always be sure to have a good map at hand and you won't have a problem. Once you get past the city, basically one road circles the island, so you'd have to work hard to lose your bearings.

Navigating your way around Honolulu

America's 11th largest city, Honolulu is approximately 12 miles wide and 26 miles long, running east-west roughly between Diamond Head crater and Pearl Harbor. It folds over seven hills laced by seven streams, and runs down to the sea.

Honolulu's most famous neighborhood, Waikiki, runs along Honolulu's central stretch of coast all the way to grassy Kapiolani Park and Diamond Head crater, Hawaii's most recognizable landmark, to the east. This well-developed strip of land is about three miles long, but extends from the coast inland only a few blocks to the man-made Ala Wai Canal.

Waikiki's primary thoroughfares run east to west. Kalakaua Avenue runs one block away from and parallel to the coast in an easterly direction, toward Diamond Head. Ala Wai Boulevard runs along Waikiki's inland (northern) edge one way toward downtown. Sandwiched in between — one block north of Kalakaua, one block south of Ala Wai — is Kuhio Avenue, which handles two-way traffic.

West of Waikiki is the Ala Moana section of Honolulu, so named for the aforementioned Ala Moana Center, Honolulu's retail and transportation hub (you can pick up almost every major bus route here; see "TheBus" later in this chapter). Drive west on Ala Moana and you pass more shopping stops — Ward Centre, the Ward Warehouse, a mall of dining options called Restaurant Row, and the historic harborfront Aloha Tower Marketplace shopping and restaurant complex — before reaching downtown Honolulu.

Situated in the blocks inland from the Aloha Tower Marketplace — basically between Nuuanu Avenue and Punchbowl Street — downtown Honolulu is comprised of a tiny cluster of high-rises that serves as the financial, business, and government center of Hawaii. Also here are the Chinatown Historic District, the oldest Chinatown in America, and some of Hawaii's most important historic landmarks, most notably Iolani (ee-oh-LAN-ee) Palace, the only royal palace on American soil.

Inland from here, and north of the Ala Wai Canal above Waikiki, residential neighborhoods make their way up the hills, creating an urban backdrop unlike any other in a major American city. Running through these neighborhoods is the freeway known as H-1, which leads to the east end of Oahu.

To avoid frustration when driving around Waikiki and downtown Honolulu, always have a map nearby that features directional indicators for the city's many one-way streets. The map on the color tear-out cheat sheet at the front of this book, which features Waikiki on one side, and the downtown and Ala Moana areas of Honolulu on the other, should do the trick. Just think of the Waikiki side as the easterly portion and the Honolulu side as the westerly portion; if you were to photocopy them and put them side by side, they'd (roughly) align to cover in large part the area where you'll be spending most of your time in the city.

If you stop a local and ask for directions, you're likely to hear a few unfamiliar terms. That's because islanders tend to give directions a bit differently than what mainlanders are used to, particularly in Honolulu:

✔ Seldom will anyone direct you north or south; instead, they'll send you either makai (ma-KAI), meaning toward the sea, or mauka (MOW-kah), toward the mountains.

✔ Instead of east and west, locals will tell you to go Diamond Head when they mean east (in the direction of the world-famous Diamond Head crater), and Ewa (EE-va) when they mean west (in the direction of the town called Ewa, beyond Pearl Harbor).

Keep these terms in mind — because if you ask a local for directions, this is what you're likely to hear: "Drive two blocks *makai* (toward the sea), then turn Diamond Head (east) at the stop light. Go one block, and turn *mauka* (toward the mountains). It's on the *Ewa* (western) side of the street."

Exploring the rest of Oahu

Once you move beyond the city, Oahu is simple to navigate. That's because just a few roads work in concert to form a rough circle.

The "Circle Island" Route starts in Honolulu, travels up the middle of the island to the north shore, curves around the island's top knob, proceeds down the eastern, or windward, coast, and around the island's eastern knob back to Waikiki and Honolulu. (Thanks to a few highway tunnels drilled through the Koolau Mountains, you can also drive directly between Honolulu and the Windward Coast without having to go all the way around the east end of the island.)

Driving to the north shore

The north shore is the epicenter of Hawaii's surf culture. Small communities and collections of simple houses serve as scant interruption for the string of fabulous beaches that line this rural coast, where the schizophrenic surf is flat as a pancake in summer and kicks up to monster proportions in winter. The charming little surf town of Haleiwa (ha-lay-EE-vah) is the north shore's main community and the heart of the culture.

I highly recommend coming here to explore, either to watch the world's most outrageous daredevil surfers in action in winter, or just to experience the laid-back vibe and play in the baby waves in summer. I discuss the beaches and other north shore highlights in Chapter 10. But getting there is half the fun.

Haleiwa sits about an hour's drive north of Waikiki, at the junction of highways 99 and 83, both called Kamehameha Highway. The easiest way to get there is to cruise north through Oahu's broad and fertile central valley, past Pearl Harbor, Schofield Barracks of *From Here to Eternity* fame, and pineapple and sugarcane fields until the sea reappears.

From Waikiki, pick up the H-1 freeway heading west. Your best bet is probably to take Ala Wai Boulevard to McCully Street north to H-1, but it all depends on where your hotel is; ask at the front desk for the most direct route.

Once you're on H-1, stay to the right, as the freeway divides abruptly. Follow the signs for H-1, then H-1/H-2. When the two roads divide, follow the H-2 up the middle of the island, heading north toward the town of Wahiawa (wa-hee-AH-va). That's what the sign will say — not north shore or Haleiwa, but Wahiawa.

The H-2 runs out and becomes a two-lane road about 18 miles out of downtown Honolulu, near Schofield Barracks. It then turns into Kamehameha Highway (first Highway 99, then Highway 83) at Wahiawa. Kam Highway, as islanders call it, will be your road for the rest of the trip to Haleiwa.

Keep in mind that you can also meander your way to the north shore by driving along the lush Windward Coast and around Oahu's peak. In fact, I highly recommend driving the full circle and making a day of it. If you're in a hurry to get to the north shore, take the central route and follow the Windward Coast back south. If you'd rather enjoy one or two of the windward side's magnificent beaches on the way north (see Chapter 10), do that in the morning, and come back to Waikiki via the less scenic central route. For windward driving directions, see "Exploring the Windward Coast" later in this chapter.

Heading to East Oahu

At some point you're likely to find yourself heading beyond Diamond Head, either bound for Hanauma Bay, one of Hawaii's finest snorkel spots (and best for first-timers), or Sea Life Park, or just to take in some very groovy desert-meets-the-sea scenery. You can reach east Oahu simply by heading east on the H-1, which dumps you onto the Kalanianaole (ka-lan-ee-an-OW-lay) Highway (Highway 72), the main thoroughfare that takes you around the elbow of Oahu.

Cruising along the scenic Windward Coast

Stand in the heart of Waikiki with your back to the ocean. To your right you'll see a mountain range called the Koolaus (koo-OO-laus); on the other side of them is the east coast of Oahu. This windward-facing coast is the wettest side of the island, and therefore its most lush and gorgeous. Lined with suburban beach communities and some breathtakingly beautiful beaches, it's well worth seeing.

Three highways will get you from the city to the Windward Coast in about 20 minutes or so: the Pali Highway (Highway 61), the Likelike (lee-kay-LEE-kay) Highway (Highway 63), and the brand-new H-3 freeway, all of which cut right through the mountains. Your best bet from Waikiki is to take the H-1 to the Pali Highway. Once you go through the tunnel, turn left on Kamehameha Highway (Highway 83); this coastal highway will be your roadway for the rest of the trip, whether you choose to follow it all the way to Haleiwa (about 1½ hours without stops), whether you're heading to the Polynesian Cultural Center (the South Pacific cultural theme park about an hour from Waikiki), or whether you're simply enjoying the ultra-lush scenery and some of best beaches in the islands. (See Chapter 10 for specific suggestions.)

Dominating the west side of Oahu is the island's second mountain range, the Waianae (wah-ee-AN-eh) mountains. Beyond this ridge is the hot, dry leeward side of the island. You're by no means prohibited from heading there, but there's not much to see, and locals prefer to keep this one area of heavily touristed Oahu to themselves. I suggest honoring their wishes and concentrating your efforts on exploring the other parts of this wonderfully multifaceted island instead.

Letting somebody else do the driving

Oahu is the one island that's easy to visit if you can't — or won't — drive yourself. Oahu's islandwide public transportation system — TheBus — was just named America's Best Transit System by the American Public Transit Association, so you can count on it being extremely user-friendly. The Waikiki Trolley is also available for getting around town.

While TheBus can take you anywhere you want to go on Oahu, I don't recommend using it to reach areas beyond the city. Not only will you spend a total of 3½ to 4½ hours on the bus getting there and back, but the waits can be extremely long at lonely north shore bus stops. If you don't want to rent a car for the duration of your stay, I strongly encourage you to rent one for your day of north shore and windward coast exploring. Or use one of the tour companies I mention in Chapter 10 that can take you around the island.

TheBus

TheBus is an excellent transit deal. The service is good, the buses are clean, and the cost is low. The one-way fare to ride TheBus is $1 per one-way ride, 50 cents for school-age children, which will get you anywhere you want to go on the island. Service begins daily at 3:30 a.m. and runs until 1:30 a.m. Buses run about every 5 to 15 minutes during the day and every 30 minutes in the evening.

If you plan use TheBus as your main mode of transportation, consider a $10 Visitor Pass, which allows you unlimited rides for four consecutive days. Visitor Passes can be purchased at any ABC convenience store in Waikiki (you can't blink without tripping over an ABC store in Waikiki) as well as at the ABC store at Ala Moana Center.

TheBus operates dozens of bus lines, but you'll only need to concern yourself with the handful that pass through Waikiki. Two-way Kuhio Avenue is the main thoroughfare for bus routes through Waikiki.

Virtually all of the city's major bus routes converge at the Ala Moana Shopping Center, just west of Waikiki. TheBus makes three stops at the mammoth mall: two on the ocean side of the mall on Ala Moana Boulevard, and one on the mountain side, on Kona Street. Read the posted sign at the stop to make sure that the line you want is going where you want to go. Or, if you prefer to iron things out beforehand, call TheBus at ☎ 808-848-5555 to determine which stop is the right one for your destination.

TheBus

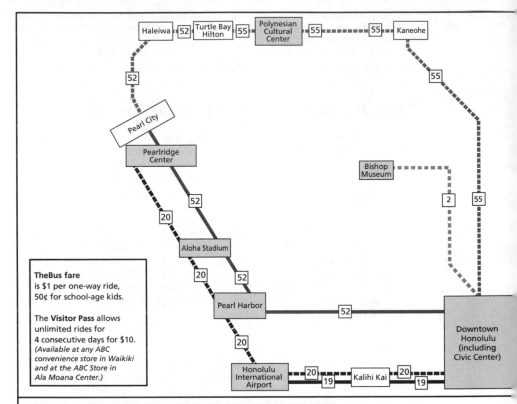

TheBus fare
is $1 per one-way ride,
50¢ for school-age kids.

The **Visitor Pass** allows
unlimited rides for
4 consecutive days for $10.
(*Available at any ABC
convenience store in Waikiki
and at the ABC Store in
Ala Moana Center.*)

BUS ROUTES TO MAJOR ATTRACTIONS FROM WAIKIKI

Ala Moana Center: Bus no. 8, 19, 20, 47, or 48 toward downtown Honolulu.

Aloha Tower Marketplace: Bus no. 19, 20, or 47 toward downtown Honolulu.

Battleship Row, Pearl Harbor: Take no. 20 or 47 in the downtown Honolulu direction past the airport and get off across the street from the *Arizona* Memorial. Or take any bus to Ala Moana Center, and transfer to the no. 52 to Pearl Harbor.

Bishop Museum: Bus no. 2 to downtown Honolulu; get off at Kapalama Street, walk one block inland to Bernice Street and museum.

Chinatown: Bus no. 2 or 13 to downtown Honolulu.

Circle Island tour: Bus no. 52 or 55.

The Contemporary Museum & Punchbowl Crater (National Cemetery of the Pacific): Bus no. 2 or 13 to downtown Honolulu to corner of Beretania and Alapai streets (across from police station); walk toward ocean on Alapai Street to Hotel Street and pick up bus no. 15.

Diamond Head Crater: Bus no. 22 or 58.

Hanauma Bay: Bus no. 22 in the Diamond Head direction to East Oahu.

Honolulu Academy of Arts: Bus no. 2 or 13 to downtown Honolulu to the corner of Beretania Street and Ward Avenue.

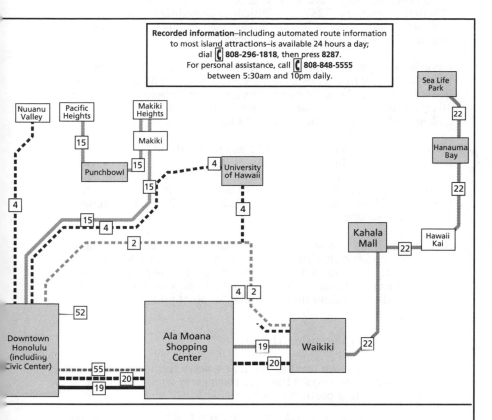

Recorded information–including automated route information to most island attractions–is available 24 hours a day; dial 808-296-1818, then press 8287. For personal assistance, call 808-848-5555 between 5:30am and 10pm daily.

Honolulu Zoo: Bus no. 8, 19, 20, 47, or 58 toward Diamond Head.

Iolani Palace & Mission Houses Museum: Bus no. 2 and 13 to downtown Honolulu; get off at the corner of Punchbowl and Beretania streets toward the ocean to King Street.

Kapiolani Park & Kodak Hula Show: Bus no. 2, 19, or 20 toward Diamond Head to Kapiolani Park; walk to the Waikiki Band Shell for the hula show.

Polynesian Cultural Center: Any bus toward downtown Honolulu to Ala Moana Center; transfer to bus no. 55.

Restaurant Row: Bus no. 19, 20, or 47 toward downtown Honolulu.

Sea Life Park: Bus no. 22 or 58 in the Diamond Head direction to East Oahu.

Waikiki Aquarium: Bus no. 2 toward Diamond Head.

Waimea Valley & Adventure Park: Any bus to Ala Moana Center and transfer to no. 52.

Ward Centre & Ward Warehouse: Bus no. 8, 19, 20, or 47 toward downtown Honolulu.

*Two-way Kuhio Avenue is the main thoroughfare for bus routes through Waikiki.
DIRECTIONAL KEY:
"toward downtown Honolulu" = **west**
"toward Diamond Head" = **east**

Recorded information is also available around the clock; dial ☎ **808-296-1818,** then press **8287.** In addition to providing a summary of general information — including the major Waikiki bus lines — this information line offers automated route information to major island attractions.

If you'd like help planning a specific route, or if you have other questions pertaining to TheBus system, call ☎ **808-848-5555,** where a real live information specialist can help you out daily between 5:30 a.m. and 10 p.m. Have your departure and destination points handy when you call, as well as the time of day you'd like to travel.

If you're planning on relying on TheBus to get around, I highly recommend visiting TheBus's excellent Web site at www.thebus.org and familiarizing yourself with the system before you leave home. It offers timetables and maps for all routes, plus directions to many local attractions and a list of upcoming events. (Taking TheBus is sometimes easier than parking.)

Also, don't hesitate to ask the front desk or concierge at your hotel for assistance in navigating TheBus system. Chances are very good that they know the system well, and they'll be glad to help. And don't be shy about asking the bus drivers for help. In general, they're very friendly and helpful, and they'll be glad to point you in the right direction.

A few etiquette tips for using TheBus:

✔ When the bus you want approaches, wave to the driver to indicate that you want to board the bus. Back away from the stop if you don't want that particular bus.

✔ You must have the exact fare when you board the bus because the drivers don't make change. You can use either dollar bills or change.

✔ To transfer to another line, ask the driver of the first bus you board for a free transfer when you board. You can't use a transfer to pick up the same line going in the same direction, nor can you use a transfer to go back to where you came from.

✔ To open the rear door of the bus, push on the door or step on the first step when the green light is lit. Be sure to hold the door open as you get off the bus so that your fellow riders don't get hit by the slamming door.

Taking the Waikiki Trolley

The **Waikiki Trolley** (☎ **800-824-8804** or 808-591-2561; Internet: www.waikikitrolley.com) is an open-air, motorized trolley similar to a San Francisco cable car. It may be the most fun you can have on public transportation. The trolley runs along three lines:

✔ The **Red (Honolulu City) Line** runs daily from 8:30 a.m. to 4:30 p.m. It makes a loop around Waikiki and downtown Honolulu every 20 minutes, stopping at key attractions such as the Royal Hawaiian Shopping Center, the Waikiki Aquarium, Aloha Tower

Marketplace, the Bishop Museum, Ward Centre, Ala Moana Center, and other prime stops.

✔ The **Yellow (Shopping and Dining) Line** runs daily from 8:50 a.m. to 11 p.m., following a similar loop but making different stops. (Don't be misled by the name of this line; you have to take the Red Line if you want to visit Hilo Hattie's or the Aloha Tower Marketplace.)

✔ The **Blue (Ocean Coast) Line** makes its rounds daily from 8:30 a.m. to 4:30 p.m., connecting Waikiki with Hanauma Bay and Sea Life Park.

A few odd rules exist about getting on and off the Blue Line at Hanauma Bay, however, so call and ask for specifics before you use this option to get to and from the marine preserve for a day of snorkeling.

Pricing is a tad complex. Basically, you can purchase three kinds of jump-on, jump-off passes:

✔ A **one-day two-line pass** costs $18 for adults, $8 for kids 4 to 11 and allows you to hop on and off two of the three lines all day long, as much as you want: either the Red and Yellow *or* the Blue and Yellow.

✔ A **one-day all-line pass** costs $30 for adults and $10 for kids 4 to 11 and allows you to use all three lines on an unlimited basis all day long.

✔ A **four-day all-line pass** give you unlimited trolley privileges for four consecutive days for $42 adults, $12 kids 4 to 11.

I like using the trolley; it's a fun way to do some open-air sightseeing. The four-day pass is a good deal, relatively speaking; still, you're proba-bly better off using TheBus to get around for that many days, as the trolley routes are simply too limited — and a four-day bus pass is a mere ten bucks.

You can also use the **Yellow Line** on a one-way basis in the evenings between 5 and 11 p.m. to get to and from dinner or shopping, as it trav-els around Waikiki and to a number of restaurant hot spots, namely the Hard Rock Cafe, Ala Moana Center, and Ward Centre. The one-way fare is $2; it's $5 for an all-evening pass.

You have to purchase your trolley tickets before you board the trolley. The main customer service kiosk is at the **Royal Hawaiian Shopping Center,** in the heart of Waikiki at Kalakaua and Seaside avenues. If this isn't convenient, call one of the numbers listed in this section and ask the friendly operator for the location nearest you.

At press time, you could save big by purchasing your trolley tickets online in advance, either by getting a second one-day pass for 50 percent off with the purchase of one at full price, or by getting a second four-day pass free with the purchase of one at full price. It's well worth checking www.waikikitrolley.com to see if these deals are still available.

Quick Concierge

American Express

At Commerce Tower, 1440 Kapiolani Blvd., Suite 104, Honolulu (☎ 808-946-7741); it's open Monday through Friday from 8 a.m. to 5 p.m. Also in the Tapa Tower at **Hilton Hawaiian Village,** 2005 Kalia Rd., at Ala Moana Boulevard (☎ 808-951-0644), open daily 7 a.m. through 11 p.m.; and at the **Hyatt Regency Waikiki,** 2424 Kalakaua Ave. (☎ 808-926-5441), open daily from 8 a.m. to 9 p.m. (financial services to 8 p.m.).

Baby-Sitters & Baby Stuff

Any hotel should be able to refer you to a reliable baby-sitter with a proven track record. **Dyans Rentals** (☎ 808-845-2080) rents cribs, strollers, highchairs, playpens, infant seats, and the like; they'll deliver whatever you need to wherever you're staying, and pick it up when you're done.

Doctors

Straub Doctors on Call (☎ 808-971-6000; Internet: www.straubhealth.org) offers around-the-clock care at their 24-hour health clinic on the ground floor of the Sheraton Princess Kaiulani Hotel, 120 Kaiulani Ave., just north of Kalakaua Avenue in the heart of Waikiki. They also have additional walk-in clinics at the Hyatt Regency Waikiki, 2424 Kalakaua Ave. (☎ 808-971-8001; open Mon–Fri 7:30 a.m.–4 p.m.), the Hawaiian Regent Hotel, 2552 Kalakaua Ave. (☎ 808-923-3666; open Mon–Fri 8 a.m.–4:30 p.m.), and the Kahala Mandarin Oriental, 5000 Kahala Ave. (☎ 808-739-8909; open Mon–Fri 9 a.m.–1 p.m.). They accept more than 150 health plans, so pack your insurance card. House calls can be arranged. Walk-in health care is also available at the **Urgent Care Clinic,** above Planet Hollywood at 2155 Kalakaua Ave., between Beach Walk and Lewers Street, suite 308 (☎ 808-597-2860; open daily 7 a.m.–11 p.m.).

Emergencies

Dial **911** from any phone, just like back home.

Hospitals

Nearest to Waikiki is **Straub Clinic and Hospital,** 888 S. King St., at Ward Avenue (☎ 808-522-4000; Internet: www.straubhealth.org); the Emergency Room entrance is on Hotel Street. Also offering 24-hour emergency care is **Queens Medical Center,** 1301 Punchbowl St., between Beretania Street and Vineyard Boulevard (☎ 808-538-9011; Internet: www.queens.org).

Information

The **Hawaii Visitors and Convention Bureau** operates an office on the fourth floor of the Royal Hawaiian Shopping Center, 2233 Kalakaua Ave., at Royal Hawaiian Avenue in the heart of Waikiki (☎ 800-464-2924 or 808923-1811; Internet: www.gohawaii.com), open Mon-Fri from 8 a.m. to 4:30 p.m. Tons of info is available on the Web site. The **Oahu Visitors Bureau,** 733 Bishop St., Makai Tower, Suite 1872, downtown Honolulu (☎ 877-525-OAHU or 808-524-0722; Internet: www.visit-oahu.com), offers good island-specific information on their Web site, and you can order a good vacation planner by calling the **877** number. You can stop into either of these offices while you're in town to pick up information, but chances are you won't have to; plenty of information is available right at the airport. Just stop at the information desk near baggage claim and pick up a copy of *This Week Oahu, 101 Things to Do on Oahu,* and other free tourist publications; they're packed with good maps. All of Waikiki's hotels, from budget to deluxe, also overflow with printed info, and the staffs are generally well-informed and helpful.

Newspapers/Magazines

The *Honolulu Advertiser* (www.honoluluadvertiser.com) and *Honolulu Star-Bulletin* (www.starbulletin.com; for sale at press time) are Oahu's daily papers. The *Honolulu Weekly* (www.honoluluweekly.com) is the best source for entertainment listings and information on what's happening around town; it's available free at restaurants, clubs, shops, and newspaper racks around Oahu. *Honolulu* magazine is a popular glossy monthly.

Pharmacies

Long's Drugs, Hawaii's biggest drugstore chain, has convenient locations at Ala Moana Center, 1450 Ala Moana Blvd. (☎ 808-941-4433), and at other locations around town. The city's only 24-hour store is at 1330 Pali Hwy., at Vineyard Boulevard, downtown Honolulu (☎ 808-536-7302).

Police

The **Waikiki City Police Station** is in the Waikiki Beach Center at 2425 Kalakaua Ave., between Kaiulani and Uluniu streets on the ocean side of the street (☎ 808-529-3801). **Honolulu Police Department Main Station** is at 801 S. Beretania St., west of Ward Avenue (☎ 808-529-3111; Internet: www.honolulupd.org). Of course, if you have an emergency, dial **911** from any phone.

Post Offices

The Waikiki branch is at 330 Saratoga Rd., just south of Kalakaua Avenue, adjacent to Fort DeRussy Park. To find the location nearest you, call ☎ 800-275-8777 or visit new.usps.com.

Taxes

Hawaii's sales tax is 4 percent. Expect taxes of about 11.42 percent to be added to your hotel bill.

Taxis

Oahu's major cab companies offer island-wide, 24-hour radio-dispatched service. Call **Aloha State Cab** (☎ 808-847-3566); **City Taxi** (☎ 808-524-2121); **TheCab** (☎ 808-422-2222); or **Star Taxi** (☎ 808-942-7827; Internet: www.hawaii-oahu.com/taxi.html). See "Advice for Travelers with Disabilities" in Chapter 4 for wheelchair-accessible transportation.

Transit Info

For information on routes and schedules, call **TheBus** at ☎ 808-848-5555, or 808-296-1818 for recorded route information (press 8287). Point your browser to www.thebus.org for online info.

Weather and Surf Reports

For the weather, call ☎ 808-973-4380. For marine conditions and sunrise/sunset times, call ☎ 808-973-4382. For surf reports, call ☎ 808-973-4383 or the Surf News Network Surfline at ☎ 808-596-7873.

Chapter 9

Dining around Oahu

*O*nce the land of overcooked fish and frozen peas, Hawaii has become a culinary mecca in recent years, attracting worldwide attention for both its unique brand of European-influenced Pacific Rim cooking — known as Hawaii Regional cuisine — and its population of increasingly recognizable star chefs. Honolulu, as you might expect, is ground zero for this fabulous foodie revolution — so expect to eat well while you're here. Of course, the good stuff doesn't come cheap — but even if you're looking for affordable options, great choices abound.

If you're a foodie who's looking to splurge on one *really* fabulous meal while you're in Hawaii, you need to know only two names: **Chef Mavro** and **Alan Wong's.** These are the two finest restaurants in the entire Pacific, hands down — and the unassuming masters behind them deserve megastar status on the world culinary map. Alan Wong's cooking brings all the goals of Hawaii Regional cuisine to their ultimate realization, while George Mavrothalassitis adds an inspired Provençal touch that's pure genius. You're in for a transcendent dining experience at either restaurant — and I highly recommend squeezing both in, if you can manage it.

Oahu's Best Restaurants

In the restaurant listings that follow, the emphasis is on Waikiki and Honolulu, because a) that's where you're likely to spend most of your time; and b) that's where most of Oahu's restaurants are located. You will also find some excellent options for north shore and windward coast dining for those days you spend touring the rest of the glorious island.

Restaurants In & Around Waikiki

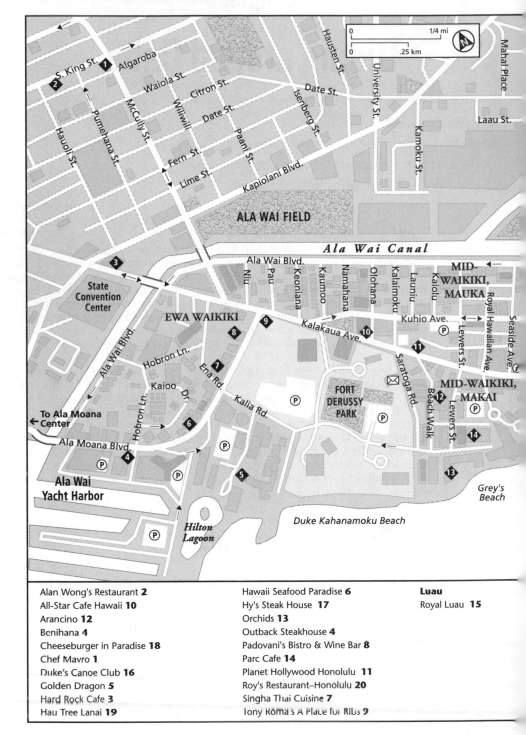

		Luau
Alan Wong's Restaurant **2**	Hawaii Seafood Paradise **6**	Royal Luau **15**
All-Star Cafe Hawaii **10**	Hy's Steak House **17**	
Arancino **12**	Orchids **13**	
Benihana **4**	Outback Steakhouse **4**	
Cheeseburger in Paradise **18**	Padovani's Bistro & Wine Bar **8**	
Chef Mavro **1**	Parc Cafe **14**	
Duke's Canoe Club **16**	Planet Hollywood Honolulu **11**	
Golden Dragon **5**	Roy's Restaurant–Honolulu **20**	
Hard Rock Cafe **3**	Singha Thai Cuisine **7**	
Hau Tree Lanai **19**	Tony Roma's A Place for Ribs **9**	

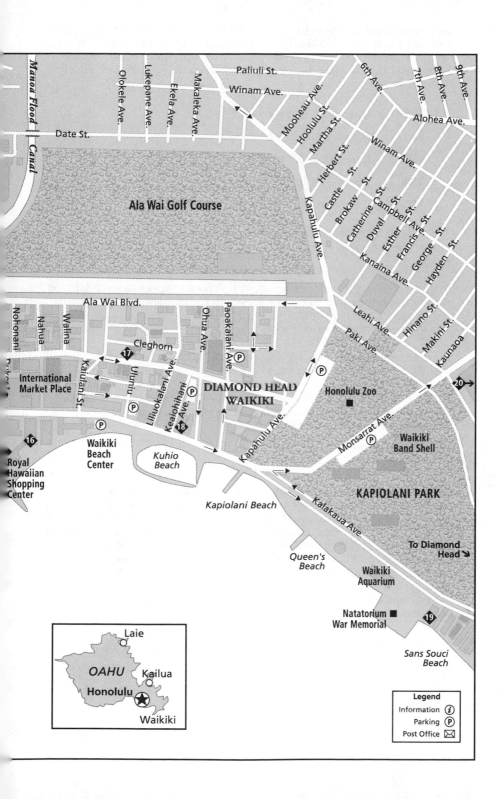

Each restaurant review is followed by a number of dollar signs, ranging from one ($) to five ($$$$$). The dollar signs give you an idea of what a complete dinner for one person — including appetizer, main course, one drink, tax, and tip — is likely to set you back. The price categories go like this:

$	Cheap eats — less than $15 per person
$$	Still inexpensive — $15 to $25
$$$	Moderate — $25 to $40
$$$$	Pricey — $40 to $70
$$$$$	Ultraexpensive — more than $70 per person

Of course, it all depends on how you order, so stay away from the surf and turf or the north end of the wine list if you're watching your budget.

To give you a further idea of how much you can expect to spend, I also include the price range of main courses in the listings. (Keep in mind that prices can change at the whim of the management, so call before you go to confirm the price range.)

The state adds about 4 percent in sales tax to every restaurant bill. A 15 to 20 percent tip is standard in Hawaii, just like back home.

As you plan where you'd like to eat, use the "Menus & Venues" worksheet at the back of this book to organize your choices.

Ahi's Restaurant

$–$$ Windward Coast   Seafood/Local

This legendary windward coast spot is a wonderful place to break for a casual bite during your circle island drive. A genuine Hawaii-style restaurant housed in a simple rural bungalow tucked among the trees, Ahi's is the embodiment of true island spirit and harks back to a time before prepackaged, prefab Hawaii set the tone. The highlight of a basic fish-and-steak menu is the shrimp, prepared any of four ways: cocktail, scampi, tempura, or deep-fried (a combo plate is available if you can't decide). A few naysayers complain that it's not as good as the original (which succumbed to fire a few years back), but I find that this newer place captures the funky old vibe beautifully.

53-146 Kamehameha Hwy. (Hwy. 83), Punaluu (south of the Polynesian Cultural Center). ☎ *808-237-8474 or 808-293-5650. Reservations not taken. Main courses: $6.50–$15; complete meals $2.50–$4 extra. No credit cards. Open: Lunch and dinner Mon–Sat.*

Alan Wong's Restaurant

$$$$–$$$$$ Honolulu Hawaii Regional

If there is one master of true Hawaii Regional cuisine above all others, it is Alan Wong — and his restaurant offers a world-class experience. Koa, rattan, and other tropical touches maintain a real Hawaiian ambience in the warmly contemporary dining room, which serves as an ideal show-case for Wong's masterful elevation of the local culinary tradition. Expect perfectly prepared island fish bursting with clean, fresh flavors; Asian accents galore (the seaweed-wrapped tempura bigeye ahi with soy mustard is magnificent); and modernist takes on island favorites: ahi tartare is adorned with truffled ponzu and grated chili daikon, while luau pork accompanies baby romaine, poi, and anchovy dressing in a delightful twist on a classic Caesar. Service is appropriately sophisticated yet completely unpretentious, rounding out the best-of-show dining experience.

1857 S. King St. (1½ blocks west of McCully Street), 5th Floor, Honolulu. ☎ *808-949-2526. Internet:* www.alanwongs.com. *Reservations highly recommended. To get there: Take Kalakaua west from Waikiki and turn right on S. King St. Main courses: $24–$30. 5- and 7-course tasting menus: $65–$85. AE, DC, JCB, MC, V. Open: Dinner nightly.*

Arancino

$$ Mid-Waikiki Northern Italian

If Arancino can draw island residents into the heart of Waikiki, you know it has to be good. This intimate and affordable trattoria-style Italian restaurant is hugely popular with Japanese visitors, mainlanders, and locals alike, all of whom bond over their love of good Italian food. Creative pizzas and pastas, homemade risottos, and fresh island seafood comprise a simple but very appealing menu that delivers on all counts. With burnished terra-cotta walls, tile floors, and red-checked cloths on the tables, the charming room is equally inviting, and friendly service caps the good news. Don't be surprised if you find a patient line when you arrive — but the excellent value is worth the wait.

255 Beach Walk (just south of Kalakaua Ave.), Waikiki. ☎ *808-923-5557. Reservations not taken. Main courses: $8.50–$15. AE, CB, DC, JCB, MC, V. Open: Lunch and dinner daily.*

Brew Moon

$$ Ala Moana Eclectic

A comfortable-chic setting, satisfying contemporary pub food, and even better microbrews earned Brew Moon "Best New Restaurant" kudos from *Honolulu Weekly* in 1999. This trendy spot won't exactly wow the gourmands among you, but the casual eats are nicely prepared and boast an island flair. Even the award-winning beers (which include a homemade root beer) have an island edge: Witness Hawaii "5" ale, a smooth copper-toned amber that washes down the coconut shrimp, fire-roasted ribs, sesame-seared ahi, and veggie stir-fry perfectly. A full selection of salads, sandwiches, burgers, and creative pizzas complements the array of small plates, making this a good place to come with a group and share. Tiki torches flicker on the lanai once the sun goes down, and live music sets a festive mood three or four nights a week.

In Ward Centre, 1200 Ala Moana Blvd. (between Kamakee and Queen sts.), Honolulu. ☎ 808-593-0088. Internet: www.brewmoon.com. *Reservations recommended. Main courses: $15–$25 (most less than $17). AE, DC, MC, V. Open: Lunch and dinner daily.*

Chai's Island Bistro

$$$$ Downtown Euro Pacific Rim

Chef/owner Chai Chaowasaree (whose Singha Thai cuisine is recommended later in this chapter) uses this attractive California-style restaurant as his outlet for cross-cultural innovation, and it's a winner. The pan-Asian influences lean heavily on the Thai tradition, as evidenced by grilled beef salad on organically grown greens with lemongrass garlic dressing, and grilled fresh island mahimahi dressed in a zippy red curry sauce. Those with more timid palates will enjoy the Continental-style plates, such as grilled beef tenderloin in a shiitake-Chianti demi-glace, plus Mediterranean-influenced pastas and risottos. The umbrella-covered patio is a delight despite its parking-lot view. The food is a tad too pricey, but nightly entertainment by some of Hawaii's best musicians — including, at press time, the excellent duo Hapa on Thursday and Friday and the legendary Brothers Cazimero on Wednesday — softens the blow.

Aloha Tower Marketplace, 1 Aloha Tower Dr., just south of downtown Honolulu. ☎ 808-585-0011. Internet: www.hawaiisrestaurants.com/chaisislandbistro. *Reservations recommended. To get there: Take Ala Moana Blvd. west from Waikiki. Main courses: $11–$20 at lunch, $29–$40 at dinner. Chef's 3-course dinner: $46. AE, DC, DISC, JCB, MC, V. Open: Lunch and dinner daily.*

Cheeseburger in Paradise

$ Diamond Head Waikiki American

The Waikiki branch of this wildly successful Maui burger joint doesn't have the spectacular on-the-water location that the original one has, but the burgers are just as good. Located just across the street from a prime stretch of beach, this is the perfect spot for takeout or a casual sit-down meal. The tropical-style gourmet burgers are big, juicy, and served on fresh-baked buns. Vegetarians can opt for the terrific garden burger, a tofu burger, or a meal-sized salad. Chili dogs, onion rings, cheese fries, and a full bar with a groovy tropical drinks menu complete the picture. You can even launch your beach day here with hearty omelets, French toast, eggs Benedict, and other morning favorites.

2500 Kalakaua Ave. (at Kealohilani Ave., 3 blocks west of Kapahulu Ave.), Waikiki. ☎ 808-923-3731. Internet: www.chzyburger-waikiki.com. *AE, DISC, MC, V. Main courses: $5–$11. Open: Breakfast, lunch, and dinner daily.*

Chef Mavro

$$$$$ Honolulu   Hawaii   Regional

Chef Mavro may even edge out Alan Wong's (see earlier in this chapter) as one of the two finest restaurants for a haute Hawaiian meal. In fact, if forced to decide, I might choose Mavro's first. Marseilles transplant and James Beard award–winner George Mavrothalassitis has long been considered one of Hawaii's finest chefs, and he brings a one-of-a-kind Provençal-Mediterranean accent to the Hawaii Regional table. Chef Mavro prepares ethereally light cuisine with an unfailing sense of culinary balance; with only a few worthwhile exceptions, he uses no butter or cream. The *onaga* (longtailed snapper) baked in a Hawaiian salt pastry crust and served with a ratatouille-herb sauce is a signature delight. I haven't found a dish yet that doesn't improve on the description. The dazzling menu even goes a delightful step further, pairing each and every dish with the perfect glass of wine. It's a faultless dining experience from start to finish — just ask *Gourmet* magazine, which raved that Mavro's has bestowed upon Hawaii "a dining experience comparable to a three-star restaurant's in France."

1969 S. King St. (at McCully St.), Honolulu. ☎ 808-944-4714. Reservations highly recommended. To get there: Take McCully St. north to King St. Main courses: $27–$38. 3- to 6-course tasting menus: $46–$77 ($64–$106 with wine). Open: Dinner Tues–Sun.

Cholo's Homestyle Mexican

$ North Shore   Island Style Mexican

Yummy fresh island fish tacos, burritos, and fajitas make this laid-back restaurant one of my favorite Hawaii dives. It's cheap, ultra-casual, and super friendly — everything you want in a north shore noshing spot. The cheery hole-in-the-wall dining room is a tad cramped, but service is just as attentive at the outdoor tables. The combo plates are a bargain-basement deal, and veggie and *carne asada* options are available for avowed fish-o-phobes.

At the North Shore Marketplace (in back), 66-250 Kamehameha Hwy., Haleiwa. ☎ 808-637-3059. A la carte items: $3–$7. Combo plates: $5–$12. No credit cards. Open: Lunch and dinner daily.

Compadres Mexican Bar & Grill

$$ Honolulu   Mexican

Look forward to high-quality south-of-the-border fare as well as the best margaritas in town at this lively cantina. The extensive menu features all the standards and then some, including eight kinds of enchiladas, a half-dozen quesadillas, and even four variations on the chiles relleno. The fresh fish tacos vary daily but never disappoint, and you can't go wrong with the huevos rancheros. The tortilla chips are light and greaseless, the guacamole is fresh and chunky, and the combos are big enough to satisfy two, making Compadres an all-around good deal.

At Ward Centre, 1200 Ala Moana Blvd. (between Kamakee and Queen sts.), Honolulu. ☎ 808-591-8307. Reservations recommended. Main courses: $9–$20 (most less than $15). AE, DC, JCB, MC, V. Open: Lunch and dinner daily.

Duke's Canoe Club

$/$$$ Mid-Waikiki   Steaks/Seafood (American/Hawaii Local in the Barefoot Bar)

Duke's is everything that Waikiki dining should be, complete with sarong-wearing cocktail waitresses, open-air beachfront dining, and tiki torches in the sand. This inviting restaurant manages to be all things to all people: a kid-friendly choice for families, a romantic lair for lovers, a magnet for Hawaiian music fans, and a hot spot for party hoppers. The menu deserves high marks, too, from the fresh-caught local fish (with a half-dozen preparations to choose from) to the succulent prime rib. I particularly love the "poke" rolls, made with sushi-grade ruby-red ahi, to start. Duke's is also well-loved for its Barefoot Bar, with a mile-long drinks menu, budget-friendly food, and top-notch nightly entertainment. It's a great place to watch the sunset.

At the Outrigger Waikiki on the Beach, 2335 Kalakaua Ave. (between the Royal Hawaiian Shopping Center and the Sheraton Moana Surfrider), Waikiki. ☎ 808-922-2268. Internet: www.hulapie.com. *Reservations recommended for dinner. Barefoot Bar menu (served all day): $7–$10. Main courses: $14–$22 at dinner (salad bar included). AE, DC, DISC, MC, V. Open: Breakfast, lunch, and dinner daily.*

Golden Dragon

$$$ Ewa Waikiki Canton   Chinese

The Golden Dragon makes dining out on Chinese food a special event. The tranquil and exotically elegant space sets the stage for a memorable restaurant experience. The classic Cantonese cuisine is always superbly prepared and presented with an elegant flourish. Lazy Susans on the tables encourage sharing, but a number of fixed-price meals mean that even couples can sample generously from the wide-ranging menu. The Imperial Beggar's chicken — wrapped in lotus leaves, enveloped in clay, and baked to perfection — and sublime Peking duck require 24 hours' advance notice; consider the lobster tail stir-fried in curry sauce, another signature dish, if you didn't plan so far ahead. For a really unique finish, the lovely tea lady will even read your fortune, if you like.

In Hilton Hawaiian Village, 2005 Kalia Rd. (at Ala Moana Blvd.), Waikiki. ☎ 808-946-5336. Reservations recommended. Main courses: $11–$31 (most less than $20). Prix-fixe menus: $29.50–$47. AE, CB, DC, DISC, JCB, MC, V. Open: Dinner Tues–Sun.

Hau Tree Lanai

$$$ Diamond Head Waikiki   Eurasian/Continental

Shaded by an ancient hau tree that twinkles with tiny lights at dinner-time, this informal outdoor terrace on the sand is one of the most romantic beachfront restaurants in all of Hawaii. The A-1 location surpasses the food at any time of day — but, frankly, it would be hard for any chef to live up to this magical setting. Breakfast is best: Throw caution to the wind and start the day with the sausage sampler — three kinds of local sausage and a side of fluffy poi pancakes — or the eggs Benedict, which wears a perfect hollandaise. Lunchtime features burgers, sandwiches, and salads, while the fresh island fish preparations are the standouts at dinner. Live music enhances the romantic mood on weekends and during the Friday lunch hour.

In the New Otani Kaimana Beach Hotel, 2863 Kalakaua Ave. (across the street from Kapiolani Park), Waikiki. ☎ *808-921-7066. Internet:* www.kaimana.com. *Reservations recommended. Main courses: $7.50–$15 at breakfast and lunch, $19–$32.50 at dinner. AE, CB, DC, DISC, JCB, MC, V. Open: Breakfast, lunch, and dinner daily.*

Hawaii Seafood Paradise

$$ Ewa Waikiki   Chinese Seafood

Eating at this quirky, unpretentious restaurant is a great culinary adventure; seafood fans should make a particular point of it, because the bounty hardly gets better than this. You can dine as cheaply or as lavishly as you want; specialties range from gloriously simple heads-on salt-and-pepper shrimp to rare shark's fin soup and braised abalone. The huge menu also offers an array of excellently prepared Cantonese and Szechuan standards, including a to-die-for Peking duck (no advance order necessary), for those who don't want a meal from the sea. A few of the best items on the menu have no English translation, so don't be afraid to ask questions. The decor is *way* too pink, but other than that, you can't lose.

In the Holiday Inn Waikiki, 1830 Ala Moana Blvd. (between Ena Rd. and Hobron Lane). ☎ *808-946-4514 or 808-946-4624. Reservations recommended for dinner. Main courses: $7–$23 (most less than $16; specialties may go as high as $42). AE, JCB, DC, MC, V. Open: Breakfast, lunch, dinner, and late night (to 3 a.m.) daily.*

Hy's Steak House

$$$$ Waikiki   Steaks/Seafood

I just love Hy's — it's the only place in town that still serves a great steak and flaming bananas Foster in true old-world style. This dark and clubby steak house is the perfect setting for classics like oysters Rockefeller, beef Wellington, lamb chops à la Hy's (perfectly broiled and served with tropical fruit chutney), and Chateaubriand for two. A number of surf-and-turf combos are available to choose from, plus a good selection of seafood options (including calamari, ahi, and *kiawe* (mesquite)-charred scallops). I suggest starting with the Caesar salad show (prepared tableside with all of the classic flourishes) and crowning the meal with a flambéed dessert, such as cherries jubilee or the aforementioned bananas Foster.

In the Waikiki Park Heights, 2440 Kuhio Ave. (near Uluniu Ave.). ☎ *808-922-5555. Internet:* www.gtesupersite.com/hyssteakhse. *Reservations highly recommended. Main courses: $15.50–$40. AE, DC, DISC, JCB, MC, V. Open: Dinner nightly.*

Downtown & Ala Moana Restaurants

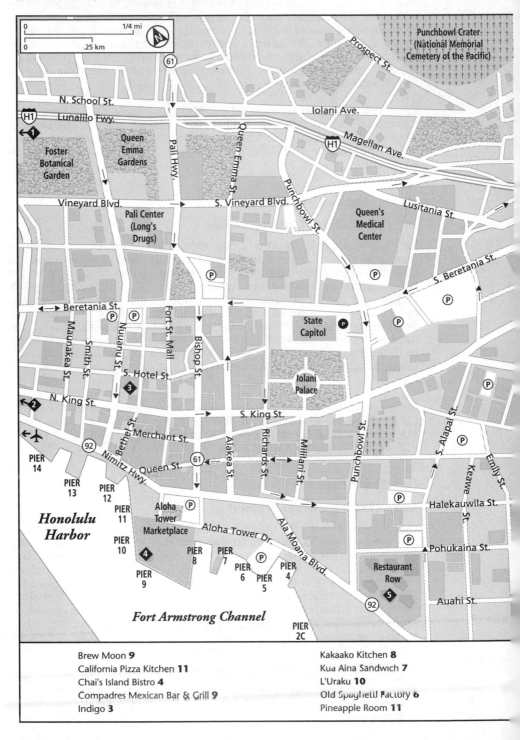

Brew Moon **9**	Kakaako Kitchen **8**
California Pizza Kitchen **11**	Kua Aina Sandwich **7**
Chai's Island Bistro **4**	L'Uraku **10**
Compadres Mexican Bar & Grill **9**	Old Spaghetti Factory **6**
Indigo **3**	Pineapple Room **11**

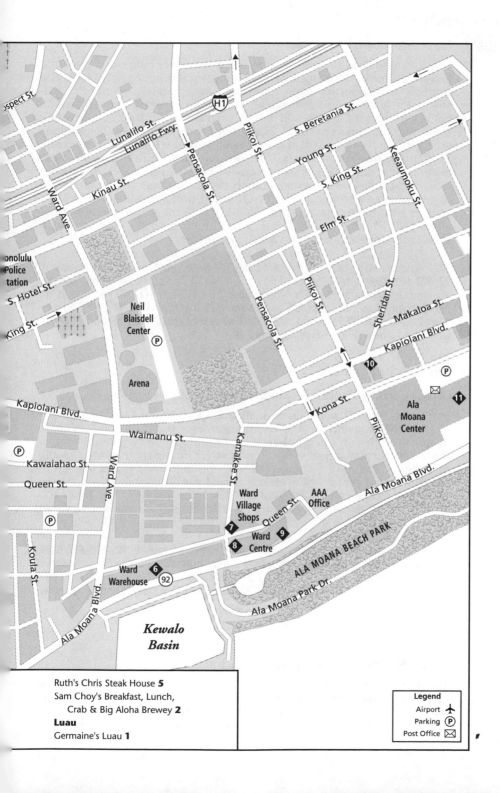

Ruth's Chris Steak House **5**
Sam Choy's Breakfast, Lunch,
    Crab & Big Aloha Brewey **2**
Luau
Germaine's Luau **1**

Legend
Airport ✈
Parking Ⓟ
Post Office ✉

Indigo

$$$ Downtown Eurasian

This intimate downtown restaurant is a wonderful choice for a romantic midpriced meal. Boasting a casual-chic plantation-goes-SoHo look, the tropical-contemporary main room sets an appealing scene. But call ahead for a table on the magical lanai, which overlooks a charming pocket park; dark woods and rattan, oversize palm fronds, a trickling water fountain, and conspiratorially dim candlelight make this outdoor dining room feel as if it had been transplanted wholesale from exotic Thailand or deepest Malaysia. Chef/owner Glenn Chu's east-meets-west menu is best described as pan-Asian — Chinese and Thai traditions are most apparent — with serious French twists: Witness such taste treats as goat cheese wontons in a four-fruit sauce, and Mongolian lamb chops sauced with minted tangerines. This is excellent, surprisingly harmonious hybrid cuisine. Light eaters or the chronically indecisive can choose to make a meal of dim sum–style plates.

1121 Nuuanu Ave. (between S. King and S. Hotel sts.), downtown Honolulu. ☎ *808-521-2900. Internet:* www.indigo-hawaii.com. *Reservations recommended. To get there: Take Ala Moana Blvd. from Waikiki to Bethel St.; turn right, then left on Pauahi St., then left on Nuuanu Ave. Valet parking $4 after 5:30 p.m. Main courses: $6–$15 at lunch, $12.50–$20 at dinner. DC, DISC, JTB, MC, V. Open: Lunch and dinner Tues–Fri, dinner only Sat.*

Jameson's by the Sea

$$-$$$$ North Shore Steaks-Seafood-American

Don't come to this north shore institution for the food — come for the tropical cocktails and breathtaking oceanfront setting. The food isn't bad, by any stretch — it's just not very memorable, especially in the face of those spectacular sunset views. The upstairs dining room offers capably prepared surf-and-turf choices in the evening, but I prefer the more casual outdoor patio, which makes a great spot for sandwiches, salads, and other casual eats throughout the day, to be accompanied by a celebratory fruity drink or ice-cold beer at cocktail (and sunset-viewing) hour.

62-540 Kamehameha Hwy., Haleiwa (just north of town). ☎ *808-637-4336. Reservations recommended for upstairs dining room (also taken for downstairs Mon–Tues, when upstairs is closed). Main courses: $8–$15 in downstairs bar, $19–$30 in upstairs dining room. AE, DC, DISC, JCB, MC, V. Open: Lunch and dinner daily.*

Kakaako Kitchen

$ Ala Moana Hawaii Local/American

This contemporary dine-and-dash elevates takeout to gourmet status. The huge menu can please even the most finicky eaters with choices ranging from Chinese *char siu* chicken salad with crispy wontons to an all-American oven-roasted turkey sandwich with sage dressing and machies.

The island-style chicken linguine in chile-hoisin cream is a standout, but you can also come by for a juicy beef or homemade veggie burger, home-style pot roast, sandwiches ranging from seared ahi to grilled pastrami, and daily vegetarian specials. Breakfast stars include omelets, corned-beef hash, and fresh-baked scones. You order at the counter, pay, pick up your utensils, then choose a table in the simple but bright indoor space or on the lanai; a server will deliver your freshly made, affordable, and tasty meal in short order. Beware the workday lunch hour, which can be maddening.

At Ward Centre, 1200 Ala Moana Blvd. (entrance 1 block north, on Auahi St. at Kamakee St.), Honolulu. ☎ 808-596-7488. Main courses: $5–$7 at breakfast, $6–$9 at lunch and dinner. MC, V. Open: Breakfast and lunch daily, dinner Mon–Sat.

Kua Aina Sandwich

$ Ala Moana/North Shore   Island Style/American

This north shore legend has pleased many a city dweller — who used to have to drive an hour for the ultimate burger — by opening a second Ala Moana–area location. Cheeseburger in Paradise (see earlier in this chapter) wins on atmosphere, but Kua Aina (KOO-ah EYE-na) boasts the better burger. The gourmet sandwiches are equally as good, especially the mahimahi with a green-chile sauce and cheese. Whatever you order, don't forget a side of the spindly fries, which elevate the fried spud to new levels. A low crowd-to-table ratio makes take-out a good idea at the perpetually packed north shore location; the larger Honolulu branch offers more seating.

In Honolulu: In the Ward Village Shops, 1116 Auahi St. (at Kamakee St., directly behind Ward Centre), Honolulu. ☎ 808-591-9133. Sandwiches and burgers: $4–$6. No credit cards. Open: Lunch and dinner daily. On the North Shore: 66-214 Kamehameha Hwy., Haleiwa. ☎ 808-637-6067. Reservations not taken. Sandwiches and burgers: $4–$6. No credit cards. Open: Lunch and early dinner (to 8 p.m.) daily.

L'Uraku

$$$–$$$$ Ala Moana   Euro-Japanese

As soon as you enter L'Uraku, you'll see that you're in for something different: The room's clean, corporate lines are interrupted by a welcoming touch of whimsy — a collection of umbrellas festively painted with impulsive brush strokes and suspended from the ceiling, creating the impression of an upside-down garden in bloom. It's a warm, colorful setting in which you can sit back and enjoy Hiroshi Fukui's unique European-Japanese hybrid cuisine, a welcome departure from the same-old-seared-ahi syndrome that threatens Hawaii kitchens. The dishes are light, fresh, and bursting with spirited flavor: Citrus-ponzu-butter sauce and fresh grated daikon add zest to filet mignon, while a balsamic reduction and onion chive pesto give an inspired Mediterranean edge to miso butterfish and peppered shrimp. Service is impeccable, and plates are beautifully presented in the Japanese tradition.

At Uraku Tower, 1341 Kapiolani Blvd. (near Piikoi St.), Honolulu. ☎ *808-955-0552. Internet:*www.hawaiisrestaurants.com/luraku. *Reservations highly recommended. To get there: Take Ala Moana Blvd. east from Waikiki; turn right onto Piikoi St., just beyond the Ala Moana Center, then right on Kapiolani Blvd. and pull into free lot. Main courses: $9–$15 at lunch, $17–$27 at dinner. 4-course dinner tasting menu: $34, $47 with wine. Open:AE, CB, DC, JCB, MC, V. Lunch and dinner daily.*

Orchids

$$$$$ Waikiki International   Seafood

There's no arguing with the fabulousness of the Halekulani's classic French restaurant, La Mer — but oceanside Orchids is equally fabulous, less expensive, and better suits the Hawaii mood. Everything about Orchids is sigh-inducing: the gorgeous alfresco setting; the spectacular ocean and Diamond Head views; the seamless service; and an impressive surf-and-turf menu that offers time-tested classics to traditionalists and globe-hopping innovations for adventurous spirits. Chef Jean-Pierre Maharibatcha was born in Vietnam and grew up in the south of France, so you'll find elements of both cultures in his cooking. It's very pricey — the wine list alone will cause you to do a double-take — but if you have something to celebrate, this is a wonderful place to do it. Live music adds to the romantic vibe nightly and during the legendary Sunday brunch.

In the Halekulani, 2199 Kalia Rd. (at the beach end of Lewers St.), Waikiki. ☎ *808-923-2311. Reservations essential. Main courses: $15–$21 at lunch, $25–$36 at dinner. AE, CB, DC, JCB, MC, V. Open: Breakfast, lunch, and dinner Mon–Sat; brunch and dinner Sun.*

Padovani's Bistro & Wine Bar

$$$$–$$$$$ Ewa Waikiki   Continental

If you want a fabulous meal but you'd rather do without the pervasive Asian accents, book a table at intimate, elegant, classic Padovani's. You'll know this place is first class as soon as you lay eyes on the sumptuous decor and impressively laid tables. Island influences pop up on occasion, but Philippe Padovani generally sticks to a French-Mediterranean repertoire: pan-fried Sonoma duck liver, for example, roasted quail in garlic-thyme jus, and prime beef tenderloin in a porcini sauce. The wine list is probably the most exciting in town — no less than 50 vintages are offered by the glass alone — and desserts like ginger crème brulée and Hawaiian Vintage chocolate mousse provide a timeless finish. If you'd like a more casual meal — or you simply want to spend less — head to the wine bar, where that same fab list is accompanied by classic cart service and an incredible after-dinner scotch and liqueurs list.

In the Doubletree Alana Waikiki, 1956 Ala Moana Blvd. (between Kalakaua Ave. and Ena Rd.). ☎ *808-946-3456. Reservations recommended. Main courses: $12–$18 at lunch, $17–$35 at dinner. Three-course prix-fixe dinner: $45. Open: Lunch Mon–Fri, dinner nightly.*

Parc Cafe

$$–$$$ Mid-Waikiki Island American

Drawing locals and in-the-know visitors alike with its high-quality buffet spreads, this smart little hotel restaurant offers one of Honolulu's best dining values. Don't let the buffet concept scare you away — this is winning gourmet cuisine. The theme changes by day and meal; my favorite is the fabulous Hawaiian buffet (available at Wednesday and Friday lunch and Wednesday dinner), which offers a well-prepared introduction to the local dining tradition. The nightly (except Wednesday) prime-rib buffets boast succulent beef and rotisserie chicken along with a wide array of accompaniments; on Friday, Saturday, and Sunday, fresh seafood and a wok station broaden the appeal. The breakfast spread features such luxuries as an omelet station, and the Sunday brunch is suitably lavish and includes a made-to-order sushi station.

In the Waikiki Parc, 2233 Helumoa Rd. (at Lewers St., east of the Halekulani). ☎ 808-921-7272. Internet: www.waikikiparc.com. *Reservations recommended. All-you-can-eat buffets: $13 at breakfast, $16–$17 at lunch, $19–$26 at dinner, $26 at Sunday brunch. Parents pay $5–$12 for kids 5–12, based on $1-per-year ratio. AE, CB, DC, JCB, MC, V. Open: Breakfast, lunch, and dinner Mon–Sat; brunch and dinner Sun.*

Pineapple Room

$$$ Ala Moana Hawaii Regional

Culinary star Alan Wong (see Alan Wong's, earlier in this chapter) has made a surprising addition to his stable of successes: a genuine, all-day department-store restaurant — and it's a winner. Dining at the warm, comfortable Pineapple Room offers a wonderful opportunity to sample the master chef's impressive cuisine in more casual preparations and in a more laid-back atmosphere than what you find at his namesake restaurant — and at a lower price tag to boot. Sure, you can blow a wad of cash on dinner here, but you don't have to. Opt for a round of affordable family-style appetizers instead (almost all under $10), such as luau pork nachos, crispy fried salt-and-pepper shrimp, vine-ripened Waimea tomato salad, and one of the day's wood-fired pizzas. The breakfasts are the best in town, and lunch offers a gourmet take on the shopping break.

On the third floor of Liberty House, Ala Moana Center, 1450 Ala Moana Blvd. (at Atkinson Dr., just west of Waikiki). ☎ 808-945-8881. Reservations recommended for dinner. Main courses: $8–$20 at breakfast and lunch, $18–$30 at dinner. Afternoon tea (daily 3–5 p.m.): $15. Three-course dinner prix-fixe: $38–$45. Six-course dinner sampling menu: $52. AE, DC, JCB, MC, V. Open: Breakfast Sat–Sun, lunch daily, dinner Mon–Sat.

King of the food courts

I hesitate to recommend that you waste too much of your island time in — gulp — a mall, but I have to make an exception for the Makai Market Food Court at the **Ala Moana Center,** 1450 Ala Moana Blvd., between Piikoi Street and Atkinson Drive (☎ **808-955-9517;** Internet: www.alamoana.com). It's one of the coolest food courts in the country. About 25 different vendors populate this busy, noisy, colorful complex on the ground floor of the rambling mall, from take-out bowls of Japanese noodles to Korean barbecue to sit-down Italian. Great for a quick, affordable meal — or if you and the rest of the family just can't agree on what to eat.

Roy's Restaurant–Honolulu

$$$ Hawaii Kai Hawaii Regional

Roy Yamaguchi is the Wolfgang Puck of Hawaii. No, Roy isn't the sole mastermind behind the Hawaii Regional cuisine concept, but he is responsible for bringing it an international audience. The flagship restaurant of his worldwide chain is a full 20 minutes east of Waikiki, and many of his peers have surpassed Roy in the kitchen in recent years. Still, the original Roy's is worth visiting if you want to see what the fuss was all about. You can go whole hog or keep costs down by ordering from the wide selection of appetizers and creative wood-oven pizzas, virtually all less than $10. The menu changes nightly, but count on such signatures as Szechuan-spiced baby-back ribs, crispy crab cakes in spicy sesame butter, and several inventively prepared fresh catches. Tables are big and comfortable, and service is friendly and impressively attentive. Kids are welcome, and Roy's is particularly well-suited to groups, making it an ideal choice for a multigenerational family meal.

In Hawaii Kai Corporate Plaza, 6600 Kalanianaole Hwy. (Hwy. 72 at Keahole St.), east of Honolulu in Hawaii Kai. ☎ 808-396-7697. Reservations highly recommended. Appetizers and pizzas: $5–$10. Main courses: $16–$28. AE, CB, DC, DISC, JCB, MC, V. Open: Dinner nightly.

Sam Choy's Breakfast, Lunch, Crab & Big Aloha Brewery

$$$ Honolulu Hawaii Regional/Seafood

This informal island-style restaurant and crab house is a huge favorite for its gargantuan portions and fun, energetic atmosphere. I love Sam for his mammoth morning meals and lunches; with appetite ragin' full on, I invariably head here straight off my transpacific flight for a piled-high fried poke (ahi) lunch or a monster Lava burger (topped with crabmeat and Swiss cheese). Thoughts invariably turn to crab at dinner: The variety changes with the season, but you can expect a national atlas of choices, from Kona to Alaskan to Maryland crabmeat, in preparations that range from steamed legs to rich chowder to delectable cakes. The food is great, but come for the whole festive experience; you're welcome — nay, expected — to roll up your sleeves and get messy with the shellfish. Sam's own Big Aloha beer is brewed on site.

580 Nimitz Hwy. (on the way to the airport), Honolulu. ☎ 808-545-7979. Internet: www.samchoy.com. *Reservations recommended. Main courses: $4–$12 at breakfast, $6.50–$30 at lunch (most less than $14), $15–$35 at dinner (most less than $26). AE, DC, DISC, JCB, MC, V. Open: Breakfast, lunch, and dinner daily.*

Eating with the Chain Gang

The local **Hard Rock Cafe** is just west of Waikiki at 1837 Kapiolani Blvd., at Kalakaua Avenue (☎ 808-955-7383). This branch has everything you've come to expect from the long-lived Hard Rock chain — a lively atmosphere, a good burgers-and-fajitas fare, and wall-to-wall rock memorabilia — but with the appropriate tropical twist, of course. **Planet Hollywood Honolulu** is right nearby, in Waikiki, at 2155 Kalakaua Ave., at Beach Walk (☎ 808-924-7877), if you're in the mood for more theme-restaurant madness — but the sports buffs among you might prefer the **All-Star Cafe Hawaii**, in King Kalakaua Plaza, 2080 Kalakaua Ave., at Olohana St. (☎ 808-955-8326).

California Pizza Kitchen, in the Ala Moana Center, 1450 Ala Moana Blvd. (☎ 808-941-7715), is a friendly, affordable, and familiar choice, where the individual-sized pizzas come in what seem like a million varieties. Another great family destination — and a bargain to boot — is the **Old Spaghetti Factory,** at the Ward Warehouse, 1050 Ala Moana Blvd., between Ward Avenue and Kamakee Street (☎ 808-591-2513). It's fun, festive, and cheap — and what kid doesn't love spaghetti?

If it's a prime cut of beef and a martini you're in the mood for but you can't get into Hy's (see the listing earlier in this chapter), don your best aloha shirt and head to **Ruth's Chris Steak House,** at Restaurant Row, 500 Ala Moana Blvd., at Punchbowl Street (☎ 808-599-3860).

Just a stone's throw from Waikiki, **Outback Steakhouse,** 1765 Ala Moana Blvd., at Hobron Lane (☎ 808-951-6274), makes a more affordable and casual choice for big beef, and it's a great place to take the kids. The national rib shack **Tony Roma's A Place for Ribs** is also conveniently located, at 1972 Kalakaua Ave., near Ala Moana Boulevard at Pau Street (☎ 808-942-2121).

When I was a kid, I loved nothing more than a night at **Benihana** — and I'll wager good money that your kids would agree. The local branch is at Hilton Hawaiian Village, 2005 Kalia Rd., at Ala Moana Boulevard (☎ 808-955-5955). You'll sit family style with other diners at a long table while a show-stopping chef performs culinary razzle-dazzle, slicing, dicing, and grilling scallops, lobster, fresh island fish, chicken, or steak right before your eyes, Japanese style. Benihana is more than a meal — it's full-tilt entertainment.

Singha Thai Cuisine

$$$ Ewa Waikiki Thai

This spiffy restaurant serves up imaginative Thai-Hawaiian hybrid cuisine that wins fans among Asian-food addicts and novices alike. Thai-born chef Chai Chaowasaree's complete dinners for two to five are family-style feasts — perfect for introducing first-timers to this rich, flavorful cuisine, as well as elements of Hawaii Regional cuisine that the chef has incorporated into his cooking. Highlights of the varied menu include yummy blackened ahi rolls; fresh island fish in a light black-bean sauce; a kaleidoscope of curries; and excellent seafood dishes. Dishes are presented prettily, and service is first-rate. Graceful Thai dancers perform nightly from 7 to 9 p.m.

1910 Ala Moana Blvd. (at Kalia Road, below California Pizza Kitchen), Waikiki.
☎ *800-482-THAI or 808-941-2898. Internet: www.singhathai.com. Reservations recommended. Free validated parking at neighboring Canterbury Place. Main courses: $12–$30 (most less than $20). Complete dinners: $30. AE, CB, DC, DISC, JCB, MC, V. Open: Lunch Mon–Fri, dinner nightly.*

Luau!

None of Oahu's luaus are on par with those offered on the neighbor islands, especially Maui's Old Lahaina Luau. Still, you might want to try one of the following choices if you're in the mood to luau while you're here. In addition to the choices I list here, also consider the nightly (except Sunday) luau at the **Polynesian Cultural Center;** see Chapter 10 for more information.

Reservations are almost always required for luaus, so be sure to call at least a day or two in advance (a few days ahead if you want to guarantee admission).

Germaine's Luau

Head west to Germaine's private-beachfront backyard-style luau grounds to party with nearly 1,000 of your closest friends (for the evening, anyway) at this touristy, but appealing, feast. Entertainment begins with a Pacific Ocean flourish, as dancers arrive via outrigger canoe. The vibrant floor show plays liberally with Polynesian tradition, but incorporates thrilling Samoan fire-knife dancers (always a big crowd-pleaser). You can watch dinner being unearthed from its underground oven (*imu*), and then feast on an all-you-can-eat luau pig and traditional sides (plus chicken teriyaki and potato salad for less adventurous diners). Come for the cheeky fun, not the mediocre food.

Many of the map books handed out by the major rental-car companies include a discount coupon for Germaine's Luau tickets, so check yours.

In the Campbell Industrial Park, 91-121 Olai St., west of Barbers Point Naval Air Station, 24 miles (or a 30- to 40-minute drive) west of Waikiki via H-1.
☎ *800-367-5655 or 808-949-6626. Internet: www.germainesluau.com.*

Admission: $49 adults, $39 teens 13–20, $27 kids 6–13. Prices include free shuttle service to and from Waikiki, plus unlimited soft drinks and 3 drink coupons for adults. Times: Nightly at 6 p.m.

Royal Luau

Waikiki's only luau takes place in a magical beachfront setting at the historic Pink Palace, the Royal Hawaiian — and it's the perfect setting for a luau with a touch of elegance. This may not be the most authentic luau in the islands, but it's intimate and romantic to the max. The food is good if not wholly traditional, the setting is beautiful, and the hour-long Royal Polynesian Extravaganza is exactly that. It's easy to forgive this luau its few faults as soothing Hawaiian melodies dance on the tradewinds and Diamond Head rises iconically in the background. The luau is on Monday nights only, so plan accordingly.

At the Royal Hawaiian, 2259 Kalakaua Ave. (at the end of Royal Hawaiian Ave.), Waikiki. ☎ 808-923-7311 or 808-931-7194. Admission: $78 adults, $48 kids 5–12; discounts for Royal Hawaiian guests. Price includes unlimited mai tais. Time: Mon at 6 p.m.

Chapter 10

Fun On and Off the Beach

● ●

In This Chapter

▶ Heading to Oahu's best beaches

▶ Renting snorkel gear, taking a surfing lesson, catching an ocean cruise, and many more ways to enjoy the waves

▶ Seeing Oahu's top sights and attractions, either on your own or on a guided tour

▶ Finding the top hunting grounds for shoppers

▶ Kicking back — or partying hearty — once the sun goes down

● ●

*O*ahu is the place to rev up and have some fun. This island boasts more than you could see or do in the span of five vacations, much less one — so save the kicking-back portion of your vacation for the next island.

Then again, there are those wonderful white sands and warm turquoise waters. . . .

Hitting the Beaches

 When you're at the beach, maintain a healthy respect for the ocean. Big waves can come seemingly out of nowhere and travel far upshore in a matter of minutes. Never turn your back on the ocean, and always remember to get out of the water when the swells come. Take extra care to heed this advice in winter, when the surf is at its least predictable.

 Never leave valuables in your rental car while you're at the beach. Theives prey on tourists, and they'll have no trouble getting into your car to take whatever you've left there.

Beaches & Attractions Around Oahu

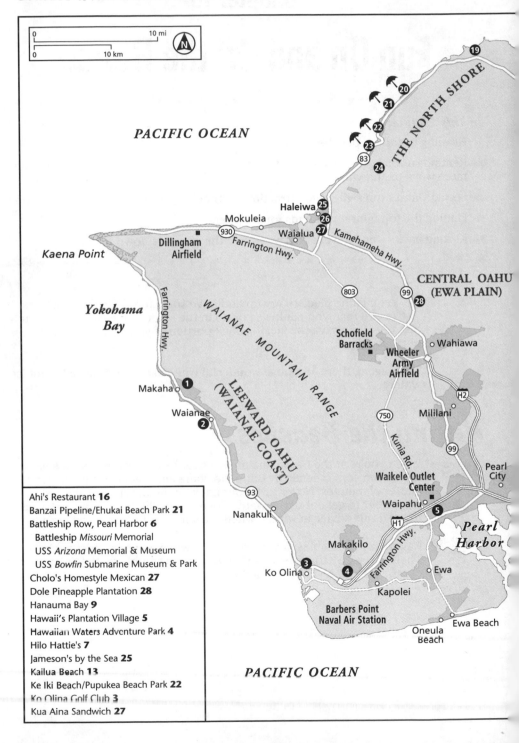

Ahi's Restaurant **16**
Banzai Pipeline/Ehukai Beach Park **21**
Battleship Row, Pearl Harbor **6**
  Battleship *Missouri* Memorial
  USS *Arizona* Memorial & Museum
  USS *Bowfin* Submarine Museum & Park
Cholo's Homestyle Mexican **27**
Dole Pineapple Plantation **28**
Hanauma Bay **9**
Hawaii's Plantation Village **5**
Hawaiian Waters Adventure Park **4**
Hilo Hattie's **7**
Jameson's by the Sea **25**
Kailua Beach **13**
Ke Iki Beach/Pupukea Beach Park **22**
Ko Olina Golf Club **3**
Kua Aina Sandwich **27**

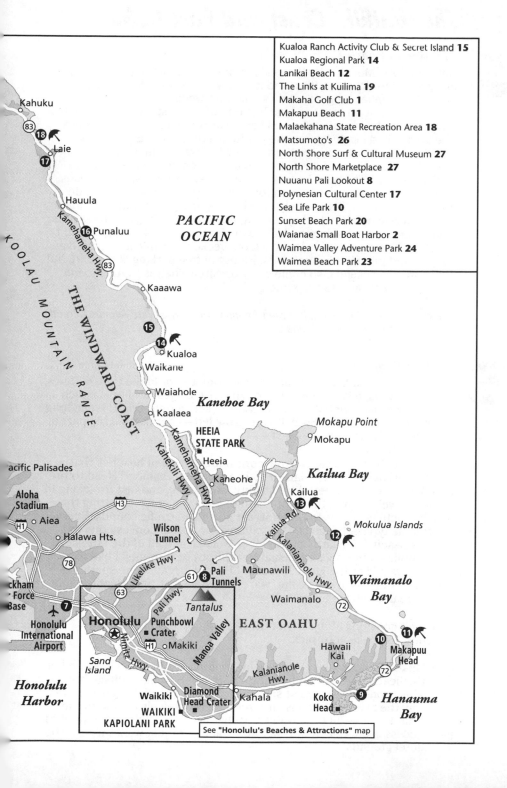

Kualoa Ranch Activity Club & Secret Island **15**
Kualoa Regional Park **14**
Lanikai Beach **12**
The Links at Kuilima **19**
Makaha Golf Club **1**
Makapuu Beach **11**
Malaekahana State Recreation Area **18**
Matsumoto's **26**
North Shore Surf & Cultural Museum **27**
North Shore Marketplace **27**
Nuuanu Pali Lookout **8**
Polynesian Cultural Center **17**
Sea Life Park **10**
Sunset Beach Park **20**
Waianae Small Boat Harbor **2**
Waimea Valley Adventure Park **24**
Waimea Beach Park **23**

Kahuku

83
18
Laie
17

Hauula

PACIFIC
OCEAN

16 Punaluu
83

K O O L A U

T H E   W I N D W A R D   C O A S T

Kaaawa

15
14 Kualoa
Waikane

Waiahole
Kaalaea

Kanehoe Bay

HEEIA
STATE PARK
Heeia

Mokapu Point
Mokapu

acific Palisades
Kaneohe

Kailua Bay

Aloha
Stadium
H3
Aiea
Halawa Hts.

Kailua
13

Wilson
Tunnel

Mokulua Islands
12

78

Likelike Hwy.

61
8 Pali
Tunnels

Maunawili

Waimanalo
72

Waimanalo Bay

ckham
Force
Base
7
63

Pali Hwy.

Tantalus

EAST OAHU

Honolulu
International
Airport

Honolulu
Punchbowl
Crater
H1
Makiki

Manoa Valley

Hawaii
Kai

10
11
Makapuu
Head
72

*Sand
Island*

Kalanianole
Hwy.

*Honolulu
Harbor*

Waikiki
Diamond
Head Crater
WAIKIKI
KAPIOLANI PARK

Kahala
Koko
Head
9

*Hanauma
Bay*

See **"Honolulu's Beaches & Attractions"** map

M O U N T A I N   R A N G E
Kamehameha Hwy.
Kahekili Hwy.
Kamehameha Hwy.
Kailua Rd.
Kalanianaole Hwy.
Nimitz Hwy.

The Waikiki Coast and East Oahu

Ala Moana Beach Park

Gold-sand Ala Moana ("by the sea") is the city's most popular beach playground for local families, and it's easy to see why. Stretching for more than a mile along Honolulu's coast between downtown and Waikiki, the long, man-made beach is one of the best-sheltered beaches on Oahu, so the water's calm and safe year-round for even little ones. The area called Magic Island, the peninsula that extends from Ala Moana Park, is especially well-protected thanks to a man-made breakwater that cuts the surf down to zero and offers great views of the Waikiki skyline. The park boasts concessions, lifeguards, bathhouses, tennis courts, a nice paved path for joggers, picnic tables, and wide-open grassy lawns. It's the only beach along this coast that's not lined with high-rise hotels, which gives it a nice, open feeling, and the sands are set far enough back from Ala Moana Boulevard that traffic doesn't interfere. The ambience is laid-back on weekdays, while a fun, festive party mood prevails on weekends. Plenty of free parking is at hand, but it fills up on weekends, so come early or catch TheBus to Ala Moana Center and walk across the street.

Along Ala Moana Boulevard, between Atkinson Drive and Ward Avenue (directly across the street from Ala Moana Center).

Waikiki Beach

Probably the most famous beach on the planet — or in the United States, at least — Waikiki is ground zero for Hawaii's biggest and best beach party. Five million global visitors a year descend onto this 1½-mile-long sunny crescent of sand. Sure, it gets crowded — but that's a big part of what makes Waikiki such a blast.

Waikiki is actually a long, narrow continuous string of beaches that extends between Ala Wai Harbor to the west and Diamond Head to the east. Each one is wonderful for surfing, swimming, and just frolicking in the mini swells — and the tight chain of high-rise hotels abutting the beaches actually helps to block street noise and traffic sounds. Every imaginable type of beach toy is available for rent at concessions that line the beach. Lifeguards patrol all of Waikiki, and all of the hotels have public restrooms and casual beachfront restaurants. I like to think of Waikiki as the giant Jacuzzi of Hawaii, because the sparkling turquoise water is always calm, warm, crystal-clear, and great for floating the real-life stress away.

You can't go wrong along any of these easily accessible Waikiki beaches. Just take your pick:

✔ **Duke Kahanamoku** (ka-ha-na-MOW-koo) **Beach** is the west end of the beach, the section fronting the Hilton Hawaiian Village hotel. This is one of the widest sections of Waikiki sand. Because of the way the massive hotel is situated, the beach feels almost private (but it isn't — all of Hawaii's beaches are accessible to the public). Access is off Kalia Road via Paoa Place — or just walk through the hotel grounds.

✔ **Gray's Beach,** the arc of sand between the Halekulani and the Sheraton Moana Surfrider hotels, is my favorite stretch of Waikiki Beach. It's everybody else's too, particularly the area in front of the historic Royal Hawaiian and Moana hotels — so bring your beach chair and stake a claim because this is where the party begins. (If you're lucky enough to be staying at the Royal or the Moana, the hotel will provide you with a beach chair.) Waikiki's waters are at their calmest and shallowest here. The beach has a number of access points, including a beach access pathway off of Kalia Road, just to the left of the Halekulani and to the right of the Waikiki Parc hotel (as you face the coast); walk to the left to get to the wider sands. (Or, better yet, just parade through one of the hotels, such as the Royal, the Outrigger, or the Moana.)

✔ **Kuhio Beach,** which begins just to the east of the Sheraton Moana Surfrider at the end of Kaiulani Avenue, continues the festive party atmosphere. Since fewer hotels separate Kalakaua Avenue from the beach, this one affords the quickest access to the Waikiki shoreline. This is where the majority of concessionaires are set up, so head to Kuhio Beach if you want to rent a boogie board, catch an outrigger canoe ride, or take a surfing lesson (for more on what's available, see "Water Fun for Everyone" later in this chapter). The swimming is good here, but some deep pools exist (heed the "Watch out for Holes" signs, as you could suddenly find yourself in very deep water), and the surf kicks up a bit a few hundred yards offshore (where the line of surfers are). To the east of the Moana between Kaiulani and Uluniu avenues is the Waikiki Beach Center, which houses restrooms, showers, and the Waikiki police substation. At the end of Kapahulu Avenue, a seawall marks a favorite boogie-boarding spot that draws local daredevils when the swells kick up.

✔ **Queen's Beach,** directly across from Kapiolani Park (between the zoo and the aquarium), is the easiest place to park along Waikiki. This is also the quietest stretch of beach, since no hotels line the road, and a grassy, palm-dotted lawn backs the sand. Head here if you'd like to get away from the crowds, as Queen's Beach tends to be much less crowded than its sister sands to the west. The facilities include showers, restrooms, barbecue grills, picnic tables, volleyball courts, and a pavilion. The middle section of the beach (in front of the pavilion) is a popular gay hangout.

✔ **Sans Souci Beach** is the easternmost section of Waikiki, the bit that fronts the New Otani Kaimana Beach Hotel and the other small hotels and condos at the foot of Diamond Head. This is the locals' favorite stretch of Waikiki thanks to its beautiful setting (Diamond Head makes a gorgeous backdrop) and intimate, low-key vibe. It's also on the quiet side, with easy-access parking along Kalakaua Avenue and beach showers. The swimming here is excellent — a shallow reef close to shore keeps the waters calm and protected from big waves — but the beach is rather small, so I prefer the areas farther west along the coast.

Honolulu's Beaches & Attractions

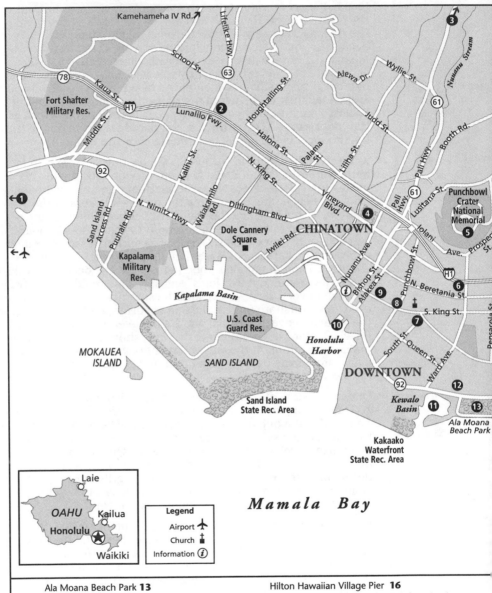

Ala Moana Beach Park **13**
Ala Moana Center **14**
Aloha Tower Marketplace **6**
Bishop Museum **2**
The Contemporary Museum **26**
Diamond Head Crater **23**
Foster Botanical Garden **4**
Hanauma Bay **25**
Hawaii Maritime Center **10**
Hawaii's Plantation Village **1**
Hawaiian Waters Adventure Park **1**
Hilo Hattie's **1**

Hilton Hawaiian Village Pier **16**
(departure point for Atlantis Submarines)
Honolulu Academy of Arts **6**
Honolulu Zoo **21**
Ilikai Sports Center **15**
International Market Place **18**
Iolani Palace **9**
Kawaiahao Church **8**
Kewalo Basin **11**
Ko Olina Golf Club **1**
Kodak Hula Show **22**
(at the Waikiki Band Shell)

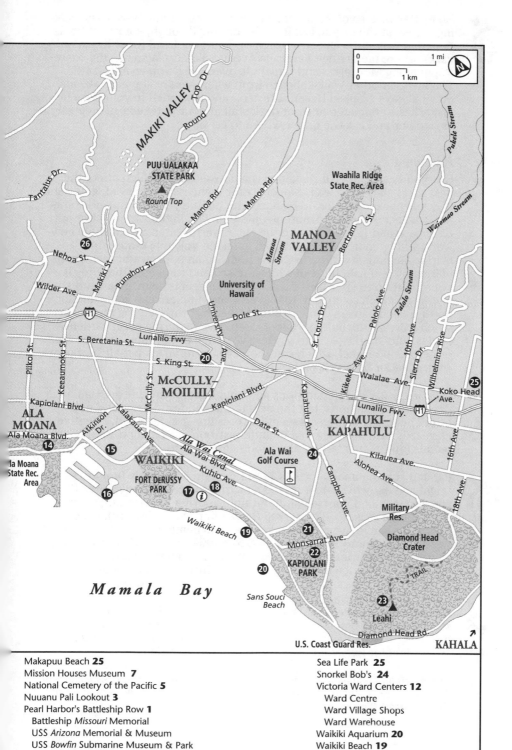

No matter where you're staying in Waikiki, you should have easy walking access to the beach. But if you're driving through, your best bet is to park down at the Queen's Beach or Sans Souci end (near Kapiolani Park), where meters line Kalakaua Avenue. You can also usually snare a spot along Monserrat and Kapahulu avenues. If you want to catch TheBus to another Waikiki beach from where you're staying, take any one that says "Waikiki Beach & Hotels" and is headed in your direction; just ask the concierge or front-desk staff at your hotel where the nearest stop is, and ask the driver where to get off.

Hanauma Bay

Everybody should visit Hanauma (ha-now-ma) Bay, which offers the best snorkeling in Hawaii, especially for novices. The curved, gold-sand beach is packed blanket-to-blanket with people year-round, and sometimes it seems there are more people than fish in the water — but put on a mask and gaze down into the clear, warm water, and a whole new world will open up to you. Cradled in an old volcanic crater, this marine life conservation district is home to an underwater metropolis of friendly reef fish, most of which are so used to people that they'll swim right up to your face mask. The inner reef is calm, clear, and shallow — so much so, in fact, that even nonswimmers can wade and look down. Serious divers come to shoot "the slot" through the reef to Witch's Brew, a turbulent, 70-foot-deep cove featuring coral gardens, turtles, and sharks — but I suggest you stick to the safe, shallow, well-protected inner reef, which can keep even veteran seen-it-all snorkelers enthralled for hours on end.

Excellent snorkeling conditions and abundant marine life are Hanauma Bay's main attractions, but the beach is a wonderful draw all on its own. The lovely golden crescent features fine-grained sand, attentive lifeguards, and facilities that include restrooms, a pavilion, snorkel-gear rentals ($6), picnic tables, and a food concession.

Parking at Hanauma Bay costs $1 per car and is severely limited, so go bright and early to snare a spot (8 a.m. isn't too early); arrive after 10 a.m. and you may find yourself shut out until another car leaves. You can also take TheBus No. 22 (marked Hawaii Kai – Sea Life Park), which runs down Kuhio Avenue and takes about 45 minutes to reach Hanauma Bay. Or call Tommy's Tours (☎ 808-373-5060), which offers round-trip shuttle service from most Waikiki hotels for $20 per person, $10 for kids 3 to 6; the price includes gear and an instructional briefing for first-time snorkelers. Call a day in advance to schedule your pickup.

Even though snorkel gear is available at Hanauma Bay, I much prefer to stop by Snorkel Bob's on the way to Hanauma Bay to pick up higher quality gear, which is well worth the extra two or three dollars; see "Water Fun for Everyone" later in this chapter for details.

In Koko Head Regional Park, off Kalanianaole Highway (the exit is well marked). ☎ *808-396-4229. Admission: $3; free for kids under 12. Open: Wed–Mon 6 a.m. – 7 p.m.; closed Tues.*

Makapuu Beach

The most famous bodysurfing beach in Hawaii is beautiful gold-sand Makapuu (ma-ka-POO-oo) Beach, which is cupped between stark black cliffs on Oahu's easternmost point. This local favorite has starred in countless TV shows, from *Hawaii Five-O* to *Magnum P.I.*, and is well worth a visit just to take in its great natural beauty. In summer, the ocean is fine for swimming and boogie-boarding — but come just to watch in winter. Makapuu's big, pounding winter waves draw expert bodysurfers in droves but are simply too dangerous for regular swimmers. The wave-riders can be thrilling to watch in action, though. If you come to play in the summer waves, boogie boards are fine, but leave any boards with skegs (bottom fins) at home. Facilities include restrooms, beach showers, lifeguard, barbecue grills, and picnic tables.

On Kalanianole Highway across from Sea Life Park. To get there: Drive east on H-1, which becomes Kalanianaole Highway; go past Hawaii Kai, up the hill to Hanauma Bay, past the Halona Blow Hole, and along the coast. The next big, gold, sandy beach you see ahead on the right is Sandy Beach (too rough for regular folks year-round); Makapuu's small free lot is just a few minutes farther around the bend.

Along the windward coast

If you have the time, I highly recommend spending a day at the beach along this stunning, uncrowded, residential coast. Come midweek and you'll find these beaches almost deserted, which offers a nice change of pace from Waikiki. They're even a pleasant relief on weekends, when local families set the tone.

Plan on arriving for your day of east shore beachgoing early, as the windward Koolau mountains block the afternoon sun — and you don't want to end up sitting in the shade on a beautiful day!

Kailua Beach

The windward coast's premier beach park is a two-mile-long gently sloping golden strand with dunes, palm trees, panoramic views, gentle waves, and a gorgeous green-mountain backdrop. With excellent swimming, water that's about 78°F year-round, and good facilities, it's ideal for families — and your kids will love the bodysurfing and boogie-boarding here. Set up your toddlers in the freshwater shallows in the middle of the park, near the mouth of the stream, and they'll be happy as clams all day. Facilities include picnic tables, barbecues, restrooms, a volleyball court, a bike path, an open-air cafe (which may be closed on weekdays), and plenty of free parking; lifeguards are usually on hand. Kayak and windsurf rentals are often available, too, as this is also Oahu's premier windsurfing beach.

At the end of Kailua Road, Kailua. To get there: Take the Pali Highway (Highway 61) to Kailua, where it becomes Kailua Road as it proceeds through town; at Kalaheo Avenue, turn right and follow the coast to the park.

Lanikai Beach

This is one of the most tranquil and beautiful beaches in the entire state and my favorite place to spend a beach day on the entire island. It's almost always excellent for swimming, snorkeling, and kayaking, plus a little easy wave-jumping on occasion. The beach is long and narrow, with gold sand as soft as talcum powder and lightly rippled turquoise water. Two tiny offshore islets provide the perfect panoramic finish. Unfortunately, the tradeoff for all this unspoiled beauty is an utter lack of facilities, so bring your own water, snacks, and beach toys.

Off Mokulua Drive, Kailua. To get there: Follow the directions to Kailua Beach Park, above; just past Kailua Beach Park, turn left at the T intersection and drive uphill on Aalapapa Drive, a one-way street that loops back as Mokulua Drive; park on Mokulua Drive and walk down any of the eight public access lanes to the shore.

Kualoa Regional Park

Farther north on the windward coast is one of Hawaii's most scenic beach parks, a 150-acre coco palm–fringed peninsula on Kaneohe Bay's north shore, at the foot of spiky green mountains. The biggest beach park on the windward side, it has a broad, grassy lawn that's great for picnicking. The long, narrow white-sand beach is ideal for swimming, beachcombing, kite-flying, or just enjoying the natural beauty of this once-sacred Hawaiian shore (it's listed on the National Register of Historic Places), but keep in mind that it can get pretty windy out here. The waters are shallow and safe for swimming year-round. It doesn't offer much in the way of facilities, but lifeguards are on duty.

Offshore is Mokolii (mow-ko-LEE-ee), the picturesque mini-isle more commonly known as Chinaman's Hat (because it looks like one). At low tide, people like to wade out to the island, which has a small sandy beach; it's just a bad idea to walk on the reef, however, so if you're going to go, swim it instead. Chinaman's Hat is a bird preserve, so tread gently to avoid spooking the red-footed boobies.

On Kamehameha Highway (Hwy. 83), Kualoa (about halfway up the coast, north of Waikane). Parking: There's a free lot.

Malaekahana State Recreation Area

Big, brawny Malaekahana (ma-lie-ka-HA-na) Beach is a nearly mile-long white-sand crescent with sheltered waters that are excellent for swimming year-round, and waves that are great for beginning bodysurfers in summer. On any weekday, you may be the only one here; should someone intrude on your privacy, however, you can take an easy swim out to Goat Island, a bird sanctuary (you can wade it, but don't — it's bad for the reef). Stands of trees offer daytime shade, and restrooms, barbecue grills, picnic tables, outdoor showers, and tons of free parking are at hand.

On Kamehameha Highway (Highway 83), 2 miles north of the Polynesian Cultural Center, Laie. The beach is hidden from the road, so look carefully for the main gate; as soon as you enter you'll come upon the wooded beach park. Parking: There's a free lot.

On the north shore

This is surf country, where daredevils gather from around the world to ride monster waves in surf season, basically from late September through April. Don't even think about going into the water in winter, as the rip currents along this shore are killers. The north shore coast is season-ally schizophrenic: The monstrous surf recedes entirely in summer, leaving glassy ponds and idle surfboards.

 The waves may kick up even in the fairest months, so don't go near the water in any season if the lifeguards have put out the red warning flags, or if you just suspect that conditions might be too rough for all but easy swimming.

Sunset Beach Park

This surprisingly small beach is one of those legendary surf spots, the kind that draw fearless wave riders from around the world in winter, when the waves grow to huge, thundering peaks — sometimes as high as 15 to 20 feet. Come to watch the board-riding daredevils, who put on a jaw-dropping show. This is a great place to people-watch: It's a blast to eye the local surfers, the sunbathing beauties, and even your fellow vacationers catching a glimpse of the action. Weekends are best for prime spectating. The summer surf is fun for frolicking, and the beach is virtually empty midweek. No facilities are available, save for a small parking lot; join the other cars on the shoulder if it's full.

On Kamehameha Highway (Highway 83), Pupukea.

Banzai Pipeline/Ehukai Beach Park

The Japanese word *banzai* means "10,000 years"; it's used as a toast or battle cry, meaning "go for it." (As you may remember from high-school history class, the Japanese liked to invoke it during WWII suicide missions.) In the late 1950s, filmmaker Bruce Brown was shooting one of the first surf movies ever made, *Surf Safari,* at Ekuhai Beach Park when he saw a bodysurfer ride a huge wave. Brown yelled "Banzai!", and the name stuck. The Banzai Pipeline section of the beach is about 100 yards to the left of the Ehukai Beach Park sign as you face the ocean — but you won't need to look hard to find it in surf season. When the winter surf rolls in and hits the shallow coral shelf offshore, the waves that form are so steep that the crest of the wave falls forward, forming a near-perfect tube, or "pipeline," just like in the opening credits of *Hawaii Five-O*. Hang-ten fanatics flock here from around the globe all winter long to master this holy grail of surf challenges, but the wild, wild Pipeline is one tough cookie. If you want to watch top-flight, pro-level wave-riding action, a winter weekend visit to the Pipeline is well worth the long drive from Waikiki — heck, the crowd alone is enough to keep you entertained for hours. Needless to say, head elsewhere to swim.

Off Kamehameha Highway on Ke Nui Road (which parallels the highway one mile north of Pupukea), just south of Sunset Beach. Parking: Small lot.

Ke Iki Beach/Pupukea Beach Park

This secret beach is my other Oahu favorite, along with Lanikai (see the "Along the windward coast" section earlier in this chapter). Unlike most north shore beaches, Ke Iki is hidden from the road by private homes, so most visitors don't know about it — but this white-sand beach of sloping dunes is well worth seeking out. It's big, wide, open, and virtually empty year-round. Ke Iki is a wonderful place for swimming and wave jumping in summer; stay out of the water entirely in winter, however, when the big swells come. At the lava-dotted east end of the sand is a collection of warm tidepools where you can lie back and take in the natural glory of it all. Sorry, no facilities.

On Kamehameha Highway (Highway 83), Haleiwa. To get there: From Haleiwa town, take the second left after the Foodland at Pupukea Road, then turn left again; park along the shoulder and walk down the graded public access path (marked with the "No Parking Beyond this Point" sign).

Waimea Beach Park

This legendary beach is yet another world-famous surfing mecca, a gorgeous one-of-a-kind sandy bowl whose placid fair-weather waves are excellent for swimming, snorkeling, and bodysurfing in summer. But what a difference a season makes: Winter waves pound the narrow bay, sometimes rising a phenomenal 50 feet to the sky — wow! Yes, no-fear bravehearts (or certifiable nutcases, depending on your point of view) do come to take on these record-breakers — and it's well worth the drive to see them in action. Waimea turns into a rollicking beach party when the surf is up and the crowds come to watch. Visit on weekdays to avoid the crowds, weekends to join in. Facilities include lifeguards, restrooms, and showers. The small lot fills up when the crowds come, so just pull over to the shoulder with everybody else.

On Kahehameha Highway (Highway 83), just outside the entrance to Waimea Valley Adventure Park, about 3 miles north of Haleiwa. TheBus: no. 52 or 55. A safety tip: Don't get too distracted by the waves and forget to pay attention when parking or crossing the road.

Water Fun for Everyone

If you want to rent boogie boards, surfboards, snorkel gear, kayaks, and other beach toys, you won't have a problem doing so on Oahu. In fact, you won't even need to leave Waikiki Beach, as beach boys have rental huts set up right on the sand; they'll even take you out on outrigger canoe rides that anybody can join in. For details, see "Catching a wave" later in this section. You can also rent beach chairs, life vests, and boogie boards from Snorkel Bob's, which you can read about in the following section.

If you'd like to learn how to kayak while you're on Oahu, the best place to do it is at Waimea Valley Adventure Park, which offers both river and bay paddles. See "Exploring the rest of the island" later in this chapter for details.

Offshore snorkeling

Hanauma Bay (see the section "Hitting the Beaches" earlier in this chapter) is not only Oahu's best snorkel spot, but one of the finest snorkel spots in all of Hawaii. You say you've never snorkeled before? Doesn't matter — even nonswimmers can wade into this calm, shallow, fish-stocked natural swimming pool and enjoy the underwater scenery.

While you can rent gear right at Hanauma Bay — or on Waikiki Beach if you want to do some fish-finding there — I suggest renting instead from **Snorkel Bob's,** on the way to Hanauma Bay at 702 Kapahulu Ave., at Date Street (across from the Ala Wai Golf Course), Honolulu (☎ **808-735-7944;** Internet: www.snorkelbob.com). Snorkel Bob's can rent you much better-quality gear than you'll get elsewhere — and it's well worth spending the few extra bucks for a mask that doesn't leak and a snorkel that doesn't fill with water. The best-quality gear — the "Ultimate Truth" — rents for $9 a day, or $29 a week. Prescription masks are available to those near-sighted snorkelers who'd actually like to see the little fishes without getting their glasses wet. Snorkel Bob's is open every day from 8 a.m. to 5 p.m. There's no need to reserve in advance, but you can book your gear online at www.snorkelbob.com. When you stop by to pick up your gear, the staff can also recommend other local snorkel spots that are currently offering calm conditions and good underwater sightseeing.

One of the best things about renting gear from Bob is that you can rent a set of snorkel gear at the start of your trip, carry it with you as you travel throughout the islands, and then return it to another Snorkel Bob's location on Maui, the Big Island, or Kauai. (All shops offer 24-hour gear return service.) I highly recommend doing this, even if you intend to go on snorkel cruises or kayak trips that provide gear.

Safety is key when snorkeling. Always snorkel with a buddy, and keep an eye on each other at all times. Come up every few minutes to check your bearings in relation to the shoreline and make sure there's no boat traffic coming your way. Don't touch anything underwater: undersea coral is delicate and easily damaged and can also leave you with nasty cuts. And always, always check surf conditions before you set out (a local surf-and-snorkel shop can usually help you here). You should also inquire about the specific currents and tides of the area you plan to snorkel — as well as any potentially dangerous spots to avoid.

Enjoying on-deck adventures — ocean cruising

All of Oahu's cruise-boat operators combine whale-watching with their regular activities in season (humpback whales migrate to Hawaii's warm waters each winter, roughly December through March or early April). If you're on Oahu during these months, be sure to set out on a cruise — because there's nothing like seeing these mammoth creatures up close and personal.

Snorkeling without getting your hair wet

You can dip into Hawaii's spectacular underwater world even if you don't swim by taking a submarine ride with **Atlantis Submarines** (☎ **800-548-6262** or 808-548-6262; Internet: www.goatlantis.com/hawaii). Atlantis's state-of-the-art subs deliver you a mile offshore and deep beneath the surface to see not only clouds of tropical fish and sea critters, but also sunken ships, the remains of two airliners, and ongoing work on the University of Hawaii's reef enhancement project. Shuttle boats to the sub leave from Hilton Hawaiian Village Pier, on the beach at 2005 Kalia Rd. (at Ala Moana Boulevard). The two-hour tours cost $89 to $99 for adults, $39 for kids (children must be at least 36 inches tall); select midday trips are discounted to $59 for adults. A word of warning: The ride is perfectly safe, but skip it if you suffer from serious claustrophobia.

Dolphin Excursions

Cruise the west shore of Oahu in a Zodiac, a 23-foot motorized inflatable rubber raft, with a maximum of 13 other passengers in search of friendly pods of spinner dolphins, probably the cutest creatures of the Pacific seas. These low-slung, intimate boats are great for getting close to the water and the dolphins — and I can say from experience that there's nothing like seeing humpback whales from such an intimate vantage point in whale-watching season (between late December and early April). The cruises sometimes encounter larger bottlenosed and spotted dolphins as well as year-round pilot whales. It's an excellent experience for adventurous spirits; the bravest among you can pay an extra 20 bucks for a "tow," in which you don a mask and snorkel and are towed behind the boat so that you can glide with the dolphins in their underwater habitat. Apparently, David Hasselhoff is a fan, if that carries any weight with you.

Boats depart from Waianae Small Boat Harbor, Farrington Hwy. (Hwy. 93), Leeward Oahu. ☎ *808-239-5579. Internet:* www.dolphinexcursions.com. *Half-day adventure: $60 adults, $35 first child, $45 each additional child. Prices include free shuttle from Waikiki and picnic lunch.*

Dream Cruises

If you'd like to take a dolphin-watching cruise but Dolphin Excursions' Zodiac (see the preceding listing) sits a little too close to the action for you, catch a ride aboard Dream Cruises' far more substantial catamaran, the *Rainbow I,* which cruises the west shore's Yokohama Bay in order to catch spinner dolphins in playful action. Dream Cruises also offers whale-watching in season; a kid-friendly snorkel-sail off Waikiki, a day of water play that includes an off-the-boat water slide for creative entrances; and dinner-and-dancing cruises aboard the *American Dream* yacht with sunset cocktails and great views of the Waikiki skyline — all good, touristy fun.

Cruises depart from Kewalo Basin, off Ala Moana Blvd. just west of Ala Moana Beach Park. ☎ *800-400-7300 or 808-592-5200. Internet:* www.dream-cruises. com. *Prices: $22–$63 adults, $15–$38 kids 17 and under. Rates include Waikiki hotel transfers and grilled breakfast, lunch, brunch, or dinner, depending on the cruise.*

Honolulu Sailing Co.

This very reliable company offers half- and full-day sailing and snorkeling cruises off the Waikiki shoreline aboard their 54-foot sailing yacht *Escapade*. You can also set up an exclusive sail trip or multi-day charter aboard this or one of the other members of the top-quality, A-1 sailing 38- to 67-foot fleet. You can even learn to sail or arrange a nautical wedding.

Cruises depart from Pier 2, Honolulu Harbor, off Ala Moana Blvd. ☎ *800-829-0114 or 808-239-3900. Internet:* www.honsail.com. *Half- and full-day snorkel-sails: $60–$95 adults, half-price for kids. Beginning sailing lessons $350 for one, $390 for two.*

Royal Hawaiian Cruises

For the smoothest ride in the Pacific, hop aboard the *Navatek I*, a high-tech 140-foot SWATH (Small Waterplane Area Twin Hull) vessel that promises even the most perpetually queasy passengers a seasick-free ride. The *Navatek* offers a number of different cruises, from scenic lunch cruises and in-season morning whale watches (with breakfast) to the finest dinner cruises on the Waikiki coast, featuring a romantic candlelit setting, a multi-course sit-down dinner, and top local entertainers.

Cruises depart from Pier 6, Honolulu Harbor, Aloha Tower Dr. (just off Ala Moana Blvd./Nimitz Hwy. intersection, next to the Aloha Tower Marketplace), Honolulu. ☎ *808-848-6360. Internet:* www.royalhawaiiancruises.com. *Cruise prices: $45–$120 adults, $26.50–$72 kids 2–11. Prices include breakfast, lunch, or dinner, depending on cruise. Ask about dinner cruises with add-ons like shuttle service to and from Waikiki, and "Prestige Club" packages featuring preferred seating, champagne and cocktails, and chauffered limo pick-up.*

Catching a wave

Book your surfing lesson, or your windsurfing lesson (see the following section), for early in your stay. That way, if conditions aren't right on your scheduled day, you'll have plenty of time to reschedule.

Learning to surf

If you've always dreamed of learning to surf, Waikiki is the perfect place to do it. The Waikiki beach boys swear that they can teach anybody to stand up on a surfboard and catch a wave, as long as they have the basic swimming skills. If you want to learn, go early to the section of Waikiki Beach called Kuhio Beach, next to the Sheraton Moana Surfrider (see "Hitting the Beaches" earlier in this chapter). Both **Aloha Beach Service** and **Hawaii Beach Boys Services** offer surfing lessons for about $35 an hour, plus surfboard rentals to experienced wave riders for $8 for an hour, $12 two hours, $25 for all day (for use on Waikiki Beach only). The small waves are also great for bodysurfing and boogie-boarding, and both surf shacks will be happy to rent you the appropriate gear. Regular catamaran and outrigger canoe rides are offered from this stretch of sand as well, usually for about ten bucks a head; the beach boys will call out for participants when they're ready to go out. (FYI: If you're expecting Waikiki's beach boys to be strapping young lads on break between semesters, think again. Most of these perma-tanned fellows haven't been "boys" since the Nixon administration.)

If you're more serious-minded about learning to surf, book a lesson at least a day in advance with the **Hans Hedemann Surf School** (☎ 808-924-7778; Internet: www.hhsurf.com), whose pro instructors teach private and group lessons in surfing and bodyboarding off the Diamond Head end of Waikiki. Prices start at $50 for an hour-long lesson.

For experienced surfers only

If you're already a skilled surfer, stop at any surf shop to check the latest wave conditions. A good surfing spot for advanced surfers is the Cliffs, at the base of Diamond Head. The 4- to 6-feet waves churn here, allowing for high-performance surfing — and the views of Diamond Head are great. Call or stop at the **Hans Hedemann Surf School** in the Diamond Head Beach Hotel, 2947 Kalakaua Ave. (☎ 808-924-7778; Internet: www.hhsurf.com), to rent a board and check conditions. Surfboards are available for rent at **Local Motion,** 1958 Kalakaua Ave., near McCully Street at the west end of Waikiki (☎ 808-979-7873; Internet: www.localmotionhawaii.com), as well as on the beach at Waikiki (see Aloha Beach Service and Hawaii Beach Boys Services in the preceding section).

Of course, if it's winter and you really know what you're doing — or you simply want to watch those who do — visit one of the north shore beaches (see "Hitting the Beaches" earlier in this chapter). Head to **Surf 'n' Sea,** 62-595 Kamehameha Hwy., Haleiwa (☎ 808-637-9887). Do not — I repeat, do not — get in the water on the north shore in winter unless you are appropriately skilled to handle the big waves.

You call also check conditions on the **Surf News Network Surfline** (☎ 808-596-SURF [808-596-7873]).

Windsurfing

Kailua Beach, on the Windward Coast, is the best place to learn to windsurf — and the folks to learn from are **Naish Hawaii** (☎ 800-767-6068 or 808-262-6068; Internet: www.naish.com), the domain of champion and pioneer windsurfer Robbie Naish. Beginning, intermediate, and advanced lessons are available, with prices starting at $55 for one, $75 for two for private 1½-hour lessons (includes use of equipment for 1½ hours following the lesson), $35 per person for a three hour group clinic (includes use of equipment for a half-hour following the lesson). There's no minimum age requirement, but you must weigh at least 75 pounds. (Naish has taught kids as young as eight or nine.) You can expect to be up and sailing (in one direction, anyway) in three to four hours; it takes 12 to 20 hours to become actually good at it. Equipment rentals are available for experienced windsurfers.

Scuba diving

Oahu is a wonderful place for wreck diving. One of the more famous wrecks in Hawaii is the *Mahi,* a 185-foot former minesweeper with an abundant marine population. Schools of lemon butterfly fish, eagle rays, green sea turtles, manta rays, and white-tipped sharks cruise by, and eels slither from the wreck.

For nonwreck diving, Kahuna Canyon, a massive underwater amphitheater, is among the island's best offshore summer dive spots. But your best bet may be to discuss with your outfitter the best places to go. Whether you're a first-timer in search of a resort course or a veteran diver just looking for a ride, the outfitter to contact is **Aaron's Dive Shop,** 602 Kailua Rd., Kailua (☎ **888-84-SCUBA** or 808-262-2333; Internet: www.hawaii-scuba.com), Hawaii's oldest and largest dive shop, in business for more than three decades. Aaron's offers boat and beach dive excursions at all of Oahu's top dive spots, plus night dives, cave dives, photography dives, and more. Prices for two-tank dives start at $100, with equipment. They can also offer uncertified introductory dives, or certify you in three days if you're ready to commit.

What to See and Do on Dry Land

You may be able to save money on a few of your big-ticket Oahu activities by booking them through Maui-based **Tom Barefoot's Cashback Tours** (☎ **888-222-3601**; Internet: www.tombarefoot.com), which also books activities on Oahu. Tom Barefoot is a very reliable activities center that's willing to split its commissions with you so that everybody comes out ahead. You'll save 7 percent with select activities and outfitters (those marked with a blue dolphin on the Web site, which include some of those I recommend later in this section) if you pay with a credit card, 10 percent if you send a check — which could add up to substantial savings, especially if you're bringing the entire family along. At press time, you could save on admission fees at Sea Life Park, Hawaiian Waters Adventure Park, Waimea Valley Adventure Park, and Hawaiian Ocean Thrills (all listed later in this section), but you should check the Web site for current offerings.

Taking a guided tour

If your mobility is limited, or if you have limited time and want an introductory look at the big picture, you might want to hook up with a guided tour. If you've rented a car and can get around easily, though, I consider going out on your own the preferable option, since most tour operators do little more than whiz by the major sights in tour buses — including some places you might actually want to spend some time — or charge you an arm and a leg to take you places like the *Arizona* Memorial, which is absolutely free to tour if you show up on your own.

If you intend to visit the National Cemetery of the Pacific at Punchbowl Crater (see "Visiting Honolulu's top attractions" later in this chapter), don't go with a tour if you want to look around and pay your respects. Tour buses are not allowed to disembark passengers in the Punchbowl; they can merely drive through.

Polynesian Adventure Tours (☎ **800-622-3011** or 808-833-3000; Internet: www.polyad.com) offers a range of guided tours in mini-vans, big-windowed mini-coaches (good for small groups and big views), and full-size buses. First launched to take visitors along Maui's Heavenly Road to Hana, Polynesian Adventure's tours tend to be a little more action-oriented than those offered by competing companies. They also tend to offer multiple variations on each theme. Offerings range from city sightseeing and outlet-shopping tours to circle island tours that include a beach picnic (recommendable if you don't have a car and your other alternative is to skip visiting the rest of this multifaceted island altogether) to full-day excursions to the Polynesian Cultural Center (see "Exploring the rest of the island" later in this chapter). Check the Web site to peruse the full range of options.

Book your Polynesian Adventure Tour online to get a 10 percent price break.

Roberts Hawaii (☎ **800-831-5541** or 808-539-9495; Internet: www.roberts-hawaii.com) is Hawaii's biggest name in narrated bus tours. Roberts offers a similar slate of tours as Polynesian Adventure, plus add-ons such as sightseeing cruises, luaus, and dinner shows.

If you're 55 or older, Roberts Hawaii will give you a 10 percent discount on all tours.

Roberts also offers day excursions to the neighbor islands, but the itineraries are so intense that sites tend to whiz by in a blur. If you can't sleep there, don't bother.

E Noa Tours (☎ **800-824-8804** or 808-591-2561; Internet: www.enoa.com), operators of the Waikiki Trolley (see "Letting Somebody Else Do the Driving" in Chapter 8), also offers a range of guided minibus tours around the city and around the island. E Noa's tours tend to be smaller than those offered by their competitors, and are usually cheaper since the tours are intimate enough that the driver also serves as your tour guide.

Guided city walks

The **Mission Houses Museum,** 553 S. King St., at Kawaiahao Street in downtown Honolulu (☎ **808-531-0481;** Internet: www.lava.net/~mhm/main.htm), offers a terrific three-hour walking tour of Honolulu's historic downtown on Thursday and Saturday mornings at 9:30 a.m. A guide takes you first through the Mission Houses site (where American missionaries set up house to convert the natives in the 1820s) and then through the surrounding capitol and historic district, taking in such sights as Iolani Place, the statue of King Kamehameha the Great (the Big Island boy who grew up to unite the independent Hawaiian isles into a single kingdom), and the Royal Tomb of King William Lunalilo. Tickets are $15 for adults, $13 for seniors, $11 for college students and teens 13 to 18, $10 for kids 4 to 12. Reservations are required; the tour is well worth booking if you're a history buff.

You're welcome to stop in to tour the museum, which tells the story of the arrival of Protestant missionaries in the 19th century and the subsequent cultural sea change in the islands, on your own. Three restored mission buildings are open for exploring Tuesday through Saturday between 9 a.m. and 4 p.m. Admission is $8 for adults, $6 for seniors, $4 for college students and teens 13 to 18, $3 for kids 4 to 12.

Guided eco-walks

Mauka Makai Excursions (☎ 877-ECO-OAHU or 808-593-3525; Internet: www.oahu-ecotours.com) offers half- and full-day tours revealing a hidden side of Oahu that even most island residents haven't seen. The emphasis is on archaeology and ancient history, but Mauka Makai's tours are also a great choice for nature walkers. On the half-day "Legends and Myths" tour, guide Dominic Aki can show you hidden petroglyphs, the ruins of a royal palace tucked away in a bamboo forest, an ancient temple presiding over modern suburbia, and other cultural treasures, complete with fascinating narrative. Full-day tours go farther afield and also include shore fishing, snorkeling, or other beach activities. Full-day trips are $62.50 for adults, $52 for kids 6 to 17; half-day trips are $36 adults, $26 for kids, including hotel pickup.

Visiting Honolulu's top attractions

Bishop Museum

If you come inside to visit just one museum while you're in Hawaii, make it this one. The state museum of cultural history houses the world's greatest collection of natural and cultural artifacts from Hawaii and the Pacific. If your time is limited, head straight to the Hawaiian Hall, which provides a wonderful introduction to island life and culture. You'll see the great feathered capes of kings, the last grass shack in Hawaii, preindustrial Polynesian art, and even the skeleton of a 50-foot sperm whale. Hawaiian Hall gallery tours are offered daily at 10 a.m. and noon; catch one for the most informed overview of the gallery. A terrific traditional hula show is also offered every day at 11 a.m. and 2 p.m., garden tours are offered daily at 12:30 p.m., and various Hawaiian crafts like lei-making, feather-working, and quilting are demonstrated daily from 9 a.m. to 2 p.m. Call for the current schedule of planetarium shows.

1525 Bernice St., just off the Lunililo Freeway (H-1) at Kalihi Street (also known as Likelike Hwy.), Honolulu. ☎ 808-847-3511; 808-848-4136 for planetarium info. Internet: www.bishop.hawaii.org. Admission: $14.95 adults, $11.95 kids 4–12 and seniors. Open: Daily 9 a.m.–5 p.m.

The Contemporary Museum

Housed in a beautiful 1925 estate in one of Honolulu's most exclusive residential communities, TCM is worth visiting as much for the hilltop house and its panoramic views as for its impressive collection of postwar art. The emphasis is on works by Hawaiian artists, but not exclusively so; modern artists ranging from Jasper Johns to Jim Dine to William Wegman are also well represented, and a highlight of the collection is David Hockney's environmental installation inspired by Ravel's *L'Enfant et Les Sortilèges*. The grounds are gorgeous and feature an impressive sculpture garden. The cafe is one of Honolulu's best-kept secrets, so plan on lunch as part of your visit.

2411 Makiki Heights Dr., Honolulu. ☎ 808-526-0232. Internet: www.tcmhi.org. *To get there: Take Kalakaua Avenue to Beretania Street and make a left; go one block to Makaki Street, turn right, and follow it up the hill; turn left on Makiki Heights Drive and proceed to the museum. Admission: Adults $5, seniors and students $3, free for kids 12 and under. The third Thurs of each month is free for everyone. Open: Tues–Sat 10 a.m.–4 p.m., Sun noon–4 p.m.*

Diamond Head Crater

Called Mt. Leahi (lee-AH-hi) by the Hawaiians, Waikiki's most famous landmark is a mountain that just about anyone with a little stamina can climb. The easy but steep 1.4-mile, 1½-hour round-trip climb is a lot of fun — and the 360° views from the top are spectacular.

To prepare for your hike to the top, wear a reasonable pair of walking shoes (sneakers or Tevas are fine), and get your hands on a flashlight (you'll walk through several dark tunnels), a bottle of water, and a camera. If you don't have a flashlight or your hotel can't lend you one (most can, precisely for this purpose), you can buy one at just about any ABC store (you can hardly walk a block in Waikiki without tripping over an ABC store). If you have binoculars, bring them along.

Go early, before the afternoon sun starts beating down. The trailhead begins in the parking lot on the crater's inland side and proceeds along a paved walkway (with handrails) that turns rocky as it ascends the slope. You'll pass old World War I and II pillboxes, gun emplacements, and tunnels built as part of the Pacific defense network. Yes, you'll be climbing lots of steps, but it's well worth the effort — once you reach the observation post up top, the views are indescribable.

Access road at Monsarrat (also called Diamond Head Avenue) and 18th avenues. To get there: Follow Kalakaua Avenue to Kapiolani Park; turn north on Monsarrat Avenue and follow it around to the back of Diamond Head. Just past Kapiolani Community College, turn right and go ⁶⁄₁₀-mile to the parking lot. Admission: Free! Open: Daily 6 a.m.–6 p.m.

Foster Botanical Garden

This intimate, leafy oasis amid the high-rises of downtown Honolulu is a living museum of plants — some rare and endangered — collected from the tropical regions of the world. Of special interest are 26 "Exceptional

Trees" protected by state law, a large palm collection, a primitive cycad garden, and a hybrid orchid collection. It's easy to tour the garden in a half-hour or so. The garden suggests that you bring insect repellent, as this is a buggy place. Guided tours are offered weekdays at 1 p.m.; call ☎ **808-522-7066** for reservations.

50 N. Vineyard Blvd. (at Nuuanu Ave., across the street from Zippy's), downtown Honolulu. ☎ *808-522-7065. Internet:* www.co.honolulu.hi.us/parks/hbg/ fbg.htm. *Admission: $5 adults, $3 teens 13–18, $1 kids 6–12. Open: Daily 9 a.m.– 5 p.m.*

Hawaii Maritime Center

If you're interested in Hawaii's rich maritime heritage, or you're just nostalgic for the long-gone cruise-ship days, stop at this harborfront museum for an hour-long visit. The museum tells the islands' complete maritime story, from the ancient journey of Polynesian voyagers to Hawaii's whaling era to the high-style Matson Line days of the 1940s and '50s. Outside, the famous *Hokulea,* a reconstruction of the double-hulled sailing canoe that the ancients used to reach Hawaii, is moored next to the *Falls of Clyde,* a four-masted, full-rigged 1878 schooner.

Pier 7, Honolulu Harbor, Aloha Tower Dr. (off Nimitz Hwy., next to Aloha Tower Marketplace), Honolulu. ☎ *808-536-6373. Internet:* www.holoholo.org/ maritime. *Admission: $7.50 adults, $4.50 kids 6 to 17. Open: Daily 10:30 a.m. – 5 p.m.*

Hawaiian Ocean Thrills

Satisfy your inner speed demon at this water adventure park, where you have a chance to take the wheel of a Formula One race boat, zipping around a quarter-mile ocean track. You can also play on bumper boats, cruise aboard a catamaran, ride high-powered jet skis or manpowered pedal-boats, swim in an ocean pool complete with waterslides, and more. You pay one price (with or without the Formula One racing), which allows you to enjoy all of the available activities on and off HOT's manmade "floating island" for the duration of your morning or afternoon stay (see "Times" later in this listing). Lounging areas, a snack bar, and shower and changing areas are at your disposal.

Adventures depart from either Kewalo Basin or Sand Island; confirm when booking. ☎ *800-831-5541 or 808-539-9400. Internet:* www.roberts-hawaii. com/hot.htm. *Adventure and Grand Prix packages: $59–$89 adults, $39–$49 kids 6–14. Prices include bus transfers from Waikiki and boat to the HOT island. Times: Daily 9 a.m.–1 p.m., 1– 5 p.m.*

Honolulu Academy of Arts

This museum is home to one of the finest collections of Asian art in the country, a top-notch collection of American and European masters, and terrific ancient and Pacific art. See what's on when you're in town, as the temporary exhibits can range from treasures from ancient Egypt to the world's greatest collection of aloha shirts. Guided one-hour tours are offered Tuesday through Saturday at 11 a.m. and Sunday at 1:15 p.m.

*900 S. Beretania St. (between Victoria St. and Ward Ave.), downtown Honolulu.
☎ 808-532-8701 or 808-532-8700. Internet:* www.honoluluacademy.org. *Admission: $7 adults; $4 seniors and students; free for kids 12 and under. Open: Tues–Sat 10 a.m.–4:30 p.m., Sun 1–5 p.m.*

Honolulu Zoo

Located in the heart of Waikiki's lovely Kapiolani Park, this 43-acre zoo is a real charmer. Globe-trotting highlights include the Karibuni Reserve, an African savanna habitat with exotic African mammals roaming around in the open, separated from visitors by hidden rails and moats; a wonderful South American aviary filled with colorful toucans and other eye-catching birds; and the Tropical Forest exhibit, a draw for horticultural buffs as well as animal lovers. The Children's Zoo features friendly critters who love to be petted, including a llama, a monitor lizard, and a pot-bellied pig.

In Kapiolani Park, 151 Kapahulu Ave. (at Kalakaua Ave.), Waikiki. ☎ 808-971-7171. Internet: www.honoluluzoo.org. *Admission: $6 adults, $1 kids 6–12, free for kids 5 and under; Family Pass $25. Open: Daily 9 a.m.–4:30 p.m.*

For a real treat, take the Zoo by Moonlight two-hour family walking tour, which offers you a behind-the-scenes look at zoo life after the gates close and the sun goes down. The cost is $9 per person, and tours are usually offered in the evenings surrounding the full moon; call for the exact schedule.

Iolani Palace

I highly recommend visiting this royal palace, the official residence of the last monarchs of Hawaii: King David Kalakaua (ka-la-COW-ah) and his sister, Queen Liliuokalani (li-lee-uh-ka-LA-nee). The Italian Renaissance structure can only be seen on a docent-led 45-minute tour, which tells the fascinating story of the coming of Western ways to the islands, the rebirth of Hawaiian culture in the last years of royal rule, and the story of the monarchy's final defeat in a bloodless coup.

King Kalakaua (often called the "Merrie Monarch") built the place, and it served as the royal home from 1882 until the Hawaiian monarchy was forcibly ended in 1893, when Queen Liliuokalani was dethroned by U.S. Marines at the demand of white sugar planters and missionary descendants. (Liliuokalani wrote the famous Hawaiian ballad "Aloha Oe" while under house arrest here.) Some areas are unfurnished, but others are complete enough to give you an idea what life in and around the palace was like; the well-schooled tour guides are excellent at filling in the blanks.

Tours sell out regularly, so you must call ahead and reserve your tour spots. Call at least a day ahead, a few days in advance if you don't want to be disappointed. (It took me three tries before I was able to make my first visit.) Leave the little ones behind, however, as they'll be less than enthralled.

Starting in September 2000, visitors will be able to take a self-guided tour through the lower galleries, which house jewelry belonging to the king and queen, royal gowns, the re-created chamberlain's office, and other period goodies that have previously not been on display. It's a wonderful collection that you should make time to see, as it really rounds out the Iolani experience.

At S. King and Richards sts., downtown. ☎ ***808-522-0832.*** *Internet:* alaike. lcc.hawaii.edu/openstudio/iolani. *Admission: $15 adults, $5 kids 5–12; kids under 5 not admitted. Guided tours: You must be booked on a 45-minute guided tour to enter the palace. Every 15 minutes Tues–Sat 9 a.m.–2:15 p.m. Tickets should be picked up 30 minutes prior to your tour (you can watch a video on the Hawaiian monarchy and the palace or tour the new galleries while you wait).*

If you're a history buff who'd like to see more of downtown Honolulu's historic attractions, hold on to your Iolani Palace brochure, which will point you to other sites in the immediate surrounding area, including **Kawaiahao Church,** at the intersection of Punchbowl and King streets, the proud stone Protestant church erected under missionary guidance in 1842. You might also entertain a visit to the **Mission Houses Museum,** 553 S. King St., at Kawaiahao Street (☎ **808-531-0481;** Internet: www. lava.net/~mhm/main.htm), whose visitor center and preserved 19th-century missionary campus (established by American missionaries in order to convert the natives in the 1820s) are open for self-guided touring from Tuesday through Saturday between 9 a.m. and 4 p.m. Admission is $8 for adults, $6 for seniors, $4 for college students and teens 13 to 18, $3 for kids 4 to 12.

Kodak Hula Show

When the Eastman Kodak Company withdrew its 60-year sponsorship of this legendary 1¼-hour hula show, everyone mourned — then rejoiced when a package-tour operator came to its rescue soon thereafter. The Kodak Hula Show isn't exactly a bastion of high culture — it's more '50s nostalgic than anything else — but people just love it. It's a good bit of fun, and you will learn how to interpret some basic hula moves in the process. The bleachers seat 2,000, and you'll have a good view no matter where you sit, but arrive by 9:15 a.m. for the best photo ops.

At the Waikiki Band Shell in Kapiolani Park, 2805 Monserrat Ave. (between Kalakaua and Paki aves.), Waikiki. ☎ ***808-627-3379*** *or 808-945-1818. Admission: Free! Showtimes: Tues, Wed, and Thurs at 10 a.m.*

Nuuanu Pali Lookout

Sometimes gale-force winds howl through this misty mountain pass, so hold on to your hat. But if you walk up from the parking lot to the precipice, you'll be rewarded with a stunning view of the luxuriant windward coast. Bring a jacket or sweater with you, as it's windy and cool up here year-round, even when it's 85°F and sunny at the beach.

Near the summit of Pali Hwy. (Hwy. 61); take the Nuuanu Pali Lookout turnoff.

Punchbowl Crater/The National Cemetery of the Pacific

This collapsed volcanic cone in the middle of Honolulu offers some of
the most spectacular views in the city. But most people don't come for
the views (although you shouldn't miss them; the observation platform
is on the ocean side of the crater) — they come to honor the 35,000 vic-
tims of three American wars whose theaters were Asia and the Pacific:
World War II and the Korean and Vietnam wars. Among the graves are
many unmarked ones bearing only the date December 7, 1941 — the day
Pearl Harbor was bombed and the United States entered the Last Great
War. Some of the honorees are destined to be unknown forever; others
are world-famous, like war correspondent Ernie Pyle. The Courts of the
Missing's white stone tablets bear the names of 28,788 Americans missing in action in WWII.

*2177 Puowaina Dr. (at the end of the road), Honolulu. ☎ 808-532-3720. To get there:
Take Ward Ave. to Prospect St. to Puowaina Dr. Admission: Free. Open: Daily 8
a.m.–6:30 p.m., to 5:30 p.m. Oct–Feb.*

Waikiki Aquarium

The small but first-class Waikiki Aquarium is a must for anybody who
wants to know what they're actually seeing when they're snorkeling. It
features tanks full of an amazing variety of marine life found in the offshore waters; a fascinating jellyfish tank; a Hawaiian reef habitat with
sharks and eels; a kid-friendly touch tank with urchins and sea cucum-
bers; and habitats for the endangered Hawaiian monk seal and green sea
turtle. You can watch the monk seals being trained and fed Wednesday
at 1:30 p.m., Thursday at 10 a.m., and Friday through Tuesday at 2:30
p.m. — but always call ahead to check; I myself have been disappointed
by a last-minute schedule change.

*2777 Kalakaua Ave. (across from Kapiolani Park on the ocean side of the road),
Waikiki. ☎ 808-923-9741. Internet: www.waikikiaquarium.com. Admission: $7
adults; $5 seniors, students with ID, and active-duty military; and $3.50 kids 13–17;
free for kids under 12. Open: Daily 9 a.m.–5 p.m.*

In Pearl Harbor

If you'd like to see all of Pearl Harbor's sights, arrive early and plan on
spending the better part of a day here.

To reach Pearl Harbor, drive west on the H-1 freeway or Nimitz Highway
(reachable via Ala Moana Boulevard) past the Honolulu International
Airport; take the USS *Arizona* Memorial exit (no. 15-A). Follow the
green-and-white highway signs to the free parking lots.

Shuttle service is available from Waikiki daily between 6:50 a.m. and
4:30 p.m. for $5 per person round-trip; to schedule pickup at your
hotel, call ☎ 808-839-0911 24 hours in advance. If you'd rather take
TheBus, pick up no. 20 or 47 (see Chapter 8 for complete information
on TheBus system). Either way, expect the ride to take about an hour
from Waikiki (it's about a half-hour if you drive yourself).

Battleship Missouri Memorial

The newest addition to Pearl Harbor's Battleship Row memorial fleet is this 58,000-ton, 887-foot battleship — the last one the U.S. Navy built — which served in three wars, but is most famous for being the site of Japanese surrender to Douglas MacArthur and the Allied forces in 1945. Decommissioned in 1955, the Missouri went back into action to the Gulf War before its final retirement to Hawaii in 1998.

Once you check in at the visitor center at the USS *Bowfin* (see the listing later in this section), you'll be shuttled by trolley to Ford Island for ship boarding. You're free to explore the mammoth battleship from bow to stern after you watch a short informational film, which is a blast: You can see the biggest guns the Navy ever built, climb up the flying bridge, visit the officer's quarters, and experience how sailors lived at sea. I highly recommend hooking up with one of the hour-long guided tours (no reservations necessary), which offer the best insights. Allow about three hours in total for your visit if you plan on working in a tour.

On Battleship Row, Pearl Harbor; check in at the Visitor's Center of the USS Bowfin. ☎ *877-MIGHTY-MO, 888-USS-MISSOURI, or 808-423-2263. Internet:* www.ussmissouri.com. *Admission: $14 adults, $10 kids 4–12. Hour-long guided tours $6 extra per person. Open: Daily 9 a.m.–3:55 p.m.*

Serious WWII buffs, or anybody in need of transportation, might want to consider the VIP tour of the *Missouri*, which includes transportation to and from Waikiki, automatic check-in that allows you to fly right by ticket lines, and a guided tour that also includes exclusive access to areas not open to regular guests. VIP tours are $29 for adults, $19 for kids 4 to 12.

USS Arizona Memorial and Museum

On December 7, 1941, while moored in Pearl Harbor, this 608-foot battleship was bombed in a Japanese air raid. The USS *Arizona* sank in nine minutes without firing a shot, taking 1,177 sailors and Marines to a fiery death — and plunging the United States into World War II.

Today, launches take you out to the stark white 184-foot memorial that spans the sunken hull of the *Arizona,* which lies 6 feet below the surface of the sea. The memorial contains the ship's bell, recovered from the wreckage, and a shrine room with the names of the dead carved in stone.

Try to arrive early at the visitor center (which is operated jointly by the National Park Service and the U.S. Navy) to avoid the huge crowds, as advance reservations are not taken and waits of an hour or two are common. While you're waiting for the shuttle to take you out to the ship — you'll be issued a number and time of departure, which you must pick up yourself — you can explore the small but arresting museum, which features personal mementoes, photos, and historic documents. A 20-minute film precedes your trip to the ship. Allow about three hours for your visit, and be sure to remain respectfully silent when you're on the actual memorial.

On Battleship Row, Pearl Harbor. ☎ **808-422-0561.** *Internet:* www.nps.gov/usar. *Admission: Free! Shirts and shoes required. Open: Daily 7:30 a.m.–5 p.m. (boat shuttles run 8 a.m.– 3 p.m.).*

USS Bowfin Submarine Museum and Park

The USS *Bowfin* is one of only 15 World War II submarines still in existence today. You can go below deck of this famous submarine — nicknamed the "Pearl Harbor Avenger" for its successful retaliatory attacks on the Japanese — and see how the 80-man crew lived during wartime. The museum holds an impressive collection of submarine-related artifacts, the Waterfront Memorial honors submariners lost during World War II, and the mini-theater shows a constant run of sub-related videos.

11 Arizona Memorial Drive (next to the USS Arizona Memorial Visitor Center), Pearl Harbor. ☎ **808-423-1341.** *Internet:* www.aloha.net/~bowfin. *Admission: $8 adults, $6 seniors, $3 kids 4–12 (kids under 4 are not allowed on the submarine, but can visit the museum and mini-theater). Open: Daily 8 a.m.–5 p.m. (last tour at 4:30 p.m.).*

You can save money on USS *Missouri* and USS *Bowfin* admission by purchasing a combination ticket when you arrive at their shared visitor center at the *Bowfin.* Combo tickets are $18 for adults (seniors included), $9 for kids 4 to 12.

In nearby East Oahu

Sea Life Park

This marine-themed park is Hawaii's very own version of Sea World, and it's lots of fun. Highlights include a sea lion feeding pool; the quarter-million-gallon Hawaiian Reef Tank, brimming with tropical fish plus a few sharks and stingrays; performing seals, dolphins, and penguins strutting their smarts and skill in choreographed shows, which run every 45 minutes (it takes about two hours to see all four); and a pirate-themed play area for the little ones. The chief curiosity, though, is the world's only "wholphin," a genuine genetic cross between a false killer whale and an Atlantic bottle-nosed dolphin. On-site marine biologists operate a recovery center for endangered marine life that allows you to visit with rehabilitated Hawaiian monk seals and seabirds.

41-202 Kalanianaole Hwy. (Hwy. 72), Waimanalo. ☎ **808-259-7933.** *Internet:* www.atlantisadventures.com. *To get there: Take H-1 east to Highway 72; once the road has narrowed to two lanes, it's just past Sandy Beach on the left. Parking: $3. Admission: $24 adults, $12 kids 4–12. Open: Daily 9:30 a.m.–5 p.m.*

Shuttle service to Sea Life Park is available from select Waikiki hotels for $5 per person; call the above number to arrange pickup.

Sea Life Park offers a couple of add-on programs that allow you to get up-close and personal with the park's residents. Seawalker gives you the opportunity to actually dive into the Hawaiian Reef Tank with a guide for 15 minutes, no previous diving experience necessary; the cost is $89 per person, and you must be 12 or older to participate. Splash University allows you to interact with dolphins in a shallow-water environment (read: no swimming); you'll learn communication and training techniques, and even be allowed to feed your new friends. The cost for Splash U. is $79 for adults, $67 for kids 40 inches tall through age 12. Call ☎ 808-259-2500 to enroll in either or both of these special programs.

Exploring the rest of the island

West Oahu

Hawaii's Plantation Village

This impeccably restored 50-acre outdoor museum offers a genuine look back in time to Hawaii's plantation days, when sugar planters from America — and the field workers they attracted from countries around the world, including Japan, China, Portugal, the Philippines, Puerto Rico, and Korea — shaped the land, economy, and culture of territorial Hawaii. You can only explore the village on an hour-long guided tour, which takes you through more than two dozen faithfully restored camp houses, a Buddhist temple and a Shinto shrine, a plantation store, and even a sumo-wrestling ring.

In the Waipahu Cultural Garden Park, 94-695 Waipahu St. (at Waipahu Depot Rd.), Waipahu. ☎ *808-677-0110. To get there: Take H-1 west to the no. 7 (Waikele) exit; turn south onto Paiwa St., pass 4 traffic signals, turn right onto Waipahu St., and go ¾-mile. Admission: $5 adults, $4 seniors, $3 kids 5–18. Open: Mon–Fri 9 a.m.–4:30 p.m., Sat 10 a.m.–4:30 p.m.; escorted tours offered hourly on the hour; last tour at 3 p.m.*

Hawaiian Waters Adventure Park

This new-in-1999, 25-acre water-theme amusement park is the place to play if the beach just isn't enough for you. Highlights include an inner-tube cruise along an 800-foot "river"; two phenomenal seven-story water-slides; a multilevel playpool that's fun for the whole family; mind- and body-bending tube slides and rides; a wave pool that's as big as a foot-ball field (and better for bodysurfing, I might add); and more waterlogged fun. Adults have their own "spa" area for relaxing and hot-tubbing. There's something for even the littlest ones here, but you have to be at least 48 inches tall to enjoy everything. Locker rooms, changing rooms, showers, and a well-endowed food court are on hand.

400 Farrington Hwy. (Hwy. 90), Kapolei. ☎ *808-674-9283. Internet:* www. hawaiianwaters.com. *To get there: Take H-1 west to exit no. 1 (Campbell Industrial Park/Barbers Point Harbor). Admission: $30 adults, $10 seniors 60 and over, $20 kids 3–11; free for kids under 3. Open: Daily from 10:30 a.m.; closing times vary between 4 and 6 p.m., depending on day and season.*

You can order a package ticket that includes round-trip bus transportation to Hawaiian Waters from Waikiki by calling ☎ 808-674-9283, ext. 107.

Along the windward coast

Kualoa Ranch Activity Club and Secret Island

This 4,000-acre former working cattle ranch is now a gorgeous outdoor playground (parts of *Jurassic Park* were filmed here). Five separate full-day adventure packages are on offer, including such activities as helicopter rides, horseback riding, mountain biking, rifle shooting, jet skiing, kayaking, windsurfing, snorkeling, freshwater fishing, and more. The beach activities, in particular, are terrific: You'll be shuttled out to a private area that's decked out like a country club with hammocks on the beach, volleyball courts, ping-pong tables, horseshoe pits, and beach pavilions; if you don't want to kick back here, you can catch a catamaran ride out to Kaneohe Bay for snorkeling. Reservations are required, and you'll need to talk to an agent in advance to sort out the package that's right for you.

49-560 Kamehameha Hwy. (Hwy. 93), Kaaawa. ☎ *800-231-7321 or 808-237-7321. Internet:* www.kualoa.com. *To get there: Take H-1 to the Likelike Hwy. (Hwy. 63); turn left at Kahekili Hwy. (Hwy. 83) and continue on to Kaaawa. Activity packages: $69–$139 adults, half-price 3–11. Open: Daily 9 a.m.–3 p.m.*

Polynesian Cultural Center

This remarkable cultural theme park allows you to tour the vast Pacific in just a single day. Seven Pacific island villages — representing Fiji, New Zealand, Marquesas, Samoa, Tahiti, Tonga, and Hawaii — let you experience first-hand each island or island group's lifestyle, traditions, songs, dance, costumes, and architecture as you tour the 42-acre park.

You can "travel" through this living-history museum/theme park either on foot or in a poleboat navigated along a man-made freshwater lagoon system. Each village is "inhabited" by native students from Polynesia who attend Hawaii's Bright Young University. Operated by the Mormon Church, the park also features a variety of stage shows celebrating the music, dance, history, and culture of Polynesia. An IMAX theater offers two gorgeous movies telling the story of Polynesian migration. An all-you-can-eat luau is served every evening (sorry, no alcohol) capped by a two-hour Polynesian entertainment extravaganza.

The whole thing may sound hokey, and it is — to a degree. But it's extremely well done and teaches a fascinating cultural lesson about the peoples of Polynesia and their cultural distinctions. Still, it's a lot to take in, and most people will find that the regular daytime activities are satisfactory. My recommendation is that you come for just the day and save your luauing for a neighbor island, where the feasts are better quality and you won't be required to maintain your theme-park stamina from noon 'til night. If you do want to stay for the entire affair, you'll have to choose between the different price packages, whose options include quality of food, quality of seating, and souvenirs. Since a visit is an all-day affair even if you don't stay for the evening show (straight-admission guests are kicked out at 6:30 p.m.), plan to arrive before 2 p.m.

55-370 Kamehameha Hwy. (Hwy. 83), Laie. ☎ *877-572-2347, 800-367-7060, or 808-293-3333. Internet:* www.polynesia.com. *To get there: Take the Pali Hwy. (Hwy. 61) or the Likelike Hwy. (Hwy. 63) to the windward coast and turn left on Kamehameha Hwy (Hwy, 83). Basic admission: $27 adults, $16 kids 5–11. Admission, IMAX, and show: $35 adults, $20 kids. Buffet and luau packages: $65–$155 adults, $4–$105 kids, depending on which package you choose. Open: Mon–Sat 12:30 p.m.–9:30 p.m. (box office opens at noon); regular exhibits close at 6:30 p.m.*

Even if you have a rental car, you might want to take an alternate method of transportation to the Polynesian Cultural Center if you're planning to spend the day and evening, as the drive back to Waikiki at 10 p.m. can be a real drag after an exhausting day at the park. You can book bus, minibus, and limo transportation starting at $15 per person through the PCC by calling ☎ 877-572-2347.

On the north shore

Little more than a collection of faded clapboard storefronts with a picturesque harbor, the north shore town of Haleiwa (ha-lay-EE-va) has evolved into ground zero for Hawaii's surf culture and a major roadside attraction filled with art galleries, restaurants, surf shops, and boutiques. This beach town really comes alive in winter, when the timid summer waves swell to monster proportions and draw big-wave surfers — and the people who love to watch them risk their necks — from around the world.

Haleiwa is definitely worth a stop to soak in some surf-style atmosphere. Shoppers will find an hour or two worth of good browsing to be had, and your kids will love the wild and wacky surf shops. For directions on getting here, see "Getting around Oahu" in Chapter 8.

If you're heading up to the north shore via the Central Oahu route, you might want to make a pit stop at the **Dole Pineapple Plantation,** 64-1550 Kamehameha Hwy. (Highway 99), Wahiawa (☎ **808-621-8408;** Internet: www.doleplantation.com), located just north of the point where the H-2 dumps you onto the Kam Highway, about 40 minutes from Waikiki. The two draws of this ticky-tacky tourist attraction are a) the world's largest maze (pineapple shaped, no less), which you can take a shot at navigating for $4.50 adults, $2.50 kids; and b) three words: pineapple ice cream. The shop is open daily from 9 a.m. to 6 p.m.

If you're captivated by surf lore, or you just want to see what all the fuss is about, stop into the **North Shore Surf and Cultural Museum,** tucked into the North Shore Marketplace at 66-250 Kamehameha Hwy. (across from Twelve Tribes) in Haleiwa (☎ **808-637-8888**). Oahu's only surf museum is a fun place to spend 20 minutes. The collection of memorabilia includes everything from vintage surfboards to old beach movie posters to trophies won by surfing's biggest legends. Spend a few minutes in the back video room watching surfing's finest moments (and biggest washouts) caught on film. It's definitely worth the price of admission — free, but donations are gladly accepted. The museum is open daily from 10 a.m. to 6 p.m., but call ahead, because "once in awhile somebody doesn't make it" to open up. Surf's up, anyone?

After you've finished browsing the museum, stop in at **Strong Current Surf Design**, also in the North Shore Marketplace (☎ **808-637-3406; Internet:** www.strongcurrenthawaii.com), the place for surf memorabilia and gear. You can't miss Strong Current — just look for the vintage Woody station wagon parked in front of the store.

In addition to Strong Current and Haleiwa's other surf shops, browsers will find enough to keep them busy for a good couple of hours. A few highlights, also located in the North Shore Marketplace (Haleiwa's biggest concentration of shopping ops), are **Silver Moon Emporium** (☎ **808-637-7710**), for lacy, silky, and elegantly flowing women's clothing; and **I Am Paradise** (☎ **877-295-2862** or 808-637-6888; Internet: www.iamparadise.com) for black pearl jewelry that is both elegant and affordable.

To really get into Haliewa's surf city groove, stop into **Matsumoto's,** at 66-087 Kamehameha Hwy., for a taste of Hawaii's favorite sweet treat: shave ice (never "shaved ice"), the island version of a snow cone. Shave ice comes in a generous cup (don't get the cone — you'll be sorry!) sweetened with your choice of syrup: strawberry, root beer, banana, passion fruit — it really doesn't matter, because they all come out rainbow-colored and tasting vaguely the same. I highly recommend doing as the locals do and ordering yours with a scoop of ice cream and sweet red azuki beans nestled in the middle — yum! I never pass up an opportunity to visit Matsumoto's, and you shouldn't, either. Don't be daunted by the long line, as it moves fast.

If you're coming up to the north shore in winter to catch the surfers in action — and you should, if you're on the island — you'll want to head to **Waimea Beach Park,** the **Banzai Pipeline,** and **Sunset Beach**; see "Hitting the Beaches" at the start of this chapter for details.

For recommendations on where to head for food and sunset cocktails while you're in the Haleiwa area, see "Oahu's Best Restaurants" in Chapter 9.

Waimea Valley Adventure Park

Waimea Valley is the ideal place for a family outing — because it takes a whole family to do everything there is to do here. This scenic 1,800-acre river valley is a botanical extravaganza, with gorgeous gardens and groves blooming with flora from all over the world. A small collection of native birds and animals is on hand, including the endangered Hawaiian nene geese, the state bird. The park is also a great cultural discovery ground, with remnants of old Hawaiian settlements and authentic demonstrations of the ancient hula, games, and crafts. The highlight is the cliff-diving shows, in which expert divers take death-defying leaps into a pool fed by a 45-foot waterfall — very cool. You can ride through the park on a tram with narration, hopping on and off as you like, or walk through on your own.

But that's not all — not by a long shot. Adventure seekers can skip the more prosaic attractions and head right for the thrills. You can learn to kayak on one-hour guided and unguided river and ocean kayaking tours, you can ride roughshod along 16 separate mountain-biking trails on 1¾-hour backcountry tours; you can scoot through three separate obstacle courses on a fat-wheeled ATV; or you can take a 1½-hour ride through stunning north shore foothills on horseback. If you're just coming to explore the park, allow about four hours; if you're coming for some adventuring as well, reserve your adventure package in advance, dress accordingly, and plan on spending the whole day.

59-864 Kamehameha Hwy., Haleiwa. ☎ *808-638-8511. Internet:* www. atlantisadventures.com. *Admission: $24 adults, $12 kids 4–12. Extra charges apply for kayaking, horseback riding, ATV riding, and mountain biking. Open: Daily 10 a.m.–5:30 p.m.*

Hitting the links and courts

Golf

Oahu has a handful of championship courses, but hard-to-get tee times and inaccessibility from Waikiki makes this my least favorite island to tee off on. Still, if you're on Oahu and in the mood, these courses are your best bets.

Stand-by Golf (☎ **888-645-2665;** Internet: www.standbygolf.com) offers up to 50 percent off greens fees to bargain hunters and last-minute duffers at 39 courses around Oahu. What's available is dependent upon when you call and where you're staying on the island, but since Stand-by has access to so many island courses, you'll have a good chance of finding a tee time to your liking, and maybe even saving a few bucks in the process.

Another great information resource on Oahu's golf courses is **808Golf. com** (☎ **808-947-5785;** Internet: www.808golf.com), whose extensive Web site offers comprehensive course descriptions and the opportunity to book tee times right online. The folks at 808Golf.com can even grant you discounts at select courses.

Also keep in mind that most hotels have prearrangements with certain courses, so you might want to check with the concierge or activities desk at your hotel before you try another route.

Ko Olina Golf Club

Located on Oahu's arid west side, this 6,324-yard, par-72 Ted Robinson–designed course is a standout with rolling fairways, multi-tiered greens, and no fewer than 16 water features. The signature hole is the picturesque 12th, a par-3 with an elevated tee sitting on a rock garden, plus its very own cascading waterfall. Wait until you get to the 18th hole; you'll see and hear water all around you. You'll have no choice but to play the left and approach the green over the water. This course isn't overly difficult, but you'd better be on your game once the wind picks up. Facilities include a driving range, locker rooms, Jacuzzi/steam rooms, and a restaurant and bar. Book in advance, as the course is always crowded. Men are asked to wear collared shirts.

92-1220 Aliinui Dr., Ewa Beach. ☎ *808-676-5300. Internet:* www.koolinagolf. com. *To get there: Take H-1 west until it becomes Farrington Hwy. (Hwy. 93); exit at Ko Olina and turn left onto Aliinui Dr. Greens fees: $145, $75 after 2:30 p.m., $45 after 4 p.m.*

The Links at Kuilima

This Arnold Palmer and Ed Seay–designed north shore course is the most spectacular golf course on the island. With rolling terrain, only a few trees, and lots of wind, the front nine holes play like a Scottish course, while the back nine have narrower tree-lined fairways and lots of water (including wonderful ocean views from the 17th hole). Several holes skirt a wetlands preserve, giving the course a tranquil vibe and beautiful native flora and fauna. This is a really fun place to play, and five sets of tees on every hole accommodate golfers of all abilities. Facilities include a pro shop, driving range, putting and chipping green, and snack bar.

57-049 Kuilima Dr., Kahuku. ☎ *808-293-8574. Internet:* www.kuilima.com. *To get there: Follow directions to Haleiwa outlined under "Exploring the rest of Oahu" in Chapter 8; proceed through town and follow Hwy. 83 to the Turtle Bay Country Club. Greens fees: $125, $95 after noon, $65 after 2 or 2:30 p.m. (depending on the season).*

Hilton hotel guests only pay $75, $45 after 2 or 2:30 p.m., at the Links at Kuilima.

Makaha Golf Club

Ask any local duffer and they're bound to name this as one of their favorite courses on the island — everybody does. Designed by William Bell, the challenging par-72, 7,077-yard course is one of Oahu's longest, most difficult, most beautiful, and best maintained. But don't let the rugged beauty of wrinkled cliffs or the luxuriant valley setting distract your attention from the challenges: 8 water hazards, 107 bunkers, and frequent and brisk winds that you'll have to play into on three holes, minimum. Facilities include a pro shop, a driving range, bag storage, and a particularly fine clubhouse with food service.

84-626 Makaha Valley Rd., Waianae (45 miles west of Honolulu). ☎ *800-757-8060 or 808-695-9544. To get there: Take H-1 west until it turns into Hwy. 93, which will wind up the leeward coast; turn right on Makaha Valley Road and follow it to the fork, and the course will be on the left. Greens fees: $125, $90 after noon, $50 after 2 p.m.; also inquire about heavily discounted rates for guests of select resorts.*

Tennis

The **Ilikai Sports Center** at the Renaissance Ilikai Waikiki Hotel, 1777 Ala Moana Blvd., at Hobron Lane (☎ 808-949-3811), has six courts, both hard-surface and grass (the grass courts are lit for night play), open to the public for $10 per hour. Call at least a day in advance to reserve a court. Equipment rental, lessons, and repair service are also available.

A shopper's guide to Honolulu

Honolulu is the crux of commerce in the Pacific — people fly in from as far away as Tahiti to do their Christmas shopping here. Most of the city's shopping is conveniently concentrated in a few big malls and shopping centers.

Additionally, browsers shouldn't neglect Waikiki's main drag, **Kalakaua Avenue,** as well as Kuhio Avenue one block to the north. Both avenues and the side streets that connect them are lined with an eclectic mix that ranges from haute couture boutiques to tacky souvenir stalls. Kalakaua is becoming the Rodeo Drive of Hawaii, lined as it is with shops like **Prada, Versace, Bulgari, Celine,** and others. These runway names cater largely to the Japanese crowd, who apparently find this stuff affordable compared with what they pay in Tokyo. You'll find that many of the stores along Kalakaua are open until late into the evening.

Malls

Ala Moana Center

With more than 200 shops — and counting — this monster-size mall is the largest open-air shopping center in the United States. With a selection of stores that ranges from **Sears** and **JC Penney** to **Fendi** and **Gucci,** there really is something for everybody here.

Among the standouts are three department stores: **Liberty House,** Hawaii's biggest department-store chain, is part of the Federated/Macy's group; in addition to surpassing the Macy standard in most departments, this flagship store boasts a wonderful Hawaiian crafts department (Kuu Home on the fourth floor) and a phenomenally good restaurant, the **Pineapple Room** (see Chapter 9). Also worth seeking out is the endlessly entertaining **Shirokiya,** a Japanese department store with a divine food department. **Neiman-Marcus** is a bastion of high-society elegance, and it boasts its own fine restaurant, Mariposa.

One of the great things about Ala Moana is that you can meet all of your practical needs here, since the mall is home to everything from **LensCrafters** to the U.S. Post Office, and shop for aloha wear at **Reyn's** (one of my favorites for island prints), footwear at a terrific branch of **Nordstrom Shoes,** and meet just about any other need you have. It's a must for mall lovers.

1450 Ala Moana Blvd. (between Piikoi Street and Atkinson Drive), Honolulu. ☎ *808-955-9517. Internet:* www.alamoana.com.

Aloha Tower Marketplace

This waterfront restaurant and dining complex is better for dining (**Chai's Island Bistro** is here; see Chapter 9) and views than it is for actual shopping, as most of the stores are ticky-tacky. The choices are more tourist-oriented than those at neighbors Ala Moana Center, Ward Centre, and

Ward Warehouse. Expect lots of gift boutiques and T-shirt shops. It's a great place to stroll, but don't expect the find of a lifetime. The few stand-outs include **Martin & MacArthur** for handcrafted Hawaiian furniture and art objects; and **Beyond the Beach** for a surprisingly good collection of surf apparel. If you're looking for a java fix, the **Bad Ass Coffee Company** will do the trick. They want you here so badly that the marketplace even offers free shuttle service from select Waikiki hotels; ask your concierge or call for pickup points and times.

At Honolulu Harbor between piers 8 and 11 (just past the point where Ala Moana Boulevard meets Nimitz Highway), Honolulu. ☎ *808-566-2337. Internet:* www.alohatower.com.

Royal Hawaiian Shopping Center

Located in central Waikiki, this mall is the heart of Honolulu's European designer shopping. It's where you'll find **Chanel, Cartier, Hermès, Versace, Van Cleef & Arpels,** and other big-ticket boutiques. You'll find the Waikiki Trolley service desk here as well, plus the local branch of the Hawaii Convention and Visitors Bureau (see Chapter 8).

2201 Kalakaua Ave. (at Seaside Avenue), Waikiki. ☎ *808-922-0588 or 808-922-2299. Internet:* www.hawaiishopper.com/RHSC.

Victoria Ward Centers

What used to be two simple two-story sister shopping centers has bloomed into a five-center mini-empire of quality mid-priced shopping. Of the two original malls, Ward Centre is largely dedicated to dining, but has a few standouts, most notably **Borders Books & Music,** which boasts an excellent Hawaiian music department; **The Gallery at Ward Centre,** which carries a notable collection of works by Hawaii artists (Doug Young's city landscapes are particularly noteworthy, and relatively affordable); and the **Honolulu Chocolate Company,** makers of fine island-made chocolates from island-grown cocoa beans. **Ward Warehouse's** good choices include the **Nohea Gallery,** a constant favorite for its terrific collection of high-quality Hawaii-made crafts; and **Mamo Howell,** for both traditional and contemporary muumuus in Mamo's wonderful signature fabrics.

Attention, bargain hunters: At the Ward Village Shops (across Auahi Street from Ward Centre) is the **Crazy Shirts Outlet,** where Hawaii's biggest and best souvenir T-shirt emporium sells excellent quality seconds and leftovers for a fraction of the retail prices. Best of all, it's attractive and well-run — no shuffling through masses of unorganized Ts in dusty bins.

Ala Moana Blvd. and Auahi St. between Ward Ave. and Queen St., just west of the Ala Moana Center. ☎ *808-591-8411. Internet:* www.victoriaward.com.

Other shopping of note

Hilo Hattie's has been Hawaii's first name in aloha wear for decades, and I'm happy to report that both the quality and selection is better than ever. The flagship store is out toward the airport at 700 N. Nimitz

Hwy., at Pacific Street (☎ 808-536-6500; Internet: www.hilohattie.com). You'll find a big children's department, as well as macadamia nuts, Hawaii-grown coffees, and lots of other souvenirs to choose from. One of their best recent inventions are Hawaiian print car seatcovers, which are selling like hotcakes — be the first on your block to have 'em! A more manageable location is at Ala Moana Center, where the selection tends toward the high end (☎ 808-973-3266).

Hilo Hattie runs a free shuttle service every 20 minutes between 8:20 a.m. and 3:30 p.m. daily from various Waikiki locations to their main Nimitz store. You can stay as long as you want and return directly to Waikiki, or make pit stops at Aloha Tower Marketplace and another mall, the Dole Cannery, along the way. Call ☎ 808-537-2926 for details.

For the best selection of vintage aloha shirts, visit **Bailey's Antiques and Aloha Shirts,** 517 Kapahulu Ave. (across from the Ala Wai Golf Course), north of Kapiolani Park in the Kapahulu section of Honolulu (☎ 808-734-7628). A '50s-era cotton or silkie in A-1 condition can cost upwards of $600, but some cheapies are on hand, too; prices begin around $20. Besides, browsing is a big part of the fun. You'll also find hula-girl lamps, vintage costume jewelry, and other bits of kitsch, all priced at top dollar — but a joy to discover, anyway.

Contemporary aloha wear is everywhere, but my favorite prints and styles are made by **Reyn's** (www.reyns.com). Reyn's has a number of boutiques throughout Hawaii, including one at the Ala Moana Center, plus a charming shop on the lobby level of the Sheraton Waikiki hotel.

In addition to top-flight choices like the **Kuu Home** department at Liberty House and the **Nohea Gallery** at Victoria's Ward Centre (see earlier in this section), some of the finest stops for Hawaiian-made gifts are museum shops: The **Academy Shop** at the Honolulu Academy of Arts, 900 S. Beretania St., between Victoria and Ward avenues in downtown Honolulu (☎ 808-523-8703), and both **Native Books and Beautiful Things** and **Shop Pacifica** at the Bishop Museum, 1525 Bernice St. at Kalihi Street, also downtown (☎ 808-847-3511); and **The Contemporary Museum Gift Shop,** 2411 Makiki Heights Rd., in the Tantalus section of Honolulu (☎ 808-523-3447). The Academy Shop, Native Books, and Shop Pacifica are great choices for traditional Hawaiiana, crafts, and books, while the Contemporary Museum shop focuses on (what else?) contemporary arts and crafts. Native Books and Beautiful Things also has a larger location downtown at 222 Merchant St., at Alakea Street (☎ 808-599-5511).

Nothing says "aloha" like a lei. If you'd like to skip the overpriced, less-than-interesting selections available in most tourist 'hoods, head to Chinatown in downtown Honolulu, where the aroma of flowers being woven into beautiful treasures fills the air. The stretch of Maunakea Street between Beretania and King streets and the adjacent block of Beretania Street are lined with lei shops on both sides of the street. The designs of the leis made here are almost always exceptional, and the prices are the best on the island. Wander through all the shops before you decide which lei you want, and feel free to ask questions about any unfamiliar tropical flowers and styles.

Living It Up After the Sun Goes Down: Nightlife

Your best bet for finding out what's going on around town is to pick up a copy of *Honolulu Weekly* (www.honoluluweekly.com), available free at restaurants, clubs, shops, and newspaper racks around Oahu. Also check the daily papers, particularly *Honolulu Advertiser* (www.honoluluadvertiser.com). But most important, don't forget to make use of that most valuable of resources: your hotel concierge. He or she is always up on what's happening around town, whether you're looking for a hot Polynesian revue or a cool nightclub.

If the Brothers Cazimero are putting on a show while you're in town, don't miss it. This legendary musical duo is one of Hawaii's most beloved and gifted acts; their contemporary Hawaiian music exudes aloha. Check the papers or ask your concierge if they're playing anywhere in town.

If you're in the party mood and ready to luau, see Chapter 9.

The really big shows

The shows listed in this section are Waikiki staples. Still, performers move around from time to time, and schedules, prices, and other parameters do change — so always call ahead.

Don Ho

Perennial favorite Don "Mr. Mellow" Ho still packs in the crowds, just like he's been doing for four decades now. (He has a Dick Clark thing going on, though, so you wouldn't know his age by looking at him.) Hawaii's best-known singer is engaging to the core, singing nostalgic numbers like "Tiny Bubbles" and "I'll Remember You" in an intimate nightclub setting. You can often get tickets on the day of show, but you're better off planning ahead (it's usually sold out by showtime). If you (or your teenager) get lucky, Don's daughter, the rising teen pop queen Hoku, may make one of her frequent appearances (although she probably spends more time in the company of folks like N'Sync these days).

At the Hana Hou Supper Club, Waikiki Beachcomber hotel, 2300 Kalakaua Ave. (at Duke's Lane), Waikiki. ☎ **877-693-6646** *or 808-923-3981. Internet:* www.donho.com. *Showtimes: Sun–Thurs 7 p.m. (dark Fri and Sat). Tickets: Dinner show $52 adults, $26 kids 6–12. Cocktail show (with 1 drink) $32 adults, kids 6–12.*

At press time, ticket-buyers who made their reservations online at www.donho.com qualify for heavily discounted rates: $42 for the dinner show and $27 for the cocktail show, plus a special show-only rate of $20.

Magic of Polynesia

This extravaganza is downright Vegas-worthy. Master illusionist John Horikawa performs mind-boggling feats of magic on an elaborate stage set, aided by a large costumed cast and state-of-the-art lighting and sound. This is a first-class production, and the audience eats it up. This show sells out regularly, so reserve seats a day or two in advance.

At the Waikiki Beachcomber hotel, 2300 Kalakaua Ave. (at Duke's Lane), Waikiki. ☎ *877-971-4321 or 808-971-4321. Internet:* www.waikikibeachcomber.com. *Showtimes: Most nights 6:30 p.m. and 8:45 p.m. (call for exact schedule). Tickets: $35–$130 adults, $24–$90 kids 5–12, depending on service (cocktail or dinner).*

Society of Seven

Waikiki's longest-running nightclub act (inching up on three decades now) still puts on one of the best shows in Waikiki. Expect a lively blend of skits, impersonations, show tunes, '50s and '60s pop hits, and more.

In the Outrigger Main Showroom, Outrigger Waikiki on the Beach, 2335 Kalakaua Ave. (between the Royal Hawaiian Shopping Center and the Sheraton Moana Surfrider), Waikiki. ☎ *808-922-6408 or 808-923-7469. Internet:* www.outriggerentertainment.com. *Showtimes: Mon 8:30 p.m., Tues–Sat 6:30 p.m. and 8:30 p.m. Tickets: $34.50–$62 adults, $17–$40.50 kids, depending on type of service you choose (cocktail, buffet dinner, sit-down dinner).*

The Yes! International Review

Acts from around the world perform magic, illusion, acrobatics, juggling, mime, Polynesian dancing, and more. Expect lots of kid-friendly audience participation.

At the Polynesian Palace, 227 Lewers St. (between Kalakaua Ave. and Helumoa Rd.), Waikiki. ☎ *808-922-6408 or 808-923-7469. Internet:* www.outriggerentertainment.com. *Tickets: $34.50–$55 adults, $17–$36 kids, depending on type of service you choose (cocktail, buffet dinner, sit-down dinner).*

Cocktails, music, and dancing

Hands down, our favorite spot for sunset cocktails is the **House Without a Key** at the Halekulani hotel, 2199 Kalia Rd. (at the beach end of Lewers St.), Waikiki (☎ **808-923-2311**; Internet: www.halekulani.com). On an oceanfront patio shaded by a big kiawe tree, you can sip the best mai tais on the island, listen to masterful steel guitar music, and watch a traditional hula dancer (often former Miss Hawaii Kanoe Miller) sway with the palms. It's romantic, nostalgic, and simply breathtaking. Afterward, move indoors to the Lewers Lounge, where light jazz continues the romantic tone.

Another top spot for Hawaiian music and orchid-adorned cocktails is the oh-so-romantic **Banyan Veranda** at the Sheraton Moana Surfrider, 2365 Kalakaua Ave. (on the beach, across from Kaiulani St.), in the heart of Waikiki (☎ **800-325-3535**). We just love this Victorian-style beachfront hotel, situated around a hundred-year-old banyan tree — the perfect setting for some soft island sounds.

Nothing separates you from the sand at the **Royal Hawaiian's Mai Tai Bar,** 2259 Kalakaua Ave., at the end of Royal Hawaiian Avenue (☎ 808-923-7311), giving this one of the most lovely views of Waikiki Beach. The Mai Tai Bar maintains an all-Hawaiian music program, which adds to the magical mood.

There's always something cooking at **Duke's Canoe Club,** at the Outrigger Waikiki on the Beach, 2335 Kalakaua Ave. (between the Royal Hawaiian Shopping Center and the Sheraton Moana Surfrider), Waikiki (☎ 808-923-0711). This lively spot is the quintessential beachfront bar and restaurant, with tiki torches in the sand, a tropical party vibe, and a mammoth drink menu to suit the scene. It's crowded in the evening, but that's part of the fun. The Hawaiian entertainment is always top-notch — and best of all, it usually starts around 4 p.m.

The Sheraton Waikiki, 2255 Kalakaua Ave. (at Royal Hawaiian Ave., west of the Royal Hawaiian), Waikiki (☎ 808-922-4422), is home to **Esprit,** Waikiki's only dance club. You'll find an oceanfront setting, live rock, and a lively scene every night of the week.

Over at the **Paradise Lounge** at Hilton Hawaiian Village, 2005 Kalia Rd. (at Ala Moana Blvd.), Waikiki (☎ 808-949-4321), live music and mai tais set an idyllic island mood. If the multi-award-winning **Olomana** is in the house, as they often are on Friday and Saturday, don't miss it.

If you're at the Diamond Head end of Waikiki, head to the **Sunset Lanai** at the New Otani Kaimana Beach Hotel, 2863 Kalakaua Ave., across the street from Kapiolani Park (☎ 808-923-5555). Shaded by a giant light-festooned hau tree and practically on the sand, it's no wonder that this magical spot is a favorite Waikiki watering hole. Live Hawaiian music heightens the ambience at weekend sunset hours. And if you're around on Friday at lunchtime, stop in at the Hau Tree Lanai (adjacent to the Sunset Lanai) for some entertainment from the legendary Arthur Lyman, one of the leaders of the big exotica boom of the '50s and '60s. Arthur really swings!

Hawaii's finest musicians have a new home: **Chai's Island Bistro,** Aloha Tower Marketplace, 1 Aloha Tower Dr., just south of downtown Honolulu (☎ 808-585-0011), where the pricey dinners are more than worth the price of admission to see such stellar acts as the excellent duo Hapa on Thursday and Friday and the legendary Brothers Cazimero on Wednesday. The calendar here is always jam-packed with top-quality talent, so don't miss it.

Sailing into the sunset

Nothing closes a perfect day in paradise like a sunset cruise. If you're looking for a place to cruise into the sunset, do it on Oahu, where the Waikiki skyline and Diamond Head come together in an unforgettable backdrop. Both Dream Cruises and Royal Hawaiian Cruises offer a number of packages you can choose from; see "Enjoying on deck adventures — ocean cruising" earlier in this chapter for complete details.

Part IV
Maui

"Did you want to take the Schwinn bicycle dive, the
Weber gas grill dive, or the Craftsman riding lawn
mower dive?"

In this part . . .

Maui's popularity as a vacation destination makes planning your trip before you leave home essential. The chapters in this part will help you map out everything you need for an unforgettable Maui vacation.

Chapter 11

The Lowdown on Maui's Hotel Scene

*P*repare yourself — Maui isn't cheap. High demand means that both
resort hotels and condos can — and do — garner ridiculously high
rack rates for accommodations, making it the priciest of Hawaii's islands
in the accommodations category.

Take heart, however: Some good bargains are available, especially in the
condo market. I list some of the best values under "Maui's Best Hotels,
Condos, and B&Bs" in this chapter, but those of you looking for budget
accommodations may find the widest array of options by going through
one of the condo rental agencies listed at the end of this chapter.

You may be able to save more money on Maui than anywhere else in
Hawaii by purchasing an all-inclusive package deal, especially if you're
looking for an upscale vacation. In the package market, Maui's popularity may work in your favor: Packagers scoop up huge numbers of Maui
hotel rooms, precisely because they know they'll be able to resell them.
Packagers buying rooms in bulk are able to negotiate substantial price
breaks with accommodations providers — hotels and condos — that
they can then pass on to their clientele — you. Of course, I can't guarantee what the prices will be when you book, but it's worth the extra effort
to see what's available, even if you're booking the rest of your vacation
on your own (some packagers can arrange land-only vacations if you
already have your plane tickets covered). See "The Ins and Outs of Travel
Packages" in Chapter 5 for tips on where to look for the package deal
that's right for you.

Choosing Your Location

The commercial hub of Maui is **Kahului** (ka-hoo-LOO-ee); just east of Kahului is **Wailuku,** Maui's appealingly funky county seat (and a burgeoning antique center). These two Central Maui communities are Maui's largest, but visitors almost never stay there — although Maui's finest B&B, the impeccable Old Wailuku Inn, is located here; see "Maui's Best Hotels, Condos, and B&Bs" later in this chapter.

Instead, most visitors stay on one of Maui's two major resort coasts: West Maui and South Maui. Both are comprised of smaller beach resorts and communities, each with its own distinct personality.

West Maui

Look at a map of Maui — the island faintly resembles the head and shoulders of a person in left profile. If you go with this geographical Rorschach test, the West Maui coastline serves as the island's forehead (and Kahului is on Maui's "neck"). In winter this coast is a little greener — and a little wetter — than the South Maui coast. Some of the best beaches on the island fringe West Maui; eastward, the beautifully jagged mountain peaks of the West Maui mountains rise in the distance.

Of the communities along this resort coast, only Lahaina is a real town; the others are really just a collection of condos or hotels, each targeted to a different audience and anchored by a few fancy resorts or a high-end mini-mall. The following communities start at the southern end of West Maui and move northward along the **Honoapiilani** (ho-no-ah-pee-ee-LA-nee) **Highway** (Highway 30).

The historic port town of **Lahaina** is not really all that historic anymore; in fact, it has superceded Waikiki as the tacky tourist center of Hawaii. The blocks are lined with bustling waterfront restaurants, tourist-targeted galleries and shops, and aggressive activity centers that catcall onto the street, begging to book your activities for you (or, if they can, talk you into "sitting through" a timeshare presentation). The predominant vibe is that of one big, surf-oriented street party. Some people love the freewheeling ambience, lively energy, and oceanfront setting. Lahaina also has two more things going for it: some of Maui's best accommodations values, and an extremely convenient location. Expect to drive to the beach, though.

Three miles north of Lahaina is **Kaanapali** (kah-na-PA-lee), Hawaii's first master-planned family resort. Kaanapali's chain of resort hotels and condos fronts a gorgeous golden beach and exudes a nice sense of continuity. All are linked by a landscaped parkway and a walking path along the sand, with a very nice shopping and dining complex sitting at its midpoint. Kaanapali is pricey, but not quite as expensive as Kapalua or Wailea; in fact, it's home to my favorite midpriced resort, the Kaanapali Beach Hotel, and some of Maui's best midrange condos.

Two condo communities, **Kahana** and **Napili,** sit off the highway a few minutes north of Kaanapali, offering great deals for those who want an affordable place to stay *and* a nice oceanfront setting. Apartment-style units offer good value for families or anyone who wants homelike amenities that give you the freedom to cook a meal for yourself or wash your own socks. Restaurants and supermarkets are right at hand. The only down side is a lack of personality — expect homogeneous, bulk-contracted condo complexes.

North of Kahana may be Hawaii's most beautiful master-planned community, **Kapalua,** the exclusive domain of two gracious luxury hotels, fabulous gold-sand beaches, and world-class golf. Kapalua is a marvelous place to settle in and unwind, if you have the bucks to do it. But keep in mind that, situated as it is at the far north end of the Honoapiilani Highway, Kapalua isn't the most convenient base in the world; even Lahaina is a half-hour drive to the south. It also tends to get more rain than other Maui resorts, even those a few minutes south on the West Maui coast.

South Maui

South Maui is the island's hottest, driest, and sunniest coast. Actually western-facing, but well-protected from the elements by peninsula-like West Maui, South Maui receives only about 15 inches of annual rainfall, and temperatures stay around 80°F year-round.

If you drive south from Central along Piilani Highway (Highway 31) or Kihei Road (Highway 310), you'll first reach Kihei and then Wailea; which one you choose will be entirely dependent on your budget.

Centrally located **Kihei** (KEY-hay) is Maui's bargain coast. Its main drag is South Kihei Road, which is bordered by a continuous string of condos and mini-malls on one side, and a series of sandy beaches on the other. Kihei isn't charming or quaint; it feels more like Southern California than Hawaii at times, especially when the traffic is bumper to bumper along Kihei Road. What Kihei lacks in physical appeal, though, it more than makes up for in sunshine, affordability, and convenience. Choose another base if you can afford it, though.

Just a few minutes south of Kihei, **Wailea** (why-LAY-ah) sits at the opposite end of the budget-deluxe continuum. This ritzy, well-manicured neighborhood is home to Maui's best luxury resort spreads, enough championship golf courses to keep you busy for a week, five outstanding beaches, and the Wailea Tennis Center (known as Wimbledon West). The strip is well-developed and tightly packed, but my favorite Wailea resorts remain worlds unto themselves. Even though Kapalua is unarguably more beautiful, Wailea is no slouch — and I prefer its more accessible location and wider range of hotel choices. You'll even find some midrange and upscale condos in this appealing nabe.

Maui's Best Hotels, Condos, & B&Bs

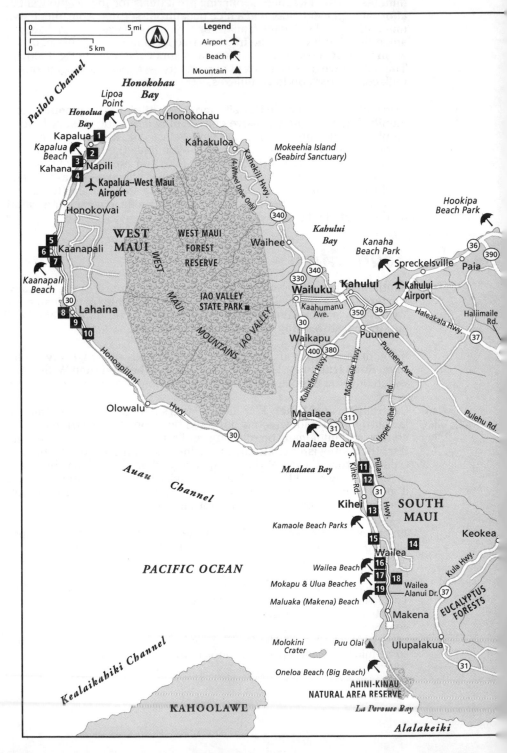

Legend

Airport ✈
Beach 🏄
Mountain ▲

Pailolo Channel

Honokohau Bay

Lipoa Point

Honolua Bay

Kapalua **1**

Kapalua Beach

Kahana **3**

Napili **4**

✈ Kapalua–West Maui Airport

Honokowai

WEST MAUI

WEST MAUI FOREST RESERVE

Honokohau

Kahakuloa

Mokeehia Island (Seabird Sanctuary)

Kahekili Hwy (4-Wheel Drive Only)

340

Kahului Bay

Waihee

340

Kanaha Beach Park

Spreckelsville

Hookipa Beach Park

36

390

Paia

Kaanapali **5** **6** **7**

Kaanapali Beach

30

Lahaina **8** **9** **10**

Honoapiilani Hwy

WEST MAUI MOUNTAINS

IAO VALLEY STATE PARK

IAO VALLEY

330

Wailuku

Kahului

✈ Kahului Airport

350

36

Haleakala Hwy

Haliimaile Rd.

37

Kaahumanu Ave.

Puunene

30

Waikapu

400 380

Puunene Ave.

Kuihelani Hwy

Mokulele Hwy

Upper Kihei Rd.

Pulehu Rd.

Olowalu

30

Maalaea

311

Maalaea Beach

31

Auau Channel

Maalaea Bay

S. Kihei Rd.

Piilani Hwy

11 **12**

31

Kihei **13**

Kamaole Beach Parks

15

Wailea **14**

SOUTH MAUI

Keokea

PACIFIC OCEAN

Wailea Beach **16**

Mokapu & Ulua Beaches **17** **18**

Maluaka (Makena) Beach **19**

Wailea Alanui Dr.

37

Kula Hwy

EUCALYPTUS FORESTS

Makena

Molokini Crater

Puu Olai ▲

Ulupalakua

31

Oneloa Beach (Big Beach)

AHINI-KINAU NATURAL AREA RESERVE

La Perouse Bay

Kealaikahiki Channel

KAHOOLAWE

Alalakeiki

Ann & Bob Babson's Bed & Breakfast & Sunset Cottage **14**
Aston at the Maui Banyan **13**
Aston Maui Islander **8**
Best Western Pioneer Inn **9**
Four Seasons Resort Maui at Wailea **17**
Grand Wailea Resort & Spa **17**
Hana Oceanfront Cottages **20**
Heavenly Hana Inn **21**
Kaanapali Alii **7**
Kaanapali Beach Hotel **6**
Kahana Sunset **4**
Kapalua Bay Hotel & Villas **2**
Kea Lani Hotel Suites & Villas **19**
Koa Resort **11**

Mana Kai Maui **15**
Maui Coast Hotel **12**
Napili Kai Beach Club **3**
Noelani Condominium Resort **4**
Old Wailuku Inn at Ulupono **10**
Palms at Wailea **18**
Plantation Inn **8**
Punahoa Beach Apartments **12**
Renaissance Wailea Beach Resort **16**
Ritz-Carlton Kapalua **1**
Sheraton Maui **5**
Westin Maui **7**
The Whaler on Kaanapali Beach **6**
What a Wonderful World B&B **14**

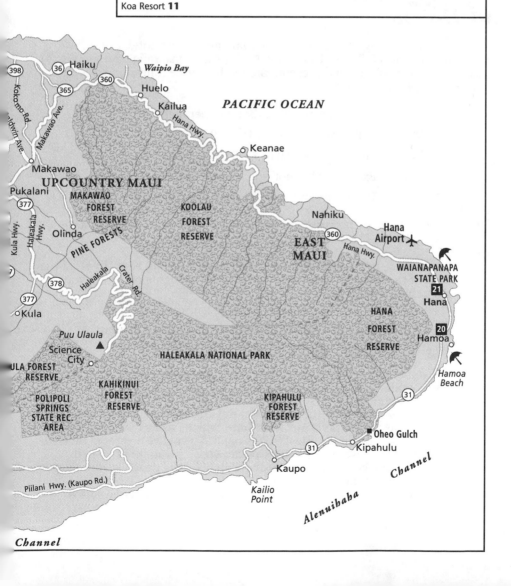

Rural Maui: Upcountry and Hana

A few visitors also like to stay way out in **Hana,** in easternmost Maui, for the ultimate escape; or in cool, inland **Upcountry Maui** to be nearer to Haleakala (ha-lay-ah-KA-la) National Park. You don't have to stay there to enjoy these areas; both are reachable on day trips from the West and South Maui resorts (although the Hana trip, in particular, makes for a monster day). If you're contemplating a visit or a stay either upcountry or in Hana, check out the section called "Staying Off the Beaten Path" at the end of this chapter.

Maui's Best Hotels, Condos, and B&Bs

In the following listings, you'll see that each resort hotel, condo, and B&B name is followed by a number of dollar signs, ranging from one ($) to five ($$$$$). Each represents the median price range for a double room per night, as follows:

$	Super-cheap — less than $75 per night
$$	Still affordable — $75 to $150
$$$	Moderate — $150 to $225
$$$$	Expensive but not ridiculous — $225 to $300
$$$$$	Ultra-luxurious — more than $300 per night

So that there are no surprises at checkout time, don't forget that the state adds 11.42 percent in taxes to your hotel bill.

You can use the worksheet "Sweet Dreams: Choosing Your Hotel" at the back of this book to help you organize your thoughts on where you might like to stay.

Ann & Bob Babson's Bed & Breakfast & Sunset Cottage

$–$$ South Maui (Kihei)

For something more cozy and homelike than your average nondescript Kihei condo, book a room or a cottage with these fine folks, who have four accommodations on their lovely half-acre, all with private baths, TV, and phones. Two rooms in the main house also feature mini-fridges and ceiling fans; best is the skylit Molokini Suite, which has its own deck with hot tub — quite luxurious for just $120 a night. The petite two-room Hibiscus Hideaway (for two, max) boasts ocean views, while the two-bedroom/two-bath cottage features a complete kitchen. The beach is about a mile away, but since the house sits at 400 feet elevation, you'll have fab ocean views from all decks. The warm and friendly Babsons go above and beyond to make sure their guests feel at home and have a great time. They have three cats, though, so book elsewhere if you're allergic.

3371 Keha Dr. (in Maui Meadows), Kihei. ☎ *800-824-6409 or 808-874-1166. Fax: 808-879-7906. Internet:* www.mauibnb.com. *Parking: Free! Rates: $90–$120 double (continental breakfast included Mon–Sat), $125–$155 cottage. 5-night minimum (7-night minimum in cottage). Deals: 10% discount for stays of 7 nights or longer (excluding cottage). MC, V.*

Aston at the Maui Banyan

$$–$$$ South Maui (Kihei)

Skip the standard hotel rooms, if you can, and go straight for a condo unit — which offers much more value for your dollar — at this very nice apartment-like complex situated across Kihei Road from Kamaole (kam-a-OH-lay) Beach Park II. The roomy, open-plan 1- to 3-bedroom units are all nicely outfitted and well maintained. They feature comfy, contemporary-style furniture, full kitchens with microwave, washer/dryers, and furnished lanais. Light daily maid service is included, and two pools, tennis courts, and a Jacuzzi are on site. The building sits perpendicular to the coast, so partial ocean views are the best you can do — most upper units overlook the parking structure or the building next door. Still, this is a great value if you can score one of the many price breaks.

2575 S. Kihei Rd., Kihei. ☎ *800-922-7866 or 808-875-0004. Fax: 808-874-4035. Internet:* www.aston-hotels.com. *Parking: Free! Rack rates: $130–$155 double, $160–$220 1-bedroom, $215–$295 2-bedroom, $340–$400 3-bedroom. Deals: Excellent opportunities for discounts. Internet-only ePriceBreaker rates can result in substantial savings (doubles as low as $103 at press time). Ask for AAA, senior (50-plus), and corporate discounts, and other special rate programs. Qualify for 25% discount if you stay at Aston properties for 7 or more nights with Aston's "Island Hopper" program. AE, CB, DC, DISC, JCB, MC, V.*

Aston Maui Islander

$–$$ West Maui (Lahaina)

This well-managed plantation-style complex offers one of Maui's best deals. A few hotel rooms (with coffeemaker and mini-fridge) are on offer, but most of the spacious units are apartment-style studios and one- and two-bedrooms (some of which can be linked to form a three-bedroom), all with fully outfitted kitchens (some with microwaves). About half have been renovated with pretty textiles, bamboo furnishings, and cream-colored walls that brighten them up considerably; even the unrenovated units are fine, but ask for a newer one for maximum value. The grounds are tropically lush and feature coin-op laundry, tennis courts, barbecues, and a pool. The larger units are perfect for families; your kids will love the heart-of-Lahaina location, and you'll appreciate the tranquil ambience that results from a peaceful side-street location (a rarity in Lahaina). The complex is very quiet in general, but ask for a unit away from the highway for minimum intrusion.

Lahaina & Kaanapali Hotels & Condos

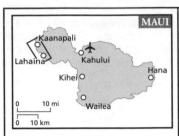

Aston Maui Islander **8**
Best Western Pioneer Inn **7**
Kaanapali Alii **5**
Kaanapali Beach Hotel **2**
Plantation Inn **6**
Sheraton Maui **1**
Westin Maui **4**
The Whaler on Kaanapali Beach **3**

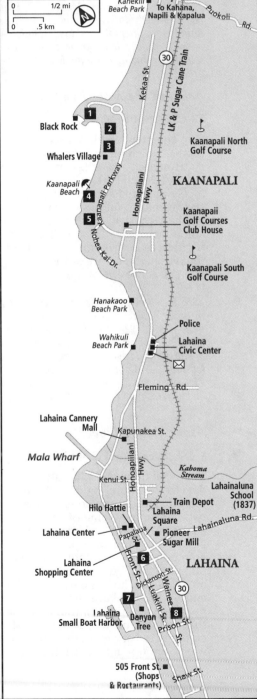

660 Wainee St. (between Dickenson and Prison sts.), Lahaina. ☎ *800-922-7866, 800-367-5226, or 808-667-9766. Fax: 808-667-2792. Internet:* www.aston-hotels. com. *Parking: $3. Rack rates: $98–$108 double, $118–$142 studio, $138–$162 1-bedroom, $198–$227 2-bedroom, $248–$276 3-bedroom. Rates include continental breakfast on your first morning. Deals: Excellent opportunities for discounts. Internet-only ePriceBreaker rates can result in substantial savings (doubles as low as $85 at press time). Ask for AAA, senior (50-plus), and corporate discounts, and other special rate programs. Qualify for 25% discount if you stay at Aston properties for 7 or more nights with Aston's "Island Hopper" program. AE, CB, DC, DISC, JCB, MC, V.*

Best Western Pioneer Inn

$$ West Maui (Lahaina)

This delightfully restored 1901 whaler's inn overlooking Lahaina Harbor blends a genuine old-time ambience with proven Best Western comforts, and it's a winning combination. Rooms are small and on the dark side, but they're cool, pretty, and comfortable, with paisley textiles, modern tiled baths, and coffeemakers (deluxe rooms also have wet bars with mini-fridge). The quietest rooms face the garden courtyard pool or the massive banyan tree next door; a few have harbor views that heighten the maritime experience. Front Street–facing rooms are noisy, but shaded and furnished lanais give you a ringside seat for the sidewalk party. It has an appealing indoor-outdoor restaurant and bar on-site; the beach is a drive away, but the town couldn't be more convenient. All in all, not Maui's roomiest or quietest place to stay, but a real charmer.

At Lahaina Pier, 658 Wharf St. (at Front St.), Lahaina. ☎ *800-457-5457 or 808-661-3636. Fax: 808-667-5708. Internet:* www.pioneerinnmaui.com *or* www. bestwestern.com. *Parking: $5. Rack rates: $110–$130 standard double, $145–$175 deluxe double, $150–$165 suite. Deals: Discounts for AAA and AARP members as well as seniors (55-plus); inquire about family rates and other special packages. AE, DC, DISC, JCB, MC, V.*

Four Seasons Resort Maui at Wailea

$$$$$ South Maui (Wailea)

I prefer the excitement of the Grand Wailea (see the following listing), but this is a better choice for those in search of peaceful relaxation and understated elegance. The guest-to-staff ratio is 2 to 1, and it shows — service is out of this world. The big, bright, airy rooms are done in a casually elegant natural palette and feature cushy furnishings, grand and gorgeous bathrooms, big lanais (nearly all with ocean views), and all the little luxuries. The gorgeous grounds overflow with first-rate facilities, and the stunning beach is one of Maui's finest. If you prefer to lounge poolside, you can recline in comfort under a shaded cabana, and a pool attendant will even bring you chilled towels and spritz you with Evian if you dare break a sweat. The kids will be duly pampered in an excellent activities program. Vacation doesn't get better than this.

3900 Wailea Alanui Dr., Wailea. ☎ ***800-334-6284*** *or 808-874-8000. Fax: 808-874-2244. Internet:* www.fshr.com. *Rack rates: $305–$745 double, suites from $575. Parking: Free! Deals: Ask about Under the Sun packages (including car and breakfast), plus romance, golf, fifth night free, room-and-car, bed-and-breakfast, and other packages. AE, DC, DISC, JCB, MC, V.*

Grand Wailea Resort & Spa

$$$$$ South Maui (Wailea)

I didn't want to love this outrageous resort, but I couldn't help myself. This monument to monied excess won me over with its lush, art-filled grounds and exclusive tropical-theme-park vibe; the 50,000-foot Spa Grande, the ultimate temple to the pampered life; and Hawaii's best water playground, a fantasy of falls, rapids, slides, grottos, hidden hot tubs and swim-up bars — the world's only water-powered elevator merely puts the finishing touch on the ultimate pool complex. If you manage to make it out to the beach, you'll find one of Maui's best (equal to the Four Seasons'). Rooms are huge and elegantly appointed, with luxurious marble baths. Restaurants, lounges, and shops abound, and service is first rate, making this the place to stay if you can afford to live large. And bring the kids — they'll think they've died and gone to heaven, especially once they see the whopping 20,000-square-foot kids' camp. Minimalists, on the other hand, should book elsewhere.

3850 Wailea Alanui Dr., Wailea. ☎ ***800-888-6100*** *or 808-875-1234. Fax: 808-879-2442. Internet:* www.grandwailea.com. *Parking: included in $10-per-night resort services fee, which also includes free local and 800 calls, in-room coffee, and other resort extras. Valet parking: $8. Rack rates: $410–$710 double, suites from $1,200. Deals: Excellent air-inclusive prices are often available through Pleasant Hawaiian Holidays and other packagers (see "The Ins and Outs of Travel Packages" in Chapter 5). AE, CB, DC, DISC, JCB, MC, V.*

Kaanapali Alii

$$$$ West Maui (Kaanapali)

If you want luxury living *and* condo conveniences, this high-rise beachfront complex is the place for you. These are Maui's finest (and priciest) condos, but they're worth it. Each is privately owned, so decor varies, but owners are held to a high standard. Apartments are universally large (between 1,500 and 1,900 square feet) and come with fully equipped gourmet kitchens, huge living room and dining room, two TVs and VCR; two full baths, even in the one-bedrooms; washer/dryer; and private lanais. The luxuriant grounds feature a fitness room, tennis, a heated pool with hot tub and poolside snack service, and a beach activities center. Among the resort-like amenities are daily maid service; concierge, bell, valet, and room service; and even grocery delivery and a resident tennis pro.

50 Nohea Kai Dr., Kaanapali. ☎ *800-642-6284 or 808-667-1666. Fax: 808-661-1025. Internet:* www.kaanapali-alii.com. *Parking: Free! Rack rates: $265–$360 1-bedroom, $325–$590 2-bedroom. Three-night minimum. Deals: Phenomenal discounts are often available through Pleasant Hawaiian Holidays, so check (see "The Ins and Outs of Travel Packages" in Chapter 5). AE, MC, V.*

Kaanapali Beach Hotel

$$$ West Maui (Kaanapali)

The Kaanapali Beach is the last hotel left in Hawaii that gives you a real resort experience in this price range. It's older and not luxurious, but it boasts a genuine spirit of aloha that's absent in so many other hotels. Set beachfront around a wide, grassy lawn with a whale-shaped pool, three low-rise wings house spacious, just-upgraded rooms; still rather motel-like, they're nevertheless perfectly comfortable and feature all the conveniences, plus lanais overlooking the pretty yard or beach. Tiki torches, hula, and music create an irresistible Hawaiian ambience every evening, and the service is some of the friendliest around. An extensive Hawaiiana program goes beyond the standard hula lessons to include *lauhala* weaving, lei-making, and cultural tours. A kids' program, three restaurants, and coin-op laundry are also on site. One of my all-time favorites! *Travel & Leisure's*, too: The magazine dubbed this Hawaii's top hotel for value, and third-best hotel value in the world, in 1999.

2525 Kaanapali Pkwy., Kaanapali. ☎ *800-262-8450 or 808-661-0011. Fax: 808-667-5978. Internet:* www.kaanapalibeachhotel.com. *Self-parking: $5. Valet parking: $7. Rack rates: $170–$265 double, $215–$595 suite. Deals: Free breakfast, free car, free night, golf, and romance packages are almost always available, as well as senior (50-plus) and corporate discounts. AE, CB, DC, DISC, JCB, MC, V.*

Kahana Sunset

$$–$$$ West Maui (Kahana/Napili)

These oceanfront condos are an excellent value, one of Maui's best. The attractive wooden complex stair-steps down pretty terraced grounds to a petite but perfect white-sand-fringed swimming cove. The apartments are roomy enough to accommodate families, especially the two-bedrooms, which boast two full bathrooms. Every unit has nice island-style furniture; a complete kitchen with dishwasher, microwave, and even an icemaker on the fridge; washer/dryer; A/C and ceiling fans; VCR and sleeper sofa in the living room; and big lanais with terrific views. Nestled between the coastline and the road above, the complex is much more private than many on this condo coast. On-site are a lovely heated pool and Jacuzzi, barbecues, and beach showers. What's more, daily maid service (not a given in condos) makes it actually feel like vacation.

4909 Lower Honoapiilani Hwy., at the northern end of Kahana (8 miles north of Lahaina). ☎ *800-367-7052, 800-669-1488, or 808-669-8011. Fax: 808-669-9170. Internet:* www.kahanasunset.com *or* www.premier-hawaii.com. *Parking: Free! Rack rates: $100–$200 1-bedroom, $150–$295 2-bedroom. Three-night minimum. Deals: Car-and-condo packages, special rates, and Internet offers often available, so always mine for discounts. AE, MC, V.*

Kapalua, Napili & Kahana Accommodations & Dining

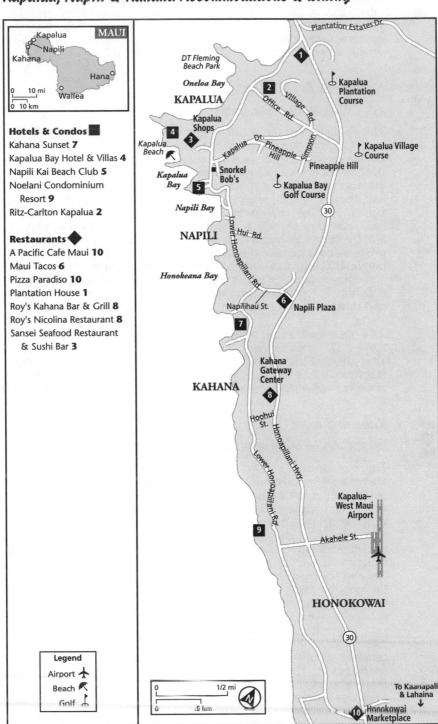

MAUI

Kapalua
Napili
Kahana
Hana
Wailea

0   10 mi
0   10 km

Hotels & Condos ■
Kahana Sunset **7**
Kapalua Bay Hotel & Villas **4**
Napili Kai Beach Club **5**
Noelani Condominium
   Resort **9**
Ritz-Carlton Kapalua **2**

Restaurants ◆
A Pacific Cafe Maui **10**
Maui Tacos **6**
Pizza Paradiso **10**
Plantation House **1**
Roy's Kahana Bar & Grill **8**
Roy's Nicolina Restaurant **8**
Sansei Seafood Restaurant
   & Sushi Bar **3**

Legend
Airport ✈
Beach 🏖
Golf ⛳

Plantation Estates Dr.

DT Fleming
Beach Park
Oneloa Bay

KAPALUA

Kapalua
Plantation
Course

Village Rd.
Office Rd.

Kapalua
Shops

*Kapalua
Beach*

Kapalua Dr.
Pineapple Hill

Kapalua Village
Course

Pineapple Hill

*Kapalua
Bay*

Snorkel
Bob's

Kapalua Bay
Golf Course

Napili Bay

30

NAPILI

Lower Hui Rd.

Lower Honoapiilani Rd.

Honokeana Bay

Napilihau St.

Napili Plaza

KAHANA

Kahana
Gateway
Center

Hoohui
St.

Honoapiilani Hwy.

Lower Honoapiilani Rd.

Kapalua–
West Maui
Airport

Akahele St.

HONOKOWAI

30

To Kaanapali
& Lahaina
↓

Honokowai
Marketplace

0   1/2 mi
0   .5 km

N

Kapalua Bay Hotel & Villas

$$$$$ Kapalua

The standard rooms are just a step above dowdy here, but a downright phenomenal setting brings loyal guests coming back for more. Sprawling over 18 oceanfront acres, the lush grounds command gorgeous views in every direction, the beach cove (named "Best in America" more than once) is virtually private and excellent for swimming, and golf and tennis facilities don't get any better. Additional facilities include two pools, a fitness center, a full-service beach activities desk, a great kids' program, and easy access to classes at the Kapalua Art School. The amenity-laden one- and two-bedroom villas — freestanding luxury homes with full kitchen, washer/dryer, and multiple lanais — make a great choice for families who have the necessary cash. Villa guests also enjoy three private pools.

1 Bay Dr., Kapalua. ☎ ***800-367-8000,*** *800-782-9488, or 808-669-5656. Fax: 808- 669-4605. Internet:* www.kapaluabayhotel.com *or* www.luxurycollection.com. *Parking: Free! Rack rates: $360–$610 double; suites and villas from $1,000. Deals: Excellent package deals often include golf, family, and romance options, so be sure to inquire. AE, CB, DC, JCB, MC, V.*

Kea Lani Hotel Suites & Villas

$$$$$ Wailea

This fanciful Moorish palace is just as pricey as Maui's other luxury resorts, but it gives you so much more for your money: namely, a giant one-bedroom suite, complete with a gorgeous living room with full entertainment center — VCRs and CD and DVD players, plus a second TV in the bedroom — a wet bar with coffeemaker and microwave; a mammoth marble bath with a soaking tub big enough for two, double sinks, separate shower, and terrific toiletries; and a furnished lanai that's ideal for an alfresco breakfast. The villas are even more luxurious, boasting a gourmet kitchen, a gas barbecue and plunge pool on the private patio, and a prime on-the-sand location. Amenities include three swimming pools and two Jacuzzis, an excellent spa (second only to the neighboring Grand Wailea's), a fitness center, a full beach activities center, a wealth of daily activities and kids' programs, and excellent dining, including one of my favorite Maui restaurants, Nick's Fishmarket (see Chapter 13). A first-rate choice on every level.

4100 Wailea Alanui Dr., Wailea. ☎ ***800-882-4100*** *or 808-875-4100. Fax: 808-875-1200. Internet:* www.kealani.com. *Parking: Free! Rack rates: $305–$615 suite; $1,450–$2,050 2- or 3-bedroom villa. Deals: Ask about Kea Lani's fifth-night-free deal, which is regularly on offer. AE, CB, DC, DISC, JCB, MC, V.*

Koa Resort

$–$$ South Maui (Kihei)

These nice condos sit right across the street from the ocean, and make a good choice for active families on tight budgets: On site are two tennis courts, a very nice swimming pool, a hot tub, and an 18-hole putting green. The spacious, privately owned one-, two-, and three-bedroom units are fully equipped and have plenty of room for even a large brood. Each comes with a full kitchen — complete with dishwasher, microwave, and coffeemaker — a large lanai, ceiling fans, and washer/dryer. The smaller units have showers only, so ask for one with a tub if it matters. Also, for maximum peace and quiet, ask for a unit removed from Kihei Road.

*811 S. Kihei Rd. (between Kulanihakoi St. and Namauu Pl.), Kihei. Reservations c/o Bello Realty (Maui Beach Homes). ☎ **800-541-3060** or 808-879-3328. Fax: 808-875-1483. Internet:* www.bellomaui.com. *Parking: Free! Rack rates: $85–$105 1-bedroom, $100–$130 2-bedroom, $135–$180 3-bedroom. No credit cards.*

Mana Kai Maui

$$ South Maui (Kihei)

Situated on a beautiful white-sand beach with excellent snorkeling, this eight-story hotel-condo hybrid is one of my favorite affordable choices. About half of the units are hotel rooms, which are smallish but offer great value. The larger apartments feature full kitchens, nice island-style furnishings, like-new kitchens and baths, and open living rooms that lead to small lanais with ocean views. All units have some age on them, but they're clean and comfortable, thanks to daily maid service. A coin-op laundry is located on each floor, a restaurant and lounge is downstairs, and a nice pool and a grassy lawn with beach chairs complement that fabulous beach. Management is friendly and conscientious. But the Mana Kai's real best-kept secret is its location: It lies on Wailea's doorstep, on the prettiest, most quiet end of Kihei, away from the strip-mall fray.

*2960 S. Kihei Rd., Kihei (just before Wailea). ☎ **800-367-5242** (800-663-2101 from Canada) or 808-879-2778. Fax: 808-879-7825. Internet:* www.crhmaui.com. *Parking: Free! Rack rates: $93–$137 double, $172–$242 1-bedroom, $213–$297 2-bedroom. Deals: Excellent car-and-condo packages usually on offer; also ask about other available specials. Discounts available on monthly stays. AE, MC, V.*

Maui Coast Hotel

$$$ South Maui (Kihei)

Newly refurbished after a $2½ million renovation, this affordable hotel is recommended for its great package deals and its central (if rather unpretty) location, about a block from the beach and a walk away from restaurants, shopping, and nightlife. This isn't the Four Seasons, however, so don't expect luxury — but the nicely freshened rooms feature good-value extras, including sitting areas, coffeemakers, mini-fridges, A/C and ceiling fans, and furnished lanais. Add room service, free use of laundry facilities, two pools (one for the kids) with poolside service, two Jacuzzis, a restaurant, and tennis courts (with lights for night play), and you end up with a full-service hotel at a bargain price. The suites offer families excellent value, especially if you can find a package to suit you.

South Maui Accommodations & Dining

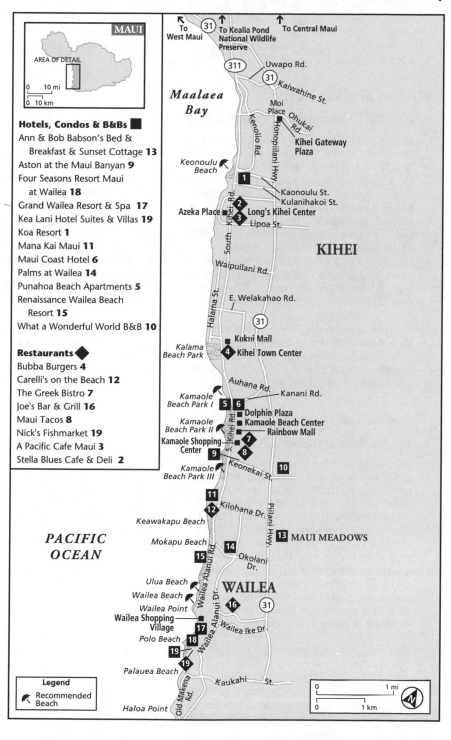

MAUI

AREA OF DETAIL

0   10 mi
0   10 km

Hotels, Condos & B&Bs ■
Ann & Bob Babson's Bed &
   Breakfast & Sunset Cottage **13**
Aston at the Maui Banyan **9**
Four Seasons Resort Maui
   at Wailea **18**
Grand Wailea Resort & Spa **17**
Kea Lani Hotel Suites & Villas **19**
Koa Resort **1**
Mana Kai Maui **11**
Maui Coast Hotel **6**
Palms at Wailea **14**
Punahoa Beach Apartments **5**
Renaissance Wailea Beach
   Resort **15**
What a Wonderful World B&B **10**

Restaurants ◆
Bubba Burgers **4**
Carelli's on the Beach **12**
The Greek Bistro **7**
Joe's Bar & Grill **16**
Maui Tacos **8**
Nick's Fishmarket **19**
A Pacific Cafe Maui **3**
Stella Blues Cafe & Deli **2**

To West Maui
31
To Kealia Pond National Wildlife Preserve
To Central Maui

Maalaea Bay

311
31
Uwapo Rd.
Kaiwahine St.
Moi Place
Ohukai Rd.
Kenolio Rd.
Homapiliani Hwy.
Kihei Gateway Plaza

Keonoulu Beach

1

Kaonoulu St.
Kulanihakoi St.
Azeka Place
South Kihei Rd.
2
3   **Long's Kihei Center**
Lipoa St.

KIHEI

Waipuilani Rd.

E. Welakahao Rd.
31
Halama St.
Kukui Mall ■
Kalama Beach Park
4   Kihei Town Center
Auhana Rd.
Kanani Rd.
Kamaole Beach Park I
5   6
Dolphin Plaza ■
Kamaole Beach Park II
Kamaole Beach Center ■
Rainbow Mall
7
Kamaole Shopping Center ■
9
8
Kamaole Beach Park III
Keonekai St.
10

PACIFIC OCEAN

11
12   Kilohana Dr.
Keawakapu Beach
Piilani Hwy.
13   **MAUI MEADOWS**
Mokapu Beach
14
Okolani Dr.
15
Ulua Beach
WAILEA
Wailea Beach
16
31
Wailea Point
Wailea Alanui Dr.
Wailea Shopping Village ■
17   Wailea Ike Dr.
Polo Beach
18
19
19
Palauea Beach
Kaukahi St.
Old Makena Rd.
Haloa Point

Legend
🏖 Recommended Beach

0   1 mi
0   1 km
N

2259 S. Kihei Rd. (at Ke Alii Alanui Dr.), Kihei. ☎ 800-426-0670, 800-895-6284, or 808-874-6284. Fax: 808-875-4731. Internet: www.westcoasthotels.com. *Parking: Free! Rack rates: $165–$215 double, $215 1-bedroom suite, $309 2-bedroom suite. Deals: Multiple extra-value packages are almost always available, including an option that gives you a room for as little as $145 (at press time), plus a free rental car or a sixth night free. AE, DC, DISC, JCB, MC, V.*

Napili Kai Beach Club

$$$–$$$$ West Maui (Kahana/Napili)

Make yourselves right at home at this terrific complex of bright one- and two-story units embracing its own, wonderful white-sand snorkeling beach. All but the handful of basic hotel rooms have top-notch kitchenettes (all with microwave, some with dishwasher), while the hotel rooms have mini-fridge and coffeemaker. Most units offer air-conditioning, but not all, so ask if you want it (you'll only need it in summer); otherwise, ceiling fans pick up the slack. The complex has a nice restaurant and bar, a beach pagoda serving daytime snacks and drinks, daily maid service, four pools and a hot tub, barbecues, a fitness room, dry cleaning as well as self-serve laundry, and two putting greens (great for practicing your tee-offs for nearby Kapalua's championship greens). There's free coffee every morning, and tea every afternoon. This place has a very loyal following, so book way in advance.

5900 Honoapiilani Rd., Napili (at the extreme north end of Napili, next to Kapalua). ☎ 800-367-5030 or 808-669-6271. Fax: 808-669-0086. Internet: www.napilikai. com. *Parking: Free! Rack rates: $185–$230 double, $200–$295 studio, $360–$435 1-bedroom suite, $535–$660 2-bedroom suite. Deals: Ask about room/car and bed-and-breakfast packages. AE, MC, V.*

Noelani Condominium Resort

$$ West Maui (Kahana/Napili)

I stand by all of my recommendations — but that doesn't mean I don't get a teensy bit nervous when my boss says she's going to take me up on one. So I was thrilled when she came home from Maui confirming my own observations — that this top-notch oceanfront condo is a stellar value and a great place to stay. All of the well-maintained apartments sport kitchens, VCRs, ceiling fans (no A/C), and spectacular ocean views; all but the studios have dishwashers and washer/dryers, too (laundry is available for studio dwellers). Best is the Antherium building, where apartments have ocean-facing lanais just 20 feet from the surf. Concierge and midweek maid service, two freshwater pools (one heated for night swimming), and an oceanfront Jacuzzi round out the good value. Next door is a sandy cove that's popular with snorkelers, but you might find yourself driving to a prettier beach; at these prices, you won't mind.

4095 Lower Honoapiilani Rd., Kahana. ☎ 800-367-6030 or 808-669-8374. Fax: 808-669-7904. Internet: www.noelani-condo-resort.com. *Rack rates: $107–$135 studio, $147–$165 1-bedroom, $197–$207 2-bedroom, $237–$267 3-bedroom. Three-night minimum (7-night minimum Dec 15–April 15). Parking: Free! Deals: Check for 5% Internet booking discount, 10% discount on monthly stays, weekly discounts for seniors and AAA members, and honeymoon specials. AE, MC, V.*

Old Wailuku Inn at Ulupono

$$–$$$ Central Maui

If you're charmed by the notion of old-time Hawaii, book into this exquisite 1920s home, located in the historic town of Wailuku. Innkeepers Tom and Janice Fairbanks have painstakingly restored the house (a cross between Craftsman and plantation style), transforming it into one of the finest inns at which I've ever had the privilege to stay. Each of the seven guest rooms is impeccably decorated with a Hawaiian heirloom quilt on the bed and top-quality everything, including an oversize luxury bathroom. Janice has used her impeccable eye to fill the home with island-style bamboo and Asian antiques. If it sounds a bit formal, don't worry: the furnishings are oversized, cushy, and invite you to kick back and make yourself at home. A wide lanai is perfect for alfresco lounging. The beach is a drive away, but the central location puts all of Maui within easy reach — plus, for those in an acquisitive mood, Wailuku is lined with antiques shops.

2199 Kahookele St. (at High St.), Wailuku. ☎ *800-305-4899 or 808-244-5897. Fax: 808-242-9600. Internet:* www.mauiinn.com. *Parking: Free! Rack rates: $120–$180 double. Rates include full gourmet breakfast. 2-night minimum. AE, DC, DISC, JCB, MC, V.*

Palms at Wailea

$$$ South Maui (Wailea)

This newly renovated villa-style apartment complex is an excellent choice if a sunny Wailea location appeals to you but you just don't want to shell out for one of those ridiculously expensive resorts. The smart, upscale complex boasts contemporary Southwestern-style buildings spread over tidy greens. The modern apartments are quality-furnished and feature all of the expected amenities, including fully outfitted kitchen, fully furnished lanai, VCR, and washer/dryer. On site is a very nice pool and hot tub, and championship Wailea golf and tennis facilities are right at hand. Daily maid service and concierge-style desk service are part of the package. Guests have easy access to excellent Ulua Beach, located just across the street.

3200 Wailea Alanui Dr., Wailea. ☎ *800-688-7444 or 808-879-5800. Fax: 808-874-3723. Internet:* www.outrigger.com. *Parking: Free! Rack rates: $215–$235 1-bedroom, $240–$275 2-bedroom. Deals: Almost nobody pays rack with Outrigger, the king of package deals. Better-than-average discounts for AAA and AARP members and seniors (50-plus), plus corporate, government, and military discounts. First night free, bed-and-breakfast, room-and-car, and other packages regularly on offer. AE, DC, DISC, JCB, MC, V.*

Plantation Inn

$$–$$$ West Maui (Lahaina)

This charming Victorian-style hotel in the heart of Lahaina offers both in-town convenience and old-fashioned romance. It's actually of 1990s vintage, but modern extras like ceiling fans and A/C, soundproofing (a plus in downtown Lahaina), VCR, fridge, and private bathroom (some with shower only) don't detract from the period appeal. Deluxe rooms have lanais, and a few have kitchenettes. No. 17 is a standout for romantics, with a writing desk and a canopy bed, while light and spacious no. 20 features a terrific kitchen and makes an excellent family suite. The inn wraps around a nice large tiled pool and deck with a hot tub. On site are coin-op laundry facilities and Gerard's, a topnotch French restaurant. The staff is excellent. You'll have to drive to a good beach, but Lahaina Harbor is a walk away (great for early-morning snorkel cruises).

174 Lahainaluna Rd. (between Wainee and Luakini sts.), Lahaina. ☎ *800-433-6815 or 808-667-9225. Fax: 808-667-9293. Internet:* www.theplantationinn.com. *Parking: Free! (A rarity in Lahaina.) Rack rates: $145–$185 double, $225 suite. Rates include continental breakfast plus. Deals: Discounts on dinner at Gerard's. Ask about 3- and 7-night honeymoon and anniversary packages. AE, CB, DC, DISC, JCB, MC, V.*

Punahoa Beach Apartments

$–$$ South Maui (Kihei)

With the best location in Kihei, this friendly little complex is a bona-fide beachfront bargain. The setting — off noisy, traffic-congested Kihei Road, on a quiet side street that faces the ocean — is fabulous: A grassy lawn extends down to the sand, where great offshore snorkeling awaits, and a popular surfing spot sits just next door. Markets and restaurants are but a stroll away. The apartments aren't fancy, but they're nicer than you'd expect for the money; each has a fully equipped kitchen and a lanai with great ocean views. There's no A/C, but at these prices, you'll live. Guests keep coming back, so reserve your bargain unit as far in advance as possible.

2142 Iliili Rd. (off S. Kihei Rd., near Kamaole Beach Park I), Kihei. ☎ *800-564-4380 or 808-879-2720. Fax: 808-875-3147. Parking: Free! Rack rates: $79–$116 studio, $98–$167 1-bedroom, $108–$161 2-bedroom. 5-night minimum. AE, MC, V.*

Ritz-Carlton Kapalua

$$$$$ West Maui (Kapalua)

Situated at the end of the road in Kapalua, the Ritz is a destination resort by default alone. But you won't need to hop in the car every day in search of fun, because everything is right at hand: a small but fabulous beach and activities galore, including Kapalua's world-class golf challenges. The natural setting is breathtaking, the rooms live up to the chain's usual high standard, the dining is excellent (especially the superb sushi bar), the amenities are extensive (including an outstanding kids' program, so bring 'em along), and the service is unsurpassed. Designed to look like a grand plantation house, the hotel is airy and graceful. On the down side, I think it's too formal for Hawaii (not the place to parade through the lobby in your cutoffs) and so sprawling that you may wear yourself out just finding your room. Still, you get what you pay for here — and, frankly, it's less overpriced than so many of Maui's resorts are these days.

1 Ritz-Carlton Dr., Kapalua. ☎ *800-241-4333 or 808-669-6200. Fax: 808-665-0026. Internet:* www.ritzcarlton.com. *Self-parking: Free! Valet parking: $10. Rack rates: $305–$575 double, suites from $550. Additional $10-per-night resort fee covers such amenities as shuttle service, use of fitness center, kids' program, and other extras. Deals: Romance, golf, and other packages often available. AE, CB, DC, DISC, JCB, MC, V.*

Sheraton Maui

$$$$$ Kaanapali

This expansive resort hotel boasts the best location on Kaanapali Beach: on a spectacular stretch of sand at the foot of Black Rock, one of Maui's best offshore snorkel spots. Much like its Kauai sister, this Sheraton is ideal for those who don't care for the forced formality or over-the-top excesses that often go hand-in-hand with resort vacations. The Sheraton Maui has an easygoing, open style; big rooms that are simple yet comfortable — and feature nice extras like mini-fridges and coffeemakers; and great facilities for families and fitness buffs, including a lagoonlike pool, a nice fitness center, and an open-air spa. A class of oversize rooms is dedicated to families. Restaurants and bars, a nightly torch-lighting and cliff-diving show, a year-round kids' program, tennis, and lots of other extras further the appeal.

2605 Kaanapali Pkwy., Kaanapali. ☎ *800-782-9488 or 808-661-0031. Fax: 808-661-0458. Internet:* www.sheraton-maui.com *or* www.sheraton.com. *Parking: $12. Rack rates: $340–$520 double, suites from $625. Deals: Promotional rates and/or package deals are almost always available, so be sure to ask. Also ask for AAA-member and senior discounts. AE, CB, DC, DISC, ER, JCB, MC, V.*

The Whaler on Kaanapali Beach

$$$ Kaanapali

Not only would I stay at this beachfront midrise condo complex again, but I'd move in here if I could. The Whaler was built in the '70s and still sports a few "Me Decade" hallmarks, but in a good way — it feels like the kind of place where Jack Lord would keep his neighbor island bachelor pad. The relaxing atmosphere starts in the clean-lined, open-air lobby and continues in the impeccably kept apartments. They're privately owned and individually decorated, but all have fully equipped kitchens, VCR, marble baths, and big, blue-tiled lanais. Many one-bedrooms have two full bathrooms, making them great for small families or shares. Most units have some kind of ocean view, but the garden views are also pleasant. Luxuries include daily maid service, plus bell and concierge services. The grounds are private and well-manicured, and on-site extras include an oceanfront pool and spa, an exercise room, and great dining and shopping at neighboring Whalers Village.

2481 Kaanapali Pkwy., Kaanapali. ☎ *800-367-7052 or 808-661-4861. Fax: 435-655-4844 or 808-661-8315. Internet:* www.the-whaler.com. *Parking: Free! Rack rates: $195–$225 studio, $245–$420 1-bedroom, $450–$550 2-bedroom. Deals: Car-and-condo packages, special rates, and Internet offers often available, so always mine for specials and off-season discounts. AE, MC, V.*

What a Wonderful World B&B

$ South Maui (Kihei)

Tucked away in a lovely, quiet subdivision, this beautifully done redwood house is one of Maui's best B&B bargains — and it's family-friendly to boot. Host Eva Tantillo has both travel agent and hotel management experience, and it shows — she knows what guests want, and provides it. You have four units to choose from, all with private bath and phone, each warmly and comfortably decorated in a contemporary style: two large one-room suites with private entrances, one with a kitchenette; and two two-room suites, one with mini-kitchen and one with complete facilities. Guests are welcome to use the barbecue, laundry facilities, and hot tub, and encouraged to take in the great views on the lanai. Privacy is a keynote, but Eva is always happy to offer guidance. Kamaole Beach Park II is a half-mile away, and a number of other excellent beaches — and dining and shopping — are within very easy reach.

2828 Umalu Pl., Kihei. ☎ ***800-943-5804*** *or 808-879-9103. Fax: 808-874-9352. Internet:* `www.thesupersites.com/wonderfulworld`*. Parking: Free! Rack rates: $69–$99 double or suite. Rates include full family-style breakfast. Deals: Wedding, honeymoon, and special-occasion packages available. AE, MC, V.*

No Room at the Resort?

Maui boasts a terrific collection of resort properties, more than I have room to discuss in detail here. The best of the bunch are reviewed earlier in this chapter, but two deserve honorary mention.

Westin Maui

$$$$–$$$$$ This hotel isn't quite as fabulous as the Grand Wailea, but it's considerably cheaper, and your kids will be in water-hog heaven here, too, thanks to an 87,000-square-foot "Aquatic Playground" complete with swim-through grottos, waterfalls, and a 128-foot water slide. Rooms are on the smallish side, but a prime stretch of Kaanapali Beach and a wealth of facilities are on hand to keep active travelers busy and happy at this fantasy resort. *2365 Kaanapali Pkwy., Kaanapali.* ☎ ***888-625-4949*** *or 808-667-2525. Internet:* `www.westinmaui.com`*.*

Renaissance Wailea Beach Resort

$$$$$ A package-deal favorite, the Renaissance is smaller and boasts more open space than most of Maui's other luxury resorts, particularly its Wailea neighbors. It makes a lovely choice for those who'd like the conveniences of a resort but prefer a more intimate setting. *3550 Wailea Alanui Dr., Wailea.* ☎ ***800-992-4532*** *or 808-879-4900. Internet:* `www.renaissancehotels.com`*.*

Home Sweet Vacation Condo

Well-developed Maui abounds with condo developments, above and beyond my favorites listed in this chapter. Many complexes aren't handled by a single management company; instead, real-estate agencies tend to handle individual rentals throughout a variety of complexes in a given area. So if you want more choices, your best bet is to contact one of the following agencies, which can match you up with the unit that meets your needs and budget.

For a complete selection of upscale condos throughout sunny, luxury-minded Wailea, reach out to **Destination Resorts Hawaii (☎ 800-367-5246** or 808-879-1595; Internet: www.destinationresortshi.com). Destination Resorts generally handles first-class properties boasting lots of deluxe amenities. Prices start as low as $150 or so for a studio, and go as high as $700 per night for a spacious three-bedroom. One of the nice things about this company is that they operate less like a real-estate agency and more like a full-service agent catering to vacationers, regularly offering car, romance, fifth night free, golf, tennis, and other money-saving packages. If you're a golfer looking for a homelike bargain, Destination Resorts can garner you a good deal of fairway-convenient space for your money.

Those of you looking for cheaper sleeps on the South Maui coast should contact **Bello Realty (☎ 800-541-3060** or 808-879-3328; Internet: www.bellomaui.com). In addition to handling the Koa Resort, one of my favorite inexpensive places to stay on Maui (listed earlier in this chapter), Bello represents affordable condos throughout the Kihei/Wailea area, with prices starting as low as $55 in the low season, $70 in the high season. I've received lots of good feedback from vacationers who've used Bello and come away with an excellent beachfront bargain and good service results, so I'm quite confident about the quality and values that Bello offers.

Condominium Rentals Hawaii (☎ 800-367-5242, 800-663-2101 from Canada, or 808-879-2778; Internet: www.crhmaui.com) also books condos throughout Kihei, and handles the **Mana Kai** (see earlier in this chapter). The car-and-condo packages and other regular specials on offer can really up the value-to-dollar ratio on their units.

Another agency worth trying is **Maui Beachfront Rentals (☎ 888-661-7200** or 808-661-3500; Internet: www.mauibeachfront.com), which can book you into a range of good apartments along West Maui's condo coast. One of their best values for budget-minded couples are the studios at the **Napili Bay,** which start at as low as $89. They might even be able to save you a few dollars on rentals at two of my favorite Kaanapali Beach condo complexes, **The Whaler** and **Kaanapali Alii** (both reviewed earlier in this chapter).

Hawaii Condo Exchange (☎ 800-442-0404 or 323-436-0300; Internet: wwte.com/condos) is a Southern California–based agency that acts as a consolidator for condo properties throughout the islands. They represent a number of properties on Maui, including some otherwise hard-to-get Kapalua villas.

Staying Off the Beaten Path

Situated at the far east end of the winding Hana Highway (Highway 36/360), isolated from the rest of the island by a three-hour drive, **Hana** makes a dreamy place to kick back and stay awhile, surrounded by little but lush natural beauty. One of Maui's most popular attractions is the drive along the winding 50-plus-mile route, one of the most beautiful scenic drives in the world. (I cover it in detail later, in Chapter 14.)

Most people drive to Hana and back again in a day, an entirely doable trip. It makes for one long day, however, as the curving highway has only one lane in each direction and 50 or so one-lane bridges. What's more, since the drive itself boasts so many wonderful stops, simply getting there can turn into an all-day event. So consider booking a place to stay at the end of the road in lush and lovely Hana for a couple of nights. It's a good idea, except for a few down sides: Many of the area's B&Bs and rentals require a two-night stay at least (sometimes longer); you'll find virtually nowhere to eat except the overpriced Hotel Hana-Maui's very mediocre dining room; and, in general, Hana accommodations are not cheap. (I advise against staying at the trouble-plagued Hana-Maui. Although this luxury resort has great bones, it's plagued by long-term neglect and unseemly high rates. Here's hoping some management company swoops in and turns the place around soon.)

If you would like to stay out in Hana, I personally recommend two places as my absolute local favorites:

✔ The **Heavenly Hana Inn** ($$–$$$$; ☎/Fax **808-248-8442**) is a gorgeous Japanese-style inn originally built in the 1950s and gut-renovated in the '90s — with no dollar or attention to detail spared. This place is utterly beautiful, luxuriously comfortable, and totally serene. Every room exhibits stunning woodwork and the impeccable taste of the innkeepers. The suites boast sitting rooms, little lanais, big baths with deep soaking tubs, and platform beds bedecked in lavish textiles and deep, cushy futons. The two outside acres are landscaped Japanese style with a bamboo fence, tiny bridges over a meandering stream, and lava-rock paths. The two-course continental breakfast is an expanded gourmet feast served kaiseki style, and elegant dinners can be prepared to order with advance notice.

✔ Another marvelous choice: the **Hana Oceanfront Cottages** ($$$; ☎ **808-248-7558**; Internet: www.hanaoceanfrontcottages.com). Housed in two brand-new plantation-style buildings built by friendly California refugees Dan and Sandi Simoni, the two one-bedroom units are fully outfitted for Hana living. Each comes complete with a living room, a fully appointed kitchen (no worrying about that pesky where-to-dine problem), brand-new, super-comfortable furniture (including beautifully made beds), a full bath, and a big lanai with ocean views. Paradise-like Hamoa Beach, East Maui's finest swimming beach, is just steps away.

Other wonderful one-of-a-kind options — too many to list here — are available in Hana and in the wonderful rural territory along the road to Hana. Additionally, some folks also like to stay in Maui's cool, misty upland, on the slopes of the sleeping volcano at Maui's core, for easy extended access to magical, barren Haleakala National Park.

Your best bet for booking one of these off-the-beaten-path stays is **Hawaii's Best Bed & Breakfasts** (☎ **800-262-9912** or 808-885-4550; Internet: www.bestbnb.com), which has a wonderful selection of B&Bs, inns, and vacation rentals that they have personally inspected and approved in all of the areas mentioned above. Hawaii's Best holds all of the property owners they represent to a very high standard, so you can be assured of quality lodgings if you book with them. All of their properties are the cream of the crop, but I particularly love **Maluhia Hale** (ma-loo-HEE-ah HA-lay)**,** which has one of the most charming cottages I've ever seen, and **Huelo Point Flower Farm,** a lush and private little Eden by the sea, both along the road to Hana. **Ekena** is an elegant 1,700-square-foot apartment on the lower level of a gorgeous country home right in Hana. On the slopes of Haleakala, consider the **Silver Cloud Ranch,** which commands some of the most glorious views on Maui, or one of their wonderful country cottages.

Bed & Breakfast Honolulu (☎ **800-288-4666** or 808-595-7533; Internet: www.hawaiibnb.com) also offers vacation rentals in Hana, in Kula on the slopes of Haleakala, and around the island.

Chapter 12

Settling in on Maui

● ●

In This Chapter

▶ Getting from the airport to your hotel without a hassle

▶ Finding your way around Maui and its major resort areas

▶ Getting weather reports, prescriptions filled, traveler's checks cashed, and more — an easy-reference list of important local contacts

● ●

*M*aui is a little more difficult to manage than the other islands — instead of uniting to circle the island, all of the major roads meet and criss-cross on the flat land between the island's two volcanoes. Still, getting around is not overly complicated; with a good map in hand, you're golden.

You'll most likely arrive at the island's centrally located main gateway, Kahului (ka-hoo-LOO-ee) Airport, in Central Maui.

Arriving at Kahului Airport

Kahului Airport (☎ 808-872-3893) is conveniently located three miles from the town of Kahului, Maui's main community, at the end of Keolani Place (just west of the intersection of Dairy Road and the Haleakala Highway). **Aloha Airlines** and **Hawaiian Airlines** provide both interisland and direct mainland service to Kahului. **American, Canadian, Delta, TWA,** and **United** all serve Kahului directly from the mainland as well. Nearly all of the island's highways are accessible just outside the airport, ready to whisk you to wherever you'll be staying.

Open-air Kahului Airport is easy to negotiate. The airport is small (and will remain so even after the announced expansion is complete), and the route from your gate to the baggage claim is clearly marked.

While almost everyone arrives at Kahului Airport, Maui does have two single-strip airports served by commercial propeller carriers — one in Kapalua, in West Maui, and another one in Hana. If you're interested in avoiding busy Kahului altogether, contact **Island Air** (☎ 800-323-3345, 800-652-6541, or 808-484-2222; Internet: www.alohaair.com) or **Pacific Wings** (☎ 888-575-4546 or 808-873-0877; Internet: www.pacificwings.com).

Maui Orientation

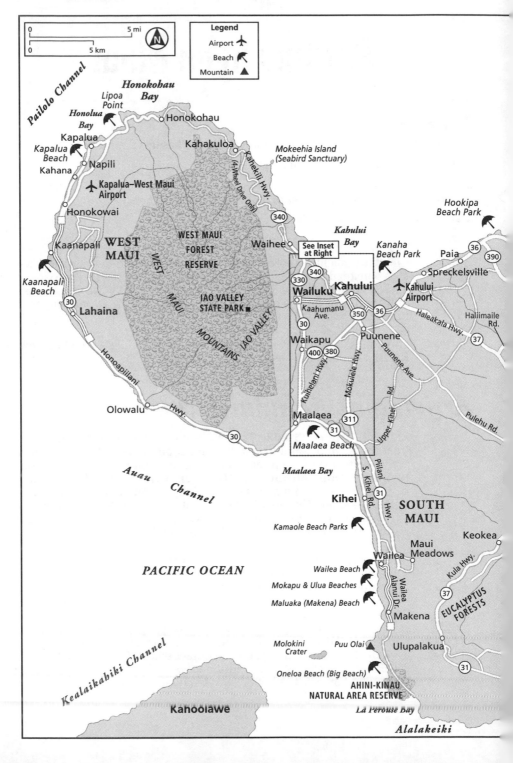

0   5 mi
0   5 km

Legend
Airport ✈
Beach 🏖
Mountain ▲

Pailolo Channel

Honokohau Bay

Lipoa Point

Honolua Bay

Honokohau

Kapalua

Kapalua Beach

Kahana

Napili

Kahakuloa

Mokeehia Island (Seabird Sanctuary)

✈ Kapalua–West Maui Airport

Honokowai

WEST MAUI

Kahekili Hwy. (4-Wheel Drive Only)

Kaanapali

WEST MAUI FOREST RESERVE

Waihee

Kahului Bay

Kanaha Beach Park

Paia

36

390

Hookipa Beach Park

Kaanapali Beach

30

Lahaina

WEST MAUI MOUNTAINS

IAO VALLEY STATE PARK ■

IAO VALLEY

See Inset at Right

340

330

Wailuku

Kahului

Kaahumanu Ave.

350

36

✈ Kahului Airport

Spreckelsville

Haleakala Hwy.

Haliimaile Rd.

37

30

Waikapu

400 380

Puunene

Kuihelani Hwy.

Mokulele Hwy.

Puunene Ave.

Upper Kihei Rd.

Pulehu Rd.

Honoapiilani Hwy.

Olowalu

30

Maalaea

311

31

Maalaea Beach

Maalaea Bay

Auau Channel

PACIFIC OCEAN

S. Kihei Rd.

Piilani Hwy.

Kihei

31

SOUTH MAUI

Keokea

Kamaole Beach Parks

Maui Meadows

Wailea

Wailea Beach

Mokapu & Ulua Beaches

Maluaka (Makena) Beach

Wailea Alanui Dr.

Kula Hwy.

37

EUCALYPTUS FORESTS

Makena

Molokini Crater

Puu Olai ▲

Ulupalakua

31

Oneloa Beach (Big Beach)

AHINI-KINAU NATURAL AREA RESERVE

Kealaikahiki Channel

Kahoolawe

La Perouse Bay

Alalakeiki

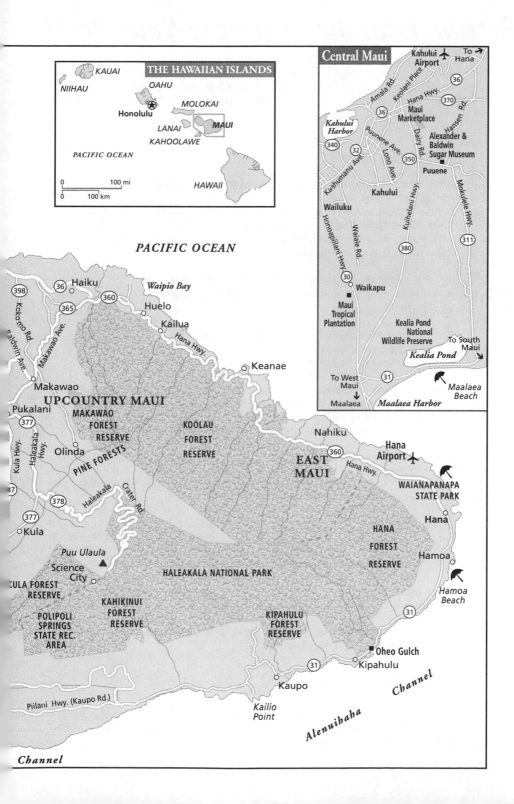

THE HAWAIIAN ISLANDS

KAUAI

NIIHAU

OAHU

MOLOKAI

Honolulu

LANAI   MAUI

KAHOOLAWE

PACIFIC OCEAN

HAWAII

0   100 mi
0   100 km

Central Maui

Kahului
Airport   To
Hana

Amala Rd.

Keolani Place

Hana Hwy.   36

370

36

Maui
Marketplace

Hansen Rd.

Kahului
Harbor   32

Puunene Ave.

Dairy Rd.

Alexander &
Baldwin
Sugar Museum

340   340

Kaahumanu Ave.

Lono Ave.

350   Puunene

Makulele Hwy.

Kuihelani Hwy.

Kahului

Wailuku

Honoapiilani Hwy.

Waiale Rd.

380   311

30   Waikapu

Maui
Tropical
Plantation

Kealia Pond
National
Wildlife Preserve   To South
Maui

To West
Maui   31   Kealia Pond

Maalaea   Maalaea Harbor   Maalaea
Beach

PACIFIC OCEAN

398   36   Haiku

365   360   Waipio Bay

Kokomo Rd.   Huelo

Baldwin Ave.   Makawao Ave.   Kailua

Hana Hwy.

Keanae

Makawao

UPCOUNTRY MAUI   KOOLAU
FOREST
RESERVE

Pukalani   MAKAWAO
FOREST
RESERVE   Nahiku

377

Kula Hwy.   Haleakala Hwy.   Olinda

PINE FORESTS   EAST
MAUI   Hana
Airport

378   Haleakala   Crater Rd.   Hana Hwy.   WAIANAPANAPA
STATE PARK

377

Kula   HANA
FOREST
RESERVE   Hana

Puu Ulaula   Hamoa

Science
City   HALEAKALA NATIONAL PARK   Hamoa
Beach

KULA FOREST
RESERVE   KAHIKINUI
FOREST
RESERVE   31

POLIPOLI
SPRINGS
STATE REC.
AREA   KIPAHULU
FOREST
RESERVE   Oheo Gulch

31   Kipahulu

Piilani Hwy. (Kaupo Rd.)   Kaupo

Kailio
Point   Channel

Alenuihaha

Channel

Getting from the Airport to Your Hotel

All of the big car-rental names have cars available at Kahului, and I suggest that you arrange for one in advance (for more on this subject, see "Arranging for Rental Cars" in Chapter 6). If you'd rather not drive yourself, I'll give you some alternative transportation options in this section.

Driving yourself

After collecting your bags from the automated carousels, step outside to the curbside rental-car pickup area at the ocean end of the terminal (to your right as you exit the building). Either go over to the counter if your rental company is represented, or wait for the appropriate shuttle van — they circle the airport at regular intervals — to take you a half-mile away to your rental-car check-out desk.

All of the rental-car agencies offer map booklets at the counter that are invaluable for getting around the island. If the agent doesn't offer one up, ask for it.

Getting from the airport to your hotel can be a bit of a trial, since Kahului is Maui's main business district and all of Maui's main highways intersect just outside the airport.

If you're heading to **West Maui,** take the Kuihelani (koo-ee-hay-LA-nee) Highway (Highway 380) to the Honoapiilani (ho-no-ah-pee-ee-LA-nee) Highway (Highway 30). The Honoapiilani Highway curves around the knob that is West Maui, leading to Lahaina, Kaanapali, Kahana, Napili, and finally Kapalua. To pick up the Kuihelani Highway, exit the airport at Keolani Place and turn left onto Dairy Road, which turns into the highway you want. Expect it to take 30 minutes to reach Lahaina, 40 minutes to reach Kaanapali, and 50 to 60 minutes to reach Kapalua, maybe a little longer if there's traffic.

If you're heading to **South Maui,** exit the airport at Keolani Place and turn left onto Dairy Road, then left onto Puunene (poo-oo-NAY-nay) Avenue (Highway 350), which takes you immediately to the Mokulele (mow-koo-LAY-lay) Highway (Highway 311), which leads directly south. Just north of Kihei, the Mokulele ends; you can choose to continue on the highway — now called Piilani (pee-ee-LA-nee) Highway (Highway 31) — which will take you through Kihei and to Wailea along the speediest route, with frequent exits along the way. If you're staying at the north end of Kihei, though, exit the Mokulele Highway onto South Kihei Road, Kihei's main drag.

Taking a taxi

As long as you arrive before 10 p.m., you won't need to arrange for a taxi to pick you up at the airport before you leave home; just go out to the well-marked curbside area and pick up the next available one.

If you want to arrange for pickup ahead of time, call **Maui Airport Taxi** (☎ 808-877-0907), **Kihei Taxi** (☎ 808-879-3000), or **Wailea Taxi** (☎ 808-874-5000). Expect to pay $45 to $60 depending on your West Maui destination, and about $26 to $32 to the Kihei/Wailea area. Don't forget to tack on a 10 to 15 percent tip, of course.

Catching a shuttle ride

If you're not renting a car, the cheapest way to get to your hotel is via airport shuttle. **SpeediShuttle** (☎ 808-875-8070 or 808-661-6667; Internet: www.speedishuttle.com) can take you between Kahului Airport and any of the Maui resort areas between 4:45 a.m. and 11:30 p.m. daily. Rates vary depending on your destination and the number of people riding with you, but figure on about $24 for two to Wailea, $36 for two to Kaanapali, and about $50 to Kapalua. You can either set up your airport pickup in advance or use the courtesy phone in baggage claim to summon a van (dial 65). Call at least 24 hours before your departure flight to arrange pickup.

If you're arriving between 10 a.m. and 4 p.m. and staying in the Lahaina-Kaanapali area, take the **Trans Hawaiian Maui Airporter Shuttle** (☎ 800-231-6984, 800-533-8765, or 808-877-7308; Internet: www.transhawaiian.com), which runs every half-hour. The per-person cost is $13 one way, $19 round-trip. No reservations are necessary; just look for the white vans that stay outside baggage claim. Book your return trip to the airport at least 48 hours in advance.

You'll find a $2-off coupon on round-trip airport shuttle service at www.transhawaiian.com. Print it out and present it to the driver upon boarding.

Getting around Maui

To really see the Valley Island, you have to drive it yourself. Maui has only a handful of major roads, but they all meet in a complicated web in the center of the island, and untangling them can take some effort. Be sure to study a good island map and know exactly where you're going before you set out.

Navigating your rental car around the valley isle

If you get in trouble on Maui's highways and you don't have your cell-phone with you, look for the flashing blue strobe lights on 12-foot poles; at the base are emergency call boxes (programmed to dial 911 as soon as you pick up the handset).

Starting out in Central Maui

Kahului, in Central Maui, is where the major airport is, and where you'll arrive. Kahului isn't a vacation destination, but a real town with Wal-Marts, car lots, malls, and so on. Still, you will occasionally find yourself in Kahului as you head to other areas of the island because this is where Maui's highways intersect.

Kahului's main drag is **Kaahumanu** (ka-ah-hoo-MA-noo) **Avenue** (Highway 32). If you're heading to the town of Wailuku, either for some antiquing or to visit Iao Valley (see Chapter 14), just follow Kaahumanu Avenue west for about 10 minutes and — *voila* — you're there.

Reaching the West and South Maui resorts

If you're heading to any of Maui's beach resort areas, either in West Maui or South Maui, you first have to head south through the Central Maui corridor (often referred to as Maui's "neck").

To reach West Maui, you take the **Kuihelani Highway** (Highway 380) south from Kahului to the **Honoapiilani Highway** (Highway 30). The Honapiilani Highway actually starts in Wailuku (it meets up with the end of Kaahumanu Avenue to make a neat inverted "L" there) and runs directly south to Maalaea (mah-LAY-ah), a windy harborfront village at the south end of Central Maui — where you may be picking up a snorkel cruise to Molokini or visiting the state-of-the-art Maui Ocean Center aquarium (see Chapter 14 for details). Past Maalaea, the south-bound Honoapiilani Highway begins to follow the curve of the land, turning abruptly west and north along the coast toward Lahaina.

All of West Maui's resort communities lie directly off the Honoapiilani Highway on the ocean side of the road. As you go from south to north, you'll first reach the old whaling town of Lahaina; then Kaanapali, Hawaii's first master-planned beach resort; then two quiet beachfront condo communities, Kahana and Napili; and, at the end of the road, the Kapalua resort, a stunning manicured beauty. It's about a half-hour of easy highway driving from Lahaina to Kapalua. You were most likely introduced to these communities when you were choosing a place to stay; for further details, see "Choosing Your Location" in Chapter 11.

Be extra-alert as you drive the Honoapiilani Highway (Highway 30), since the road is rather winding and drivers who spot whales in the channel between Maui and Lanai sometimes slam on the brakes in awe, precipitating tie-ups and accidents.

From Kahului, it's basically a straight shot to South Maui, the island's hottest, driest, and sunniest resort coast. The **Mokulele Highway** (Highway 311) heads straight south across the Central Maui corridor from Kahului to the north end of Kihei, west of the Kuihelani Highway, Highway 380.

At the end of the Mokulele Highway, you have two choices: You can either pick up South Kihei Road, Kihei's main drag, which is what you should do if you're heading to a destination in the north portion of

Kihei or if you're looking for a supermarket or gas station. If you're on your way to the southern portion of Kihei — to Wailea for a round of golf, or to Makena, farther south, to hang out on a quiet beach or go snorkeling — stick to the right as the Mokulele ends and pick up the **Piilani Highway** (Highway 31), which continues south to Wailea. Near the end of the Piilani Highway, you'll veer right onto the coastal road to reach the Wailea resorts or Makena.

The Mokulele Highway (Highway 311) is often the scene of crashes involving intoxicated and speeding drivers, so be extra careful.

If you're traveling from South Maui to West Maui, or vice versa, there's no need to travel all the way back to Kahului to pick up the appropriate road. **Highway 310** (North Kihei Road) connects the Mokulele Highway (Highway 311, the road to South Maui) to the Honoapiilani Highway (Highway 30, the road to West Maui), running east–west at the south end of Maui's "neck."

Going Upcountry and to East Maui

The giant volcanic crater that dominates the main body of the island is Haleakala (ha-lay-ah-KA-la), officially preserved as Haleakala National Park. It's only about 38 miles from Kahului to the summit of Haleakala, but the drive takes about 1½ hours because of its curving nature and steep ascent (to about 10,000 feet). The drive, natch, is called the **Haleakala Highway,** which is Highway 37 as it passes through open flatlands, past turnoffs for groovy rural towns like Haliimaile (home to a great restaurant; see Chapter 13) and Makawao (a charming shopping stop). Then, just past Makawao Avenue, the Haleakala Highway becomes Highway 377 — so be sure to take the turn for it. After you pass through the little town of Kula, turn onto **Haleakala Crater Road** (Highway 378), which will deliver you to the summit.

If you don't take the Haleakala Crater Road turnoff, you'll continue south on Highway 377, which soon connects up with Highway 37 again, here called the **Kula Highway.** If you stay on this road, it will eventually take you all the way to Hana, the small, isolated town at the east end of the island.

But the more popular route to Hana is the **Hana Highway** (Highway 360), which hugs the north cliffs of Maui for about 52 miles east of Kahului. The Heavenly Road to Hana, as it's often called, is a winding drive that borders on treacherous in each direction, crossing more than 50 one-lane bridges in the process. Still, it's one of the most spectacular scenic drives you'll ever take in your life. I'll guide you through it, mile by mile, in Chapter 14. Even if you don't head all the way to Hana, consider making a visit to charming Paia (pa-EE-ah), a hip little surf town about 10 minutes east of Kahului that has two main draws: some hip and artsy boutiquing, and the best windsurfing beach in the world, Hookipa Beach Park, which I discuss in Chapter 14.

From Kahului to Haleakala

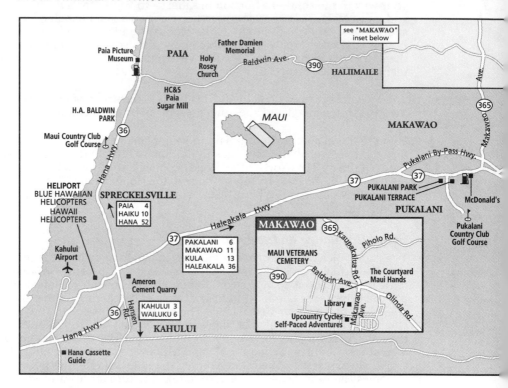

I discuss the south route to Hana — which is officially Highway 31, but most folks call it the **Kaupo** (COW-po) **Road** — in further detail in Chapter 14, but some warnings about it bear repeating here, too. While the road has been considerably improved in recent years, it's still a risky route. Before you set out on it, check with your hotel regarding current road conditions. It's usually fine if the weather has been clear — but stay away if it's been raining, as unpaved sections of the road can wash out. And check with your rental-car company before you set out; many rental contracts actually *forbid* customers from driving their car on Kaupo Road — so if you get stuck, the cost for the tow will be your responsibility.

Getting around without wheels

Your options are limited if you're not going to rent a car, as the island has no islandwide public transportation system.

Maui does have islandwide taxi service. The meter can run up fast, but a taxi will get you where you need to go if you don't have your own wheels. Call **Alii Taxi** (☎ **808-661-3688** or 808-667-2605), **Kihei Taxi** (☎ **808-879-3000**), or **Wailea Taxi** (☎ **808-874-5000**).

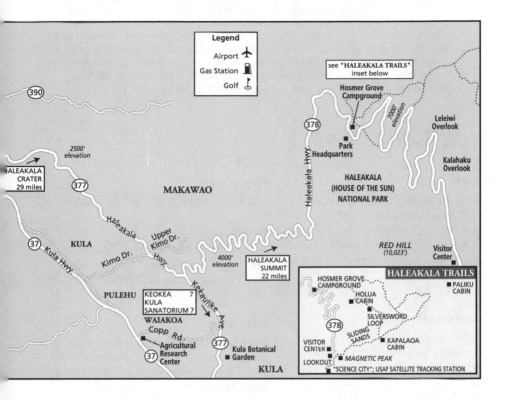

If you're going to go wheel-free on Maui, a good bet is to base yourself in Lahaina, since restaurants, shops, and attractions are right at hand. Your beach enjoyment will be limited, though; while Lahaina does have a beach, it's not the greatest.

A Kaanapali base may be the best choice for auto-free visitors — the beach is excellent here, and restaurants and shops are right at hand in Whaler's Village. A free resort shuttle connects hotels, golf, and other attractions within the resort, but most of Kaanapali's attractions are within walking distance of one another. What's more, the **West Maui Shopping Express** trolley can shuttle you between Kaanapali and Lahaina daily between about 9:30 a.m. and 10:30 p.m.; the fare is $1 per person each way. Select shuttles run north of Kaanapali, all the way to Kapalua, for $2. The same company also runs shuttle service between Whaler's Village and the Maui Ocean Center Aquarium in Maalaea as well as select points in South Maui aboard the **Whaler's Village Maui Ocean Center Trolley.** For details on both services, call ☎ **808-877-7308,** or point your Web browser to www.transhawaiian.com/shopmaui.htm.

Kapalua and Wailea also have local resort shuttles that you can rely upon to transport you between destinations within the resort — to the golf course, to local restaurants, and to resort shops. This is, however, another very limited option.

If you're coming to Maui and not renting a car, ultimately your best bet may be to call the concierge at the hotel at which you'll be staying before you leave home. He'll be able to give you a clear heads-up on how convenient the hotel or resort is to nearby restaurants, shopping, and the beach, as well as what kinds of transport are readily available for you to get to other destinations on the island. Also see the section in Chapter 14 called "Sightseeing with a Guide," which will fill you in on bus tours that can pick you up and drop you off at your hotel.

Quick Concierge

American Express

Two offices are located on Maui: one in Kaanapali at the **Westin Maui,** 2365 Kaanapali Pkwy. (☎ 808-661-7155), open daily 8 a.m. to 6 p.m.; and in South Maui at the **Grand Wailea Resort & Spa,** 3850 Wailea Alanui Dr., Wailea (☎ 808-875-4526), open daily 7 a.m. to 6 p.m.

Baby-Sitters & Baby Stuff

Any hotel or condo should be able to refer you to a reliable baby-sitter with a proven track record. If yours can't, contact **Happy Kids** (☎ 808-667-5437) or the **Nanny Connection** (☎ 808-875-4777). **Baby's Away** (☎ 800-942-9030; Internet: www.babysaway.com) rents cribs, strollers, highchairs, playpens, infant seats, and the like; they'll deliver whatever you need to wherever you're staying, and pick it up when you're done.

Doctors

West Maui Healthcare Center, Whaler's Village, 2435 Kaanapali Pkwy., second floor, Kaanapali (☎ 808-667-9721), takes walk-ins daily from 8 a.m. to 8 p.m. In South Maui, walk-in care is available from **Urgent Care Maui,** 1325 S. Kihei Rd. (at Lipoa Street, across from Star Market), Kihei (☎ 808-879-7781), which is open daily from 6 a.m. to midnight. If you need medical attention while you're out in Hana, contact the **Hana Community Health Center,** 4590 Hana Hwy. (☎ 808-248-8294).

Emergencies

Dial **911** from any phone, just like back home.

Hospitals

Around the clock emergency care is available from **Maui Memorial Hospital,** 221 Mahalani St., Wailuku (☎ 808-244-9056), in Central Maui.

Information

The Maui Visitors Bureau is located in Central Maui at 1727 Wili Pa Loop, Wailuku, HI 96793 (☎ 800-525-6284 or 808-244-3530; Internet: www.visitmaui.com). Call before you leave home to order the free *Maui: The Magic Isles* travel planner, or check the Web site for a wealth of good information. Some of Maui's resort areas have dedicated visitor associations that provide information, including the **Kaanapali Beach Resort Association** (☎ 800-245-9229 or 808-661-3271; Internet: www.maui.net/~kbra) and the **Kapalua Resort** (☎ 800-KAPALUA or 808-669-0244; Internet: www.kapaluamaui.com).

Once you land at Kahului Airport, stop over at the state-operated **Visitor Information Center** while you're waiting for your baggage and pick up a copy of *This Week Maui, 101 Things to Do on Maui,* and other free tourist publications. If you forget, don't worry — you'll find them at malls and shopping centers around the island.

In addition, all of the big resort hotels are overflowing with printed info. Even if your hotel or condo doesn't have a dedicated concierge, they should be happy to point you in the right direction, make recommendations, and give advice.

Newspapers/Magazines

The *Maui News* (www.mauinews.com) is the island's daily paper; the Web site can provide you with a great source of information before you leave home. Additionally, a number of free newspaper weeklies, such as *Maui Time* and *Maui Outdoor Adventures,* are available from racks around town.

Pharmacies

Long's Drugs, Hawaii's biggest drugstore chain, has a branch in Central Maui at 100 E. Kaahumanu Ave. (between Wharf Street and Puunene Avenue), Kahului (☎ 808-877-0041). If you're in West Maui, head to the branch at **Lahaina Cannery Mall,** 1221 Honoapiilani Hwy. (between Kapunkea and Kenui streets), Lahaina (☎ 808-667-4384). In South Maui, head to **Long's Kihei Center,** 1215 S. Kihei Rd. (just north of Lipoa Street), Kihei (☎ 808-879-2259).

Police

Maui's main headquarters are in Wailuku at 55 Mahalani St., near Maui Memorial Hospital (☎ 808-244-6400). District stations are located next to the Lahaina Civic Center, 1760 Honoapiilani Hwy., on the mountain side of the highway, just north of Lahaina (☎ 808-661-4441); and in Hana on the Hana Highway, near Ua Kea Road (☎ 808-248-8311). Of course, if you have an emergency, dial **911** from any phone.

Post Offices

In West Maui, a big branch office is next to the Lahaina Civic Center at 1760 Honoapiilani Hwy. between Kaanapali and Lahaina (on the mountain side of the highway; it's easy to spot); and in downtown Lahaina adjacent to the Lahaina Shopping Center, 132 Papalaua St. (between Front and Wainee streets). In South Maui, you'll find a post office at 1254 S. Kihei Rd., across the street from Long's Kihei Center. Satellite post offices are located around the island; to find the one nearest you, call ☎ 800-275-8777 or visit new.usps.com.

Taxes

Hawaii's sales tax is 4 percent. Expect taxes of about 11.42 percent to be added to your hotel bill.

Taxis

Call Kihei Taxi (☎ 808-879-3000), Wailea Taxi (☎ 808-874-5000), Alii Taxi (☎ 808-661-3688 or 808-667-2605), or Maui Airport Taxi (☎ 808-877-0907).

Weather & Surf Reports

For Maui's current weather and forecasts, call ☎ 808-871-5054 or 808-877-5111; the former number also offers sunrise times, and the latter number supplies forecasts for Molokai and Lanai. For marine conditions, dial ☎ 808-877-3477; for wind and surf reports, call ☎ 808-877-3611.

Chapter 13

Dining on Maui

● ●

In This Chapter

▶ Choosing among Maui's best restaurants, with complete reviews and all the details

▶ Finding the state's finest luaus if you're in the hula mood

● ●

Maui's dining scene is excellent — maybe even better than Oahu's in overall scope and innovation (although that island boasts the state's two finest restaurants; see Chapter 9). The lovely and charismatic Valley Isle has attracted so many top chefs from around the globe that choosing among their outposts can be a trying business.

Be prepared to pay for the privilege of dining on Maui, however, because restaurants on this island are *expensive*. Generally speaking, you can expect to spend more for dinner here than you will on the other islands. Maui is overflowing with restaurants, so choice isn't a problem — but you'll have to navigate a minefield of overpriced, mediocre-quality restaurants in order to get value for your dollar. The listings in this chapter offer a recommendable course of action, whether you're looking for a splurge-worthy special-occasion restaurant or a satisfying casual meal that relieves the pressure on your wallet.

Lahaina, on Maui's west shore, is the heart of the island's dining scene. Luckily, it's quite convenient — no more than a half-hour's drive or so from any of the beach resorts (45 minutes from Wailea). Many of its restaurants — even the affordable ones — boast front-row, on-the-water seats for spectacular sunset-watching. Nowhere is the minefield of mediocrity more explosive, though, so choose carefully.

Maui's Best Restaurants

In the restaurant listings that follow, each restaurant name is followed by a number of dollar signs, ranging from one ($) to five ($$$$$). The dollar signs are meant to give you an idea of what a complete dinner for one person — with appetizer, main course, a drink, tax, and tip — is likely to cost. The price categories go like this:

Maui's Best Restaurants

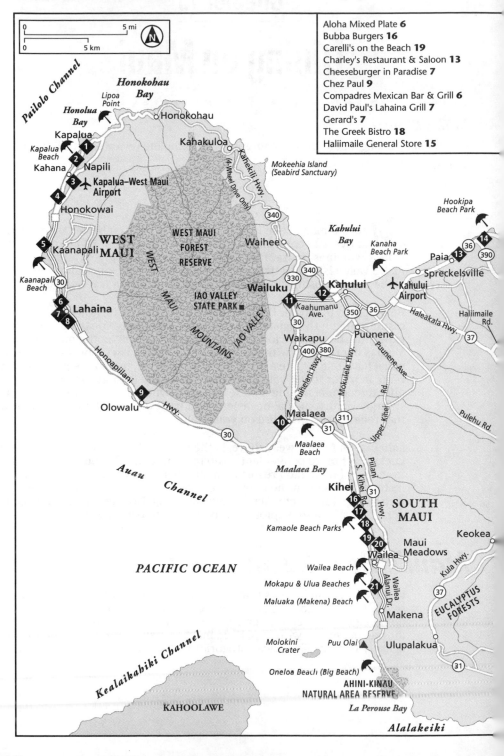

Aloha Mixed Plate **6**
Bubba Burgers **16**
Carelli's on the Beach **19**
Charley's Restaurant & Saloon **13**
Cheeseburger in Paradise **7**
Chez Paul **9**
Compadres Mexican Bar & Grill **6**
David Paul's Lahaina Grill **7**
Gerard's **7**
The Greek Bistro **18**
Haliimaile General Store **15**

Hana Ranch Restaurant **25**
Hard Rock Cafe Maui **7**
Hotel Hana-Maui Main Dining Room **24**
Hula Grill **5**
I'o **8**
Joe's Bar & Grill **20**
Kimo's **7**
Kula Lodge & Restaurant **22**
Kula Sandalwoods Restaurant **23**
Lahaina Coolers **7**
Leilani's on the Beach/Beachside Grill **5**
The Maalaea Waterfront Restaurant **10**
Mama's Fish House **14**
Maui Tacos **2**, **7**, **12** & **17**
Nick's Fishmarket **21**

A Pacific Cafe Maui **4** & **16**
Pacific'o **8**
Pizza Paradiso **4** & **5**
The Plantation House **1**
Roy's Kahana Bar & Grill/Roy's
    Nicolina Restaurant **3**
A Saigon Cafe **11**
Sansei Seafood Restaurant & Sushi Bar **1**
Stella Blues Cafe & Deli **16**
Woody's Island Grill **7**

Luaus
The Feast at Lele **8**
Maui Marriott Luau **5**
Old Lahaina Luau **6**

For detailed locations, see the following maps:
"Kapalua, Napili & Kahana Accommodations & Dining" in Chapter 11
"Lahaina Restaurants" later in this chapter
"South Maui Accommodations & Dining" in Chapter 11

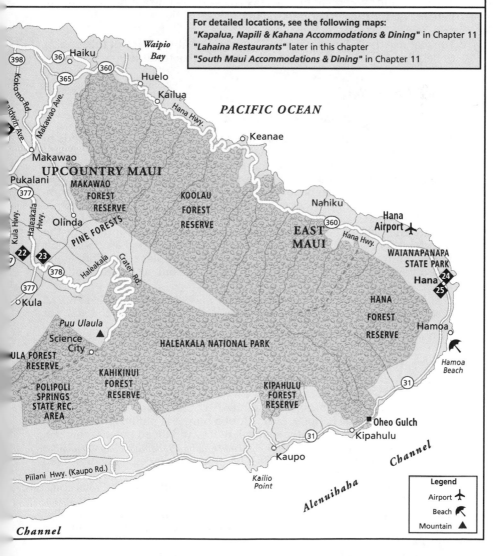

$	Cheap eats — less than $15 per person
$$	Still inexpensive — $15 to $25
$$$	Moderate — $25 to $40
$$$$	Pricey — $40 to $70
$$$$$	Ultra-expensive — more than $70 per person

Of course, it all depends on how you order, so stay away from the surf and turf or the north end of the wine list if you're watching your wallet. To give you a further idea of how much you can expect to spend, I've also included the price range of main courses in the listings. (Prices can change at any time, of course, but restaurants usually don't raise their prices by more than a dollar or two at any given time.)

The state adds 4 percent in sales tax to every restaurant bill. A 15 to 20 percent tip for the server is standard.

You can use the "Menus & Venues" worksheet at the back of this book to help keep track of the places where you'd like to dine.

Aloha Mixed Plate

$ West Maui (Lahaina) Hawaii Local

This charming, cheap patio restaurant specializes in traditional foods of Hawaii: great saimin (ramen noodle soup), teriyaki chicken, finger-lickin' Korean-style barbecue ribs, coconut shrimp, mahimahi sandwiches, stir-frys, and other local staples, plus burgers (both garden and beef). Most dishes are served as complete meals (a style called "plate lunch"), accompanied by "two scoop" rice and a scoop of macaroni salad for a sumo-sized starchfest, making them a real bargain in the process. Brought to you by the people behind the Old Lahaina Luau (the top luau in the islands), this colorful place serves up the best local food around. Don't expect gourmet — this is Hawaii's version of paper-plate eats. Still, Aloha Mixed Plate offers real value — and in an oceanfront setting to boot!

1285 Front St. (across from Lahaina Cannery Mall), Lahaina. ☎ 808-661-3322. Reservations not necessary. Main courses: $5–$10. MC, V. Open: Lunch and dinner daily.

Bubba Burgers

$ South Maui (Kihei) American

Kauai's favorite burger joint opened its first Maui outpost in 2000, and Mauians couldn't be happier. Every Bubba burger is plump and juicy and served on a toasted bun with mustard, relish, and diced onions; chicken, ginger-teriyaki tempeh, and fish burgers are also available, plus variations on the standard Bubba: the Slopper (served open-faced and smothered in Budweiser chili), the three-patty Big Bubba, and the Hubba Bubba (with a scoop of rice *and* a hot dog, all awash in chili and onions). Folks come for Bubba's quick wit as much as the food: "We cheat tourists, drunks, and attorneys." "We relish your buns." (You get the picture.) Still, the killer burgers never disappoint. Bubba serves up a mean pile of fries, too.

In Kalama Village, 1945 S. Kihei Rd. (at Auhana Rd., across from Kalama Beach Park), Kihei. ☎ 808-891-2600. Internet: www.bubbaburger.com. *Open: Lunch and dinner (to 9 p.m.) daily. Burgers: $2.50–$6. MC, V.*

Carelli's on the Beach

$$/$$$$ South Maui (Kihei)   Milanese/Neapolitan Italian

Some call the food at this chic South Maui Italian overpriced and over-rated, and it is. (Thirty bucks for pasta? Please!) What you're really paying for is the gorgeous on-the-sand setting and stupendous sunset views — and boy, are they worth it. While the kitchen can be inconsistent, the food is generally quite pleasing; I find the *specialita'della casa* to be the most satisfying dishes, most notably the seafood-heavy cioppino and the fontina-crowned grilled veal. But my favorite way to enjoy Carelli's charms is to pull up a stool at the bar, where you can nosh on a terrific wood-fired individual pizza and take in the gorgeous views (and the stylish crowd) for a lot less.

At the Maui Oceanfront Inn, 2980 S. Kihei Rd. (at the south end of Kihei, just north of Kilohana St.), Kihei. ☎ 808-875-0001. Reservations recommended (not taken for bar seating). Pizzas: $15–$16. Main courses: $26–$38. MC, V. Open: Dinner nightly.

Charley's Restaurant & Saloon

$$ Central Maui   American/International

Before I set out on any drive to Hana, I always make time to have breakfast at Charley's. This is my favorite breakfast place on Maui, thanks to overstuffed breakfast burritos, fluffy omelets, mac-nut pancakes, and eggs Benedict with perfectly puckery hollandaise. Lunch and dinner bring burgers, kiawe-smoked ribs and marlin, calzones baked fresh to order, and a variety of vegetarian delights, from veggie lasagna to bounteous salads and stir-frys. Expect nothing in the way of ambience, but service is friendly and prices are low, making Charley's worth the half-hour drive from Kihei for an affordable and unpretentious meal, even if you're not heading to Hana. The adjacent roadhouse-style bar serves up a good selection of microbrews.

142 Hana Hwy. (at Baldwin Ave.), Paia. ☎ 808-579-9453. Reservations not taken. Main courses: $6–$11 at breakfast and lunch, $7–$17 at dinner. AE, DC, DISC, MC, V. Open: Breakfast, lunch, and dinner daily.

Cheeseburger in Paradise

$ West Maui (Lahaina) American

This oceanfront burger joint is a perennial favorite thanks to an always-lively atmosphere, consistently terrific food, and million-dollar views, all at bargain-basement prices. The second-level open-air room offers a prime view from every seat and tropical-style burgers that are first class all the way — big, juicy, served on fresh-baked buns, and guaranteed to satisfy even the most committed connoisseur. Dieters and vegetarians can opt for the excellent garden and tofu burgers, a lean chicken breast sandwich, or a meal-size salad. Two full bars boasting a festive tropical-drinks menu and lively music nightly round out the party-hearty appeal. You can even launch your day oceanside with hearty omelets, French toast, eggs Benedict, and other morning faves.

811 Front St. (oceanside near the end of Lahainaluna Rd.), Lahaina. ☎ *808-661-4855. Internet:* www.chzyburger-lahaina.com. *Reservations not taken. Main courses: $5–$11. AE, DISC, MC, V. Open: Breakfast, lunch, and dinner daily.*

Chez Paul

$$$$–$$$$$ West Maui (Lahaina) Provençal French

Boasting cozy country-style decor, luscious French cuisine that could hold its own in Paris, and career waiters who care more about your needs than tomorrow's surf report, Chez Paul is a real original in a sea of chic island hotspots. Locally grown veggies and island-water catches make copious appearances, but preparations are single-mindedly rich and classic: Witness such winning dishes as fresh local fish poached in champagne with shallots, cream, and capers; crispy duck roasted with exotic island fruits and bathed in sweet-tart pineapple juice; and a brilliant filet mignon in tricolor peppercorn sauce. Save room for dessert, because the deliciously sweet treats are as beautifully presented as they should be. Be prepared for a tab that's heftier than it needs to be — but if you're willing to pay for quality, you won't be disappointed.

On Honoapiilani Hwy., Oluwalu (4 miles south of Lahaina, on the mountain side of the highway). ☎ *808-661-3843. Reservations highly recommended. $23–$40. AE, MC, V. Open: Dinner nightly.*

Compadres Mexican Bar & Grill

$$ West Maui (Lahaina) Mexican

This big, airy, comfortable, and lively restaurant serves up high-quality South-of-the-Border fare and the best margaritas on the island. The monster menu features all of your Mexican favorites, including eight kinds of enchiladas, a half-dozen quesadillas, and four variations on the chile relleno. The fish tacos are always first rate, and you can't go wrong with the huevos rancheros at any time of day. The chips are light and greaseless, the guacamole is fresh and chunky, and the combos are big enough to satisfy even Hungryman appetites, making Compadres an excellent value in an overpriced restaurant town.

Lahaina Restaurants

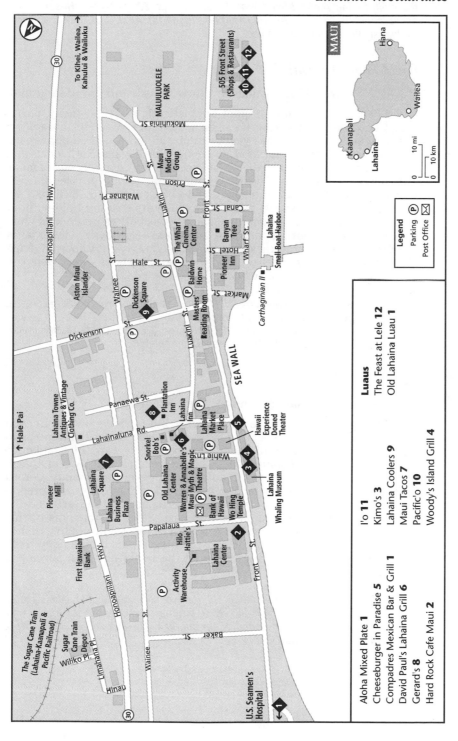

Aloha Mixed Plate **1**
Cheeseburger in Paradise **5**
Compadres Mexican Bar & Grill **1**
David Paul's Lahaina Grill **6**
Gerard's **8**
Hard Rock Cafe Maui **2**

I'o **11**
Kimo's **3**
Lahaina Coolers **9**
Maui Tacos **7**
Pacific'o **10**
Woody's Island Grill **4**

Luaus
The Feast at Lele **12**
Old Lahaina Luau **1**

In the Lahaina Cannery Mall, 1221 Honoapiilani Hwy. (on the Front Street side of the mall, facing Aloha Mixed Plate), Lahaina. ☎ 808-661-7189. Reservations accepted. Main courses: $9–$20 (most less than $15). AE, DC, JCB, MC, V. Open: Breakfast, lunch, and dinner daily.

David Paul's Lahaina Grill

$$$$–$$$$$ West Maui (Lahaina)   New American/Hawaii Regional

David Paul's is a bastion of quiet sophistication in ticky-tacky, party-hearty Lahaina. What's more, it's been named "Best Maui Restaurant" by *Honolulu* magazine for seven years running and awarded an impressive 26 (out of a possible 30) for food by dining bible Zagat's. Both locals and visitors regularly name it as their Maui favorite. It's definitely one of mine. The dining room is stylish yet delightfully homey, with pressed-tin ceilings, butter-yellow walls, original art, and a black-and-white tile floor. Chef David Paul Johnston excels at distinctive flavors that are bold without being overpowering. His signature "kalua" duck bathed in reduced plum wine sauce is rich, fork-tender, and greaseless — always a winner, as is the Kona coffee–roasted rack of lamb dressed in a light Cabernet demi-glace. The wine list is excellent, and the all-pro waitstaff offers welcome relief from Lahaina's usual surfer style.

In the Lahaina Inn, 127 Lahainaluna Rd. (1 block inland from Front Street), Lahaina. ☎ 800-360-2606 or 808-667-5117. Internet: www.davidpauls.com/maui. *Reservations highly recommended. Main courses: $26–$39. Chef's tasting menu: $85–$115. AE, DC, DISC, JCB, MC, V. Open: Dinner nightly.*

Gerard's

$$$$–$$$$$ West Maui (Lahaina)   New French

Chez Paul's has a slight edge cuisine-wise, but Gerard's boasts an even more romantic setting, especially for couples who prefer to swoon in an alfresco setting. Winner of the *Wine Spectator* Award of Excellence five years running and named "Maui's little French jewel" by *Bon Appetit* magazine, Gerard's offers refined cuisine that never disappoints. Gerard Reversade excels at seeking out the freshest local ingredients and preparing them in traditional Gallic style. My favorite among the starters is the shiitake and oyster mushrooms in puff pastry, but the foie gras terrine is a must for those who indulge. A wealth of meat and poultry dishes are at hand (including a terrific roasted quail), plus divine daily fresh fish preparations that depend on what the boats bring in. Service is appropriately attentive.

In the Plantation Inn, 174 Lahainaluna Rd. (between Wainee and Luakini streets), Lahaina. ☎ 877-661-8939 or 808-661-8939. Internet: www.gerardsmaui.com. *Reservations highly recommended. Main courses: $27–$45. AE, DC, JCB, DISC, MC, V. Open: Dinner nightly.*

The Greek Bistro

$$$ South Maui (Kihei)   Greek-Mediterranean

This pleasing indoor/outdoor restaurant offers a refreshing midpriced change of pace to the pricey French restaurants and island-style seafooders that tend to dominate Maui. The Greek menu is authentic and satisfying, and ingredients are always top quality, from the fresh veggies to the rich, crumbly feta. The yummy hummus comes with fresh-baked pita for dipping, the tabouleh is fresh and zesty with cilantro, and the phyllo-crusted spanakopita is a delectable realization of the classic spinach pie. Other consistent winners include the souvlakis, kebabs, and the Greek lasagna, chopped lamb and beef layered with cinnamon and cheeses. Dishes are generously portioned and make for great family-style sharing. Request an outside table when booking if you want one.

In Ke Nani Village, 2511 S. Kihei Rd. (across from Kamaole Beach Park II), Kihei. ☎ 808-879-9330. Reservations recommended for large parties. Main courses: $18–$25. AE, DC, DISC, JCB, MC, V. Open: Dinner nightly.

Haliimaile General Store

$$$$ Upcountry Maui   Hawaii Regional

This simple but attractive plantation-style restaurant is a great choice for those who prefer to sample top-quality island-style cooking in a refreshingly casual and pretension-free setting. Star chef Bev Gannon presents a heartier-than-average Hawaii Regional menu full of American homestyle favorites prepared with an island spin. Look for such signature satisfiers as succulent barbecued pork ribs; long-simmering coconut fish and shrimp curry; pumpkin-seed-crusted scallops accompanied by a roasted veggie enchilada in mole sauce; and New Zealand rack of lamb prepared Hunan style. The desserts are better than mom used to make; I never miss the light and tangy *lilikoi* (passion fruit) tart. Prices have crept higher than they should have, but it's still worth the 45-minute drive upcountry.

900 Haliimaile Rd., Haliimaile (ha-lee-ee-MY-lee). From the Hana Highway (Hwy. 36), take Hwy. 37 for 4½ miles to Haliimaile Rd. (Hwy. 371); turn left and drive 1½ miles to the restaurant. ☎ 808-572-2666. Reservations recommended. Main courses: $8–$15 at lunch, $18–$38 at dinner. AE, DC, DISC, MC, V. Open: Lunch Mon–Fri, dinner nightly.

Hotel Hana-Maui Main Dining Room

$$$$ East Maui   Continental-Island Fusion

This luxury resort has been passed from owner to owner and mired in the doldrums for years now — which is too bad, because it has great bones. Unfortunately, the similarly unsteady dining room is the only real restaurant in Hana, which is why I mention it here. (Nonexistent competition sets the "Best Restaurant" bar low in Hana.) The room itself is well-furnished, but one look at the beleaguered servers' uniforms tells the story: half wear bright new aloha shirts and muumuus, while the other half are stuck in last decade's overwashed wear. The island-accented fare is similarly schizophrenic — sometimes great, other times just a step above mediocre, almost always overpriced. Fine for a night, but book a stay at a place with a kitchen so you can cook for yourself during longer stays. Sandwiches, pastas, burgers, stir-frys, and the like lessen the financial and culinary risks at lunch. A kids' menu is available during the dinner hour.

In the Hotel Hana-Maui, Hana Hwy., Hana. ☎ *808-248-8211. Reservations recommended for dinner. Main courses: $10–$20 at breakfast and lunch, $22–$33 at dinner. AE, DC, MC, V. Open: Breakfast, lunch, and dinner daily.*

Hana's only other option is the more casual and affordable **Hana Ranch Restaurant** ($–$$), in town on the mountain side of Hana Highway (☎ 808-248-8255). At lunchtime, choose between the informal takeout window, serving up local fare like teriyaki chicken and hot dogs that you can enjoy at outdoor picnic tables, or the indoor all-you-can-eat lunch buffet ($10.95). The restaurant is also open for pizza on Wednesday evenings and sit-down dinner on Friday and Saturday (reservations required).

Hula Grill

$–$$$ West Maui (Kaanapali)   Steaks/Seafood (American/Hawaii Local in the Barefoot Bar)

My favorite Kaanapali restaurant features a killer on-the-beach setting and a midpriced island-style steak-and-seafood menu brought to you from Big Island star chef Peter Merriman and the people behind Waikiki's renowned Duke's Canoe Club. The tradewind-blessed patio is the ideal setting for sunset-watchers, and tiki torches make for after-dark magic. The wide-ranging menu has something for everyone, including superb wood-grilled or macadamia-crusted fresh island fish, yummy barbecued pork ribs in mango barbecue sauce, or steamed Alaskan king crab legs (with a side of top sirloin, if you like). Those on a budget can stick to the bar menu, which features Merriman's famous poke rolls (filled with seared fresh ahi), kiawe (mesquite)-fired pizzas, and creative salads and sandwiches. Hawaiian music, hula dancing at sunset, and tropical drinks dressed up with umbrellas round out the carefree island vibe. If you want a patio table, you should request one when you book.

In Whaler's Village, 2435 Kaanapali Pkwy., Kaanapali Beach. ☎ *808-667-6636. Internet:* www.hulapie.com. *Reservations recommended for dinner. Main courses: $15–$30 at dinner. Barefoot Bar menu (served all day): $7–$13. AE, DISC, MC, V. Open: Lunch and dinner daily.*

I like Hula Grill better, but sister restaurant **Leilani's on the Beach/ Beachside Grill** ($–$$$), also in Whaler's Village (☎ 808-661-4495; Internet: www.hulapie.com), makes a good choice for reliable steak-and-seafood fare and a lovely oceanfront setting. The Beachside Grill serves an affordable all-day menu similar to that at the Hula Grill's Barefoot Bar.

Going for a post-Haleakala-sunrise breakfast

Rising at o'dark thirty to drive two hours upcountry to catch the glorious sunrise from atop Haleakala crater is one of Maui's greatest pastimes (see Chapter 14). But the real treat comes after, in the form of a hearty, country-style breakfast. Happily, two wonderful breakfast stops sit at the base of the mountain, in a tiny town called Kula that you can't help but drive through on your way back to the beach.

Kula Sandalwoods Restaurant ($), on Haleakala Highway (Hwy. 377; ☎ 808-878-3523), is a family-run restaurant that starts serving home-baked pastries, omelets prepared with fresh-from-the-chicken-coop eggs and garden-fresh veggies, and eggs Benedict topped with hollandaise sauce (made from scratch) every morning at 7 a.m. All of the homestyle breakfasts and lunches are hearty and delicious. You can choose to eat in the large diner-like room, or out on the lanai if it's not too chilly.

For slightly more upscale dining, head down the road apiece to **Kula Lodge & Restaurant ($$;☎ 808-878-1535)**, whose cozy lodgelike dining room features a big stone fireplace; breakfast is served starting at 6:30 a.m. Picture windows with lush panoramic views on three sides let the outside in as you enjoy egg scrambles with bacon and sausage, French toast made with home-baked Portuguese sweetbread, and justifiably famous banana–macadamia nut pancakes.

I'o

$$$$ West Maui (Lahaina)   New Pacific

You can't get closer to the ocean than I'o's alfresco tables, some of which sit just feet from the surf (request one when you book). Overseen by award-winning chef James McDonald, I'o is a multifaceted joy, with winningly innovative fusion cuisine, first-rate service, and a top-notch, *Wine Spectator* Award of Excellence–winning wine list. The seafood-heavy menu features copious Pacific Rim accents, plus a few creative twists courtesy of the western hemisphere: The tropical seafood cocktail gets a chipotle tomatillo sauce for zest; the oysters wear star anise–accented coconut cream and Parmesan-panko crust in a pan-Asian Rockefeller; the grilled lamb tenderloin lies on a bed of wasabe-spiced mashies; and the fresh catch gets a crust of foie gras for the ultimate decadence. Each dish is paired with a recommended wine for easy ordering. Skip the silken purse appetizer, though — it's an overrated signature. A full, friendly bar makes this an all-around terrific choice.

505 Front St. (on the ocean at Shaw St.), Lahaina. ☎ *808-661-8422. Internet:* www.iomaui.com. *Reservations recommended. Main courses: $18–$30 at dinner. AC, MC, V. Open: Dinner nightly.*

If you relish the idea of an oceanfront setting but would prefer more straightforward seafood preparations, head instead to I'o's equally divine — and equally well situated — sister restaurant, **Pacific'o** ($$$$), also overseen by star chef James McDonald and located at 505 Front St. (☎ **808-667-4341**; Internet: www.pacificomaui.com), serving lunch daily as well as dinner.

Joe's Bar & Grill

$$$$ South Maui (Wailea)   New American/Hawaii Regional

I prefer Joe's over its more widely lauded sister restaurant, Haliimaile General Store. It's a little slicker than its upcountry sibling and serves a similarly pleasing menu of American home cooking with a regional twist, this time without the strong Asian influence. Top choices include the signature grilled applewood salmon, smoky and sublime; a creamy lobster and seafood pot pie with a light and flaky crust; and innovative preparations of such classics as meatloaf, rack of lamb, and center-cut pork chops. The wood-paneled room is casual and welcoming, rock 'n' roll memorabilia lines the walls (Joe Gannon managed Alice Cooper for years), and open-air views take in the tennis action below. At night, low lighting and well-spaced tables make for a surprisingly romantic ambience, and the service is top-notch.

At the Wailea Tennis Center, 131 Wailea Ike Place (between Wailea Alanui Dr. and Piilani Hwy.), Wailea. ☎ *808-875-7767. Reservations recommended. Main courses: $17–$34. AE, DC, DISC, MC, V. Open: Dinner nightly.*

Kimo's

$–$$$ West Maui (Lahaina)   Steaks/Seafood

This casual waterfront restaurant boasts a winning combination of affordable prices, good food, and great ocean views. The menu isn't quite as innovative as that of sister restaurant Hula Grill, but it still offers a reliable and satisfying selection of fresh fish preparations (a good half-dozen are available to choose from), hefty sirloins served with garlic mashed potatoes, and island favorites like koloa pork ribs with plum barbecue sauce. With Caesar salads and sides included, dinners make for a very good deal. Dessert lovers should save room for Kimo's own Hula Pie, macadamia-nut ice cream in a chocolate-wafer crust with fudge and whipped cream — a decadent island delight.

845 Front St., Lahaina. ☎ *808-661-4811. Internet:* www.hulapie.com. *Reservations recommended for dinner. Main courses: $6–$10 at lunch; $15–$24 at dinner, including Kimo's Caesar salad. Burgers at the bar (served all day) $6.50–$10. AE, MC, V. Open: Lunch and dinner daily.*

Lahaina Coolers

$$ West Maui (Lahaina)   American/Eclectic

Billing itself as "The *Cheers* of the Pacific," this lively, friendly spot serves up affordable eats at breakfast, lunch, and dinner that are a step above the standard. Despite its side-street location, this happy-hour favorite maintains an appealingly laidback tropical vibe. Start the day with an overstuffed breakfast burrito with black beans and rice or fluffy Portuguese sweet-bread french toast, lunch on one of the tropical pizzas (I love the Evil Jungle Pizza, with grilled chicken and spicy Thai peanut sauce), and finish the day with the famous fresh fish tacos or one of the homemade pastas, then follow up with $1.75 drafts and crispy calamari to munch on. The full dinner menu is served until midnight, making this a Hawaii late-night rarity.

180 Dickenson St. (between Front and Wainee streets), Lahaina. ☎ **808-661-7082.** *Main courses: $8–$18. AE, MC, V. Open: Breakfast. lunch, and dinner daily.*

The Maalaea Waterfront Restaurant

$$$$ South Maui Continental/Seafood

This decidedly unhip seafooder is a traditionalist's delight. The European-style waitstaff, which serves every dish with a professional flourish, has won the "Best Service" award from the *Maui News* for six years running, and the kitchen has topped the "Best Seafood" category three years in a row. A half-dozen fresh catches are usually on hand, and the only-at-the-Waterfront preparations include *à la meuniere;* stuffed with Alaskan king crabmeat and baked, Provençal style (sauteed with olives, peppers, and tomatoes in garlic and olive oil), and Cajun spiced. But my absolute favorite is the *en Bastille,* in which the fish is "imprisoned" (get it?) in grated potato and sauteed, then crowned with scallions, mushrooms, tomatoes, and meuniere sauce — yum! Meat and poultry are on hand for non-seafood-eaters, including a well-prepared steak Diane. The bread comes with a delectable beer cheese spread (how retro is that?), and your server will prepare your Caesar salad tableside if you ask. Book a table on the lanai before sunset for pretty harbor views.

In the Milowai Condominium, 50 Hauoli St., Maalaea (north of Kihei). ☎ **808-244-9028.** *Internet:* www.waterfrontrestaurant.net. *Reservations recommended. To get there: From Hwy. 30, take the second right into Maalaea Harbor, then turn left. Main courses: $18–$30. AE, DC, DISC, MC, V. Open: Dinner nightly.*

Mama's Fish House

$$$$$ Central Maui Seafood

Despite pay-through-the-nose prices and a touch of touristiness, Mama's is one of my favorite Hawaii restaurants. Fresh island fish simply doesn't get any better, and the tiki-room setting is an archetype of timeless Hawaii cool. The beachhouse dining room has ambience in excess, with sea breezes ruffling the tapa tablecloths and gorgeous views galore. The day's catches are the stars of the show — the menu even tells you who the winning angler was — and you choose from four preparations. My favorite is the saute of garlic butter, white wine, and capers, which lets the natural flavors of the top-notch catch shine. The service is sincere if dated ("And what will the lady have?"), but somehow it suits the mood. A lengthy list of tropical drinks (dressed with umbrellas, of course) completes the tropical-romantic picture. A kids' menu is on hand for families.

799 Poho Place, Paia (just off the Hana Highway, 1½ miles past Paia town). ☎ **808-579-8488.** *Internet:* www.mamasfishhouse.com. *Reservations highly recommended. Main courses: $13–$22 at lunch, $28–$46 at dinner. AE, DC, DISC, JCB, MC, V. Open: Lunch and dinner daily.*

Maui Tacos

$ Central Maui/West Maui (Lahaina, Napili)/South Maui (Kihei)
Island-Mexican

This growing Maui chain (which is beginning to spread to the mainland) serves up gourmet island-accented Mexican with a healthy bent in a fast-food format. All menu items are prepared using top-quality produce, lean steak, and skinless chicken; light sour cream; and vegetable oil and stocks only (no lard). Chips, beans, salsas, and guacamoles are all made fresh on the premises, making Maui Tacos a terrific choice for a quickie meal that you won't regret later. Go with one of the generously stuffed big surf burritos for maximum satisfaction — and take it to the beach for the ultimate setting.

Central Maui: In Kaahumanu Center, 275 Kaahumanu Ave., Kahului. ☎ *808-871-7726. West Maui: In Lahaina Square, 840 Wainee St. (at Lahainaluna Rd.), just off and Honoapiilani Hwy., Lahaina.* ☎ *808-661-8883. In Napili Plaza, 5095 Napilihau St. (at Honoapiilani Hwy.), Napili.* ☎ *808-665-0222. South Maui: In Kamaole Beach Center, 2411 S. Kihei Rd. (across from Kamaole Beach II), Kihei.* ☎ *808-879-5005. Internet:* www.mauitacos.com. *Main courses: $3–$8. AE, DISC, MC, V. Open: Lunch and early dinner daily.*

Nick's Fishmarket

$$$$–$$$$$ South Maui (Wailea)   Mediterranean Seafood

Wow! My favorite newcomer to the Maui dining scene is this expensive Mediterranean-accented seafooder, which gets everything just right: food, wine list, setting, and service. It's not on the beach, but the ambience is romantic to the max anyway; I prefer the vine-covered, iron furniture–dressed terrace, but the gorgeous, dimly-lit dining room doesn't disappoint, either. The on-the-simple-side preparations let the clean, fresh flavor of the top-quality seafood shine: Kona-raised lobster is perfectly steamed and shelled at your table; mahimahi is *kiawe* (mesquite)-grilled and dressed with a sweet corn relish and aged balsamic vinegar; and an elegant *opakapaka* (pink snapper) is sauteed with meaty rock shrimps and lightly dressed with lemon butter and capers. The young, elegantly dressed servers have been schooled as pros, and it shows; you'll want for nothing here. The wine list is pricey, but excellent.

In the Kea Lani Hotel & Villas, 4100 Wailea Alanui Dr., Wailea. ☎ *808-879-7224. Internet:* www.tri-star-restaurants.com. *Reservations highly recommended. Main courses: $25–$41. AE, CB, DC, DISC, JCB, MC, V. Open: Dinner nightly.*

A Pacific Cafe Maui

$$$$ South Maui (Kihei)/West Maui (Kahana)   Hawaii Regional

Like the Kauai original, this Pacific Cafe boasts an appealing atmosphere but zero view; come instead to tuck into Jean-Marie Josselin's particular brand of Hawaii Regional cuisine, which draws diners from all over the island. The excellent food is the focus; the menu changes daily, but expect a bold fusion of Asian flavors and Mediterranean techniques, multiple choices from the *kiawe* (mesquite) grill, and such signature dishes as light-as-air tiger-eye ahi tempura and garlic-sesame-crusted, pan-seared mahi — a Josselin staple, and a marvel every time. What's more, with prices soaring all over the island these days, this top-flight cuisine doesn't seem so expensive anymore.

South Maui: In Azeka Place II, 1279 S. Kihei Rd. (at the north end of Kihei, at Lipoa Rd.), Kihei. ☎ *808-879-0069. West Maui: In the Honokowai Marketplace, 3350 Honoapiilani Rd., Honokowai (south of Kahana).* ☎ *808-667-2800. Reservations highly recommended. Main courses: $22–$27; tasting menus $40–$50. DC, DISC, JCB, MC, V. Open: Dinner nightly.*

Pizza Paradiso

$ West Maui (Kahana)   Italian

This sit-down pizzeria serves up top-quality pies that manage to wow even skeptical New Yorkers (really!). In addition to a long list of create-your-own traditional toppings, Pizza Paradiso also offers a variety of theme pies, from the Maui Wowie (with ham and pineapple) to the Clam Slam (with juicy clams and tons of garlic), plus pastas; fresh, bounteous salads; and surprisingly good desserts. A terrific choice for bargain-hunting families, or anybody who needs a break from high-priced ahi for awhile. Call for free delivery if you're staying in the area.

In the Honokowai Marketplace, 3350 Honoapiilani Rd., Honokowai (south of Kahana). ☎ *808-667-2929. Full-size pizzas: $13–$23. Pastas and sandwiches: $6–$10. MC, V. Open: Lunch and dinner daily.*

Pizza Paradiso also maintains an express take-out location with counter seating in the food court at Whaler's Village, 2435 Kaanapali Pkwy., Kaanapali Beach (☎ **808-667-0333**). Free delivery is available in the Kaanapali area.

The Plantation House

$$$$ West Maui (Kapalua)   Hawaii Regional/Mediterranean

This absolutely wonderful restaurant has been around for a decade, but it's really only come into its own in the past year or so. Overlooking lux-uriant golf greens and the stunning Kapalua coastline beyond, the Plantation House may have the most glorious setting on Maui. Chef Alex Stanislaw and his team have crafted a one-of-a-kind Asian-Mediterranean fusion menu. Signature dishes include curried spinach potstickers with peanut sauce; ahi and sea bass carpaccios, pounded to paper thinness and dressed in crunchy greens and salty feta for a multitextured taste treat; and the divine Rich Forest seafood preparation, in which the fish is pressed with bread crumbs and porcini mushroom powder, sauteed, and nestled in garlic-braised spinach and mashed potatoes. Chef Alex even lends his descriptive thoughts to the impressive wine list, one of the finest on the island. Book a terrace table and come at sunset for maxi-mum enjoyment.

In the Plantation Course Clubhouse, 200 Plantation Club Dr., Kapalua. ☎ *808-669-6299. Internet:* www.theplantationhouse.com. *Reservations highly recommended for dinner. Main courses: $6–$13 at breakfast and lunch, $22–$34 at dinner. AE, DC, MC, V. Open: Breakfast, lunch, and dinner daily.*

Roy's Kahana Bar & Grill/Roy's Nicolina Restaurant

$$$–$$$$ West Maui (Kahana) Hawaii Regional

Roy Yamaguchi is the most famous name in Hawaii Regional cuisine, and his island restaurants are always terrific. There's hardly any difference between these two side-by-side siblings, which share the same executive chef and the same basic menu; Roy's Kahana has an open kitchen and a livelier atmosphere, while Roy's Nicolina is quieter, a tad more sophisticated, and boasts outdoor dining on the lanai. Thanks to an oversized menu of dim sum, appetizers, and imu-baked pizzas, it's easy to eat affordably in either dining room. The daily menu revolves around a few standards, such as sublime Szechuan baby-back ribs and blackened ahi with a delectable soy mustard butter. The service is always attentive, and Roy's well-priced private-label wines are an excellent value.

In the Kahana Gateway Shopping Center, 4405 Honoapiilani Hwy. (Hwy. 30), Kahana. **Roy's Kahana:** ☎ *808-669-6999.* **Roy's Nicolina:** ☎ *808-669-5000. Reservations highly recommended. Appetizers and pizzas: $5–$10. Main courses: $16–$28. AE, CB, DC, DISC, JCB, MC, V. Open: Dinner nightly.*

A Saigon Cafe

$$ Central Maui Vietnamese

This family-run restaurant in decidedly untouristy Wailuku serves up outstanding Vietnamese cuisine that's worth seeking out, especially if you're looking for a high-quality culinary return on your dollar. The wide-ranging menu features a dozen different soups (including a terrific lemongrass version), a complete slate of hot and cold noodle dishes, and numerous wok-cooked Vietnamese specialties starring island-grown produce and fresh-caught fish. Expect a taste sensation no matter what you order, as every authentic dish bursts with piquant flavor. Ambience is minimal, but the quality of the food, low prices, and caring service more than compensate.

1792 Main St. (between Kaniela and Nani sts.), Wailuku. To get there: Take Kaahumanu Avenue (Hwy. 32) to Main St.; it's the white building under the bridge. ☎ *808-243-9560. Reservations recommended for 4 or more. Main courses: $7–$17. MC, V. Open: Lunch and dinner daily.*

Sansei Seafood Restaurant & Sushi Bar

$$$ West Maui (Kapalua) Japanese/Pacific Rim Seafood

Sushi chef D.K. Kodama's new Honolulu outpost has crashed upon arrival — in my opinion, anyway — but his original closet-sized Kapalua location still shines brightly. Composed primarily of pan-Asian seafood dishes with multicultural touches, Sansei's winningly innovative menu has won fans around the globe; the Zagat's food bible awards it an impressive 26 out of 30 for food. Entrees are available, but I recommend assembling a family-style meal from the sushi rolls and small plates: The rock shrimp cake in ginger-lime-chili butter, topped with crispy Chinese noodles, and Thai ahi carpaccio in a red pepper–lime sauce are both standouts, but it's hard to go wrong with anything here. I love the beautifully presented flower sushi; don't miss it if you're a fishhead. Even the desserts are divine at this low-key, Japanese-style place. Book in advance so you don't miss out.

In the Shops at Kapalua, 115 Bay Dr., Kapalua. ☎ 808-669-6286. Reservations highly recommended. Sushi rolls: $4–$16. Main courses: $16–$24. AE, MC, V. Open: Dinner nightly.

Stella Blues Cafe & Deli

$–$$ South Maui (Kihei)   American

At breakfast, lunch, or dinner, this unpretentious strip-mall deli has something for everyone — vegetarians, fussy kids, and bargain-hunting travelers alike. Cozy up to the counter for a well-stuffed sandwich, which can range from egg salad to grilled chicken to a tofu wrap. At dinner, selections run the gamut from complete local-style dinners (including a pleasing lasagna) to satisfying pastas and burgers (both beef and veggie). Java hounds will find coffee drinks galore, plus a good selection of pastries to accompany the caffeine. All in all, Stella Blues is a terrific bet for those in search of a real meal deal. A kids' menu increases the dinner value for families. I recommend ignoring the unfortunate Grateful Dead theme, which is easy to overlook thanks to the quality of the eats.

In Long's Center, 1215 S. Kihei Rd. (at the north end of Kihei). ☎ 808-874-3779. Reservations not necessary. Main courses: $4–$9 at breakfast, $11–$18 at dinner. Sandwiches (served all day): $5–$9.50. DISC, MC, V. Open: Breakfast, lunch, and dinner daily.

Woody's Island Grill

$$ West Maui (Lahaina)   American-Island

Tucked away inside one of Lahaina's few top-quality aloha-wear stores, this retro-decorated surfer grill is well worth seeking out. The petite patio juts right out over the water for prime views at all hours. The menu is casual, unpretentious, and affordable, comprised largely of bounteous salads, burgers, sandwiches, and simply-grilled fish and ribs. Winners include the Chinese chicken salad, a classic accented with a trio of yummy potstickers; Cajun-spiced fish tacos; and a fine cheeseburger. This familiar cuisine isn't going to set the culinary world on fire, but everything is fresh, well-prepared, and pleasing. A full menu of creative tropical cocktails are on hand to celebrate the sunset, plus yummy fruit smoothies.

Inside Gary's Island Clothing Store, 839 Front St., Lahaina. ☎ 808-661-8788. Reservations accepted (highly recommended for sunset dining). Main courses: $8–$22. AE, MC, V. Open: Lunch and dinner daily.

Luau!

Maui is Hawaii's hands-down winner in the luau department. If you're going to attend just one, do it on this island.

Reservations are required for all of the luaus listed in this section. Make reservations as far in advance as possible — preferably before you leave home — because all of these first-rate beach parties are often fully booked a full week or more in advance (the absolute best luau in the islands — the Old Lahaina Luau — often books up two weeks in advance in high season).

Don't give up if you're trying to make last-minute plans, though; it never hurts to call and ask if a few spots have opened up. Luaus often have cancellations that allow you to slip in the back door a day or two beforehand, or even on the same day. Also, if you're booking at the last minute and you'd like more luaus to choose from, contact **Tom Barefoot's Cashback Tours** (☎ **888-222-3601;** Internet: www.tombarefoot.com), a very reliable Maui-based activities center that can hook you up with a number of other luaus on Maui, and sometimes even save you a few bucks in the process.

The Feast at Lele

This partnership between the folks behind the stellar Old Lahaina Luau (see the listing later in this section) and star chef James McDonald of I'o and Pacific'o (earlier in this chapter) is a winning new concept in luaus — and it's ideal for those who don't mind paying more for a more intimate oceanfront setting, a private table, and an excellently prepared five-course meal prepared by a culinarily lauded kitchen and served at your table over the stand-on-line all-you-can-eat buffet standard. You'll experience a lovely flower-lei greeting but no traditional imu ceremony or craft demonstrations, like at the Old Lahaina Luau, and the performance troupe is smaller, but they're held to the same exacting standards.

This feast celebrates not only Hawaii but three more Polynesian islands — Tonga, Tahiti, and Samoa. The structure here diverges from your standard luau: Each course is dedicated to an island culture — comprised of gourmet versions of foods from the native cuisine, followed by a native song and dance performance. Not only does this creative approach offer you the opportunity to sample lots of well-prepared dishes — steamed *moi* (island trout) from Hawaii; lobster, octopus, and *ogo* salad from Tonga, steamed chicken and taro leaf in coconut milk from Tahiti, and so on — but it also highlights the nuances between the unique but related Polynesian groups. What's more, since Samoa is represented, the dazzling show can both stay culturally correct and feature crowd-pleasing fire-knife dancers.

While the Feast at Lele welcomes all visitors, it tends to cater to a more sophisticated, kid-free grown-up crowd than most luaus, making it an ideal choice for romance-seeking couples or anyone wanting a more refined experience. A full wine list and tropical cocktail menu is on hand in addition to the included well cocktails, and you can expect your two dedicated servers to be friendly, knowledgeable, and attentive.

505 Front St. (on the ocean at Shaw St.), Lahaina. ☎ *808-667-5353. Internet:* www.feastatlele.com. *Times: Tues–Sat at 6 p.m. (at 5:30 p.m. Oct–Mar). Admission: $89 adults, $59 kids 2–12. Cocktails are included.*

Maui Marriott Luau

Marriott's nightly luau may not be quite the triumph that Old Lahaina's is (see the following listing), nor as innovative as the Feast at Lele (see the preceding listing), but it's fabulous fun nonetheless if you can't get into one of the other two luaus. It's a glitzy affair set beachside in Kaanapali that starts with the traditional imu ceremony (in which the night's main course, a whole roasted pig, is unearthed from its underground oven) and culminates in a full-scale, Vegas-style Polynesian revue complete with traditional hula and kid-wowing finale staring three fire-knife dancers. You're greeted with a shell lei; and, if you like, you can learn traditional craft making and play ancient island games before you line up to fill your plate from the satisfying all-you-can-eat luau spread. Take advantage of those bottomless mai tais, and you'll be doing the Hukilau (Hawaii's version of the Hokey Pokey) before you know it. Expect a rollicking good time.

At the Maui Marriott, 100 Nohea Kai Dr. (on Kaanapali Pkwy.), Kaanapali. ☎ *808-661-5828. Internet:* www.luaus.com. *Times: Nightly at 5:30 p.m. Admission: $67 adults, $27 kids 6–12, kids under 5 free. Prices include cocktails.*

Check the Web site for Internet booking discounts ($50 adults, $25 kids at press time). And call the Coconuts activity desk at ☎ **888-661-6887,** which can often offer as much as 30 percent off adult admission.

Old Lahaina Luau

Old Lahaina Luau is Hawaii's must authentic and acclaimed luau, and my absolute favorite. The oceanfront luau grounds provide a stunning setting, both the luau feast and riveting entertainment serve as a wonderful introduction to genuine island culture, and the staff exudes aloha. When you book, choose between Hawaiian-style seating, on mats and cushions set at low tables at the foot of the stage, or traditional seating, at generously proportioned common tables with comfortable wooden chairs; all tables have great views, but earlier bookings garner the best seats.

You'll be welcomed with a fresh flower lei (the yellow plumeria is the fragrant one) and greeted with a tropical cocktail. Arrive early so you'll have plenty of time to stroll the grounds — watching craftspeople at work and taking in the gorgeous views — before the imu ceremony, in which the luau pig is unearthed from the underground oven. The traditional buffet spread is excellently prepared and well labeled so you know what you're eating (although the sit-down Feast at Lele, which I describe earlier in this section, should be the choice for gourmands).

After dinner is the excellent show, which features authentic hula and traditional chants accompanied by an intelligent narrative charting the history of Hawaii from the first islanders to modern day. Don't mistake this for a deadly dull history lesson — it's compelling entertainment, and both the male and female dancers are first-rate performers (not to mention gorgeous). (Don't expect fire dancers, though, as ancient Hawaiians didn't play with fire.) It's well worth the money, and a joy from start to finish — and an excellent choice for families, groups, and couples alike.

1251 Front St. (on the ocean side of the street, across from Lahaina Cannery Mall), Lahaina. ☎ *800-248-5828 or 808-667-1998. Internet:* www.oldlahainaluau.com. *Times: Nightly at 6 p.m. (at 5:30 p.m. Oct–Mar). Admission: $69 adults, $39 kids 2–12. Prices include cocktails.*

Chapter 14

Fun On and Off the Beach

● ●

In This Chapter

▶ Locating Maui's best beaches

▶ Playing in the waves: Where to schedule dive trips, snorkel cruises, and much more

▶ Exploring Maui's top two attractions: Haleakala National Park and the Heavenly Road to Hana

▶ Discovering more great sights and activities

▶ Side-tripping to Lanai or Molokai for a bit of offbeat excitement

▶ Zeroing in on the top hunting grounds for shoppers

▶ Enjoying the lively island nightlife

● ●

*M*aui is much like a smorgasbord: Even if you have no intention of sampling everything it has to offer, you'll be wowed by the bounty of choice — and your plate is bound to be full well before you satisfy all of your cravings.

This action-packed island has something for everyone — and then some — so staying active and happy will *not* be a problem on Maui. Your biggest dilemma will likely be just trying to fit everything you want to see and do while you're here into your vacation calendar.

The Lowdown on Activity Centers

Your activities tab can really add up on Maui, especially if you have the entire family with you. A whole new cottage industry has sprung up to deal with this consumer dilemma: activity centers, which are present on all of the islands but are beyond ubiquitous on this one (especially in Lahaina, where you can barely buy an ice-cream cone without being hassled to book a snorkel cruise).

Activity centers and desks serve as middlemen in the activity-booking process. The way it works is like this: The sales reps at activity centers generally try to book you on a snorkel cruise, guided tour, sunset sail, luau, or whatever with an outfitter or activity vendor who is willing to pay them a commission for signing you up for the booking. Often, in order to entice you to book with them instead of calling an activity-provider directly, they pass on a discount on the overall ticket price — in effect, splitting their commission with you.

But there's a catch: The majority of Maui's activity centers serve as fronts for timeshare sales. Using free or heavily discounted snorkel-cruise or luau tickets as bait, they'll require you to attend a sales presentation before they hand over the savings. ("Not to buy, just to look." Yeah, *right*.) Not only will they try to sell you a Hawaii timeshare that you don't want, but — since their business is timeshares rather than activities — they're generally not the least bit interested in matching you up with the right activities for you; they'll simply book you with whomever will pay them a commission. (Many of the best activity operators, such as the Old Lahaina Luau or Trilogy Excursions, won't pay commissions to activity bookers; they're so popular that they simply don't have to.)

Do yourself a favor and avoid these hard-sell dealers altogether. Even if they can save you a few bucks on an activity, so what? You're not coming out ahead if they book you on a third-rate snorkel boat or talk you into a luau you weren't all that interested in in the first place.

But if you do need a little reliable personal assistance in making sense of Maui's wealth of activity options (or glut, depending on your perspective), you can get it. The best and most reliable activity booker on Maui is **Tom Barefoot's Cashback Tours,** in the heart of Lahaina at 834 Front St., near Lahainaluna Road (☎ **888-222-3601** or 808-661-8889; Internet: www.tombarefoot.com). This professional operation has nothing to do with timeshares — activities is their business, and their reps are pros who really know their stuff. I've always gone into the office under cover ("Hi, this is my first time in Hawaii and I've never snorkeled before but I want to go out on a cruise . . ."), and I've found the salespeoples' recommendations to be consistently good ones. Their office is filled with pictures and descriptive information on all of the activities they represent.

What's more, Tom Barefoot's offers a 10 percent discount on select activities when you pay with cash, personal check, or traveler's checks, and 7 percent if you pay by credit card. However, if you tell them that you want the top-of-the-line snorkel cruise or luau, they'll freely recommend and book you with Trilogy or Old Lahaina, even though they can't offer you a savings and won't make a dime — because they figure that a happy customer is a returning customer. You can book discounted activities before you leave home via their Web site or toll-free number.

Another highly recommendable activity booker is **Trilogy Ocean Sports,** which maintains a kiosk on Kaanapali Beach in front of the Kaanapali Beach Hotel (☎ **808-661-7789**). A sister business to Trilogy Excursions, which is universally regarded as the finest snorkel-sail operator on Maui, Trilogy Ocean Sports can book you not only onto Trilogy cruises but with other activity providers they endorse, whether you're looking for a backcountry jeep excursion or a beginning surfing lesson. They've hand-picked a top-flight group of activity providers to represent, and I've found their recommendations to be terrific.

Trilogy Ocean Sports doesn't offer discounts, so they can't save you money on activities. But they can offer you two valuable services: one-stop shopping for your activities — since they'll help you assemble an activities calendar for your stay and make all of the necessary bookings — and excellent recommendations if you're looking for an outfitter or activity provider beyond what I've recommended in the pages that follow.

Hitting the Beaches

Never leave valuables in your rental car while you're at the beach. Knowledgeable thieves like to prey on tourists, and they know how to get into your interior, trunk, and glove box in no time flat. Be especially diligent about leaving your stuff behind at your condo or in your hotel safe when you're heading off to a remote beach.

Also, if you see a red flag hoisted at any beach, don't venture into the water, as it indicates that conditions are unsafe for swimmers. Even if the waves look placid, trust the warning.

In West Maui

Honolua Bay

This sandless, smooth-rock beach doesn't have any appeal to sunbathers, but snorkelers love it for its calm, clear waters (which are protected as a marine-life conservation district), excellent coral formations, and abundance of tropical fish, especially on the west side of the bay. Despite the lack of actual beach, the setting is lovely, and it's never too crowded. In winter, stay out of the water; come instead to watch daredevil surfers ride some of the finest breaks in the islands. Sorry, no facilities.

At the northernmost end of Honoapiilani Hwy. (Hwy. 30), about 2 miles past Office Rd. (the turnoff for Kapalua); park with the other cars along the roadside and walk 200 yards to the beach.

Kapalua Beach

This gorgeous golden crescent bordered by two palm-studded points is justifiably popular for sunbathing, swimming, and snorkeling. The sandy bottom slopes gently to deep water that's so clear you can see where the gold sands turn to green, and then deep blue. Well-protected from strong winds and currents, Kapalua's calm waters are usually great for swimmers of all ages and abilities year-round, and waves come in just right for easy riding. The rocky points offer good fish-communing opportunities for both snorkelers and offshore divers. The beach is also great for offshore whale watching in winter, too. The inland side of the beach is edged by a shady path and cool lawns. Facilities include showers, restrooms, a rental shack, and outdoor showers. The small parking lot is limited to about 30 spaces, so arrive early.

On Lower Honoapiilani Rd. at the south end of Kapalua, just before the Napili Kai Beach Club. To get there: From Honoapiilani Highway, turn left just past mile marker 30, go 7/10-mile to Lower Honoapiilani Rd.; turn left and go 8/10-mile to the access point.

Maui's Best Beaches and Attractions

Legend

Airport ✈
Beach 🏄
Golf ⛳
Information ⓘ
Mountain ▲

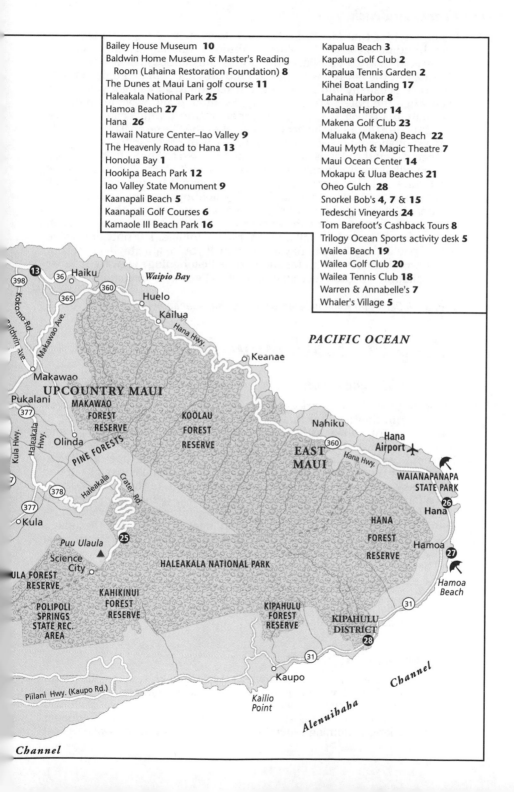

Bailey House Museum **10**
Baldwin Home Museum & Master's Reading
   Room (Lahaina Restoration Foundation) **8**
The Dunes at Maui Lani golf course **11**
Haleakala National Park **25**
Hamoa Beach **27**
Hana **26**
Hawaii Nature Center–Iao Valley **9**
The Heavenly Road to Hana **13**
Honolua Bay **1**
Hookipa Beach Park **12**
Iao Valley State Monument **9**
Kaanapali Beach **5**
Kaanapali Golf Courses **6**
Kamaole III Beach Park **16**

Kapalua Beach **3**
Kapalua Golf Club **2**
Kapalua Tennis Garden **2**
Kihei Boat Landing **17**
Lahaina Harbor **8**
Maalaea Harbor **14**
Makena Golf Club **23**
Maluaka (Makena) Beach **22**
Maui Myth & Magic Theatre **7**
Maui Ocean Center **14**
Mokapu & Ulua Beaches **21**
Oheo Gulch **28**
Snorkel Bob's **4**, **7** & **15**
Tedeschi Vineyards **24**
Tom Barefoot's Cashback Tours **8**
Trilogy Ocean Sports activity desk **5**
Wailea Beach **19**
Wailea Golf Club **20**
Wailea Tennis Club **18**
Warren & Annabelle's **7**
Whaler's Village **5**

Kaanapali Beach

It's no wonder that Maui's first resort developers chose this beach to start building on — it's absolutely fabulous. Kaanapali's four miles of grainy gold sand are now lined with hotels and condos in near Waikiki-like density, but the not-too-wide beach tends to be populated only in pockets; you can usually find an uncrowded section to spread out your towel even when the hotels are at capacity. Swimming and wave jumping are excellent, but beware the rough winter shorebreak, which can really kick up. At the north end of the beach, in front of the Sheraton, is Black Rock, the best offshore snorkel spot on Maui: The water is clear, the reef is well-protected, and the clouds of tropical fish are used to finned folks. A paved beach walk links the hotels and the open-air Whaler's Village shopping and dining complex, a great place to cure the midday munchies or tuck into a tropical cocktail. Lifeguards and beachboys from the resorts man the beach, beach-gear rental shacks are set up right on the sand, and most hotels have outdoor showers (and sometimes restrooms) you can use; restrooms are also available at Whaler's Village. The only down side is that you'll likely have to pay for parking if you're not staying here, but it'll be worth the few bucks for such prime beachgoing (a few free spaces are available, but good luck snaring one — I've never been able to).

Kaanapali Pkwy., off Honoapiilani Hwy. (Hwy. 30), Kaanapali.

Along the South Maui Coast

Kamaole III Beach Park

Three popular beach parks — Kamaole I, II, and III — face the waves across from South Kihei Road in mid-Kihei. The biggest and best is Kamaole III (or Kam-3, as the locals call it), which boasts a playground and a grassy lawn that meets the finely textured golden sand. Swimming is generally safe, but parents should make sure that little ones don't venture too far out, as the bottom slopes off quickly. Families might prefer the grassy end of the beach with shade trees, where the ocean bottom has a fairly gentle slope. Both the north and south ends have rocky fingers that are great for snorkelers, and the winter waves attract body-surfers. This west-facing beach is also an ideal spot to watch the sun go down, or look for whales offshore in winter. Facilities include restrooms, showers, picnic tables, barbecues, volleyball nets, and lifeguards. Food and beach-gear rentals are available at the malls across the street — but be careful crossing busy Kihei Road!

On S. Kihei Rd. just south of Keonekai St. (across from the Maui Parkshore and Kamaole Sands condos), Kihei.

Mokapu and Ulua Beaches

Situated at the north end of Wailea, these lovely side-by-side sister beaches boast pretty golden sand, good grassy areas for sandless picnicking, and nice facilities, including restrooms and a freshwater shower pole. The ocean bottom is shallow and gently slopes down to deeper waters, making swimming generally safe; snorkelers will find Wailea's best snorkeling at the rocky north end. When the surf kicks up, the waves are excellent for bodysurfers. Although these gems are popular with the nearby upscale condo crowd, the sand rarely gets too crowded; the parking lot is tiny, though, so come early.

On Wailea Alanui Rd. at Hale Alii Place, just south of the Renaissance Wailea (across from the Palms at Wailea condos), Wailea.

Wailea Beach

The ultra-fine gold-sand beach is big, wide, and protected on both sides by black lava points with a sandy and sloping bottom, making the clear waters excellent for swimming (and okay for snorkeling, too). The year-round waves are just right for easy board-riding or bodysurfing, but tradewinds can kick up in the afternoon, so come early. The view out to sea is gorgeous, with the islands of Kahoolawe and Lanai framing the view; this is an ideal spot to watch for humpback whales in winter. This stretch of shoreline may feel like it belongs to the ultra-deluxe resorts that line it, but it doesn't; just look for the blue "Shoreline Access" signs for easiest access. Restrooms and showers are available.

Fronting the Grand Wailea and Four Seasons resorts, Wailea. To get there: The blue "Shoreline Access" sign is between the two resorts on Wailea Alanui Dr.

Maluaka (Makena) Beach

This wonderful beach park offers a pleasing off-the-beaten-path experience for those in search of a first-rate snorkel experience, or anybody who wants a break from Maui's ever-present crowds. Short, wide, and palm-fringed, this unspoiled crescent of golden, grainy sand is set between two protective lava points and bounded by big, grassy sand dunes. Snorkelers will find surprisingly colorful coral and an impressive array of vibrantly hued reef fish at the rocky south end of beach, past the lava point. Sunbathers and casual swimmers will want to stick to the beautiful strand closer to the hotel, which is virtually empty on weekdays. Facilities include restrooms and showers.

Makena Alanui Dr., Makena (south of Wailea). To get there: Follow Wailea Alanui Dr. south through Wailea to Makena, and look for the "Shoreline Access" sign near the Maui Prince hotel; turn at the "Dead End" sign past the hotel for public access parking.

Central and East Maui

Hookipa Beach Park

Possibly the most famous windsurfing beach in the world, this small, gold-sand beach at the foot of a grassy cliff attracts top windsurfers and wave jumpers from around the globe with hard, constant winds and endless waves that result in near-perfect wave-riding conditions. Come on weekday afternoons to watch the local experts fly over the waves with their colorful sails; winter weekends host regular competitions. When the winter waves die down, snorkelers and divers explore the reef. Even then, you should be extremely careful, as these waters are rough year-round; summer mornings are best. Facilities include some rustic restrooms and showers, plus pavilions, picnic tables, and barbecues. The lower parking lot is generally reserved for windsurfers and their equipment, so park in the upper lot (see the following directions), where the high, grassy bluff offers a better perch for watching the action, anyway.

Off Hana Highway (Hwy. 36), 2 miles east of Paia, about 6 miles east of Haleakala Hwy. (Hwy. 37). To get there: Drive past the park and turn left at the entrance at the far side of the beach, at the Hookipa Lookout sign.

Hamoa Beach

This remote, half moon–shaped beach near the end of the Hana Road is one of the most breathtakingly lovely in all of Hawaii, celebrated in writing by no less than James Michener for its singular beauty. The Hotel Hana-Maui likes to maintain the beach as its own — but they have to share, so feel free to march right down the steps from the lava-rock lookout point and stake out a spot on the open sand. Even if you don't want to swim or sunbathe, come to peek at this stunner from above: You'll find surf that's the perfect color of turquoise, golden-gray sand, and luxuriant green hills serving as the postcard-perfect backdrop. The beach is generally good for swimming and wave-riding in the gentle seasons, but stick close to the shore, as this is open, unprotected ocean; it's best to stay out of the water entirely in winter. The hotel maintains minimal facilities for nonguests, including a restroom.

Off the Hana Highway (Hwy. 36), about 2½ miles past Hana town. To get there: Turn at the small white sign that says "Hamoa Beach" and go about 1½ miles to the lava-rock lookout point; you can park on the roadside or in the dirt area across the street. The stairs are just beyond the lookout point (if you reach the steep service road to the beach, you've gone too far).

Water Fun for Everyone

If your hotel or condo doesn't provide beach gear or beach toys, you won't have a problem finding a place to rent these items. In addition to top-quality snorkel gear, **Snorkel Bob's** rents boogie boards and beach chairs at its three Maui stores (see "Snorkeling," in the following section), and rental shacks on popular beaches like Kaanapali and Kapalua can rent you whatever you'll need while you're there.

You can also rent all manner of gear — from beach chairs and picnic coolers to boogie boards and surfboards to ocean kayaks — at very reasonable prices from the **Rental Warehouse,** at Duke's Surf Shop, 578 Front St. (at Prison Street), Lahaina (☎ **808-661-1970**), and in Kihei at **Rainbow Water Sports,** in Azeka Place II shopping center, 1278 S. Kihei Rd., near Lipoa Street (☎ **808-875-4050**).

Snorkeling

Maui is justifiably famous for its snorkel cruises to Molokini and Lanai (see the following section), both of which offer first-class fish spotting, some of the best in the state. But anybody who's already perused the "Hitting the Beaches" section earlier in this chapter knows that the island offers a wealth of terrific snorkel spots that are accessible from shore. Probably the best of these is Black Rock at the north end of **Kaanapali Beach;** also excellent are **Honolua Bay,** north of Kapalua; **Mokapu and Ulua Beaches,** in Wailea; and one of my lesser-known favorites, **Maluaka (Makena) Beach,** south of Wailea in Makena.

Additionally, many of the island's hotels and condo complexes sit on coves that are excellent for snorkeling. And not just the super-expensive ones; the affordable Mana Kai Maui in Kihei, for example, fronts a gem of a snorkeling area. Ask at the front desk when you check in for nearby recommendations — or even when you book, if it's really important to you.

If you want to take advantage of Maui's offshore snorkeling opportunities, you'll likely need to rent some gear. My favorite rental-gear supplier in Hawaii is **Snorkel Bob's;** they rent the best-quality gear, with friendly service and a refreshing dose of snarky good humor thrown in. Snorkel Bob's maintains three Maui locations, with two in West Maui: at 112 Front St. in Lahaina, at the north end of town near the Old Lahaina Luau (☎ **808-661-4421**); and near Kapalua in Napili Village, 5425 Lower Honapiilani Hwy. (☎ **808-669-9603**). In South Maui, you'll find Bob's at the Kamaole Beach Center at Kihei Marketplace, 2411 S. Kihei Rd., between Rainbow Mall and Dolphin Plaza (☎ **808-879-7449**).

The basic set of snorkel gear — mask, snorkel, fins — is $9 a week, but I recommend going with the deluxe package for $29 a week (reasonable daily rates are available, too). Do yourself a favor and rent the highest-quality gear — it's worth the extra bucks to get a mask that doesn't leak and a snorkel that doesn't clog. If you're nearsighted, you can rent a prescription mask that allows you to actually *see* the fish; wetsuits and life vests are also available. The shops are open daily from 8 a.m. to 5 p.m. You don't need to reserve gear in advance, but you're welcome to book your gear online at www.snorkelbob.com.

One of the best things about renting gear from Bob is that you can pick up a set of snorkel gear at the start of your trip, carry it with you as you travel throughout the islands, and then return it to another Snorkel Bob's location on Oahu, the Big Island, or Kauai. (All shops offer 24-hour gear return service.)

Any snorkel cruise or kayak outfitter will supply you with gear to use, but, as I've said before, I highly recommend renting your own set and bringing it aboard instead. Free gear is almost universally bad — and there's nothing worse than not being able to see sea turtles or other cool creatures because of a crappy mask. It's worth the extra few dollars to rent a quality mask and snorkel and fins that fit.

If, on the other hand, you'd prefer to just rent the cheapest snorkel gear you can get your hands on, head to **Rental Warehouse,** in Lahaina at Duke's Surf Shop, 578 Front St., at Prison Street (☎ **808-661-1970**), and in Kihei at **Rainbow Water Sports,** Azeka Place II, 1278 S. Kihei Rd., near Lipoa Street (☎ **808-875-4050**).

Keep these snorkel tips in mind as you don your fins and head into the water:

✔ Make mornings your offshore snorkel time on Maui, because the winds often start to kick up around noon, making surf conditions rougher and less conducive to fish-spying.

✔ Always snorkel with a friend, and keep an eye on each other.

✔ Look up every few minutes to get your bearings, check your position in relation to the shoreline, and to see if there's any boat traffic.

✔ Don't touch anything. Not only can your fingers and feet damage coral, but it can give you nasty cuts. Moreover, camouflaged fish and spiny shells may surprise you.

✔ Before you set out, check surf conditions by calling one of the local dive or snorkel shops, such as Snorkel Bob's, which can give you the latest on local conditions, and recommend alternative spots if the prime ones are too rough for snorkeling.

Ocean cruising to Molokini and Lanai — and other on-deck adventures

Maui boasts two favorite day-cruising destinations: the sunken offshore crater **Molokini,** which is hugely popular among snorkelers and divers; and the island of **Lanai,** terrific for snorkelers and sunbathers alike. (Do note, however, that only Trilogy and Paragon take their guests onshore at Lanai; other operators just anchor offshore for snorkeling in the surrounding waters.) If you're a snorkeler and you have to choose, I'd say head to Molokini first; then, if you have the time and money, follow up with a day of snorkeling around Lanai. In whale-watching season, though — from mid-December through April — go with a Lanai cruise first, as the channel that separates Maui from Lanai is a favorite hangout for wintering humpback whales.

Additionally, one cruise operator, the *Maui Princess,* offers twice-weekly sails to Maui's *other* neighboring isle, **Molokai,** for some offbeat exploring.

Dramamine or nausea-prevention wristbands are an excellent idea if you're prone to seasickness, especially aboard cruises to Lanai and Molokai. The channel is usually calm on the morning trip over but turns quite choppy as the afternoon winds kick up, often making the return trip a stomach-churning ride. A very important tip: Be sure to take the Dramamine *before* the boat gears up for the return trip to Maui. Once the return sail is under way, it's too late for the drug to do any good.

Snorkeling without getting your hair wet

There's a great way to see Maui's spectacular underwater world even if you don't swim: Take a submarine ride with **Atlantis Submarines** (☎ **800-548-6262** or **808-667-6604**; Internet: www.goatlantis.com/hawaii). From Lahaina Harbor, you'll go 125 feet beneath the surface in one of Atlantis's state-of-the-art subs to see a whole new world of sea critters, including — if you're lucky — humpback whales in season. The two-hour tours cost $79 for adults, $39 for kids (children must be at least 36 inches tall).

A word of warning: The ride is perfectly safe, but skip it if you suffer from serious claustrophobia.

Here's a way to save money on your submarine trip. At press time, you could save 7 percent (or 10 percent if you pay with a check) by booking your Atlantis submarine dive through Lahaina-based **Tom Barefoot's Cashback Tours** (☎ **888-222-3601** or **808-661-8889**; Internet: www.tombarefoot.com).

The outfitters listed in this section hardly scratch the surface of the glut of cruise operators that sail from Maui. I consider these to be the best. If you'd like additional options, contact the island's most reliable activity center, **Tom Barefoot's Cashback Tours,** which can also save you a few bucks by booking you with some of the operators I've listed, including Blue Water Rafting, Maui Classic Charters, and Paragon (at press time, at least); contact information for Tom's is listed in the section "The Lowdown on Activity Centers" earlier in this chapter. But before you book any pricey snorkel-sail trip or other ocean cruise, review the accompanying discussion of activity centers there.

All of the sail-snorkel cruises I recommend are family friendly, but Trilogy boasts the kid-friendliest crew of them all.

Blue Water Rafting

Blue Water's cruises are distinct for four reasons. First, they take small groups of guests (no more than 24) out on fast-flying, rigid-hulled inflatable boats for an exciting ride. Second, their Molokini Express cruises arrive at Molokini in between the big boats' trips, so those of you who opt for this cruise will have the perpetually overpopular crater largely to yourselves. Third, the speed and extra-maneuverability of their boats allow them to take you to South Maui's otherwise untouristed Kanaio Coast beyond Makena, where you'll visit sea caves and snorkel in pristine areas favored by sea turtles and spinner dolphins on both Kanaio-only and Molokini-combination tours. And lastly, the low-to-the-water boats put you as close as possible to said turtles and dolphins, as well as humpback whales in winter. An excellent choice for adventure-seekers in search of something different.

Cruises depart from Kihei Boat Landing, on S. Kihei Rd. just south of Kamaole III Beach Park (between Keonekai St. and Kilohana Dr.), Kihei. ☎ *808-879-7238. Internet:* www.bluewaterrafting.com. *2- to 5½-hour raft cruises: $39–$99 adults, $39–$85 kids under 12. Prices include deli lunch, plus continental breakfast on the 5½-hour tour.*

Maui Classic Charters

This company can offer you two very different kinds of Molokini snorkel-sail experiences: One aboard the *Four Winds*, a modern 53-foot, 112-person-capacity catamaran featuring a glass-bottom hull for on-ship viewing, a waterslide and three swim ladders, and barbecues; and one aboard the *Lavengro*, a 60-foot, 30-passenger schooner built in 1926 whose historic charm more than compensates for its lack of modern toys (although you will find freshwater showers and restrooms on board). A naturalist accompanies the *Four Winds'* afternoon sail-snorkel trip in whale-watching season.

Cruises depart from Maalaea Harbor (at the Hwy. 30/130 junction), Maalaea. ☎ *800-736-5740 or 808-879-8188. Internet:* www.mauicharters.com. *3½- to 6-hour Molokini cruises: $40–$72 adults, $30–$47 kids 12 and under. Prices include continental breakfast and lunch (deli-style aboard the Lavengro, barbecue aboard the Four Winds), plus beer, wine, and soda.*

Maui Princess/Lahaina Princess

The 118-foot yacht Maui Princess offers a unique day trip that's well worth planning ahead for if you're into offbeat adventures: A sail to the funky, little-touristed island of Molokai, often called the most Hawaiian island both for its number of native Hawaiian residents and rural old Hawaii vibe. You have your choice of three island tours following the 1½-hour passage: a self-guided Walking Tour, which basically means you're on your own once you land in Kauanakakai; a Cruise/Drive package, which includes a transfer to a rental car so that you have the mobility to explore for the day; and the Alii Tour, in which a local guide takes you sightseeing by van for the day. I strongly recommend opting for one of the two deluxe options (you'll feel stranded otherwise). Which one you choose all depends on what kind of traveler you are; just be sure to pick up Molokai information at the Maui Visitors Bureau (see the "Quick Concierge" in Chapter 12) before you go if you decide to explore on your own.

Molokini cruises are offered aboard the 65-foot yacht *Lahaina Princess*. These cruises are most notable because a) they're the only Molokini cruises that depart from Lahaina (rather than Molokini); b) they also include a stop at Olowalu, another good snorkel spot; and c) kids love the water trampoline for splashy ocean entrances.

The *Lahaina Princess* offers Molokini snorkel cruises only from May through November, because it's singularly occupied with whale-watching in the winter months. This snorkel-free cruise is an excellent choice for those who want to seriously watch and learn about the visiting humpback whales, as the boat carries cutting edge underwater viewing equipment as well as whale researchers and naturalists.

Cruises depart from Lahaina Harbor, Front St., Lahaina. ☎ 800-275-6969 or 808-667-6165. Internet: www.mauiprincess.com *or* www.whalewatchmaui.com. *2-hour whale-watch cruises (Dec–May): $19–$31 adults, $12.50–$17.50 kids 3–12. 6-hour Molokini snorkel/dive cruises (Apr–Nov): $69 adults, $39 kids 3–12, including continental breakfast and barbecue lunch; $109–$129 for certified divers. 9-hour Molokai adventure: $79 adults, $45 kids 3–12, for round-trip passage only; $139 for first adult, $79 for extra adults, $45 for kids 3–12 for passage plus rental car on Molokai; or $139 per person for Alii Tour, featuring narrated van tour of Molokai.*

At press time, a 10 percent online-booking discount and a 15 percent AAA-member discount were available on select (not all) Maui Princess and Lahaina Princess cruises.

Royal Hawaiian Cruises

For the smoothest ride to Lanai there is, book a ride aboard the *Navatek II,* a high-tech 82-foot, 149-passenger SWATH (Small Waterplane Area Twin Hull) vessel that promises even the most perpetually queasy passengers a seasick-free ride thanks to twin torpedolike hulls that cut through the waves rather than ride them (which just about everyone will appreciate on the often-choppy afternoon ride back across the channel). The cruise doesn't land on Lanai; rather, it takes you on a gorgeous ride to the rugged west coast, where you'll snorkel in a wonderful secluded bay. A good alternative to those for whom Trilogy's epic day on Lanai just doesn't appeal.

For a more thrilling adventure, book your Lanai cruise instead aboard Royal Hawaiian's 48-foot, 49-passenger racing boat, the *Maui Nui Explorer.* The longer version features a naturalist and Hawaiian culture expert, plus three separate snorkel spots, as does the winter whale-watch cruise.

Cruises depart from Maalaea Harbor (at the Hwy. 30/130 junction), Maalaea. ☎ 808-873-3475. Internet: www.royalhawaiiancruises.com. *3½ to 6½-hour Lanai cruises: $67–$120 adults, $60–$99 teens (12–17), $51–$79 kids 2–11. Prices include continental breakfast and/or deli lunch, depending on cruise. 2-hour whale-watch cruise (Dec 15–Apr 15): $29 adults, $21 kids 5–11.*

Royal Hawaiian also hosts two-hour sunset cruises Monday through Saturday that feature an open bar, sit-down dinner, live music, and dancing for $91 per person.

Pacific Whale Foundation Eco-Adventures

If you consider yourself to be ecologically minded, you can't do better than to give your snorkel-cruise dollars to the Pacific Whale Foundation. This nonprofit has been at the forefront of Maui-based whale research, education, and conservation since the 1970s — and they also happen to host very fine cruises. Their first-rate modern catamaran fleet offers some of the best tours of Molokini and offshore Lanai. Their Lanai snorkel-sails take in the island's less-visited bays, and the slightly pricier one includes a search for wild dolphins in its regular itinerary. The Molokai trip is as fine as any and includes a visit to a second snorkel spot,

Olowalu's Turtle Town. Not only is there always at least one naturalist on board, but the entire crew is knowledgeable, eco-conscious, and friendly; the boats (each of which carry 100 people maximum), even burn eco-friendly fuel. What's more, the cruises are great for beginning snorkelers, because guides lead fish talks and reef tours, and a wide variety of flotation devices are available. The winter whale-watching cruises are unparalleled, of course. You simply can't go wrong with these folks.

Departures from Maalaea Harbor (at the Hwy. 30/130 junction), Maalaea, and Lahaina Harbor, on Front St., Lahaina, depending on cruise. ☎ *800-942-5311 or 808-879-8811. Internet:* www.pacificwhale.org. *2-hour whale-watch cruises (Dec–Apr): $20–$30 adults, $15 kids 4–12. 5-hour Molokini cruises: $56 adults, $28 kids 4–12. 3½ to 5½-hour Lanai cruises: $37–$84 adults, $19–$42 kids 4–12. Prices include continental breakfast and/or deli lunch, depending on cruise.*

You have numerous ways to save significant bucks on Pacific Whale Foundation cruises. You'll save 10 percent if you book online. Or you can save 15 percent (and garner yourself a groovy T-shirt in the process) by becoming a PWF member, which costs $35 dollars, but still puts you ahead if you book a snorkel cruise for two (and it's deductible, since the foundation is a nonprofit).

Paragon Sailing Charters

Paragon is most notable for its state-of-the-art, high-performance catamarans, intimate gatherings (only 24 to 38 passengers, depending on the trip), and landing rights at Manele Bay, which give their Lanai trip a special edge. (Trilogy is the only other outfitter that lands on Lanai, and the only one that will take you on a tour of the island.) This quality outfitter is a nice choice if you'd like to embark on a Molokini cruise or a sunset sail, too.

Departures from Maalaea Harbor (at the Hwy. 30/130 junction), Maalaea, and Lahaina Harbor, on Front St., Lahaina, depending on cruise. ☎ *800-441-2087 or 808-244-2087. Internet:* www.sailmaui.com. *2-hour sunset cruise: $39 per person, including hors d'oeuvres and cocktails. 3-hour Coral Gardens snorkel-sail: $39 adults, $19.50 kids, including hors d'oeuvres and beer and wine. 5-hour Molokai snorkel and performance sail: $68.50 adults, $34.25 kids, including continental breakfast, buffet lunch, and beer and wine. 7-hour Lanai snorkel-sail: $129, including continental breakfast, beach picnic lunch, and cocktails.*

Check Paragon's Web site for online booking discounts (10 percent off at press time).

Trilogy Excursions

Book these trips in advance, because Trilogy — the Mercedes of Maui snorkel-sail operators — offers the island's best and most popular snorkel-sail trips, hands down. They're the most expensive, too, but they're worth every penny. The trips feature first-rate catamarans, top-quality equipment, great food, and the best crew in the business. What's more, Trilogy is the only Lanai cruise operator that's allowed to land on the island's Hulopoe Beach, a terrific marine preserve that's considered to be one of the best snorkel and dolphin-watching spots in Hawaii, for a fun-filled day of sailing and snorkeling; they're also the only ones to offer a ground tour of the island. If you really want a genuine Lanai experience, don't book with anyone else. Terrific half-day snorkel/sail trips to Molokini and unique late-morning snorkel-sail trips off Kaanapali Beach are also offered.

No matter which trip you take, you'll find that the Trilogy crews are fun and knowledgeable (there's always a naturalist on board), and the state-of-the-art boats are comfortable, well-equipped, and meticulously maintained. All trips include a continental breakfast (with home-baked cinnamon buns) and a very good barbecue lunch (shipboard on the half-day trip, ashore on the Lanai trip). You should know, however, that they may make you wear a floatation device no matter how good your swimming skills are; if this is going to bother you, ask when you book.

Departures from Maalaea Harbor (at the Hwy. 30/130 junction), Maalaea; Lahaina Harbor, on Front St., Lahaina; or Kaanapali Beach, Kaanapali, depending on cruise. ☎ *888-MAUI-800 or 808-661-4743. Internet:* www.sailtrilogy.com. *9-hour Lanai cruises: $159–$229 adults, $80–$115 kids 3–12, including barbecue lunch and island tour, with a Jeep Safari and champagne return sail on the "Ultimate Adventure." 5½ to 6½-hour Molokini or Kaanapali cruise: $89 adults, $45 kids 3–12.*

Scuba upgrades are available on most Trilogy excursions for beginning and certified divers alike ($45 to $70). If you'd like to spend more time on Lanai, ask about Lanai Overnighters, which include special rates on accommodations at the Lodge at Koele and the Manele Bay Hotel. Seasonal discounts are occasionally available, so ask when you book.

If you've always been interested in trying scuba diving but haven't gotten around to the hassles and expense of certification, you can sample a very close approximation — Snuba. With Snuba, you wear a mask and regulator that's connected via a 20-foot-long hose to an oxygen tank that floats on the surface, thereby allowing you to dive deep and simulate the scuba experience without full training. All it takes is about 15 minutes of instruction, and an instructor and two or three other first-timers are usually along for the ride. Virtually all of the snorkel cruise operators I mention in this section offer a Snuba upgrade for about 50 bucks. No advance booking is necessary — the Snuba instructor will ask on the way out if you're interested in participating. But call ahead to confirm that Snuba will be offered on your cruise if your heart's set on trying it.

Ocean kayaking

Whether you already paddle or you'd just like to learn, Maui's a great place to hit the waves in a kayak. Riding low on the turquoise water not only puts you at one with the ocean, but also allows you to visit snorkel spots where the big boats just don't go (I've had my finest sea turtle–spotting experiences while kayaking Maui's waters).

Maui's best kayaking outfitter for beginners and accomplished kayakers alike is **South Pacific Kayaks & Outfitters,** in the Rainbow Mall, 2439 S. Kihei Rd., Kihei (☎ **800-77-OCEAN** or 808-875-4848; Internet: www.southpacifickayaks.com). They offer a range of kayak tours that launch from both South and West Maui and incorporate whale-watching in winter. The excellent guides are all very knowledgeable and ecology-minded. Tour prices run from $55 to $89 per person, with custom options available.

If you're an experienced kayaker capable of setting out on your own, South Pacific can rent you single or double kayaks for $30 or $40 a day, respectively, and point you to good launching areas. Weekly rates and islandwide delivery (for an additional charge) are also available.

Winter whale-watching

More than any other Hawaiian island, Maui is your best perch for spotting Pacific humpback whales in winter. Virtually every boat that operates from Maui combines whale-watching with their regular adventures from December through April, and a good number offer dedicated whale-watch cruises in season, most notably the Pacific Whale Foundation (see "Ocean cruising to Molokini and Lanai — and other on-deck adventures" earlier in this chapter). The channel separating Maui from Lanai and Molokai is a whale-watching hot spot, so Lanai cruises, in particular, are always an excellent bet.

You don't have to shell out the bucks for a pricey cruise to see whales. In season, you can spot them right from shore. Just look out to sea — just about any west-facing beach offers you a prime whale-watching opportunity.

Follow these tips to increase your humpback-spotting chances:

   ✔ **Once you see a whale, keep watching in the same vicinity.** They often stay down for 20 minutes or so, then pop back up to take in some air and play a little. Be patient, and you're likely to be rewarded.

   ✔ **Bring your binoculars from home.** You'll see so much more with a little magnification. If you don't own any — or you just plumb forgot — you can rent some from the **Rental Warehouse/Rainbow Water Sports,** in Kihei at Azeka Place II, 1278 S. Kihei Rd., near Lipoa Street (☎ **808-875-4050**).

   ✔ Anywhere along the West Maui coast is a good bet for whale-watching. A great place to park yourself is **McGregor Point,** a scenic lookout at mile marker 9 on the Honoapiilani Highway (Highway 30), on the way to Lahaina from Maalaea. Another good West Maui whale-watching perch is the straight part of Honoapiilani Highway between McGregor Point and Olowalu (where Chez Paul is). However, do yourself — and everybody else — a favor and pull over to the side of the road before you look out to sea, as whale spotting along here has been known to cause more than a few accidents.

Catching a wave

Book your surfing or windsurfing lesson (keep reading for more information on how to do that) for early in your stay. That way, if conditions aren't right on your scheduled day, you'll have plenty of time to reschedule.

For daily reports on wind and surf conditions, call the **Wind and Surf Report** at ☎ **808-877-3611.**

Learning to surf

If you've always wanted to learn to surf, Maui is a great place to fulfill the dream, as it's known for having the easiest learning surf in Hawaii. The motto at the **Nancy C. Emerson School of Surfing** (☎ **808-873-0264;** Internet: www.maui.net/~ncesurf) is, "If a dog can surf, so can you!" — a dubious challenge, but a surprisingly comforting one, too. A pro international surfing champ, an instructor since 1973, and a stunt performer in movies like *Waterworld*, Nancy has pioneered the technique of teaching completely unskilled folks to surf in one two-hour lesson. You can, really — I've seen it happen firsthand. The instructors are professional and personable; you'll probably have your lesson on the beach behind 505 Front St. in Lahaina, where the surf breaks are big enough to learn on but not overwhelming. A beginning lesson is $95 per person for a one-hour private lesson, $70 per person for two hours with a group; I recommend going for the group option. Experienced surfers can take full- and multi-day private lessons and group clinics with Nancy's skilled instructors; check the Web site or call for rate schedules.

If you want to learn on the north shore, **Action Sports Surf School** (☎ **808-871-5857;** Internet: www.actionsportsmaui.com), offers everything from kiddie lessons to extreme tow-in and strap surfing lessons for experienced board riders.

For experienced surfers only

Expert surfers visit Maui in winter when the surf's really up. The best surfing beaches include **Honolua Bay,** north of Kapalua; **Maalaea,** just outside the breakwall of the Maalaea Harbor; and **Hookipa Beach Park** in Paia, where surfers get the waves until noon, when the windsurfers take over. If you have a bit of experience but don't want a serious challenge, head to the **505 Front Street Beach,** next to Lahaina Harbor in Lahaina, where even long-surfing locals regularly catch the easy waves.

In Lahaina, surfboards are available for rent at the **Rental Warehouse,** 578 Front St., at Prison Street (☎ **808-661-1970**). Rental Warehouse also has a South Maui location in Kihei at Azeka Place II, 1278 S. Kihei Rd., near Lipoa Street (☎ **808-875-4050**). You can rent quality boards in Central Maui from the friendly folks at **Second Wind Surf, Sail & Kite,** 111 Hana Hwy. (between Dairy Road and Hobron Avenue), Kahului (☎ **808-877-SHOP;** Internet: www.secondwindmaui.com).

Windsurfing

Expert windsurfers will want to head to Paia's world-famous **Hookipa Beach,** known all over the globe for its brisk winds and excellent waves, in the afternoons. When the winds turn northerly, **Kihei** is the spot to be; some days you can see whales in the distance behind the windsurfers. The northern end of Kihei is best: At **Ohukai Park,** the first beach along South Kihei Road, the winds are good, the water is easy to access, and a long strip of grass is available to assemble your gear. If you have enough experience to head out on your own, but you want manageable waves, head to **Kanaha Beach Park** near the airport in Kahului, which is where all of the top schools take their students to learn.

Endorsed by Robbie Naish, Hawaii's most famous windsurfer (who has his own windsurfing school on Oahu; see Chapter 10), **Hawaiian Island Surf and Sport,** 415 Dairy Rd., Kahului (☎ **800-231-6958** or 808-871-4981; Internet: www.hawaiianisland.com), offers beginning 2½-hour windsurf lessons for $69, as well as instruction in shortboard sailing for those ready to move to the next level. The island's best assortment of quality gear rentals are available as well.

Top-quality rental gear for windsurfing and kite surfing can be had from **Second Wind Surf, Sail & Kite,** 111 Hana Hwy. (between Dairy Road and Hobron Avenue), Kahului (☎ **808-877-SHOP;** Internet: www.secondwindmaui.com). They're also an excellent contact if you'd like to arrange for windsurfing lessons, for beginners and experienced windsurfers alike, as well as kiteboarding lessons for experienced wave-riders. **Action Sports Maui** (☎ **808-871-5857;** Internet: www.actionsportsmaui.com) also offers lessons in both windsurfing and kiteboarding.

Scuba diving

Molokini is one of Hawaii's top dive spots thanks to calm, clear, protected waters and an abundance of marine life at every level, from clouds of yellow butterfly fish to white-tipped reef sharks to manta rays. This crescent-shaped crater has three tiers of diving: a 35-foot plateau inside the crater basin (used by beginning divers and snorkelers), a wall sloping to 70 feet just beyond the inside plateau, and a sheer wall on the outside and backside of the crater that plunges 350 feet below the surface.

Other top dive spots include the pristine waters off the island of **Lanai,** whose south and west coasts are a dream come true for divers looking for a one-of-a-kind setting.

You need to book a dive boat to get to Molokini or Lanai. **Lahaina Divers** (☎ **800-998-3483** or 808-667-7496; Internet: www.lahainadivers.com) is a five-star PADI facility that has been lauded as one of Hawaii's top dive operators by publications like *Scuba Diving* magazine. They can take certified divers to Molokini or Lanai aboard one of their big, comfortable dive boats for two- to four-tank dives ranging in price from $110 to $175; West Maui dives start at $95. Instruction is available for divers of all experience levels, and their "Discover Scuba" package for beginners costs $99.

Or contact **Ed Robinson's Diving Adventures** (☎ 800-635-1273 or 808-879-3584; Internet: www.mauiscuba.com/erd1.htm), which caters exclusively to certified divers from South Maui. A widely published underwater photographer, Ed is one of Maui's best; most of his business is repeat customers. Ed offers personalized two-tank dives for $110 ($125 with equipment), plus three-tank adventures, Lanai trips, and sunset and night dives. Custom dives are also available, plus discounts for multiple-day dives.

Also recommendable for two-tank boat dives to Molokini and nearby Maui waters is **Mike Severns Diving** (☎ 808-879-6596; Internet: www.mikesevernsdiving.com), which takes 12 divers at a time out from Kihei in two groups of six for a quiet and crowd-free experience. The price is $120, with discounts available if you have your own equipment or schedule multi-day dives.

If you've never scuba dived before but would like to learn, contact either Lahaina Divers or **Bobby Baker's Maui Sun Divers** (☎ 877-808-3337; Internet: www.mauisundivers.com). They specialize in beginners, and they offer a whole slate of introductory dives and multiple-day starter and certification programs.

Parasailing

Are you in search of an easy thrill to suit your laidback vacation? Let **UFO Parasail** (☎ 800-FLY-4UFO or 808-661-7UFO; Internet: www.ufoparasail.com) take you soaring high above the Kaanapali waves, alone or with a friend, between mid-May and mid-December. Anybody can parasail — no experience or special skills are necessary, and tours are offered year-round. The speedboat driver does all the work; you just put on the securely attached parachute and go along for the ride. UFO has state-of-the-art equipment, including the latest in liftoff and landing technology. It costs $42 per person for a seven-minute ride at 400 feet, but if you're going up you might as well spend the extra ten bucks for the ten-minute ride at 800 feet, which includes an optional simulated freefall (is that a good thing?).

What to See and Do on Dry Land

Maui is home to two of Hawaii's most renowned attractions: Haleakala National Park, a remarkable, otherworldly crater at the heart of the island that offers some of the best sunrise-watching in the world, not to mention one-of-a-kind hiking and biking fun; and the Heavenly Road to Hana, one of the most well-known scenic drives in the United States.

Taking a guided van or bus tour

If you've rented a car and can get around easily on your own, driving yourself around the island is definitely the preferable way to go. But, if your mobility is limited, or if you're traveling alone and you don't want to make the drive to Hana on your own, or if you just want to kick back and let somebody else take the driver's seat, you might want to hook up with a guided tour.

Remember that with a guided tour, you will have little or no control over where you go and how long you stay, and your time communing with nature at some of Hawaii's finest natural spots will be limited. Still, for some people, a guided tour is the best way to see Haleakala National Park and take in the glories of the Heavenly Road to Hana.

For small-scale, local-led van tours of the Heavenly Road to Hana and Haleakala National Park's sunrise extravaganza, book your guided trip with family-owned **Ekahi Tours** (☎ **888-292-2422** or 808-877-9775, Internet: www.ekahi.com). One of the great advantages of their Hana tour is that it's a circle island tour; you'll not only drive the road to Hana, but you'll experience the otherworldly desert landscape of the little-traveled back road on the return trip, which takes you along the south coast and around the back side of the Haleakala Volcano (weather permitting). Ekahi can take you not only to Hana but to hidden Kahakuloa, a half-day tour that offers an insightful look at Maui's ancient past and rural present. Ekahi tour prices range from $65–$79 adults, $50–$60 kids under 12, depending on the tour you choose; prices include a deli lunch.

Now offering guided bus tours statewide, **Polynesian Adventure Tours** (☎ **800-622-3011** or 808-877-4242; Internet: www.polyad.com) offered the very first guided tours along the Heavenly Road to Hana, and they're still going strong in this department. In addition to the Hana option, they offer both Haleakala sunrise and sunset tours (including one with a side trip to Central Maui's Iao Valley) in mini-vans, big-windowed mini-coaches, and full-size luxury buses. Prices run $52.50 to $89 for adults, $35 to $79 for kids 3 to 11.

Book your Polynesian Adventure Tour online to get a 10 percent price break.

Roberts Hawaii (☎ **800-831-5541** or 808-521-3666; Internet: www.roberts-hawaii.com) is Hawaii's biggest name in narrated bus tours. Roberts offers a similar slate of tours as Polynesian Adventure, with comparable schedules and prices.

Roberts awards seniors 55 and older a 10 percent discount on all tours. AAA members qualify for similar savings.

If you choose to visit Haleakala National Park on a guided tour, remember to dress warmly, because it gets *cooooold* at 10,000 feet. For more on Haleakala's weather, see the complete section on the park later in this chapter.

Guide-led nature hikes and Jeep safaris

Maui's oldest and best guided hiking company is Ken Schmitt's **Hike Maui** (☎ 808-879-5270; Internet: www.hikemaui.com). Hike Maui has been universally lauded for the quality of their hikes; you can't go wrong with them. The expert guides are all trained naturalists who really know their stuff. This is a fabulous way to see beautiful Maui at its natural best.

Hike Maui offers seven hikes ranging from three to eight miles and from easy to strenuous, but most fall in the moderate category. Two Rainforest and Waterfall hikes are available: A three-mile, easy-to-moderate half-day option, and a 4½-mile, full-day moderate option, both of which take you through lush rain forests to gorgeous waterfalls; the full-day trip visits dramatic Kipahulu and includes time for swimming in the waterfall pools.

Two Haleakala Volcano hikes are available, a moderate four-mile walk and a strenuous eight-mile walk; both offer an excellent way to see this splendid national park, which can be difficult to appreciate if you don't know what your seeing. If you're an accomplished hiker and fit for it, don't miss the longer hike. It takes you all the way to the crater floor — which looks so much like the moon that the lunar astronauts trained here — for a truly otherworldly experience.

Other options include a moderate West Maui Mountain Ridge Trail that offers a good workout and fabulous views; a three-mile, marine biologist–led Coastline Hike that combines a moderate hike with an archaeological tour of ancient Hawaiian villages and some terrific snorkeling; and a five-mile, full-day, moderate Cloud Forest Hike to Polipoli State Park, where you'll spot rare birds and wildflowers.

Hikes range from $85 to $135 for adults, $65 to $110 for kids 15 and under. Prices include equipment and transportation from Central Maui (one of the company's air-conditioned vans will take you from the office to the trailhead), and a simple, healthy lunch of sandwiches and fruit. You can book as late as a couple of days in advance, but your best bet is to call before you arrive on the island for the greatest flexibility and to avoid disappointment.

If Hike Maui's schedules don't suit your needs, call **Maui Hiking Safaris** (☎ 888-445-3963 or 808-573-0168; Internet: www.maui.net/~mhs), another reputable company offering guided hikes for all levels, including waterfall hikes and guided hikes of Haleakala. Prices run from $49 to $89 per person (10 percent less for kids 13 and under).

Maui Hiking Safaris extends 10 percent discounts to hikers who book more than two weeks in advance as well as for groups of six or more.

If you'd rather explore Maui's backcountry on wheels, go off-roading with **Maui Jeep Adventures** (☎ 808-876-1177; Internet: www.mauijeepadventures.com). They'll take you out in their four-wheel-drive Jeeps on your choice of two exciting tours: the Mauka Tour, which lets you explore hard-to-reach pristine natural areas on the slopes of Haleakala; and the Makai Tour, which will show you otherwise inaccessible areas along the rugged South Maui coastline, taking in ancient rock formations, ruins of ancient villages, and incredible views along the way. The 4½-hour tours are $79 for adults, $49 for kids 5 to 10, including a picnic lunch; custom and private options are also available.

Getting a bird's eye view: flightseeing tours

Flightseeing is an excellent way to explore Maui's stunning, untouched natural areas that are simply unviewable by any other means. Maui-based helicopter tours also offer you the opportunity to see a neighbor island — Molokai, Lanai, or even the Big Island — from the air in addition to the Valley Isle itself.

There are, however, some considerations. While the companies I recommend all feature skilled pilots and helicopters with excellent safety records, the truth of the matter is that flightseeing can be risky business. Twenty-eight people have died in commercial helicopter crashes in Hawaii over the last decade, six of those in a 1998 Kauai accident, seven in a Maui crash in July 2000. Of course, just getting into your rental car and driving to dinner — or even getting into the shower in your condo with a renegade bar of soap — is far more dangerous than catching a 'copter ride. Still, you should make informed decisions.

 When reserving a helicopter tour with any company, check to make sure that safety is their first concern. The company should be an FAA-certified Part 135 operator, and the pilot should be Part 135 certified as well; the 135 license guarantees more stringent maintenance requirements and pilot training programs than those who are only Part 91 certified. And any time weather conditions look iffy, reschedule.

Blue Hawaiian Helicopters

This terrific company flies a fleet of new American Eurocopter ASTAR 350 helicopters that carry six passengers, providing each with a 180-degree view and a Bose noise-cancelling headset that lets you enjoy a surprisingly quiet ride. The pilots are well trained and knowledgeable narrators, and a state-of-the-art in-flight video is on board in case you'd like to preserve the sights and sounds of your thrill-a-minute flight for posterity. A range of available options include some or all of the following spectacular sights: the misty, green West Maui Mountains; otherworldly Haleakala Volcano; luxuriant, unspoiled East Maui and Hana; and Molokai, where you'll fly by the highest seacliffs in the world. The "Sunset Spectacular of Hana and Haleakala" includes a midflight landing at an ideal sunset-watching perch.

Tours depart from Kahului Airport. ☎ 800-745-BLUE or 808-871-8844. Internet: www.bluehawaiian.com. 30- to 100-minute tours: $105–$240 per person.

Hang gliding in Hana

All you need is an adventurous spirit to soar above the spectacular East Maui coastline with **Hang Gliding Maui** (☎ 808-572-6557; Internet: www.hanglidingmaui. com). Hang Gliding Maui offers tandem flights from the Hana Airport aboard their engine-powered, open-cockpit, ultralight aircraft the *Airborne Trike.* This is an instructional flight, where you'll learn the basics of weight-shift control, aerodynamics, and aviation safety as you soar over the breathtaking Hana coast and ride the thermals with your instructor. The cost is $95 for a half-hour flight, $165 for an hour. Reservations are required; the weight limit is 220 pounds, and flights are weather-dependent, of course.

If you book seven days or more in advance via e-mail or call and mention that you visited their Web site, Blue Hawaiian will award you a 15 percent price break.

Hawaii Helicopters

Featured on *Baywatch Hawaii,* Hawaii Helicopters flies Twinstar twin jet engine helicopters, supposedly the safest 'copters around (makes sense, what with two engines instead of one). They also feature 180-degree views from every seat, Bose noise-cancelling headsets for a quiet ride, and a five-camera video system that can record your trip for at-home viewing. Hawaii Helicopters is also notable for its wide range of multi-island options, which include a three-hour volcano tour that not only shows you Haleakala but whisks you over to the Big Island for an island-wide tour that includes Kilauea's bubbling caldera (see the "Hawaii Volcanoes National Park" section in Chapter 18 for details). There's also a 1¾-hour three-island tour that flies across the channel to take in the spectacular sea cliffs of Molokai (the highest in the world) and the rugged rock gardens of Lanai as well as Haleakala and the gorgeous wind- and rain-carved West Maui Mountains. Shorter Maui-only tours are also available.

Tours depart from Kahului Airport. ☎ *800-994-9099 or 808-877-3900. Internet:* www.hawaii-helicopters.com. *25- to 70-minute tours: $105–$200 per person. 1¾-hour Tri-Island Spectacular: $240 per person. Epic 3-hour Volcano tour: $420 per person.*

Book online to garner a 15 percent price break from Hawaii Helicopters.

Visiting Haleakala National Park

Haleakala (HA-lay-ah-KA-la) — the House of the Sun — is the massive 10,023-foot-high mountain that forms the core of the island of Maui. It's also Hawaii's second national park (after the Big Island's Hawaii Volcanoes National Park), designated as such in 1961, and Maui's biggest natural attraction.

About two million people drive to the summit of Haleakala to peer down into the crater of the world's largest dormant volcano. (Its official status is "active but not currently erupting," even though Haleakala has remained silent since 1790.) The crater is impressive: at 3,000 feet deep, 7½ miles long by 2½ miles wide, and encompassing 19 square miles, it's big enough to hold the island of Manhattan, and more than anything else resembles a barren moonscape.

This stark, rugged, otherworldly place is actually breathtakingly beautiful in its own way. Just driving up the mountain is an experience in itself: The road climbs from sea level to 10,000 feet in just 37 miles, and the views are magnificent along the entire route. At first glance, the landscape looks like nothing more than a dry and barren wasteland. But soon, a fascinating, multi-hued geologic world emerges — a surprisingly fragile one that supports a number of the world's rarest examples of flora and fauna. Among the rare endangered species that call Haleakala home are the *nene* (NAY-nay), a gray-brown Hawaiian goose that doesn't migrate, prefers rock-hard lava beds to lakes, and is now protected as the state bird; and the silvery-green, porcupiney *silversword* plant, which grows only in Hawaii, lives for about 50 years, blooms once in a beautiful purple bouquet, and dies.

Nene like to hang out around park headquarters, so you should be able to spot one or two there — if you don't hear their distinctive call ("nay! nay!") first. Kalahaku Overlook is a good place to see silverswords. (Please don't feed the nene, and leave the silverswords where you see them.)

Haleakala is never more stunning than at sunrise, a truly awesome, you've-never-really-seen-a-sunrise-until-now technicolor sight from this lofty perch; in fact, Mark Twain called watching the sun rise above Haleakala "the sublimest spectacle" of his life. A few folks may tell you that sunset is just as spectacular, but it's not. Stick around after sunrise for some excellent hiking opportunities. Or do what a lot of people do: Hop on a bike and coast down the switchbacked, view-endowed road to the base of the mountain; see "Biking down the volcano" later in this section for recommended outfitters.

The best photo ops are in the afternoon, when the sun illuminates the crater and clouds are few. Stargazing from the summit can be spectacular, so consider bringing your binoculars (or renting a pair) and making the ascent if the sky is clear.

The park actually contains two separate and distinct destinations: Haleakala Summit and the Kipahulu coast. Lush, green, and tropical, Kipahulu is a world apart from the summit — and accessible only from the east side of the island, near Hana; no road links the summit and the coast. For a discussion of Kipahulu and its biggest attraction, Oheo Gulch, see "Driving the Heavenly Road to Hana" later in this chapter.

Haleakala National Park

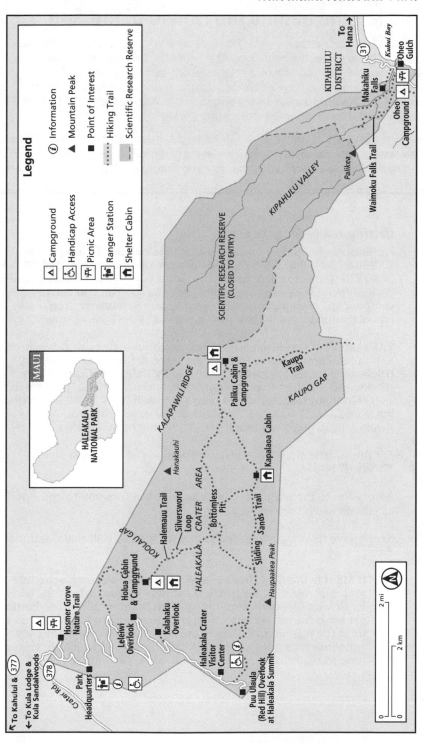

Legend

(i) Information
▲ Mountain Peak
■ Point of Interest
••••• Hiking Trail
▨ Scientific Research Reserve

Ⓐ Campground
♿ Handicap Access
🏕 Picnic Area
👤 Ranger Station
⛺ Shelter Cabin

MAUI

HALEAKALA
NATIONAL PARK

To Kahului & (377)
← To Kula Lodge &
Kula Sandalwoods
(378)
(Crater Rd.)

Park
Headquarters

Hosmer Grove
Nature Trail

Leleiwi
Overlook

Holua Cabin
& Campground

Kalahaku
Overlook

Haleakala Crater
Visitor
Center

Puu Ulaula
(Red Hill) Overlook
at Haleakala Summit

KOOLAU GAP

Halemauu Trail

Silversword
Loop

▲ *Hanakauhi*

HALEAKALA CRATER AREA

Bottomless
Pit

Sliding Sands Trail

▲ *Haupaakea Peak*

KALAPAWILI RIDGE

Paliku Cabin &
Campground

Kapalaoa Cabin

Kaupo
Trail

KAUPO GAP

SCIENTIFIC RESEARCH RESERVE
(CLOSED TO ENTRY)

KIPAHULU VALLEY

Palikea

Waimoku Falls Trail

KIPAHULU
DISTRICT

To
Hana →

Kuhui Bay

(31)

Makahiku
Falls

Oheo
Gulch

Oheo
Campground

N

2 mi

2 km

0

0

The legend behind the House of the Sun

The name *Haleakala* actually means "House of the Sun." The story of how this wild-looking volcano got such a magnificent name goes like this: One day, a mom complained that the sun sped across the sky so quickly that her tapa cloth didn't have enough time to dry. So in the pre-dawn hours of the next morning, her thoughtful son, the demi-god Maui, climbed to the top of the volcano. When the sun rose above the horizon, Maui lassoed it, bringing it to a halt in the sky.

The sun begged Maui to let go. Maui said he would, on one condition: That the sun slow its trip across the sky to give the island more sunlight. The sun agreed. In honor of the agreement, islanders dubbed the mountain "House of the Sun."

Getting ready for your visit

For information before you go, contact **Haleakala National Park** at ☎ **808-572-4400** or 808-572-4420 for a recorded message, dial ☎ **808-248-7375** to talk to a live person, or point your Web browser to the park's official Web site at www.nps.gov/hale. You can call to have camping and hiking information sent to you in advance. You'll also find lots of useful information at www.haleakala.national-park.com.

The summit of Haleakala is 38 miles, or about a 1½-hour drive, from Kahului in Central Maui. To get there, take the Haleakala Highway (Highway 37, then Highway 377) to wiggly Haleakala Crater Road (Highway 378), the heavily switchbacked road that will lead you to the 10,000-foot summit. Allow two hours to reach the summit if you're driving from Lahaina or Kihei, 2½ hours if you're arriving from Wailea or Kaanapali, 15 minutes more if you're coming from Kapalua.

For the sunrise time and viewing conditions at Haleakala summit, call ☎ **808-871-5054.**

Admission to the park is $10 per car, which allows you to come and go as you please for seven days.

Keep these tips in mind as you plan your visit to Haleakala National Park:

 ✔ **If Maui is the first Hawaiian island you're visiting, schedule your sunrise visit for the first full day of your trip.** Your body clock won't be on Hawaii time yet, so it shouldn't be too hard to get up at 3 a.m. — since it's anywhere from 5 to 9 a.m. if you're from the mainland. If Maui is the last island on your itinerary, schedule your sunrise visit for the final day of your trip, since it's time to reacclimate yourself to the at-home hour anyway.

✔ **Dress warmly, in layers, no matter what time of year you visit.**
Temperatures at the summit usually range between 40 and 65°F
but can drop below freezing any time of year once you factor in
the wind chill, especially in the predawn hours. Wear a hat and
sturdy shoes, and bring a blanket if you don't have a warm jacket.
The weather is unpredictable at the summit, so be prepared for
wind and rain in winter no matter what the time of day; don't be
fooled by the coastline conditions. Call ☎ **808-871-5054** for the
summit forecast.

✔ **Bring drinking water.** You'll need plenty of water on hand —
especially if you plan on hiking.

✔ **Remember that this is a high-altitude wilderness area.** The thinness of the air makes some people dizzy; you may also experience
lightheadedness, shortness of breath, nausea, headaches, and
dehydration. The park recommends that pregnant women and
those with heart or respiratory problems consult a doctor before
ascending to high elevations.

✔ **Fill up your gas tank before you head to Haleakala.** The last gas
is 27 miles below the summit at Pukalani. Fill up the night before if
you're going for sunrise, because it will be near impossible to find
an open gas station at 4 a.m.

Those of you who'd like to explore the park thoroughly might consider
booking a Haleakala day hike with **Hike Maui** or **Maui Hiking Safaris;**
see "Guide-led nature hikes and Jeep safaris" earlier in this chapter. If
you're interested in a stay near the park for a few nights to facilitate
more intensive park exploration, see "Staying Off the Beaten Path" in
Chapter 11.

Arriving at the park and making the drive to the summit

About a mile from the entrance is **Park Headquarters,** open daily from
7:30 a.m. to 4 p.m. It's a great place to pick up park information, including the latest schedule of guided walks and ranger talks. If, however,
you arrive before dawn, all you can do here is use the around-the-clock
restrooms; the ones here are much nicer than the ones at the summit,
so I highly recommend making a pit stop on the way up. Drinking water
is also available.

You'll pass two scenic overlooks on the way to the summit. Stop at the
one just beyond mile marker 17, **Leleiwi Overlook,** if only to get out,
stretch, and get accustomed to the heights. From the parking area, a
short trail leads to a panoramic view of the lunarlike crater. (The other
overlook, Kalahaku, is most easily accessible on the descent.)

Continue on, and you'll soon reach **Haleakala Visitor Center,** 11 miles
from the park entrance (open daily from sunrise to 3 p.m.), which
offers spectacular views and some bare-bones restrooms.

Park rangers also offer excellent, informative, and free naturalist talks
daily at 9:30, 10:30, and 11:30 a.m. from the Haleakala Visitor Center.

The actual summit — and the ideal sunrise-viewing perch — is beyond the turnoff for the visitor center, at **Puu Ulaula Overlook** (Red Hill). At Puu Ulaula, a triangular glass building serves as a windbreak and the best sunrise viewing spot. After the spectacle of sunrise, you can often see all the way to the snowcapped summit of Mauna Kea on the Big Island if it's clear. Haleakala Observatories (nicknamed Science City), which isn't open to the public, is also located here.

Hiking the park

If you want to hike the park, I strongly suggest going with a guide. This is an outlandishly huge, empty place that is best seen with someone who can lead you in the right direction and help you understand what you're seeing. Park rangers offer a range of free guided hikes; call for the latest schedule (☎ 808-572-4400) and to find out what to wear and bring (sturdy shoes and water are musts). Also consider taking one of the guided Haleakala Crater hikes offered by Hike Maui and Maui Hiking Safaris; see "Guide-led nature hikes and Jeep safaris" earlier in this chapter.

If you don't want to bother with a serious hike but just want a glimpse of the park's peculiar brand of natural beauty and fascinating fauna, take a half-hour walk down the half-mile **Hosmer Grove Nature Trail,** which anybody can do. The trail is well-marked, with placards that point out what you're seeing along the way. Ask the ranger at the visitor center to direct you to the trailhead.

If you'd like to strike out on your own along the park's more serious trails, you can preview your options online at www.haleakala. national-park.com (click on Hiking Guide) or call ahead (☎ 808-572-4400); the rangers will be happy to send you complete trail information.

Driving back down the mountain

Put your rental car in low gear on the way down so that you don't ride your breaks.

Around mile marker 24 is **Kalahaku Overlook,** the best place to spot the spiky, alienlike silversword plant, and to take in some fabulous panoramic views.

At the base of the mountain, where you'll turn onto Haleakala Crater Road from the Haleakala Highway, is Kula, the closest thing to a gateway town that Haleakala has. Kula is most notable for its two restaurants, Kula Sandalwoods and the Kula Lodge, both of which serve great post-sunrise breakfast and lunch; see the sidebar called "Going for a Post-Haleakala-Sunrise Breakfast" in Chapter 13 for specifics.

Biking down the volcano

Another great way to experience Haleakala is to cruise down it, from summit to base, on a bicycle. The guided ride is quite an experience, with stunning views the entire way. And you don't need to be an expert cyclist to do it; you just have to be able to ride a bike. In fact, you barely have to pedal — you'll coast down at a nice, leisurely pace (the constant switchbacks keep you from picking up too much speed).

A number of companies offer these trips with minor variations — some offer midday tours, others have go-at-your-own-pace options — but they generally work like this: A van picks you up at your hotel or condo anywhere between 2 and 3:30 a.m. and transports you to headquarters, where they'll outfit you with a custom-fitted bike (with a comfy seat and good brakes), a helmet, rain gear, and any other equipment you'll need for the downhill cruise. You and your fellow bikers then reboard the van, which takes you (and the bikes on an attached trailer) up to Haleakala's summit.

Just after the miracle of sunrise, you mount your bike and start down Haleakala Crater Road, usually riding single file behind a guide on the right shoulder of the road so that you don't interfere with traffic. The group generally stops for photo ops along the way. By about 10 a.m., you've come 22 miles to the end of Haleakala Crater Road. Some tours end with breakfast in Kula, while others break for breakfast and then proceed the rest of the way down the hill, to sea level.

Maui's oldest downhill company is **Maui Downhill** (☎ **800-535-BIKE** or 808-871-2155; Internet: www.mauidownhill.com). Maui Downhill offers a variety of guided Haleakala bike "safaris" at both sunrise and midday that range in price from $62 to $115 per person.

Other reliable companies include **Maui Mountain Cruisers** (☎ **800-232-MAUI** or 808-871-6014; Internet: www.mauimountaincruisers. com), whose tours run $110 to $120 per person (book online and you'll save 15 percent); and **Mountain Riders** (☎ **800-706-7700** or 808-242-9739; Internet: www.mountainriders.com), who charges $125 for the sunrise trip, $115 for the day trip.

Prices usually include hotel pickup, transport to the top, all equipment, breakfast (or lunch on a midday cruise), and dropoff. Generally, riders have to be at least 12 and at least 4'10" tall. Younger kids and pregnant women can usually ride along in the van.

At press time, Maui's most reliable activity booker, **Tom Barefoot's Cashback Tours,** 834 Front St., near Lahainaluna Road in Lahaina (☎ **888-222-3601** or 808-661-8889; Internet: www.tombarefoot.com), could save you bucks with all of the above-mentioned companies if you book through them — 10 percent discount on select activities when you pay with cash, personal check, or traveler's checks, 7 percent if you pay by credit card.

If you'd prefer a more independent — and more affordable — downhill ride, contact **Haleakala Bike Company** (☎ **888-922-2453** or 808-572-2200; Internet: www.bikemaui.com). Haleakala Bike Company will outfit you with all the gear and take you up to the top but, after a little initial guidance, will leave you to proceed down the mountain at your own pace. Tours are $49 to $69 per person, with no hotel pickup or meal included, and gear is available for kids as young as 8. The company also offers straight bike rentals.

Coasting down Haleakala can be an incredible ride, and thousands of people come home from Maui every year claiming that it was the highlight of their trip. Still, there are a few things you should know before you book one of these trips. I'm not trying to discourage you, by any means; I just want you to know exactly what to expect:

✔ Virtually all of the activity-providers advertise these trips as safe, no-strain bicycle rides that anyone can do, even grandma. However, these downhill bike tours do require some stamina, particularly in winter. Conditions can be harsh (freezing temperatures and 40mph winds are common on the mountain), you have to stay in line and keep up the pace with the other riders as cars go by (drivers are usually quite respectful, so you don't have to worry about dodging traffic), and the entire trip makes for a very long day.

✔ Summer and fall — when drive conditions and relatively mild temperatures usually prevail — are the best seasons for Haleakala downhill rides, with any time from late May through September being prime time.

✔ The better outfitters provide you with slick jumpsuits and headgear to protect you from the rain you'll almost inevitably encounter at some point along the way. But still count on getting cold and wet in winter and spring.

Driving the Heavenly Road to Hana

No road in Hawaii is more celebrated than the Hana Highway (Highway 36), the super-curvaceous two-lane highway that winds along Maui's northeastern shore, offering some of the most scenic natural sightseeing in the entire state.

The Hana Highway winds for some 52 miles east from Kahului, in Central Maui, crossing more than 50 one-lane bridges, passing greener-than-green taro patches, magnificent seascapes, gorgeous waterfalls, botanical gardens, and rain forests before passing through the little town of Hana and ultimately ending up in one of Hawaii's most beautiful tropical places: the Kipahulu section of Haleakala National Park. Kipahulu is home to Oheo (oh-HAY-oh) Gulch, a stunning series of waterfall pools that tumble down to the sea.

Despite the draws at the end of the road, this drive is about the journey — *not* the destination. The drive from end to end takes at least three hours, but you should allow all day for it. If you race along just to arrive in Hana as quickly as you can, you'll be as perplexed as so many others who just don't get it. Start out early, take it slow and easy, stop at the scenic points along the way, and let the Hana Road work its magic on you. It will — I promise.

Take these points into consideration as you plan your Hana Road trip:

✔ **Leave early.** Get up just after dawn, have an early breakfast (Charley's in Paia opens at 7 a.m.; see Chapter 13), and hit the road by 8 a.m. If you wait until mid-morning to leave, you'll get stuck in bumper-to-bumper Hana Road traffic, you won't have enough time to enjoy the sights along the way, and you'll arrive at Oheo Gulch too late in the day to take a hike or a dip. It's especially important to make the most of the daylight hours in winter, when days are shortest.

✔ **Consider booking a place to stay in Hana if you'd really like to take your time.** That way, you can head out to Hana against the traffic in the afternoon, stay for a couple of nights so that you have a full day to enjoy East Maui's attractions (including an abundance of peace and quiet), and meander back at your own pace (once again avoiding the traffic) on the morning of the third day. See "Staying Off the Beaten Path" in Chapter 11 for recommendations.

✔ **Fill up on gas before you set out.** If all else fails, make sure you stop in Paia, just east of Kahului, as the next gas is in Hana — 44 miles, 50-some bridges, and 200-plus hairpin turns down the road.

✔ **Don't bother if it's been raining heavily.** The Hana Highway is well paved and well maintained but can nevertheless be extremely dangerous when wet — and it's easy to get stuck in muddy shoulders and pull-offs.

✔ **Bring your bathing suit in warm weather.** You'll find a number of waterfall pools along the way that are ideal for a refreshing dip, and folks love to swim in Oheo Gulch's placid summer pools.

✔ **Bring mosquito repellent.** Lush East Maui is a buggy place.

✔ **Leave your mainland road rage on the mainland.** Practice aloha as you drive the Hana Road: Give way at the one-lane bridges. Wave at passing motorists. Let the locals who drive this road with jaw-dropping speed and who pass on blind curves have the right-of-way; if the guy behind you blinks his lights, let him pass. And don't honk your horn — it's considered rude in Hawaii.

In the exception to the no-horn-honking rule, if you reach a blind curve, *do* honk your horn to indicate that you're coming around the bend — and proceed slowly.

If you'd like some narration to accompany what you're seeing along the Road to Hana, pick up a **Hana Cassette Guide** on your way out of town. The 90-minute tape or CD is $20 at the Hana Cassette Guide shop in Kahului on Dairy Road (Highway 380), next to the Shell Service Station just before the Hana Highway (☎ **808-572-0550**). Along with the recorded tour you'll get a Hana Road map, and they'll even lend you a cooler or a tape player for free (with refundable deposit) if your rental car doesn't have one. They also have a recorded guide to Haleakala available for $10, and they open daily at 3 a.m. to accommodate the earliest risers.

The Heavenly Road to Hana

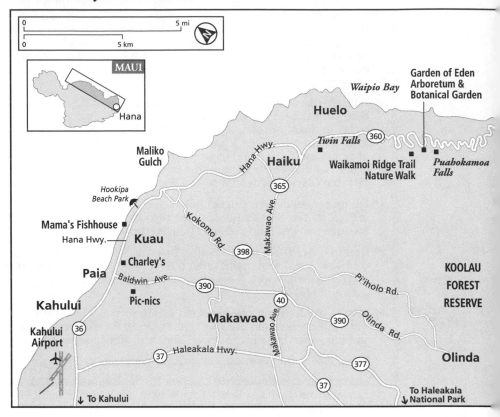

To avoid traffic, consider one of these two route-reversal strategies. While both have their problems, they might be preferable for those of you who'll be so distracted by the crowds that you won't be able to enjoy the drive:

✔ Drive directly to Oheo Gulch, at the end of the road, without stopping. Explore Hana and Oheo Gulch in the morning. Head out of Hana right after lunch and do your meandering on the way home, against traffic. The disadvantage of this strategy is that, for some, the gorgeous scenery can lose some of its magic by afternoon: You're tired, you've been in the car a long time — you know how it goes.

✔ If conditions allow, drive out along the south route, which most Mauians call the Kaupo (COW-po) Road. Once you're done exploring Kipahulu and Hana, drive home along the Hana Highway. This strategy, however, has the same tired-of-being-in-the-car problem that the previous one does. What's more, a good seven miles of the Kaupo Road remains unpaved; not only is it impassable in bad weather, but some rental-car contracts disallow you from driving on it. Lastly, if you set out on this route too late in the day (after

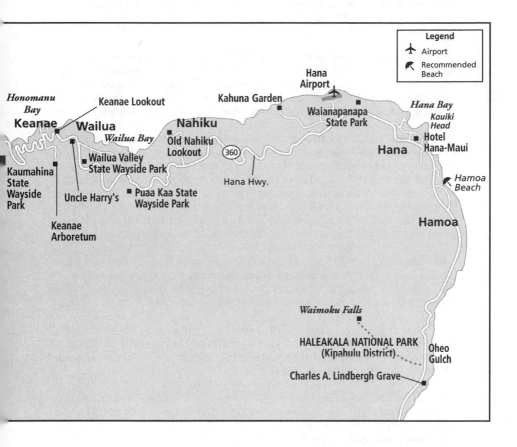

Legend
✈ Airport
✔ Recommended Beach

Honomanu Bay
Keanae Lookout
Kahuna Garden
Hana Airport
Hana Bay
Keanae
Wailua
Nahiku
Waianapanapa State Park
Kauiki Head
Wailua Bay
Old Nahiku Lookout
Hotel Hana-Maui
Hana
Wailua Valley State Wayside Park
360
Kaumahina State Wayside Park
Hana Hwy.
Hamoa Beach
Uncle Harry's
Puaa Kaa State Wayside Park
Keanae Arboretum
Hamoa
Waimoku Falls
HALEAKALA NATIONAL PARK (Kipahulu District)
Oheo Gulch
Charles A. Lindbergh Grave

lunch), the traffic you encounter on the narrow road as you near Kipahulu will make you feel like you're heading the wrong way on a one-way street — quite unnerving. Be sure to read "Heading back to the resorts" at the end of this section, which discusses the Kaupo Road more fully.

If you want to see the Hana Road but you just don't want to drive it yourself, consider taking a guided van or bus tour. See the section called "Taking a guided van or bus tour" earlier in this chapter for recommended tour operators.

Highlights worth seeking out along the way

Setting Out: A half-dozen miles east of Kahului on the Hana Highway is Paia (pa-EE-ah), a former mill town that's now a neo-hippie, boutique-dotted surf spot. **Charley's,** at Baldwin Avenue in the heart of town, makes an ideal stop for a hearty breakfast; afterward, you can bop around the corner to 30 Baldwin Ave., where **Pic-nics** (☎ **808-579-8021**) can put together a picnic for you to take on the road.

Just beyond Paia town is **Hookipa Beach Park,** one of the greatest windsurfing spots on the planet; see "Hitting the Beaches," earlier in this chapter, for details.

The road narrows to one lane in each direction and starts winding around Mile Marker 3. But it's at Mile Marker 16 that the curves really begin, one right after another. Slow down and enjoy the bucolic surroundings. After Mile Marker 16, the highway number changes from 36 to 360 and the mile markers start again at 0 (I have no idea why).

At Mile Marker 2: The first great place to stop is **Twin Falls,** on the inland side of the road; the Twin Falls Fruit Stand marks the spot. Hop over the short ladder on the right side of the red gate and walk about 3 to 5 minutes to the waterfall off to your left, or continue on another 10 to 15 minutes to the second, larger waterfall. There's a No Trespassing sign at the gate, but you'll see from the crowds that it doesn't bother most folks. If it bothers you, skip Twin Falls altogether; there's plenty more to see that's not so marked further down the road.

After Mile Marker 4: The vegetation grows more lush as you head east. This is the edge of the **Koolau Forest Reserve,** where the branches of 20- to 30-foot-tall guava trees are laden with green (not ripe) and yellow (ripe) fruit, and introduced eucalyptus trees grow as tall as 200 feet.

The upland forest gets 200 to 300 inches of rainfall annually, so you'll begin to see waterfalls around just about every turn as you head east from here. The one-lane bridges start, too, so drive slowly and be prepared to yield to oncoming cars.

After Mile Marker 6: Just before Mile Marker 7 is a forest of waving bamboo. The sight is so spectacular that drivers are often tempted to take their eyes off the road, so be very cautious. Just after Mile Marker 7 you can pull over at the **Kaaiea Bridge,** which offers a terrific view of the bamboo grove.

At Mile Marker 9: The sign says Koolau State Forest Reserve, but the real attraction is the **Waikamoi Ridge Trail,** an easy and well-marked three-quarter-mile loop. This is a great place to stretch your legs; look for the turnout on the right.

Between Mile Markers 10 and 11: At the halfway point, on the inland side of the road, is the **Garden of Eden Arboretum and Botanical Garden,** more than 500 exotic plants, flowers, and trees from around the Pacific (including lots of wild ginger and an impressive palm collection) on 26 acres. You can drive through the garden in about five minutes, walk its main loop in about 20 minutes, or stay a bit longer and follow any number of nature trails. The garden is open daily from 9 a.m. to 2 p.m., and admission is $5 per person. A fruit and smoothie stand offers refreshment at the gate.

At Mile Marker 11: Park at the bridge and take the short walk up the stone wall–lined trail to **Puohokamoa Falls,** tucked away in a fern-filled amphitheater surrounded by banana trees, colorful heliconias, and sweet-smelling ginger. The gorgeous pool of this 30-footer is a great place to take a plunge.

Just Beyond Mile Marker 12: Kaumahina State Wayside Park has portable toilets and picnic tables at the large parking area, plus a gorgeous view of the rugged coastline across the road.

Just Beyond Mile Marker 14: One of my favorite stops on the entire drive is **Honomanu Bay,** a stark rocky beach popular with net fishermen that faces a beautiful bay. Tear your eyes away and you'll find incredible golden-green cliffs forming an intense backdrop as you look inland and up. The turnoff is on the left, at the stop sign just after the mile marker; don't attempt the rutted and rocky road if it has been raining recently.

Just Beyond Mile Marker 17: Keanae Lookout is a wide spot on the ocean side of the road where you can see the entire Keanae Peninsula jutting out into the sea, with its checkerboard pattern of green taro fields and its ocean boundary etched in black lava. If time is precious, though, wait to stop after Mile Marker 19, where the view from the **Wailea Valley** viewpoint is even better.

At Mile Marker 18: The road widens, and fruit and flower stands begin to line the road. Many of these operate on the honor system: you select your purchase and leave your money in the basket. I recommend stopping at **Uncle Harry's,** just beyond Keanae School on the ocean side of the road. Harry Kunihi Mitchell was a legend in his time, an expert in native plants who devoted his life to the Hawaiian-rights and nuclear-free movements.

A Quarter-Mile After Marker 19: For the best view of the **Wailua Peninsula,** stop at the lookout and parking area on the ocean side of the road, where sun-dappled picnic tables serve up great views.

A bit farther down the road, just before the bridge on the inland side, is a pretty waterfall view.

Between Mile Markers 22 and 23: At **Puaa Kaa** (poo AH-ah KA-ah) **State Wayside Park,** the splash of waterfalls provides the soundtrack for a small park area with restrooms and a picnic area. On the opposite side of the road from the toilets is a well-marked and paved path that leads through a patch of sweet-smelling ginger to the falls and a swimming hole.

After Mile Marker 25: After the mile marker, turn toward the ocean at the steep turnoff just before the one-lane bridge, and follow the well-paved but winding road 2½ miles down to the **Old Nahiku Lookout,** one of the very few points along the entire route that lets you get close to the ocean, and the finest picnic spot on the entire route. A small grassy lawn faces rocky lava points and crashing turquoise surf for a breathtaking, up-close view. You can walk down to the rocky beach at the backside of the parking lot.

At Mile Marker 31: Turn toward the ocean on Ulaino Road and go a half-mile to **Kahanu Garden,** one of four National Tropical Botanical Gardens in Hawaii (☎ **808-248-8912;** Internet: www.ntbg.org). Surrounded by a native pandanus forest (the leaf that *lauhala* products are woven from), the garden features a remarkable collection of ethno-botanical plants from the Pacific islands (with a particular concentration on plants of value to the people of Polynesia and Micronesia), plus the foundation of Poolanihale Heiau, the largest Hawaiian temple in Hawaii. The self-guided walking tour is $5 (free for kids 12 and under) and takes 30 to 40 minutes to complete. The road that leads to the garden entrance is rough and unpaved, but not bad; still, don't bother if it's been raining.

At Mile Marker 32: The turnoff for 122-acre **Waianapanapa** (wa-ee-na-pa-NA-pa) **State Park** leads to shiny black-sand **Waianapanapa Beach,** whose bright-green jungle backdrop and sparkling cobalt water make for quite a stunning view. On hand are picnic pavilions, restrooms, trails, and fruit stands lining the road, so come down to take a peek. The beach here is not for swimming, though. A blowhole appears when the winter surf kicks up. This natural hole in the rocks is configured so that when harsh surf kicks up, water shoots through the hole like a spout — quite a neat sight.

Arriving in Hana

Postage stamp–sized Hana is a lush and charming little hamlet, but frankly, there's just not much to see in the town itself.

The few attractions include the **Hana Coast Gallery** at the Hotel Hana-Maui (☎ 808-248-8636), an excellent showcase for island-made products hewn by master craftspeople, including gorgeous woodworks. The quirky **Hasegawa General Store** (☎ 808-248-8231 or 808-248-7079) is worth stopping in for kicks (look for the Spam sushi vending machine near the entrance) or to use the ATM, but the prices on practicals and munchies are better across the road and up the hill at the **Hana Ranch Store** (☎ 808-248-8261). If you want a meal, you have two choices: the casual **Hana Ranch Restaurant,** or the **Hotel Hana-Maui Dining Room;** for details, see "Maui's Best Restaurants" in Chapter 13.

If you'd like to see more of what's available in town, pick up a copy of the **Hana Visitors Guide,** a fold-out map and pamphlet that's available free around town. If you don't run across one, stop into Hasegawa's to pick one up.

For those of you spending some time in these parts, a number of active adventures are at hand:

✔ **Hang Gliding Maui** (☎ 808-572-6557; Internet: www. hanggl idingmaui .com), which offers tandem instructional flights aboard their engine-powered ultralight aircraft; see "Flightseeing tours" earlier in this chapter for details.

✔ If you'd like to explore the lush Kipahulu District on horseback, reach out to **Oheo Stables** (☎ 808-667-2222; Internet: www. maui .net/~ray); advance reservations are a must.

✔ **Maui Cave Adventures** (☎ 808-248-7308; Internet: www.mauicave. com) offers cave-exploring hikes for every age and ability, including kids as young as 7, through Kaeleku Caverns.

Hana

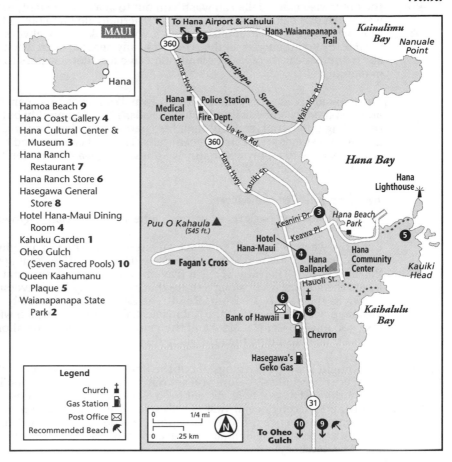

MAUI

Hana

Hamoa Beach **9**
Hana Coast Gallery **4**
Hana Cultural Center &
  Museum **3**
Hana Ranch
  Restaurant **7**
Hana Ranch Store **6**
Hasegawa General
  Store **8**
Hotel Hana-Maui Dining
  Room **4**
Kahuku Garden **1**
Oheo Gulch
  (Seven Sacred Pools) **10**
Queen Kaahumanu
  Plaque **5**
Waianapanapa State
  Park **2**

Legend
Church
Gas Station
Post Office
Recommended Beach

To Hana Airport & Kahului
Hana-Waianapanapa Trail
Kainalimu Bay Nanuale Point
360
Kawaipapa Stream
Waikoloa Rd.
Hana Medical Center Police Station Fire Dept.
Ua Kea Rd.
360
Hana Hwy.
Kauiki St.
Hana Bay
Hana Lighthouse
Puu O Kahaula (545 ft.)
Keanini Dr.
Hana Beach Park
Keawa Pl.
Hotel Hana-Maui
Fagan's Cross
Hana Ballpark
Hana Community Center
Kauiki Head
Hauoli St.
Bank of Hawaii
Kaihalulu Bay
Chevron
Hasegawa's Geko Gas
31
0   1/4 mi
0   .25 km
To Oheo Gulch

Beyond Hana: Hamoa Beach and Oheo Gulch

ROMANCE

About 2½ miles past Hana is the turnoff for Hamoa Beach, one of the most gorgeous beaches in all of Hawaii — and great for swimming, to boot (in summer, anyway). For details, see "Hitting the Beaches" earlier in this chapter.

About 10 luxuriant miles past Hana along the highway is **Oheo** (oh-HAY-oh) **Gulch,** a dazzling series of waterfall pools cascading into the sea that some folks call Seven Sacred Pools, even though there are more like two dozen. This is the Kipahulu district of Haleakala National Park, and a **ranger station** located at the back of the unpaved parking lot (☎ 808-248-7375) is staffed daily from 9 a.m. to 5 p.m. Restrooms are available, but no drinking water, so be sure to pick some up in Hana if you're out. There is no fee for visiting this area of the park.

The easy, half-mile **Kuloa Point Loop Trail** leads to the lower pools, where you can take a dip when the weather is warm and the water is placid. This well-marked 20-minute walk is a must for everyone.

Stay out of the Oheo Gulch pools in winter or after a heavy rain, when the otherwise placid falls can wash you out to sea in an instant, to the waiting sharks below. (No kidding — they actually do hang out in the brackish water at the foot of the falls.) If you do take a dip, always keep an eye on the water in the streams in any season. Even when the sky is sunny near the coast, upland rain can cause flood waters to rise in minutes.

The two-mile (each way), moderate **Pipiwai Trail** leads upstream to additional pools and 400-foot Waimoku Falls. The often-muddy but rewarding uphill trail leads through taro patches and bamboo, guava, and mango stands to the magnificent falls. The trail is unmarked but relatively easy to follow. Wear sturdy shoes, bring water, and don't attempt the trek in the rain.

Heading back to the resorts

Most visitors head back the way they came, along the Hana Highway.

But if the weather is good, you have an alternative. The Hana Highway continues past Kipahulu around Maui's southern coast, becoming the Piilani Highway (Highway 31) as it traverses the empty desert that meets the southern sea along a route that's informally but universally known as the **Kaupo** (COW-po) **Road.** The Kaupo Road ultimately meets up with Highway 37 (the Kula/Haleakala Highway), which will take you back to Central Maui and the resorts. The route is no shorter or less time-consuming than the Hana Road — just different.

You should know a few things about the Kaupo Road — and consider them very carefully — before you set out on it. For one thing, you'll find nothing at all out here, except for a few lone cows, some desert scrub, and amazing ocean views — no structures at all, let alone any modern conveniences. Those who appreciate desert beauty will find the landscape striking, but anyone else will feel like they've arrived in Mad Max territory.

Seven miles of road remain unpaved, but the entire stretch between Mile Markers 39 and 23 (the markers run west to east) is dreadful. In fact, the unpaved portion is an improvement over the other pitted nine miles, whose pavement is so lumpy that it doesn't deserve to be called pavement.

While the Kaupo Road is fine for average cars in dry weather, the road washes out with a little rain, so don't go near it if the weather has been poor. Ask around, both at your hotel and in Hana; you'll find that the news gets out. And check with your rental-car company before you set out, as many rental contracts forbid you from taking their car on this road. If you get stuck, you'll pay a hefty tow charge — but that will be the least of your problems, because you'll be stuck in the real middle of nowhere, where other cars may not pass by for hours.

All that said, I love the Kaupo Road and the little-seen side of Maui it shows. Still, before you consider it, be sure to take all of my warnings and recommendations extremely seriously. And if one person tells you that conditions are less than optimum and advises you against it, skip it — go back the way you came.

Before departing Hana, don't forget to check your gas gauge no matter which road west you're traveling, as there's nowhere to fill up along either route back to civilization. If you need gas, stop at one of the town's two service stations, Chevron and Hasegawa's Hana Geko Gas, which sit nearly side by side on the right side of the Hana Highway as you leave town.

More attractions worth seeking out

Central Maui

The following attractions are all located in Wailuku, the charming county seat directly west of far less appealing Kahului, Maui's main 'burb. Antique hounds, in particular, won't want to miss retro-minded North Market Street; see "A shopper's guide to Maui" later in this chapter.

Bailey House Museum

This 19th-century missionary and sugar planter's home is a treasure trove of Hawaiiana that includes a notable collection of pre-contact Hawaiian artifacts as well as items from post-missionary times. This little museum is well worth a half-hour stop for history buffs. It has a good gift shop, too.

2375-A Main St., just west of the Kaahumanu Ave./Honoapiilani Hwy. (Hwy. 32/30) intersection, Wailuku. ☎ *808-244-3326. Admission: $4 adults, $3.50 seniors, $1 kids 6–12. Open: Mon–Sat 10 a.m.–4 p.m.*

Hawaii Nature Center — Iao Valley

Before you head into Iao Valley to explore (directly following), don't neglect to stop into this interactive science center, which features great hands-on exhibits for kids and displays relating to the park's natural history. A must for Iao Valley visitors.

At the gateway to Iao Valley State Monument, 875 Iao Valley Rd. ☎ *808-244-6500. Internet:* www.hawaiinaturecenter.org. *Admission: $6 adults, $4 kids under 12. Open: Daily 10 a.m.–4 p.m.*

Call ahead to reserve a spot on one of Hawaii Nature Center's daily nature walks through Iao Valley.

Iao Valley State Monument

As you head west to Iao Valley, the transition between town and wild is so abrupt that most people who drive up into the valley don't realize they're suddenly in a rain forest. The walls of the canyon rise, and a 2,250-foot needle pricks gray clouds scudding across the blue sky. This is Iao (EE-ow) Valley, a place of great natural beauty and a haven for Mauians and visitors alike.

You could easily spend an entire day here, but you can see everything in a couple of hours. Two paved walkways loop the 6.2-acre park; a leisurely ⅓-mile loop walk takes you past lush vegetation and lovely views of the Iao Needle, an impressive spire jutting 2,250 feet above sea level. An architectural heritage park of Hawaiian, Japanese, Chinese, Filipino, and New England–style houses stands in harmony by Iao Stream at Kepaniwai Heritage Garden, which also makes a good picnic spot. You'll see ferns, banana trees, and other native and exotic plants in the streamside botanic garden.

On Iao Valley Rd. (at the end of Main St.), Wailuku. To get there: From Kahului, follow Kaahumanu Ave. east directly to Main St. and the park entrance. Admission: Free! Open: Daily 7 a.m.–7 p.m.

West Maui: Historic Lahaina Town

It may be hard to believe these days, overrun as Lahaina is with contemporary tourist schlock. But any of you who've read James Michener's *Hawaii* know that back in the whaling and missionary days, Lahaina was the capital of Hawaii and the Pacific's wildest port. Now it's a party town of a different kind, and has lost much of its historic vibe; but history buffs with an interest can unearth a half-day's worth of historic sites.

Your best bet is to start at the **Baldwin Home Museum,** a beautifully restored 1838 missionary home at the corner of Front and Dickenson streets, where the **Lahaina Restoration Foundation** (☎ **808-661-3262;** Internet: www.lahainarestoration.org) is headquartered in the adjacent Master's Reading Room. Stop in any day between 10 a.m. and 4:30 p.m. to pick up the free self-guided walking tour brochure and map of Lahaina's most historic sites. All within easy walking distance of one another, stops include the Brig *Carthaginian II,* a replica of the 19th-century whaling ship that brought the first missionaries to Hawaii, docked at Lahaina Harbor; the banyan tree, planted as a sapling in 1873 and now a massive 60 feet high and spanning two-thirds of an acre; an 1850s prison, the inside of which the rowdiest whalers no doubt saw on a regular basis; and a number of other interesting sites, including some lovely Buddhist missions and temples.

South Maui

Maui Ocean Center

This state-of-the-art aquarium is too pricey for its own good — it's no Monterey Bay Aquarium after all, not by a long shot — but it's still one cool place. All exhibits feature the creatures that populate Hawaii's waters, which makes this a great place to visit before you set out on a snorkel cruise. Start at the surge pool, where you'll see shallow-water marine life like spiny urchins and cauliflower coral; then move on to the reef tanks, a turtle lagoon (where you'll meet some wonderful green sea turtles), a "touch" pool featuring tidepool critters, a stingray pool populated by the graceful bottom dwellers, and a disappointing whale discovery exhibit (no live creatures) before you get to the star of the show: the 600,000-gallon main tank, which features tiger, gray, and white-tip sharks, as well as tuna, surgeon fish, triggerfish, and other large-scale tropicals. The neatest thing about the tank is that it's punctured by a clear acrylic tunnel that lets you walk right through it, giving you a real idea of what it might be like to stand at the bottom of the deep blue sea. Allow about two hours for your visit.

In Maalaea Harbor Village, at the triangle between Honoapiilani Highway (Hwy. 31) and Maalaea Road, Maalaea. ☎ *808-875-1962. Internet:* www.coralworld.com/moc. *Admission: $18 adults, $16.20 seniors, $12.50 kids 3–12. Audio tour $4 extra (at press time, a 2-for-1 audio-tour deal was in effect). Open: Daily 9 a.m.–5 p.m.*

Upcountry Maui

Maui's biggest upcountry attraction is, of course, **Haleakala National Park,** which is so big that it deserved its own dedicated section earlier in this chapter. The rural upcountry also has a handful of other appealing features, most notably Maui's only commercial winery (see the following listing) and the cowboy-turned-boutique-town of **Makawao** (see "A shopper's guide to Maui" later in this chapter).

Tedeschi Vineyards

Maui's only winery is worth visiting less for its wines — which aren't going to cause the Napa Valley to worry about the Hawaii competition anytime soon — and more for the stunning mountain drive it takes to get there, and the pretty pastoral you'll find once you arrive. Sitting on the little-visited south slopes of Haleakala at 2,000 feet elevation, these rolling, golden-hued ranchlands are like no other place you'll find on the island. The ranch dates back to the mid-19th century (the tasting room is housed in a lovely 1874 stone cottage built for a visit by King David Kalakaua), so it has a wonderful historic feeling and well-established grounds that are perfect for picnicking; buy a bottle — red, white, or sparkling — to accompany lunch, but skip the silly pineapple wine. Allow an hour each way for the drive from most resorts. Free tastings and tours make this a surprisingly popular destination.

On the Kula Hwy. (Hwy. 37), Ulupalakua. ☎ *808-878-6058. Internet:* www.maui.net/~winery. *To get there: Follow the Haleakala Hwy. south to the Kula Hwy.; once you reach Keokea, go 5.1 miles past the Henry Fong Store. Admission, tastings, and tours: Free! Open: Daily 9 a.m.–5 p.m.; tours 9:30 a.m.–2:30 p.m.*

Hitting the links and courts

Golf

Always book your tee times well in advance on popular Maui, especially in high season. Weekdays are best for avoiding the crowds and securing the tee times you want.

Stand-by Golf (☎ **888-645-2665** or 808-874-0060; Internet: www.standbygolf.com) offers up to 50 percent off greens fees to bargain hunters and last-minute duffers at select courses. What's available depends on when you call and where you're staying; give it a shot if you want to save a few bucks or get a sudden urge to hit the links.

The Dunes at Maui Lani

By all accounts, this dramatic British links-style course — Maui's newest — plays like an old pro. Inspired by the old-growth links of Ireland, Honolulu-based course architect Robin Nelson built this public course on the former home of a sand-mining operation, which has allowed the fairways to mature in record time. Several blind and semi-blind shots give this all-around enjoyable course an edge. Considering the quality of the course, the rates are a veritable bargain.

1333 Mauilani Pkwy., Kahului. ☎ *808-873-0422. Greens fees: $75, $37 after 2 p.m.*

Kaanapali Golf Courses

Both of these popular, rolling resort courses pose a challenge to all golfers, from high handicappers to near-pros. The par-71, 6,136-yard Tournament North Course is home to the Senior PGA Tour, and a true Robert Trent Jones design, with an abundance of wide bunkers, several long, stretched-out tees, the largest, most contoured greens on Maui, and one of Hawaii's toughest finishing holes. The par-71, 6,067-yard Resort South Course is an Arthur Jack Snyder design that, although shorter than the North Course, requires more accuracy on the narrow, hilly fairways. There's a tricky water hazard on the 18th, so don't tally up your scorecard until the final putt is sunk. Facilities include a driving range, putting green, clubhouse, and comprehensive golf academy.

2290 Kaanapali Pkwy. (off Hwy. 30), Kaanapali. ☎ *808-661-3691. Internet:* www.kaanapali-golf.com. *Greens fees: $107–$120 for Kaanapali resort guests, $67 after 2 p.m.; $132–$140 for non-guests, $70 after 2 p.m.*

Kapalua Golf Club

These three spectacularly sited championship courses are worth the sky-high greens fees for the views alone. Resort golf hardly gets finer — *Hawaii* magazine just named the Bay and the Plantation courses two of the top nine courses in Hawaii. An Arnold Palmer/Francis Duane design, the par-72, 6,600-yard Bay Course is a bit forgiving thanks to generous and gently undulating fairways, but even the pros have trouble with the 5th, which requires a tee shot over an ocean cove. The breathtaking — and breathtakingly difficult — Ben Crenshaw/Bill Coore–designed Plantation Course is prime for developing your low shots and precise chipping; this 7,263-yard, par-73 showstopper is home to the PGA's annual season opener. The par-71, 6,632-yard Village Course, a Palmer/Ed Seay design and the most scenic of the three courses, suits beginners and pros alike, but winds can make for a challenging day among the Cook and Norfolk pines. Facilities include locker rooms, driving range, restaurant, and a first-rate golf academy.

Off Honoapiilani Highway (Hwy. 30), Kapalua. ☎ *877-527-2582 or 808-669-8044. Internet:* www.kapaluamaui.com. *Greens fees: $110–$120 for Kapalua resort guests, $155–$200 for non-guests; $70–$80 after 2 p.m.*

Wailea Golf Club

Most difficult among Wailea's courses is the par-72, 7,070-yard Gold Course, the new home to the Senior Skins Game. This classic Robert Trent Jones, Jr., design boasts a rugged layout, narrow fairways, several tricky dogleg holes, daunting natural hazards, and only-in-Hawaii features like lava outcroppings and native grasses. Both the Blue and the Emerald are easy for most golfers to enjoy, but the par-72, 6,407-yard Emerald Course — another Trent Jones, Jr., design — is both the prettiest and easiest for high-handicappers to enjoy. The par-72, 6,700-yard Blue Course, an open course designed by Arthur Jack Snyder, has wide fairways that also appeal to beginners, but bunkers, water hazards, and undulating terrain make it a course that all can enjoy. Facilities include two clubhouses, two pro shops, restaurants, lockers, club rentals, and a complete training facility.

Off Wailea Alanui Dr., Wailea. ☎ *888-328-MAUI, 800-322-1614, or 808-875-7450. Internet:* www.waileagolf.com. *Greens fees: $90–$100 for Wailea resort guests, $120–$125 non-guests. Call to inquire about discounted afternoon rates and money-saving triple- and unlimited-play passes.*

Makena Golf Club

Robert Trent Jones, Jr., was in top form when he designed these 36 holes. The par-72, 7,017-yard oceanside South Course is considered the more forgiving of the two, but has a couple of holes you'll never forget: Running parallel to the ocean, the par-4 16th has a two-tiered green that slopes away from the player, while the par-5, 502-yard 10th is one of Hawaii's best driving holes. With tight fairways and narrow doglegs, the par-72, 6,914-yard North Course is both more difficult and more spectacular, since it sits higher up the slope of Haleakala. Facilities include clubhouse, driving range, two putting greens, pro shop, lockers, and lessons. Additional bonuses include a gorgeous rural setting and spectacular views.

5415 Makena Alanui Dr., Makena (south of Wailea). ☎ *808-879-3344. Internet:* www.makenagolf.com. *Greens fees: $140, $75 after 2 p.m.*

Tennis

Private tennis courts are available at most resorts and the nicer condo complexes around Maui.

If you need a court in West Maui, contact the **Kapalua Tennis Garden,** Kapalua Resort (☎ **808-669-5677;** Internet: www.kapaluamaui.com), which features 10 plexi-pave courts for both day and night play ($12 for non-resort guests), plus group and private instruction.

In South Maui, book a court at the **Wailea Tennis Club** (☎ **808-879-1958;** Internet: www.wailea-resort.com). Consistently chosen as one of the finest tennis facilities around, Wailea has 11 hard courts available for $25 for resort guests, $30 for non-guests, plus a full calendar of lessons, clinics, round robins, and the like.

For adventure seekers: Side-tripping to Molokai

Looking for an attention-grabbing answer to the inevitable "How was your vacation" question? Try this one on for size: "I scaled the highest sea cliffs in the world on the back of a mule to reach a leper colony in exile."

If such a reply appeals to your adventurous heart, consider breaking away from Maui for the day for a side trip to Molokai. Scruffy, rural Molokai's most famous site is **Kalaupapa National Historical Park,** the world-famous 19th-century leper colony that sits on the dorsal fin–shaped peninsula that juts out from Molokai's north shore.

Beginning in 1865, in one of history's most devastating marriages of ugly human behavior and supreme natural beauty, islanders diagnosed with Hansen's Disease (leprosy) were forcibly taken from their homes and families and exiled to this wild and completely undeveloped peninsula, which is open to the sea but isolated from the rest of Molokai by the highest sea cliffs in the world, which soar 1,700 feet to the sky in a near vertical slope. The first exiles were left with not even the tools to build shelters. Later, what few supplies that intermittently arrived would be tossed into the waters by fearful sea captains refusing to come ashore; patients would be forced to retrieve the crates by braving life-threatening ocean conditions. (Not a few patients disembarked in a similar manner.)

The horror continued unabated until Father Damien, a Belgian Catholic missionary priest, arrived in 1873. Father Damien secured the funding and supplies to build homes, hospitals, and churches for the resident exiles of Kalaupapa. Before he succumbed to Hansen's Disease himself in 1889, his efforts resulted in the development of a cohesive and established community where few thought one could ever exist.

The use of new sulphone antibiotics beginning in 1946 cured Hansen's Disease overnight and halted the threat of leprosy in Hawaii. Isolation laws were abolished in 1969, and the population of this community that contained more than 8,000 residents over 100 years has dwindled to less than 45 (all voluntary residents). At this writing, the youngest resident is 59 — so now is a good time to visit, when you can still see a community that is; within the next couple or few decades, visitors will see only a community that once was.

Kalaupapa can only be reached by mule, prop plane, helicopter, or a steep trek best attempted by the hardiest hikers. You can visit Kalaupapa between Monday and Saturday, but it is off-limits to visitors on Sunday. Kids under 16 are not admitted. You can't tour Kalaupapa on your own; you must be part of a guided tour.

Riding the Mule Train

The most popular way to reach Kalaupapa is on the world-famous **Molokai Mule Ride** (☎ 800-567-7550; Internet: www.muleride.com). If you're up for the trip, I highly recommend it; it's one of the most incredible journeys I've ever taken. The company is run by two Molokai fellows, Buzzy Sproat and Roy Horner, both of whom love showing Molokai to visitors. Their Mule Skinners will train you to ride one of their strong and sure-footed mules (mine was Elvira), then lead you 1,700 feet down the mind-bogglingly steep sea-cliff trail, which boasts some of the most breathtaking views in the world.

While you don't have to have any skill or experience to participate, this ride is *not* for the faint of heart. The practiced mules take the 26 switchbacks in heart-stopping fashion — they love to cling to the outermost edge, and you're just sure they're gonna step right off the side and take you tumbling down to the bottom. It's a rough, jarring ride in which the great risk is not the mule falling off the cliff, but you falling off the mule. You'll get dirty, sweaty, and smelly in the two-hour ride to the bottom. (I could barely see through the layer of dust on my contact lenses.)

When you reach the bottom, you'll hook up with Damien Tours (see contact information in the following section). Resident Richard Meeks or one of his guides will take you on a tour of the Kalaupapa settlement aboard a big yellow school bus, offering insights along the way that only a resident can provide.

Once your tour is done (a basic lunch is included), you'll again mount your mule, who's ready to make the punishing climb back to the top. The entire adventure lasts from just before 8 a.m. until 3:15 p.m., when you'll return to the mule barn, and costs $150 per person, or $279 per person including air flights from Maui or Oahu, plus transfers to the mule barn from the airport. Molokai Mule Ride can make all the arrangements.

Alternatives for mule-phobes

If you want to visit Kalaupapa but you don't like the sound of the mule ride, you have options. Molokai Mule Ride (see contact information in the previous section) can also arrange a number of Kalaupapa packages that don't involve four-legged beasts:

- ✔ A hike in/hike out option is $40 per person ($58 with airport transfer), including Damien Tour, or $205 including airfare from Maui or Oahu.

- ✔ A fly in/fly out option is the least time-consuming or tiring. You can fly in to the Kalaupapa Airport (the smallest airport I've ever seen) and meet up with Damien Tours, who'll drop you back at the airport after the tour for your return flight. This option is $109 per person if you're flying from Molokai's main airport, Hoolehua Airport, to Kalaupapa (you arrange your own flights to Hoolehua Airport), or $189 from Maui or Oahu.

- ✔ The hike in/fly out plan is the best option for those who want to hike the trail. Trust me on this — even the most passionate hikers find the single-day roundtrip hike to be too much. This option is $80, including the tour and return flight to Molokai Airport.

If you are going to hike the trail, wear sturdy, ankle-supporting shoes, as the terrain is extremely steep and rocky.

If you'd rather arrange your own hike-in or fly-in tour to Kalaupapa, you can. You must book your guided Kalaupapa land tour directly with **Damien Tours** (☎ 808-567-6171); call Monday through Saturday between 7 and 9 a.m. and 5 and 7 p.m. to reach a real person. The price for the four-hour tour is $30 per person, plus airfare (expect to pay about $50 round-trip from Molokai's main airport). If you're going to hike in, inquire about arranging for the necessary permit (the Molokai Visitor Association can also assist with this issue).

The following airlines offer flights to and from Kalaupapa from Maui, Oahu, and Molokai's main gateway, Hoolehua Airport, in Kaunakakai:

- ✔ **Molokai Air Shuttle** (☎ 808-567-6847 on Molokai; ☎ 808-545-4988 on Oahu)
- ✔ **Pacific Wings** (☎ 888-575-4546 or 808-873-0877; Internet: www.pacificwings.com)

You might find that booking a standard interisland flight from Maui (or Oahu) to Molokai's main airport aboard either Hawaiian Airlines or Aloha (through their subsidiary carrier, Island Air) and then hopping a flight to Kalaupapa aboard one of the above-mentioned smaller carriers gives you the greatest flexibility in terms of scheduling. See "Flying between the Hawaiian Islands" in Chapter 5 for details on interisland flights.

If you're only interested in taking a topside tour and don't care to visit Kalaupapa, consider one of the sail-and-tour options offered by the *Maui Princess.* See the section called "Ocean cruising to Molokini and Lanai — and other on-deck adventures" earlier in this chapter.

Options for overnighters and ground transportation

If you'd prefer to spend the night before your mule ride (or hike) on Molokai rather than catching a predawn flight from Maui or Oahu, Molokai Mule Ride can recommend convenient accommodations. You can also locate accommodations by contacting the **Molokai Visitors Association** (☎ 800-800-6367, 800-553-0404, or 808-553-3876; Internet: www.molokai-hawaii.com) or checking the listings on the **Visit Molokai** Web site (www.visitmolokai.com).

Even if you're flying in for the day, you may want to rent your own car rather than relying on the Mule Ride folks to shuttle you around. Flight scheduling might give you a couple of extra hours after the mule ride before your return flight to Maui, and a rental car allows you to do a little topside exploring rather than sitting at the airport. Both **Budget** (☎ 800-527-0700; Internet: www.budgetrentacar.com) and **Dollar** (☎ 800-800-1000; Internet: www.dollarcar.com) have cars available at Molokai airport.

For taxi or guided tour service on Molokai, contact **Molokai Off-Road Tours & Taxi** (☎ 808-553-3369; Internet: www.molokai.com/offroad).

A shopper's guide to Maui

When it comes to shopping opportunities, the Valley Isle is the reigning king among the neighbor islands in terms of quantity. Its status is a bit more dubious when it comes to quality, but you will find some real gems in the eclectic mix.

Central Maui: Wailuku

While Kahului is the island's hub and the place to go for practicals, the historic town of Wailuku immediately to the west offers prime hunting grounds for antique hounds. It's still a mixed bag, but an increasing number of quality shops featuring both new and used treasures can be found on North Market Street; to get there, simply go west from Kahului on Kaahumanu Avenue and turn right when you reach Market, in the heart of Wailuku.

Highlights include **Memory Lane,** 130 N. Market St. (☎ 808-244-4196) for 20th-century collectibles; **Brown-Kobayashi,** 160 N. Market St. (☎ 808-242-0804), a treasure trove of graceful and stylish finds (mostly large pieces, but make it a destination anyway); and **Bird of Paradise Unique Antiques,** 54 N. Market St. (☎ 808-242-7699), for glassware, pottery, and Hawaiiana.

In the "new" department, Wailuku's top stop is **Sig Zane,** 53 N. Market St. (☎ 808-249-8997). Mauians cheered when this Big Island designer set up this new Valley Isle outpost. Sig's distinctive, two-color all-cotton aloha wear is the height of simple style and good taste. The stunningly beautiful fabrics are sold in a variety of clean-lined, easy-to-wear styles as well as off the bolt if you'd like to take some home. If you buy one article of aloha wear to bring home, buy it here. And if you've already visited the Big Island boutique, stop in anyway, because you'll find unique patterns and colors here.

West Maui: Lahaina and Kaanapali

Lahaina's main drag, Front Street, overflows with surf-wear shops, contemporary art galleries, trendy boutiques, cheesy T-shirt shops, and much, much more — you'll tire of browsing well before you run out of places to flex your credit card.

Your best bet is to just start at one end and browse. Highlights include **Serendipity,** 752 Front St. (☎ 808-667-7070) for casual, island-style women's wear in comfortable, loose-fitting styles. **Honolua Surf Co.,** 845 Front St. (☎ 808-661-8848; Internet: www.honoluasurf.com) carries their own fabulous line of surf wear and gear. **Célébrités,** 764 Front St. (☎ 800-428-3338 or 808-667-0727; Internet: www.celebrityfineart. com), has a collection of art by and about celebrities that's the height of over-the-top conspicuous consumption, but it's a compelling browse, nonetheless.

An island of artistic integrity in the sea of Lahaina kitsch is **Na Mea Hawaii Store,** in the Masters Reading Room, 120 Dickenson St., at Front Street (☎ 808-661-5707), which sells only fine-quality island-made crafts and gifts. That doesn't mean expensive, though; you'll find a surprising number of affordable prizes among the bounty.

For marine-themed goods and educational gifts for kids, you can't do better than the surprisingly nice nonprofit **Pacific Whale Foundation** store, 143 Dickenson St., a block up from Front Street (☎ 808-667-7447; Internet: www.pacificwhale.org). Members save 15 percent off all whale- and eco-themed goodies as well as whale-watch cruises and snorkel tours that can be booked right at the shop (see "Ocean cruising to Molokini and Lanai — and other on-deck adventures" earlier in this chapter), so consider joining up for a good cause.

You'll find a second Pacific Whale Foundation shop in South Maui at Kealia Beach Plaza, 101 N. Kihei Rd., at the north end of Kihei (☎ 808-879-8660; Internet: www.pacificwhale.org).

At the far south end of Front Street, in the 505 Front St. complex, is **Lei Spa Maui** (☎ 808-661-1178; Internet: www.leispa.com), which carries a wonderful line of fragrant and rejuvenating Hawaii-made bath and body products, while therapists offer massages, body wraps, and facials.

At the opposite, north end of Front Street are a couple of shopping centers, including **Lahaina Cannery Mall,** 1221 Honoapiilani Hwy. (☎ 808-661-5304; Internet: www.lahainacannerymall.com), for practicals; **Lahaina Center,** 900 Front St. (☎ 808-667-9216; Internet: www.lahainacenter.com), a pleasant open-air mall that boasts **Local Motion** for surf wear and gear; **Hilo Hattie,** Hawaii's biggest name in affordable aloha wear; and mall standards like **The Gap.**

On the beach in Kaanapali, **Whaler's Village,** 2435 Kaanapali Pkwy. (☎ 808-661-4567; Internet: www.whalersvillage.com), has blossomed into quite an upscale shopping and dining complex, offering a surprisingly appealing open-air shopping experience. While it has become the Rodeo Drive of Maui in recent years — with **Gucci, Dior, Chanel, Prada, Louis Vuitton,** and **Versace** all represented — it also has some surprisingly excellent mid-range boutiques, including two branches of **Honolua Surf Co.,** whose stylish surf gear and wear I just love; **Sandal Tree,** for an excellent collection of women's footwear, sunhats, and handbags; a branch of **Reyn's,** the Hawaii-based company that makes my second-favorite contemporary aloha wear (after Sig Zane; see Wailuku, earlier in this section); and **The Body Shop,** in case you need to stock up on eco-friendly sunscreen.

Off the beaten path: Paia and Makawao

The hip little surf town of Paia (pa-EE-ah), just 15 minutes east of Kahului on the Hana Highway (Highway 36), makes an eclectic but appealing stop for shoppers looking for funkier goods. The boutiques sprawl in a T-shape from the intersection of the Hana Highway and Baldwin Avenue, and the choices range from the sublime to the ridiculous. On the sublime end is **Maui Crafts Guild,** on the ocean side of Hana Highway at no. 43 (☎ 808-579-9697; Internet: www.mauicraftsguild.com), an artist-owned cooperative that represents some of the finest fine artists and craftspeople on Maui; you'll find artworks and gifts in all price ranges here. At the opposite end of the spectrum is **Big Bugga Sportswear,** 18 Baldwin Ave. (☎ 808-579-6216; Internet: www.bigbugga.com), which

carries the largest men's casual wear you've ever seen in your life —
from XL to a sumo-sized 10X. In between you'll find **Moonbow Tropics,**
36 Baldwin Ave. (☎ **808-579-8592;** Internet: www.moonbowtropicsmaui.
com), which offers the finest contemporary aloha-wear lines available;
and **Paia Trading Co.,** 106 Hana Hwy. (☎ **877-218-8763** or 808-579-9472),
for good, old-fashioned vintage collectibles.

From Paia, drive toward the mountain on Baldwin Avenue (Highway
390), and in seven miles you'll reach Makawao (ma-KA-wow), a cowboy–
town–turned–New–Age–village that's another petite shopper's paradise.

The shopping is so good in Makawao that the whole *town* is a highlight.
Serious shoppers should definitely save an afternoon to explore. If you
only have an hour or so to shop, seek out **Ola's Makawao,** in the
Paniolo Building, 1156 Makawao Ave. (☎ **808-573-1334**), the town's top
gift gallery; **Hurricane,** 3639 Baldwin Ave. (☎ **808-572-5076**), a wonderful split-level boutique that carries a well-displayed selection of fine
casuals for women; and **Tropo,** next door (☎ **808-573-0356**),
Hurricane's boutique for men. **The Courtyard,** at 3620 Baldwin Ave.,
houses a number of interesting crafts shops of varying quality, plus a
fascinating glassblower's studio that's worth a peek: **Hot Island
Glassblowing** (☎ **808-572-4527**).

The highlight of Makawao is the **Hui Noeau Visual Arts Center,** a mile
outside of town at 2841 Baldwin Ave. (☎ **808-572-6560;** Internet: www.
maui.net/~hui). A tree-lined driveway leads to the 1917 estate
(designed by noted Hawaii architect C.W. Dickey) that houses the
island's most renowned artists' collective and features rotating exhibits
by both established and up-and-coming island artists, plus an excellent
shop featuring original works. The artistically active among you might
also want to inquire about workshops, demonstrations, visiting-artist
events, and other short-term opportunities for study.

Living It Up Once the Sun Goes Down

After Oahu, Maui boasts Hawaii's second-biggest after-dark scene.
Many of the island's restaurants — particularly the oceanfront ones —
do double-duty as post-dinner hotspots, often hosting lively bar
scenes, live music, and dancing. The epicenter of island nightlife is
lively Lahaina.

For the most complete calendar of what's happening while you're on
Maui, pick up a copy of the weekly *Maui Time* newspaper, available for
free at kiosks all over the island.

If you're interested in the more refined performing arts, look for a copy
of *Centerpiece,* the free bimonthly magazine published by the **Maui
Arts and Cultural Center,** the finest cultural venue in the neighbor
islands; hotel concierges usually have copies. You can also call the
center at ☎ **808-242-2787** or visit the Web site at www.mauiarts.org
for a current schedule.

The island's best sunset cruises are offered by **Royal Hawaiian Cruises** (☎ 808-873-3475; Internet: www.royalhawaiiancruises.com), which hosts two-hour dining-and-dancing cruises aboard its smooth-sailing, ultra-modern *Navatek II.* For further details, see "Ocean cruising to Molokini and Lanai — and other on-deck adventures" earlier in this chapter.

And, of course, don't forget that Maui is home to the finest examples of the ultimate island form of after-dark entertainment: the luau! I highly recommend planning to participate in one while you're on the Valley Isle. For details, see the "Luau!" section at the end of Chapter 13.

West Maui and Kaanapali

All of Lahaina takes on a real festive atmosphere as sunset nears. The restaurants along oceanfront Front Street boast stellar views and energetic bar scenes, some with live music; just stroll the street and join whatever party suits your fancy. Among the best are **Cheeseburger in Paradise,** 811 Front St. (☎ 808-661-4855), a regular forum for live-and-lively music; **Kimo's,** 845 Front St. (☎ 808-661-4811); and **Maui Brews,** in Lahaina Center at 900 Front St., next to the Front Street Theaters (☎ 808-667-7794), which offers Lahaina's largest on-tap selection and an eclectic calendar of DJ dance parties and live music that's one of the best in town.

Lahaina is also home to two nightly shows that are well worth seeking out. If you love the performing arts — and even if you don't think you do — do not pass up an opportunity to see *'Ulalena,* at the **Maui Myth & Magic Theatre,** 878 Front St. (☎ 877-688-4800 or 808-661-9913; Internet: www.ulalena.com). This incredible, Broadway-quality 75-minute live show interweaves the natural, historical, and mythological tales of the birth of Hawaii using a near-perfect mix of original contemporary music and dance, ancient chant and hula, and creative lighting, gorgeous costumes, visual artistry (including some mind-blowing puppets), and live musicianship. This universally lauded production is bold, mesmerizing, and like nothing Hawaii has ever seen before — sort of like Laurie Anderson hooks up with Cirque du Soleil in Hawaii. Lest you think it all sounds too artsy for you, *'Ulalena* has been so popular among tourists and visitors alike that two shows are performed nightly from Tuesday through Saturday, at 6 p.m. and 8:30 p.m. Tickets are $40 per person, $30 for kids 5 to 12 — yes, they'll love *'Ulalena,* too. Don't miss it!

For something completely different, spend an evening at **Warren & Annabelle's,** 900 Front St. in Lahaina (☎ 808-667-6244; Internet: www.hawaiimagic.com). This genuinely fun and surprisingly uncheesy mystery-and-magic cocktail show stars illusionist Warren Gibson and "Annabelle," a ghost from the *previous* turn of the century who plays a grand piano — and even takes your requests. Expect the requisite audience participation, of course. Tickets are $36 per person; you must be 21 or older to enter. Food and drinks are available for an additional charge. The show is very popular, so book at least a few days in advance to avoid disappointment.

At press time, an early-evening family-friendly show had been added to the Warren & Annabelle's schedule; call for details.

In Kaanapali, the name of the game is beachfront romance. Head to **Whaler's Village,** on Kaanapali Beach at 2435 Kaanapali Pkwy., where you can take an open-air seat facing the ocean at Hula Grill's **Barefoot Bar** (☎ 808-667-6636), which features Hawaiian music and hula dancing nightly at sunset. Or head next door to the Beachside Grill at **Leilani's on the Beach** (☎ 808-661-4495) where the party starts every afternoon with live music at 2:30 p.m. or so. With tiki torches flickering and the waves rolling in, you can't go wrong at either spot.

South Maui

South Maui is a tad quieter overall, but boasts a couple of hopping joints.

Hapa's Brew Haus, in the Lipoa Shopping Center, 41 E. Lipoa St. (between South Kihei Road and Piilani Highway), Kihei (☎ 808-879-9001), serves up live music and microbrews nightly from 9 p.m. to 1:30 a.m. This large, popular place is simple and lively, boasting good sound and a big dance floor. Call to see what's on: It could be jazz, blues, rock, reggae, funk, or Hawaiian.

A DJ spins Top-40 hits at chic **Tsunami,** the neighbor islands' biggest and best dance club, at the Grand Wailea Resort, 3850 Wailea Alanui Dr., Wailea (☎ 808-875-1234), where a well-heeled crowd shakes its collective booty Wednesday through Saturday from 9 p.m. to 1 a.m.

Part V
Hawaii, The Big Island

The 5th Wave   By Rich Tennant

FEW MOMENTS IN SAILING COMPARE IN MAJESTY TO THE SHRINERS SUNSET REGATTA.

©RICHTENNANT

In this part . . .

It's not called the Big Island for nothing. Measuring 4,028 square miles, the island is more than twice the size of all the other islands combined. You'll do plenty of driving here if you plan to explore the island's many attractions, and I hope that you do — this is the land of salt-and-pepper beaches, active lava flows, and tropical rain forests. The chapters in this part will help you make the most of your time in this enchanting place.

Chapter 15

The Lowdown on the Big Island's Hotel Scene

. . . .

In This Chapter

▶ Deciding where to base yourself — or how to divide your time — on the Big Island

▶ Choosing among the island's top resort hotels, condos, and B&Bs

▶ Expanding your options: Agencies that specialize in vacation-home rentals and additional condo and B&B choices

. . . .

*A*t 4,038 square miles, the Big Island really is big. Not only that, but a handful of volcanic mountains dominates the interior, making criss-crossing from coast to coast a challenge, to say the least. Therefore, if you want to visit all of the Big Island's major attractions, I strongly suggest that you choose not one but two places to stay while you're here: one on the hot, arid Kona coast, and the other on the lush, rain-forested volcano coast.

You *can* stay just on the Kona side of the island and visit Hawaii Volcanoes National Park on a day trip. Expect a long day, however: It takes at least three hours to reach the park from anywhere on the western coast. And, since the best time to visit the park when the lava is flowing is after dark, you won't get back to Kona anytime before midnight.

If you're planning to visit both sides of the island, here's a way to cut down on driving time and maximize sightseeing (or relaxation) time. I suggest scheduling your Big Island visit so that you fly in on one side of the island and fly out on the other. Either land at Kona airport and fly out of Hilo, or vice versa — it really doesn't matter. Doing so will likely cost you about fifty bucks in car-rental drop-off charges, but can save those of you visiting both coasts an extra 3- or 3½-hour drive to return to the coast you started from for your outbound flight.

Choosing Your Location

The west, or Kona, side of the Big Island is the hot, arid, beachy side, where all of the island resorts and condos are located. The misty, luxuriant east side is home to the pretty, petite city of Hilo and spectacular Hawaii Volcanoes National Park.

On the west (Kona) side

This hot, dry, almost-always-sunny side of the island is where you go when you want to hit the beach. West Hawaii may come as a shock to some — this is parched, black lava–covered land fringed by swaying palms, salt-and-pepper sand, and gorgeous Pacific waves. Still, it's a landscape of dramatic, otherworldly beauty, and some the beaches found along here are Hawaii's most gorgeous.

The Kohala Coast

This ritzy resort coast stretches for about 30 miles north from Kona International Airport. No resort coast in Hawaii boasts luxury spreads that are this sprawling or fabulously grand.

Every hotel along the Kona-Kohala Coast is part of a "resort" — Kaupulehu (cow-poo-LAY-hoo), Waikoloa, Mauna Lani, and Mauna Kea, as they progress from south to north — each of which functions something like a neighborhood, usually encompassing two resort hotels, upscale residential developments (condos, freestanding homes, or both), and golf courses. Each resort has a clearly marked gateway off Queen Kaahumanu Highway (Highway 19, the coast's main drag) and its own network of roads, plus public beach access. Waikoloa even boasts its own sizable shopping and restaurant complex.

When you're making your resort decision, take distance into consideration if you're planning to do lots of running around. Mauna Kea is at least a half-hour's drive from the airport, and 40 or 45 minutes from Kailua-Kona town — which can make popping into town for dinner more work than you'd like. Kaupulehu (where the Four Seasons and Kona Village resort hotels are), on the other hand, is only about 10 or 15 minutes from Kailua-Kona, and practically around the corner from the airport (seven miles to be exact, which qualifies as "around the corner" on this island).

Kailua-Kona

About seven miles south of the Kona International Airport, Kailua-Kona is the commercial hub of the island's West Side. It's similar to Maui's Lahaina, down to the tacky touristy shopping and open-air restaurants along Alii (ah-LEE-ee) Drive that open to spectacular ocean views. Kailua-Kona is a convenient and affordable place to stay, with lots of hotel and condo bargains. Keep in mind, however, that you'll have to drive to get to a decent beach. Go for one of the condo complexes south of town if you want easy beach access and a respite from crowds and noise.

Upcountry Kona

Drive 15 minutes inland and upland from Kailua-Kona and you'll enter a whole different world. Lush, green, cool, and quiet, this is the world-famous Kona coffee country. Charming Holualoa village serves as a great alternative to the beach resorts if you're looking to get away from it all. Views are spectacular, the streets are lined with art galleries, and you won't hear much but birdsong and the sound of the tropical fruit growing on the trees. It's an excellent choice for off-the-beaten-track types.

South Kona

A 10-minute drive south of Kailua-Kona town is South Kona, a lusher and quieter territory than Kona central. It's still convenient to everything, but much quieter, with a handful of nice hotels and condo complexes, plus an excellent B&B on the slope above the coast, Horizon Guest House. You'll have wonderful ocean views no matter where you stay in South Kona, but expect a short drive to reach a swimmable beach (although some of the best snorkel spots on the island are within easy reach).

The east (volcano) side

This east side of the island seems like the polar opposite of the Kona side — it's cool, wet, rain-forested, fragrant with tropical flowers (the Big Island is also known as the Orchid Isle), and decidedly *not* the place for a day at the beach. Stay on this side of the island if you want to dedicate some time to exploring Hawaii Volcanoes National Park, but expect a whole different kind of island experience here.

Hilo

Hawaii's largest city after Honolulu embodies Hawaii the way it used to be: It's a quaint, misty, flower-filled city with a gorgeous half-moon bay, a charmingly historic false-fronted downtown, some beautifully restored Victorian houses, and a real penchant for rain — 128 inches a year makes it one of America's wettest cities. Not everybody loves Hilo, but those of us with a passion for anything retro do. Since it's just about a 45-minute drive from the national park, Hilo makes a great base if you can't get a place to stay in Volcano Village (see the following section).

Volcano

The gateway to Hawaii Volcanoes National Park is Volcano Village, a network of charming B&Bs and vacation rentals tucked into the rain forest just outside the national park's gate. Needless to say, Volcano makes the best base for exploring the park. No matter where you stay, you'll be just minutes from the park entrance.

The Big Island's Best Hotels, Condos, and B&Bs

In the following listings, you'll see that each resort hotel, condo, or B&B name is followed by a number of dollar signs, ranging from one ($) to five ($$$$$). Each represents the median price range for a double room per night, as follows:

$	Super-cheap — less than $75 per night
$$	Still affordable — $75 to $150
$$$	Moderate — $150 to $225
$$$$	Expensive but not ridiculous — $225 to $300
$$$$$	Ultra-luxurious — more than $300 per night

So that there are no surprises at checkout time, don't forget that the state adds 11.42 percent in taxes to your hotel bill.

As you sift through the choice of places to stay, use the "Sweet Dreams: Choosing Your Hotel" worksheet at the back of the book to help keep track of potential overnighting spots.

Aston Keauhou Beach Resort

$$$ South Kona

Unveiled in early 2000 after a $15-million-plus overhaul, this hotel has been restored to like-new condition and is a great choice for culture buffs, active vacationers, or anybody in search of affordable oceanfront accommodations. Situated on a tranquil and lovely stretch of coast, the mid-rise structure boasts a central location, a genuine Hawaiian ambience, and an award-winning Hawaiiana program with a full slate of free cultural activities. The island's best snorkeling is right next door at Kahaluu Beach Park, while the hotel's own grounds feature an oceanside pool, a fitness center, and tennis courts lit for night play. A grassy oceanfront area is dedicated to the easy life, with hammocks strung between coconut palms. The rooms themselves are less distinctive but perfectly comfortable. They're fresh and pleasant, with good bedside reading lights, generous counter space and cushy towels in the bathrooms (some of which have showers only), coffeemakers, and lanais, most with some kind of ocean view. Adjoining rooms make this a good family choice, too.

78-6740 Alii Dr., Keauhou (6 miles south of Kailua-Kona). ☎ *800-922-7866 or 808-322-3441. Fax: 808-322-3117. Internet:* www.aston-hotels.com. *Parking: $5. Rack rates: $155–$270 double, $400–$420 suite. Deals: Excellent opportunities for discounts. Internet-only ePriceBreaker rates can result in substantial savings (doubles as low as $128 at press time). Ask for AAA, senior (50-plus), and corporate discounts, and other special rate programs. Qualify for 25% discount if you stay at Aston properties for 7 or more nights with Aston's "Island Hopper" program. AE, CB, DC, DISC, JCB, MC, V.*

Aston Royal Sea Cliff Resort

$$$ Kailua-Kona

Parents with kids in tow will love these apartments. They're not fancy, but they're large, well outfitted, and older but well cared for. The big five-story complex steps down a terraced cliff to an unswimmable black-sand beach, but the situation allows for spectacular views and maximum privacy. Gardens and hanging bougainvillea give the whole place a pleasant, tropical ambience. The spacious, air-conditioned apartments carry through on the vibe, with lots of rattan, sunny lanais, full kitchens with microwave, washer/dryers, and daily maid service, making for easy vacation living. Two pools (one freshwater, one saltwater), a Jacuzzi, sauna, tennis, and barbecues are all on site. The nearest beach is four miles south, but it's a winner for snorkelers.

75-6040 Alii Dr., Kailua-Kona (2 miles south of town). ☎ *800-922-7866 or 808-329-8021. Fax: 808-326-1887. Internet:* www.aston-hotels.com. *Parking: Free! Rack rates: $175–$200 studio, $200–$255 1-bedroom apartment, $230–$630 2-bedroom apartment or villa. Deals: Excellent opportunities for discounts. Internet-only ePriceBreaker rates can result in substantial savings. Ask for AAA, senior (50-plus), and corporate discounts, and other special rate programs. Qualify for 25% discount if you stay at Aston properties for 7 or more nights with Aston's "Island Hopper" program. AE, CB, DC, DISC, JCB, MC, V.*

Carson's Volcano Cottages

$$ Volcano

Warm and wonderful innkeepers Tom and Brenda Carson offer an accommodation for everyone just outside Hawaii Volcanoes National Park: three charming guest rooms with private entrances and private baths for travelers looking for good value; three ultra-romantic tin-roofed cottages, each with full kitchen; and two dedicated family cottages with full kitchen and TV. All units brim with island-style charm and feature cozy beds with goose-down comforters, plush terry robes, daily maid service (the family cottages are serviced every second or third day). Some cottages feature wood-burning stoves (a wonderful extra on cold nights) and/or private hot tubs; my favorite is the magical Koa Cabin, which boasts both, plus wonderful Jadite dinnerware (Martha Stewart's fave) and other mid-century collectibles. The property also features a hot tub tucked under the ferns for everybody's use. The bountiful breakfast buffet is a hearty, delicious feast — good carbo pumping for your day at the park.

501 Sixth St. (near Pearl St.), Volcano. ☎ *800-845-5282 or 808-967-7683. Fax: 808-967-8094. Internet:* www.carsonscottage.com. *Parking: Free! Rack rates: $105–$115 double, $125–$155 suite, $125–$170 cottage. Full breakfast buffet included. Deals: Ask about weekly, monthly, and off-season rates. AE, DISC, MC, V.*

The Big Island's Best Hotels, Condos & B&Bs

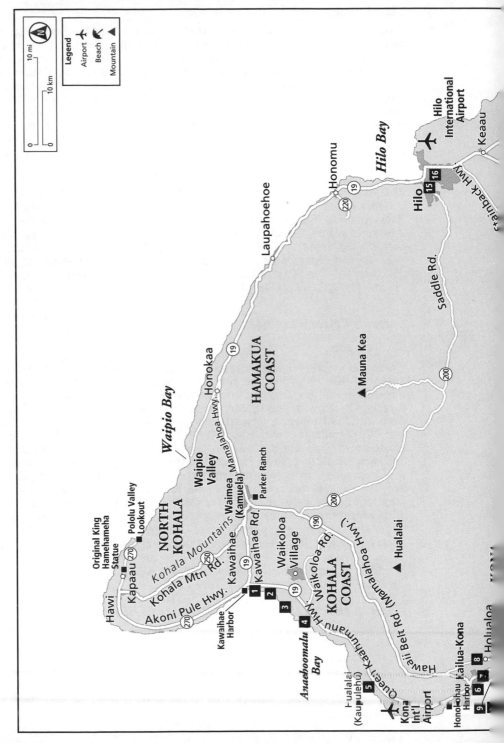

Legend
Airport ✈
Beach 🏄
Mountain ▲

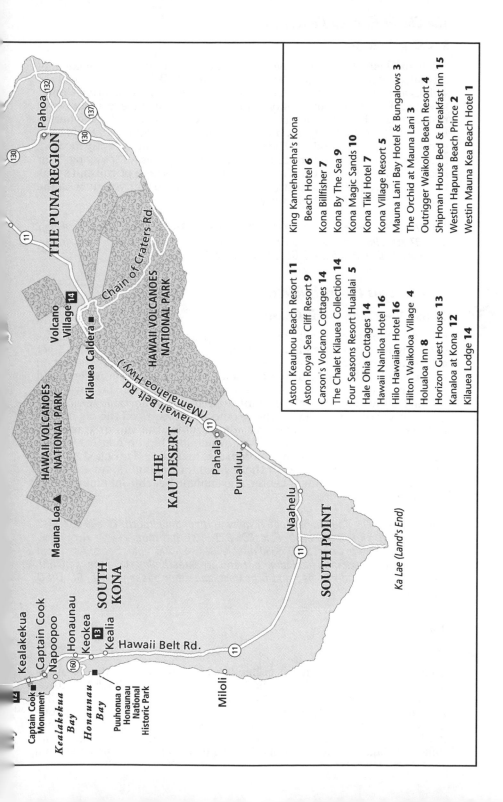

Aston Keauhou Beach Resort **11**
Aston Royal Sea Cliff Resort **9**
Carson's Volcano Cottages **14**
The Chalet Kilauea Collection **14**
Four Seasons Resort Hualalai **5**
Hale Ohia Cottages **14**
Hawaii Naniloa Hotel **16**
Hilo Hawaiian Hotel **16**
Hilton Waikoloa Village **4**
Holualoa Inn **8**
Horizon Guest House **13**
Kanaloa at Kona **12**
Kilauea Lodge **14**

King Kamehameha's Kona
  Beach Hotel **6**
Kona Billfisher **7**
Kona By The Sea **9**
Kona Magic Sands **10**
Kona Tiki Hotel **7**
Kona Village Resort **5**
Mauna Lani Bay Hotel & Bungalows **3**
The Orchid at Mauna Lani **3**
Outrigger Waikoloa Beach Resort **4**
Shipman House Bed & Breakfast Inn **15**
Westin Hapuna Beach Prince **2**
Westin Mauna Kea Beach Hotel **1**

The Chalet Kilauea Collection

$–$$$$$ Volcano

Brian and Lisha Crawford have built a mini-empire outside the gates of Hawaii Volcanoes National Park. They own a B&B for every budget, as well as a selection of vacation rentals (see "Home Sweet Vacation Home" later in this chapter) and not one but two of the tiny village's handful of restaurants. I think their luxury suites are overpriced and a bit too heavy-handed to be called elegant, but the rest of their accommodations offer good value for your dollar. All are well-maintained, conveniently located, nicely outfitted, and feature comfortable public spaces for lounging. Your best bet is either to peruse the comprehensive Web site or call and speak to the friendly folks, who will gladly take the time to pair you up with the accommodation that's right for you.

988 Wright Rd., Volcano. ☎ *800-937-7786 or 808-967-7786. Fax: 800-577-1849 or 808-967-8669. Internet:* www.volcano-hawaii.com. *Parking: Free! Rack rates: $45–$395 double or suite. AE, DC, DISC, JCB, MC, V.*

Four Seasons Resort Hualalai

$$$$$ West Side (Kona Coast)

Here it is: the finest resort hotel in the islands, the Hope diamond of the glittering Four Seasons chain — island-style luxury simply doesn't get any better. Low-rise clusters of clean-lined oceanfront villas are nestled between a lovely sandy beach and a fabulous Jack Nicklaus–designed golf course (for guests only — so start dialing, duffers!). You'll want for nothing in the huge, casually elegant, supremely comfortable rooms; the ground-level ones even have private outdoor showers off the big marble bathrooms so you can shower *au naturel* under the sun or stars. The beautiful beach can be too rough for swimming, but no matter — three oceanfront pools more than compensate, including a stocked snorkel pond (with friendly stingrays!) that's ideal for beginners. An exclusive spa, a state-of-the-art fitness center, and sublime beachfront dining round out the experience.

100 Kaupulehu Dr., Kaupulehu-Kona (7 miles north of the airport). ☎ *800-332-3442, 888-340-5662, or 808-325-8000. Fax: 808-325-8100. Internet:* www.fshr.com. *Parking: Free! Rack rates: $450–$650 double, $775–$5,700 suite. Deals: Ask about Under the Sun packages (including car and breakfast), plus romance, golf, fifth night free, room-and-car, bed-and-breakfast, and other packages. AE, DC, DISC, JCB, MC, V.*

Hale Ohia Cottages

$$ Volcano

This charming and tranquil collection of suites and cottages offers an ideal opportunity to both step into the past and get back to nature. The gorgeous red-shingled 1931 estate is an impeccable blend of 1930s Hawaii plantation style with modern-day sophistication. The gorgeous botanical grounds are the result of 30 years' work by a master Japanese gardener. All of the accommodations are lovely and comfortable; the Ihilani Cottage is a honeymooner's delight, with its own enclosed lanai with bubbling fountain, while the three-bedroom Hale Ohia Cottage, with its own full kitchen, is a great deal for families. The massive Master Suite (where the owner stays when he's on the island) is a steal if you can snare it. The in-room continental breakfast makes this an excellent choice for privacy seekers. Ask about the funky-romantic newest cottage, with a bedroom housed in a water tank.

On Hale Ohia Road (off Highway 11), Volcano. ☎ *800-455-3803 or 808-967-7986. Fax: 808-967-8610. Internet:* www.haleohia.com. *Parking: Free! Rack rates: $95–$135 double. Rates include continental breakfast. DC, DISC, MC, V.*

Hawaii Naniloa Hotel

$$ Hilo

Nine stories high and overlooking Hilo Bay, Hilo's biggest hotel has older motel-like rooms and a quiet, leafy setting near the pretty Liluokalani Gardens and the historic heart of town. Don't expect a lot in the way of personality or in-room amenities, but service is friendly and facilities abound: two restaurants (including a good Chinese restaurant), two lounges, shops, two pools, a spa, laundry facilities and valet service, and a nine-hole golf course. I like the Hilo Hawaiian a bit better, but this is also a perfectly reasonable choice.

93 Banyan Dr., Hilo. ☎ *800-367-5360, 800-442-5845, or 808-969-3333. Fax: 808-969-6622. Internet:* www.naniloa.com. *Parking: Free! Rack rates: $100–$160 double, $190–$800 suite. Deals: Check for AAA-member discounts as well as Internet specials. AAA members and seniors can also qualify for discounts. AE, DISC, MC, V.*

Hilo Hawaiian Hotel

$$ Hilo

This eight-story waterfront hotel on picturesque Hilo Bay features nice rooms that do the job at a fair price. It's as generic as the Hawaii Naniloa (directly preceding) and shares the same gracious setting on leafy Banyan Drive, but the rooms here are a tad nicer — more Holiday Inn than Travelodge quality, if you know what I mean. The Naniloa has more facilities, but you'll still find a pool and sundeck, a gift shop, a laundro-mat, and a restaurant and lounge here. Pay the few extra bucks for a bay view if you can swing it; you won't be disappointed.

71 Banyan Dr., Hilo. ☎ *800-367-5004 or 808-935-9361. Fax: 808-477-2329. Internet:* www.castle-group.com. *Parking: Free! Rack rates: $107–$141 double, $177–$350 suite. Deals: Check for specially discounted Internet rates (as low as $86 at press time). Also check for romance, room-and-car, free night, and other special packages. AE, CB, DC, DISC, JCB, MC, V.*

Hilton Waikoloa Village

$$$$ Kohala Coast

With 1,240 rooms spread over 62 acres, this massive hotel is too big for its own good. Just getting from your room to the lobby is a 15-minute production — so check in, park yourself, and don't be in any hurry to leave. This is a destination resort of the highest order, Hawaii's very own version of Disneyland. Its high-rise towers, water slide–riddled megapools, dolphin lagoons, and gaggle of restaurants, bars, and shops are connected by trams, boats, and art-lined walkways. This megaresort boasts so many eye-popping diversions that your kids will think they've died and gone to heaven. Mom and Dad are bound to be entertained too, thanks to a tremendous spa and championship golf — if you don't run screaming from sensory overload first. The rooms are well-appointed and comfortable, and relatively affordable considering the level of luxury you'll find here. There's no sandy beach here, though; you have to go next door for that.

69-425 Waikoloa Beach Dr., Waikoloa. ☎ *800-774-1500 or 808-886-1234. Fax: 808-885-2900. Internet:* www.hiltonwaikoloavillage.com *or* www.hilton. com. *Parking: Free! Rack rates: $260–$600 double, suites from $875. Deals: A range of packages and special offers is usually available, including romance packages, discounts on multi-night stays, free breakfast, and more. Also ask for AAA, AARP, corporate, frequent-flyer, and other discounts. AE, CB, DISC, ER, JCB, MC, V.*

Holualoa Inn

$$$ Upcountry Kona

Set on 40 pastoral acres on the slopes above Kailua-Kona, in the charmingly artsy town of Holualoa, this impeccable inn offers the ultimate tranquil escape — yet it's also conveniently located, with great beaches and all the conveniences just a 15-minute drive away. Built entirely of golden woods and outfitted in a simple Balinese style — all clean lines, rattan, and subtle colors — this gorgeous contemporary Hawaiian home boasts six spacious guest rooms, window-walls that slide away to reveal stunning panoramic ocean views, and an easygoing island vibe. The lovely pool and Jacuzzi overlook a backyard coffee farm and fruit trees (which supply the morning brew and breakfast papayas) and offer spectacular views of the coastline below. Nice extras include a gas grill with all the supplies you need to prepare a romantic dinner, wonderful common spaces for dining and lounging, and a pool table to entertain yourself on quiet evenings. Even B&B-phobes will feel right at home.

76-5932 Mamalahoa Hwy., Holualoa (a 15-minute drive uphill from Highway 19, along Hualalai Road). ☎ *800-392-1812 or 808-324-1121. Fax: 808-322-2472. Internet:* www.konaweb.com/HINN. *Parking: Free! Rack rates: $150–$195 double. Rates include substantial continental breakfast and sunset pupus. Children under 13 not accepted. Deals: 15% discount on stays of 7 nights or more. AE, DISC, MC, V.*

Horizon Guest House

$$$$ South Kona

This spanking-new bed-and-breakfast offers the ultimate in luxurious relaxation. The house is situated on 40 acres of lush pastureland at 1,100 feet elevation, offering unparalleled coastline views. The four carefully designed one-room suites are cantilevered off the end of the house for maximum privacy. Each has its own private entry and is filled with gorgeous island antiques, hand-quilted Hawaiian bedspreads, a mini-fridge, coffeemaker, cushy robes, and a furnished lanai. A dramatic 20-by-40–foot infinity pool and a romantic hot tub are situated to take full advantage of the breathtaking views. Guests have free use of laundry facilities and beach toys galore. Innkeeper Clem Classen serves a gourmet buffet breakfast in the artifact-filled main house, which also features a multi-media room with an extensive book and video library and a TV with VCR and DVD. Impeccable personalized (but completely unobtrusive) service is the elegant finish that justifies the high price tag.

On Highway 11 (just before mile marker 100), Honaunau. ☎ *888-328-8301 or 808-328-2540. Fax: 808-328-8707. Internet:* www.horizonguesthouse.com. *Rack rates: $250 double. Rate includes full gourmet breakfast. Children under 14 not accepted. Deals: 15% off bookings of 7 nights or more. Inquire about other discounts; rates can fall as low as $175. MC, V.*

Kanaloa at Kona

$$$–$$$$ South Kona

Tucked away in a quiet, attractive neighborhood, these big, well-managed oceanfront condos are a cut above the average, and ideal for families. Comfortably furnished in quality island style with Hawaiian wood accents, the apartments have all the comforts of home and then some, including dressing rooms, big kitchens loaded with appliances, huge bathrooms (plus whirlpools in oceanview suites!), and washer/dryers. Tennis courts, three pools, a Jacuzzi, and playgrounds dot the pleasant, attractively manicured ocean-facing grounds; the coast is lava rock here, however, so you'll have to drive a half-mile to Kahaluu Beach (one of Hawaii's best for snorkeling). An excellent restaurant, Edward's at Kanaloa (see Chapter 17), is on site; a big, modern, well-stocked supermarket is just up the hill, and Kailua-Kona's restaurants and shops are just a ten-minute drive away.

78-261 Manukai St., Keauhou. ☎ *800-688-7444 or 808-322-9625. Fax: 808-322-3618. Internet:* www.outrigger.com. *Parking: Free! Rack rates: $235–$265 1-bedroom, $270–$310 2-bedroom. Deals: Almost nobody pays rack with Outrigger, the king of package deals. Better-than-average discounts for AAA and AARP members and seniors (50-plus), plus corporate, government, and military discounts. First night free, bed-and-breakfast, room-and-car, and other packages regularly on offer. AE, DC, DISC, JCB, MC, V.*

Kilauea Lodge

$$ Volcano

Built in 1938 as a YMCA camp, this popular roadside lodge sits on ten wooded acres just a stone's throw from the main gate of the national park. The lodge is a real woodsy charmer, with stone pillars and beamed ceilings. Eleven comfortably outfitted rooms offer private baths, attractive artwork by local artists, lovely garden views, and individual heat controls and towel warmers (nice plusses in chilly Volcano). A phone, lending library, games, and a TV set for shared viewing are found in the common room. Two charming cottages are also available, one with two bedrooms and full kitchen that's great for families. A complete, satisfying breakfast is served in the restaurant, which is my Volcano favorite for dinner (see Chapter 17). All in all, this is an excellent choice for those who prefer hotel-style anonymity over the intimacy of many of Volcano's B&B-style stays.

19-4055 Volcano Rd. (just off Hwy. 11 at Wright Rd.), Volcano. ☎ *808-967-7366. Fax: 808-967-7367. Internet:* www.kilauealodge.com. *Parking: Free! Rack rates: $125–$145 double, $145–$155 cottage. Rates include full breakfast. AE, MC, V.*

King Kamehameha's Kona Beach Hotel

$$ Kailua-Kona

Located in the heart of Kailua-Kona town, just a stroll away from everything, this hotel can't be beat in terms of convenience. The King Kam is Holiday Inn simple, but it's clean, ocean-facing, and an ideal choice for those who don't want to have to go far for shopping and dining. Ask for a room overlooking sparkling Kailua Bay for only-in-Hawaii views. (Note that bathrooms have showers only.) The small, gold-sand beach isn't exactly your dream beach, but it will satisfy in a pinch. Other on-site extras include shops, a pool and Jacuzzi, tennis, sauna, restaurants and a poolside bar, a luau, and coin-op laundry plus valet service. Nicer beaches are just a short drive away.

75-5660 Palani Rd. (at Alii Dr.), Kailua-Kona. ☎ *800-367-6060 or 808-329-2911. Fax: 808-922-8061. Internet:* www.konabeachhotel.com. *Parking: Free! Rack rates: $120–$195 double, $350–$550 1- to 3-bedroom suite. Deals: Very good packages are usually on offer; as low as $128 — with car and breakfast — at press time. Also ask about corporate and senior rates. AE, CB, DC, DISC, JCB, MC, V.*

Kona Billfisher

$ Kailua-Kona

This is my favorite under-$100 bargain. The units aren't fancy, but you can't do better for the money — and discounts on longer stays make the rooms practically free. The management company invests in constant renovations, and the resident manager keeps everything neat and fresh. Each apartment has a full kitchen with all-electric appliances, a large lanai, decent newish furniture, and king-size beds. The one-bedrooms have sliding doors that allow you to close off the living room into another bedroom, which makes them a real deal for penny-pinching families. On-site extras include a pool, barbecues, and coin-op laundry, and the town is just a walk away. You'll have to drive to a swimmable beach, but at these prices you won't mind. Book well in advance, as this place fills up fast, usually with repeat guests.

On Alii Dr. (on the mountain side of the street, across from the Royal Kona Resort), Kailua-Kona. c/o Hawaii Resort Management. ☎ *800-622-5348 or 808-329-9393. Fax: 808-326-4137. Internet:* www.konahawaii.com. *Parking: Free! Rack rates: $70–$90 1-bedroom, $90–$105 2-bedroom/1-bath. 3-night minimum (higher rates available for shorter stays). Deals: Big discounts available on weekly and monthly stays. MC, V.*

Kona Coast Hotels, Condos, & B&Bs

Aston Keauhou Beach Resort **8**
Aston Royal Sea Cliff Resort **4**
Holualoa Inn **5**
Horizon Guest House **10**
Kanaloa at Kona **9**
King Kamehameha's Kona
    Beach Hotel **1**
Kona Billfisher **2**
Kona By The Sea **6**
Kona Magic Sands **7**
Kona Tiki Hotel **3**

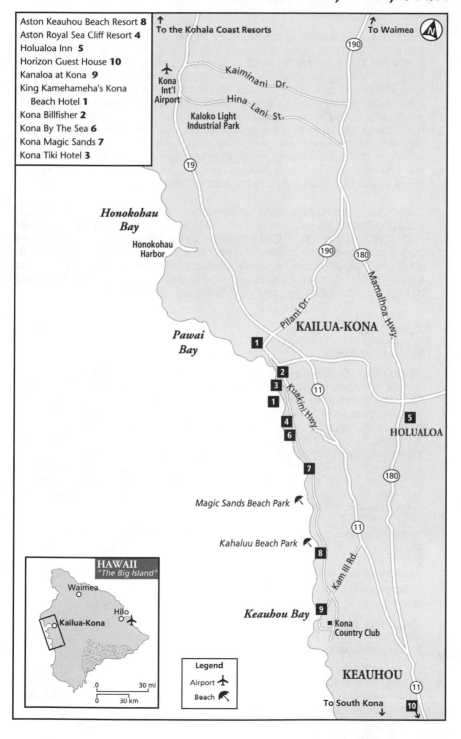

Kona By The Sea

$$$$ Kailua-Kona

The units and grounds at this deluxe oceanfront condo complex are a tad more inviting than those of its sister property, the perfectly nice Aston Royal Sea Cliff (see earlier in this chapter), but not dramatically so. The bright, spacious, nicely decorated apartments boast complete kitchens with microwave, washer/dryers, daily maid service, and large lanais (most with ocean views). On site you'll find a nice oceanfront freshwater pool, Jacuzzi, barbecues, and an activities desk that can book your island fun. One of the nice plusses exclusive to this property is the personal grocery shopping service, whereby you leave a shopping list with the manager and your staples are delivered right to your door. The white-sand beach here is lovely but unswimmable, so plan on heading four miles south to Kahaluu Beach for first-rate snorkeling.

75-6106 Alii Dr., Kailua-Kona (2 miles south of town). ☎ *800-922-7866 or 808-327-2300. Fax: 808-327-2333. Internet:* www.aston-hotels.com. *Parking: Free! Rack rates: $235–$290 1-bedroom, $290–$345 2-bedroom. Deals: Excellent opportunities for discounts. Internet-only ePriceBreaker rates can result in substantial savings. Ask for AAA, senior (50-plus), and corporate discounts, and other special rate programs. Qualify for 25% discount if you stay at Aston properties for 7 or more nights with Aston's "Island Hopper" program. AE, CB, DC, DISC, JCB, MC, V.*

Kona Magic Sands

$$ Kailua-Kona

These older studios are small (two people maximum) and not exactly luxurious, but they're great for those who want to be lulled to sleep by the rhythm of the waves. Each nicely maintained studio consists of one long, narrow room with a small kitchen at one end and a lanai at the other that practically extends out over the surf, with living and sleeping space in between. Since you're facing west, expect nothing less than killer sunset views, and front-row seats for whale-watching in winter. Coin-op laundry, a small oceanfront pool, barbecues, and a decent restaurant, Jameson's by the Sea, are on site. If that weren't enough, the building is sandwiched between two beach parks. With these perks at these prices, you won't even miss the air-conditioning.

77-6452 Alii Dr. (next to White Sands Beach), Kailua-Kona. c/o Hawaii Resort Management. ☎ *800-622-5348 or 808-329-9393. Fax: 808-326-4137. Internet:* www.konahawaii.com. *Parking: Free! Rack rates: $85–$115 studio. 3-night minimum (higher rates available for shorter stays). Deals: Big discounts are available on weekly and monthly stays. MC, V.*

Kona Tiki Hotel

$ Kailua-Kona

This friendly family-run motel is one of the best cheap sleeps in the state. Staying here is like stepping into a time warp — one where you can have a reasonable room for two, right on the ocean, for as little as 57 bucks. The rooms are budget-basic on every level, but the beds are firm and comfy, ceiling fans and mini-fridges are at hand (a few have kitchenettes for just $11 more), and every room has a lanai with front-row ocean views. New paint and carpets were in the works at press time. A basic continental breakfast is served poolside every morning, making this incredible value that much more astounding. The location is pleasant, away from the hustle and bustle of downtown. The ocean isn't swimmable from here and there are no TVs, phones, or coin-op laundry (a local laundry will pick up and deliver), but those are the sacrifices you make for such a bargain. Book way in advance, because people *loooove* this place.

75-5968 Alii Dr. Kailua-Kona (a mile south of town). ☎ *808-329-1425. Fax: 808-327-9402. Parking: Free! Rack rates: $57–$62 double, $68 double with kitchenette. Rates include continental breakfast. 3-night minimum. No credit cards.*

Kona Village Resort

$$$$$ Kohala Coast

Hawaii may have fancier and more amenity-laden resorts, but the state's only all-inclusive is really something special: a super-deluxe version of *Gilligan's Island*, where everybody stays in thatched huts and it seems perfectly natural to tuck a flower behind your ear and sip cocktails out of coconuts. This South Seas paradise of swaying palms and lagoons offers blissful escape and Robinson Crusoe–style: no TVs, phones, or fax machines around to interrupt your tropical reverie for a minute. The dark-sand beach is small but offers first-rate snorkeling, often with green sea turtles. A tenderly attentive staff is on hand to meet your needs and desires even before you know you have them, and the food is terrific at every meal. There's something going on most nights, whether it's dancing to a Hawaiian trio or the terrific Friday-night luau (see Chapter 17), and the kids' program is excellent (note that no kids' rates or programs are offered in May and September). I have, however, heard some minor complaints about maintenance recently, but management is usually quick to respond.

At the Kaupulehu resort, 7 miles north of the airport. ☎ *800-367-5290 or 808-325-5555. Fax 808-325-5124. Internet:* www.konavillage.com. *Parking: Free! Rack rates: $480–$825 double, $785–$1,015 suite. Rates include all meals, in-room refreshments, most activities, children's program, airport transfers, and more. All rates are based on double occupancy (suite rates accommodate 3); $35–$190 per person extra. Deals: Ask about honeymoon, celebration, family, car, and other packages. Also ask about specially discounted AAA and AARP rates, available Sept–Nov. AE, CB, DC, JCB, MC, V.*

Mauna Lani Bay Hotel & Bungalows

$$$$$ Kohala Coast

Hawaiian elders named this section of the sunny lava coast Mauna Lani, or "Mountain reaching Heaven" — and it's an apt name for so heavenly a resort. Mauna Lani has a finer swimming and snorkeling beach than that of any other Big Island resort hotels, and it's built like an arrow to take advantage of the prime coastal position, providing most rooms with substantial ocean views. A vast open-air lobby spilling over with tropical

The Kohala Coast Resorts

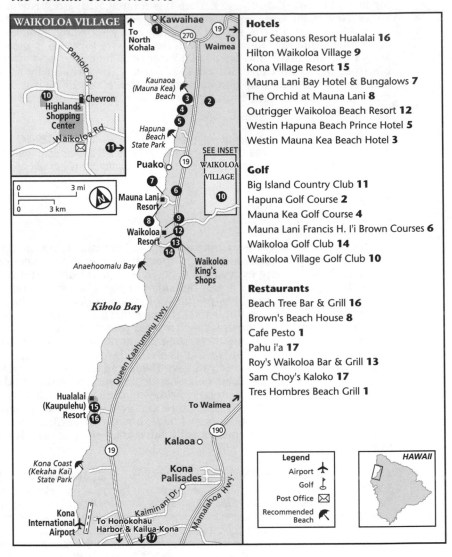

WAIKOLOA VILLAGE

Kawaihae ①
To North Kohala
270
19 To Waimea

Paniolo Dr.

⑩ Highlands Shopping Center
Chevron

Waikoloa Rd.

Kaunaoa (Mauna Kea) Beach ③ ②
④
⑤

Hapuna Beach State Park

⑪

0   3 mi
0   3 km
N

Puako ○ 19
⑦   ⑥
Mauna Lani Resort
⑧   ⑨
Waikoloa Resort ⑫
⑬
⑭

Anaehoomalu Bay

SEE INSET
WAIKOLOA VILLAGE
⑩

Waikoloa King's Shops

Kiholo Bay

Queen Kaahumanu Hwy.

Hualalai (Kaupulehu) Resort ⑮ ⑯

To Waimea
190

Kalaoa ○

19

Kona Coast (Kekaha Kai) State Park

Kona Palisades

Kona International Airport

Kaiminani Dr.

Mamalahoa Hwy.

To Honokohau Harbor & Kailua-Kona ⑰

Hotels
Four Seasons Resort Hualalai **16**
Hilton Waikoloa Village **9**
Kona Village Resort **15**
Mauna Lani Bay Hotel & Bungalows **7**
The Orchid at Mauna Lani **8**
Outrigger Waikoloa Beach Resort **12**
Westin Hapuna Beach Prince Hotel **5**
Westin Mauna Kea Beach Hotel **3**

Golf
Big Island Country Club **11**
Hapuna Golf Course **2**
Mauna Kea Golf Course **4**
Mauna Lani Francis H. I'i Brown Courses **6**
Waikoloa Golf Club **14**
Waikoloa Village Golf Club **10**

Restaurants
Beach Tree Bar & Grill **16**
Brown's Beach House **8**
Cafe Pesto **1**
Pahu i'a **17**
Roy's Waikoloa Bar & Grill **13**
Sam Choy's Kaloko **17**
Tres Hombres Beach Grill **1**

Legend
Airport ✈
Golf ⛳
Post Office ✉
Recommended Beach

HAWAII

greenery leads to serene and simple rooms that exude island style — teak floors, lauhala headboards, ceiling fans, natural-hued textiles, and lanais. VCRs, opposing vanities, seersucker robes, and twice-daily maid service add a luxury touch. Families can stay in the homelike villas, but those with bottomless bank accounts should opt for one of the incredible bungalows, which comes with its own private pool and butler. The historically and culturally sensitive resort features an extensive calendar of daily activities, plus a spa; CanoeHouse, one of the coast's most highly regarded restaurants; a first-rate tennis center; and easy access to some of Hawaii's best golf.

68-1400 Mauna Lani Dr., Mauna Lani resort. ☎ 800-367-2323 or 808-885-6622. Fax: 808-885-1484. Internet: www.maunalani.com. *Parking: Rack rates: $350–$620 double, $525–$970 villa or suite, $4,200–$4,750 bungalow. Deals: A wealth of packages is usually available; rates as low as $285, $490 for 2-room family suite, at press time. Discounted weekly rates available on villas. AE, CB, DC, DISC, JCB, MC, V.*

The Orchid at Mauna Lani

$$$$$ **Kohala Coast**

This elegant, attractive, and all-around appealing beach resort boasts gorgeous views and some of the best extras on the coast. The sports facilities are extensive (championship golf, tennis, catamaran rides), the spa is as stress-relieving as they come, and the heated oceanfront pool and Jacuzzis are open around the clock (and tiki-torchlit for maximum romance at night). The resort also offers an excellent Hawaiiana program for culture and craft buffs, and Brown's Beach House is the coast's most romantic restaurant (see Chapter 17). The spacious rooms are more boldly colorful than most, featuring an eye-catching teal palette, comfy furnishings, big lanais, and large marble baths. The beach is small but pretty, and perfect for snorkeling and kids at play. All in all, the Orchid is a tad less opulent and a bit more accessible than many other Big Island resorts, which some consider its greatest appeal. The service is top-notch, and even employees at competing resorts admit that the Orchid's concierge staff is the island's best. The only down side is that it's oddly situated in a U shape, which gives most of the rooms courtyard rather than ocean views.

1 N. Kaniku Dr., Mauna Lani resort. ☎ 800-845-9905 or 808-885-2000. Fax: 808-885-5778. Internet: www.orchid-maunalani.com *or* www.luxurycollection.com. *Parking: Free! Rack rates: $650–$3855 double, $700–$4,250 suite. Deals: Package deals are usually available, so be sure to ask; at press time, second rooms could be had for just $20 (no guarantee that this will be available when you call, of course). Also ask for AAA-member and senior discounts. AE, DC, DISC, JCB, MC, V.*

Outrigger Waikoloa Beach Resort

$$$$ **Kohala Coast**

This used to be the Kohala Coast's best value back when it was the Royal Waikoloan. The Hawaii-based Outrigger chain spent $23 million and five months reinventing it as a full-service resort; the new renovation has really lightened and upscaled the place and removed much of the budget feel from the smallish rooms, giving them an island vibe and all-new everything, including coffeemakers and mini-fridges. Still, the biggest plus remains location: The resort is situated on palm-lined A-Bay, one of the island's best bays for water sports. An excellent beach-activities desk provides easy access to snorkeling, diving, kayaking, and windsurfing; championship golf is also on hand. All in all, the resort looks great. The food service is less than impressive, and the service and trappings are not on par with its more luxury-minded neighbors — yet rates have climbed too close to their tariffs for comfort. Still, Outrigger excels in handing out packages and discounts, so if you snare a good rate, you could have the bargain of the Kohala Coast.

69-275 Waikoloa Beach Rd., Waikoloa. ☎ 800-688-7444 or 808-886-6789. Fax: 808-886-7852. Internet: www.outrigger.com. Parking: Free! Rack rates: $265–$395 double, $450–$2,000 suite. Deals: Almost nobody pays rack with Outrigger, the king of package deals. Better-than-average discounts for AAA and AARP members and seniors (50-plus), plus corporate, government, and military discounts. First night free, bed-and-breakfast, room-and-car, and other packages regularly on offer. AE, DC, DISC, JCB, MC, V.

Shipman House Bed & Breakfast Inn

$$–$$$ Hilo

Misty, flower-filled Hilo wows nostalgics with its Victorian homes and charming downtown overlooking a romantic half-moon bay. One of those century-old Victorians is this dreamy B&B, my favorite place to stay in town. Impeccably renovated and on the National Register of Historic Places, it's right in step with Hilo's old Hawaii vibe. Barbara Ann and Gary Andersen have kept the inn true to its original form, but they've haven't lost sight of its present-day purpose. It's full of modern conveniences, including full baths, ceiling fans, mini-fridges, and kimono robes in each of the five spacious, impeccably done rooms. Most romantic is Auntie Clara's, a corner room with windows on two walls overlooking a lush rain forest and bay, with a clawfoot tub in the bath. Breakfast is served on the wide veranda. Perfect for romance-seeking couples, history buffs, and national parkgoers alike — Hawaii Volcanoes is a half-hour's drive south.

131 Kaiulani St. (off Waianuenue Ave.), Hilo. ☎ 800-627-8447 or 808-934-8002. Fax: 808-934-8002. Internet: www.hilo-hawaii.com. Parking: Free! Rack rates: $140–$175 double. Rates include generous continental buffet breakfast. Rates $25 higher for single-night stays. AE, MC, V.

No Room at the Resort?

Needless to say, all of the Kohala Coast resorts are fabulous. I've listed my favorites earlier in this chapter, but the following deserve honorable mention.

Westin Hapuna Beach Prince

$$$$$ — The Mauna Kea's younger sister property is lighter, very contemporary, and very Japanese in style, and is situated on magnificent white-sand Hapuna Beach, one of my island favorites (see Chapter 18). 62-100 Kaunaoa Dr. ☎ 800-882-6060 or 808-880-1111. Internet: www.hapunabeachprincehotel.com.

Westin Mauna Kea Beach Hotel

$$$$$ — Built by Laurance Rockefeller back in the '60s, this is where old money comes to play. The Asian and Pacific art–filled resort is a bit formal and a tad dated, but the moneyed crowd doesn't seem to care. The fabulous crescent beach is virtually private and the only one that can rival the Mauna Lani Bay's sands (earlier in this chapter). 62-100 Mauna Kea Beach Dr., Mauna Kea resort. ☎ 800-882-6060 or 808-882-7222. Internet: www.maunakeabeachhotel.com.

Big Island B&B Bonanza

This wonderfully diverse island boasts a marvelous collection of bed-and-breakfasts and cozy cottages, so if you'd like more to choose from, contact Big Island–based **Hawaii's Best Bed & Breakfasts** (☎ 800-262-9912 or 808-885-4550; Internet: www.bestbnb.com), my favorite B&B agent in the islands. Hawaii's Best personally inspect and approve all of the properties they represent, and they're so tough that being represented by them is a badge of honor among island B&Bs and inns. They can offer more excellent choices in Volcano Village as well as a few Kohala Coast vacation rentals and more terrific Kona B&Bs. They also have some charming offerings in Waimea, a nice town at the heart of the Big Island's cowboy country, but I don't consider it the best base for a Big Island vacation, since it's not really close to anything.

You might also try the Web site for the **Hawaii Island B&B Association** (www.stayhawaii.com), a confederation of more than 50 bed-and-breakfasts and inns located around the island. This is another excellent place to find additional choices in Volcano, in particular; links worth pursuing include the Country Goose and Volcano Rainforest Retreat. The site offers extensive information on each property plus Web site and e-mail links; you contact and book with the innkeeper directly, though, so there's no additional charge.

Home Sweet Vacation Home

For a wealth of additional condo choices in and around Kailua-Kona and South Kona, contact **Knutson & Associates** (☎800-800-6202 or 808-329-6311; Internet: www.konahawaiirentals.com), the Kona Coast's best vacation-rental broker, representing everything from affordable condos to multibedroom oceanfront houses. All of their properties are good-quality, and the friendly agents will work with you to match you up to the rental that's right for you; they can even help you garner discounted rental-car rates through Avis.

Another good condo source, especially for budget-watching travelers, is **Hawaii Resort Management** (☎ 800-622-5348 or 808-329-9393; Internet: www.konahawaii.com). In addition to representing the previously recommended Kona Billfisher and Kona Magic Sands (earlier in this chapter), Hawaii Resort Management represents about a dozen more condo properties in the Kailua-Kona area, most with prices starting at less than $100 per night. Also inquire with these folks about discounted car rates through Avis.

If you'd prefer a luxury rental on the sunny, golf course–riddled Kohala resort coast, reach out to **South Kohala Management** (☎ 800-822-4252 or 808-883-8500; Internet: www.southkohala.com), which offers first-rate condos and townhomes in the Mauna Kea, Mauna Lani, and Waikoloa resorts. At press time, they also represented a wonderful two-bedroom oceanfront pad that's worth checking out if you're looking for something upscale.

If you'd like a full-scale vacation home outside the gates of Hawaii Volcanoes National Park, contact the folks behind the Chalet Kilauea Collection (earlier in this chapter), who also offer seven very nice vacation homes in the Volcano area. All are extremely well furnished, well maintained, and well priced, ranging from $135 nightly for a cozy one-bedroom cottage to $275 for a fully equipped three-bedroom home that sleeps six (plus $15 for each additional person over two). Call ☎ **800-937-7786** or 808-987-7786, or point your browser to www.volcano-hawaii.com.

Chapter 16

Settling in on the Big Island

● ●

In This Chapter

▶ Getting from the airport to your hotel

▶ Finding your way around the Big Island

▶ Getting weather reports, prescriptions filled, traveler's checks cashed, and more — an easy-reference list of important local contacts

● ●

*Y*ou will need a rental car on the Big Island. Not having one will leave you dependent on what your resort has to offer — or worse, relegate you to the confines of touristy Kailua-Kona.

All of the major car-rental firms have cars available at both island airports: Kona International Airport, on the arid, beachy west side of the island; and Hilo International Airport, on the east, or volcano, side of the island. Arrange for one before you arrive; in most cases, you'll be charged top dollar at the airport counter (or run the risk of their being out of stock entirely).

Arriving on the West Side at Kona Airport

Keahole-Kona International Airport (☎ **808-329-3423**) is located seven miles north of Kailua-Kona, just off Queen Kaahumanu Highway (Highway 19). Kona is served direct from the mainland by three airlines: **United Airlines, Hawaiian Airlines,** and **TWA;** otherwise, you can arrive on an interisland flight, from another Hawaiian island, via Aloha or Hawaiian airlines.

This small, open-air airport is a breeze to navigate. After collecting your bags from the automated carousels, step outside and head across the street to the clearly marked car-rental counters. Most of the big car-rental companies have their lots right at the airport, so once you finish your business at the counter, you can walk right to your car.

If your company has an off-site lot (**Alamo** is one of the few major companies that does), wait at the curb for the appropriate shuttle van (they circle the airport at regular intervals), which will take you to the nearby lot, where you'll pick up your car.

While you're at the rental counter, be sure to pick up a map booklet from the agent; all of the car-rental agencies offer them, and they're invaluable for getting around the island. They often include money-saving coupons for attractions as well. If the agent doesn't offer one, ask.

If you're heading to Kailua-Kona, turn right out of the airport onto Queen Kaahumanu (ka-a-hoo-MA-noo) Highway (Highway 19). Clearly marked turnoffs will take you down to the town's main drag, Alii (ah-LEE-ee) Drive, about seven miles to the south. If you're continuing on to South Kona or Keauhou (kay-A-ho), stay on Highway 19 for another seven or so miles; for Keauhou, turn toward the coast on Kamehameha III Road.

If you're heading to a Kohala Coast resort, turn left out of the airport onto Queen Kaahumanu Highway (Highway 19) and proceed to one of the following:

- ✔ **Kaupulehu** (cow-poo-LAY-hoo), home to the Four Seasons and Kona Village, is seven miles north of the airport, or a 10-minute drive.

- ✔ **Waikoloa** (why-ko-LO-ah), home to the Outrigger Waikoloa Beach Resort and Hilton Hawaiian Village, is 18 miles north, or a 20- to 25-minute drive.

- ✔ **Mauna Lani,** home to The Orchid and the Mauna Lani Bay Hotel and Bungalows, is about 23 miles north, or a half-hour drive.

- ✔ **Mauna Kea** has its entrance 28 miles north of the airport, or a 40-minute drive.

Look for the gateway to your resort on the ocean side of the road; the only one that's on the right side of the road is the turnoff for the Westin Hapuna Prince Beach Hotel, just before Mauna Kea's entrance. They tend to be marked in a rather understated way, so look carefully.

If you're staying at one of the Kohala Coast resorts, you can usually arrange for the resort shuttle to pick you up at the airport. You can then pick up your prearranged rental car right at the hotel. Call the concierge at your hotel for details before you arrive.

If you're not renting a car and your hotel doesn't offer shuttle service, taxis are readily available at the airport's curbside, so there's no need to arrange for one in advance. Expect the cost to be about $21 to Kailua-Kona, more if you're heading to one of the Kohala Coast resorts.

Arriving on the East Side at Hilo Airport

Hilo (HEE-low) **International Airport** (☎ **808-934-5840** or 808-934-5838) is two miles east of downtown Hilo, at the junction of Kamehameha Avenue and Kanoelehua Avenue (Highway 11).

After collecting your bags, step outside and proceed straight to the rental car check-out desk, where you'll pick up your car. Be sure to pick up a map booklet at the rental counter, as they're invaluable for getting around the island. If the agent doesn't offer one up, ask.

If you're staying in Hilo, turn right out of the airport onto Kanoelehua Avenue (Highway 11), which will lead you right to Banyan Drive and the Hilo Hawaiian and Hawaii Naniloa hotels. To reach downtown and the waterfront, turn left onto Kamehameha Avenue just before Banyan Drive.

If you're heading to Volcano, turn left out of the airport onto Kanoelehua Avenue (Highway 11). Highway 11 will take you the 27 miles (a 45-minute or so drive), to Volcano Village, at the entrance of Hawaii Volcanoes National Park.

Taxis line up in a queue right at the airport's curbside, so there's no need to arrange for one in advance. Expect to pay $8 or $9 to a Hilo destination, plus tip.

Driving around the Big Island

You really do need a car to see the Big Island. An islandwide bus system, the **Hele-On Bus** (☎ **808-961-8744**), is available, but all it really does is transport passengers (mostly locals) between Kailua-Kona and Hilo.

If you're not going to have a car at hand, contact your hotel concierge or condo front desk and ask about local shuttle services. A few shuttles service the Kailua-Kona area and the South Kona coast. In addition, most of the Kona-Kohala Coast resorts offer free resort shuttles that transport guests within the resort, to golf courses, neighboring hotels, and any other nearby facilities. If you plan on relying on a resort shuttle, though, expect to be largely confined to your resort.

The Big Island only has a handful of main roads, all of which basically stick to the perimeter of the island because of the volcanic mountains that dominate the interior: most notably Mauna Kea to the north, and Mauna Loa in the lower middle (both of which rise so far above sea level that their peaks often sport snow even in July). Thus, it's pretty hard to get lost on this island.

The most important thing to keep in mind is the island's sheer size — they don't call this the Big Island for nothing, after all. Driving from coast to coast — from Kailua-Kona to Hilo, say, or from Volcano to the Kohala Coast — takes 3 to 3½ hours; circling the entire island takes between 6 and 7 hours' drive time. Distances are often longer than they seem on this island, much like they are in the southwest U.S. — so be sure that you have a realistic idea of how far you need to travel before you set out. If you're not sure, check with the concierge or the front-desk staff of your hotel or condo before you set out.

Big Island Orientation

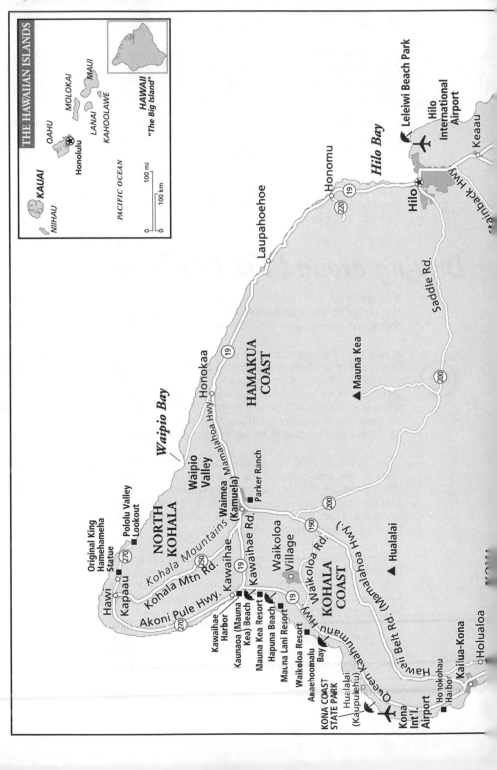

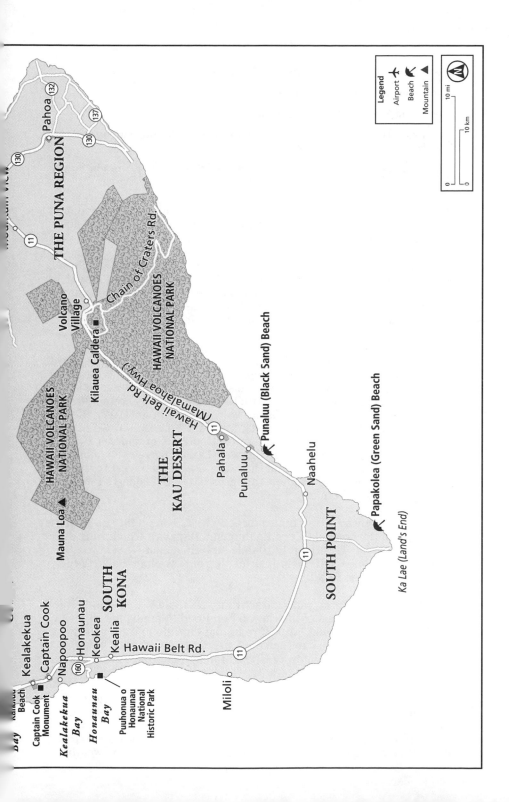

Legend
Airport ✈
Beach 🏖
Mountain ▲

10 mi

10 km

THE PUNA REGION

Pahoa

132

137

130

130

11

Chain of Craters Rd.

Volcano Village

Kilauea Caldera

HAWAII VOLCANOES NATIONAL PARK

Hawaii Belt Rd. (Mamalahoa Hwy.)

HAWAII VOLCANOES NATIONAL PARK

Mauna Loa ▲

THE KAU DESERT

Pahala

Punaluu

Punaluu (Black Sand) Beach

11

Naahelu

Papakolea (Green Sand) Beach

SOUTH POINT

Ka Lae (Land's End)

11

SOUTH KONA

Kealakekua

Captain Cook

Napoopoo

Honaunau

Keokea

160

Kealia

Hawaii Belt Rd.

11

Miloli

Kealakekua Bay

Honaunau Bay

Puuhonua o Honaunau National Historic Park

Captain Cook Monument

Beach

Bay

Here are some estimated circle island drive times:

- ✔ **From Kailua-Kona to the Waikoloa Resort:** 35 minutes
- ✔ **From Waikoloa Resort to Waimea:** 25 minutes
- ✔ **From Waimea to Hilo:** 1 hour
- ✔ **From Hilo to Volcano Village (gateway to Hawaii Volcanoes National Park):** 45 minutes
- ✔ **From Hawaii Volcanoes National Park to Kailua-Kona via South Point:** 2¾ to 3 hours

If you're a driver who sticks to the conservative side of the speed limit or it's a rainy day, expect drive times to be a slightly longer. And don't forget to factor in pit stops.

If you arrive at Kona Airport, the first of the Big Island's main highways you'll encounter is **Queen Kaahumanu Highway** (Highway 19), which runs along the Kona-Kohala coast for 33 miles, from Kailua-Kona at the south to the industrial port of Kawaihae at the north. All of the major Kohala Coast resorts and beaches are accessible from this main coastal highway.

The Big Island has one main highway that circles the island: the **Hawaii Belt Road,** also known as the **Mamalahoa Highway,** which is labeled **Highway 11** as it runs south from the sunny, arid resort town of Kailua-Kona around the island's southern tip (a 60-mile drive); another 36 miles through Volcano (gateway to Hawaii Volcanoes National Park); then about 27 miles north to Hilo, a misty, funky-cool bayfront town that's the second-largest city in the state (after Honolulu, of course). Go north from Hilo and it becomes **Highway 19** as it travels north along the misty and ruggedly beautiful Hamakua Coast, then west to the upland cowboy town of Waimea, the heart of the Big Island's ranch-land, for a total of 54 miles.

In Waimea, Highway 19 continues directly west, connecting up with the north end of the coastal Queen Kaahumanu Highway, which runs down the Kohala Coast. This roughly 10-mile stretch of east — west road connecting Waimea and the industrial port of Kawaihae (ka-WHY-high) is called **Kawaihae Road.**

An interior road offers a more direct route between Waimea and Kailua-Kona: The continuation of the Hawaii Belt Road (Mamalahoa Highway) is **Highway 190,** a scenic "upper" road that cuts along the western slope of Mauna Kea back to the coast, meeting up with the Queen Kaahumanu Highway (Highway 19) right in Kailua-Kona — thus completing the loop.

One more road links east to west: **The Saddle Road** (Highway 200) is so named because it crosses the "saddle" between Mauna Kea and Mauna Loa volcanoes as it runs from Highway 190 south of Waimea direct to Hilo. Your rental-car agreement will most likely ask you to avoid it, and for good reason: It's rough and narrow, and the weather conditions can be tough to handle. So don't take the Saddle Road — stick to the main highways instead.

You're also supposed to avoid **South Point Road,** the road that runs from the Mamalahoa Road at the south end of the island directly south, to the southernmost point in the United States. While this road is far less treacherous, you're best off avoiding it — because if you do get stuck, you'll end up coming home with a souvenir in the form of a hefty tow bill.

Also stay off of the steeply graded **Waipio Valley Road,** at the north end of the Hamakua Coast, which is not meant for cars — and you will get stuck here.

For a more complete discussion of the major resort areas as well as Hilo and Volcano, check out the section called "Choosing Your Location" in Chapter 15.

If you drive north from the intersection of the Kohala Coast's Queen Kaahumanu Highway and the Kawaihae Road, you'll enter North Kohala, the peninsula that extends off the northern end of the island. The drive north along the **Akoni Pule** (ah-KO-nee POO-lay) **Highway** (Highway 270) offers a peek at a different side of the Big Island, one where lava cedes to gorgeous rolling ranchlands. It's a beautiful hour-long drive that leads to some wonderful wilderness activities that I discuss in detail in Chapter 18. You can circle back from the town of Hawi (HA-vee) at North Kohala's tip along the **Kohala Mountain Road** (Highway 250), ending up back on the Kawaihae Road just west of Waimea.

Quick Concierge

American Express

American Express has one office on the Big Island, on the Kohala Coast at the **Hilton Waikoloa Village,** 425 Waikoloa Beach Dr., off Hwy. 19 in the Waikoloa Resort (☎ 808-886-7958), open daily 7 a.m. to 5 p.m.

Baby-Sitters and Baby Stuff

Any resort, hotel, or condo should be able to refer you to a reliable babysitter with a proven track record. **Baby's Away** (☎ 800-931-9030; Internet: www.babysaway.com) rents cribs, strollers, highchairs, playpens, infant seats, and the like; they'll deliver whatever you need to wherever you're staying, and pick it up when you're done.

Doctors

Hualalai Urgent Care is in Kailua-Kona at 75-1028 Henry St. (behind Borders Books and Music, across the street from Safeway; ☎ 808-327-4357).

Emergencies

Dial **911** from any phone, just like back home.

Hospitals

Kona Community Hospital, on the South Kona coast on Haukapila Street, off Highway 11, in Kealakekua (☎ 808-322-9311), has 24-hour emergency facilities. On the east side of the island, head to the emergency room at **Hilo Medical Center,** 1190 Waianuenue Ave. (just west of Rainbow Drive), Hilo (☎ 808-974-4700).

Information

The **Big Island Visitors Bureau** has two island offices: One on the Kohala Coast at the Kings' Shops, 250 Waikoloa Beach Dr., in the Waikoloa resort (☎ 808-886-1655); and another in Hilo at 250 Keawe St., at Haili Street (across from Pescatore's restaurant), downtown (☎ 808-961-5797). You can find plenty of information before you leave home on the Big Island's official Web site at www.bigisland.org. Or, if you'd like information specifically on the island's west side, contact the **Kona Kohala Resort Association** (☎ 800-318-3637 or 808-886-4915; Internet: www.kkra.org).

Chances are good that you'll find all of the information you need even before you leave the airport. Just wander over to the information kiosks while you're waiting for your baggage and pick up copies of *This Week Big Island* and *101 Things to Do on the Big Island,* and the other free tourist publications and brochures you'll find there. They're also available all over the island (particularly at malls and shopping centers).

Also, don't hesitate to ask the staff at your resort or condo for help or advice if you need it. These knowledgeable folks are usually more than happy to point you in the right direction and make recommendations.

Newspapers/Magazines

The Big Island has two daily papers: *West Hawaii Today* (www.westhawaiitoday.com), and the *Hawaii Tribune Herald* (www.hilohawaiitribune.com), which predominately serves Hilo and environs. In addition, the *Hawaii Island Journal* is a free weekly newspaper that's a good source for event and entertainment listings; it's easy to find in free racks around the island.

Pharmacies

Long's Drugs, Hawaii's biggest drugstore chain, has two branches in Kailua-Kona: one at 78-6831 Alii Dr., north of Judd Trail (☎ 808-322-5122); and one at 75-5595 Palani Rd., on the ocean side of Highway 19 (☎ 808-329-1380). In Hilo, you'll find branches of Long's at 555 Kilauea Ave., between Kukueu and Osorio streets (☎ 808-935-3357); and in the Prince Kuhio Shopping Plaza, 111 E. Puainako St., east of Highway 11 (☎ 808-959-5881).

Police

Island headquarters is at 349 Kapiolani St. (between Kukuau and Hualalai streets), Hilo (☎ 808-935-3311). The Kona Police Station is at 74-5221 Queen Kaahumanu Hwy. (Highway 19), just south of Kaloko Light Industrial Park (☎ 808-326-4646). Of course, if you have an emergency, dial **911** from any phone.

Post Offices

The Kailua-Kona branch offices are at 74-7577 Palani Rd. (past Highway 11, almost to the shoreline) and 78-6831 Alii Dr. (near Judd Trail). In Hilo, head to 1299 Kekuanaoa Ave. (past the airport; follow it as it loops around). A downtown branch is at 152 Waianuenue Ave., between Keawe and Kinoole streets. Satellite post offices are located around the island; to find the one nearest you, call ☎ 800-275-8777 or visit new.usps.com.

Taxes

Hawaii's sales tax is 4%. Expect taxes of about 11.42% to be added to your hotel bill.

Taxis

On the west side of the island, **Paradise Taxi** (☎ 808-329-1234) serves the Kailua-Kona area, while **Aloha Taxi** (☎ 808-329-7779 or 808-325-5448) serves the Kohala Coast. In Hilo, call **Ace One** (☎ 808-935-8303) or **Hilo Harry's Taxi** (☎ 808-935-5839).

Weather, Surf, and Volcano Reports

For conditions in and around **Hilo,** call ☎ 808-935-8555. For **islandwide weather,** ☎ 808-961-5582. For **wind and marine** forecasts, call ☎ 808-935-9883. For **volcano eruption** information, dial ☎ 808-985-6000.

Chapter 17

Dining around the Big Island

. . . .

In This Chapter

▶ Choosing among the Big Island's best restaurants, with complete reviews and all the details

▶ Finding a luau if the party mood strikes you

. . . .

*T*he Big Island is home to some wonderful restaurants — including a handful of special-occasion oceanfront spots that are just right for some grand island-style wooing. But you don't have to spend a fortune to eat well; in fact, the Big Island is home to some of my favorite affordable and ethnic restaurants in the state.

On the down side, things are a little spread out on this oversized rural island (as you've no doubt already noted), so choose your dining spots carefully — you don't want to make a reservation for dinner and realize that the restaurant is an hour's drive from where you're staying. I've worked to include the best restaurants in and around all of the major resort and visitor areas in which you'll be staying. Still, you may find that your choices are limited; around Hawaii Volcanoes National Park, for example, there simply isn't more than a handful of restaurants from which to choose, period. If you want additional choices, your concierge, front-desk staff, or innkeeper will usually be happy to make recommendations.

If you're staying at a Kohala Coast resort, you'll find that the resort restaurants are almost universally overpriced. So I've included a few worthy local favorites near the resorts, for those of you who weary of paying a minimum of thirty bucks for an entree or $16 for a room-service burger little Johnny isn't going to finish anyway.

The Big Island's Best Restaurants

In the restaurant listings in this chapter, each restaurant review is followed by a number of dollar signs, ranging from one ($) to five ($$$$$). The dollar signs are meant to give you an idea of what a complete dinner for one person — including appetizer, main course, one drink, tax, and tip — is likely to set you back. The price categories go like this:

The Big Island's Best Restaurants

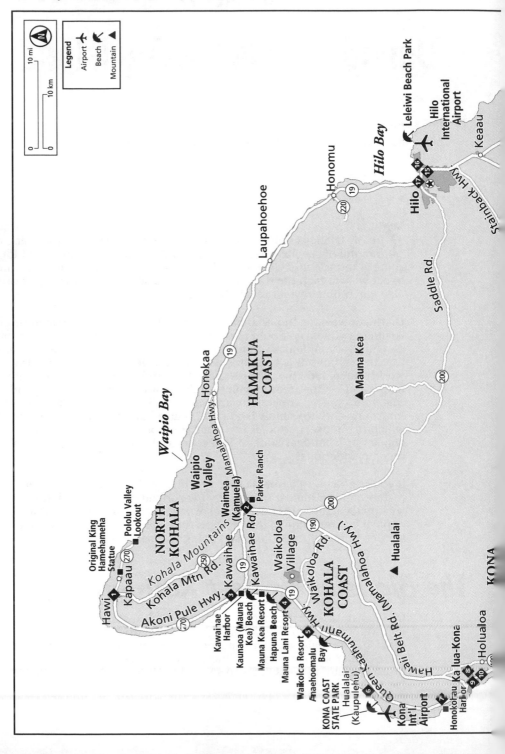

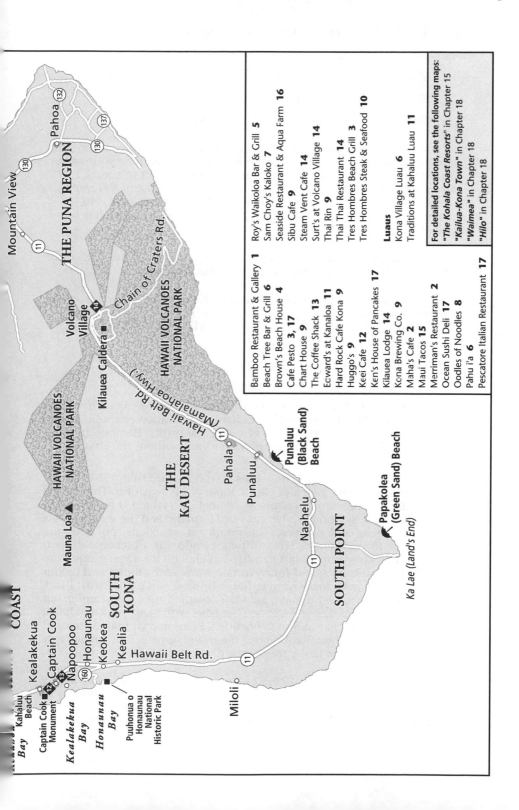

Mountain View

Pahoa

THE PUNA REGION

Volcano Village

Kilauea Caldera

Chain of Craters Rd.

HAWAII VOLCANOES NATIONAL PARK

HAWAII VOLCANOES NATIONAL PARK

Mauna Loa

THE KAU DESERT

Hawaii Belt Rd. (Mamalahoa Hwy.)

Pahala

Punaluu

Punaluu (Black Sand) Beach

Naahelu

Papakolea (Green Sand) Beach

SOUTH POINT

Ka Lae (Land's End)

SOUTH KONA

Kealia

Keokea

Honaunau

Napoopoo

Captain Cook

Kealakekua

Kahaluu Beach

Captain Cook Monument

Kealakekua Bay

Honaunau Bay

Puuhonua o Honaunau National Historic Park

Hawaii Belt Rd.

Miloli

COAST

Bamboo Restaurant & Gallery **1**
Beach Tree Bar & Grill **6**
Brown's Beach House **4**
Cafe Pesto **3, 17**
Chart House **9**
The Coffee Shack **13**
Ecward's at Kanaloa **11**
Hard Rock Cafe Kona **9**
Huggo's **9**
Keei Cafe **12**
Ken's House of Pancakes **17**
Kilauea Lodge **14**
Kona Brewing Co. **9**
Maha's Cafe **2**
Maui Tacos **15**
Merriman's Restaurant **2**
Ocean Sushi Deli **17**
Oodles of Noodles **8**
Pahu i'a **6**
Pescatore Italian Restaurant **17**

Roy's Waikoloa Bar & Grill **5**
Sam Choy's Kaloko **7**
Seaside Restaurant & Aqua Farm **16**
Sibu Cafe **9**
Steam Vent Cafe **14**
Surt's at Volcano Village **14**
Thai Rin **9**
Thai Thai Restaurant **14**
Tres Hombres Beach Grill **3**
Tres Hombres Steak & Seafood **10**

Luaus
Kona Village Luau **6**
Traditions at Kahaluu Luau **11**

For detailed locations, see the following maps:
"The Kohala Coast Resorts" in Chapter 15
"Kailua-Kona Town" in Chapter 18
"Waimea" in Chapter 18
"Hilo" in Chapter 18

$	Cheap eats — less than $15 per person
$$	Still inexpensive — $15 to $25
$$$	Moderate — $25 to $40
$$$$	Pricey — $40 to $70
$$$$$	Ultra-expensive — more than $70 per person

Of course, it all depends on how you order, so stay away from the surf and turf or the north end of the wine list if you're watching your wallet. To give you a further idea of how much you can expect to spend, I've also included the price range of main courses in the listings. (Keep in mind that prices can change at the whim of the management, but restaurants usually don't raise their prices by more than a dollar or two at any given time.)

The state adds 4 percent in sales tax to every restaurant bill. A 15 to 20 percent tip is standard in Hawaii, just like back home.

Just dying to take home a **Hard Rock Cafe Kona** T-shirt? The Big Island branch of the rock-and-burger chain is in the heart of Kailua-Kona at the Coconut Grove Marketplace, 75-5815 Alii Dr. (☎ **808-329-8866**).

Bamboo Restaurant & Gallery

$$–$$$ North Kohala   Hawaii Local/Pacific Rim

This wonderful restaurant provides the perfect excuse to venture up to pastoral North Kohala. Housed in a delightful plantation-era building and done up in well-worn rattan and retro-tropical prints, Bamboo bubbles over with old Hawaii appeal — like Trader Vic's without the kitsch.

The pleasing menu features delicious island cuisine that, refreshingly, doesn't bother with "gourmet" or "culinary" pretensions. This is real food, well prepared with local pride: Almost everything is fresh-caught or locally grown by Kohala fishermen and farmers, and the owners grow their own herbs and flowers. The quality is excellent, portions are generous, and Pacific and Thai influences add zip. Chicken sate pot-stickers are handwrapped and pan-fried in chili oil for a spicy signature treat. Island fish is prepared four winning ways, and a moist and tender herb-marinated pork tenderloin is flame-broiled and paired with black tiger shrimp and green papaya salad. The lunch menu is simpler but equally satisfying, and eggs Bamboo (Benedict with kalua pork and lilikoi hollandaise) is a winner at Sunday brunch. Passion-fruit margaritas and live slack-key guitar music round out the island appeal. Plan on an early dinner so that you can enjoy the scenic drive in daylight.

On Akoni Pule Hwy. (at Hwy. 270/250 intersection), Hawi (a 30- to 45-minute drive from most Kohala Coast resorts). ☎ 808-889-5555. Internet: www.bamboorestaurant.com. *Reservations highly recommended for dinner. Main courses: $5–$11 at lunch, $8–$24 at dinner. DC, MC, V. Open: Lunch and dinner Tues–Sat, Sun brunch.*

Beach Tree Bar & Grill

$$$–$$$$ Kohala Coast   Pacific Rim/International

Kudos to the Four Seasons for creating such an unpretentious, and relatively affordable, beachfront spot. This casually lovely outdoor patio restaurant sits right on the sand, and every generously sized, comfortable table is angled to make the most of the surf and sunset views; Hawaiian music and hula make an already enchanting setting simply exquisite at sunset. The regular menu focuses on informal pan-Asian dishes like Thai-style rock shrimp spring rolls, coconut-marinated sweet chile tiger prawns (yum!), and a classic Caesar topped with barbecued chicken for a extra kick. But the Beach Tree really shines on all-you-can-eat nights, when the staff mounts a bountiful, top-quality themed spread. Monday is Asian night and Wednesday is dedicated to Italian, but the hands-down winner is Saturday's Surf, Sand, and Stars Barbecue, a traditional cookout featuring fresh island fish, steak, ribs, oysters, clams, and snow-crab claws grilled over an open flame.

At the Four Seasons Resort Hualalai, 100 Kaupulehu Dr., Kaupulehu-Kona (7 miles north of Kona Airport). ☎ *808-325-8000. Reservations recommended for dinner (highly recommended on buffet nights). Main courses: $7–$15 at lunch, $13–$25 at dinner; all-you-can-eat buffets $34–$44 adults, $15 kids 6–12. AE, DC, DISC, JCB, MC, V. Open: Lunch, afternoon pupus, and dinner daily.*

Book your table at the Beach Tree's Surf, Sand, and Stars Barbecue in advance, as this festive Saturday-night beach party is a hugely popular weekly event.

Brown's Beach House

$$$$$ Kohala Coast   Hawaii Regional/International

On-the-beach dining experiences don't come finer than Brown's, an excellent alfresco restaurant that consistently shines in all categories: food, service, and setting. What was in the past an overly complex interpretation of Hawaii Regional cuisine is still cross-pollinated in a global-minded kitchen, but the innovations have been toned down a few notches to great effect. Pueblo corn-crusted mahimahi is accompanied by spicy purple Molokai sweet potatoes and orange miso vinaigrette in a surprisingly successful marriage of Southwest and island flavors that no longer overwhelms, while macadamia-nut-crusted lamb chops wear a just-right touch of honey-mustard. I prefer the food at Pahu i'a (later in this chapter), but the one-of-a-kind ambience here is pure magic. Reserve a table close to the spotlit surf for the ultimate in romance (and bring a light wrap to ward off the ocean breeze, which can wear a nip after dark).

In the Orchid at Mauna Lani, 1 North Kaniku Dr., Mauna Lani resort. ☎ *808-885-2000. Reservations highly recommended for dinner. Main courses: $10–$22 at lunch, $28–$39 at dinner. AE, DC, DISC, JCB, MC, V. Open: Lunch and dinner daily.*

Cafe Pesto

$$–$$$ Hilo/Kohala Coast   Pizza/Italian/Island

These casual favorites are a long-standing hit with locals and visitors alike. The well-prepared pastas and Pacific Regional specialties are pleasing, but the pizza is the real star — and the real value — of the menu. Both branches serve up top-flight gourmet brick-oven-baked pies featuring fresh organic herbs, island-grown produce, and a thick, slightly sweet golden crust. My favorite is the pizza luau, with kalua-style pork, sweet onions, and fresh pineapple, but you can choose from a full slate of creative combinations as well as a build-your-own option. I find the food to be consistently better at the original Hilo branch (which also boasts a lovelier setting), but the second branch, at the northernmost end of the Kohala Coast, provides a great escape for families tired of feeding on resort food.

Hilo: In the S. Hata Building, 308 Kamehameha Ave. (at Mamo St.). ☎ *808-969-6640. The Kohala Coast: In the Kawaihae Shopping Center at Kawaihae Harbor, at Akoni Pule Hwy. and Kawaihae Rd., Kawaihae (at the Hwy. 19/270 junction).* ☎ *808-882-1071. Internet:* www.cafepesto.com. *Reservations recommended for dinner. Pizzas: $8–$18. Main courses: $8–$12 at lunch, $15–$24 at dinner. AE, CB, DC, DISC, JCB, MC, V. Open: Lunch and dinner daily.*

Chart House

$$$$ Kailua-Kona   Steaks/Seafood

Alii Drive boasts a string of on-the-water restaurants — and most of them barely surpass mediocre on any other score but setting. So I cast aside my no-chain-restaurants rule of thumb in favor of this familiar steakhouse, which is the best of the bunch by far. The proven Chart House formula — reliable surf-and-turf plates, a skilled bartender manning a well-stocked bar, and a spectacular oceanfront perch — is in top form here. The chain-standard menu — filet mignon, black Angus sirloin, flown-in king-crab legs and lobster tails, the always-satisfying salad bar — includes a few fresh island catches, but otherwise expect the usual Chart House comforts. A kids' menu is available, making this a good family choice to boot.

In Waterfront Row, 75-5770 Alii Dr., Kailua-Kona. ☎ *808-329-2451. Internet:* www.chart-house.com. *Reservations recommended. Main courses: $16–$34. AE, DISC, MC, V. Open: Dinner nightly.*

The Coffee Shack

$ South Kona   American

This bare-bones roadside charmer prepares some of South Kona's best eats. Take a seat on the pleasant terrace (which boasts ocean views beyond the banana trees) for table service, or pony up to the friendly counter to order takeout. You can start the day with a first-class eggs Benedict or thick French toast, or come by at lunch for the best sandwich on the coast: Top-notch fillings range from smoked Alaskan salmon to fresh local veggies to warmed corned beef and black forest ham, and you have them applied to any one of six kinds of fresh-baked bread. The thick-crusted, generously topped pizzas are even better than Cafe Pesto's. The wait service can be slow, but you're on vacation, so sit back and take it in stride — and consider it a blessing that you have more time to take in the million-dollar view.

On Hwy. 11, between mile markers 108 and 109, a mile south of Captain Cook (about 10 minutes south of Keauhou). ☎ *808-328-9555. Breakfast and sandwiches: $5–$9. Pizzas: $10–$16. AE, MC, V. Open: Breakfast and lunch Mon–Sat.*

Edward's at Kanaloa

$$$–$$$$ South Kona   Mediterranean

Not much more than a covered pier reaching out to sea, Edward's is one of the most romantic restaurants in Hawaii. The tables for two sit so close to the melodious surf that the outermost ones have to be pulled in when the waves kick up. Sunset is breathtaking, and tiki torches make magic after dark. The food wins high praise, too: Edward's broadly Mediterranean cuisine — a Provençal flair here, a taste of Verona there — is rich, flavorful, and delicious. I love to start with the escargot medley, deftly seasoned with fresh herbs and accompanied by mushrooms, asparagus spears, and artichoke hearts. In addition to the requisite fresh island fish preparations, ricotta-stuffed squid dressed in *herbes de provence* and tomato caper sauce is a standout. The food isn't inexpensive, but it's not overpriced, either, like so many other restaurants boasting a winning combination of cuisine, service, and views. The wine list is short but also reasonably priced.

At Kanaloa at Kona, 78-261 Manukai St., Keauhou. ☎ *808-322-1003 or 808-322-1434. Internet:* www.edwardsatkanaloa.com. *Reservations required. To get there: From Hwy. 11, turn right on Kamehameha III Rd. (between mile markers 117 and 118), then right on Manukai Street. Main courses: $5–$10 at breakfast, $9–$14 at lunch, $17–$30 at dinner. AE, DC, MC, V. Open: Breakfast, lunch, and dinner daily.*

Huggo's

$$$$ Kailua-Kona   Seafood

Happy, hopping Huggo's serves reliably fine seafood to a jovial crowd drawn in by the festive vibe and remarkable Kailua Bay views. Fresh fish is the specialty, as it should be — they could practically cast a line over the side of the deck. The kitchen isn't going to set the world on fire with its culinary creativity, but the simplicity can be refreshing when so many restaurants smother the freshness and flavor of top-quality local catches with heavy-handed preparations. Garlic chicken, prime rib, and New York steak are on hand for the fish-o-phobic. There's live music nightly, and the lively bar prepares an extensive tropical cocktail menu — perfect for a place that exists to celebrate sunset.

75-5828 Kahakai Rd., off Alii Drive (behind Snorkel Bob's and next to the Royal Kona Resort), Kailua-Kona. ☎ *808-329-1493. Reservations highly recommended. Main courses: $7–$17 at lunch, $17–$30 at dinner. AE, CB, DC, DISC, JCB, MC, V. Open: Lunch Mon–Fri, dinner nightly.*

Keei Cafe

$$–$$$ South Kona   Island/Eclectic

Keei (KAY-ee) Cafe prepares some of the Big Island's finest food — but you would never guess it based on appearances. You'll have to look hard for the restaurant, which isn't so much hidden as just utterly nondescript. Inside, the tidy room boasts zero ambience, but it's comfortable and casual, and service is friendly — and the island-style meals are excellent. Expect hearty Asian-slanted dishes in pleasantly light sauces and accompanied by fresh, crisp vegetables, such as half-roasted chicken in red Thai curry, or marvelous fresh Kona catches in a puckery picatta sauce. Keei Cafe offers one of the best dining values in the state — it's easy to pay a lot more for a lot less elsewhere in Hawaii. Note that the owners are contemplating a possible move just a few minutes up the highway sometime in 2001, so it's best to confirm the location when you call.

83-4587 Mamalahoa Hwy. (on the ocean side of Hwy. 11, at mile marker 106), Captain Cook. ☎ *808-328-8451. Reservations highly recommended. Main courses: $9–$19. No credit cards. Open: Dinner Tues–Sat.*

Ken's House of Pancakes

$ Hilo   Coffee Shop

The classic coffee shop goes Hawaiian at Ken's — and stays open around the clock. This cheery place is your average all-American diner, where the food is familiar and pleasingly prepared, and the old-fashioned service comes with a dash of island-style aloha. Ken's is a three-meals-a-day-plus kind of place: Start your day bright and early with French toast or a macadamia-nut waffle (topped with passion-fruit or coconut syrup, if you wish); come back at noon for a garden-fresh salad or a flame-broiled burger; stop in for a roast turkey, teriyaki chicken, or kalbi rib dinner; and drop by for a late-night piece of pie and a cup of Kona joe.

1730 Kamehameha Ave. (at Kanoelehua Ave.), Hilo. ☎ *808-935-8711. Reservations not taken. Main courses: $2–$11. AE, DC, DISC, JCB, MC, V. Open: Daily 24 hours.*

Kilauea Lodge

$$$$ Volcano   Continental

My favorite Volcano restaurant is dressed like a cozy old-world hunting lodge and tucked away in the rain forest just outside the national park. The large, high-ceilinged room is appealingly attractive, with country-style furniture polished to a high sheen and a roaring stone fireplace; knowledgeable and warmly welcoming servers dressed in beautiful island prints by renowned Big Island designer Sig Zane (see "A shopper's guide to the Big Island" in Chapter 18); and a skilled bartender whose martinis could pass muster on Manhattan's Upper East Side. Chef/owner Albert Jeyte specializes in hearty old-world cuisine: Sure, a well-prepared fresh catch is always on offer, but Jeyte's heart lies with such richly flavored dishes as venison medallions, which arrive pan-seared, brandy-flamed, and sporting a yummy Nicole sauce; duck l'orange, roasted with orange wedges, pepper, and garlic and dressed in an apricot mustard glaze; and *hasenpfeffer*, succulent braised rabbit in a red-wine sauce. Dinners come with soup, salad, and fresh-baked bread, which makes the excellent fare an excellent value, too.

19-4055 Volcano Rd., (just off Hwy. 11 at Wright Rd.), Volcano. ☎ *808-967-7366. Internet:* www.kilauealodge.com. *Reservations recommended. Main courses: $16–$35 (most less than $29). AE, MC, V. Open: Dinner nightly.*

Kona Brewing Co.

$–$$ Kailua-Kona   Island/Pizza

Kona Brewing Co. is Hawaii's finest microbrewery, specializing in flavorful hand-crafted brews with island-rooted names like Longboard Lager, Fire Rock Pale Ale, and Pahoehoe Porter. You can enjoy them fresh from the tap at this pleasingly casual pub, along with equally well-prepared island-style pub grub: hand-tossed pizza crusts topped with top-quality Parmesan and mozzarella, locally grown herbs, and a range of creative ingredients, from traditional pepperoni to *lilikoi* (passion fruit) barbecue chicken; hearty salads with crisp island-grown veggies; and generously stuffed sandwiches on the brewery's own focaccia. A nice selection of *pupus* (appetizers) are on hand for those who merely want to pull up to the blond-wood bar for some munchies and a brewski. Inside service is available, but snare a table on the pretty tropical patio if you can. Friendly service rounds out the affordable, easygoing appeal.

In the North Kona Shopping Center, at Kuakini Hwy. (1 block inland from Alii Dr.) and Palani Rd. ☎ *808-334-2739. Internet:* www.konabrewingco.com. *Reservations taken only for parties of ten or more. To get there: Heading toward the ocean on Palani Rd., turn left on Kuakini Hwy., then right into the shopping center. Sandwiches and salads: $6–$9. Pizzas: $7–$21. DC, JCB, MC, V. Open: Lunch and dinner daily.*

Maha's Cafe

$ Waimea   Island/Sandwiches

Maha's alone makes a trip to Waimea well worth the effort. This cozy country cottage is one of the Big Island's best restaurants. Simple home-style cooking is raised to new heights by Maha's magic touch. I still dream about Maha's oven-roasted turkey sandwich: Served on dark squaw bread with homemade mushroom stuffing and cranberry sauce, this open-faced symphony of sandwich shouldn't be relegated to holiday time. Other choices are similarly ethereal: honey-smoked ahi with *lilikoi* salsa; roasted lamb with spicy mango chutney; and fresh fish with local taro and sweet potato. Don't skip dessert even if you don't usually indulge, because the fresh-baked sweets are divine.

In front of Waimea Center, 65-1148 Mamalahoa Hwy. (Hwy. 19), near Hwy. 190 junction (next to McDonald's), Waimea. ☎ *808-885-0693. Internet:* www.hawaiinow.com/mahas. *Reservations not taken. Main courses: $5.50–$8. Afternoon tea: $12. MC, V. Open: Breakfast, lunch, and afternoon tea Wed–Mon.*

Maui Tacos

$ Hilo Island-Mexican

The only Big Island branch of this burgeoning Hawaii chain (which is beginning to spread to the mainland) serves up gourmet Mexican with a healthy bent in a fast-food format. All of the menu items are prepared using top-quality produce, lean steak, skinless chicken, light sour cream, and vegetable oil and stocks only (no lard). Chips, beans, salsas, and guacamoles are all made fresh on the premises. A terrific choice for a quickie meal that you won't regret later. Go with one of the generously stuffed big surf burritos for maximum satisfaction.

In Prince Kuhio Plaza, 111 E. Puainako St. (at Kanoelehua Ave./Hwy. 11), Hilo. ☎ *808-959-0359. Internet:* www.mauitacos.com. *Main courses: $3–$8. DISC, JCB, MC, V. Open: Lunch and dinner Mon–Sat, lunch only Sun (to 6 p.m.).*

Merriman's Restaurant

$$$$ Waimea Hawaii Regional

One of the original purveyors of Hawaii Regional cuisine, chef Peter Merriman's cozy cowboy-country enclave has matured into a still-pleasing — and still hugely popular — culinary institution. Residents and visitors alike happily make the long drive upcountry (20 minutes from the Kohala Coast, about an hour from Kona or Hilo) to feast on Merriman's winning cuisine, the long-lasting success of which lies in its simplicity: Waimea-raised beef and lamb, fish caught daily in Kona waters, and organically grown local veggies are used in uncomplicated yet innovative preparations that let the fresh natural flavors of the top-quality ingredients shine through. Wok-charred ahi, Pahoa corn–and-shrimp fritters, and slow-roasted chicken are among the many standouts on the perpetually pleasing menu. Meals are more affordably priced than most of this caliber, and lunch is a downright bargain. The only down side is the Big '80s-reminiscent pastel interior, which is nicely maintained but nevertheless sorely in need of an update.

In Opelo Plaza, Hwy. 19 (at Opelo Road, on the Kona side of town), Waimea. ☎ *808-885-6822. Reservations recommended. Main courses: $8–$14 at lunch, $20–$35 at dinner. AE, MC, V. Open: Lunch Mon–Fri, dinner nightly.*

Ocean Sushi Deli

$$ Hilo Japanese

Sushi lovers who visit Hilo shouldn't miss this plain and simple sushi restaurant, which makes the most of the bounty of the sea, both island-caught and flown in fresh from Japan. Always of A-1 quality, the fish is skillfully prepared by master sushi chefs and served with aloha by a young, friendly, and attentive waitstaff. Creative rolls are a forte, and combination plates are a bargain. The restaurant is very popular at dinnertime, so make reservations or be prepared for a wait. Across the street, at no. 250, is sister restaurant Tsunami Grill and Tempura, which excels at noodle bowls, bentos, tempura, katsu, and other Japanese comfort foods; the sushi-phobic members of your party can order non-fish items from the Tsunami menu at Ocean Sushi Deli.

239 Keawe St. (near Haili St., next to Pescatore), Hilo. ☎ *808-961-6625. Reservations recommended for dinner. 2-piece sushi and rolls: $2–$7.50. Complete meals: $4–$20. DC, JCB, MC, V. Open: Lunch and dinner Mon–Sat.*

Oodles of Noodles

$$–$$$ Kailua-Kona   Pan-Asian/International

Oodles isn't just any Formica-countered quickie noodle stand — rather, it's the domain of top Hawaii Regional chef Amy Ota, who has reinvented noodle dishes for discriminating diners with resounding success. Noodles are the unifying theme on a creative global-gourmet menu that runs the gamut from Vietnamese *pho* (beef noodle soup) to pasta primavera with grilled vegetables to wok-seared ahi noodle casserole to the world's best macaroni and cheese. Save room for the surprisingly scrumptious desserts, which are often the finest feature of an all-around pleasing meal. The hip, warm-hued restaurant has doubled in size in recent years, but its popularity among locals and visitors alike means that you might still encounter a wait for a table.

In the Crossroads Shopping Center (the Safeway Center), 75-1027 Henry St. (at Hwy. 11 and Palani Rd.), Kailua-Kona. ☎ *808-329-9222. Reservations accepted for parties of 6 or more. Noodle bowls: $9–$16. Main courses: $14–$22. AE, DC, DISC, JCB, MC, V. Open: Lunch and dinner daily.*

Pahu i'a

$$$$$ Kohala Coast   Euro-Pacific Fusion

Done in an elegant haute-plantation style and open to the tradewinds and ocean views, this ultra-romantic candlelit dining room is the Big Island's most beautiful restaurant — and the sublime food and faultless service live up to the setting in every respect. The regularly changing menu features only the finest regional ingredients, and both Pacific-born and continental preparations take inspired turns in the capable kitchen — for example, while a thick-cut ahi steak wears a Szechuan pepper crust, the threat of excessive spice is undone by a light and aromatic Kau orange citrus sauce. I'm clearly not alone in considering Pahu i'a phenomenal on all fronts — it scores no lower than 27 (out of a possible 30) *in every category* in the restaurant bible *Zagat.* Be prepared, because it's dreadfully hard to get in — but your efforts will be well-rewarded, so book well ahead (before you leave home, if possible) or opt for an early or late meal.

At the Four Seasons Resort Hualalai, 100 Kaupulehu Dr., Kaupulehu-Kona (7 miles north of the airport). ☎ *808-325-8000. Reservations essential. Main courses: $25–$48 at dinner. AE, DC, DISC, JCB, MC, V. Open: Breakfast and dinner daily.*

Pescatore Italian Restaurant

$$$ Hilo   Italian

Hilo's top fine-dining spot is an old-world restaurant with wood-paneled walls, ornately cushioned chairs, and delicate lace curtains on the windows. The traditionally Southern Italian, seafood-heavy menu stars excellent scalloppines, primaveras, and puttanescas. Dishes are consistently well-prepared and pleasing: Ahi carpaccio is sliced paper thin and dressed in fine extra-virgin olive oil to heighten the fresh flavor, the seafood Fra Diavolo is a spicy bounty of fresh seafood in zesty marinara, and the veal is always a tender triumph. Service is attentive, and the wine list is affordable. The lunch menu is simpler but no less satisfying.

235 Keawe St. (at Haili St.), Hilo. ☎ *808-969-9090. Reservations recommended for dinner. Main courses: $5–$10 at lunch, $16–$22 at dinner. AE, DISC, MC, V. Open: Lunch and dinner daily, breakfast Sat–Sun.*

Roy's Waikoloa Bar & Grill

$$$–$$$$ Kohala Coast   Hawaii Regional

The Waikoloa branch of Roy Yamaguchi's high-profile, high-end restaurant chain is not quite as winningly casual as the other Roy's throughout Hawaii (particularly my favorite, Roy's Poipu Grill on Kauai), but this brightly lit restaurant is a great place to sample the original Hawaii Regional cuisine nonetheless. Roy's food is more overtly Asian than what you'll find in many other Hawaii Regional restaurants (like Merriman's, earlier in this chapter). The menu revolves around a few standards, such as sublime Szechuan baby-back ribs and blackened ahi with a delectable soy mustard butter, supplemented by a long sheet of daily specials. It's easy to eat affordably here thanks to an oversized menu of dim sum, appetizers, and imu-baked pizzas, and the wines bottled under Roy's own label are affordable and surprisingly good. Service is a little too attentive, but it's a minor complaint.

In the King's Shops, 250 Waikoloa Beach Dr., Waikoloa resort. ☎ *808-886-4321. Internet:* www.roysrestaurant.com. *Reservations highly recommended. Appetizers and pizzas: $5–$10. Main courses: $16–$28. AE, CB, DC, DISC, JCB, MC, V. Open: Lunch and dinner daily.*

Sam Choy's Kaloko

$$$ Kailua-Kona   Hawaii Regional

You might already know Big Island boy Sam Choy from the Food Network and other TV appearances. The jolly, wide-girthed chef — the most down-home of all of Hawaii's star chefs — launched his dining empire at this plain industrial-park diner, and it's still going strong. Award-winning dishes like seafood *laulau* (fresh island fish and veggies steamed in ti leaves); roasted half-duck in orange sauce and mac nuts; and *poke* (PO-kay), cubed raw ahi or marlin seasoned with onions, soy, and seaweed and seared (Sam's signature dish), are always served in Samoan-sized portions in the truck-stop-basic room. Dinners are accompanied by salad and soup large enough to be a meal unto themselves; no wine list is offered, but you can BYOB. Since the ambience is zero and quality can be uneven if Sam isn't in the house (which he's usually not), I prefer to skip dinner and go for the gargantuan island breakfasts — always starch and protein fests — and local-style lunches.

In the Kaloko Light Industrial Park, 73-5576 Kauhola St., 3 miles north of Kailua-Kona. ☎ *808-326-1545. Reservations highly recommended for dinner. To get there: At the "Kaloko Light Industrial Park" sign on Hwy. 19, turn toward the mountain onto*

Hinalani St., right again on Kanalani St., then the second left onto Kauhola St. Complete meals: $3–$11 at breakfast and lunch, $13.50–$28 at dinner. DISC, MC, V. Open: Breakfast and lunch daily, dinner Tues–Sat.

Seaside Restaurant & Aqua Farm

$$ Hilo   Seafood

Enterprising aquaculture farmers, the Nakagawa family has struck on a winning concept: a simple, satisfying restaurant overlooking well-stocked fish ponds, into which the chef himself drops a line to fulfill the night's dinner orders. Seaside is a refreshing alternative for fish lovers who'd like a break from the ahi and mahimahi — not to mention the high prices — so prevalent on Hawaii menus. Farm-raised mullet, catfish, and golden perch are steamed in a ti leaf with lemon and onion, a wonderfully unfussy preparation that lets the flavor of the state's freshest-caught fish star on the plate. *Aholehole* (Hawaiian flagtail bass), fried and served whole, is another house specialty. Dinners come complete with salad, veggies, rice, apple pie, and tea or coffee for an excellent value. Chicken and steak are available for non-fish eaters, as are more familiar island fishes like ahi, mahi, and ono. A genuine island dining experience, complete with aloha-friendly service. Reserve ahead so that the angler knows how big to make the day's catch.

1790 Kalanianaole Ave. (at Lokoaka St., 2.6 miles east of Banyan Dr.), Hilo. ☎ *808-935-8825. Reservations highly recommended. Complete dinners: $9–$25 (most $17–$21). MC, V. Open: Dinner Tues–Sun.*

Sibu Cafe

$$ Kailua-Kona   Indonesian

Tucked away in an inoffensive Alii Drive mini-mall, affordable Sibu offers flame-grilled satays (including a terrific all-veggie version), rich and flavorful curries, fresh stir-frys, and a creative list of daily specials that offer a welcome change of pace from Kona's ubiquitous and overpriced surf-and-turf fare. Both the Balinese chicken with peanut sauce and the garlic shrimp linguine with black pepper and green chili more than justify their longstanding popularity. The closet-sized dining room is colorful but otherwise devoid of ambience, so I recommend grabbing a well-shaded courtyard table, where the table service is equally attentive.

In the Banyan Court Mall, 74-5695 Alii Dr. (near Kailua Pier, on the mountain side of the street), Kailua-Kona. ☎ *808-329-1112. Reservations not taken. Main courses: $10–$14. No credit cards. Open: Lunch and dinner daily.*

Steam Vent Cafe

$ Volcano   Sandwiches

This gourmet deli is your best choice for a quickie bite in Volcano. The sandwiches and salads are pre-prepared but still crisp and fresh, and the all-day pastries are scrumptious.

Java lovers, take heed: The main attraction is a state-of-the-art self-serve espresso and cappuccino machine that makes a potent cup of brew precisely to your specifications in 20 seconds — it even fresh-grinds the beans and steams the milk with the touch of a button. The tiny storefront also carries postcards, little gifts, rain ponchos, and flashlights for nighttime lava treks, and an ATM is on hand if you need to replenish your cash supply.

At Volcano Village Square, Haunani and Old Volcano rds. (just off Hwy. 11 between mile markers 26 and 27, behind the Volcano Store), Volcano. ☎ 808-985-8744. Sandwiches and salads: $5–$10. AE, DC, MC, V. Open: Breakfast, lunch, and early dinner daily.

Surt's at Volcano Village

$$$ Volcano   Asian/Continental

Surt's wouldn't garner much notice in a more competitive restaurant landscape, but it makes a perfectly fine choice for a meal in rural Volcano. The menu is rather odd: It's not Euro-Asian, but half European and half Asian. The dishes are rich and heavy, which wouldn't pass muster in arid, beachy Kona but works just fine in chilly Volcano. Western specialties include creamy beef stroganoff, and a satisfying steak Diane whose red wine–dijon sauce compensates for a so-so New York steak. On the east side of the menu, you'll find beef panang that's tender and spicy, and rich, colorful curries. The room is upcountry charming and comfortable, with butter-yellow walls and affable, outgoing service, and a nice wine list is on hand.

At Volcano Village Square, Old Volcano and Haunani rds. (just off Hwy. 11 between mile markers 26 and 27, next to the Volcano Store), Volcano. ☎ 808-967-8511. Reservations recommended at dinner. Main courses: $8–$15 at lunch, $12–$22 at dinner. AE, DC, MC, V. Open: Lunch and dinner daily.

Thai Rin

$$ Kailua-Kona   Thai

An oasis of good value in a town that falls short more often than not, this affordable and authentic spot features an expansive menu of well-prepared Thai favorites. The noodle dishes and multicolored curries are universally pleasing, and include a pad Thai that borders on greatness. Thai Rin's version of chicken with cashew nuts — a dish my husband usually won't let me order because he considers it too pedantic (rightly, most of the time) — is light, flavorful, and overflowing with a bounty of fresh veggies. The menu features lots of seafood choices, of course — to be expected in the deep-sea-fishing capital of the Pacific. The dining room is plain, high-ceilinged, and simple, but patio tables offer views of the bay across Alii Drive. Service is graciously attentive from start to finish.

75-5799 Alii Dr., in the heart of Kailua-Kona. ☎ 808-329-2929. Reservations accepted. Lunch specials: $4–$8. Main courses: $5–$17 (most less than $13). AE, DC, DISC, JCB, MC, V. Open: Lunch and dinner daily.

Thai Thai Restaurant

$$ Volcano   Thai

I was thrilled to find this wonderful Thai restaurant in Volcano Village, which doesn't exactly brim with quality dining spots. An attractive high-ceilinged room with Thai decorative touches, pretty table linens, and Thai pop music on the sound system sets the stage for simple, freshly prepared ethnic specialties. The menu is on the smallish side, but every dish I tasted was a winner: the tom yum soup was clear and well-spiced with lemongrass and kaffir lime leaves; the masaman curry was rich with coconut milk and potatoes; and a stir-fry starred crisp Asian veggies and jumbo shrimp. The green papaya salad makes an excellent way to start a wholly satisfying meal.

19-4084 Old Volcano Rd., Volcano. ☎ *808-967-7969. Reservations accepted. Main courses: $9–$13. MC, V. Open: Lunch Mon–Fri, dinner nightly.*

Tres Hombres Beach Grill/Tres Hombres Steak & Seafood

$$ Kohala Coast/Kailua-Kona   Mexican

Set on the second floor of a harborfront center at the very north end of the Kohala Coast, this cheerful tropical Mexican restaurant is perfectly situated for watching outrigger canoe clubs paddle out to sea from the nearby launch. The food is only a step above average-quality gringoized Mexican grub, but I like Tres Hombres anyway. A welcome alternative to the generally overpriced resort dining, this fun, easygoing, surf-style restaurant features a nice Trader Vic's–style bar with a big, creative tequila and tropical drinks menu; a simply furnished outdoor patio; and an affordable menu with an island flair: fresh mahimahi tacos, mammoth surf burritos, sizzling fajitas, and more, all sizably portioned and satisfying. A second, slightly more upscale branch is now conveniently located in Kailua-Kona, ideally suiting the resort town's party mood.

The Kohala Coast: In the Kawaihae Shopping Center at Kawaihae Harbor, at Akoni Pule Hwy. and Kawaihae Rd., Kawaihae (at the Hwy. 19/270 junction). ☎ *808-882-1031. Reservations accepted for parties of 5 or more. Kailua-Kona: 75-5864 Walua Rd. (at Alii Dr.).* ☎ *808-329-2173. Reservations accepted. Main courses: $8–$20. MC, V. Open: Lunch and dinner daily.*

Luau!

My favorite luau on the Big Island has always been the wonderful Friday-night-only Kona Village Luau — although the brand-new and culture-rich Traditions at Kahaluu, just launching at press time, promises to give Kona Village a run for its money.

The Kona Village Luau should *always* be reserved as far in advance as possible, as it sells out sometimes weeks in advance. It's not a bad idea to book the Traditions at Kahaluu luau ahead, either, to avoid disappointment.

Kona Village Luau

This ultra-deluxe Polynesian-style resort is the ideal place for a luau, and you'd be hard-pressed to find a better one. The food is excellently prepared and well labeled (so you know what you're eating), and the traditional *imu* (underground pig roasting) ceremony is well narrated, so you get the cultural gist. The South Pacific revue is fast-moving and lots of fun, if not nearly as authentic as the one you'll see at the new Traditions at Kahaluu luau (I don't think there were cowboy hulas in old Hawaii). The fire dancer is a show-stopper, of course, and everyone involved is a first-rate entertainer. The setting isn't oceanfront, but it's lovely nonetheless; the luau is large-scale, but manages to feel friendly and intimate; and service is attentive and aloha friendly. Reservations are required, so book as far in advance as possible.

At Kona Village, in the Kaupulehu resort, 7 miles north of the airport on the Kohala Coast. ☎ *800-367-5290 or 808-325-5555. Admission: $74 adults, $45 kids 6–12; $21.50 kids 2–5. Beer and house wine included. Included in the rates for Kona Village guests. Time: Fri at 6 p.m.*

Traditions at Kahaluu

This brand-new luau, just launched in September 2000, promises to be a winner. It takes place at the Keauhou Beach Resort, a newly renovated oceanfront hotel that takes its job as cultural ambassador seriously — so you can expect an experience that's not only fun but rich in Hawaiian culture and history. The evening launches in a gorgeous oceanfront setting with ancient Hawaiian living-history demonstrations that extend well beyond the *imu* (pig unearthing) ceremony to include net-throw fishing, taro-pounding (to create poi, the starchy purple staple of the Hawaiian diet), tapa-cloth making, and *lauhala* weaving; you and your kids can even learn to play *konane* (Hawaiian checkers) and other ancient island games. The authentic luau feast is an all-you-can-eat buffet spread — complete with roasted-in-the-ground kalua pig, chicken long rice, haupia coconut pudding, and the like — served in a beautiful coconut grove set up to serve as the open-air dining room. There are no fire-knife dancers in the after-dinner show (Hawaiians never played with fire), but you won't be disappointed by the quality of the authentic live entertainment — the hula troupe has won multiple championships at the Merrie Monarch Hula Festival, the World Series of hula.

At the Aston Keauhou Beach Resort, 78-6740 Alii Dr., Keauhou (6 miles south of Kailua-Kona). ☎ *877-532-8468 or 808-322-3441. Admission: $67.50 adults, $22.75 kids 12 and under. One mai tai or soft drink included (full cash bar available). Times: Sun and Thurs at 6 p.m.*

Chapter 18

Fun On and Off the Beach

● ●

In This Chapter

▶ Locating the Big Island's best beaches

▶ Enjoying the waves: Where to rent snorkel gear, schedule first-time dives or sportfishing trips, and much more

▶ Exploring Hawaii's number-one attraction: Hawaii Volcanoes National Park

▶ Discovering more great sights and attractions

▶ Zeroing in on the top hunting grounds for shoppers

▶ Enjoying yourself on this rural isle once the sun goes down

● ●

*T*he Big Island's biggest attraction — indeed, the biggest attraction in all of Hawaii — is Hawaii Volcanoes National Park, one of the most exciting and unusual parks in the entire national park system. But the Big Island is no one-trick pony; it boasts a wealth of wonderful and one-of-a-kind attractions that you won't want to miss.

Keep in mind that the Big Island really is big — about the size of Connecticut, with virtually all of the main attractions located along the island's perimeter. If you circle the island in the course of a day, you'll find that it takes about six hours to make the drive — which makes visiting the national park from your Kona hotel, say, quite an arduous trip. Therefore, you may seriously want to consider dividing your stay on the island between the two coasts — a few nights on the sunny, arid Kona-Kohala coast followed by a few nights on the lush, misty Hilo-Volcano coast, or vice versa — and plan your island activities and sightseeing accordingly. For more on this subject, see Chapter 15.

Hitting the Beaches

Don't fall into the trap that so many of your fellow visitors to the Big Island do — namely, coming home complaining that the island has only ugly dark-sand beaches, not the pretty white ones that you always assumed would line the shores of Paradise.

The Big Island's Best Beaches & Attractions

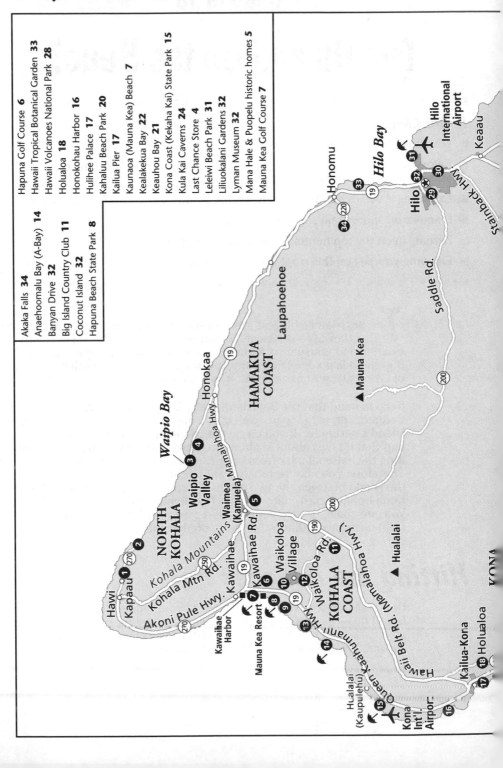

Akaka Falls **34**
Anaehoomalu Bay (A-Bay) **14**
Banyan Drive **32**
Big Island Country Club **11**
Coconut Island **32**
Hapuna Beach State Park **8**

Hapuna Golf Course **6**
Hawaii Tropical Botanical Garden **33**
Hawaii Volcanoes National Park **28**
Holualoa **18**
Honokohau Harbor **16**
Hulihee Palace **17**
Kahaluu Beach Park **20**
Kailua Pier **17**
Kaunaoa (Mauna Kea) Beach **7**
Kealakekua Bay **22**
Keauhou Bay **21**
Kona Coast (Kekaha Kai) State Park **15**
Kula Kai Caverns **24**
Last Chance Store **4**
Leleiwi Beach Park **31**
Liliuokalani Gardens **32**
Lyman Museum **32**
Mana Hale & Puopelu historic homes **5**
Mauna Kea Golf Course **7**

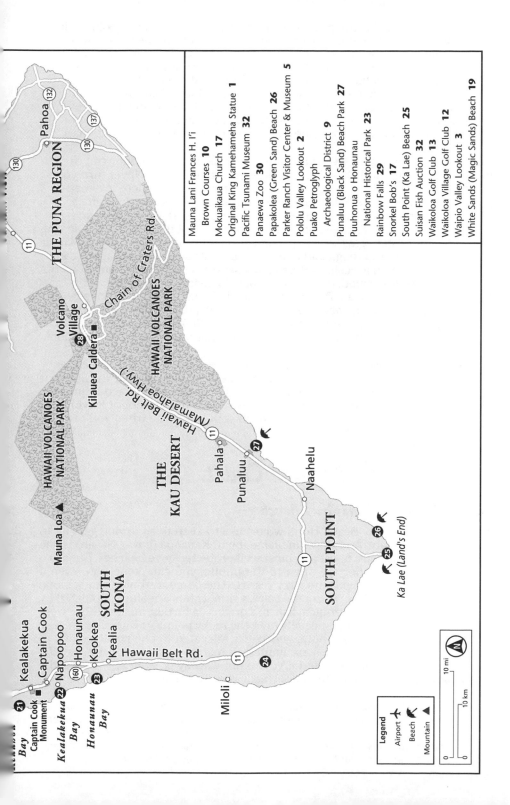

Mauna Lani Frances H. I'i
Brown Courses **10**
Mokuaikaua Church **17**
Original King Kamehameha Statue **1**
Pacific Tsunami Museum **32**
Panaewa Zoo **30**
Papakolea (Green Sand) Beach **26**
Parker Ranch Visitor Center & Museum **5**
Pololu Valley Lookout **2**
Puako Petroglyph
Archaeological District **9**
Punaluu (Black Sand) Beach Park **27**
Puuhonua o Honaunau
National Historical Park **23**
Rainbow Falls **29**
Snorkel Bob's **17**
South Point (Ka Lae) Beach **25**
Suisan Fish Auction **32**
Waikoloa Golf Club **13**
Waikoloa Village Golf Club **12**
Waipio Valley Lookout **3**
White Sands (Magic Sands) Beach **19**

THE PUNA REGION

Pahoa

Volcano Village

HAWAII VOLCANOES NATIONAL PARK

HAWAII VOLCANOES NATIONAL PARK

Chain of Craters Rd.

Kilauea Caldera

Hawaii Belt Rd. (Mamalahoa Hwy.)

THE KAU DESERT

Mauna Loa

SOUTH KONA

Kealakekua
Captain Cook
Captain Cook Monument
Napoopoo
Honaunau
Keokea
Kealia
Kealakekua Bay
Honaunau Bay
Bay

Miloli

Hawaii Belt Rd.

Pahala

Punaluu

Naahelu

SOUTH POINT

Ka Lae (Land's End)

Legend
Airport
Beach
Mountain

0   10 mi
0   10 km

The Big Island is the youngest island in the Hawaii chain, geologically speaking; as it matures over the next few millennia, the shores will pumice into the fine white sands you're used to. But if it's unusual-looking beaches you're after, the Big Island features the most eye-popping collection you'll ever see: black-sand ones, salt-and-pepper ones, lava-covered ones, even a green-sand one. What's more, the island also happens to already boast some of the dreamiest white sands in Hawaii — it's just a matter of knowing where to find them. (Hint: Do not pass go, do not collect $200 — go directly to Hapuna.)

Always make safety your top priority at the beach, whether you're swimming, snorkeling, surfing, or even taking a stroll. Never turn your back on the ocean, as big waves can come out of nowhere in a matter of minutes. Some beaches, like the popular Hapuna, on the Kohala Coast, regularly have lifeguards on duty, while others, like the Kohala Coast's Kaunaoa, have none. At beaches without lifeguards, keep an eye out for posted signs warning of dangerous currents or conditions. Winter surf is generally rough and unpredictable, although some beaches can be counted on for calm waters in any season. Others have dangerous rip currents year-round, making swimming inadvisable for all but the strongest swimmers. Do your homework: Check out the following beach descriptions, and, once you're on the Big Island, get daily weather reports (in and around Hilo, call ☎ 808-935-8555; for the rest of the Big Island, call ☎ 808-961-5582) and make inquiries on local surf conditions.

Never leave valuables in your rental car while you're at the beach, or you may lose them to a thief who can be in and out of your car before you've finished slathering on your sunscreen. Remote beaches, in particular, are magnets for thieves. Be especially diligent about leaving your stuff behind at your condo or in your hotel safe when you're heading off to a remote beach.

Along the Kohala Coast

Kaunaoa (Mauna Kea) Beach

The Mauna Kea Beach Hotel would like to keep this curving gem all to itself, no doubt. And who can blame them? Kauanoa (cow-a-NO-ah) is one of the Big Island's finest and most well-protected cove beaches. But since all Hawaii beaches are open to the public, you can come, too, even if you're not staying at the ritzy resort. The gorgeous beige sands slope gently into the bay, where the calm, warm waters are often populated by schools of colorful tropical fish and green sea turtles, making this a wonderful snorkel spot (especially near the rocky points). Swimming is excellent year-round. Non–hotel guests are relegated to one small section of the beach, and facilities are limited to restrooms and showers (no lifeguard). Don't be surprised if you're not warmly greeted at the gate; the hotel prefers to keep the public-access crowd small.

At the Mauna Kea Resort, off Queen Kaahumanu Hwy. (Hwy. 19), 28 miles north of Kona Airport (about 2½ miles south of Kawaihae, where Hwy. 19 turns inland toward Waimea). To get there: Turn west at the Mauna Kea Beach Hotel entrance and ask for a beach pass from security; follow the road to the public beach parking area, at the end of the road (through the hotel and past registration).

Arrive at Mauna Kea Beach early, because public beach-access parking is extremely limited.

Hapuna Beach State Park

Wow! If forced to choose, I'd name this as my favorite beach in all of Hawaii. This gorgeous gal is endowed with all the assets: glorious turquoise surf, a half-mile-long crescent of powdery-fine white sand backed by green lawns that allow you to picnic without getting sand in your lunch, and the best facilities on the coast. Hapuna is simply magical, especially in the gentle seasons, when the beach is widest, the ocean is calmest, and crowds — locals and visitors alike — come out to swim, play, and ride the easy waves. One of the best things about this stunning beach is that it's a blast even when it is crowded; and even though the Hapuna Beach Prince Hotel is tucked away at the north end, you barely notice it. Venture nearer to the hotel only if you're looking to snorkel; the cove at its base is your best bet. The excellent facilities include restrooms, showers, pavilions, picnic tables, barbecues, Hapuna Harry's for snacks and beach toys, and plenty of parking. Beware the waves in winter, though, when the big surf can be very dangerous.

Off Queen Kaahumanu Hwy. (Hwy. 19), about 27 miles north of Kona Airport (3 miles south of Kawaihae, where Hwy. 19 turns inland toward Waimea).

Anaehoomalu Bay (A-Bay)

This popular beach — called Anaehoomalu (ah-na-ay-ho-o-MA-loo), or A-Bay for short — is the most beautiful of the Big Island's salt-and-peppery beaches. It's long, curvaceous, and boasts pretty fine-grained sand and a lovely grove of swaying coconut palms. The beach fronts the Outrigger Waikoloa Beach Resort but it's easily accessible, and it's so nice that even locals come. The sand slopes gently from shallow to deep water; swimming, kayaking, and windsurfing are all terrific here, and the snorkeling is very good at the end nearest the hotel. At the far edge of the bay is a rare-turtle cleaning station, where snorkelers and divers can watch endangered green sea turtles line up, waiting their turn to have small fish clean them; the hotel's friendly beach boys usually have the area marked so you can make your way out to see the action. Facilities include restrooms, showers, and plenty of parking, plus excellent beach-gear rentals at the north (hotel) end of the beach.

At the Waikoloa Resort, just off Queen Kaahumanu Hwy. (Hwy. 19), 18 miles north of Kona Airport. To get there: Turn west at the stone gate marked Waikoloa then left at the stop sign, and follow the road to the parking lot.

On the Kona–Keauhou Coast

Kona Coast (Kekaha Kai) State Park

If you really want some sand to yourself, head to this remote beach park, which is separated from civilization by nearly two miles of vast lava fields. The road that reaches the beach is a bit rough going (see the directions that follow), but what awaits at the end is worth the drive for solitude seekers: a half-dozen long, curving, unspoiled gold-sand beaches, with well-protected coves that are great for swimming in the gentle seasons. Even if a few other folks are around, you'll find plenty of stretches of sand that you can have all to yourself. Stay out of the water in winter, when the swells come, but you may want to visit anyway to kick back on the sand and see the surfers in action. Facilities are minimal — nothing more than a few picnic tables and portable toilets — so be sure to bring your own drinking water.

Off Queen Kaahumanu Hwy. (Hwy. 19), 2¾ miles north of Kona Airport. To get there: Turn left at the sign and follow the bumpy road 1¾ miles to the coast. The speed limit is 15 mph, but you'll find yourself going 10 mph unless you've rented a 4-wheel drive (not necessary); take it slow and watch for potholes. Open: Thurs–Tues 9 a.m.–7 p.m.

White Sands (Magic Sands) Beach

This petite white-sand pocket of beach is an oddity on this lava-rock coast in more ways than one: Not only are darker and coarser beaches more common on this coast, but the beach itself sometimes vanishes completely, washed away by high tides or winter waves or during storms. It usually reappears in short order, just like it never went away. The small waves are great for just-learning boogie boarders and bodysurfers; on calm summer days, the water is good for swimming and snorkeling, too. Facilities include restrooms, showers, and a small parking lot. All in all, White Sands isn't worth traversing long distances to seek out, but it's conveniently situated for those staying in the Kailua-Kona or Keauhou areas.

Adjacent to Kona Magic Sands condos, 77-6452 Alii Dr., 4½ miles south of Kailua-Kona.

Kahaluu Beach Park

Kahaluu (ka-ha-LOO-oo) isn't exactly the prettiest beach in the islands: It's narrow, salt-and-peppery, close to the road (a situation softened by a collection of coconut palms that serve as a buffer), and almost always blanket-to-blanket crowded. But don't skip it, because this is one of the finest snorkeling beaches in all of Hawaii, with a shore that gently slopes to shallow, well-protected turquoise pools that are so clear and rich with marine life that all you have to do is wade in and look down. If you're a first-time snorkeler, this is the place to learn — but even advanced fish-watchers will be thrilled with the schools of brilliantly colored tropical fish that weave in and out of the well-established reef. You may even spot a sea turtle or two here (I have, more than once!). Great facilities are on hand, including a parking lot, beach-gear rentals, a covered pavilion, and a snack bar. Come early to stake out your spot. Riptides sometimes kick up in winter, though, so check the lifeguard warning flags (red means stay out of the water).

On Alii Dr., 5½ miles south of Kailua-Kona.

While snorkel gear is available for rent at Kahaluu Beach, you'll get much better quality gear by renting at Snorkel Bob's, just a few minutes up the road in Kailua-Kona; for details, see "Snorkeling" under "Water Fun for Everyone" later in this chapter.

On the Hilo–Volcano Coast

Leleiwi Beach Park

If you get a beautiful beach day while you're in Hilo, head to picture-perfect Leleiwi (lay-lay-EE-vee) Beach. This lovely palm-fringed cove of black-lava tidepools fed by freshwater springs and rippled by gentle waves is a photog's delight — and the ideal place to take a dip. The shallow pools are generally calm and ideal for little ones, especially in the protected inlets at the center of the park. Sea turtles make this the locals' favorite snorkel spot. Facilities include restrooms, showers, and picnic pavilions.

On Kalanianaole Ave., 4 miles west of Hilo.

Punaluu (Black Sand) Beach Park

If you're driving the south route between Volcano and Kona, stop here if you want to set your eyes on a genuine black-sand beach, the only one that's still accessible (the others have been blocked by lava flows). Stay out of the water year-round as the offshore currents are strong (although you're likely to see some daredevil surfers taking on the waves), but the sands are great for sunbathing and picnicking (keep your distance from the turtles who often come on shore to nest). If you do venture into the water, do it in summer, and be extremely careful. Picnic pavilions and restrooms are located across the road.

Off the Hawaii Belt Road (Hwy. 11), about 30 miles south of Volcano Village. (The turnoff is well-marked.)

At Land's End

Ka Lae (South Point) & Papakolea (Green Sand) Beach

The southernmost point in the United States is Ka Lae, or South Point. There's not much down here, except some rocky cliffs and remarkable ocean views, but I love coming anyway: Standing at this dramatic, desolate, windswept place (hold on to your hat!) actually feels like you're standing at the ends of the earth.

Also down at South Point is Green Sand Beach, worth seeing for its olive-green sands (actually crushed olivine, a green semiprecious mineral found in eruptive rocks and meteorites). It's a bear to reach, however, so most people don't bother. You need a four-wheel-drive and a hearty constitution to traverse the 2½-mile path from the Kaulana Boat Ramp to the cliffs overlooking the beach. You can also walk it, if you wear sturdy shoes and bring water. The trail is relatively flat, but you're usually walking into the wind as you head toward the beach. After about 30 or 40 minutes, you'll see an eroded cinder cone by the water; continue to the edge, where the green sands lie below.

I highly recommend that you just take in the view from the cliff above the beach (which is actually very good), as the trail to the sand is difficult and treacherous, requiring you to drop down (and climb back up) four to five feet in spots. If the surf's up, don't even think about it — and stay out of the water anywhere along South Point entirely.

At the end of South Point Rd., 12 miles south of Mamalahoa Hwy. (Hwy. 11).

 South Point Road is paved, but don't venture down it if it's been raining, and don't venture off it at all. And check your rental car agreement before you go; many car-rental companies prohibit you from driving down to South Point. (If you get stuck, you'll also be stuck with a hefty tow bill.)

Water Fun for Everyone

While there are some accessible beaches on the east (Hilo-Volcano) coast (see the preceding section), it is the west (Kona-Kohala) coast that is the exclusive domain of water sports on the Big Island.

Snorkeling

The Big Island boasts wonderful opportunities for snorkeling, possibly the best in all the islands. One of Hawaii's absolute best snorkel spots is **Kealakekua Bay** (kay-ah-lah-ka-KOO-ah) Bay. The coral in this underwater marine life preserve is the most beautiful I've ever seen, and the calm, clear waters teem with a kaleidoscope of colorful reef fish, octopuses, and Moray eels; what's more, a pod of playful spinner dolphins often comes by to say hi. (The bay sports a white obelisk on the north shore, marking the spot where Captain James Cook (credited with "discovering" the Hawaiian islands by Western-biased history books) lost his life to a group of annoyed islanders in 1778.) The bay can only be reached by snorkel cruise or kayak, however; see the sections later in this chapter called "On-deck adventures: ocean cruising" (Fair Wind is my favorite snorkel-cruise operator) and "Ocean kayaking" for details on getting there.

The Kona and Kohala coasts also boast a bunch of wonderful offshore snorkel beaches that allow you to simply wade in and see the colorful fishes. The best on the coast is **Kahaluu Beach Park,** but you might also have some fish- and turtle-spotting luck at **Anaehoomalu Bay, Kaunaoa Beach, White Sands Beach,** at the north end of **Hapuna Beach,** or even right at the foot of your hotel, if you're lucky enough to be staying at a beachfront resort (the Mauna Lani Bay Hotel is a particularly good choice for snorkelers without budget constraints; see Chapter 15).

All of the Big Island's dive shops arrange snorkel cruises and/or take experienced snorkelers out on their dive trips; Jack's Diving Locker will even take a limited number of snorkelers out on their night dives with manta rays. See "Scuba diving" later in this chapter for details.

One of the locals' favorite snorkeling spots is in South Kona, in the cove right next to the Puuhonua o Honaunau National Historical Park (see "More attractions worth seeking out" later in this chapter). It's not the kind of place that you'll want to set up beach camp for the day, but it is a great spot to snorkel, with an abundance of colorful reef fish and sea turtles. To get there, follow Highway 11 south from Kailua-Kona to mile marker 103 (about 22 miles); turn at the sign onto Highway 160 and follow it 3½ miles downslope to the national park and coast. Come early in the day before the waves kick up, bring your own gear, and turn right before you get to the entrance kiosk; the road will take you down to the boat ramp and snorkel area. (The kind guard in the booth will point you in the right direction if you miss the turn.)

Since so much of the Big Island's best snorkeling is accessible from shore, you'll need to rent some gear if you don't have your own. I suggest heading to **Snorkel Bob's** (☎ **808-329-0770**) at the south end of Kailua-Kona town. The address is 75-5831 Kahakai St., but it's actually on Alii Drive (Kailua-Kona's main drag) right in front of Huggo's restaurant.

The basic set of snorkel gear — mask, snorkel, and fins — is just $9 a week, but I go with the deluxe package for $29 a week — it's worth the extra bucks for a mask that doesn't leak and a snorkel that doesn't clog. If you're nearsighted, you can rent a prescription mask so you can actually see the little fishes, plus boogie boards, life vests, wet suits, beach chairs, and so on. The shop is open every day from 8 a.m. to 5 p.m. There's no need to reserve gear in advance, but plan-ahead types can book their gear online at www.snorkelbob.com.

I highly recommend renting gear from Snorkel Bob's even if you intend to go on a snorkel cruise to Kealakekua Bay that provides gear. I've gone on enough of these trips to say confidently that free gear is universally awful — and there's nothing worse than your fellow snorkelers spotting sea turtles or other groovy critters that you can't see through a bad mask. This is especially true where children are concerned. Invest in a comfortable mask that fits your kid to a T, and you'll be helping ensure his safety as well as his enjoyment of the sport.

If you so choose, you can have a set of snorkel gear fitted on the Big Island, carry it with you and use it as you travel throughout Hawaii, and then return it to another Snorkel Bob's location on Oahu, Maui, or Kauai. (All shops offer 24-hour gear return service.)

Safety is key when snorkeling. Before you go out, make sure to grease up with SPF-30 or higher sunscreen, especially on your back; wearing a T-shirt can help somewhat, but you'll still need to put on sunscreen. Always snorkel with a buddy, and keep an eye on each other at all times. Come up every few minutes to check your bearings in relation to the shoreline and make sure there's no boat traffic coming your way.

Snorkeling without getting your hair wet

There's a great way to see Hawaii's spectacular underwater world even if you don't swim: Take a submarine ride with **Atlantis Submarines** (☎ 800-548-6262 or 808-329-3175; Internet: www.goatlantis.com/hawaii). You'll head a mile offshore and dive to 100 feet beneath the surface in one of Atlantis's state-of-the-art subs to see a whole new world of sea critters that hang out at one of the most well-populated and phenomenal coral reefs in the world. Shuttle boats to the sub leave from Kailua Pier in the heart of Kailua-Kona town; check in is at the Atlantis Gift Shop across Alii Drive. The two-hour tours cost $79 for adults, $39 for kids (children must be at least 36 inches tall).

Attention, bargain hunters: You may be able to save 7 percent (or 10 percent if you pay with a check) by booking your Atlantis submarine dive through Maui-based **Tom Barefoot's Cashback Tours** (☎ 888-222-3601; Internet: www.tombarefoot.com).

A word of warning: The ride is perfectly safe, but skip it if you suffer from serious claustrophobia.

Don't touch anything underwater: coral is delicate and easily damaged and can also leave you with nasty cuts. And always, always check surf conditions before you set out (a local surf-and-snorkel shop can usually help you here). You should also inquire about the specific currents and tides at the area you plan to snorkel — as well as any potentially dangerous spots to avoid.

On-deck adventures: ocean cruising

When the Pacific humpback whales make their annual visit to Hawaii from Alaska from December to March, they swim right by the Big Island. In season, virtually all cruise boats combine whale-watching with their regular adventures — which means that you can get two adventures for the price of one!

If you'd like to go sportfishing off the world-famous Kona Coast, see the section called "Hooking the Big One in the sportfishing capital of the world" later in this chapter.

Body Glove Cruises

The 51-foot, 100-passenger trimaran *Body Glove* runs cruises to Pawai Bay, north of Kailua-Kona, a marine preserve with excellent snorkeling and dolphin-watching opportunities year-round. The year-round morning cruise features 2½ hours of snorkel time, while the afternoon cruise (offered from April to November) features 1½ hours of snorkeling. Both the 15-foot water slide and high-dive board will get you into the drink immediately, and are real kid-pleasers. Scuba upgrades with PADI-certified instructors and dive masters are available as well. In winter, the afternoon sail becomes a three-hour whale watch, complete with a naturalist on board.

Cruises depart from Kailua Pier, off Alii Dr., Kailua-Kona. ☎ *800-551-8911 or 808-326-7122. Internet:* www.bodyglovehawaii.com. *3- to 4½-hour snorkel-sails and whale-watch trips (in season): $48–$72 adults, $29–$42 kids 6–17. Morning cruises include continental breakfast and buffet deli lunch; afternoon sails include snacks.*

At press time, you could save 7 percent (or 10 percent if you pay with a check) by booking your Body Glove cruise through Maui-based **Tom Barefoot's Cashback Tours** (☎ 888-222-3601; Internet: www.tombarefoot.com).

Captain Dan McSweeney's Year-Round Whale-Watch Learning Adventures

Do you have your heart set on whale-watching, even though you missed whale season? Or maybe you're visiting in winter, but you just want to spot humpbacks with the most qualified expert around? Then contact Captain Dan McSweeney, a professional whale researcher for more than 25 years, who leads excellent whale-watching tours along the Kona Coast year-round. Sure, you'll only spot the visiting humpbacks from December through April — but you can see pilot whales, sperm whales (which grow even larger than the mammoth humpbacks!), false killer and pygmy killer whales, melon headed whales, and beaked whales, as well as five kinds of dolphins, in any month. Knowledgeable and engaging, Captain Dan and his crew are experts at knowing where to look for these wonderful creatures so that you can watch them, undisturbed, in their natural habitat (he frequently drops an underwater video camera and/or microphone into the water so that you can see them clearly and listen to their whale songs). What's more, he professes to have a 99 percent success rate at finding humpbacks in season. But if, for some reason, you don't see any whales at all on your trip, Captain Dan will take you out again for free — not a bad guarantee! Terrific for visitors of all ages.

Cruises depart from Honokohau Harbor, off Queen Kaahumanu Hwy. (Hwy. 19), 2½ miles south of Kona Airport. ☎ *888-942-5376 or 808-322-0028. Internet:* www.ilovewhales.com. *3-hour cruises: $49.50 adults, $29.50 kids 11 and under. Prices include snacks.*

Captain Zodiac Raft Expeditions

Captain Zodiac leads snorkel cruises to Kealakekua Bay aboard 16-passenger, 24-foot fiberglass-bottom rubber boats (zodiacs), the inflatables pioneered by Jacques Cousteau, which have minimal environmental impact, sit low to the water, and cruise fast over the waves for a thrill-a-minute ride. On the way to Kealakekua — one of the best snorkel spots in all of Hawaii, and accessible only by boat (see "Snorkeling" earlier in this chapter) — you'll search for spinner dolphins and green sea turtles (plus humpback whales in season), then spend more than an hour snorkeling in the bay. On the return, if conditions permit, the captain will take you exploring sea caves that only these small, easily maneuverable boats can reach. An excellent choice for adventuresome types.

Cruises depart from Honokohau Harbor, off Queen Kaahumanu Hwy. (Hwy. 19), 2½ miles south of Kona Airport. ☎ 808-329-3199. Internet: www.captainzodiac. com. *4-hour tours: $69.75 adults, $56.25 kids 3–12. Deli lunch included.*

Both Captain Zodiac and Fair Wind (see the following listing) advise that pregnant women and those with back problems should skip the inflatable raft trips.

Fair Wind Snorkel Cruises & Orca Raft Adventures

Family-owned and -operated since 1971, this terrific company offers my favorite sail-and-snorkel cruises to Kealakekua Bay. They take a hundred or so passengers out aboard their 60-foot catamaran, the *Fair Wind II*, a state-of-the-art, impeccably maintained boat complete with easy-access water stairs (so you can literally walk into the water), a 15-foot waterslide (a big hit with the kids), and freshwater showers. The morning cruise offers the best conditions (before the afternoon winds kick up) and 2½ hours of snorkeling (as opposed to 1½ hours of snorkeling on the afternoon cruise. (Note that a full-length version, with 2½ hours of snorkeling, is offered in select seasons.) Scuba upgrades are available on most cruises (call ahead).

Fair Wind also offers high-speed cruises to Kealakelua aboard their 28-foot inflatable Orca rafts (very similar to Captain Zodiac's). Fair Wind's Orca rafts do have canopy tops, though, which offer some shelter from the hot Kona sun. You'll have about 1½ hours of snorkel time, and do similar sea-cave and lava-tube exploring as you would with Captain Zodiac.

Book ahead, because these cruises fill up fast.

Catamaran cruises depart from Keauhou Bay, off Hwy. 11 at the end of Kamehameha III Rd. (between mile markers 117 and 118), 10 minutes south of Kailua-Kona. Orca cruises depart from Kailua Pier, off Alii Dr., Kailua-Kona. ☎ 800-677-9461 or 808-322-2788. Internet: www.fair-wind.com. *3- to 4½-hour Fair Wind cruises: $48–$83 adults, $31–$46 kids 6–17. Morning and deluxe afternoon cruises include continental breakfast and barbecue lunch; regular afternoon cruises include snacks. 3- to 4-hour Orca raft cruises: $50–$67 adults, $40–$57 kids 6–17. Raft cruises include light snacks.*

If you've always been interested in trying scuba but haven't gotten around to the hassles and expense of certification, you can sample a very close approximation — Snuba — aboard Fair Wind's cruises. With Snuba, you wear a mask and regulator that's connected via a 20-foot-long hose to an oxygen tank that floats on the surface, thereby allowing you to dive deep and simulate the scuba experience without full training. All it takes is about 15 minutes of instruction, and an instructor and two or three other first-timers are usually along for the ride. No advance booking is necessary — the Snuba instructor will ask on the way out if you're interested in participating — and the charge is usually about $50 extra. Still, you may want to call ahead to confirm that Snuba will be offered on your cruise if your heart's set on trying it.

Kamanu Charters

If you'd like to snorkel in untouristed Pawai Bay but you'd prefer a more intimate experience than Body Glove offers, go instead with the *Kamanu,* a late-model 36-foot catamaran that limits its crowds to about two dozen per sail. An excellent choice for first-time snorkelers (instruction is provided) and non-swimmers, as a wide array of alternative flotation devices is available.

Cruises depart Honokohau Harbor, off Queen Kaahumanu Hwy. (Hwy. 19), 2½ miles south of Kona Airport. ☎ *800-348-3091 or 808-329-2021. Internet:* www. kamanu.com. *3½-hour cruises: $50 adults, $30 kids 12 and under. Tropical lunch included.*

Ocean kayaking

Kayaking is another great way to explore Kealakekua Bay, especially if you'd prefer an up-close, unmotorized relationship with the water and the marine life around you. It's quite easy to learn, as long as you know how to swim: Just get on your sit-on-top kayak, find your balance and stroke, and paddle. Nevertheless, I highly recommend taking a guided kayak tour if you're inexperienced, as there are nuances to launching your kayak, dealing with surf, and getting on and off your kayak in open water. Hawaiian-owned and -operated **Aloha Kayak Co. (☎ 877-322-1444;** Internet: www.alohakayak.com) offers 2½- to 4-hour guided tours for $45 to $65 for adults, $20 to $32.50 for kids under 12, including all equipment and snacks.

If you're experienced, you can rent single kayaks for $25 a day, tandem kayaks for $40, with all gear (including a cooler and car rack). The friendly guys at the shop will point you to the best launch spots. Weekly rates are available, as well as snorkel-gear rentals. Most convenient to Kealakekua Bay is the Honalo location, on the ocean side of Highway 11 at 79-7428 Mamalahoa Hwy., across from the 114 mile marker and Teshima's restaurant (☎ **808-331-8558** or 808-322-2868).

Scuba diving

With calm, warm waters (75 to 81°F), 100-plus-feet visibility, and an open drop-off that supports a wealth of colorful marine life of all shapes and sizes, the Kona-Kohala Coast offers some of the best scuba diving in the world (including excellent opportunities to swim with manta rays). Conditions are so good, in fact, that scuba mags regularly name it among the best diving destinations in the world.

One of Kona's best and most popular dive operators is **Eco Adventures,** based at King Kamehameha's Kona Beach Hotel, 75-5660 Palani Rd. (at Alii Dr.), Kailua-Kona (☎ **800-949-3483** or 808-329-7116; Internet: www.eco-adventure.com). Eco-Adventures offers dives to more than 75 dive sites along the coast, including one-, two-, and three-tank day dives, night dives with manta rays, and long-distance charters. They also offer a full slate of instructional courses ranging from introductory courses for beginners to instructor-certification courses. Daily two-tank dives start at $97. The Discover Scuba Diving trip, which operates sort of like a tandem parachute jump in which you're with an instructor the entire time so you only have to learn the basics to give it a go, is ideal for beginners ($117 per person).

Another very highly regarded outfitter is **Jack's Diving Locker,** 75-5819 Alii Dr., Kailua-Kona (☎ **800-345-4807** or 808-329-7585; Internet: www.jacksdivinglocker.com), chosen by readers of *Rodale's Scuba Diving* magazine as the best dive shop in the Indo-Pacific in 1999 and 2000. Two-tank boat dives start at $90, guided shore dives start at $50, and night dives with manta rays are $95.

Jack's also offers a full slate of introductory dives, and is the best dive shop on the island for kids who'd like to learn: Skin-diver programs are available for kids ages 8 and up, while open-water instruction is offered to kids 12 and older.

Kona Coast Divers, 75-5614 Palani Rd., Kailua-Kona (☎ **808-329-8802;** Internet: www.konacoastdivers.com), is another good bet, especially for wallet-watching divers: Two-tank boat dives start at $79.50, and night dives with manta rays at $64.50. At press time, a coupon was available online for an additional $5 off any product or service costing more than $60, so check to see if it's still available.

Red Sail Sports (☎ **877-RED-SAIL** or 808-886-2876; Internet: www.redsail.com) operates watersports and dive centers from the Hapuna Beach Prince Resort and Hilton Waikoloa Village hotels, and hosts two-tank dives and night dives aboard their 38-foot Delta dive boat (the *Lani Kai*) to a number of unique sites accessible from the Kohala Coast; prices run $69 to $99. Red Sail also offers a one-day introductory scuba instruction package — including pool instruction, one- or two-tank boat dive, and all equipment — for $114 to $134 per person.

Also keep in mind that both Body Glove and Fair Wind offer scuba upgrades for divers aboard their cruises to Palani Bay and Kealakekua Bay, respectively; see "On-deck adventures: ocean cruising," earlier in this chapter.

Adventures in parasailing

Are you in search of an easy thrill to suit your easygoing vacation? Let **UFO Parasail** (☎ **800-FLY-4UFO** or 808-325-5UFO; Internet: www.ufoparasail.com) take you soaring high above the waves, alone or with a friend. Anybody can parasail — no experience or special skills are necessary, and tours are offered year-round. The speedboat driver does all the work; you just put on the securely attached parachute and go along for the ride. UFO has state-of-the-art equipment, including the latest in liftoff and landing technology. It costs $42 per person for a seven-minute ride at 400 feet, but if you're going up you might as well spend the extra ten bucks for the ten-minute ride at 800 feet, which includes an optional simulated freefall.

Freshwater fluming

I'm not a huge fan of this adventure, but I seem to be alone on this score — everybody else I talk to loves it. Back in the old plantation days, North Kohala kids used to grab old inner tubes in the heat of summer and go "fluming" down the Kohala Sugar Plantation's freshwater irrigation system, past rain forest, over ravines, under waterfalls, and through cool, drippy dark tunnels. Decades later, the surreptitious fun has been legitimized as **Flumin' da Ditch — the Kohala Mountain Kayak Cruise** (☎ **808-889-6922;** Internet: www.kohalakayaks.com).

The three-hour trip goes like this: You drive up to the Hawi office, at the intersection of the Akoni Pule Highway (Highway 270) and Hawi Road (Highway 250) at the north end of the North Kohala peninsula (about an hour north of Kailua-Kona), where you're outfitted with a life vest (hardly needed) and a dry jacket (the water is pretty darn cold). You'll board a four-wheel-drive van for a rough ride through the plantation fields, accompanied by knowledgeable narration on the area and irrigation system. Once you reach the water, you'll board a double-hulled inflatable kayak that you may be recruited to paddle (two people paddle each four-person boat, with one guide dedicated to every two boats). The local guide will "talk story" about the history, culture, and flora of the area; for the best experience, do what you can to get yourself a spot in the guide's boat.

For me, "fluming" brought to mind sitting in a fake log at Six Flags, experiencing shriek-inducing drops down steep hills and an exciting splash at the end, so perhaps it's no wonder that I was disappointed. This is more a gentle adventure than a thrill-a-minute one — no match for kayaking alongside spinner dolphins in Kealakekua Bay. But if you like your adventure easygoing and pillowy soft, or you have little ones or older folks in tow, chances are good that you'll love this trip. Prices are $89 for adults, $68 for kids ages 5 to 18. Wear a swimsuit and/or bring a change of clothes, as you will get wet.

These trips fill up fast, so book your Flumin' da Ditch trip at least three to four days in advance, more if you're a larger party.

Hooking the Big One in the sportfishing capital of the world

If you want to catch fish, you've come to the right place. Big-game fish, including monster blue, black, and striped marlin; spearfish; ahi, aku, and albacore tuna, mahimahi, ono (also known as wahoo); and other good-eating fish roam the deep, warm Kona waters, including barracuda and shark. These waters are known as "fish rich," which means that there are no guarantees, but few anglers come away empty-handed. While more than 100 charter boats depart from four harbors along the island's west coast, the epicenter for Hawaii sportfishing is Honokohau Harbor, located off the Queen Kaahumanu Highway (Highway 19) 2½ miles south of the Kona Airport.

The best way to arrange a charter is through a charter boat booking agency, and the best in Kona is **The Charter Desk at Honokohau Marina** (☎ **888-KONA-4-US** or 808-329-5735; Internet: www.charterdesk.com). The Charter Desk's booking agents are real pros — they know the best boats in Honokohau Harbor, and they'll sort through the more than 50 different available boats, fishing specialties, and personalities to match you up with the boat and crew that's right for you. When you book with the Charter Desk, you can be sure that your boat captain is USCG licensed and the boat is fully insured.

Most big-game charter boats carry six passengers maximum. Half-day and full-day charters are available, and boats supply all equipment, bait, tackle, and lures. You're not required to be licensed. Prices start at around $70 for a half-day share charter (where you share the boat with strangers); private charters start at $250 for a half-day, about $400 for a full day.

Understand that if you go for a share, you'll have to rotate rods, so you won't get a full four hours of fishing in on a half-day charter; therefore, on a time-for-dollar basis, it's probably a better bet to book your own boat, especially if two or three of you are along to split the costs.

In addition, you might also consider booking your boat through **Hawaii Fishing Adventures & Charters** (☎ **877-388-1376**; Internet: www.sportfishhawaii.com), which represents about a half-dozen boats based at Honokohau Harbor, or **Charter Services Hawaii** (☎ **800-567-5662**; Internet: www.konazone.com). If you're an experienced angler and prefer to book with a boat captain directly, consider the **Anxious** (☎ **808-326-1229**; Internet: www.alohazone.com). If you're interested in sportfishing fun that employs easy-to-use light tackle (which offers the advantage of more strikes with action), contact Captain Del Dykes of **Reel Action Light-Tackle Fishing** (☎ **808-325-6811**), who can take you out spinning, bottom fishing, or trolling for smaller catches, or fly fishing for giant tuna or marlin if you're looking for a real thrill.

Keep these tips in mind as you book and before you set out on a Hawaii sportfishing charter:

✔ Island custom aboard fishing boats is that the fish go with the captain and crew. The fish never goes to waste — it's either eaten or sold for food. If you'd prefer to have your catch for dinner or mounting over the TV, it's usually not a problem — just be sure to tell the agent when you book. If you're interested in mounting, your captain can usually answer all of your questions. Agents and captains are also concerned about conservation, so tag and release is an option, if you prefer.

✔ Clients usually bring their own snacks and beverages, plus sunscreen, a hat, and sunglasses. If you want the boat to supply food and drinks, let the agent know when you book (and expect an extra charge, of course).

✔ If you enjoy yourself, don't forget to tip! Just like in a restaurant,
15 percent is standard; base your reward on the effort of the crew,
not on your luck in the fishing grounds. The custom is to give the
tip to the captain, who will disperse it among crew members.

What to See and Do on Dry Land

I've said it before and I'll say it again: Visiting Hawaii Volcanoes
National Park is one of the most thrilling things you can do not only on
this trip, but possibly in your lifetime. I know that coming within spit-
ting distance of an active volcano was definitely one of the highlights of
my life. But there's so much to see and do on the Big Island that the
excitement doesn't end there. Do what you can to budget plenty of
time to see at least a few faces of this wonderfully multifaceted island.

Sightseeing with a guide

If your mobility is limited, or if you're short on time and you want an
introductory look at the big picture, you might want to hook up with a
guided tour. If you've rented a car and can get around easily on your
own, though, driving yourself is definitely the preferable way to see the
island. Not only will you have no control over where you go and how
long you stay, but if the volcano is active, you'll kick yourself for not
being able to stay at the park to see the glowing red flow after dark
(prime viewing time).

Big Island guided tours also tend to be way too ambitious. Trust me —
there's no better way to ruin a trip to the Big Island than by spending it
on a tour bus. If you're going to take a guided bus tour of Hawaii
Volcanoes National Park, do yourself a favor and plan your trip around
taking the more detailed one that departs from nearby Hilo, rather than
the deadly-long Circle Island tour that leaves from Kona and incorpo-
rates more than five hours of driving and a good half-dozen stops into
an endurance-challenging 9- to 12-hour day (and ultimately short-
shrifts the national park in the process). Or, better yet, if you don't
mind a little hiking in your trip, book the 12-hour Volcanoes Adventure
offered by conservation-minded outfitter **Hawaii Forest & Trail,** which
travels full circle from the Kona-Kohala Coast and offers more insight
into the park and its geology and history than you're likely to glean in a
three-day visit on your own (see "Guide-led nature tours," later in this
chapter).

Polynesian Adventure Tours (☎ **800-622-3011** or 808-829-8008;
Internet: www.polyad.com) offers a range of guided tours in mini-vans,
big-windowed mini-coaches (good for small groups and big views), and
full-size buses. First launched to take visitors along Maui's Heavenly
Road to Hana, Polynesian Adventure's tours tend to be a little more
action-oriented than those offered by competing companies. Expect to
spend $44 to $65 per person ($36 to $55 for kids 3 to 11) depending on
the tour you choose and your departure point.

Book your Polynesian Adventure Tour online to get a 10 percent price break.

Roberts Hawaii (☎ **800-831-5541** or 808-521-3666; Internet: www. roberts-hawaii.com) is Hawaii's biggest name in narrated bus tours. Roberts offers a similar slate of tours as Polynesian Adventure, with comparable schedules and prices.

If you're 55 or older, Roberts Hawaii will give you a 10 percent discount on all tours. AAA members qualify for similar savings.

If you do opt for a guided tour that takes you around the entire island, remember: It will be chillier on the east coast than it is on the west coast, so bring a jacket or sweater when you visit the volcano. Rain gear and/or an umbrella is also a good idea, as are sturdy closed-toe walking shoes.

Guide-led nature tours

If you want to experience the Big Island's multifaceted natural world, I highly recommend going out with a guide. An expert guide can really help you appreciate the majesty of this fantastic island, and even take you into areas that you couldn't otherwise reach on your own. Even if hiking and nature-exploring isn't part of your daily life, don't worry — you won't be required to be in racing shape. All of the following terrific tour companies offer adventures for every level of experience and ability.

My absolute favorite Big Island outfitter is **Hawaii Forest & Trail** (☎ **800-464-1993** or 808-331-8505; Internet: www.hawaii-forest.com). I first explored the Big Island with naturalist and educator Rob Pacheco way back in 1995, and it was one of the best — and most fun — nature experiences of my life, so I'm thrilled to see his first-rate business growing and widening its options for visitors.

Rob or one of his well-trained guides takes small groups (usually no more than ten, often smaller) out for day trips in plush four-wheel-drive vehicles to some of the Big Island's most remote and pristine natural areas (some of which Hawaii Forest & Trail has exclusive access to). All of the guides are well-schooled in natural history, ecology (both native and introduced flora and fauna), vulcanology, and island culture and history; additionally, Rob himself is a serious birder.

Both half-day and full-day trips are available; they're all personalized to a group's interest and ability levels, and often feature easy or moderate walking (ask when you book if you're concerned). Regularly scheduled half-day adventures include the Valley Waterfall Adventure, which takes you into private lands on the Kohala Coast to discover hidden waterfalls and killer views along a three-mile hike; the Kahua Cloud Forest Adventure, a magnificent hiking-and-driving excursion to a historic ranch and tropical rain forest situated at 8,000 feet elevation; and my absolute favorite, the Kohala Mule Trail Adventure, in which island-born guide Wally Ching, one of the most genuine and generous folks I've ever met, takes visitors down a steep 500-foot trail on sure-footed mules to explore the stunningly pristine, history-rich, and otherwise inaccessible Pololu Valley.

Full-day adventures include the Volcanoes Adventure, a 12-hour trip from the Kona-Kohala Coast to the splendid Hamakua Coast and Hawaii Volcanoes National Park that is the best introduction to the active volcano and vulcanology that there is; if you only have one day to see the volcano, this is the way to do it. Another hugely popular full-day adventure is the eight-hour Mauna Kea Summit & Stars trip, in which your guide takes you to the summit of Mauna Kea (at 13,796 feet), one of the best and most famous stargazing spots in the world, for an incredible lesson in astronomical observation. A number of rain-forest and bird-watching adventures to private lands are also available.

Call or check the Web site for details and schedules for these and other adventures. Prices for half-day trips cost $89 to $95 per person ($79 to $85 for kids 12 and under), while full-day trips run $135 to $145 per person ($99 for kids 12 and under). Rates include food and all the gear you'll need. All trips depart from the Kona-Kohala Coast; some include pick-up and drop-off, while others have a predesignated meeting point. Reservations should be made at least a week in advance. Note that certain trips have restrictions based on age, weight, or health; be sure to confirm these with the Hawaii Forest & Trail representative when you book. Once you arrive, you can also stop at the Hawaii Forest & Trail Headquarters and Outfitting Store at 74-5035B Queen Kaahumanu Hwy. (Hwy. 19, on the mountain side of the highway across from Honokahou Harbor, behind the Chevron Station), Kailua-Kona, where you can book trips and pick up outdoor equipment and nature-related gear and books.

If, for some reason, Hawaii Forest & Trail doesn't meet your needs, or doesn't go where you want to go, try **Hawaiian Walkways** (☎ **800-457-7759** or 808-775-0372; Internet: www.hawaiianwalkways.com). This reliable outfitter offers a variety of regularly scheduled full- and half-day hikes led by excellent, enthusiastic guides. Their trips include the Waipio Waterfall Adventure, a wonderful half-day hike that takes you along the rim of the Big Island's best-loved unspoiled valley; plus a Kona Cloud Forest Botanical Walk; a Forest Waterfall Adventure at Parker Ranch, the Big Island's biggest cattle ranch; and their own Kilauea Volcano Hike into Hawaii Volcanoes National Park. Prices range from $75 to $135 per person, depending on the trip you choose; all gear, food, and beverages are provided. Custom trips are also available ($135 per person).

At press time, Hawaiian Walkways was offering a 10 percent discount to groups of four or more, kids 12 and under, and repeat customers.

The folks behind Flumin' da Ditch (see "Freshwater fluming" earlier in this chapter) also run very fun **HMV Tours** (☎ **808-889-6922;** Internet: www.kohalakayaks.com) of the spectacular North Kohala peninsula — a hidden treasure that few visitors ever see — led by island-born locals who really know what's what. These three-hour Hummer safaris take you into unspoiled lands rife with ancient rain forests and home to secret historical sites and hidden waterfalls that were previously inaccessible to the public, mixing knowledgeable narration and off-road excitement along the way. Prices are $99 for adults, $68 for kids.

If you prefer to do your road-ruling and off-road touring on two wheels, contact **Kona Coast Cycling Tours** (☎ **808-327-1133;** Internet: www.cyclekona.com), which offers guided mountain-biking tours in the Big Island's upcountry areas and Kohala Mountains for $74 to $134 per person. While some trips are dedicated to accomplished bikers, a few are geared to beginners, intermediates, and kids.

Getting a bird's-eye view: flightseeing tours

Flightseeing is a great way to explore this large, dynamic isle, which boasts sheer cliffs, pristine valleys, gorgeous waterfalls, expansive lava fields, and remote beaches that are otherwise inaccessible. And, of course, there's no better way to see that spectacular bubbling volcano, especially if the current flow is too far from civilization to see from accessible points in the national park.

As I mention in Chapter 14, you should consider the risks of flightseeing before you sign on. While all of the companies I recommend feature skilled pilots and helicopters with excellent safety records, the truth of the matter is that flightseeing is risky business. Twenty-eight people have died in commercial helicopter crashes in Hawaii over the last decade, six of those in a 1998 Kauai accident, seven in a Maui crash in July 2000. Of course, just getting into your car and driving to dinner is far more dangerous than catching a 'copter ride. Still, you should make informed decisions when booking.

When reserving a helicopter tour with any company, check to make sure that safety is their first concern. The company should be an FAA-certified Part 135 operator, and the pilot should be Part 135 certified as well; the 135 license guarantees more stringent maintenance requirements and pilot training programs than those who are only Part 91 certified. And if weather conditions look iffy, reschedule.

Blue Hawaiian Helicopters

This excellent flightseeing company flies a fleet of shiny new American Eurocopter ASTAR 350 helicopters that carry six passengers, providing each with a 180° view and a Bose noise-cancelling headset that lets you enjoy a surprisingly quiet ride. The pilots are well trained and knowledgeable narrators, and a state-of-the-art in-flight video is on board in case you'd like to preserve the sights and sounds of your thrill-a-minute flight for posterity. Blue Hawaiian offers the Circle of Fire volcano tour for Hilo-based travelers, plus two tours from the Kohala Coast: a gorgeous Kohala Coast Adventure that shows you the secret fluted valleys, majestic peaks, and rugged coastline of the island's northernmost point; and the Big Island Spectacular, which takes you over the entire island, from rugged coast and misty peaks to rain forest and volcano, all within two hours.

Spelunking for everyone!

One of the Big Island's best volcano adventures isn't anywhere near Hawaii Volcanoes National Park — it's on the southwest slopes of Mauna Loa, near South Point, at **Kula Kai Caverns.** You can tour this spellbinding labyrinth of thousand-year-old lava tubes and caves with a knowledgeable guide, who will fill you in on the volcanic activity that formed these secret places and the plants and critters that subsequently adapted to their drippy, cool, dark environment.

These exciting tours also offer novices an opportunity to experience caving for the first time and allow experienced spelunkers to try something completely new. The easy half-hour Walking Tour is suitable for everyone, and costs $12 for adults, $8 for kids 5 to 12. Longer and more adventuresome caving trips run from one hour to a half-day, and prices range from $45 to $75 per person. If you're not sure what tour you're up for, call for assistance; at least one spelunking tour is suitable for kids as young as 8 or 9.

Kula Kai Caverns is located 40 miles south of Kailua-Kona (☎ **808-929-7539** or 808-929-9725; Internet: www.kulakaicaverns.com). To get there, turn off Highway 11 between the 79 and 78 mile markers onto Kula Kai Road; after 1.4 miles, turn right onto Lauhala Road and look for the thatch-roofed "office" on the right. But before you go, be sure to call and make a reservation (a few days' advance notice is a good idea). All gear is included in the prices, but wear sturdy shoes (hiking boots, if you have them).

Tours depart from Waikoloa Heliport or Hilo Airport. ☎ *800-745-BLUE or 808-961-5600. Internet:* www.bluehawaiian.com. *40- to 50-minute tours: $140–$145 per person. 2-hour tour: $305 per person.*

If you book seven days or more in advance via e-mail or call and mention that you visited their Web site, Blue Hawaiian will award you with a 15 percent price break.

Mauna Kea Helicopters

Here's another reliable company, in business since 1986 and flying a fleet of American Eurocopter Astar helicopters, plus one McDonnell Douglas 500D, which give everybody a window seat and two-way communication with the pilot. Choose between tours that show you active Kilauea Volcano (leaving from either Hilo or the Kohala Coast) or the North Shore Valleys and Waterfalls tour, which focuses on the island's lush, misty, ancient face.

Tours depart from the Mauna Lani Helipad or Hilo Airport. ☎ *800-400-HELI or 808-885-6400. Internet:* www.maunakeahelicopters.com. *45- to 60-minute tours: $140–$165 per person. 2-hour tours: $265–$310 per person.*

Online bookings made through Mauna Kea's Web site are discounted as much as 20 percent. Additionally, free shuttle services from the Kohala Coast resorts to the Mauna Lani Helipad are available.

Seeing Hawaii Volcanoes National Park

The top natural attraction in the islands, Hawaii Volcanoes National Park is the only rain forest in the U.S. National Park system — and the only national park that's home to a live, lava-pumping volcano.

This phenomenal park stands testament to 70 million years of volcanic activity, plate tectonics, and evolution. It encompasses two volcanoes, **Mauna Loa** and **Kilauea,** and spans 217,000 acres that reach from sea level to Mauna Loa's towering summit at 13,677 feet, and both vast fields of black lava and ancient rain forest.

While both volcanoes are classified as active, Mauna Loa hasn't erupted since 1984. Kilauea, on the other hand, is the most active volcano in the world. An amazing geological phenomenon, it has been erupting nonstop since January 3, 1983. Most volcanic flows last a while — several months, maybe — but 18 years is simply unheard of in the annals of scientific history. Until now, of course.

When most people think of active volcanoes, they think of Mount St. Helens: A calm mountain suddenly blowing its stack, belching out raging, destructive torrents of fire. Hawaii's volcanoes, however, are much more mellow geologic creatures: They're shield volcanoes, which erupt gradually — in a sort of gloopy, Jell-O–like fashion — rather than in one big, fiery explosion. Thus, they allow for excellent, safe viewing most of the time, giving you plenty of time to calmly move out of the way if a blob of lava starts inching toward you. Leave it to Hawaii to have such laid-back volcanoes!

The most recent lava flow — the one you'll be able to see, if you're lucky — follows a seven-mile-long tube from the Puu Oo (POO-oo OH-oh) vent to the sea, where it spills into the ocean in a steaming stream. The hardened lava trail has extended the shoreline seaward, adding more than 560 acres of new land to the Big Island by early 2000 — and even more by the time you get here.

At press time, the lava flow was still going strong, and despite an 11-day pause in September 1999, shows no signs of stopping anytime soon, vulcanologists say. But neither Mother Nature nor Madame Pele (Pell-ay), Hawaii's volcano goddess (who is said to reside in Kilauea's steaming Halemaumau Crater), run on a fixed schedule. The volcano could be shooting fountains of lava hundreds of feet into the air, or it could be shut down on the day you arrive in the park (or the day after this book goes to press, for that matter) — there are no guarantees.

What's more, just because the lava is flowing doesn't mean that you'll be able to witness it firsthand. On many days, the lava flows right by accessible roads and within reach of hiking trails; you can get as close as the heat will allow, and even watch it dump into the sea — quite a dramatic sight. At other times the lava changes course, flowing miles away from any accessible points, visible only in the distance (or from

Hawaii Volcanoes National Park

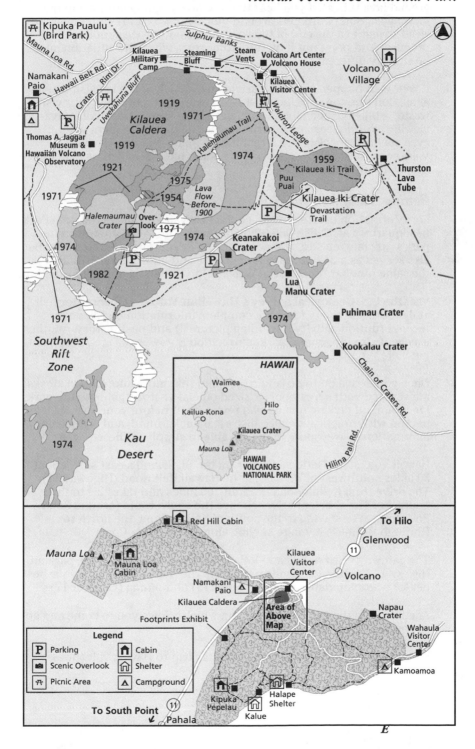

Kipuka Puaulu (Bird Park)

Mauna Loa Rd.

Sulphur Banks

Kilauea Military Camp

Steaming Bluff

Steam Vents

Volcano Art Center
Volcano House

Volcano Village

Hawaii Belt Rd.

Rim Dr.

Crater

Namakani Paio

Uwekahuna Bluff

Kilauea Visitor Center

1919

Kilauea Caldera

1971

Waldron Ledge

Halemaumau Trail

1919

Thomas A. Jaggar Museum & Hawaiian Volcano Observatory

1921

1975

1954

1974

1959

Kilauea Iki Trail

Puu Puai

Thurston Lava Tube

1971

Lava Flow Before 1900

Kilauea Iki Crater

Devastation Trail

1971

1974

Halemaumau Crater

Over-look

1971

Keanakakoi Crater

1974

1982

1921

Lua Manu Crater

1971

1974

Puhimau Crater

Southwest Rift Zone

Kookalau Crater

Chain of Craters Rd.

HAWAII

Waimea

Hilo

Kailua-Kona

Kilauea Crater

Mauna Loa

Kau Desert

1974

HAWAII VOLCANOES NATIONAL PARK

Hilina Pali Rd.

Red Hill Cabin

To Hilo

Glenwood

Mauna Loa

Mauna Loa Cabin

Kilauea Visitor Center

11

Namakani Paio

Volcano

Kilauea Caldera

Area of Above Map

Napau Crater

Footprints Exhibit

Wahaula Visitor Center

Legend

P Parking		Cabin
Scenic Overlook		Shelter
Picnic Area		Campground

Kamoamoa

Kipuka Pepelau

Halape Shelter

Kalue

To South Point

11

Pahala

E

the air via helicopter) or not at all (on occasion it sticks to underground lava tubes). If you hear that the flow is going strong and the viewing is good (word gets around quickly in Volcano), don't hesitate: Head straight to the end of the road. You won't be disappointed — I promise. And don't put it off until tomorrow, when the situation might be entirely different.

If your visit happens to land during a period when the lava isn't visible at all, don't be too disappointed — or, worse yet, consider your visit a waste. While I've been lucky enough to have some spectacular lava-viewing experiences, my favorite day in the park was spent without even seeing a speck of red. Trust me on this — visiting Hawaii Volcanoes National Park is a one-of-a-kind, once-in-a-lifetime experience even without the lava show.

Getting ready for your visit

For information before you go, contact Hawaii Volcanoes National Park headquarters at ☎ **808-985-6000,** or point your Web browser to the park's official Web site, at www.nps.gov/havo. The telephone number also serves as a 24-hour eruption update and information hotline. Dial the same number (or visit the Web site) to obtain camping information.

Visit the U.S. Geological Survey's **Hawaiian Volcano Observatory** site at hvo.wr.usgs.gov for more complete information on Kilauea's recent eruption activity (including pictures!) and past history. Another excellent site for general park information is www.hawaii.volcanoes.national-park.com.

Once you arrive on the island, you'll find that most information kiosks are stocked with a free booklet-sized official visitor's guide to the park. I recommend picking one up and reviewing it before your visit, as it's packed with practical details, historical background, and sightseeing information — way more than I am able to supply in these pages.

Hawaii Volcanoes National Park is on the Big Island's east side, about 30 miles southwest of Hilo along the Hawaii Belt Road (Highway 11). The drive from Kailua-Kona is about 100 miles and takes 2½ to three hours. For the shortest drive, choose the south route (around South Point) if you're staying to the south of Kailua-Kona, the north route (through Waimea) if you're staying along the Kohala Coast.

The gateway town of Volcano Village, on the north side of the park off Highway 11 just about a mile or so from the park entrance, is your best bet for accommodations (see Chapter 15) and dining (Chapter 17).

Admission to the park is $10 per car, which allows you to come and go as you please for seven days.

Keep these tips in mind as you plan your trip to Hawaii Volcanoes National Park:

✔ You really need two or three full days to explore the park thoroughly, so I recommend booking yourself a stay in Volcano Village, the park's gateway community, or the small and pretty city of Hilo, about a 45-minute drive away. But don't stay away if you can't dedicate so much time; you can see a lot of the park if a day is all you have, as long as you don't mind taking the whirlwind tour.

✔ No matter how long you have to visit, do yourself a favor and plan on staying until after dark at least one evening. That's when, if you're lucky, you'll be able to witness nothing less than the miracle of creation as erupting Kilauea volcano spews red-hot, glowing lava.

✔ If you're staying on the west (Kona-Kohala) coast and you can only see the park on a day trip, you might consider visiting with a guide-led nature tour — such as the one offered by **Hawaii Forest & Trail,** or the park hike that **Hawaiian Walkways** offers — in order to maximize your volcano experience. Otherwise, without a knowledgeable guide at hand to show you the highlights and explain what you're seeing, you might find that you're unable to get a real handle on the park in just a day. Trust me — an expert guide is well worth the dough you'll spend. Or, if you only want to catch a glimpse of the volcano from your perch on the Kona-Kohala Coast, consider taking a helicopter tour that flies over the volcano. See "Guide-led nature tours" and "Getting a bird's-eye view: flightseeing tours" earlier in this chapter.

✔ The most adventurous among you may want to rent a four-wheel-drive SUV when you book your rental car on the Big Island, as a few areas of the park are accessible only by four-wheel-drive. If you don't, however, don't sweat it — I never have, and I've seen more of the park than most visitors. You won't feel limited.

✔ I just can't say it strongly enough — I've seen way too many of you running around the park soaking wet or freezing your buns off in shorts and T-shirts. Remember: It's always colder here than it is at the beach, so dress accordingly. If you're coming from the Kona side of the island in summer, expect it to be at least 10 to 20 degrees cooler at the volcano than it is there; bring a sweater or a light jacket and long pants. It's probably even slightly cooler than it is in Hilo thanks to a higher elevation (4,000 feet), so anticipate a drop. In the cooler seasons, wear layers, and be prepared for temperatures to be in the 40s or 50s. Always have rain gear on hand, especially in winter. Sturdy close-toed shoes are a good idea year-round, and a necessity if you're going to walk on the lava flow, as sneakers sometimes melt on the lava.

✔ No matter what the weather forecast may be, always bring a hat, sunglasses, and sunscreen. Take it from me, who came away with quite a sunburn on a day that started with a downpour — the weather can change at any time. Bring drinking water, too, as it isn't readily available in most areas of the park.

✔ Pregnant visitors might want to skip the national park altogether, as it's not a good idea to expose yourself or your baby to the sulfuric fumes that are ever-present in the park. Those with heart or breathing problems may also want to stay away, although my asthmatic husband has never had a problem in four visits. Otherwise, the park is perfectly safe for visitors. Some people claim that long-term exposure to vog, the smoglike haze caused by the gases released when molten lava pours into the ocean, can cause bronchial ailments — but sulfuric fumes are actually far less dangerous than urban industrial fumes.

Getting your bearings once you arrive

Make your first stop the **Kilauea Visitor Center,** just beyond the park entrance, open daily from 7:45 a.m. to 5 p.m. Here you can get up-to-the-minute reports on the eruption and good viewing points, check out exhibits that show you how volcanoes work and introduce you to the plants and animals of the park, watch a 20-minute film on eruptions (shown hourly), and review a schedule of the day's activities (posted on the bulletin board). While you're there, impress the rangers with your knowledge of Hawaii's volcano vocabulary:

✔ The smooth, ropy lava that looks like swirls of chocolate frosting is called **pahoehoe** (pa-ho-ay-HO-ay). It results from a fast-moving flow that curls as it flows.

✔ The rough, chunky lava that looks like a chopped-up parking lot is called **aa** (AH-ah). It's caused by lava that moves slowly, pulling apart as it overruns itself.

An easy, 45-minute guided summit walk leaves from Kilauea Visitor Center daily at 9:45 p.m. It offers an excellent introduction to the park and its flora, fauna, and volcanic geology, so I highly recommend launching your first day in the park with it. I've also found that the guide is happy to make instructive recommendations on planning your time.

Be sure to use the restroom if you're heading into the depths of the park, because they're not readily available in the wild.

Exploring the park

For the best park overview, follow 11-mile **Crater Rim Drive,** which loops around the perimeter of Kilauea Crater and serves as the park's main road, passing through rain forest and lava desert and taking you past all of the park's well-marked scenic spots and points of interest. The drive takes about an hour if you don't make any stops, but what's the point in that? Allow at least three hours, plus hiking time.

If you haven't already done so on the morning guided summit walk, before you even get in your car at the visitor center to make the drive, walk across the street and through the Volcano House for a railside panoramic view of the **Kilauea Caldera** and its vast, black steaming floor. Before you enter the building, look to your right for the marked steam vents, which illustrate the underground action with a cloud of warm, wet air escaping from the earth (notice how all the rain-forest ferns have gravitated to the moisture).

I recommend following the Crater Rim Drive counterclockwise (west) from the visitor center so that you can stop at the **Thomas A. Jaggar Museum,** open daily from 8:30 a.m. to 5 p.m., early in your drive. This little museum is well worth a half-hour of your time for the insight it offers into the park's geologic complexities, island evolution, and volcano observing; there's even a great telling of the Pele legend in murals. (Jaggar was a scientist and volcano observer who arrived to head the observatory in 1912; he was instrumental in both making the Big Island's volcanoes the most closely watched volcanoes in the world and petitioning to establish the area as a national park, a status it achieved in 1916.)

Natural highlights along the Crater Rim Drive include the **Steam Vents** along the Steaming Bluff, where clouds of warmth rise from vents in the active earth. At **Halemaumau** (ha-lay-MOW-mow) **Overlook,** walk to the crater's edge and peer into the vast, still-sulfuric crater that is the legendary home of Pele, Hawaii's tempestuous goddess of volcanoes (evidenced by Halemaumau's still-wild steam vents, perhaps?). Across the road is **Keanakakoi Crater,** whose short trail leads to colorful eruption fissures — very cool! — and the backside of the Halemaumau crater. As you drive the road, you'll see that the flows are dated — 1959, 1974, 1982 — which really brings home the reality of volcanic destruction.

You'll also pass numerous scenic overlooks and trailheads, and I highly recommend that you hit the trail at least once during your visit; the following offer some highlights to seek out.

The **Thurston Lava Tube** is the coolest spot in the park. This short (⅓-mile), easy, well-maintained loop trail leads you into a small rain-foresty crater, luxuriant with giant ferns and native birds, and to a cave in the lava flow that hot lava once ran through. (Similar tubes are currently carrying hot lava underground closer to the current rift.) It's all drippy and cool, with naked roots hanging down. You can hike through the short tube and exit out the other side (bring your flashlight if you have one).

My absolute favorite is the **Kilauea Iki Trail,** a four-mile, two-hour moderate hike that starts across the road from the Thurston Lava Tube and descends about 400 feet to and across the floor of the Kilauea Iki Crater, which last erupted in 1959. Crossing the black, steaming crater floor is a wild, otherworldly, magnificent trip, and offers the park's best opportunity to put yourself in the heart of the matter.

Another result of Kilauea Iki's 1959 eruption is **Devastation Trail.** This brief and easy half-mile walk with the ominous name shows you what a volcanic eruption can do to a flourishing rain forest. The petrified landscape is quite astounding — it looks like a tree graveyard. Anybody can manage this walk; the trailhead is on Crater Rim Drive at Puu Puai Overlook.

Watching the red-hot lava in action

If the volcano is erupting and the flow is accessible, don't miss the chance to watch it snake down the side of the mountain and pour into the sea. Nighttime offers the best viewing conditions. At sunset, head down Chain of Craters Road to the end, where the lava flow has blocked the road. If conditions are good and the lava flow is accessible, park rangers position barricades across the hardened lava fields that will lead you to it. You can't miss it — just follow the crowds and the red-orange glow. Stay on the marked trail and heed the rangers; you'll be perfectly safe if you do. Take water, a flashlight, and your camera, and wear sturdy, hard-soled shoes for the rough and uneven trail (sneakers often melt on the hot lava). Watching the glowing lava gurgle and bubble down the mountain is bound to be the highlight of your trip.

If you'd like a respite from all the devastation, follow the **Kipuka Puaulu (Bird Park) Trail,** an easy one-mile loop that takes you through a thriving forest of native trees. The trailhead is off Highway 11 to the northeast of the main park area, on the Mauna Loa Road. (The park map makes it easy to find.)

Both the Devastation and Kipuka Puaulu trails are excellent walks to take between 4 and 5 p.m., as that's when the park's resident pheasants emerge from their daytime nests to poke around and see what's going on.

The park has enough fascinating hiking trails to keep you busy and interested for days on end. Your best bet is, again, to start your day at the Kilauea Visitor Center, where you can learn about guided walks and day-hike options. Remember to always check conditions with the park rangers before you set out on any hike. If you're interested in getting a preview of accessible trails, visit www.hawaii.volcanoes.national-park.com and click on Hiking Guide.

Once you circle back around to the Kilauea Visitor Center, stop in next door at the Volcano Art Center (www.bishop.hawaii.org/vac), which serves as one of the top showcases for island artists. Don't miss it if you're interested in local arts and crafts — from native-wood jewelry boxes to hand-crafted jewelry to first-rate paintings and photographs — as the works you'll find here are first-rate.

More attractions worth seeking out

Along the Kona-Kohala Coast

In addition to these sights, you may want to head upcountry from Kailua-Kona town on Hualalai Road to the charmingly funky gallery-lined town of **Holualoa,** which offers a nice peek at Kona's world-famous coffee-growing country; see "A shopper's guide to the Big Island" later in this chapter for further details on what you'll find there.

Kailua-Kona Town

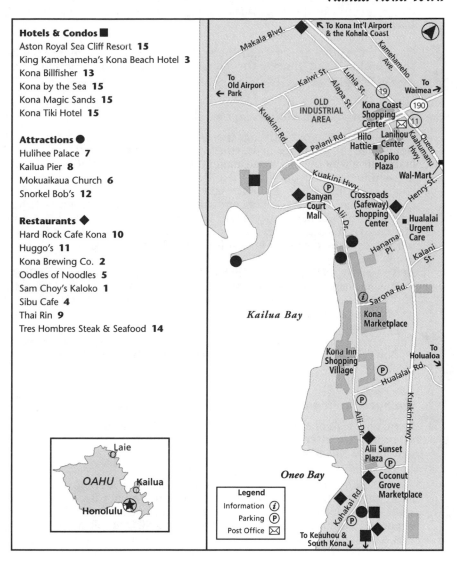

Hotels & Condos ■
Aston Royal Sea Cliff Resort **15**
King Kamehameha's Kona Beach Hotel **3**
Kona Billfisher **13**
Kona by the Sea **15**
Kona Magic Sands **15**
Kona Tiki Hotel **15**

Attractions ●
Hulihee Palace **7**
Kailua Pier **8**
Mokuaikaua Church **6**
Snorkel Bob's **12**

Restaurants ◆
Hard Rock Cafe Kona **10**
Huggo's **11**
Kona Brewing Co. **2**
Oodles of Noodles **5**
Sam Choy's Kaloko **1**
Sibu Cafe **4**
Thai Rin **9**
Tres Hombres Steak & Seafood **14**

Legend
Information ⓘ
Parking Ⓟ
Post Office ⊠

Hulihee Palace

The ancient port town of Kailua-Kona is more like a modern mall than anything else these days, lined with waterfront restaurants and tourist-friendly shopping. But if you have an interest in Hawaii's history, you may want to take 15 minutes or so to explore Hulihee Palace. Built in 1838, this beautifully restored two-story New England–style mansion of lava rock and coral mortar served as the vacation home of Hawaii's royalty. It features gleaming koa antiques as well as ancient artifacts collected by the Daughters of Hawaii. There's a cute gift shop, too. ■

75-5718 Alii Dr., Kailua-Kona (in the heart of town). ☎ *808-329-1877. Internet:* www. daughtersofhawaii.org. *Admission: $5 adults, $4 seniors, $1 kids under 12. Open: Daily 9 a.m.–4 p.m.*

Once you're done exploring the palace, head across the street to handsome **Mokuaikaua Church,** the oldest Christian church in Hawaii. The 112-foot steeple is still the tallest structure in Kailua-Kona.

Puako Petroglyph Archaeological District

Petroglyphs, lava-rock carvings that tell the story of the pre-contact past (much like the paintings inside the great pyramids of Egypt), serve as a fascinating window to Hawaii's ancient history. These pictures of daily life — dancers and paddlers, families and chiefs, poi pounders and canoes — appear throughout the islands, but most of them are found on the Big Island. The largest concentration is here, at this 233-acre site just north of the Mauna Lani resort. The easy and well-marked 1.4-mile **Malama Trail** leads you to rock art that's graphic and easy to see. Early morning or late afternoon is best for petroglyph viewing.

At the Mauna Lani resort, 23 miles north of Kona Airport. To get there: Take Queen Kaahumanu Hwy. (Hwy. 19) to the Mauna Lani turnoff and drive toward the coast on North Kaniku Dr., which ends at a parking lot; the trailhead is marked by a sign and interpretive kiosk.

The petroglyphs are thousands of years old and can be easily destroyed, so don't walk on them or attempt to take a rubbing; stick to photos, please.

Puuhonua o Honaunau National Historical Park

If you only visit one historic site while you're in Hawaii, make it this one. No other site better illustrates what ancient life in the islands was like — and, boy, is this place cool.

With its fierce, haunting totem-like idols, this sacred site on the ocean looks mighty intimidating. To ancient Hawaiians, though, it was a welcome sight — especially for defeated warriors and *kapu* (taboo) breakers, because Puuhonua O Honaunau (poo-oo-ho-NOO-ah oh ho-NOW-now) was a designated sanctuary. A massive rock wall defines the refuge; as long as the troubled Hawaiians made it inside the wall, they were absolved. In addition to the sanctuary itself, this visually stunning ancient site on the black-lava coast is also home to fascinating archaeological preservations and reconstructions, including royal grounds that were home to the *alii* (chiefs) of the Kona Coast in pre-modern times; an ancient temple re-creation; royal fishponds and burial sites (some pretty powerful chiefs called this area home); and much more. Heck, the old rock wall alone is worth a visit: Separating the royal compound from the *puuhonua* (sanctuary) and standing ten feet high and 17 feet thick in spots, it was built entirely without mortar, by simply fitting stones together — a remarkable achievement considering that it's been standing since about 1550.

The historic site is tons of fun to explore. At the park entrance, you'll get a self-guided tour map that leads you to 16 important sites. The trail takes about an hour to follow, and serves as a great window into pre-contact Hawaiian culture — not only in such fierce life lessons as war and sanctuary, but also basic living, from fish-raising and -netting to the basic rules of *konane* (ancient Hawaiian checkers). Wear shoes or sandals with good traction, and you can crawl around on the oceanfacing lava flats — fun! I highly recommend that you launch your visit, however, with a half-hour ranger-led orientation talk, held in the amphitheater at 10 a.m., 10:30 a.m., 11 a.m., 2:30 p.m., 3 p.m., and 3:30 p.m. All in all, allow two to three hours for your visit.

*At the end of Hwy. 160, Honaunau (about 22 miles south of Kailua-Kona). To get there: Turn off Mamalahoa Hwy. (Hwy. 11) at Hwy. 160, between mile markers 103 and 104, and proceed the 3½ miles to the park entrance. ☎ **808-328-2326** or **808-328-2288**. Internet:* www.nps.gov/puho. *Admission: $2 adults, free for kids 16 and under. Open: Visitor center, daily 8 a.m.–5:30 p.m.*

Off the beaten path: North Kohala

If you look at a map of the Big Island, you'll see that a mountainous peninsula protrudes from the very top of the island. That's **North Kohala,** the last bastion of plantation life on the Big Island until not too long ago. If you want to experience the Old Hawaii vibe, this is the place to do it.

The hour-long drive along the Akoni Pule (ah-KO-nee POO-lay) Highway (Highway 270) from Kawaihae (at the north end of the Kohala Coast, where Highway 19 turns inland toward Waimea) to the end of the road at the island's north tip is one of my favorite drives in all of Hawaii. It takes you past gorgeous rolling ranchlands with remarkable ocean vistas and through two charming old plantation towns, **Hawi** (HA-vee) and **Kapaau** (ka-PA-ow), both of which have been transformed into small but rewarding shopper's havens (see "A shopper's guide to the Big Island" later in this chapter for details).

As you drive through Kapaau, look to the mountainside of the road, where you can't miss the **Original King Kamehameha Statue** standing guard outside the New England–style courthouse–turned–senior center in the heart of town. This unspoiled territory was the birthplace of King Kamehameha the Great, the great chief who united the Hawaiian islands as one kingdom back in 1810. This 8-foot, 6-inch bronze statue was cast in Europe in 1880 and was lost at sea before being ultimately rescued and erected here.

Once you're finished browsing Hawi and Kapaau, if it's a nice day and you're enjoying your North Kohala drive, continue a few miles to the end of Highway 270, where you'll find the **Pololu Valley Lookout,** a gorgeous scenic overlook that takes in a panoramic view of foaming waves and sheer seacliffs. (If you'd like to take a fascinating guided mule ride down and around this luxuriant, untouched valley with its own black-sand beach, see "Guide-led nature tours" earlier in this chapter.)

After all this sightseeing, you're bound to be hungry — so don't miss retro-charming **Bamboo,** in Hawi, for lunch; see Chapter 17 for details.

Waimea (Kamuela)

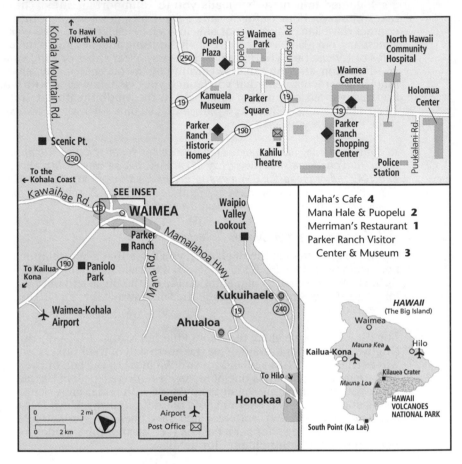

The Interior: Waimea

Smack-dab in the middle of the north road between the west and east sides of the island is Waimea, the heart and soul of Hawaii's *paniolo* (cowboy) country.

As you drive along Highway 19 east from the Kohala Coast to Waimea, most of the rolling, grassy ranchland you see is part of **Parker Ranch** (www.parkerranch.com), Hawaii's biggest ranch and one of the largest cattle ranches in the entire United States (rather remarkable, if you think about it).

If you're interested in learning just how cattle roping came to find a home in Hawaii, spend a half-hour at the **Parker Ranch Visitor Center and Museum,** in the Parker Ranch Shopping Center at the junction of highways 19 and 190 (☎ 808-885-7655), which chronicles the ranch's history from 1847 until today, capturing the essence of day-to-day life on the ranch along the way. The museum is open daily from 9 a.m. to 5 p.m. (the last ticket is sold at 4 p.m.). Admission is $5.

The Parker Ranch also has two historic homesites that you can tour, **Mana Hale** and **Puopelu** (☎ **808-885-5433** or 808-885-7311), both open from 10 a.m. to 5 p.m. daily. These beautifully restored ranch homes (once the home of ranch founding father John Parker and his Hawaiian princess bride) are filled with gorgeous furnishings (lots of native koa in Mana Hale, European heirlooms at Puopelu). To get there, turn south at the 19/190 junction in Waimea and go ¾-mile to the sign that says "Parker Ranch Historic Homes & Art Collection." Curators are available to show you around and fill you in on ranch history and gossipy lore. Allow an hour or so for your visit.

If you'd like to learn more about *paniolo* past and present and the associated activities that are available both in Waimea and around the island, point your Web browser to www.rodeohawaii.com, where you'll find a comprehensive site detailing cowboy-related sightseeing and shopping, rodeo schedules, and more.

The Hamakua Coast

If you drive east from Waimea or north from Hilo (see the following listing), you'll reach more off-the-beaten-path territory: the mist-shrouded Hamakua Coast, where you'll find some wonderful natural attractions and the one-horse town of **Honokaa,** which still boasts a weathered old-plantation charm.

Akaka Falls

Tucked away in a misty, fragrant rain forest, this dramatic 420-footer is one of Hawaii's most scenic waterfalls. You can reach it via an easy mile-long paved loop, which takes you past bamboo and flowering ginger and down to an observation point, where you'll have a perfect view. You'll also see nearby Kahuna Falls, which is a mere 100 feet tall. Be on the lookout for rainbows.

At the end of Akaka Falls Rd. (Hwy. 220), Honomu (8 miles north of Hilo). To get there: From Hwy. 19, turn left at Honomu and head 3.6 miles inland.

Hawaii Tropical Botanical Garden

This lush, Edenlike 40-acre valley makes a magical stop for horticultural buffs, or anybody who wants to experience the extraordinary flora of the Hawaiian Islands. The spectacular collection of more than 2,000 species of tropical plants runs the gamut from delicate orchids to towering torch ginger to hundred-year-old mango, coconut, and banyan trees, all of which thrive in the protected valley's rich volcanic soil. Stay for an hour, or come to bask in the natural tranquility of the garden all day.

On the 4-mile Scenic Route off Hwy. 19, Onomea Bay (8 miles north of Hilo; look for the blue "4-MILE SCENIC ROUTE" sign on the ocean side of the highway). ☎ 808-964-5233. Internet: www.htbg.com. Admission: $15 adults, $5 kids 6–16. Open: Daily 9 a.m.–5 p.m. (last admission is at 4 p.m.).

Waipio Valley

This gorgeous tropical valley at the end of the road on the Hamakua Coast is very difficult to reach — which is precisely what makes it so spectacular. From the black-sand bay at its mouth, remote Waipio sweeps back six breathtaking miles, boasting green-as-can-be taro patches rustling in the wind between sheer cliffs reaching almost a mile high.

You don't have to hike down into the remote valley to admire it. Just take Highway 19 to Honokaa, then turn onto the Kukuihaele Highway (Highway 240), which leads right to the **Waipio Valley Lookout.** This grassy park on the edge of Waipio Valley's sheer cliffs has splendid views of the luxuriantly green valley below. Featuring some old redwood picnic tables and rudimentary facilities, this is the ideal spot to unpack a picnic while you take in the magnificent view.

The more ambitious among you can hike down the paved path into the valley, or catch a ride with the **Waipio Valley Shuttle** (☎ 808-775-7121), which offers a 90-minute narrated tour. The shuttle runs from the Last Chance Store (a quarter-mile before the lookout) Monday through Saturday at 9 a.m., 11 a.m., 1 p.m., and 3 p.m. Tickets are $36.40 for adults, $15 for kids 4 to 11.

 You can also explore the valley aboard a mule-drawn wagon with **Waipio Valley Wagon Tours** (☎ 808-775-9518; Internet: www.waipiovalleywagontours.com). This touristy 1½-hour tour is also fully narrated and departs from the Last Chance Store. Tours are offered Monday through Saturday at 9:30 a.m., 11:30 a.m., 1:30 p.m., and 3:30 p.m. Tickets are $40 for adults, $20 for kids ages 3 to 12.

 If you'd like to take one of the aforementioned guided tours of the Waipio Valley, make advance reservations to avoid disappointment; call a week in advance to book a mule tour.

 Don't take your rental car down the steep road that leads into the Waipio Valley — you will not get back up the steeply graded hill. What's more, most rental-car contracts prevent it, so if you do get stuck, you'll also end up with a hefty tow bill (not to mention a wasted day).

Hilo

I love this pretty bayfront city and its wonderfully nostalgic atmosphere. Although Hilo is Hawaii's second-largest city (after Honolulu), it really feels like a sort of funky old plantation town. Some people just don't understand Hilo's appeal; I've found that you have to be something of a retro-romantic to appreciate it.

Some of you may want to spend a couple of days here. Hawaii Volcanoes National Park is only a 45-minute drive away, so Hilo makes a good base from which to explore it (see Chapter 15 for accommodations recommendations). It's also worth exploring for its interesting shopping opportunities (see "A shopper's guide to the Big Island," later in this chapter).

Hilo

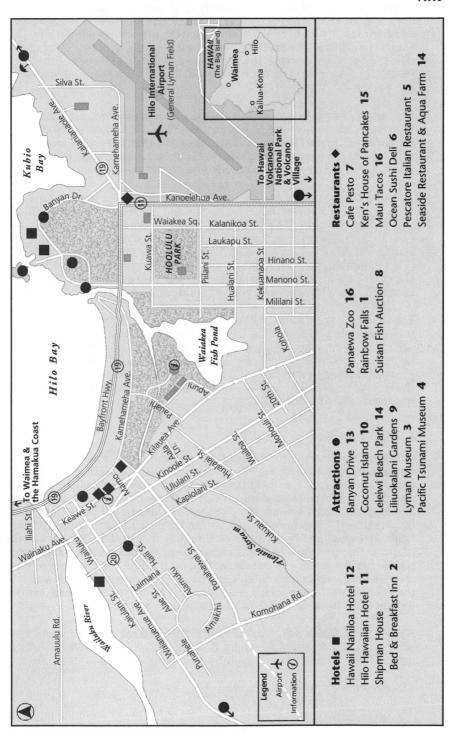

Hotels ■
Hawaii Naniloa Hotel **12**
Hilo Hawaiian Hotel **11**
Shipman House
Bed & Breakfast Inn **2**

Attractions ●
Banyan Drive **13**
Coconut Island **10**
Leleiwi Beach Park **14**
Liliuokalani Gardens **9**
Lyman Museum **3**
Pacific Tsunami Museum **4**

Panaewa Zoo **16**
Rainbow Falls **1**
Suisan Fish Auction **8**

Restaurants ◆
Cafe Pesto **7**
Ken's House of Pancakes **15**
Maui Tacos **16**
Ocean Sushi Deli **6**
Pescatore Italian Restaurant **5**
Seaside Restaurant & Aqua Farm **14**

Legend
✈ Airport
ⓘ Information

But even if you just drive through on your way to the park, take a few minutes to cruise or stroll down **Banyan Drive,** the shady lane that curves along the waterfront, offering fabulous Hilo Bay views. (A number of the banyan trees along here were planted as saplings by such celebrities as Amelia Earheart and Babe Ruth.) If it's a clear day, take the short walk across the concrete arch bridge in front of the Hawaii Naniloa Hotel to **Coconut Island,** if only for a panoramic look at this pretty little city.

Also along Banyan Drive is **Liluokalani Gardens,** the largest formal Japanese garden this side of Tokyo. This 30-acre park, named for Hawaii's last monarch, Queen Liluokalani, is postcard-pretty, complete with bonsai, carp ponds, pagodas, and a moon gate bridge. It's free and open 24 hours, so stop by to spend a moment in old Japan.

Just beyond the park, near the corner of Kamehameha Avenue (Hilo's main drag) and Banyan Drive, is the Suisan Fish Market, home to the **Suisan Fish Auction** (☎ 808-935-8511 or 808-935-9349; Internet: www.suisan.com). Wholesalers and retailers arrive daily (except Sunday) at around 7 a.m. to start bidding on the night's catches that Hilo's fisherman have brought in, and early-rising visitors and locals alike show up to watch the wheeling-and-dealing excitement. Who knows? You might even watch a restaurateur negotiate for your dinner.

The following are a handful of additional attractions you might want to seek out while you're in Hilo. If Hilo's charms win you over — and they just might — pick up a copy of the free *Explore Hilo* walking tour pamphlet, which is available all over town and the island. If, for some reason, you don't run across it, pick one up at the **Big Island Visitors Bureau** office at 250 Keawe St., at Haili Street, across from Pescatore's restaurant (☎ 808-961-5797).

Lyman Museum

Comprised of two major exhibit halls and a historic missionary home, this museum should be high on the priority list for culture and history buffs. The first-rate Earth Heritage and Island Heritage galleries tell the islands' native natural and cultural story; other permanent collections include notable collections of Hawaiian and Chinese art. Next door is the fully restored 1839 home of David and Sarah Lyman, a hybrid New England–Hawaiian-style house — the oldest wooden house on the island — that perfectly exemplifies missionary times, which transformed Hawaii permanently and served as the foundation for the unique east-meets-west island culture that prevails today. No other site in Hawaii tells the story so well. Excellent guided tours of the home are offered on open days at 9:30, 10:30, and 11:30 a.m., and at 1, 2, 3, and 4 p.m.

276 Haili St. (at Kapiolani St.), Hilo. ☎ *808-935-5021. Internet:* www.lymanmuseum. org. *Admission: $7 adults, $5 seniors, $2.50 kids. Open: Mon–Sat 9 a.m.–4:30 p.m.*

Pacific Tsunami Museum

This compelling small museum and education center chronicles the tsunamis (tidal waves) that devastated — and subsequently reshaped — Hilo in 1946 and 1960. Exhibits that tell both scientific and personal stories are on hand; some of the guides are even survivors, with their own tales to tell. Well worth an hour or 45 minutes of your time.

130 Kamehameha Ave., downtown Hilo. ☎ *808-935-0926. Internet:* www.tsunami.org. *Admission: $5 adults, $4 seniors, $2 students. Open: Mon–Sat 10 a.m.–4 p.m.*

Panaewa Zoo

This cute-as-a-button 12-acre rain-forest zoo — the only tropical rain-forest zoo in the U.S. — is a good bet if you have the little ones in tow. Some 50 species of birds, reptiles, and mammals are on hand, from Hawaiian owls to Bengal tigers.

On Stainback Hwy. (off Hwy. 11), Panaewa (just south of Hilo). ☎ *808-959-7224. Internet:* www.hilozoo.com. *Admission: Free! Open: Daily 9 a.m.–4 p.m.*

Rainbow Falls

This 80-footer isn't quite as towering or dramatic as Akaka Falls (see "The Hamakua Coast," earlier in this chapter), but the sight of the waterfall spilling into a pool surrounded by wild ginger is just lovely. Go in the morning, around 9 or 10 a.m., to see Rainbow Falls at their best.

On Waianuenue Ave. (Hwy. 200), Hilo. To get there: Follow Bayfront Hwy. (Hwy. 19) to Waianuenue Ave. and turn inland; the falls are on the right past the Kaumana Dr. intersection.

Hitting the links

Without question, the Kohala Coast is home to the finest golf courses on the Big Island — and among them are some of the finest golf challenges in the world. This vast island boasts far more golfing opportunities than I can list here; if you want more options, either on this coast or elsewhere around the island, contact the **Big Island Visitors Bureau** (☎ **808-886-1655** on the Kohala Coast, or 808-961-5797 in Hilo).

Probably the best golf course on the Big Island is the Hualalai Golf Course at the Four Seasons Resort Hualalai; some clubbers in the know, in fact, consider it to be the finest course in the state. Unfortunately, you have to be a resort guest to play it — but for committed duffers, this Jack Nicklaus–designed championship course is reason enough to pay the sky-high room rates. It also happens to be the finest resort hotel in all of Hawaii, if you ask me; see Chapter 15 for more information.

Book your tee times well in advance, especially in high season.

Stand-by Golf (☎ **888-645-2665** or 808-322-2665; Internet: www.standbygolf.com) offers up to 50 percent off greens fees to bargain hunters and last-minute duffers at select courses. What's available depends on when you call and where you're staying; give it a shot if you want to save a few bucks or you get a sudden urge to hit the links.

Big Island Country Club

The island's newest course is this 6,114-yard Pete and Perry Dye design, situated at 2,500 feet elevation above the Kohala Coast, offering welcome relief from the perennially hot coastal weather. Seven water features come into play on nine holes along this popular, immaculately kept, dramatically situated, and justifiably popular course. The mountain and ocean views are incredible. An excellent bargain on a pricey golf coast.

71-1420 Mamalahoa Hwy. (Hwy. 190), near Waikoloa Rd. ☎ 808-325-5044. Greens fees: $59, $49 after 11 a.m.

Hapuna Golf Course

This 6,029-yard links-style championship course is widely considered to be one of Arnold Palmer and Ed Seay's finest courses. Boasting indigenous vegetation and a design that blends seamlessly with the surrounding landscape, it has been honored as Most Environmentally Sensitive Course by *Golf Magazine* and Course of the Future by the U.S. Golf Association. The course extends from the coastline to 700 feet above sea level, with pastoral mountain scenery to one side and sweeping ocean views on the other. The elevation changes keep play challenging, as do the higher-elevation winds and a series of daunting bunkers. Facilities include a practice green, driving range, pro shop, restaurant, and fitness center.

Adjacent to the Westin Hapuna Beach Prince, 62-100 Kauanoa Dr. (off Hwy. 19 near mile marker 69). ☎ 808-880-3000 or 808-880-1111. Internet: www.hapunabeachprincehotel.com. Greens fees: $105 for Westin resort guests, $185 for non-guests; $60 for guests, $95 for non-guests after 3 p.m.

Mauna Kea Golf Course

This 6,365-yard Robert Trent Jones, Sr., grande dame has been around since 1964, but it's still at the top of its game — just ask the editors of *Hawaii* magazine, who recently named it the second-best course in the state (after the Kiele Course at Kauai Lagoons; see Chapter 22). Its combination of breathtaking natural beauty, stunning oceanfront setting, and championship-level challenge make it one of Trent Jones' finest designs anywhere, and one of the best courses in the state. The signature hole is the 3rd, a par-3 shocker with 200 yards of ocean standing between tee and green, that the legendary architect called his favorite hole of all time. Facilities include practice green, driving range, lockers and showers, pro shop, and restaurant.

In the Mauna Kea resort, 62-100 Mauna Kea Beach Dr. (off Hwy. 19). ☎ 808-882-5400 or 808-882-7552. Greens fees: $105 for Westin resort guests, $185 for non-guests; $60 for guests, $95 for non-guests after 3 p.m.

Mauna Lani Frances H. I'i Brown Courses

Carved out of rugged black lava flows, both of these 6,335-yard championship courses are real winners. You'll really know you're playing Big Island golf here — as a matter of fact, the dramatic oceanfront South Course is so otherworldly that it looks like it might be set on the moon. Long home to the Senior Skins, it's one of Hawaii's most difficult golf challenges and boasts an unforgettable ocean hole, the 221-yard, par-3 7th. The intense drama of the seasoned North Course is toned down by its rolling greens and wealth of old-growth greenery, which gives it a Scottish feel; don't be surprised if you have to wait for feral goats to clear the fairways before you take your shot. Facilities include two driving ranges, putting green, pro shop with rentals, restaurant, and on-course refreshment carts.

In the Mauna Lani resort, 68-150 Hoohana St. (off Hwy. 19). ☎ ***808-885-6655.*** *Internet:* www.maunalani.com/golf. *Greens fees: $90–$115 for Mauna Lani resort guests, $150–$210 for non-guests.*

Waikoloa Golf Club

The beautiful, sporty par-70, 5,958-yard Beach Course is another one dramatically set in the lava, and reflects designer Robert Trent Jones, Jr.'s motto: "Hard par, easy bogey." Most golfers remember the par-5, 505-yard 12th hole, a sharp dogleg with bunkers in the corner and an elevated tee surrounded by lava. Designed by Tom Weiskopf and Jay Morrish, the par-72, 7,074-yard Kings' Course is a links-style challenge — and a real shotmaker's course — with six major lakes and about 75 bunkers that often come into play thanks to ever-present tradewinds. Facilities include golf shop, restaurant, practice facility, and golf academy.

In the Waikoloa Resort, 18 miles north of Kona Airport. ☎ ***877-WAIKOLOA,*** *808-885-6060 (Beach Course), or 808-886-7888 (Kings' Course). Internet:* www.waikoloaresort.com. *Greens fees: $95 for Waikoloa resort guests, $185 for non-guests.*

Waikoloa Village Golf Club

This semi-private course on the slopes of Mauna Kea is a real gem, worth seeking out for its beautiful views, great game, and relatively affordable fees. Robert Trent Jones, Jr., designed this 5,490-yard challenge (with a par 72 for each of the three sets of tees) with his trademark sandtraps, slick greens, and great fairways. Facilities include pro shop, putting and chipping greens, driving range, locker rooms with showers, restaurant, club rentals, and private instruction.

On Waikoloa Rd., Waikoloa Village (off Hwy. 19, 18 miles north of Kona Airport). To get there: Turn toward the mountain at the WAIKOLOA sign (not into the resort) and go about 6 miles. ☎ ***888-796-GOLF*** *or 808-883-9621. Internet:* home1.gte.net/ wvgolf/wvgc.htm. *Greens fees: $85, $50 after 1 p.m.*

A shopper's guide to the Big Island

For such a rural island, the Big Island has a shockingly good shopping scene. Since the island is home to Hawaii's greatest stores of natural materials, Big Island–based artists and artisans generate some of the best art and crafts in Hawaii, from traditional *lauhala* weaving (rare to find) to gorgeous koa-wood gifts. But you need to know where to look, because if you don't venture past Kailua-Kona, you'll think that all this island has to sell is blatant tourism.

Kailua-Kona and South Kona

Kailua-Kona is a carnival of T-shirts, tacky trinkets, and silly souvenirs, with a little beachwear and a few quality gift items thrown into the mix for good measure. **Alii Drive** is the heart of the action; all you need to do is start at one end and browse. The best of what's to offer can be found at the **Kona Inn Shopping Village,** in the heart of town on the ocean side of the road, where one standout among the 50-plus shops is the **Honolua Surf Co. (☎ 808-329-1001;** Internet: www.honoluasurf. com) which has my favorite surf wear in the islands. But my top stop in Kona is **Hula Heaven,** also in the Kona Inn Shopping Village, 75-5744 Alii Dr. (☎ 808-329-7885), which features a one-of-a-kind mix of vintage treasures and quality new aloha wear. Don't miss it!

If you're looking for an offbeat beach read, head to the **Middle Earth Book Shoppe,** tucked away on the inland side of the street at 75-5179 Alii Dr. (☎ 808-329-2123).

Hilo Hattie, Hawaii's biggest name in aloha wear, has an outpost in Kailua-Kona at 75-5597A Palani Rd. (at Kuakini Highway, next to Burger King; ☎ 808-329-7200; Internet: www.hilohattie.com). Hilo Hattie is geared to the tourist market, carrying inexpensive, colorful wear that has improved in quality and style in recent years, plus a wide selection of souvenirs like macadamia nuts, Hawaii-grown coffees, and groovy Hawaiian-print seat covers. A good stop for gifts.

Farther south on Highway 11, in the Kealakekua area, is **Peavian Logic,** 79-7491 Mamalahoa Hwy. (☎ 808-324-4000), a worthwhile stop for unusual gifts, cards, clothing, and more.

Upcountry Kona: Holualoa

One of my favorite places to shop in all of Hawaii is the artsy, funky upcountry village of Holualoa, sitting 1,400 feet above Kailua-Kona on the slopes of Hualalai mountain. To get there, head south from Palani Road on Highway 11; turn up the mountain at the clearly marked Hualalai Road turnoff. The curving three-mile drive up the mountain takes about 10 minutes; once you reach the top, turn left on Mamalahoa Highway, the coffee country town's gallery-lined main street.

The first shop you'll reach, even before you make the turn onto Mamalahoa Highway, is **Kimura's Lauhala Shop (☎ 808-324-0053),** where the dying Hawaiian art of *lauhala* weaving still thrives, thanks to Kimura's group of weavers. Look carefully, however, to separate the island-made crafts from the increasing number of imported Polynesian imports.

Farther along Mamalahoa Highway, the highlights include the **Holualoa Gallery** (☎ 808-322-8484; Internet: www.lovein.com/holualoagalleryblue.htm), which showcases original works by a bevy of local fine painters, sculptors, photographers, and jewelers. The **Ululani Group** gallery (☎ 877-787-3611 or 808-322-7733; Internet: www.ululani.com) specializes in top-quality original works and lithos, while the **Studio 7 Gallery** (☎ 808-324-1335), a wonderful multi-roomed Japanese-style gallery, showcases prints, sculpture, multimedia art, jewelry, and gorgeous pottery and crafts, all with a signature Asian simplicity. Another worthwhile stop is the **Country Frame Shop Gallery** (☎ 808-324-1590; Internet: www.hawaiicolors.com), which features the bold and insightful paintings of artist Darrell Hill, plus some striking original print sundresses.

North Kohala

If you're interested in high-quality Hawaiian crafts, especially those made of gorgeous island woods — of which native koa wood is the most highly prized — head up the Akoni Pule Highway (Highway 270) to the North Kohala towns of **Hawi** (HA-vee) and **Kapaau** (ka-PA-ow), both of which are worth browsing. All of the stops are right along the highway.

As you shop around the islands, you'll see gorgeous koa wood boxes, vessels, furniture, and accessories in finer galleries. Prices are high (a small keepsake box can easily run more than $100) thanks to a quickly diminishing supply of the wood. The Big Island has the finest koa craftsmen, as it's home to the largest existing stand of koa.

Interesting stops include the **Kohala Koa Gallery,** inside the Bamboo Restaurant in Hawi (☎ 888-KOA-WOOD or 808-889-0055), which features two floors of koa furniture, jewelry boxes, and other gorgeous island-made gift items. Stop into **Double Joy Designs** (☎ 808-889-0645), a second-floor closet where Claire Trester displays her stunning jade jewelry; unfortunately, she keeps irregular hours, so your best bet is to call ahead if your heart's set on visiting.

If you don't mind shelling out big bucks for heirloom-quality crafts carved from koa and other woods by Hawaii's best master carvers and woodworkers, visit the **Ackerman Gallery** in Kapaau (☎ 808-889-5971; Internet: www.ackermangalleries.com). Boasting the best selection of woodcrafts in the islands, as well as Gary Ackerman's own Impressionist-style paintings, it's worth a look even if you can't buy. The second location, a little farther up the street across from the King Kamehameha Statue, is a lovely gift gallery with more affordable wood crafts, plus home accessories and jewelry (I bought a string of Hawaii-strung Japanese black pearls on my last visit).

Another excellent stop in Kapaau is the **Kohala Book Shop** (☎ 808-889-6400), Hawaii's largest used bookstore and one of the most browsable book shops in the islands, featuring everything from to rare out-of-print editions to new books by Hawaii authors to gently used beach reads.

Hilo

Boasting an appealing mix of fine and funky shops, this charming old Hawaii city is a wonderful place to browse. Shopping is centered in the wooden storefronts along oceanfront Kamehameha Avenue, on Keawe Avenue one parallel block inland, and on the side streets in between. Note that many of Hilo's shops are closed on Sunday, so plan accordingly.

If you want to come home with just one article of aloha wear, buy it at **Sig Zane,** 122 Kamehameha Ave. (☎ 808-935-7077), whose distinctive, two-color all-cotton aloha wear is the height of simple style and good taste. The stunningly beautiful fabrics are sold in a variety of clean-lined, easy-to-wear styles, and even off the bolt if you'd like to take some home. Best of all, you won't look at a Sig Zane shirt or dress once you get home and say, "What was I *thinking*?" My husband and I receive regular compliments on the mainland for our Sig Zane wear; I can't recommend this marvelous shop enough.

My second-favorite stop in Hilo is the **Mauna Kea Galleries,** 276 Keawe St. (☎ 877-969-HULA or 808-969-1184; Internet: www.maunakeagalleries. com), which boasts a wonderful collection of vintage Hawaiiana prints, photos, and other collectibles, many of them surprisingly affordable. **Basically Books,** 160 Kamehameha Ave. ☎ 800-903-MAPS or 808-961-0144; Internet: www.basicallybooks.com), is your stop for all kinds of Hawaii books and maps.

Aloha-wear queen **Hilo Hattie** has a second Big Island outpost at Prince Kuhio Plaza, 111 E. Puainako St., at Highway 11 (☎ 808-961-3077) — but if you're going to buy aloha wear while you're in Hilo, you might as well do it at Sig Zane.

In the Volcano Area

On Highway 11, the road from Hilo to Volcano, you'll find **Dan De Luz Woods** just past mile marker 12 (take the first right past the mile marker; ☎ 808-935-5587), where the master bowl turner creates gorgeous works in koa, sandalwood, mango, and other island woods.

While you're at Hawaii Volcanoes National Park, take a few minutes to stop into the **Volcano Art Center Gallery,** next to the Kilauea Visitor Center (☎ 808-967-7565), a marvelous showcase for some of the island's best artists and craftspeople, and a real delight to browse.

Living It Up After the Sun Goes Down

This marvelous island has a wealth of stuff to see and do — more than you can take in during the course of a single vacation, as you can see from this chapter — but it all tends to come to a screeching halt at sunset.

If you're staying on the west side of the island, make sunset the highlight. Enjoy a leisurely dinner at an oceanfront restaurant, then call it a night. The waterfront restaurants in Kailua-Kona all make great sunset perches, as do the Kohala Coast resorts, which offer beachfront spots for sunset cocktails and dinner. See Chapter 15 for recommendations. (Hint: Edward's at Kanaloa is ideal for South Kona romance.)

A top sunset draw on the Kona Coast is **Captain Beans' Polynesian Cruises** (☎ **800-831-5541** or 808-329-2955; Internet: www. robertshawaii.com). This adults-only two-hour sunset cruise sails from Kailua Pier nightly and features dinner, dancing, and a full-scale Polynesian revue aboard a 150-foot catamaran. It's real cheesy, but lots of fun, nonetheless. Tickets are $52 to $63 per person, including your meal, well cocktails, the show, and transportation to and from most hotels and condos on the Kona and Kohala Coast (prices vary depending on the pickup point).

Substantially less touristy are the sunset cruises that **Red Sail Sports** (☎ **877-RED-SAIL** or 808-886-2876; Internet: www.redsail.com) operates aboard their 50-foot catamaran, the *Noa Noa,* from Anaehoomalu Bay at the Waikoloa resort on the Kohala Coast. The two-hour sail costs $53 for adults, $26.50 for kids 3 to 12, including appetizers and a full bar. An extra plus: You're likely to spot humpback whales in the winter whale-watching season.

If the volcano is acting up and you're staying on the east side of the island, nighttime is the right time to see the lava pumping — so get yourself to the end of Chain of Craters Road at Hawaii Volcanoes National Park. See the complete park section earlier in this chapter for details, including where to get the latest eruption reports.

Of course, for the most animated after-dark entertainment, head to — you guessed it — a luau! The Big Island has two excellent options; check out the section at the end Chapter 15 for more information.

Part VI
Kauai

In this part . . .

*K*auai, with its lush, tranquil beauty, is the perfect tropical island getaway. In these chapters, you'll discover all that this wonderful island has to offer, from pristine white-sand beaches to dramatic seaside cliffs to gorgeous tropical gardens.

Chapter 19

The Lowdown on Kauai's Hotel Scene

In This Chapter

▶ Deciding where to base yourself on Kauai

▶ Choosing among the island's top resort hotels, condos, and B&Bs

▶ Expanding your options: agencies that specialize in vacation-home rentals and additional condo and B&B choices

Kauai boasts fewer accommodations choices than its three big-sister islands, and only a handful of full-fledged resorts. But it does offer condos in every price range, some fine B&Bs (including one of Hawaii's very few oceanfront B&Bs), and even a complex of historic plantation cottages that are ideal for both families and lovers of prewar style.

Rates tend to be pretty reasonable on Kauai; in fact, this island features some of Hawaii's best lodging values. Still, Kauai is an increasingly popular destination, and travelers are booking rooms earlier and earlier each year. So try to reserve your accommodations as soon as possible to avoid missing out on your first choice.

Choosing Your Location

Kauai has three major resort areas: The Coconut Coast, on the east shore; the north shore; and Poipu Beach, on the south shore.

The Coconut Coast

Of all of Kauai's resort areas, the island's east shore makes the most convenient base for exploring the island. The Coconut Coast is just about a ten-minute drive north of Lihue (li-HOO-ay), Kauai's largest town and the center of island life and commerce, which means that lots of conveniences are right at hand. It's also at the midpoint of the main highway, which connects the north shore to the south shore, so it can't be more centrally located.

The groves of coconut trees that pepper the area lend it a nice Hawaiian vibe — helping to make up for the mini-malls that line the highway along here. A gorgeous mountain backdrop and leftover island-style plantation buildings also help to make what could have been a suburban-generic resort coast actually rather charming. And the region's main beach, Lydgate State Beach Park, is a winner.

This area is really geared toward value-conscious travelers, with an accommodations stock comprised mostly of mid- and budget-priced, family-friendly condos, so it's a good bet if you're in the market for a deal. However, while the east shore doesn't get as much rain as the north shore, it's not as consistently dry and sunny as the south shore, either; in winter, you should expect a bit more rain than you might get in Poipu. Also expect more traffic and noise than what you'd find in Poipu.

The north shore

Kauai's north shore is as breathtaking as Hawaii gets. It boasts a string of stunning beaches; two charming towns for exploring, Hanalei and Kilauea; a sophisticated and well-manicured resort, Princeville, tucked away on a peninsula so you can enjoy it or ignore it as you see fit; stretches of taro fields as far as the eye can see; and cliffs so beautiful that they starred as Bali Hai in the film version of *South Pacific*. Spend as much time up here as you can. No place on the island is as soothing to the spirit as this verdant, almost magical coast.

So why don't I tell everyone to stay up here, you ask? First of all, the north shore is quite removed; Lihue is a full hour's drive away. Second, the number of accommodations choices is limited. Third, the north shore gets lots of rain, especially in winter. The rain is what keeps this coast so lush and stunning, but it can really put a damper on your vacation. Another turnoff is the winter surf, which can be too turbulent for most swimmers.

Still, the north shore's stunning natural beauty more than makes up for its shortcomings, and I highly recommend staying up here. Your best bet is to come in summer or autumn, when the weather is usually excellent. Choose Princeville if you like world-class golf, spa offerings, and other modern amenities. But if you're turned off by manicured resort living, skip Princeville in favor of a Hanalei Colony Resort condo (see "Kauai's Best Hotels, Condos, and B&Bs" later in this chapter) or a vacation rental in island-charming Hanalei, Anini Beach, or Haena (see "Home Sweet Vacation Home" at the end of this chapter).

Poipu Beach

Excellent year-round weather, great beaches, a wealth of ocean activities, terrific golf and tennis, and an easy-access location for both sightseeing and airport convenience make Poipu Beach an excellent place to stay, and Kauai's all-around best choice in terms of convenience, climate, activities, and natural beauty. You can't go wrong here, no matter what your budget or what kind of accommodations you're looking for — whether luxury resort, oceanfront B&B, or bargain-priced condo.

The beach is particularly family friendly, and the whole area is surprisingly relaxing considering its popularity. It's probably Hawaii's best resort development, simply because it hasn't been overdeveloped — there's still plenty of open space to enjoy. And while Poipu might not quite be the stunner that the north shore is (what is?), its sunny, vibrant setting — red earth, lush greenery, turquoise waves, blond sand, clear blue skies — can hold its own in any natural-beauty category. The only marks in the negative column are the 1½-hour drive to the north shore, and tiny Koloa, a one-horse plantation town that's become a bit too ticky-tacky for its own good; still, it's so small that it's easy to ignore.

Farther afield: Waimea

The southwest town of Waimea is a good 45 minutes from Lihue and nearly two hours from the north shore. But it's worth mentioning not only because Waimea is sunny nearly year-round, but because it's also home to one of my favorite places to stay in all of Hawaii, a charming group of fully restored plantation-era beachfront cottages that will charm the pants off even the most committed modernist. These cottages are great for a family reunion or a get-away-from-it-all vacation. You should know, however, that you'll have to drive to the beach (the dark-sand beach at Waimea is not suitable for swimming), and you'll spend a lot of time in the car if you plan on exploring the island thoroughly. But one of the most beautiful spots on the island, Waimea Canyon, is nearby, as well as the departure point for most Na Pali cruises.

Kauai's Best Hotels, Condos, and B&Bs

In the following listings, you'll see that each resort hotel, condo, or B&B name is followed by a number of dollar signs, ranging from one ($) to five ($$$$$). Each represents the median price range for a double room per night, as follows:

$	Super-cheap — less than $75 per night
$$	Still affordable — $75 to $150
$$$	Moderate — $150 to $225
$$$$	Expensive but not ridiculous — $225 to $300
$$$$$	Ultra-luxurious — more than $300 per night

Also, don't forget that the state adds 11.42 percent in taxes to your hotel bill.

Kauai's Best Hotels, Condos & B&Bs

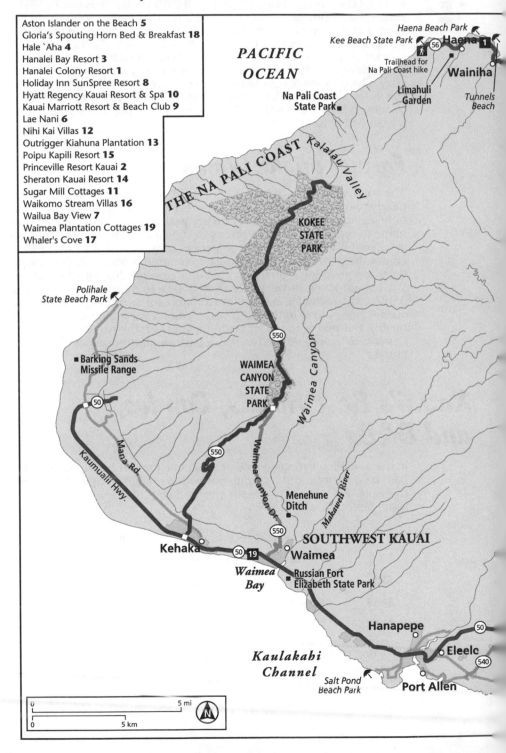

Aston Islander on the Beach **5**
Gloria's Spouting Horn Bed & Breakfast **18**
Hale `Aha **4**
Hanalei Bay Resort **3**
Hanalei Colony Resort **1**
Holiday Inn SunSpree Resort **8**
Hyatt Regency Kauai Resort & Spa **10**
Kauai Marriott Resort & Beach Club **9**
Lae Nani **6**
Nihi Kai Villas **12**
Outrigger Kiahuna Plantation **13**
Poipu Kapili Resort **15**
Princeville Resort Kauai **2**
Sheraton Kauai Resort **14**
Sugar Mill Cottages **11**
Waikomo Stream Villas **16**
Wailua Bay View **7**
Waimea Plantation Cottages **19**
Whaler's Cove **17**

PACIFIC
OCEAN

Haena Beach Park
Kee Beach State Park
Haena
Wainiha
Trailhead for
Na Pali Coast hike
Limahuli
Garden
Tunnels
Beach
Na Pali Coast
State Park

THE NA PALI COAST
Kalalau Valley

KOKEE
STATE
PARK

Polihale
State Beach Park

550

Barking Sands
Missile Range

WAIMEA
CANYON
STATE
PARK

Waimea Canyon

50

550

Kaumualii Hwy.

Mana Rd.

Waimea Canyon Dr.

Makaweli River

Menehune
Ditch

550

SOUTHWEST KAUAI

Kehaka

50 19

Waimea

Waimea
Bay

Russian Fort
Elizabeth State Park

Kaulakahi
Channel

Salt Pond
Beach Park

Hanapepe

Eleele

540

Port Allen

50

0   5 mi
0   5 km

N

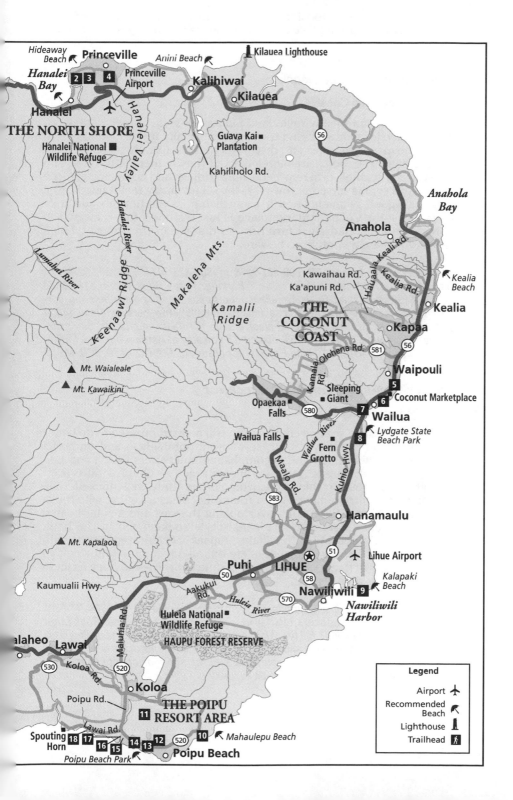

Hideaway Beach

Princeville

Anini Beach

Kilauea Lighthouse

Hanalei Bay

Princeville Airport

2 3 4

Kalihiwai

Kilauea

Hanalei

THE NORTH SHORE

Hanalei National Wildlife Refuge

Guava Kai Plantation

Kahiliholo Rd.

56

Hanalei Valley

Hanalei River

Lumahai River

Keenaawi Ridge

Makaleha Mts.

Anahola Bay

Anahola

Kawaihau Rd.

Ka'apuni Rd.

Hauaala Keali Rd.

Kealia Rd.

Kealia Beach

Kamalii Ridge

THE COCONUT COAST

Kealia

Kapaa

▲ Mt. Waialeale

▲ Mt. Kawaikini

Olohena Rd.

Kamalu Rd.

581

56

Waipouli

5

Sleeping Giant

Coconut Marketplace

Opaekaa Falls

580

7 6

Wailua

Wailua Falls

Wailua River

Fern Grotto

Lydgate State Beach Park

8

Kuhio Hwy.

Maalo Rd.

583

Hanamaulu

▲ Mt. Kapalaoa

Puhi

51

Lihue Airport

Kaumualii Hwy.

50

LIHUE

58

Kalapaki Beach

Aakukui Rd.

Huleia River

570

Nawiliwili

9

Nawiliwili Harbor

Huleia National Wildlife Refuge

HAUPU FOREST RESERVE

alaheo

Lawai

530

Koloa Rd.

Maluhia Rd.

520

THE POIPU RESORT AREA

11

Koloa

Poipu Rd.

Lawai Rd.

Spouting Horn

18 17

16 15

14 13

12

520

10

Mahaulepu Beach

Poipu Beach Park

Poipu Beach

Legend	
Airport	✈
Recommended Beach	✦
Lighthouse	⌘
Trailhead	⚐

The "Sweet Dreams: Choosing Your Hotel" worksheet at the end of this book gives you a great place to jot down ideas about where you might want to stay.

Aston Islander on the Beach

$$–$$$ Coconut Coast

This pleasant and freshly renovated plantation-style hotel complex is a great choice for value-minded travelers, especially if you can hook into one of the many packages and discounts that are usually on offer (most visitors can). The rooms are motel-like, but they're fresh, attractive, and boast pretty textiles, firm new beds, mini-fridges, and coffeemakers (the oceanfront rooms have microwaves, too). The nicely maintained property has a good swimming beach, a smallish pool and hot tub, and coin-op laundry; the Coconut Marketplace is just a stone's throw away. The only down side? Bad lanai furniture. And some of the rooms labeled "oceanview" are a stretch, so beware.

*484 Kuhio Hwy., Kapaa. ☎ **800-922-7866** or 808-822-7417. Fax: 808-822-1947. Internet:* www.aston-hotels.com. *Parking: Free! Rack rates: $140–$188 double, $230 junior suite. Deals: Excellent opportunities for discounts. Internet-only ePriceBreaker rates can result in savings of up to 45% (doubles as low as $73 at press time). Ask for AAA, senior (50-plus), and corporate discounts, and other special rate programs. Qualify for 25% discount if you stay at Aston properties for 7 or more nights with Aston's "Island Hopper" program. AE, CB, DC, DISC, JCB, MC, V.*

Gloria's Spouting Horn Bed & Breakfast

$$$$ Poipu Beach

Attention romance-seeking couples: You will be hard-pressed to do better than Gloria's, one of Hawaii's very few oceanfront B&Bs — and among its finest. The very friendly and accomplished innkeepers Gloria and Bob Merkle welcome guests (mostly youngish, active couples) into their attractive and comfortable home, which offers three well-stocked, well-furnished, and ultra-romantic guest rooms. Each has a wet bar with fridge and coffeemaker; VCR; a lanai overlooking the surf and a solar-heated pool at ocean's edge; and a Japanese-style soaking tub in the bath. Breakfasts are elaborate buffet affairs, sunset is celebrated nightly with an open bar and *pupus,* and snacks are out all day long — you won't go hungry here. Worth every penny, and people know it — so book as far in advance as possible.

*4464 Lawai Beach Rd. (just before Spouting Horn Park), Koloa. ☎/Fax: **808-742-6995.** Internet:* www.gloriasbedandbreakfast.com. *Parking: Free! Rack rates: $250 double. Rates include full breakfast and afternoon drinks and hors d'oeuvres. 3-night minimum. Higher rates and minimum-stay requirements at Christmas. Deals: $25 per-night discount for weekly stays. Ask Gloria about discounted car-rental rates and interisland airfares. No credit cards.*

Hale 'Aha

$$ North Shore

This lovely home fronts 500 feet of world-class fairway, but even golf-o-phobes who prefer personal touches over anonymous conformity will enjoy this friendly B&B. Ruth Bockelman and her daughter Teresa offer four rooms and suites, all comfortably outfitted, decorated in pretty pastels, and impeccably maintained. The stellar 1,000-square-foot Penthouse Suite is well-outfitted enough to keep even the most demanding visitors content for a month, but the substantially cheaper Honeymoon Suite is a great value for those who'd like a few extra luxuries without breaking the bank. The generous breakfast borders on a full spread, with baked dishes and fresh fruit smoothies. You won't get ocean views, but a secluded white-sand beach is nearby. If you dislike manicured resort areas, pastels, or personal attention, don't bother.

3875 Kamehameha Dr., Princeville. ☎ *800-826-6733 or 808-826-6733. Fax: 808-826-9052. Internet:* www.pixi.com/~kauai*. Parking: Free! Rack rates: $110–$120 double, $175–$275 suite. Rates include continental breakfast. 3-night minimum. Children under 14 not accepted. Deals: Discounts on greens fees at Princeville's two championship golf courses. MC, V.*

Hanalei Bay Resort

$$$–$$$$ North Shore

This first-rate condo resort is an excellent north shore choice. It overlooks the same fabled Bali Hai cliffs and gorgeous golden beach that the ritzy Princeville Hotel does (see the listing later in this chapter), but for a substantial savings, especially if you have the family in tow. The apartments are nicely done and boast plenty of room to spread out, plus rattan furnishings and big lanais; all but the most basic units are between 1,100 and 2,100 square feet and come with a full kitchen, washer/dryer, and an extra TV in every bedroom. The lush grounds feature two freshwater pools and tennis courts. The restaurant is just fine, and the lounge is a stellar place to sip a sunset cocktail. The property is part time-share, so beware — you will be invited to an "orientation" (read: sales) meeting, but it's easy to ignore.

5380 Honoiki Rd., Princeville. ☎ *800-827-4427 or 808-826-6522. Fax: 808-826-6680. Internet:* www.hanaleibaykauai.com*. Parking: Free! Rack rates: $170–$250 double or studio, $320–$350 1-bedroom, $400–$525 2-bedroom/2-bath, $725 2-bedroom/ 3-bath; $530–$1,061 prestige suite. Deals: Always ask about packages or other special offers. Discounted greens fees at Princeville area golf courses. AE, DC, JCB, MC, V.*

Hanalei Colony Resort

$$–$$$ North Shore

This small, lovely, low-rise condo resort is *the* place to stay if you're looking to experience Kauai's pristine north shore in all its lush, remote glory. It's well past Hanalei town, near the end of the road — perfect if you're looking to get away from it all, less than ideal if you're planning to do lots of exploring. But you couldn't ask for a more idyllic setting, with lush gardens and a perfect golden beach just steps from your door. Each of the two-bedroom, one-bath apartments is pleasantly furnished in island style and has a lanai, a complete kitchen, ceiling fans (A/C isn't necessary), and great views (mountain views are just as fab as ocean views). The atmosphere is quiet and relaxing — no TVs or phones to interfere with the waves and birdsong. Even the kids won't miss the TV — the resort has plenty of beach gear at hand, plus a large pool and Jacuzzi, lawn and board games, and more to keep them happy.

5-7130 Kuhio Hwy., Haena (2 miles past Hanalei town, near the end of the road). ☎ *800-628-3004 or 808-826-6235. Fax: 808-826-9893. Internet:* www.hcr.com. *Parking: Free! Rack rates: $145–$265 2-bedroom/1-bath (to $320 at Christmastime). Deals: Seventh night free; also ask about car-and-condo, honeymoon, and other package deals. AE, MC, V.*

Holiday Inn SunSpree Resort

$$$ Coconut Coast

With a wonderful beachfront location, newish rooms, lots of amenities (including a mini-fridge, coffeemaker, and Sony Playstation in every room), and a well-rounded kids' program, this Holiday Inn resort is a terrific choice for families — or anybody looking for a reasonably priced vacation, for that matter. What the resort lacks in personality it makes up in moderate prices and excellent amenities. It fronts Lydgate Beach, the best beach on the Coconut Coast, which has a playground and a protected natural pool that's ideal for young swimmers and first-time snorkelers. On-site extras include two pools, a Jacuzzi, and a coin-op laundry. The regular doubles are on the small side, so book a suite (with pullout sofa), or a freestanding family-size cottage, if you're traveling with the kids.

3-5920 Kuhio Hwy., Kapaa. ☎ *800-HOLIDAY, 888-823-5111, or 808-823-6000. Fax: 808-823-6666. Internet:* www.holidayinn-kauai.com. *Parking: Free! Rack rates: $150–$175 double, $195–$225 suite, $275 cottage. Deals: Room-and-car and other promotional packages regularly available (at press time, $135 double with car). Ask for AAA- and AARP-member discounts. Also check Internet:* www.holiday-inn.com *for Weekender, Great Rates, and other low rates (as low as $105 at press time). AE, CB, DC, DISC, ER, JCB, MC, V.*

Hyatt Regency Kauai Resort & Spa

$$$$$ Poipu Beach

I have one big complaint about this hotel: I never get to stay here. It's always too full of contented vacationers who adore the high plantation style, the easygoing vibe, the first-rate facilities (which include the sigh-inducing 25,000-foot Anara Spa, one of the best in the state), and the pleasingly sunny south shore location. One of Hawaii's best luxury hotels, the Hyatt is fabulous in an understated way; everyone feels comfortable here. The most distant guest rooms are a good five-minute hike from the lobby — but once you get there, you'll find oversized, elegant rooms with tropical accents, luxurious marble baths, and spacious lanais (most with ocean views). Because the ocean is rough here, the hotel offers a fantasy mega-pool complex, plus five acres of swimming lagoons with islands and a man-made beach. The restaurants are elegant and satisfying (particularly award-winning Dondero's for Italian), and the kids' and guest activity programs are terrific. You won't want for anything here. Needless to say, book well ahead.

1571 Poipu Rd., Koloa. ☎ *800-55-HYATT or 808-742-1234. Fax: 808-742-1557. Internet:* www.kauai-hyatt.com *or* www.hyatt.com. *Valet parking: $5 (free selfparking). Rack rates: $335–$565 double, $825–$3,100 suite. Deals: Multiple packages almost always on offer; ask about sixth night free, romance packages, customizable Hyatt Vacations packages (which can often include tee times, spa treatments, luaus, and more), Sunshine on Sale, and other special deals. AE, CB, DC, DISC, JCB, MC, V.*

Kauai Marriott Resort & Beach Club

$$$$ Lihue

This expansive resort manages to be big and splashy without going over the top — there's an air of fantasy about the place, but it's grounded in reality. Water is one of its finest features: lagoons, waterfalls, and fountains are featured throughout; the five-acre pool is the largest on the island; and the resort fronts a picture-perfect stretch of beach. The rooms are characterless but comfortable. Great golf is nearby at the world-class Kauai Lagoons courses (see Chapter 22). You can't be more centrally located — in fact, Lihue Airport may be just a tad too close. Facilities abound, including a branch of Duke's Canoe Club with a killer beachfront setting. All in all, this is a fine choice if you can't get into the Hyatt or the Sheraton, or if Princeville is just too pricey for you.

3610 Rice St. (on Kalapaki Beach, near Nawilwili Harbor), Lihue. ☎ *800-228-9290 or 808-245-5050. Fax: 808-245-5049. Internet:* www.marriott.com. *Valet parking: $7 (free self-parking). Rack rates: $270–$370 double, from $599 suite. Deals: Special promotions are almost always available; ask about romance, golf, breakfast, car, and other packages. AE, CB, DC, DISC, JCB, MC, V.*

Lae Nani

$$$ Coconut Coast

I just love this pleasant and unpretentious tropical condo complex. It's quiet, easygoing, and situated right on a wonderful stretch of beach. The individually decorated one- and two-bedroom apartments are comfortable and spacious, with large living rooms, adjacent dining areas, complete kitchens, cooling ceiling fans, and well-furnished lanais. The two-bedroom/two-baths can easily accommodate six, as long as two don't mind sleeping in the living room; even my one-bedroom unit had a second bath. There's a pool, tennis courts, barbecues, and coin-op laundry on-site, and daily maid service makes it feel like real vacation. I was very pleased with Premier's great package deals and friendly meet-and-greet airport service, but Outrigger's units are just fine, too; your best bet is to check with both management companies and see where you get the best price.

*410 Papaloa Rd. (next to the Coconut Marketplace), Kapaa. **Premier Resorts:** ☎ 800-367-7052. Fax: 808-822-1022. Internet:* www.premier-kauai.com. *Parking: Free! Rack rates: $195–$250 1-bedroom, $230–$305 2-bedroom. Deals: Specials usually on offer; rates as low as $130 at press time. AE, MC, V. **Outrigger Resorts:** ☎ 800-688-7444 or 808-822-4938. Fax 808-822-1022. Internet:* www.outrigger.com. *Parking: Free! Rack rates: $220–$270 1-bedroom, $240–$330 2-bedroom. Deals: Almost nobody pays rack with Outrigger, the king of package deals. Better-than-average discounts for AAA and AARP members and seniors (50-plus), plus corporate, government, and military discounts. First night free, bed-and-breakfast, room-and-car, and other packages regularly on offer. AE, CB, DC, DISC, JCB, MC, V.*

Nihi Kai Villas

$$–$$$ Poipu Beach

This beautifully maintained Mediterranean-style condo complex is just a block from the finest stretch of Poipu Beach and an excellent choice on all fronts. It's lovingly and meticulously run by Grantham Resorts, a Poipu-based company about whom I've heard nothing but praise, and the tropical-style apartments are gorgeous. Each boasts a full kitchen (with microwave), ceiling fans, washer/dryer, full cable (most have VCRs), lots of windows, and at least one lanai (usually two). Everything is top-notch, from the big, comfy furniture to the well-cushioned wool carpet underfoot. The grounds are well landscaped and quiet, boasting two tennis courts, paddleball, barbecues, and two nice pools.

1870 Hoone Rd., Poipu Beach. ☎ 800-325-5701, 800-742-1412, or 808-742-2000. Fax: 808-742-9093. Internet: www.grantham-resorts.com. *Parking: Free! Rack rates: $149–$169 1-bedroom, $139–$225 2-bedroom, $275–$300 3-bedroom. Ask about minimum-stay requirements (usually 5 nights). Deals: Discounts on car rentals available. DC, DISC, MC, V.*

In addition to the highly recommendable Nihi Kai Villas and the more budget-oriented Waikomo Stream Villas (later in this chapter), Grantham Resorts manages a wealth of other excellent condo properties in the Poipu Beach area, as well as full-scale vacation homes. For more information, see "Home Sweet Vacation Home" later in this chapter.

Outrigger Kiahuna Plantation

$$$ Poipu Beach

The only Poipu condos to sit right on the sand, this low-rise complex maintains an air of privacy and retro Hawaiian style. Two- and three-story plantation-style buildings pepper 35 spacious, gardenlike acres fronting a wonderful stretch of swimmable beach. The individually decorated one- and two-bedroom apartments feature full kitchens, daily maid service, VCR, and private lanais. Coin-op laundry, barbecues, and the terrific Piatti Italian restaurant (*buon gusto!*) are on site, while a first-class tennis center with pool and Poipu Shopping Village are just across the street. Rack rates are too high, but discounts abound.

2253 Poipu Rd., Poipu Beach. ☎ 800-688-7444 or 808-742-6411. Fax: 808-742-1698. Internet: www.outrigger.com. *Parking: Free! Rack rates: $199–$425 1-bedroom, $340–$480 2-bedroom. 2-night minimum. Deals: Almost nobody pays rack with Outrigger, the king of package deals. Better-than-average discounts for AAA and AARP members and seniors (50-plus), plus corporate, government, and military discounts. First night free, bed-and-breakfast, room-and-car, and other packages regularly on offer. AE, CB, DC, DISC, JCB, MC, V.*

Poipu Kapili Resort

$$$ Poipu Beach

This quiet, upscale cluster of condos is outstanding in every way but one: The ocean is across the street and the nearest sandy beach is a block away, even though the waves are right out your window. I like the home-away-from-home amenities and comforts in the very nice apartments, as well as the beautifully manicured grounds with an especially lovely pool, barbecues, tennis courts (lit for night play), and an herb garden (you're welcome to take samples to cook with). The tropical-style apartments are large (one-bedrooms are nearly 1,200 square feet, two-bedrooms a massive 1,820 square feet), and have full kitchens, ceiling fans, private lanais, VCRs, and CD players; the two-bedrooms also have washer/dryers (a coin-op laundry is on the grounds).

2221 Kapili Rd., Koloa. ☎ 800-443-7714 or 808-742-6449. Fax 808-742-9162. Internet: www.poipukapili.com. *Parking: Free! Rack rates: $180–$260 1-bedroom, $245–$500 2-bedroom. Ask about minimum-stay requirement (usually 5 nights mid-Dec–April). Higher rates may apply in holiday season. Deals: Seventh night free May–mid-December. Discounts for longer stays in high season. Ask about car-and-condo, adventure, honeymoon and anniversary, senior, and other packages. MC, V.*

Princeville Resort Kauai

$$$$$ North Shore

Thankfully, the Big '80s marble-and-chandelier decor that was all wrong for Hawaii has given way to a more subdued natural-colors-and-fibers palette that's much more at home in the islands — and with such comfortably elegant new decor, the always-fabulous Princeville graduates to nearly faultless. The north shore setting is breathtaking, and the tiered hotel steps down the cliffs above Hanalei Bay to take spectacular advantage of the views. Each sizable room is outfitted with original art, oversized windows (no lanais, though), bedside control panels for everything, and a "magic" shower window that you can switch in an instant from opaque to clear, allowing you to take in those awesome views even as you shampoo. It offers world-class golf (the Prince Course was named best in Hawaii by *Golf Digest* in 1999 and 2000), a first-rate spa and fitness center, a kids' program, a resort shuttle, first-rate dining, and a wonderful reef for snorkeling. Needless to say, you'll want for nothing here.

5520 Ka Haku Rd., Princeville. ☎ 800-325-3589 or 808-826-9644. Fax: 808-826-1166. Internet: www.princeville.com *or* www.luxurycollection.com. *Parking: $12. Rack rates: $380–$535 double, $625–$3,600 suite. Deals: Package deals are usually available, so be sure to ask. Also ask for AAA-member and senior discounts. AE, DC, DISC, JCB, MC, V.*

Sheraton Kauai Resort

$$$$ Poipu Beach

This very nice Sheraton is an excellent choice for visitors who like the advantages a resort hotel can offer, but don't care for the forced formality that often goes along with it. The resort brims with aloha sprit and an easygoing style that's reminiscent of old Hawaii. You'll have a choice of three buildings: one nestled in tropical gardens with koi-filled ponds; one facing a fabulous stretch of palm-fringed, white-sand beach (my favorite, of course); and one ocean-facing wing that boasts great sunset views. Whichever you choose, you'll get a spacious, comfortably decorated room; most in the Ocean Wing have a sofabed, making them suitable for small families. Amenities include an oceanfront pool, a kids' pool, and Jacuzzi; a fitness center; tennis courts; a handful of restaurants (kids 12 and under eat free with paying grown-ups in Shells, the signature restaurant); and a glass-walled lounge that's lovely at sunset.

2440 Hoonani Rd., Poipu Beach. ☎ 800-782-9488 or 808-742-1661. Fax: 808-742-4041. Internet: www.sheraton-kauai.com or www.sheraton.com. Valet parking: $5; self parking included in $10-per-night "resort fee", which also includes continental breakfast, mai tai hour, free local and toll-free calls, and unlimited use of fitness center. Rack rates: $285–$485 double, $575–$850 suite. Deals: Promotional rates and/or package deals are almost always available, so be sure to ask. Also ask for AAA-member and senior discounts. AE, CB, DC, DISC, ER, JCB, MC, V.

Sugar Mill Cottages

$–$$ Poipu Beach

These nine new studio apartments are my favorite Kauai bargains. Chet and Tish Hunt built this simple plantation-style complex on a pleasant residential parcel just a five-minute stroll from Brennecke's Beach, everybody's favorite stretch of Poipu sand. Each spanking-new studio for two boasts pretty textiles, cooling slate floors, an attractive bath (shower only), a kitchenette with all the tools to prepare a full meal, dining table, and TV and VCR. Three have phones (the others share), so request one when you book if you want it. Also request the kitchen that's right for you, as they vary from petite to nearly full-size. Every three units share a free laundry room, and each unit has its own beach cooler, towels, chairs, mats, and toys, plus access to a swimming pool and tennis. This is an excellent place to stay, but with no on-site manager, the cottages are best for independent types.

2391 Hoohu Rd. (at Pe'e Road), Poipu Kai. ☎ 877-742-9369 or 808-742-9369. Fax: 818-742-6432. Internet: www.accommodationspoipu.com. Parking: Free! Rack rates: $75–$85 double. AE, DC, DISC, MC, V.

Waikomo Stream Villas

$$ Poipu Beach

Here's another excellent deal — this one perfect for families, or anyone hoping for all the comforts of home at bargain-basement prices. These huge, well-managed, and attractive one- and two-bedroom apartments have everything you could possibly need — fully equipped kitchen, VCR, CD player, ceiling fans, sofabed, washer/dryer, and private lanai, plus a second bath and cathedral ceilings in the two-bedrooms — at *very* affordable prices. The beautifully landscaped complex boasts both adults' and kids' pools, tennis courts, and a barbecue area; right next door is the Robert Trent Jones–designed Kiahuna Golf Course, so pack your irons and woods. The beach is a five- to seven-minute walk away — a worthy sacrifice for the kind of savings you'll realize here. Value-conscious travelers who need their space can't do better for the dough.

2721 Poipu Rd., Poipu Beach. ☎ *800-325-5701, 800-742-1412, or 808-742-2000. Fax: 808-742-9093. Internet:* www.grantham-resorts.com. *Parking: Free! Rack rates: $99–$129 1-bedroom, $119–$149 2-bedroom. 3-night minimum. Ask about minimum-stay requirements (usually 5 nights). Deals: Inquire about "value" units, which book for as little as $85. Discounts on car rentals available. DC, DISC, MC, V.*

Wailua Bay View

$$ Coconut Coast

These one-bedroom, one-bath apartments on the beach aren't fancy, but they offer good value if your budget is tight. Every one has at least a partial ocean view, plus a complete kitchen (with microwave and dishwasher), ceiling fans, washer/dryer, TV with VCR, air-conditioning in the bedroom, and a large lanai. A sleeper sofa in the living room makes each unit spacious enough for a budget-minded family of four who don't mind sharing. Facilities include a small pool and barbecues. Apartments closest to the road can be noisy, so book oceanview for maximum quiet. It's not my first choice (I'd go with Waikomo, directly preceding, first), but it's a good bet if you want cheap.

320 Papaloa Rd., Kapaa. ☎ *800-882-9007 or 808-823-0112. Fax: 425-391-9121. Internet:* www.wailuabay.com. *Parking: Free! Rack rates: $99–$110 double. $70 cleaning fee charged for stays of less than 5 nights. Deals: Seventh night free Apr 15–Dec 15. Discounted monthly rates available. MC, V.*

Waimea Plantation Cottages

$$$ Waimea

Choose one of these historic 1930s plantation workers' cottages, set among a beachfront grove of coconut palms in perpetually sunny Waimea, and you'll feel as if you've stepped back to an island time when the living was easy. These beautifully restored bungalows are authentically outfitted with tropical-style furniture and fabrics; each has a furnished lanai, ceiling fans, a full kitchen, and oodles of period charm. On-site is a pool, coin-op laundry, and a nice restaurant, the Waimea Brewing Company. The only down sides are the black-sand beach, which is lovely but not swimmable, and the remote location. Still, it's a real retro delight — and an ideal place to get away from it all. One of my all-time Hawaii favorites.

9400 Kaumualii Hwy., Waimea. ☎ *800-992-7866 or 808-338-1625. Fax: 808-338-2338. Internet:* www.aston-hotels.com. *Parking: Free! Rack rates: $160–$220 1-bedroom, $210–$280 2-bedroom, $245–$310 3-bedroom; inquire about pricing on*

4- and 5-bedroom houses. Deals: Excellent opportunities for discounts. Internet-only ePriceBreaker rates can result in savings of up to 45%. Ask for AAA, senior (50-plus), and corporate discounts, and other special rate programs. Qualify for 25% discount if you stay at Aston properties for 7 or more nights with Aston's "Island Hopper" program. AE, CB, DC, DISC, JCB, MC, V.

Whaler's Cove

$$$$$ Poipu Beach

Condo living hardly gets better than this. The individually decorated apartments are pricey but worth the dough. They're elegant, oversized, and held to a high standard; each has a full modern kitchen, a large lanai, washer/dryer, and ceiling fans throughout; most have Jacuzzi tubs in the master bath. One of my favorites is no. 230, a two-bedroom duplex done in a beautiful Asian bamboo style. The contemporary and stylish complex was smartly designed to give each unit an ocean view. Hotel-like amenities include bell service, concierge, and daily housekeeping. A very nice oceanside pool is on-site, plus a hot tub and sauna. You'll have to drive to the beach, but there's good swimming (often with sea turtles) from a rocky cove.

2640 Puuholo Rd., Poipu Beach. ☎ 800-225-2683, 800-367-7052, or 808-742-7571. Fax: 808-742-1185. Internet: www.whalers-cove.com. Parking: Free! Rack rates: $310–$450 1-bedroom, $380–$550 2-bedroom. Deals: Ask about seventh night free, honeymoon, car-and-condo, and other package deals. AE, MC, V.

No Room at the Inn?

If you're a B&B fan and you want more options, contact **Hawaii's Best Bed & Breakfasts** (☎ 800-262-9912 or 808-885-4550; Internet: www.bestbnb.com), which can book a room for you in a Kauai inn that they have personally inspected and approved, as well as vacation rentals. Hawaii's Best holds all of the property owners they represent to a very high standard, so you can be assured of quality lodgings if you book with them.

Home Sweet Vacation Home

Kauai has lots of fabulous apartments, condos, and full homes that are rentable by the day, the week, or the month, and many are just steps from the ocean. Vacation rentals can be a fabulous deal; they often cost no more than your average resort room, but you get a whole house for your money, brimming with conveniences and privacy; sometimes, they're even cheaper, especially once you factor in the extra bucks you inevitably hand out at resorts for room service, poolside cocktails, and the like. Vacation rentals are also the only available option if you want to base yourself in the north shore's most appealing residential communities, such as Anini Beach, Hanalei, or Haena.

I've had great luck renting through **Kauai Vacation Rentals** (☎ 800-367-5025 or 808-245-8841; Internet: www.kauaivacationrentals.com), which handles top-quality vacation rentals all over the Garden Isle. They have a particularly fab selection on the lush north shore; renting a home on this quiet coast is a great way to enjoy the area's awesome nature, especially for those who favor being on their own over the sometimes smothering atmosphere of a big resort. KVR has something for everybody; prices start at $650 a week for a cozy cottage for two ($475 for a studio condo) and reach into the thousands for luxurious multibedroom beachfront homes. You can check out the complete list of options on their extensive Web site, many with links to lengthy descriptions and photos. One of my favorites is the ultracharming Ursula Taylor home, a modern two-bedroom done in traditional plantation style; it's perfectly located, just across the street from idyllic Hanalei Bay and a walk from charming Hanalei town, and goes for as little as $1,200 a week.

Another agency that represents an extensive collection of north shore vacation rentals is **Hanalei North Shore Properties** (☎ 800-488-3336 or 808-826-9622; Internet: www.planet-hawaii.com/visit-kauai).

For the best deal on the sunny Poipu Beach area, either on a condo or a full-on vacation home, don't hesitate for a moment: Pick up the phone and call **Grantham Resorts** (☎ 800-325-5701, 800-742-1412, or 808-742-2000; Internet: www.grantham-resorts.com). In addition to managing the front desks and the majority of the units at Nihi Kai Villas and Waikomo Stream Villas (see "Kauai's Best Hotels, Condos, and B&Bs" earlier in this chapter), Grantham handles Poipu-area rental units in eight other condo developments as well as 20 (and counting) Poipu-area vacation homes (including some beachfront ones that turned me pea-green with vacation envy on my visit to Poipu). Owner Nancy Grantham sets exacting standards for all of her rentals, and she offers extremely fair prices. When you rent a Grantham apartment or home, you know you're getting high quality and top value for your dollar; you can't go wrong with them. You can peruse their full list of properties on their extensive Web site. Additionally, they can book car rentals at preferred rates.

Gloria Merkle, the innkeeper behind magical Gloria's Spouting Horn B&B (see "Kauai's Best Hotels, Condos, and B&Bs" earlier in this chapter), also offers vacation-rental cottages, condos, and homes around the island through **Makai Properties** (☎ 808-742-6995 or 808-742-7561; Internet: www.makaiproperties.com). Also look into **Garden Island Rentals,** which handles Kapaa Shore and other properties (www.kauaiproperties.com).

Also keep in mind that **Hawaii's Best Bed & Breakfasts** (see "No Room at the Inn?," directly preceding) represents some excellent vacation homes on Kauai.

Chapter 20

Settling in on Kauai

● ●

In This Chapter

▶ Landing at Lihue Airport and getting to your resort hotel, condo, or B&B

▶ Learning your way around the island of Kauai

▶ Getting weather reports, prescriptions filled, traveler's checks cashed, and more — an easy-reference list of important local contacts

● ●

Kauai is an easygoing, and easily manageable, island. You will need a rental car to get around, so plan on booking one before you arrive (see "Arranging for Rental Cars" in Chapter 6). No matter where you're coming from, you'll arrive at Kauai's Lihue (li-HOO-ay) Airport.

Arriving at Lihue Airport

Lihue Airport (☎ 808-246-1440) sits on Kauai's east shore just north of Lihue town, at the end of Ahukini Road (east of Kuhio Highway). Lihue is served by three airlines: **United Airlines** from the mainland, and **Aloha Airlines** and **Hawaiian Airlines** with interisland service.

Open-air Lihue Airport is very small and easy to negotiate; the baggage claim is just a short walk from the gate. After collecting your bags from one of the two automated carousels, step outside and either walk across the street to pick up your rental car (most companies — including Hertz, Avis, and National — have their desks and lots on-site), or head to the well-marked curbside rental car pickup area to wait for the appropriate rental agency shuttle van (**Alamo** is among the rental companies with off-site lots).

All of the rental-car agencies offer map booklets at the rental counter, which are invaluable for getting around the island. If they don't offer one up, ask.

Kauai Orientation

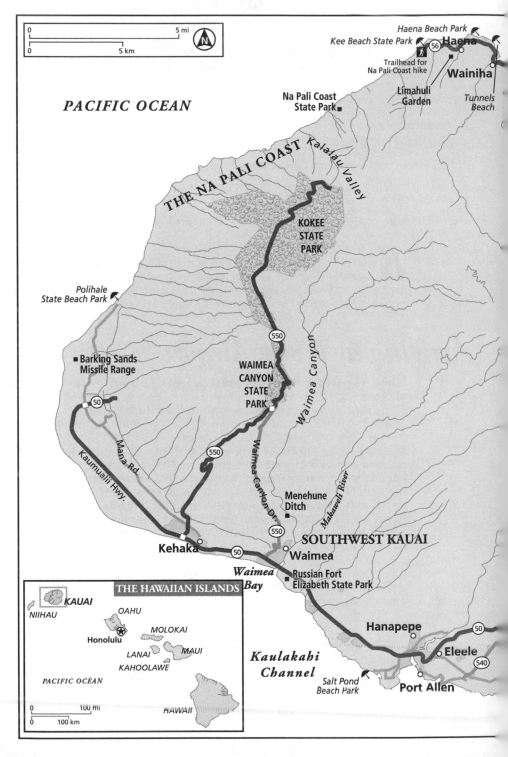

0 ___ 5 mi
0 ___ 5 km

PACIFIC OCEAN

Haena Beach Park
Kee Beach State Park
Trailhead for
Na Pali Coast hike
Limahuli
Garden

56 Haena
Wainiha
Tunnels
Beach

Na Pali Coast
State Park

THE NA PALI COAST   Kalalau Valley

KOKEE
STATE
PARK

Polihale
State Beach Park

550

WAIMEA
CANYON
STATE
PARK

Waimea Canyon

Barking Sands
Missile Range

50

Mana Rd.

550

Waimea Canyon Dr.

Makaweli River

Kaumualii Hwy.

Menehune
Ditch

550

SOUTHWEST KAUAI

Kehaka

50

Waimea

Waimea
Bay

Russian Fort
Elizabeth State Park

Hanapepe

50

Eleele

540

Kaulakahi
Channel

Salt Pond
Beach Park

Port Allen

THE HAWAIIAN ISLANDS

KAUAI
NIIHAU
OAHU
MOLOKAI
Honolulu
LANAI   MAUI
KAHOOLAWE
PACIFIC OCEAN

HAWAII

0 ___ 100 mi
0 ___ 100 km

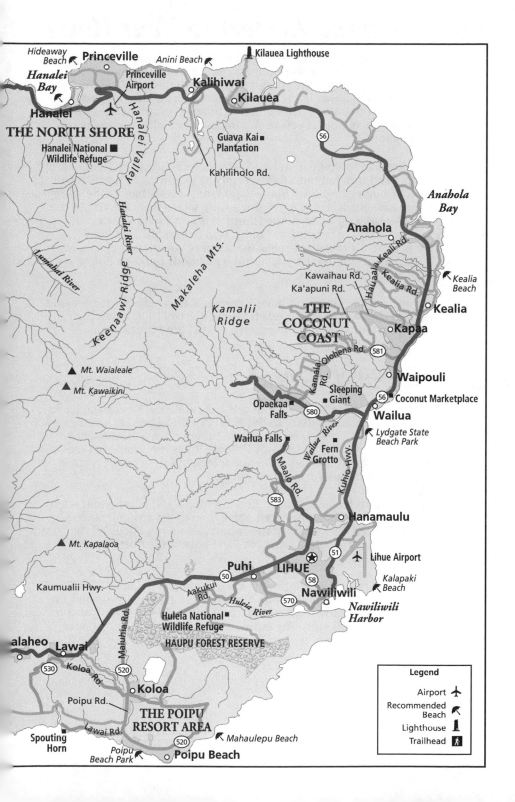

Hideaway Beach 🏖 **Princeville**

Hanalei Bay

Anini Beach 🏖

Princeville Airport

Kalihiwai

🗼 **Kilauea Lighthouse**

Hanalei

THE NORTH SHORE

Hanalei National ■ Wildlife Refuge

Hanalei Valley

Hanalei River

Kilauea

Guava Kai ■ Plantation

Kahiliholo Rd.

56

Lumahai River

Keenaawi Ridge

Makaleha Mts.

Anahola Bay

Anahola

Kawaihau Rd.
Ka'apuni Rd.

Hauaala Keali Rd.

Kealia Rd.

🏖 *Kealia Beach*

Kamalii Ridge

THE COCONUT COAST

Kealia

Kapaa

▲ *Mt. Waialeale*

▲ *Mt. Kawaikini*

Opaekaa Falls ■

580

Kamala Rd.

Olohena Rd.

581

Waipouli

Sleeping
● Giant

56 □ Coconut Marketplace

Wailua

Wailua Falls ■

Wailua River

Fern
■ Grotto

🏖 *Lydgate State Beach Park*

Maalo Rd.

Kuhio Hwy.

583

Hanamaulu

▲ *Mt. Kapalaoa*

51

✈ *Lihue Airport*

Puhi

50

⭐ **LIHUE**

58

Kalapaki
🏖 *Beach*

Aakukui Rd.

570 **Nawiliwili**

Kaumualii Hwy.

Huleia River

Nawiliwili Harbor

Huleia National ■ Wildlife Refuge

HAUPU FOREST RESERVE

Maluhia Rd.

alaheo **Lawai**

530

Koloa Rd.

520

Koloa

Poipu Rd.

THE POIPU RESORT AREA

Lawai Rd.

520

Spouting Horn ■

🏖 *Mahaulepu Beach*

Poipu Beach Park 🏖

Poipu Beach

Legend

✈ Airport

🏖 Recommended Beach

🗼 Lighthouse

🚶 Trailhead

Getting from the Airport to Your Hotel

If you're heading to the Coconut Coast or the north shore, turn right immediately out of the airport onto Kapule Highway (Highway 51), which eventually merges into Kuhio Highway (Highway 56) a mile down the road. Kuhio Highway leads to the Coconut Coast and the north shore. Expect it to take 10 to 15 minutes to reach your Coconut Coast base, and about an hour if you're staying in Princeville or Hanalei on the north shore.

If you're heading to Poipu Beach or Waimea, follow Ahukini Road out of the airport and turn left onto Kuhio Highway (Highway 56), which will take you through Lihue. Stay in the right lane; in less than a mile, merge right onto Kaumualii Highway (Highway 50), which will take you to the south and southwest areas of the island. It doesn't follow the coast, however, so if you're heading to Poipu, turn left on Maluhia Road (Highway 520); it's about ten miles from where you picked up Highway 50. You can expect it to take you about a half-hour to reach Poipu; it's 45 minutes or so to Waimea.

If, for some reason, you don't have a car, taxis are available at curbside. Expect it to cost $30 to $35 to reach Poipu, $12 to $18 to reach the Coconut Coast, or $60 to $80 to reach a north shore destination.

Getting around Kauai

You pretty much have to drive yourself around Kauai. The island has a public transportation system, **Kauai Bus** (☎ **808-241-6410;** Internet: www.kauaigov.org/kauaibus.htm), but it operates a minimal fleet and is geared to serving locals, not visitors. Taxis are available (see "Quick Concierge" at the end of this chapter), but they're not really a viable means for regular transport, either.

Kauai is a compact island — only 25 miles long by 33 miles wide — and easy to negotiate. Still, it does take some time to get around, since no roads cut through the middle of the island and no road goes all the way around, thanks to the unpassable Na Pali Coast at the northwest corner of the island.

The island has two major highways, each beginning in Lihue, Kauai's biggest town and commercial hub. They each run basically around the perimeter of the island — one north, one south — dead-ending at the Na Pali Coast on each side. The entire drive, from end to end, would take about three hours.

The two major highways are:

✔ **Kuhio Highway** (Highway 56), which follows the coast north from Lihue, leading through the Coconut Coast communities of Wailua, Waipouli, and Kapaa (ka-PA-ah) to the north shore, where it passes by charming Kilauea (turn off at the Shell Station, where the sign says "KILAUEA LIGHTHOUSE," if you'd like to explore) and, five miles beyond, the carefully manicured Princeville resort. Then — 31 miles, and about an hour's drive, beyond Lihue — Kuhio Highway runs directly through Hanalei, probably my favorite little town in all of Hawaii, and Haena, less a town than a collection of homes and vacation rentals tucked away in the tropical brush, before dead-ending at Kee (KEH-eh) Beach, where the Na Pali Coast begins.

✔ **Kaumualii** (cow-moo-a-LEE-ee) **Highway** (Highway 50) heads from Lihue south, passing through the undistinguished towns of Kalaheo (ka-la-HAY-oh) and Hanapepe (ha-na-PAY-pay) before reaching the little cowboy town of Waimea (where you can pick up the road that climbs inward and upward to Waimea Canyon; see Chapter 22 for details); at this point, you will have traveled 23 miles, or about 45 minutes, west of Lihue. After Waimea, the road curves north again before winding up in the far west at Polihale (po-lee-HA-lay) Beach, dead-ending at the other side of the Na Pali Coast.

Highway 50 doesn't hug the coast like its northern counterpart — it runs roughly four miles inland until Hanapepe — so Maluhia Road (Highway 520) cuts south to reach Poipu (po-EE-poo) Beach, Kauai's most popular resort, about 10 miles west of Lihue.

Kauai doesn't have what you'd call traffic, especially compared with places like Los Angeles (or even Honolulu, for that matter). Still, since the main highways only have one lane traveling in each direction, traffic can bottleneck in certain spots, especially along the Coconut Coast, largely from drivers turning in and out of the mini-malls and shops that line that stretch of highway.

What's more, the roads are curvy (especially once you start heading toward the north shore), and the speed limit doesn't top 50 mph anywhere on the island. Thus, don't let the short distances quoted fool you; it *will* take a full hour to reach the north shore from Lihue, and 20 minutes or so longer if you're traveling the additional eight miles beyond Hanalei. Allow 1½ hours to reach Hanalei from Poipu.

Quick Concierge

American Express

Sorry, there's no branch office on Kauai; be sure to do your business while you're on one of the other islands.

Baby-Sitters & Baby Stuff

Any hotel, and most condo management offices, should also be able to refer you to a reliable baby-sitter with a proven track record. **Baby's Away** (☎ 800-996-9030; Internet: www.babysaway.com) rents cribs, strollers, highchairs, playpens, infant seats, and the like; they'll deliver whatever you need to wherever you're staying, and pick it up when you're done.

Doctors

Walk-ins are accepted at the **Kauai Medical Clinic**, 3420-B Kuhio Hwy. (next to Wilcox Hospital; see "Hospitals"), Lihue (☎ 808-245-1500). On the north shore, head to **Hale Le'a Family Medicine**, on Oka Street (turn right off Kilauea Lighthouse Road), Kilauea (☎ 808-828-1418). You can also contact **Physicians Exchange** for a recommendation at ☎ 808-245-1831.

Emergencies

Dial **911** from any phone, just like back home.

Hospitals

Wilcox Memorial Hospital, 3420 Kuhio Hwy., Lihue (☎ 808-245-1100; Internet: www.wilcoxhealth.org), has a 24-hour emergency room located at the north end of Lihue next to Wal-Mart.

Information

The **Kauai Visitors Bureau** is located at 4334 Rice St., Suite 101, Lihue, HI 96766 (☎ 800-262-1400 or 808/245-3971; Internet: www.kauaivisitorsbureau.org). Call before you leave home to order the free *Kauai Vacation Planner*, or check the Web site for lots of good information. You can also stop in while you're in town to pick up information, but chances are you won't have to; plenty of information is available right at Lihue Airport. Just meander over to the information kiosks while you're waiting for your baggage and pick up a copy of *This Week Kauai, 101 Things to Do on Kauai,* and other free tourist publications; they're packed with good area maps. If you forget, don't worry — they're available from magazine racks all over the island. The **Poipu Beach Resort Association** (☎ 888-744-0888 or 808-742-7444; Internet: www.poipu-beach.org) can send you a Poipu area vacation planner before you leave home or answer specific questions once you arrive.

Newspapers/Magazines

The daily island paper is *The Garden Island,* available online at www.kauaiworld.com. The *Kauai Beach Press* is a free biweekly, available around town, that focuses on arts, entertainment, and dining.

Pharmacies

Long's Drugs, Hawaii's biggest drugstore chain, has a branch in Lihue at 3-2600 Kaumualii Hwy. (☎ 808-245-7771), as well as one on the Coconut Coast next to Safeway in the Kauai Village Shopping Center, 4-831 Kuhio Hwy., Kapaa (☎ 808-822-4915). There's also a pharmacy just north of downtown Lihue at **Wal-Mart**, 3-3300 Kuhio Hwy. (☎ 808-246-1599).

Police

Kauai's main headquarters is at 3060 Umi St. (at Rice Street) in downtown Lihue (☎ 808-241-6711). If you have an emergency, dial **911** from any phone.

Post Office

The main post office is at 4441 Rice St., Lihue (just off Kuhio Highway, near the Kauai Museum). Satellite post offices are all around the island; to find the branch nearest you, call ☎ 800-275-8777.

Taxes

Hawaii's sales tax is 4 percent. Expect taxes of about 11.42 percent to be added to your hotel bill.

Taxis

For islandwide service, call **Kauai Taxi Company** (☎ 808-246-9554) or **City Cab** (☎ 808-245-3227), both of which have six- and seven-passenger vans or limos available. For service in and around Princeville and Hanalei, call **North Shore Cab** (☎ 808-826-6189). For Poipu area service, dial up **Poipu Taxi** (☎ 808-639-2044). Always arrange for pickup *well* in advance.

Weather & Surf Reports

For current weather, call ☎ 808-245-6001. For marine conditions, call ☎ 808-245-3564.

Chapter 21

Dining on Kauai

● ●

In This Chapter

▶ Choosing among the Garden Island's top restaurants, with complete reviews and all the details

▶ Finding a luau when you're in the party mood

● ●

*T*he gorgeous Garden Isle has used its not-so-subtle charms to woo some of Hawaii's top chefs over to its shores, so prepare to dine well. For reasons that escape me, Kauai has an excess of quality Italian and great burgers — not that I'm complaining, mind you. But your options aren't limited there. Whether you're looking for a romantic candlelit dinner, quality seafood in an oceanfront setting, or just a great island-style burger, great choices abound.

Kauai's Best Restaurants

In the following restaurant listings, you'll see that each restaurant review is followed by a number of dollar signs, ranging from one ($) to five ($$$$$). The dollar signs are meant to give you an idea of what a complete dinner for one person — including appetizer, main course, one drink, tax, and tip — is likely to set you back. The price categories go like this:

$	Cheap eats — less than $15 per person
$$	Still inexpensive — $15 to $25
$$$	Moderate — $25 to $40
$$$$	Pricey — $40 to $70
$$$$$	Ultraexpensive — more than $70 per person

Of course, it all depends on how you order, so stay away from the surf and turf or the north end of the wine list if you're on a tight budget. To give you a further idea of how much you can expect to spend, I've also included the price range of main courses in the listings.

The state adds 4 percent in sales tax to every restaurant bill. A 15 to 20 percent tip is standard in Hawaii, just like back home.

Kauai's Best Restaurants

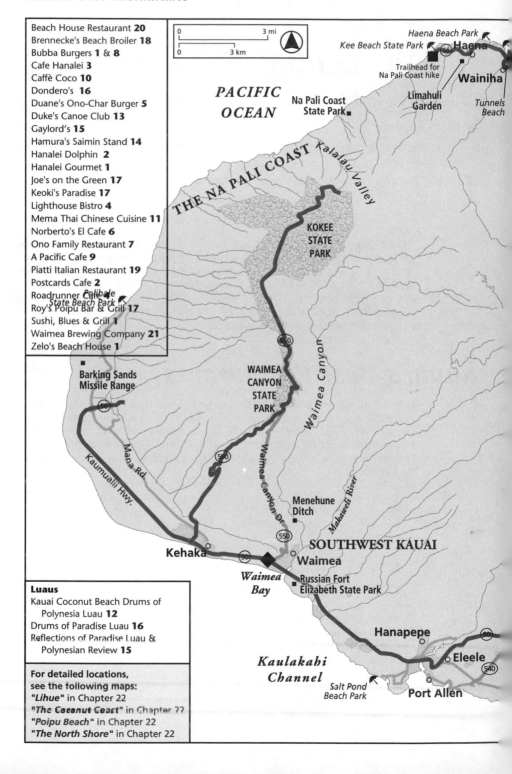

Beach House Restaurant **20**
Brennecke's Beach Broiler **18**
Bubba Burgers **1** & **8**
Cafe Hanalei **3**
Caffè Coco **10**
Dondero's **16**
Duane's Ono-Char Burger **5**
Duke's Canoe Club **13**
Gaylord's **15**
Hamura's Saimin Stand **14**
Hanalei Dolphin **2**
Hanalei Gourmet **1**
Joe's on the Green **17**
Keoki's Paradise **17**
Lighthouse Bistro **4**
Mema Thai Chinese Cuisine **11**
Norberto's El Cafe **6**
Ono Family Restaurant **7**
A Pacific Cafe **9**
Piatti Italian Restaurant **19**
Postcards Cafe **2**
Roadrunner Cafe **8**
Roy's Poipu Bar & Grill **17**
Sushi, Blues & Grill **1**
Waimea Brewing Company **21**
Zelo's Beach House **1**

Luaus
Kauai Coconut Beach Drums of
    Polynesia Luau **12**
Drums of Paradise Luau **16**
Reflections of Paradise Luau &
    Polynesian Review **15**

**For detailed locations,
see the following maps:**
"Lihue" in Chapter 22
"The Coconut Coast" in Chapter 22
"Poipu Beach" in Chapter 22
"The North Shore" in Chapter 22

PACIFIC
OCEAN

Haena Beach Park
Kee Beach State Park
Trailhead for
Na Pali Coast hike
Haena
Wainiha
Limahuli
Garden
Tunnels
Beach

Na Pali Coast
State Park

THE NA PALI COAST Kalalau Valley

KOKEE
STATE
PARK

550

Waimea Canyon

WAIMEA
CANYON
STATE
PARK

Waimea Canyon Dr.

Barking Sands
Missile Range

50

Mana Rd.

Kaumualii Hwy.

550

Menehune
Ditch

Makaweli River

550

SOUTHWEST KAUAI

Kehaka

50

Waimea

Waimea
Bay

Russian Fort
Elizabeth State Park

Kaulakahi
Channel

Salt Pond
Beach Park

Hanapepe

Eleele

540

Port Allen

0   3 mi
0   3 km

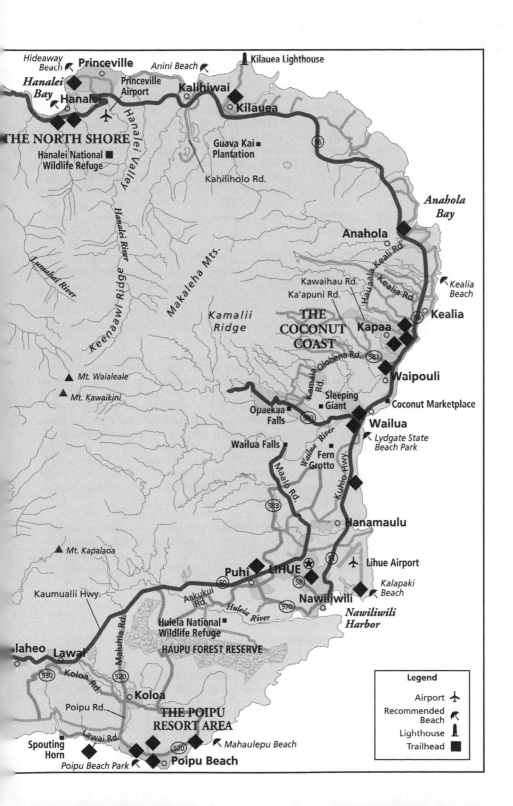

Hideaway Beach · **Princeville** · Anini Beach · Kilauea Lighthouse
Hanalei Bay · **Hanalei** · Princeville Airport · **Kalihiwai** · **Kilauea**
THE NORTH SHORE
Hanalei National Wildlife Refuge
Guava Kai Plantation
Kahiliholo Rd.
Hanalei Valley · *Hanalei River*
Lumahai River
Keenaawi Ridge
Makaleha Mts.
Anahola Bay
Anahola
Kawaihau Rd.
Ka'apuni Rd.
Kealia Beach
Kamalii Ridge
THE COCONUT COAST · **Kapaa** · **Kealia**
Olohena Rd.
▲ Mt. Waialeale
▲ Mt. Kawaikini
Sleeping Giant
Opaekaa Falls
Waipouli
Coconut Marketplace
Wailua
Lydgate State Beach Park
Wailua Falls
Wailua River
Fern Grotto
Kuhio Hwy.
Maalo Rd.
Hanamaulu
▲ Mt. Kapalaoa
Puhi · **LIHUE**
Lihue Airport
Kalapaki Beach
Kaumualii Hwy.
Aakukui Rd.
Huleia River
Nawiliwili
Nawiliwili Harbor
Huleia National Wildlife Refuge
HAUPU FOREST RESERVE
Maluhia Rd.
Lawai · **laheo**
Koloa Rd.
Koloa
Poipu Rd.
THE POIPU RESORT AREA
Lawai Rd.
Spouting Horn
Mahaulepu Beach
Poipu Beach Park · **Poipu Beach**

Legend
Airport ✈
Recommended Beach
Lighthouse
Trailhead ◼

Beach House Restaurant

$$$$ Poipu Beach   Regional

The open-air, on-the-ocean setting makes this my favorite special-occasion restaurant in Hawaii. The long, Japanese-style room is lined with shoji-like windows that make sunset a celebration every night and let in a symphony of surf after dark. The first-rate food lives up to the setting in every way. Even though star chef Jean-Marie Josselin (of A Pacific Cafe fame; see the listing later in this chapter) isn't involved anymore, his longtime first-in-command, Linda Yamada, oversees a kitchen excelling in creative island dishes that bring out the best in land and sea, from fresh-caught fish and island-raised beef to locally harvested organic greens and salt. The menu changes nightly, but count on such winners as macadamia nut–crusted mahimahi in citrus miso sauce, or mint-coriander marinated rack of lamb roasted with a goat cheese–garlic crust — yum! Excellent cocktail menu, too.

5022 Lawai Rd. (off Poipu Road, toward Spouting Horn), Koloa. ☎ *808-742-1424. Internet:* www.the-beach-house.com. *Reservations highly recommended. Main courses: $22–$28. AE, DC, DISC, MC, V. Open: Dinner nightly.*

Brennecke's Beach Broiler

$$ Poipu Beach   American/Seafood

"Right on the Beach, Right on the Price." If you have kids in tow, skip the Beach House in favor of this fun, casual restaurant, which boasts ocean views galore. The fresh fish specials attract locals and visitors alike — always a good sign of consistent quality. Well-priced and well-prepared seafood and prime rib dinners (all of which include the creamy New England–style chowder or the appealing salad bar) are guaranteed to make mom and dad fans, while the best burgers in Poipu will keep the kids wanting to come back every night. This longtime favorite is so welcoming and laid-back that you can come in straight off the beach for baby-back ribs, *kiawe* (mesquite)-broiled seafood kebabs, or surprisingly good veggie selections. Great sunset mai tais, too.

2100 Hoone Rd. (across the street from Poipu Beach Park), Poipu Beach. ☎ *888-384-8810 or 808-742-7588. Internet:* www.brenneckes.com. *Reservations recommended for dinner. Lunch and light-bite menu (served all day): $8–$14. Early dinner specials (nightly 4–6 p.m.): $6.50–$19. Complete sunset dinners (nightly 4–10 p.m.): $16.50–$23. AE, CB, DC, DISC, MC, V. Open: Lunch and dinner daily.*

Bubba Burgers

$ Coconut Coast/North Shore   American

"Bubba refuses to serve any burger costing less than a can of dog food." "The food is hot, the service is cold, and the music's TOO DAMN LOUD." Quick wit — and commercial appeal — aside, Bubba serves up one mean hamburger. It's served on a toasted bun with mustard, relish, diced onions, and lots of attitude — and boy, is it yummy. Bubba burgers are plump and juicy, so have a pile of napkins ready and waiting. Chicken,

ginger-teriyaki tempeh, and fish burgers are also available, plus variations on the standard Bubba: the Slopper (served open-faced and smothered in Budweiser chili), the three-patty Big Bubba, and the Hubba Bubba
(with a scoop of rice *and* a hot dog, all smothered in chili and onions).
Come to Bubba for your burger fix — boy, you'll be glad you did!

The Coconut Coast: 4-1421 Kuhio Hwy., Kapaa. ☎ *808-823-0069. Internet:* www.
bubbaburger.com. *Open: Lunch and early dinner (to 8 p.m.). The North Shore:
On Kuhio Highway (across from the Ching Young Center), Hanalei.* ☎ *808-826-7839.
Open: Lunch and early dinner (to 6 p.m.). Burgers: $2.50–$6. MC, V.*

Cafe Hanalei

$$$$ North Shore   Eclectic

Most think of La Cascata as Princeville's premier special-occasion restaurant, but it's really Cafe Hanalei that satisfies the perfect Bali Hai mood.
A romantic indoor-outdoor setting, breathtaking Hanalei Bay and Na Pali
views, a marvelously modern seafood-rich menu with alternating Asian
and Mediterranean accents (including plenty to satisfy steak-lovers'
needs too), and first-rate service that just won't quit all add up to the
ideal dining experience. Book a table on the casually elegant terrace for
the ultimate dinner for two. Dine on Tuesday, Wednesday, Saturday, or
Sunday for an additional bonus: an à la carte sushi menu. Satisfying
through and through.

At Princeville Resort Kauai, 5520 Ka Haku Rd., Princeville. ☎ *800-325-3589 or
808-826-9644. Internet:* www.princeville.com. *Reservations highly recommended. Main courses: $20–$34. AE, DC, DISC, JCB, MC, V. Open: Breakfast, lunch,
and dinner daily.*

Caffè Coco

$$ Coconut Coast   Eclectic/International

The eclectic cafe-cum–art gallery is an equally charming spot for a muffin
and latte or low-budget romantic dinner with a bring-your-own bottle of
Merlot. The worldwise, everything-from-scratch cuisine is inventive and
wonderful, from the morning's breakfast burritos and omelets to fresh
fish and roast chicken specials served all day. The kitchen prepares all of
its own baked goods, juices, salsas, curries, and chutneys. Order at the
counter during the day, or sit down for a full-service dinner in the fra-
grant flower-and-fruit garden, under flickering tiki torches that set an idyl-
lic island mood. An excellent choice for vegetarians, but far from
exclusively so. Service is Hawaiian style, so dine elsewhere if you're in a
hurry (which you shouldn't be).

*4-369 Kuhio Hwy., next to Bambulei (on the inland side of the street, behind the
green storefront across from Kintaro Restaurant), Wailua (just south of the Coconut
Marketplace).* ☎ *808-822-7990. Reservations recommended for larger parties.
Main courses: $5–$8 at breakfast, $6–$17 at lunch and dinner. MC, V. Open:
Breakfast, lunch, and dinner Tues–Sun.*

Dondero's

$$$$ Poipu Beach Regional Italian

The menu changes seasonally at this super-elegant Italian restaurant, but you can always count on a practiced, beautifully prepared regional menu with an emphasis on the classics. Dishes are prepared with homegrown herbs picked fresh from the kitchen garden. The setting is sublime, whether you choose to dine indoors — in a beautiful marble-tiled setting reminiscent of Tuscany with exquisite Franciscan artwork — or on an outdoor patio that says "only in Hawaii." You'll pay too much — but who cares when the food, wine list, ambience, and service are this top-notch? A winner in the celebratory category.

At the Hyatt Regency Kauai Resort & Spa, 1571 Poipu Rd., Koloa. ☎ *808-742-6260. Reservations highly recommended. Main courses: $17–$32. AE, CB, DC, DISC, JCB, MC, V. Open: Dinner nightly.*

Duane's Ono-Char Burger

$ North Shore Burgers

Bubba (see the listing earlier in this chapter) would just cringe if I called him "establishment," but compared with Duane's, he's the Wal-Mart of Kauai burgers. Little more than a roadside stand with a few picnic tables and some resident wild chickens, Duane's sets the standard for island-style burgers. I dream about the Local Girl, a juicy patty topped with teriyaki, Swiss cheese, pineapple, mayo, and lettuce on a bun — a perfect packet of juicy goodness. Sublime fries, shakes, and floats round out the lunchtime experience. Stop by on the way to the north shore, or pick up a takeout beach lunch (Kealia Beach in Kapaa is just a few minutes' drive to the south).

4-4350 Kuhio Hwy. (next to Whaler's General Store, on the ocean side of the street), Anahola. ☎ *808-822-9181. Burgers: $4–$7. MC, V. Open: Lunch daily.*

Duke's Canoe Club

$/$$$ Lihue Steaks/Seafood (American/Hawaii Local in the Barefoot Bar)

The Kauai Duke's isn't as magical as the Waikiki branch, but it's appealing nonetheless. Thanks to a wide-ranging menu and a wonderful beach-front setting, this big, bustling, tropical restaurant is appealing to families and cuddly couples alike. The dependable menu has something for everyone, from fresh-caught fish prepared a half-dozen ways to finger-lickin'-good ribs dressed in mango barbecue sauce. Come for sunset if you can, and ask for a beachfront table when you reserve; the view over Kalapaki Beach is fabulous, but some of the tables miss out. The Barefoot Bar, which spills out onto the sand and boasts its own waterfall (fake, of course), is the island's best spot for tropical noshing at reasonable prices.

At the Kauai Marriott Resort & Beach Club, 3610 Rice St. (on Kalapaki Beach, near Nawilwili Harbor), Lihue. ☎ 808-246-9599. Internet: www.hulapie.com. Reservations recommended for dinner. Barefoot Bar menu (served all day): $6.50–$10. Main courses: $14–$22 at dinner (salad bar included). AE, DC, DISC, MC, V. Open: Lunch and dinner daily.

Gaylord's

$$$$ Lihue   Continental

The more contemporary Beach House (see the first listing) is my first choice in the romance category, but if you're in the mood for love and prefer to do your wooing in a classic Old Hawaii setting, step back in time at Gaylord's. One of Hawaii's loveliest restaurants is situated a few minutes inland from Lihue, in a 1930s manor home that's retro-romantic to the max — you can even take a Clydesdale-drawn carriage ride around the beautiful plantation-era estate before you dine. Choose from a menu of competently prepared but otherwise undistinguished continental classics with a Pacific flair; the slow-roasted baby-back ribs are a Gaylord's specialty. The deserts are appropriately rich, and the wine list is suitably pricey. Go for Sunday brunch to experience the special-occasion mood without the big price tag.

At Kilohana Plantation, Kaumualii Hwy. (Highway 50), 1 mile west of Lihue. ☎ 808-245-9593. Internet: www.gaylordskauai.com. Reservations recommended. Main courses: $8–$12 at lunch, $17–$28 at dinner, $9–$14 at Sunday brunch. AE, DISC, MC, V. Open: Lunch and dinner Mon–Sat, brunch and dinner Sun.

Hamura's Saimin Stand

$ Lihue   Local

I've eaten lots of memorable gourmet meals in Hawaii — but none make me yearn for repeat visits like this nondescript lunch counter does. Located on an industrial side street just off Lihue's main drag, Hamura's serves up Hawaii's best *saimin* (ramen-style noodle soup). Cozy up to one of the U-shaped counters and order off the posted menu. The *saimin* here comes in a variety of sizes and with a variety of extras, like veggies and hard-boiled egg. Other offerings include succulently broiled beef and chicken skewers (a steal at $1 a stick) and Chinese pretzels, which are like hard funnel cakes (I like to put them in my *saimin* — a cultural travesty, I'm sure). Don't be put off by the friendly but brisk service; you'll feel at home — and be done eating — in no time. This cultural adventure is a culinary marvel.

2956 Kress St. (1½ blocks off Rice Street; turn at the Aloha Furniture Warehouse), Lihue. ☎ 808-245-3271. Reservations not taken. Main courses: $1–$6. No credit cards. Open: Lunch and dinner daily.

Hanalei Dolphin

$$$ North Shore Seafood

Fresh-off-the-boat seafood and a nicely romantic tropical-garden setting on the banks of the Hanalei River make Hanalei Dolphin a very pleasing choice for cocktails and dinner. This isn't sophisticated fare; rather, it's refreshingly simple. Choose from a wide selection of the day's catches, which come charbroiled or Cajun-style, with salad and rice, pasta, or steak fries on the side. Alaskan king crab is always on hand, but why bother? Go with one of the stellar island catches, such as ruby-red ahi, moist and tender *onaga* (red snapper), or mackerel-like *ono* (wahoo). Starters include such retro classics as shrimp cocktail and stuffed mushroom caps, while sweet finishes include old-fashioned delights like strawberry cheesecake and ice-cream pie. Steak and chicken are available for nonfish eaters.

5-5016 Kuhio Hwy., Hanalei. ☎ *808-826-6113. Reservations not taken. Sandwiches and salads: $6–$8 at lunch. Complete dinners: $11.50–$28. MC, V. Open: Lunch and dinner daily.*

If you're staying in full-scale digs with your own kitchen, visit Hanalei Dolphin's adjacent **Hanalei Dolphin Fish Market** (☎ **808-826-6113**), where you can choose from a wide range of unprepared fresh catches to grill up back at your vacation rental. Barbecue-ready steaks are on hand, too. Open daily from 11 a.m. to 8 p.m.; look for the entrance to the market at the back of the building.

Hanalei Gourmet

$$ North Shore American

This unpretentious restaurant in the heart of Hanalei town is a great choice for an informal bite at any time of day. Breakfast standards and lunchtime burgers, sandwiches, and salads give way to dinner specialties like pan-fried Asian-style crab cakes, macadamia-nut fried chicken, and charbroiled pork chops (deliciously seasoned with locally harvested salt that has its own hearty, wonderfully distinct flavor). Service is super-friendly, and super-easygoing — but the north shore is not the place to be in a hurry, anyway. Choose a table on the veranda if the TV set over the bar interferes with your Hanalei reverie.

In the Old Hanalei School at Hanalei Center, 5-5161 Kuhio Hwy., Hanalei. ☎ *808-826-2524. Main courses: $5–$8 at lunch, $10.50–$22 at dinner. AE, DISC, MC, V. Open: Breakfast, lunch, and dinner daily.*

Joe's on the Green

$ Poipu Beach American

Facing the greens of the Kiahuna Gold Course, this patio restaurant is a lovely and relaxing place to start the day. The small but satisfying morning menu features first-rate huevos rancheros (with a terrific fresh-made salsa), fluffy banana–macadamia nut pancakes, and corned beef hash and scrambled eggs served in crisp potato skins — an anti-dieter's delight. Lunchtime brings bountiful salads of island-grown greens, and burgers, sandwiches, and the like. Clad in an Aloha shirt, Joe works this modest indoor-outdoor restaurant as if it were the main dining room at Caesar's Palace; it's not, but the food's well prepared, the setting is lovely, and the prices are low, low, low.

At the Kiahuna Golf Club, 2545 Kiahuna Plantation Rd. (turn inland from Poipu Road, next to the Poipu Shopping Village), Poipu Beach. ☎ 808-742-9696. Reservations not necessary except for Thursday dinner. Main courses: $5–$9 at breakfast, $6.50–$9 at lunch. MC, V. Open: Breakfast and lunch daily, dinner Thurs.

Keoki's Paradise

$/$$$ Poipu Beach Steaks/Seafood (American/Hawaii Local in the Cafe)

Keoki's offers loads of alfresco allure, with flickering tiki torches, aloha-friendly ambience and service, and live Hawaiian music on weekends. It isn't on the oceanfront like its sister restaurant, Duke's Canoe Club (see earlier in this chapter), but it boasts a similarly lively tropical vibe and a lengthy menu highlighted by top-quality fresh fish prepared at least a half-dozen ways. Plenty of carnivore-friendly options are on hand, too, plus a decadent Hula Pie to finish. All dinners come with Keoki's surprisingly good Caesar salad, which makes meals a very good deal. The bar-area cafe serves cheaper, more casual fare all day — including fish tacos, island-style ribs, and quesadillas — plus the requisite fruity cocktails.

In the Poipu Shopping Village, 2360 Kiahuna Plantation Dr. (at Poipu Road), Poipu Beach. ☎ 808-742-7534. Reservations recommended. Cafe menu: $5–$10. Main courses: $15–$24 at dinner (with salad). AE, MC, V. Open: Lunch and dinner daily (cafe menu served all day).

Lighthouse Bistro

$$–$$$ North Shore Mediterranean/Eclectic

My longstanding favorite in Kilauea is Roadrunner Cafe (see the listing later in this chapter). But if you're simply not in the mood for Mexican after communing with nature at the Kilauea Lighthouse — or after spending your loot next door at Kong Lung, Kauai's top shopping stop — this attractive restaurant is a relaxing lunchtime option. The menu is a tad generic — pastas, salads, island fish — so I was pleasantly surprised with the high quality and tastiness of the burrito-like ahi wrap. My fellow diners were equally pleased with selections that ranged from a bounteous Caesar salad to a fresh grilled mahi sandwich. A nice wine list is on hand at dinner.

In the Kong Lung Center, 2484 Keneke St., Kilauea. From Kuhio Highway, turn right at the sign for Kilauea Lighthouse (at Menehune Food Mart and gas station), then right onto Keneke Street. ☎ 808-828-0480. Reservations recommended at dinner. Main courses: $6.50–$9 at lunch, $11–$23 at dinner. MC, V Open: Lunch and dinner daily.

Mema Thai Chinese Cuisine

$$ Coconut Coast Thai/Chinese

Tucked away in a nondescript mini-mall, Mema is well worth seeking out thanks to a mammoth, culturally cross-bred menu and a dining room that's more appealing than most at this price level. The menu leans heavily toward the Thai classics, including a satisfyingly spicy lemongrass soup, a better-than-most Pad Thai, and coconut milk–rich curries that border on the sublime. Best is the house speciality: panang curry made with kaffir lime leaves, garlic, and other seasonings. Service is thoughtful, too, making Mema a winner with well-rounded appeal.

In the Kinipopo Shopping Village, 4-361 Kuhio Hwy. (just north of Haleilio Road on the mountain side of the street), Wailua. ☎ 808-823-0899. Reservations accepted. Main courses: $8–$18. AE, DC, DISC, MC, V. Open: Lunch and dinner Mon–Fri, dinner Sat–Sun.

Norberto's El Cafe

$–$$ Coconut Coast Mexican

This cool, dark Mexican restaurant marries fresh-grown island greens and fish with traditional south-of-the-border recipes, resulting in Mexican fare that's both top-quality and pleasingly authentic. Vegetarians and carnivores alike will enjoy the Hawaiian taro leaf enchiladas — corn tortillas stuffed with the spinach-like island staple, dressed in a zesty Spanish sauce, and baked to cheesy perfection. The rellenos are another excellent choice, and the crisp corn chips are accompanied by a fresh-made salsa that will make your taste buds sit up and take notice. Frankly, I haven't been disappointed with any of Norberto's eats. Service is attentive and friendly, and Mexican beers are on hand.

4-1373 Kuhio Hwy., downtown Kapaa. ☎ 808-822-3362. Reservations accepted. A la carte items and complete dinners: $3.25–$15.50. AE, MC, V. Open: Dinner Mon–Sat.

Ono Family Restaurant

$ Coconut Coast American/Local

Service isn't exactly what I'd call friendly at this colorfully rustic, local-style restaurant in the heart of Kapaa, but the hearty homestyle breakfasts make Ono's a fortifying place to launch a day of beachgoing or sightseeing. The coffee is strong, and the home cooking is indeed *ono* (Hawaiian for "delicious"). The menu features a full slate of fluffy omelets, pancakes, and other breakfast standards, including several variations on eggs Benedict, all of which come topped with a perfectly puckery hollandaise. Classic burgers and crispy fries are midday standouts.

4-1292 Kuhio Hwy. (on the ocean side of the street), downtown Kapaa. ☎ 808-822-1710. Main courses: $4.50–$7.50 at breakfast, $5.10–$8.20 at lunch. AE, DC, DISC, JCB, MC, V. Open: Breakfast and lunch daily.

A Pacific Cafe

$$$$ Coconut Coast   Hawaii Regional

Jean-Marie Josselin was one of the forces behind Hawaii's culinary revolution, and his first restaurant is still one of the state's finest showcases
of haute Hawaiian Regional cooking. Josselin may be a Frenchman, but
he's captured the island style perfectly. Tucked away in a Coconut Coast
shopping center, the pretty, unassuming room bustles with energy and
verve, just like Josselin's cooking. The menu changes daily, but expect a
bold fusion of Asian flavors and Mediterranean techniques, plus lots of
choices from the *kiawe* (mesquite)-fired grill. Don't miss such signature
dishes as light-as-air tiger-eye ahi tempura with soy wasabi and Chinese
mustard dipping sauces, and "firecracker" salmon on a Thai chile sauce
bed — a perfect marriage of hot and sweet. A sublime — and thoroughly
enjoyable — dining experience every time. Don't miss it if you can help it.

In the Kauai Village Shopping Center, 4-831 Kuhio Hwy., Kapaa. ☎ *808-822-0013.
Reservations highly recommended. Main courses: $22–$27; tasting menus $40–$50.
DC, DISC, MC, V. Open: Dinner nightly.*

Piatti Italian Restaurant

$$$ Poipu Beach   Italian-Mediterranean

If Dondero's (see the listing earlier in this chapter) is too pricey or formal
for your tastes, Piatti makes an excellent alternative. Housed in a former
plantation house, this lovely restaurant of gleaming woods and bamboo
is a bit too bright to be really called romantic; book a seat on the garden-
facing patio for maximum ambience. The top-notch Mediterranean-style
Italian fare is prepared with herbs and greens grown right out in the back
garden. Sauces and pestos are fresh and savory, risottos are appropri-
ately rich, and many of the pastas are homemade. You can keep the bill
down by sticking with the antipasti, pizzas, and pastas, or go all out on
lovingly prepared entrees like fork-tender filet mignon wrapped in pro-
sciutto, grilled, and elegantly presented in a red wine sauce.

*In the Kiahuna Plantation, 2253 Poipu Rd. (across from Poipu Shopping Village),
Poipu Beach.* ☎ *808-742-2216. Reservations recommended. Main courses:
$11–$27. AE, DC, MC, V. Open: Dinner nightly.*

Postcards Cafe

$$$ North Shore   International

This historic plantation house on the edge of Hanalei wears two hats: one
as a hugely popular vegetarian-minded breakfast place, the second as a
globe-hopping seafood restaurant. Choose a seat in the schoolhouse-
simple but exceedingly charming dining room, or out on the wide
veranda for alfresco dining. Morning choices include a well-blended
homemade granola and creative variations on scrambled eggs; don't be
surprised if you have to wait for a table. Dinnertime is when the creative
kitchen pulls out the pan-cultural stops, from yummy taro fritters topped
with tropical salsa to Indian-spiced potato-phyllo pockets (much like

samosas) to blackened fresh-caught fish in macadamia butter or peppered pineapple sage. I've always loved Postcards for its innovative yet unfussy preparations and the freshness of the local ingredients; the friendly service doesn't hurt either. No wine list, but you're welcome to BYOB for a minimal corkage fee.

5-5075A Kuhio Hwy., Hanalei. ☎ *808-826-1191. Reservations recommended for dinner. Main courses: $5–$13 at breakfast, $15–$23 at dinner. AE, DC, MC, V. Open: Breakfast and dinner daily.*

Roadrunner Cafe

$$ North Shore   Island-Style Mexican

This hole-in-the-wall spot is worth seeking out for its gourmet island take on traditional Mexican cuisine. The cross-pollinated dishes are prepared with fish plucked from Hawaiian waters, pork raised on the island, and produce grown in Kilauea soil. The divine salsa is just spicy enough to allow the flavors of the home-roasted tomatoes and fresh-cut cilantro to shine through; ditto for the fresh, chunky guacamole. Standouts include spit-roasted chicken enchiladas in a rich tomatillo sauce, fish tacos with delectable pineapple salsa, and perfectly battered chiles rellenos. The concrete-block room is more than a little rough, but hand-painted murals add color and friendly service brings out its rustic charm. No alcohol is served, but you can BYOB (the Menehune Mart, at Kuhio Highway and Kilauea Lighthouse Road, sells brewskis). Or just go for one of the light and refreshing agua frescas, blended from hand-picked island fruit.

2430 Oka St., Kilauea. From Kuhio Highway, turn right at the sign for Kilauea Lighthouse, then right onto Oka Street. ☎ *808-828-8226. Reservations accepted. Main courses and combo plates: $8–$14. MC, V. Open: Breakfast, lunch, and early dinner Mon–Sat (to 8 p.m., Sat to 8:30), breakfast and lunch Sun.*

Roy's Poipu Bar & Grill

$$$–$$$$ Poipu Beach   Hawaii Regional

More casual than the other Roy's throughout Hawaii, Roy's Poipu is my favorite of the famous chain. Star chef Roy Yamaguchi's take on Hawaii Regional cuisine is more overtly Asian than what you'll find at the Mediterranean-accented A Pacific Cafe (see the listing earlier in this chapter). Thanks to an extensive grazing menu of dim sum, appetizers, and imu-baked pizzas, it's easy to eat inexpensively here; my husband and I got no guff at all from the waitstaff for building a meal from the starter menu. Signature dishes include luscious Szechuan baby-back ribs (better than dessert!) and blackened ahi with a delectable soy mustard butter. The service is friendly and easygoing, in keeping with the ambience, and the wines bottled under Roy's own label are affordable and surprisingly good. In sum, a winner that lives up to its reputation in every way.

In the Poipu Shopping Village, 2360 Kiahuna Plantation Dr. (at Poipu Rd.), Poipu Beach. ☎ *808-742-5000. Internet:* www.roysrestaurant.com. *Reservations highly recommended. Appetizers and pizzas: $5–$10. Main courses: $16–$28. AE, CB, DC, DISC, MC, V. Open: Dinner nightly.*

Sushi, Blues & Grill

$$$ North Shore   Japanese/Island Eclectic

The name may be awkward, but neither raw fish nor live entertainment gets any better on Kauai than at this loftlike second-floor restaurant and sushi bar. Sushi and Blues (as it's commonly called) features a first-rate sushi chef who's a master with ultra-fresh fish, much of it caught in island waters or flown in from Japan; a big bar with an extensive vodka, gin, martini, sake, and beer list; a kitchen that prepares very good island-style seafood and steaks for sushi-phobes; and gorgeous Bali Hai views. The restaurant hosts live jazz and blues or dance music three or four nights a week; call for the schedule. It's very chic for Kauai (in fact, this spot wouldn't be out of place in L.A. or Manhattan), but feel free to come in your shorts and Ts — everybody does.

In Ching Young Village, 5-8420 Kuhio Hwy., Hanalei. ☎ *808-826-9701. Reservations recommended. Sushi combos and main courses: $15–$23. MC, V. Open: Dinner nightly.*

Waimea Brewing Company

$$ Waimea Island   Eclectic

This terrific addition to the sunny west side is an ideal spot for a late lunch or early dinner after a day spent at Waimea Canyon or Kokee State Park (see Chapter 22). Housed in an attractively restored 1940s plantation house, the restaurant is easygoing and kid friendly. Order up a micro-brewed Na Pali Pale Ale or a Pakala Porter along with a slate of munchies to share, family style. The accents are international, from buffalo wings and quesadillas to island-favorite noodle dishes and Korean-style kalbi beef short ribs. Burgers, sandwiches, and foods that go well with brew fill out a surprisingly satisfying menu.

At Waimea Plantation Cottages, 9400 Kaumualii Hwy., Waimea. ☎ *808-338-9733. Internet:* www.wbcbrew.com. *Reservations recommended for larger parties. Sandwiches and small plates: $5–$9. Main courses: $12–$18. MC, V. Open: Lunch and dinner daily.*

Zelo's Beach House

$$ North Shore   Steaks/Seafood/California

Despite its location blocks from the ocean, Zelo's is the embodiment of north shore beach culture. This hip, happy spot bursts with life and surfer-dude charm. Don't expect anything approaching gourmet fare, but the large, appealing menu of seafood, pastas, steaks, fresh fish tacos, and California-style eats is uniformly pleasing. The casual vibe makes Zelo's a great place to just hang out between meals, too: Choose from a huge selection of frosty tropical drinks, microbrews, and martinis.

5-8420 Kuhio Hwy. (at Aku Road), Hanalei. ☎ *808-826-9700. Internet:* www.
zelosbeachhouse.com. *Reservations recommended for parties of six or more. Main courses: $6–$12 at lunch, $7.25–$23 at dinner (most less than $18). MC, V. Open: Lunch and dinner daily.*

Luau!

Kauai doesn't excel in the luau department. All of the island's luaus are lacking in one way or another (usually in the food department), and not one is even in the ballpark with Maui's Old Lahaina Luau or Feast at Lele (see Chapter 13), or the Big Island's Kona Village Luau (Chapter 17). Save your luau-going for those islands if you're heading there. Otherwise, the following are your best bets.

Reservations are almost always required for luaus, so be sure to call in advance (a few days ahead if you want to guarantee admission).

Kauai Coconut Beach Drums of Polynesia Luau

Usually considered to be Kauai's best, this Coconut Coast luau (run by packager Pleasant Hawaiian Holidays) loves to tout its Kahili Award, presented by the Hawaii Visitors and Convention Bureau for authenticity. Don't put _too_ much stock in that, however; come instead for the family-friendly fun. Set among a grove of coconut palms, the tiki-torchlit luau grounds are attractive, and the hula-focused production numbers are entertaining. A nightly _imu_ ceremony is performed (in which the luau pig is unearthed from an underground oven), but the rest of the food is mediocre at best.

At the Kauai Coconut Beach Resort, Kuhio Highway, Kapaa. ☎ _808-822-3455. Internet:_ www.kcb.com/kcb/kcb_luau.htm. _Reservations highly recommended. Admission: $55 adults, $33 teens (12–17), $23 kids (3–11). Prices include open bar. $5 extra for premium seating. Times: Nightly at 5:30 p.m._

Tuesday and Thursday are Family Fun Nights at the Kauai Coconut Beach Luau, when children 10 and under enter free with a paying adult. Confirm when you reserve that this policy is still in effect. At press time, you could also save 7 percent on the price of admission (or 10 percent if you pay with a check) by booking your Kauai Coconut Beach luau tickets through **Tom Barefoot's Cashback Tours** (☎ **888-222-3601;** Internet: www.tombarefoot.com).

Drums of Paradise Luau

This lively Poipu Beach luau is the most sophisticated among the Kauai choices, and my favorite. The tropical garden setting is lovely; the bountiful spread, which includes a full _imu_ ceremony, is the best of the luau feasts; and the lively floor show features Hawaiian and Tahitian dances as well as Samoan fire dancers in a loosely threaded narrative that tells the story of ancient Polynesian history and migration to the islands.

At the Hyatt Regency Kauai Resort & Spa, 1571 Poipu Rd., Koloa. ☎ _808-742-1234. Internet:_ www.hyatt.com. _Reservations essential. Admission: $62.50 adults, $41.50 teens (13–20), $31.25 kids (6–12). Prices include open bar. Times: Sun and Thurs at 6 p.m._

Reflections of Paradise Luau and Polynesian Review

This all-you-can-eat buffet of both traditional luau foods and familiar favorites such as teriyaki beef and chicken is prepared by Gaylord's (see "Kauai's Best Restaurants" earlier in this chapter), so the food isn't bad; don't expect restaurant quality, though. The luau is held on the lovely grounds of a historic 1930s plantation house in the lush heart of the island, and it features a traditional *imu* ceremony starring a kalua-roasted pig, plus a full-on Polynesian Revue. It's not the most authentic presentation, but it's fun, and the kids will love the fire-knife dancer. Expect lots of silly audience participation.

Kilohana Carriage House at Kilohana Plantation, Kaumualii Highway (Highway 50) 1 mile west of Lihue. ☎ *808-245-9593. Internet:* www.gaylordskauai.com. *Reservations required. Times: Mon, Tues, and Thurs at 6:30 p.m. Admission: $52 adults, $48 seniors over 55 and teens 14–18, $25 kids 6–13, free for kids 5 and under. Prices include mai tais and fruit punch.*

Chapter 22

Fun On and Off the Beach

• •

In This Chapter

▶ Finding Kauai's best beaches

▶ Enjoying the waves: Where to rent snorkel gear, schedule first-time dives or kayaking trips, and more

▶ Exploring the spectacular Na Pali Coast from land or water

▶ Seeing Kauai's top sights and attractions

▶ Locating the island's top hunting grounds for shoppers

▶ Having fun on the quiet isle once the sun goes down

• •

*I*f any island was made for kicking back, Kauai is it — so don't knock yourself out trying to stay busy on this idyllic, easygoing place.

That said, you'll find plenty of wonderful things to do on Kauai — especially if you're the type of traveler who prefers communing with nature over seeking out man-made attractions and entertainment.

Hitting the Beaches

Kauai is the oldest of the Hawaiian islands, geologically speaking — which means that it has had plenty of time to fashion some world-class beaches. Lined with powdery white sands and dotted with swaying palms, the island's stunning shoreline is skirted by crystal-clear waters and numerous well-developed reefs for snorkeling.

 Always make safety your top priority at the beach, whether you're swimming, snorkeling, surfing, or even taking a stroll. Always check on the local surf conditions before you head out. And *never* leave valuables in your rental car while you're at the beach. Thieves prey on tourists, and they can get inside your car quicker than you can spread out your beach towel. Leave good stuff behind at the condo or in the hotel safe if you're heading off to the beach.

Kauai's Best Beaches & Attractions

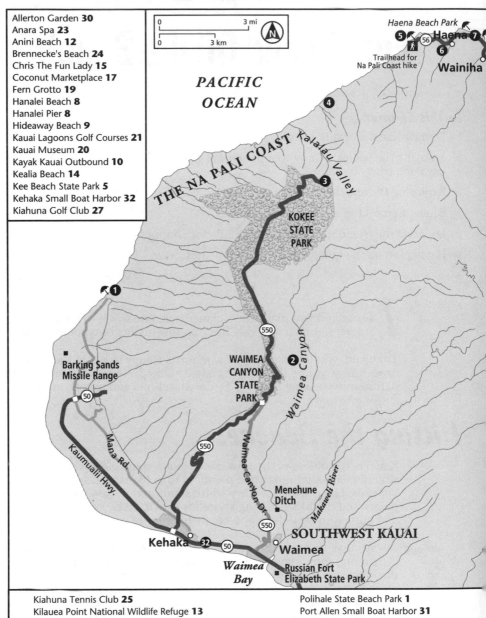

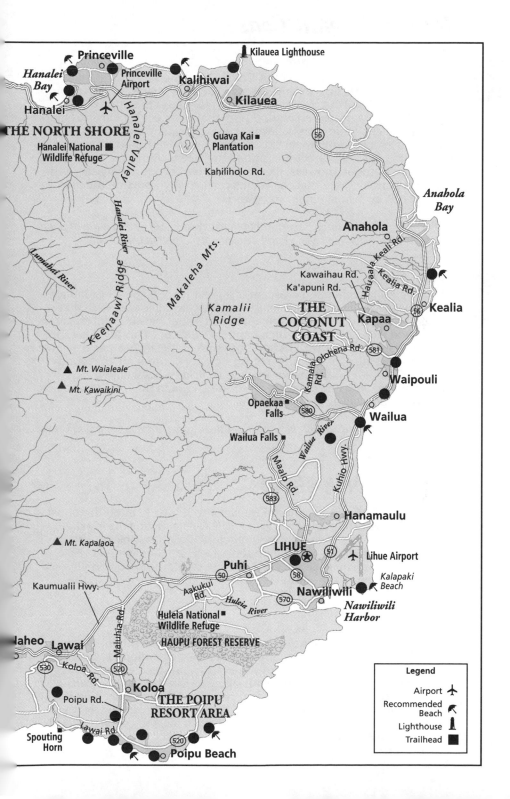

Princeville

Hanalei Bay

Princeville Airport

Kalihiwai

Kilauea Lighthouse

Hanalei

Kilauea

THE NORTH SHORE

Hanalei National Wildlife Refuge

Guava Kai Plantation

56

Kahiliholo Rd.

Anahola Bay

Anahola

Kawaihau Rd.

Ka'apuni Rd.

Kealia

THE COCONUT COAST

Kapaa

56

Kamalii Ridge

Olohena Rd.

581

Waipouli

▲ Mt. Waialeale

▲ Mt. Kawaikini

Opaekaa Falls

580

Wailua

Wailua Falls

Maalo Rd.

583

Hanamaulu

▲ Mt. Kapalaoa

LIHUE

51

Lihue Airport

Puhi

50

58

Kalapaki Beach

Kaumualii Hwy.

Aakukui Rd.

Nawiliwili

570

Huleia River

Nawiliwili Harbor

Huleia National Wildlife Refuge

HAUPU FOREST RESERVE

Jaheo

Lawai

Koloa Rd.

530

520

Koloa

Poipu Rd.

THE POIPU RESORT AREA

Lawai Rd.

Spouting Horn

520

Poipu Beach

Legend

Airport ✈

Recommended Beach

Lighthouse

Trailhead ■

On the Coconut Coast

Lydgate State Beach Park

My favorite beach on the Coconut Coast offers the safest swimming and the best snorkeling on the eastern shore, and makes an all-around great place to hang out for a day. A rock wall breaks the open ocean waves, forming a protected natural pool that's perfect for kids and first-time snorkelers. Wide, grassy lawns that are ideal for picnicking and kite-flying lead downhill to an expanse of fine-grained sand, with dramatic vistas in either direction. Among the nice facilities are a pavilion, restrooms, outdoor showers, picnic tables, barbecues, lifeguards, and plenty of parking. Note that the waves can be rough outside the protected pool, even in summer, so beware.

At the Holiday Inn Sunspree Resort, Kuhio Highway (Hwy. 56) 5 miles north of Lihue (just south of Wailua River State Park). Look for the turnoff at Leho Road.

Kealia Beach

This long, wide, half-moon crescent is a great place to play in summer. Gorgeous golden sands fringe white-crested turquoise waters that are suitably calm, particularly at the north end — but beware winter and year-round late-day swells, which can really kick up. This local favorite is particularly popular with casual bodysurfers. Kealia is a perfect spot for those seeking solitude, since there's plenty of room for everybody to spread out, even on summer weekends. Bring a blanket and a lunchtime picnic, as no facilities are on-site. Park in the dirt lot, and don't leave any valuables in your car.

On Kuhio Highway (Hwy. 56) just north of Kapaa town, across from the Kealia Country Store.

On the north shore

Welcome to the finest beaches in Hawaii — but bear in mind that most of Kauai's north shore beaches aren't safe for swimming during the winter months. The swells come just before Christmastime and stay usually through March, turning up the waves to full height and the undertow to unmanageable levels for most regular folks. So do yourself a favor and head to the south shore if you want to take a dip in the winter months.

Anini Beach

Tucked away in a million-dollar residential neighborhood, this secret beach is one of the most beautiful — and safest — swimming beaches on Kauai. The three-mile-long gold-sand beach is shielded from the open ocean by the longest, widest fringing reef in the islands. With shallow water less than five feet deep, it's the very best beach on Kauai for beginning snorkelers, and boasts the most well-protected north shore waters in winter. The grassy park has picnic and barbecue facilities, restrooms, and a boat-launch ramp. A real gem!

The Coconut Coast

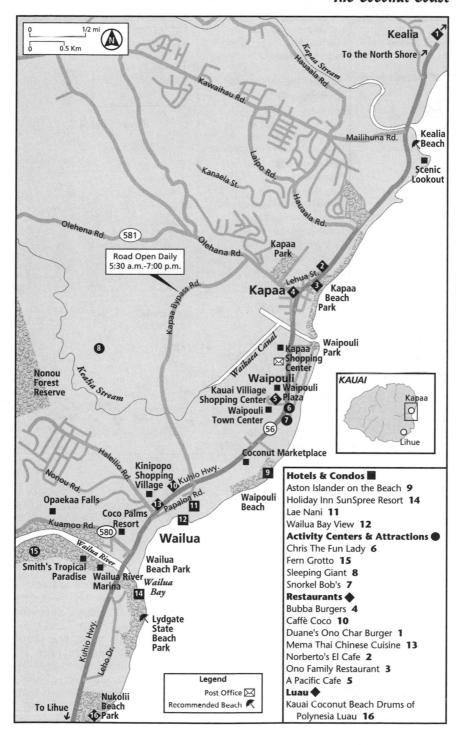

Kealia **1**
To the North Shore ↗

Kealia Beach
Scenic Lookout

Mailihuna Rd.

Kawaihau Rd.

Kapaa Stream
Hauaala Rd.

Laipo Rd.

Kanaela St.

Hauaala Rd.

Olehena Rd.
581
Olehana Rd.

Road Open Daily
5:30 a.m.-7:00 p.m.

Kapaa Park

Lehua St.
Kapaa **4**   **2** **3**
Kapaa Beach Park

Kapaa Bypass Rd.

Waipouli Park

Waikaea Canal

Kapaa Shopping Center ✉

Nonou Forest Reserve

Keahu Stream

8

Waipouli
Kauai Villiage Shopping Center   Waipouli Plaza **5**
Waipouli Town Center   **6**
56   **7**

KAUAI
Kapaa
Lihue

Coconut Marketplace   **9**

Kinipopo Shopping Village   **10**   Kuhio Hwy.
Haleilio Rd.
Nonou Rd.

Opaekaa Falls
Kuamoo Rd.   **580**
Coco Palms Resort   Papaloa Rd.   **11**   **12**   **13**

Waipouli Beach

Wailua

15
Smith's Tropical Paradise   Wailua River Marina   Wailua Beach Park   *Wailua River*   *Wailua Bay*   **14**

Lydgate State Beach Park

Kuhio Hwy.
Leho Dr.

To Lihue ↓   Nukolii Beach Park   **16**

Legend
Post Office ✉
Recommended Beach ✔

Hotels & Condos ■
Aston Islander on the Beach **9**
Holiday Inn SunSpree Resort **14**
Lae Nani **11**
Wailua Bay View **12**
Activity Centers & Attractions ●
Chris The Fun Lady **6**
Fern Grotto **15**
Sleeping Giant **8**
Snorkel Bob's **7**
Restaurants ◆
Bubba Burgers **4**
Caffè Coco **10**
Duane's Ono Char Burger **1**
Mema Thai Chinese Cuisine **13**
Norberto's El Cafe **2**
Ono Family Restaurant **3**
A Pacific Cafe **5**
Luau ◆
Kauai Coconut Beach Drums of Polynesia Luau **16**

The North Shore

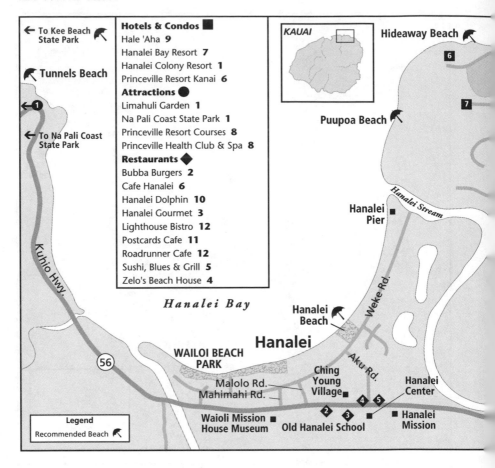

Off Kuhio Highway (Hwy. 56) past the turnoff for Kilauea. To get there: As you head toward the north shore, ignore the first exit called Kalihiwai Road and turn right at the second exit (west of mile marker 25); at the fork, follow Anini Beach Road (left) to beach park.

Hideaway Beach

It may take a little work to reach this super-secret spot, but it's well worth the effort, especially for romance-seeking couples. The perfectly named Hideaway Beach is a gorgeous pocket of beach in the Princeville Resort where the snorkeling is great, the sand is powder-fine, and the atmosphere is as tranquil as it gets. Even if a few other souls find their way there, everyone is happily content to keep to themselves. Fair warning: Getting to Hideaway is not for the faint of heart. From the parking lot, walk down the dirt path that runs between the two chain-link fences on the right; the path will take you to a steep staircase that leads down to the beach. It has no facilities, of course, so bring what you need.

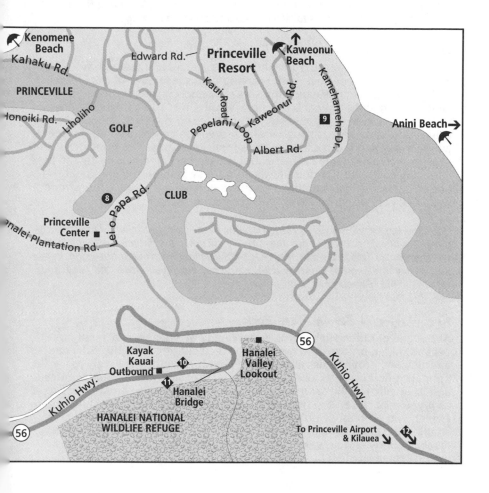

Kenomene Beach

Kahaku Rd.

Edward Rd.

PRINCEVILLE

Honoiki Rd.

Liholiho

GOLF

Princeville Resort

Kaui Road

Pepelani Loop

Kaweonui Rd.

Kaweonui Beach

Kamehameha Dr.

9

Anini Beach→

Albert Rd.

8

Lei o Papa Rd.

CLUB

Princeville Center ■

analei Plantation Rd.

56

Kayak Kauai Outbound ■

10

11

Hanalei Bridge

HANALEI NATIONAL WILDLIFE REFUGE

56

Hanalei Valley Lookout

Kuhio Hwy.

Kuhio Hwy.

To Princeville Airport & Kilauea ↘

12

In the Princeville Resort off Kuhio Highway (Hwy. 56), just east of Princeville Shopping Center. To get there: Go 2 miles to the entrance of the hotel; just before the gatehouse, turn into the public parking lot on your right.

Hanalei Beach

Half-moon Hanalei Bay has to be one of the most beautiful beaches anywhere. Gentle waves roll up the wide, golden sand; towering coco palms sway to the rhythm of the tradewinds; waterfalls vein volcanic ridges in the distance, some three miles inland. Like the tab of a giant jigsaw-puzzle piece, the bay takes a sizeable bite out of the coastline a full mile inland. It's an excellent spot for swimming in summer; in winter, stick to the westernmost curve of the bay, where the water is relatively calm even when winter swells hit. Facilities include a pavilion, restrooms, picnic tables, and parking. This beach is always packed with both local residents and visitors, but the bay is big enough for everyone to enjoy; you can usually find a spot to yourself just by strolling down the shoreline.

Off Kuhio Highway (Hwy. 56), Hanalei. To get there: Turn right on Aku Road (just after Tahiti Nui), which leads to Weke Road and the main parking lot.

Tunnels Beach

If I had to pick one beach above all others on Kauai, it would have to be Tunnels. Postcard-perfect, with swaying palms, a shelter of ironwoods, and gold sand rimming a curving shore, Tunnels is one of the most beautiful stretches of beach in all of Hawaii. Go at sunset, when golden rays butter a wide-open blue sky and bounce off the green steepled ridges. The sand here is rougher and more pumice-textured than elsewhere, but somehow it's all the more luxurious for it. The ironwoods provide welcome shade in the heat of the tropical summer. Protected by a fringing coral reef, Tunnels is excellent for swimming and snorkeling — one of my best snorkeling days _ever_ was here — but beware the winter waves, of course. No facilities mar the pristine scene.

Off Kuhio Highway (Hwy. 56) beyond Hanalei, ⁹⁄₁₀-mile past Hanalei Colony Resort, down an unmarked drive. To get there: Turn right down the dirt alley with the large wooden double gate at the end; it's just after the yellow "Narrow Bridge" sign. Park in the alley or along the highway with everybody else, walk down the alley, and turn left at the "Beach Path" sign.

Kee (KAY-eh) Beach State Park

At the end of Kuhio Highway is a real dandy of a beach — a small crescent of golden-brown sand nestled between soaring volcanic cliffs and an ironwood grove. This remote little spot is not quite as lovely as Tunnels, but it comes close — and it boasts easier access and facilities, and is equally terrific for swimming and snorkeling. You'll really feel as if you're at the end of the world out here, even if you're not alone (which you probably won't be). A well-developed reef keeps the water shallow and calm, making the inlet great for kids and snorkelers of all levels; nobody should venture out beyond the reef, though. Facilities include some rustic restrooms, showers, and lots of parking, but no lifeguard.

At the end of Kuhio Highway (Hwy. 56), about 7½ miles past Hanalei.

Kee is where you pick up the trailhead into the Na Pali Coast. It takes about three hours to hike the first two miles in (that's as far as I suggest you go) and back, so the heartier among you may want to plan on it; see the section called "What to See and Do on Dry Land" for further details.

In the Poipu Area

Poipu Beach Park

Nobody should miss this big, wide beach park. It's the perfect beach playground, where grassy lawns with leafy shade trees skirt abundant white sand at the water's edge. It's actually a series of crescents, with the two most prominent ones divided by a sandbar: On the left, a lava-rock jetty protects a sandy-bottom pool that's perfect for small kids; on the right, the open bay is great for more advanced swimmers, snorkelers, and surfers. The swimming is excellent, with small tidepools for exploring and great reefs for snorkeling and diving. Amenities include lots of top-notch facilities — including nice bathrooms, outdoor showers, picnic pavilions, plenty of parking, and a good restaurant and snack bar (Brennecke's Beach Broiler; see Chapter 21) just across the street. Poipu attracts a daily crowd of visitors and local residents, but the density seldom approaches Waikiki levels, except on holidays.

To reach Poipu Beach Park from Kaumualii Highway (Hwy. 50), turn south on Maluhia Road and follow it to Poipu Road. Go past Poipu Shopping Village and turn right on Hoowili Road, which will take you to the beach.

Farther down from Poipu Beach Park, past the grassy area at the east end of the beach, is an unprotected lava-rock cove known as Brennecke's Beach, which is terrific for boogie boarding and bodysurfing. Be careful, though, especially late in the day, as the waves can get rough.

Lawai Beach (Beach House) Beach

This small, rocky white-sand beach just to the west of the Beach House Restaurant isn't the most beautiful on the south shore, but snorkelers will love it. The water is warm, shallow, clear, and delightfully populated with clouds of tropical fish. Plenty of streetside parking is available, plus some nice restrooms and showers just across the street and a grassy lawn in front of the Beach House.

On Lawai Road next to the Beach House Restaurant, Poipu Beach. To get there: From Kaumualii Highway (Hwy. 50), turn south on Maluhia Road (Hwy. 520) and continue south on Poipu Road. At the "WELCOME TO POIPU BEACH" sign, go to the right, toward Spouting Horn; it's a mile or two down, across from the Lawai Beach Resort (look for the restaurant on your left).

Mahaulepu Beach

Here is one of the finest stretches of untouched sands in Hawaii. With two miles of grainy, red-gold sand tucked among rocky cliffs, sand dunes, and a forest of casaurina trees, this idyllic stretch is perfect for beachcombing, sunbathing, or just cuddling up with your cutie and watching the endless waves roll in. Swimming and snorkeling are risky, except in the reef-sheltered shallows about 200 yards west of the sandy parking lot. No facilities are on site — just lots of pristine natural beauty. Best of all, you're likely to have it all to yourselves. Mahaulepu makes a wonderful place to get away from it all and discover Hawaii at its natural best. Bring a picnic for maximum romance.

Off Poipu Road, 3 miles past the Hyatt Regency Kauai Resort and Spa and 2 miles from the end of Poipu Road (the unpaved stretch is called Weliweli Road). To get there: Turn right at the T intersection; stop and register at the security hut, drive 1 mile to the big sand dune, turn left, and drive a ½-mile to the small lot under the trees.

Poipu Beach

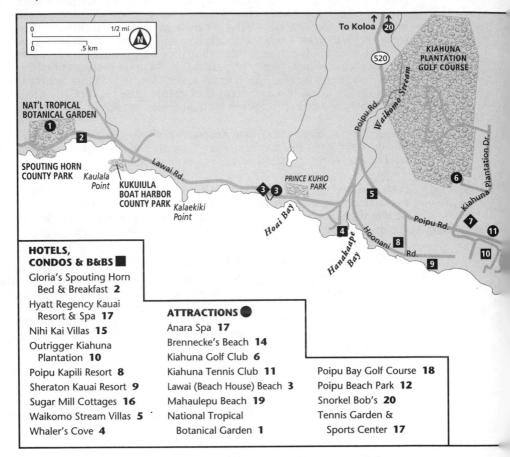

HOTELS, CONDOS & B&BS ■

Gloria's Spouting Horn
   Bed & Breakfast **2**

Hyatt Regency Kauai
   Resort & Spa **17**

Nihi Kai Villas **15**

Outrigger Kiahuna
   Plantation **10**

Poipu Kapili Resort **8**

Sheraton Kauai Resort **9**

Sugar Mill Cottages **16**

Waikomo Stream Villas **5**

Whaler's Cove **4**

ATTRACTIONS ●

Anara Spa **17**

Brennecke's Beach **14**

Kiahuna Golf Club **6**

Kiahuna Tennis Club **11**

Lawai (Beach House) Beach **3**

Mahaulepu Beach **19**

National Tropical
   Botanical Garden **1**

Poipu Bay Golf Course **18**

Poipu Beach Park **12**

Snorkel Bob's **20**

Tennis Garden &
   Sports Center **17**

Both Poipu Beach Park and Mahaulepu Beach are ideal spots for offshore humpback whale-watching in winter. Between December and April, all you have to do is look out to sea. With a little luck, you'll spot the gentle giants breaching and spy-hopping to their hearts' content in the warm Kauai waters.

On the west shore

Polihale State Beach Park

If it's raining everywhere else on Kauai, just get in your car and head west. Keep going, to the end of the road, where you'll find a mini-Sahara where the sun (almost) always shines. Polihale is a wonderful place to get away from it all. It holds Hawaii's biggest beach — 17 miles long and as wide as three football fields. The golden sands wrap around Kauai's northwestern shore from just beyond Waimea all the way to the edge of the Na Pali Coast. Some of the stretches of sand are accessible

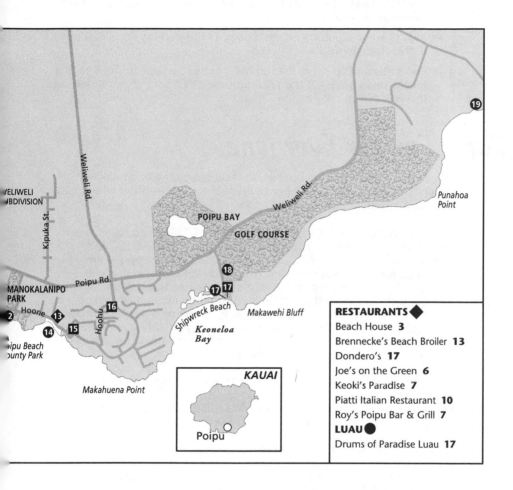

WELIWELI
SUBDIVISION

Weliweli Rd.

Kipuka St.

POIPU BAY

GOLF COURSE

Weliweli Rd.

Punahoa
Point

19

Poipu Rd.

MANOKALANIPO
PARK

Hoone **13**

2

14   **15**

Hoohu

16

18

Shipwreck Beach

17 **17**

Makawehi Bluff

*Keoneloa
Bay*

Makahuena Point

ipu Beach
ounty Park

KAUAI

Poipu

RESTAURANTS ◆
Beach House **3**
Brennecke's Beach Broiler **13**
Dondero's **17**
Joe's on the Green **6**
Keoki's Paradise **7**
Piatti Italian Restaurant **10**
Roy's Poipu Bar & Grill **7**
LUAU ●
Drums of Paradise Luau **17**

from the highway, but I like the remote area out past the cane fields best. The safest place to swim is Queen's Pond, a small, shallow, sandy-bottomed protected inlet that's usually calm, except when the high winter surf washes over the reef — stay out of the water altogether then. Restrooms, showers, picnic tables, and pavilions are scattered throughout the park, but no lifeguards are on hand.

At the end of Kaumualii Highway (Hwy. 50), a 40-minute drive west of Poipu. To get there: Drive past the Barking Sands Missile Range and follow the signs through the sugarcane fields to Polihale. The road isn't paved but it's flat and well graded, so just take it slow; it's about a 5-mile drive. Queen's Pond is at the 3.4-mile mark along the cane road, where the road curves near a large monkeypod tree; take the fork to the left and park almost immediately, then walk north along the beach until you come to a hollow in the rock; pass through it to the beach.

Be careful at Polihale year-round, as this is open ocean, and swimming is dangerous. Strong swimmers can bodysurf with caution in summer, but everybody should stay out of the water in winter. Here are a few more tips you should keep in mind when visiting Polihale State Beach Park:

✔ Rental cars are burgled on occasion out here, so don't leave any valuables in your car.

✔ Always wear flip-flops or reef shoes as the midday sand can be hotter than a griddle.

✔ Don't attempt to drive the unpaved cane road out to the beach if recent rains have left the road muddy — it's easy to get stuck, and this is far from civilization.

Water Fun for Everyone

If you want to rent boogie boards, snorkel gear, kayaks, and other beach toys, Kauai has a number of reliable outlets — all of which can book organized activities for you, too.

On the Coconut Coast, **Chris The Fun Lady,** 4-746 Kuhio Hwy. (across the street from Waipouli Town Center), Kapaa (☎ 808-822-7759; Internet: www.christhefunlady.com), considers her operation a one-stop vacation stop. Not only does Chris Gayagas offer rental gear — she even has mopeds for rent — but she can also book your activities for you; just stop in, and she'll do all the calling for you and issue your tickets right there. There's no extra fee for booking activities through Chris (the outfitters pay the commission, not you). She can offer good advice on which captains are keeping their cruise boats in top-notch condition, which luau you might like best, and so on.

My favorite place to rent snorkel gear is **Snorkel Bob's** on the Coconut Coast at 4-734 Kuhio Hwy. (right next to Chris the Fun Lady on the ocean side of the street), Kapaa (☎ 808-823-9433); and at Poipu Beach at 3236 Poipu Rd., just south of Old Koloa Town (☎ 808-742-2206).

Snorkel Bob's rents the best-quality snorkel gear. The basic set — mask, snorkel, fins — is just $9 a week, but I highly recommend going with the deluxe package for $29 a week (reasonable daily rates are available, too). If you're nearsighted, you can even rent a prescription mask so that you can actually see while you're underwater, plus boogie boards, life vests, wetsuits, beach chairs, and so on. The people at Bob's shop can also sign you up for select activities — snorkel cruises, helicopter rides, bike tours, and luaus — with their favorite vendors (their choices are, in general, very good ones). Both shops are open every day from 8 a.m. to 5 p.m. There's no need to reserve in advance, but advance bookings are available online at www.snorkelbob.com.

You can rent a set of snorkel gear from Snorkel Bob's at the start of your trip, carry it with you as you travel throughout the islands (you get attached to this stuff, you know), and then return it to another Snorkel Bob's location on Oahu, Maui, or the Big Island. (All shops offer 24-hour gear return service.) I suggest doing this, even if you intend to go on snorkel cruises or kayak trips that provide gear. Free gear is almost always awful — and I don't want you to miss out on spotting sea turtles and other groovy critters because you're fussing with a clogged snorkel or a leaking mask.

On the north shore, rent your gear from the friendly folks at **Kayak Kauai Outbound,** a mile past Hanalei Bridge on Highway 56 (look for them on the ocean side of the road, across from Postcards Cafe) in Hanalei (☎ **800-437-3507** or 808-826-9844; Internet: www.kayakkauai. com). They have a second shop on the Coconut Coast, in the south parking lot of the Coconut Marketplace, on Kuhio Highway (Highway 56) in Wailua (☎ **808-822-9179**). Kayak Kauai rents snorkel gear, body- and surfboards, river and ocean kayaks, and even camping and back-packing gear (see the kayaking section later in this chapter for details on their guided kayak trips).

Offshore snorkeling

Kauai does offer a number of snorkel cruises, but unless you're going to combine snorkeling with a Na Pali sightseeing trip (see the following section), I say save your money. Kauai is best known for its offshore snorkeling, which anybody can do — it only requires that you have a modicum of swimming ability and some good gear (see the preceding section for rental locations).

My absolute favorite offshore snorkeling in Hawaii is off Kauai's north shore. **Anini, Hideaway, Tunnels, and Kee beaches** are all world-class, boasting crystal-clear water and a mind-boggling abundance of colorful fish.

While placid throughout the summer months, most of Kauai's north shore beaches become too rough for swimming during the winter, when swells kick up and the undertow starts churning. Anini Beach is well-protected enough to stay calm year-round. Kee Beach is the second-most reliable in terms of calm winter waves.

For little ones or first-time snorkelers, head to the Coconut Coast's **Lydgate State Beach Park,** where a lava-rock wall forms a natural pool that stays calm even as the waters churn around it. The calm coves at **Poipu Beach Park** make another excellent choice for beginners, whether they're six or 60.

Lawai Beach isn't picture-postcard pretty, but it's my favorite place to snorkel in the Poipu area. You may even spot some little critters darting in and out of detritus left by Hurricane Iniki, such as concrete blocks and spare tires, the remnants of nearby hotels devastated by the 1992 storm.

For details on all of the beaches I've discussed here, see the section called "Hitting the Beaches" earlier in this chapter.

I can't say it enough: Safety is key when snorkeling. Always snorkel with a buddy, and keep an eye on each other at all times. Come up every few minutes to check your bearings in relation to the shoreline and make sure there's no boat traffic close by. Don't touch anything underwater: Coral is delicate and easily damaged and can also leave you with nasty cuts. And always, always check surf conditions before you set out (a local surf-and-snorkel shop can usually help you here). You should also inquire about the specific currents and tides at the area you plan to snorkel — as well as any potentially dangerous spots to avoid.

Cruising the Na Pali Coast and other on-deck adventures

You can see the most spectacular coastline in all of Hawaii, Kauai's remote Na Pali Coast, one of three ways: by helicopter tour (see "Getting a bird's-eye view: flightseeing tours" later in this chapter), by hiking in (see "Exploring Kauai's top attractions"), or by catching a boat ride around the bend. I like the approach from sea best, which is simply breathtaking. Most cruises combine snorkeling with sightseeing.

Kauai serves as an excellent vantage from which to see the Pacific humpback whales make their annual visit to Hawaii from Alaska between December and April. In season, most cruise operators combine whale-watching with their regular adventures.

The water can be very choppy as you cruise the north shore — especially in winter, but not exclusively so. Mornings are usually calm, but the surf tends to kick up later in the day. Those of you with sensitive tummies should take Dramamine or other motion-sickness meds well before you set out on one of these expeditions — once you're out on the sea, it's too late for the drugs to have any benefit. You won't enjoy yourself, and a perfectly good (and expensive) trip will be ruined. Also available are nausea-prevention wristbands, which can be found at any drugstore, and which seem to benefit many users.

You may be able to save a few bucks on your Na Pali Coast or other cruise by booking it through Maui-based **Tom Barefoot's Cashback Tours** (☎ 888-222-3601; Internet: www.tombarefoot.com), which also books activities on Kauai. Tom Barefoot is a very reliable activities center that's willing to split its commissions with you so that everybody comes out ahead. You'll save 7 percent with select outfitters (those marked with a blue dolphin on the Web site, which include some of those I recommend in the following sections) if you pay with a credit card, 10 percent if you send a check — which could add up to big savings, especially if you're bringing the entire family along.

Bluewater Sailing & Express

Most snorkel trips and commercial cruises are aboard double-hulled catamarans, but Bluewater offers a unique option for exploring the Na Pali Coast: The new *Northwind,* a 42-foot custom-built, all-aluminum Navy reconnaisance hull powerboat, which can carry up to 20 passengers. Their half-day (five-hour) Na Pali cruise includes a deli lunch, soft drinks, and snorkeling, while their four-hour sunset version offers snacks and beverages only (no snorkeling).

Half-day snorkel trips and sunset sails in the warm waters off southwestern Kauai are also offered aboard Bluewater's traditional mono-hulled sailboat, the *Lady Leanne II,* a 42-foot Pierson ketch-rigged yacht that can carry 15 passengers max.

The folks behind Bluewater have been plying Kauai's waters since 1964, so they really know what they're doing, and they have a sterling reputation. The crew is friendly and knowledgeable, pointing out all the important landmarks and providing solid background information on the local history, geology, and marine life as you go.

All Northwind cruises and winter Lady Leanne sails depart Port Allen Small Boat Harbor, Highway 541 (halfway between Poipu and Waimea; look for check-in office after the turnoff from Highway 50). Summer Lady Leanne cruises depart from Hanalei Pier, Hanalei. ☎ *808-828-1142. Internet:* www.bluewater.ws *or* www.sail-kauai.com. *Half-day sail-snorkels: $105–$110 adults, $85 kids 5–12. Sunset cruises: $60–$90 adults, $55–$65 kids.*

Capt. Andy's Sailing Adventures

Capt. Andy runs the *Spirit of Kauai,* a late-model 55-foot, 49-passenger Gold Coast catamaran, as well as the 65-foot, 85-passenger Super Cat catamaran the *Hula Kai,* on a number of regular trips. Both boats are sleek and comfy, excelling at both speed and stability. Choose from morning, afternoon, and full-day Na Pali Coast trips, which include sailing, snorkeling, dolphin-watching, and lunch; plus both Na Pali and Poipu sunset cruises, which include cocktails. Call or check the Web site for the current schedule, as the Na Pali schedule is truncated in winter.

Most cruises depart Port Allen Small Boat Harbor, Highway 541 (off Highway 50 halfway between Poipu and Waimea). Poipu sunset cruises depart from Kukuiula Harbor, Poipu Beach. ☎ *808-335-6833. Internet:* www.sailing-hawaii.com. *Prices: $59–$139 adults, $40–$99 kids 5–12.*

Captain Sundown

Captain Sundown is the only operator to offer cruises year-round from the north shore, which is much closer to the Na Pali Coast but has a severe limitation on permits. Their 40-foot sailing catamaran carries only 15 passengers, so this is an excellent choice for those looking for an intimate trip. Options include year-round Na Pali sails, with an emphasis on snorkeling in summer, whale-watching in winter; plus a sunset sail option that offers a stunning view of the Bali Hai cliffs (soft drinks are included; you're welcome to BYOB). All trips include an exciting short paddle out to the boat in a Hawaiian Outrigger canoe. Reserve well in advance, because these small-capacity trips often book up a week or more in advance.

Trips depart from Hanalei Beach, Hanalei. ☎ *808-826-5585. Internet:* www.captainsundown.com. *Prices: $68–$135 per person.*

Check Captain Sundown's Web site for special Internet booking deals; at press time, 10 percent price breaks were available for Visa and MasterCard bookings.

Liko Kauai Cruises

This Hawaiian-owned and -operated company offers three- and four-hour combination Na Pali Coast/snorkel/dolphin-watching/cave tours, with lunch. It all happens on a comfortable 49-foot twin-hulled catamaran (with padded seating, a nice plus). In addition to seeing whales in season, you'll peek into sea caves and lush valleys, glimpse waterfalls and miles of white-sand beaches, and make stops along the way for snorkeling. The narration is in-depth, culturally as well as naturally oriented, and very good. Prices include a deli-style lunch and sodas to wet your whistle throughout the tour. A sunset sail option is also available.

Cruises depart from Kehaka Small Boat Harbor, Waimea; office at 9875 Waimea Rd., Waimea. ☎ *888-SEA-LIKO or 808-338-0333. Internet:* www.liko-kauai.com. *Prices: $75–$95 adults, $45–$65 kids 4–14.*

Ocean and river kayaking

Kauai is an excellent place for kayaking, whether you're a beginner, an expert, or fall somewhere in between. First-timers don't have to brave the open ocean; rather, they can paddle down the Huleia River into Huleia National Wildlife Refuge, the last stand of Kauai's endangered birds (it's the only way the nature refuge can be explored), or follow the winding Hanalei River out to beautiful Hanalei Bay. More-skilled kayakers can set out for the majestic Na Pali Coast for some real excitement.

My favorite kayak outfitter in Hawaii is **Kayak Kauai Outbound,** a mile past the Hanalei Bridge on Highway 56 (look for them on the ocean side of the road, across from Postcards Cafe) in Hanalei (☎ **800-437-3507** or 808-826-9844; Internet: www.kayakkauai.com). A second shop is on the Coconut Coast, in the south parking lot of the Coconut Marketplace, on Kuhio Highway (Highway 56) in Wailua (☎ **808-822-9179**).

Kayak Kauai offers a range of guided river tours and sea kayaking trips. The five-hour Secret Falls river tour ($80 adults, half price for kids under 12) down the lush, peaceful, slow-moving Wailua River is excellent for families with kids. This fun, unhurried tour includes some of Kauai's most beautiful natural scenery and even includes a short hike and an opportunity for the quintessential tropical dream: to play in cool, clear waterfall pools, complete with a rope swing for the ultimate splash.

My favorite trip, the three-hour Blue Lagoon adventure, serves as the perfect introduction to ocean kayaking. You'll paddle down the Hanalei River (a national wildlife refuge), which serves as the perfect place to get your paddling rhythm down, and into Hanalei Bay for a taste of catching the ocean waves. In addition to teaching you the kayaking basics, the excellent guides share their extensive natural-history knowledge, which makes this a great choice even for those with a bit of experience. This tour sometimes includes snorkeling as well.

Rental packages are available for those of you who'd like to set out on you own (which you can do if you have a modicum of experience). Convenient roof racks are available, and the friendly staff will be happy to get you started by pointing you to the location that best suits your abilities and stamina. Single kayaks start at $26 per day, doubles start at $48. The staff will also help you launch onto the Hanalei River from their own boat launch out back.

On the south shore, **Outfitters Kauai,** at Poipu Plaza, 2827A Poipu Rd., (☎ **808-742-9667** or 808-742-7421; Internet: www.outfitterskauai. com), has its own full slate of guided kayaking trips. They offer sea tours for skilled kayakers (including a kayak trip along the Na Pali Coast), as well as a guided paddle along the Huleia and Wailua rivers for less experienced folks just looking for some fun. Kayak rentals are also available.

Chris The Fun Lady, 4-746 Kuhio Hwy. (across the street from Waipouli Town Center), Kapaa (☎ **808-822-7759;** Internet: www.christhefunlady. com), rents all the gear you need for river kayaking at competitive prices. Chris can tell you which kayaking areas suit your experience level (even if you're a first-timer), where to avoid the crowds and big boats, where to find secret waterfalls you can swim in, and more insider tips. She can also set you up for a guided river tour, if you like; call for details.

Catching a wave

If you've always wanted to surf the ocean waves, now's your chance, because Poipu Beach makes a great place to learn the moves. Contact **Margo Oberg's Surfing School** (☎ 808-742-8019 or 808-639-0708), the domain of seven-time world-champion surfer Margo Oberg. One of Margo's accredited instructors will teach you the basics — yep, including how to stand up — on dry land, so by the time you hit the water, you'll look like a pro (or not like an idiot, at least). These guys swear that they can get anybody up and riding a wave by the end of a lesson. The price is $45 for the 1½-hour lesson, including equipment; book at least a day in advance. Lessons are also available for more advanced surfers.

If you already have some basic moves, you can rent a surfboard from the **Nukumoi Surf Co.,** across the street from Poipu Beach at Brennecke's Beach Center (☎ **808-742-8019**). Nukumoi also rents boogie boards, which come in handy at the Brennecke's section of Poipu Beach (see "Hitting the Beaches" earlier in this chapter).

If you want to learn to surf on the north shore, reach out to **Windsurf Kauai** (☎ **808-828-6838**), which offers surfing lessons in Hanalei Bay as well as windsurfing lessons from Anini Beach, an excellent — and beautiful — place to learn the basics, whether you're 6 or 60. A 1½- to 2-hour surf lesson is $60, while a 3-hour windsurf lesson is $75. You can book windsurf lessons a day in advance; surf lessons require further notice, and depend on conditions.

On the north shore, surfboards and boogie boards are available for rent at the **Hanalei Surf Company,** in the heart of Hanalei at the Hanalei Center (directly across from Zelo's), 5-5161 Kuhio Hwy. (☎ 808-826-9000). Hanalei Bay is the island's most popular surf spot in winter, but it's strictly for experts — so stay out of the water when the waves are up unless you *really* know what you're doing.

For scuba divers (and those who want to be)

Diving on Kauai is dictated by the weather. In winter, when heavy swells and high winds hit the island, diving is generally limited to the more protected south shore. Once the winter swells disappear and the easygoing summer conditions move in, the magnificent north shore opens up for divers, where you'll find a kaleidoscopic marine world that's one of the most diverse in Hawaiian waters.

I recommend booking a two-tank dive off a dive boat. **Bubbles Below Scuba Charters** (☎ 808-332-7333; Internet: www.aloha.net/ ~kaimanu) specializes in highly personalized small-group dives, with an emphasis on marine biology. They offer up to two dives daily, plus one night dive, with most trips departing from Port Allen Small Boat Harbor on the south shore. The daytime dives usually feature two locations, depending on conditions. The night dive is particularly awesome, often featuring octopus and other nocturnal sea creatures. Prices are $100, with all equipment and snacks.

Attention, experienced divers: Twice weekly in summer (May through September) the folks at Bubbles Below also offer a full-day, three-tank trip to the "forbidden" island of Niihau, 90 minutes by boat from Kauai. It's quite an adventure, as the marine life in this seldom-visited area is astounding. Don't go if you're the least bit uncomfortable with vertical dropoffs, in huge underwater caverns, in possibly choppy surface conditions, and in significant currents. You should also be willing to share water space with the resident sharks. The all-day trip is $235, including tanks, weights, dive computer, lunch, drinks, and a marine guide. Dive Kauai, which I describe later in this section, offers a similar Niihau trip, so you might want to call and compare your options.

If you've never scuba-dived before but would like to learn while you're on Kauai, **Fathom Five Divers,** 3450 Poipu Rd., Koloa (☎ 808-742-6991; Internet: www.fathomfive.com), is the company to call. In business for more than 15 years, this PADI five-star IDC facility offers charters for experienced divers and first-timers alike. They offer no-experience-necessary introductory trips — both tank boat and shore dives — for $95 to $135 per person, including class, dives, and all gear. They also offer full-on four- or five-day certification courses for $369. Their daytime and night dives for experienced divers are comparable in price to Bubbles Below's.

If you want to explore a wider range of dive sites — including those off the north, east, and west shores — contact **Dive Kauai Scuba Center,** 976 Kuhio Hwy., Kapaa (☎ 800-828-3483 or 808-822-0452; Internet:

www.divekauai.com). In fact, they offer so many different dives that you should call for options and prices, which range from $78 to $135 for one- and two-tank shore and boat dives. Dive Kauai also offers a "Discover Scuba" introductory program for $98 to $125, as well as a full slate of certification and refresher courses.

What to See and Do on Dry Land

The most enticing thing about Kauai is its natural beauty — so get in your car and explore. Take Kuhio Highway up to the north shore — my favorite drive in all of Hawaii — just surveying the beauty as you go. Stop to take in the beautiful vistas along the way, have lunch and explore laid-back Hanalei town, kick back at one of the fabulous beaches along this shore (see "Hitting the Beaches" earlier in this chapter), and watch the sunset at the end of Kilauea Lighthouse Road (23 miles north of Lihue, 7 miles east of Hanalei; turn off at the Menehune Mart). It's the best sightseeing you can do on Kauai.

Sightseeing with a guide

If you're a movie buff — or if you just want a local to show you this gorgeous island — call **Hawaii Movie Tours** (☎ 800-628-8432 or 808-822-1192; Internet: www.hawaiimovietour.com), which offers the finest guided sightseeing tour of Kauai, hands down. It's comprehensive, in-depth, and — most importantly — just plain fun.

Hawaii Movie Tours will show you more of Kauai in the course of a day (including private areas and estates not open to the public) than you could take in on your own if you toured the island yourself for a whole week. And the movie angle serves as great context — you'll realize you've been seeing Kauai on the silver screen for years without knowing it! Remember *Blue Hawaii? Honeymoon in Vegas? Jurassic Park? Fantasy Island?* Yep — all Kauai!

Two movie tours are available:

✔ The five-hour Land Tour covers the island from the south shore to the north shore, and a wealth of moviemaking and TV history in the process, from Mitzi Gaynor washing that man right outta her hair in *South Pacific* to Indiana Jones battling Nazi evildoers in *Raiders of the Lost Ark*. You'll move from gorgeous locale to gorgeous locale in a brand-new 15-passenger van that's like a mini movie theater on wheels, complete with surround sound. Insightful commentary and sightseeing stops are supplemented by video clips. The tour-guide-led sing-a-longs of movie and TV themes are a tad corny, but trust me — you'll get into the spirit. This is a terrific tour, and well worth the money. Tickets are $85 for adults, $72 for kids 11 and under; lunch is included.

✔ The Deluxe Tour is a full-day extravaganza that includes not only a land tour but also a helicopter flightseeing tour, a cruise along the Wailua River to the Fern Grotto (featured in films ranging from *The Wackiest Ship in the Army* to the Harrison Ford/Anne Heche clinker *Six Days/Seven Nights*), and a three-hour luau once the sun goes down. This tour is $295 per person, which isn't really bad once you realize that they feed you twice — and you learn the price of helicopter rides alone (see the following section).

Both movie tours sell out regularly, so call well in advance to book your spots and avoid disappointment (a month in advance isn't too early in the high season). Also, do yourself a favor and schedule a Hawaii Movie Tour for early in your trip. That way, you can go back to that hidden beach or lush garden you fell in love with for some quality time on another day. Tickets can be booked for specific dates right on the Web site (check for Internet specials, which are sometimes on offer).

If you want a more general sightseeing tour of the island, or you don't want to drive yourself to destinations like Waimea Canyon or the north shore, contact **Polynesian Adventure Tours** (☎ **800-622-3011** or 808-246-0122; Internet: www.polyad.com), which offers a range of guided tours in minivans, big-windowed mini-coaches (good for small groups and big views), and full-size buses. Only go with these folks if you have no other way to get around; otherwise, they're not going to show you anything that you can't show yourself without the high price tag. In fact, they'll show you less, because these tours are only designed to give you an overview look at each of the stops. You'll have to go back on your own if you want to really explore or take time to commune with nature — which is why I suggest that you guide yourself around in the first place.

Book your Polynesian Adventure Tour online to get a 10 percent price break.

Getting a bird's-eye view: flightseeing tours

If you're going to choose one island on which to take a flightseeing tour, do it on Kauai. Kauai is the helicopter capital of Hawaii. So much of the Garden Isle's pristine natural world — hidden waterfalls, lush valleys, mist-shrouded peaks, the rugged interior of the thrilling Na Pali Coast, the spectral hues of Waimea Canyon's deepest ravines — is inaccessible by any other means. Helicopter rides are expensive, but they are worth the splurge if you want to take home memories above and beyond those of less adventuresome visitors. Most companies can even make a videotape of your ride for you to take home and relive again and again in the comfort of your living room.

There are, however, some considerations. While all of the companies I recommend feature skilled pilots and helicopters with excellent safety records, the truth of the matter is that flightseeing is risky business.

Twenty-eight people have died in commercial helicopter crashes in Hawaii over the last decade, six of those in a 1998 Kauai accident, seven in a Maui crash in July 2000. Of course, just getting into your rental car and driving to dinner — or even getting into the shower in your condo with a renegade bar of soap — is many times more dangerous than catching a 'copter ride. Still, you should make informed decisions when booking.

When reserving a helicopter tour with any company, check to make sure that safety is their first concern. The company should be an FAA-certified Part 135 operator, and the pilot should be Part 135 certified as well; the 135 license guarantees more stringent maintenance requirements and pilot training programs than those who are only Part 91 certified. And if weather conditions look iffy, reschedule.

Be sure to book your flight in advance (at least a week before in high season). All flights depart from Lihue Airport.

Island Helicopters

Island is one of the most well-established and safest helicopter tour operators in the business. Owner Curt Lofstedt has more than 25,000 hours of flying under his belt — and since he tackled 'Nam, you can feel pretty safe in his hands. He personally selects and trains professional pilots with an eye to both their flying skills and their ability to show you Kauai. All flights are in either the four-passenger Bell Jet Ranger III or the six-passenger American Eurocopter ASTAR, both with extra-large windows, all forward-facing seats, and stereo headsets to hear the pilot's personal narration, which is strong on island culture and history. You'll get a free pre-produced video of the tour highlights, but custom videos are not available.

☎ **800-829-5999** *or 808-245-8588. Internet:* www.islandhelicopters.com. *1-hour island tour: $197.50 per person.*

At press time, Island was offering 25 percent off plus a free video of your flight if you book their Grand Deluxe tour directly through them (not through an activities desk or agent); 35 percent if you book your tour online.

Jack Harter

A Kauai pioneer, Jack was the guy who started the sightseeing-via-helicopter trend — so, needless to say, he knows this island well. He flies four-passenger Bell Jet Rangers, which give everybody a great forward view and lots of leg and shoulder room, plus openable windows (great for the photographers among you). Jack's signature 90-minute tour hovers over the sights a bit longer than the 1-hour flight, so you can get a good look, but the 60-minute tour pretty much covers the island without whizzing by the big attractions in a blur. If you're a shutterbug who's counting on getting some good shots from above, though, go with the longer flight.

☎ **888-245-2001** or 808-245-3774. Internet: www.helicopters-kauai.com.
1-hour tour: $165 per person; 90-minute tour: $235 per person.

Ohana Helicopter Tours

Founded and run by part-native-Hawaiian, Kauai-born pilot Bogart
Kealoha, Ohana flies three six-passenger American Eurocopter 350BA
ASTAR 'copters, all with forward-facing seats and colorful pilot narration
via individual headsets. A wonderful choice for an insider's view of the
Garden Isle.

☎ **800-222-6989** or 808-245-3996. Internet: www.ohana-helicopters.com.
50-minute tour: $146 per person; 65-minute tour: $186 per person.

At press time, you could save 7 percent (or 10 percent if you pay with
a check) by booking your Ohana helicopter adventure through Tom
Barefoot's Cashback Tours (☎ **888-222-3601;** Internet: www.
tombarefoot.com).

Will Squyres Helicopter Tours

Will flies a six-passenger American Eurocopter ASTAR 350 BA helicopter,
which has custom bubble windows to allow for maximum views and side-
by-side seats (so nobody sits backwards and everybody gets a window
seat). Squyres and his pilots have each flown several thousand hours
over Kauai since 1984. They're experts on the island, and it shows in their
colorful, in-depth commentary.

☎ **888-245-4354** or 808-245-8881. Internet: www.helicopters-hawaii.com.
1-hour tour: $149 per person. Personalized video: $25.

At press time, online bookings garner you a 10 percent price break.

Exploring Kauai's top attractions

Allerton Garden

This National Tropical Botanical Garden is the height of cultivated tropical beauty in Hawaii. A former turn-of-the-century private estate that has
been transformed into a nationally chartered research facility for the
study and conservation of tropical botanics, the Allerton Garden is
simply amazing. It's home to an extraordinary collection of tropical fruit
and spice trees, rare introduced and native Hawaiian plants, hundreds
of varieties of flowers, a marvelous palm collection, a series of Green
Giant–sized Moreton Bay fig trees that were featured in *Jurassic Park,* and
some prime examples of landscape gardening featuring outdoor "rooms"
and gravity-fed fountains that would have turned William Randolph
Hearst green with envy. You can only visit the garden on a docent-led
guided tour; it's a fascinating, well-spent 2½ hours for serious green
thumbs and novices alike (really — I loved it, and I can't identify common
house plants) that's well worth the price tag. Be sure to look for the

secret beach that you'll pass at the start of the tour — it was one of the most awe-inspiring views I've ever seen.

Adjacent **McBryde Garden** features the largest collection of native Hawaiian plants in the world (many of them rare and endangered) in a much more natural setting. I suggest starting with the Allerton tour first, and then coming back for this one if you want more (which you just may). You might also want to consider visiting **Limahuli Garden**, another National Tropical Botanical Garden on the north shore (see the listing later in this chapter).

On Lawai Road (across the street from Spouting Horn), Poipu Beach. ☎ *808-742-2623. Internet:* www.ntbg.org/allerton.html. *2½-hour tours: $30. Kids under 5 not allowed (they wouldn't enjoy it anyway). Tour times: Allerton Garden, Tues–Sat at 9 a.m., 10 a.m., 1 p.m., and 2 p.m.; McBryde Garden, Mon 9 a.m. and 1 p.m.*

Reservations are required to visit the Allerton and McBryde gardens. Reserve your tour at least a week in advance in peak months of July, August, and September. Wear comfortable walking shoes and long pants, and bring insect repellent (you'll need it).

Fern Grotto

One of Kauai's oldest ("since 1947") and most popular attractions is this tacky-touristy trip filled with Hawaiian song and hula — but it's a good bit of fun nonetheless. Flat-bottomed boats take visitors up the Wailua River to a natural amphitheater filled with ferns that's the source of many Hawaiian legends (and a popular site for weddings). Mark my words: Within ten minutes of the launch, you'll be on your feet doing the Hukilau (Hawaii's version of the Hokey Pokey) along with everybody else. The Fern Grotto is lovely, but you'll see more stunning natural beauty just by heading to the north shore, so you have to be in the mood for the cheeky laughs as well as the ferns. It doesn't matter which boat operator you take; both offer just about the same experience for the same price. Allow 90 minutes for the entire trip.

Wailua Marina, at the mouth of the Wailua River. To get there: Turn off Kuhio Highway (Hwy. 56) into Wailua Marine State Park. Smith's Motor Boats: ☎ *808-821-6892. Waialeale Boat Tours:* ☎ *808-822-4908. Tickets: $15 adults, $7.50 kids 2–12. Reservations recommended. Open: Daily 9 a.m.–3:30 p.m.*

Kauai Museum

The biggest and best museum on the neighbor islands is housed in an attractive Greco-Roman-style building in downtown Lihue. If you're interested in the history of Kauai and neighboring Niihau (or if you just have a rainy day), it's definitely worth a stop. Among the holdings is a wealth of artifacts tracing the Garden Island's history from the beginning of time through contact — when Capt. James Cook "discovered" Kauai in 1778 — and the present. A short video presentation sets the context for what you'll see. The main room houses well-curated rotating exhibitions; I saw a fascinating photo exhibit documenting the reclamation of Kahoolawe, a Hawaiian island used as a U.S. military bombing target until it was returned to the Hawaiian people in the 1990s, a couple of years back. You won't need more than an hour to see the entire museum — maybe 90 minutes if you're really interested. The gift shop is one of the island's top stops for Kauai-made crafts. Free guided tours are offered Tuesday at 10 a.m.

4428 Rice St. (across from the post office), Lihue. ☎ *808-245-6931. Internet:* www.kauaimuseum.com. *Admission: $5 adults, $4 seniors, $3 students 13–17, $1 kids 6–12. Open: Mon–Fri 9 a.m.–4 p.m., Sat 10 a.m.–4 p.m.*

Kilauea Point National Wildlife Refuge

I just love this place. Sitting at the northernmost tip of the Hawaiian Islands and jutting out 200 feet above the deep blue surf, this nationally protected 203-acre headland habitat is a magnet for magnificent seabirds and landbirds alike. Park your car, pay your entrance fee, and walk an easy ³⁄₁₀-mile to the rocky headland, whose only structure is the Kilauea Lighthouse, serving as a beacon for ships arriving from Asian and South Pacific waters since 1913. Year-round you can spot red-footed boobies, Kauai's most visible seabird, which roost in the surrounding trees; the magnificent great frigatebird, with 7½-foot wings; and the endangered nene, or Hawaiian goose, the state bird of Hawaii. Depending on the time of year, you might also spot red- and white-tailed tropicbirds; Laysan albatross, famous for their elaborate courtship rituals; or wedgetailed shearwaters, which like to winter at sea. Informative placards make identification easy, even for novices. Look out to sea for spectacular views; if you get lucky, you might also spot sea turtles, spinner dolphins, and Hawaiian monk seals in the waters below. Call for the schedule of interpretive programs and guided hikes. Well worth a half-hour of your north shore time.

At the end of Kilauea Lighthouse Road, 1 mile north of Kilauea. To get there: From Kuhio Highway (Hwy. 56), turn right at the sign for Kilauea Lighthouse (at Menehune Mart and gas station, 23 miles north of Lihue). ☎ *808-828-1413. Internet:* pacific.fws.gov/pacific/wnwr/kkilaueanwr.html. *Admission: $2. Open: Daily 10 a.m.–4 p.m.*

The wildlife refuge closes its gate at 4 p.m. daily, but don't let that stop you from parking along Kilauea Lighthouse Road to watch one of Hawaii's most magnificent sunsets. No doubt you'll have company, both locals and in-the-know visitors, as you look west to watch the sun sink into the horizon beyond Hanalei Bay, brilliantly illuminating the luxuriant Bali Hai cliffs with its warm orange rays in the process.

Kokee State Park

Keep going upland and inland through Waimea Canyon, known as the Grand Canyon of the Pacific (see the listing later in this section), all the way to the top, where you'll find a high-altitude treat: Kokee (ko-KAY-eh) State Park. It's a whole different world up here at 4,000 feet: Kokee is a cloud forest at the edge of an upland bog known as the Alakai Swamp, where the breeze has a bite and trees look like the ones back home. Days are cool, wet, and mild, with intermittent bright sunshine — sort of like the Oregon Coast on a good day. The forest is full of beautiful native plants and imports, like ohia, rare stands of koa, hibiscus, eucalyptus, and redwoods. Pigs, goats, and black-tailed deer thrive in the forest, as do a wealth of native birds.

Before you get out of the car, head two miles above Kokee Lodge to Kalalau Lookout, the spectacular climax of your drive through Waimea Canyon and Kokee. The panoramic view is simply breathtaking. Then head back down to the park itself. Before you explore, stop at the Kokee Natural History Museum, a small, vital museum where you can learn about the forest and bog before you see it. If you want a bite to eat, Kokee Lodge is open for continental breakfast and lunch right next door.

After your museum visit, pick up the nature trail that starts behind the building at the rare Hawaiian koa tree (you'll see lots of expensive gifts, such as boxes and bowls, made out of this gorgeous wood in shops throughout the islands). The easy, self-guided walk is your best introduction to this rain forest, and it's great for those who'd rather not take on a tougher trail. The ¹⁄₁₀-mile walk takes about 20 minutes if you stop and look at all the plants that are identified along the way.

If you'd like to explore deeper into the park, you have 45 miles of well-maintained trails to choose from. Pick up an official park trail map at the museum (50 cents), which also sells more extensive hiking and trail guides that you can also pre-order via the Web site. Check the site for a list of recommendable self-guided hikes, plus a calendar of guided hikes, called "Wonder Walks" (offered from June through September), and other interpretive programs.

At the end of Kokee Road, 16 miles north of Waimea; from Kaumualii Highway (Highway 50), turn north on Highway 550, Waimea Canyon Drive, which eventually becomes Kokee Road. ☎ *808-335-9975. Internet:* www.aloha.net/~kokee. *Admission: Free! Open daily 24 hours; lodge, daily 9 a.m.–3:30 p.m.; museum, daily 10 a.m.–4 p.m.*

Here are a few tips to keep in mind when preparing for a visit to Kokee:

✔ No matter how hot and dry it is down at the beach, bring a jacket with you up to Kokee Average daytime temperatures range from 45°F in January to 68°F in July. Also bring rain gear and an umbrella if you have it — especially if you're visiting between October and May — as the annual rainfall up here is 70 inches. You can call the museum to check current conditions.

✔ Wear good shoes, as it can be damp and muddy — hiking boots are preferable (if you don't have them, sneakers will do).

✔ The best time to visit Kokee is early in the morning. That's when you have the best chance of seeing the panoramic view of Kalalau Valley from the lookout, before clouds obscure the valley and peaks. Early morning is also the best time to spot native birds.

> ✔ If you're going to hike, check trail conditions (posted on a bulletin board at the museum) before you set out. Stay on established trails, as it's easy to get lost here. Get off the trail well before dark. Carry water and rain gear, and wear sunscreen.

Limahuli Garden

If you've already visited the gorgeous Allerton Garden on the south shore (see the listing earlier in this section) and you want more, head to this north shore branch of the National Tropical Botanical Garden, where you'll find 17 lush Edenlike acres featuring lava-rock terraces of taro and other native and introduced species. This small, almost secret garden is ecotourism at its best. You're welcome to explore the garden on your own along a ¾-mile loop (be prepared — it's steep in some areas), which takes about 1½ hours. Or you can schedule a 2½-hour guided tour if you want botanical insight into what you're seeing. Wear comfortable walking shoes; umbrellas are available for your use in case it rains.

Near the north end of Kuhio Highway (Hwy. 56), ¼ mile before Kee Beach (look to your left, toward the mountain). ☎ *808-826-1053. Internet:* www.ntbg.org. *Reservations required for guided tours. Admission: $10, or $15 for the guided tour. Open: Tues–Fri and Sun 9:30 a.m.–4 p.m.*

Na Pali Coast State Park

Na Pali Coast State Park is the most spectacular place in the Hawaiian Islands. This 22-mile stretch of green-velvet fluted cliffs wraps around the northwest shore of Kauai. Seven valleys crease the soaring cliffs; hidden within are waterfalls, remote beaches, and other wonders of nature that are too beautiful to be real — and more than difficult to reach. You can see it one of three ways: On a commercial cruise for a from-the-sea perspective (see "Cruising the Na Pali Coast and other on-deck adventures" earlier in this chapter); via helicopter ride for an on-high view (see "Getting a bird's-eye view: flightseeing tours"); or by trekking in on your own two feet from the end of the road on the north shore.

The hike into this breathtakingly beautiful park, along the Kalalau Trail, may be too tough for most. First, you'll need a permit to walk the length of it (keep reading for more information); second, it winds for 11 grueling miles through the remote park, and takes about eight hours each way. I suggest hiking in just the first two miles, to Hanakapiai Beach, which is what most visitors do. Even this first stretch isn't easy — it's graded but never level, it's rocky the entire way, and the first mile's all uphill. You can, however, get a big payoff in terms of views by just hiking in the first half mile, which gives a good taste of the breathtaking natural beauty beyond. The trailhead is well marked, so this initial stretch is often crowded. Expect it to take between 60 and 90 rough-going minutes to reach the beach.

If you reach the two-mile mark and you want to see more, you can also hike another two miles inland from the beach to Hanakapiai Falls, a 120-foot cascade. This trail is more difficult, however, and it shouldn't be tackled if it's muddy (I saw people coming out who had been literally knee-deep in mud). Allow another three hours round-trip to the falls.

Kalalau trailhead at the end of Kuhio Highway (Hwy. 56) at Kee Beach, about 7½ miles past Hanalei. ☎ *808-274-3444. Internet:* www.hawaii.gov/dlnr/dsp/ NaPali/na_pali.htm.

If you're planning to hike the Kalalau Trail, keep these tips in mind as you plan your adventure:

- ✔ Wear good, supportive shoes (tennis shoes or hiking boots).

- ✔ Don't attempt even the first half-mile if the trail is too muddy.

- ✔ If you're going any farther than the first half-mile, bring plenty of water, plus a hat and sunscreen; snacks and insect repellent are a good idea, too.

- ✔ Use the PORTA-POTTIES at the parking lot before you hit the trail, because you'll find no facilities along it.

- ✔ If you get as far as Hanakapiai Beach, try to resist taking a dip, as currents are strong year-round, and drownings occur here regularly. Don't even think about it in winter.

- ✔ You are not allowed to go more than two miles down the trail without a permit. If you want to go farther, you'll need to get a day-use permit from the State Parks Office at 3060 Eiwa St., room 306, Lihue (☎ 808-274-3444); the office is open weekdays 8 a.m. to 3:30 p.m. (closed for lunch 11:45 a.m. to 1 p.m.). Permits were free at press time, but a schedule of fees may be instituted in the near future.

Sleeping Giant

If you squint your eyes as you drive down Kuhio Highway past the 1,241-foot-high Nounou Ridge, which forms a dramatic backdrop to the Coconut Coast towns of Wailua and Waipouli, you just may see the fabled Sleeping Giant. At the 7-mile marker, look toward the mountain. It's easy to spot: The geologic giant lies on his back, with his head pointing north and slightly east, his feet south and slightly west, and he's got his great mouth open in a mammoth yawn. As island legend goes, he's a giant named Puni who fell asleep after a great feast, but he reminds me of Gulliver and the Liliputians. You're welcome to climb the big guy if you like; the Sleeping Giant Trail offers an easy family hike to a fabulous panoramic view. From the parking lot, posted signs lead you over the 1¾-mile trail, which ends at a picnic table and shelter. Wear sunscreen and bring water — and a picnic, if you like.

Trailhead on Haleilio Road, off Kuhio Highway (Highway 56) between Wailua and Kapaa, just past mile marker 6. Turn toward the mountain off Kuhio Highway and follow Haleilio Road for 1.2 miles to the parking area at telephone pole no. 38.

Waimea Canyon

The great gaping gulch that Mark Twain dubbed the "Grand Canyon of the Pacific" is quite a sight — no other island offers anything like it. The nickname is apt, for the valley and its reddish lava beds remind everyone who sees it of Arizona's Grand Canyon. Kauai's version is bursting

with ever-changing color, just like its namesake, but it's much smaller —
only a mile wide, 3,567 feet deep, and 12 miles long. You can stop by the
road and look at it (it makes a great stop on your way to Kokee State Park;
see the previous section), hike down in it, or swoop through it in a helicopter (see "Getting a bird's-eye view: flightseeing tours" earlier in this
chapter).

As you climb north — and up in elevation — the first good vantage point
you'll reach is Waimea Canyon Lookout, located between the 10- and
11-mile markers on Waimea Canyon Road. Take a peek; you'll see why the
canyon got its nickname. A few more lookout points dot the route, each
offering spectacular views; Puu Hina Hina Lookout, located between the
13- and 14-mile markers at 3,336 feet in elevation, is a particular jewel.

If you want to hike in, your best bet is the Canyon Trail, which leads to
the east rim for a breathtaking view into the canyon. Park your car at the
top of Halemanu Valley Road, located between the 14- and 15-mile markers on Waimea Canyon Road, about a mile down from the Kokee Natural
History Museum. Walk down the not-very-clearly marked trail on the
3.6-mile round-trip, which takes about two to three hours and leads to
Waipoo Falls and back. I suggest going in the afternoon — following your
visit to Kokee is best — when the late afternoon light illuminates the
canyon magnificently.

*About 11 miles north of Waimea; turn north from Kaumualii Highway (Hwy. 50) onto
Waimea Canyon Drive (Hwy. 550).*

One of the best views of Waimea Canyon is from the seat of a bike —
coasting 12 miles down the miraculously multihued canyon.
Outfitters Kauai (☎ 808-742-9667 or 808-742-7421; Internet: www.
outfitterskauai.com) offers group rides from rim to sea level on
safe, comfortable cruiser bikes fitted with power brakes. A guide
knowledgeable in local flora and fauna leads the way, and you'll stop
periodically for photo ops and to learn about what you're seeing. This
4½-hour adventure is a fun, leisurely way to enjoy the canyon (and it's
a much easier trip than the similar tour of Haleakala Crater offered on
Maui). The sunrise trip is awe-inspiring, but the sunset tour is almost
as magical and a great option for late-day bloomers. The price is $70
per person, including all gear and snacks, and you have to be 10 or
older to join in the fun. Outfitters Kauai also has bikes for rent if you'd
prefer to pedal around the island on your own.

Hitting the links and courts

Golf

Always book your tee times well in advance — before you leave home,
preferably — especially in high season.

Stand-by Golf (☎ 888-645-2665 or 808-553-8222; Internet: www.
standbygolf.com) offers up to 50 percent off greens fees to bargain
hunters and last-minute duffers at nine courses on Kauai. What's available depends on when you call and where you're staying; give it a shot
if you want to save a few bucks or get a sudden urge to hit the links.

Lihue

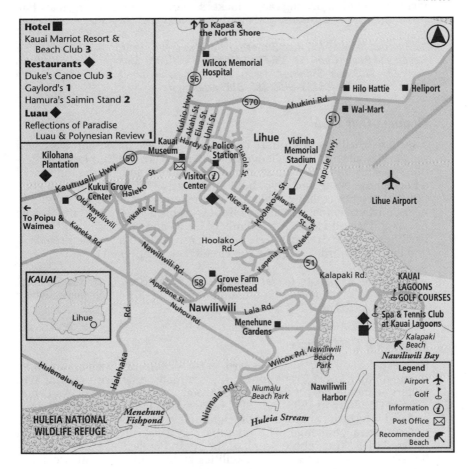

Hotel ■
Kauai Marriot Resort &
    Beach Club **3**
Restaurants ◆
Duke's Canoe Club **3**
Gaylord's **1**
Hamura's Saimin Stand **2**
Luau ◆
Reflections of Paradise
    Luau & Polynesian Review **1**

↑ To Kapaa &
the North Shore

Wilcox Memorial
Hospital

⑤⑥

⑤⑦⓪   Ahukini Rd.

Hilo Hattie   Heliport

⑤①   Wal-Mart

Kauai Hardy St. Police
Museum   Station   Lihue   Vidinha
                                                Memorial
                                                Stadium

Kuhio Hwy. Akahi St. Elua St. Umi St.

Kilohana
Plantation

⑤⓪

Kaumualii Hwy.   St.   Haleko

Kukui Grove
Center   Pikake St.

Old Nawiliwili Rd.

← To Poipu &
Waimea   Kaneka Rd.

Visitor ⓘ
Center

Rice St.   Hoolako St. Halau St. Haoa St. Peleke St.

Piaole St.   Kapule Hwy.

Lihue Airport

Nawiliwili Rd.

Hoolako
Rd.

Kapena St.

⑤①

Apapane St.   ⑤⑧   Grove Farm
                                Homestead

Kalapaki Rd.   **KAUAI
                                LAGOONS
                                GOLF COURSES**

KAUAI

Lihue ○   Rd.   Nuhou Rd.

Nawiliwili   Lala Rd.
                        Menehune ■
                        Gardens

Spa & Tennis Club
at Kauai Lagoons

Kalapaki
Beach

Nawiliwili Bay

Hulemalu Rd.   Haleheka

Wilcox Rd. Nawiliwili
            Beach
            Park

Legend

Airport ✈

Golf ⛳

Niumala Rd.   Niumalu
                    Beach Park   **Nawiliwili
                                        Harbor**

Information ⓘ

Post Office ✉

**HULEIA NATIONAL
WILDLIFE REFUGE**   *Menehune
                            Fishpond*   *Huleia Stream*

Recommended
Beach ↖

Kauai Lagoons Golf Courses

Kauai Lagoons often appears on lists of top resort courses in the U.S.; in 2000, *Golf Digest* awarded Kauai Lagoons its gold medal, calling the Kiele Course "one of the four finest courses in the country." Both of the Jack Nicklaus–designed courses are excellent: the Mokihana Course is an 18-hole Scottish-style links course that's ideal for recreational golfers, while the Kiele Championship Course offers an exciting blend of tournament-quality challenge and high-traffic playability — perfect for low handicappers.

The Kiele winds up with one of Hawaii's most difficult — and rewarding — holes, a 431-yard, par-4 played straightaway to an island green surrounded by water; but the signature is the par-4, 330-yard 16th, a short but demanding ocean cliff shot whose green isn't even visible from the tee. (The trick is to hit your tee shot toward the coconut trees on the right side of the fairway.)

The two courses share one of the largest practice facilities in the islands; facilities include a driving range, lockers, showers, restaurant, snack bar, pro shop, practice greens, golf clubhouse, and golf club and shoe rental.

3351 Hoolaulea Way (off Rice Street), Lihue (turn at the sign for the Kauai Marriott Resort and Beach Club). ☎ *800-634-6400 or 808-241-6000. Mokihana course greens fees: $85–$100, $65–$80 after 11 a.m., depending on where you're staying. Kiele Course greens fees: $125–$150, $95–$105 after noon.*

Kiahuna Golf Club

This par-70, 6,353-yard Robert Trent Jones, Jr.–designed course is a real only-in-Hawaii gem. Its challenging layout plays around four large archaeological sites, ranging from an ancient Hawaiian temple to the remains of a Portuguese home and crypt built in the early 1800s. The Scottish-style links course has rolling terrain, undulating greens, sand bunkers galore, near-constant winds, a swath of rainbow-colored vegetation, and terrific ocean and island views. A good mix of locals and visitors man the tees. Facilities include driving range, practice greens, and a terrific breakfast-and-lunch restaurant, Joe's on the Green (see Chapter 21).

2545 Kiahuna Plantation Dr. (at Poipu Road), Poipu Beach. ☎ *808-742-9595. Internet:* www.kiahunagolf.com. *Greens fees: $65–$75, depending on where you're staying; $60 after 11 a.m., $40 after 2 p.m.*

Poipu Bay Golf Course

Not yet a decade old, this 6,959-yard, par-72 oceanfront links-style course designed by Robert Trent Jones, Jr., is already a favorite among avid golfers — including, no doubt, Tiger Woods, who won the PGA's Grand Slam of Golf here in 1998 and 1999. Fairways and greens are undulating, and water hazards are located on eight holes; the prevailing tradewinds add an extra challenge. The champs play this rugged beauty, often referred to as "the Pebble Beach of the South Pacific," like a British Isles links course — smart and low. Facilities include an excellent pro shop, plus a restaurant, driving range, and putting greens.

2250 Ainako St. (across the street from the Hyatt Regency Kauai), Poipu Beach. ☎ *800-858-6300 or 808-742-8711. Internet:* www.kauai-hyatt.com/golf. *Greens fees: $155, $110 after 12:30 p.m.*

Princeville Resort Golf Courses

Nestled in the glorious environs of Kauai's north shore, these two much-heralded Robert Trent Jones, Jr., designs are the real stars of the Kauai show. One of the most breathtaking — and toughest — golf courses in all of Hawaii, the Prince sits on 390 acres carefully sculpted to offer ocean views from every hole. Golfers in the know often name it the best layout in the state, and *Golf Digest* lauded it as the number-one course in Hawaii. Some holes have a waterfall backdrop to the greens, others shoot into the hillside, and the famous par-3 seventh requires that you tee off over a stunning wide-mouthed gorge – dead against the wind, no less. Needless to say, accuracy is key here; if you miss the fairway, chances are good that your ball's in the drink.

The Makai is more forgiving, but don't kick back just yet. It's actually three nine-hole courses in one — the Ocean, the Woods, and the Lakes — with the Lakes being the most spectacular and the Ocean being the most thrilling, thanks to a seventh hole that requires you to shoot from one ocean promontory to the other, with the blue Pacific roiling below.

Facilities include a health club and spa, a restaurant and bar, clubhouse, golf shop, and driving range.

In the Princeville Resort, off Kuhio Highway (Hwy. 56) at mile marker 27. ☎ *800-826-1105 or 808-826-5070. Internet:* www.princeville.com/play. *Prince course greens fees: $165 ($110–$130 for Princeville guests). Makai course greens fees: $120 ($95–$100 for Princeville guests).*

Tennis

Most resorts and many condo complexes have their own well-maintained courts, some even lit for night play. If yours doesn't, all of the following have courts that are open to the public. Be sure to reserve ahead, and expect to pay court fees between $10 and $25.

In Lihue, the **Spa & Tennis Club at Kauai Lagoons,** 3351 Hoolaulea Way (next to the Kauai Marriott Resort and Beach Club; ☎ **808-246-2414**), has eight courts to choose from, plus private lessons and a daily clinic.

At Poipu Beach, the **Tennis Garden & Sports Center** at the Hyatt Regency Resort and Spa, 1571 Poipu Rd. (☎ **808-742-1234**), has four plexi-pave courts, plus group clinics, round robins, private lessons for all levels, and an excellent pro shop. There's also the **Kiahuna Tennis Club,** on Poipu Road just past the Poipu Shopping Village (☎ **808-742-9533**), which has ten courts in an exceptionally lovely setting.

On the north shore, the **Princeville Tennis Club** (☎ **808-826-3620** or 808-826-9823; Internet: www.princeville.com/play) has six courts available, plus pro instruction in clinics or private lessons, and a full-service pro shop.

Horseback riding

There's no better way to admire Kauai's remarkable natural scenery than from high in the saddle. In the Poipu area, **CJM Country Stables** (☎ **808-742-6096**; Internet: www.cjmstables.com) offers a number of guided 2- to 3½-hour rides along the beach, some of which work in a break for a swim and a picnic. Prices run $65 to $90 per person, and all levels of riders are accepted.

Personally, I think the spectacular north shore makes even better quarter-horse stomping grounds. **Princeville Ranch Stables** (☎ **808-826-7777** or 808-826-7473; Internet: www.princevilleranch.com) can take you out on a whole host of guided rides, from a casual yet magical three- or four-hour waterfall picnic ride to horsemanship lessons for serious riders. Prices range from $55 for 1½ hours in the saddle to $125 if you want to participate in a full-on cattle drive. They also offer guided hikes, plus sunset dinner and wagon rides that are a great adventure for the entire family.

Always book horseback adventures with plenty of advance notice — before you leave home is best — and always inquire about age, height, weight, and other restrictions.

Getting pampered at the spa

This is your vacation, after all — so what better time to succumb to the soothing treatments that a day at the spa can offer? If you have such a plan, you've come to the right place, because Kauai is home to two first-rate spas — one on the south shore, the second conveniently located on the north shore.

The 25,000-foot, state-of-the-art **Anara Spa,** at the Hyatt Regency Kauai Resort & Spa, 1571 Poipu Rd., Poipu Beach (☎ 808-742-1234; Internet: www.kauai-hyatt.com/anara), is one of Hawaii's finest spa facilities. "Anara" is an acronym for "A New Age Restorative Approach," which sets the tone for Anara's touchy-feely, homeopathic-minded mission — and God bless 'em for it. This phenomenal facility is the perfect place to spend the day — and the spa's masterminds know it, which is why they designed a full slate of spa packages that run anywhere from 1½ hours to a complete day of head-to-toe pampering. You'll spend an arm and a leg here, but it's worth every penny. Stand-alone services are available as well. This place is always booked up, so reserve well ahead.

On the north shore, **Princeville Health Club & Spa** (☎ 808-826-5030; Internet: www.princeville.com) isn't quite so extensive, mission-oriented, or eye-catching, but its facilities are comfortable, its spa menu appropriately lengthy, and its technicians first-rate. Prices are lower, too — $90 for a 60-minute massage, as opposed to $100 for a 50-minute rubdown at Anara.

A shopper's guide to Kauai

The Garden Isle isn't exactly what you'd call a shopper's destination, so don't come expecting to give your credit card an aerobic workout. Still, a few hidden gems make the Garden Isle sparkle, especially for those in search of gifts with a Hawaiian flair.

In Lihue

One of the best resources for Kauai-made crafts and gifts is the shop at the **Kauai Museum,** across from the post office at 4428 Rice St., downtown Lihue (☎ 808-245-6931; Internet: www.kauaimuseum.com). In addition to astonishing native-wood bowls that have been carved and polished to a high sheen, the shop boasts a nice collection of budget-friendly koa gifts like barrettes, bracelets, and key rings, all made from the gorgeous native wood. The little shop also has a good selection of books, lauhala bags, coconut products, and more. You can only reach the shop through the museum entrance, but the door attendant will let you in for free if you want to skip the permanent collection and head straight for the saleable stuff.

The Kauai outpost of **Hilo Hattie,** Hawaii's biggest name in aloha wear, is at 3252 Kuhio Hwy., at Ahukini Road (the turnoff for the airport; ☎ 808-245-4724; Internet: www.hilohattie.com). Geared to the tourist market, Hilo Hattie carries inexpensive, colorful wear that has substantially improved in quality and style in recent years.

On the Coconut Coast

Kuhio Highway is dotted with mini-malls boasting practical stops and familiar shops, from Safeway to the Sunglass Hut. Most prominent is the **Coconut Marketplace,** 484 Kuhio Hwy., between the Wailua River and Kapaa (☎ 808-822-3641). This open-air mall features a largely unimpressive collection of 70 or so shops, mostly of the gift variety. Highlights include **Ship Store Galleries,** which features a compelling collection of 19th-century nautical antiques among the contemporary art; the **Happy Kauaian** for its unabashed collection of tacky souvenirs; and Kauai's own **Lappert's Ice Cream,** a must-stop for ice-cream lovers. Free entertainment, either hula or live music, is offered at the centerstage daily at 5 p.m.

If it's a rainy day and you want to kill some time by catching a flick, see what's on at the Coconut Marketplace Cinemas by calling ☎ 808-821-2324.

One of my favorite shopping stops in all of Hawaii is **Bambulei** (☎ 808-823-8641), which takes a little effort to find, but stick with it, especially if you're a retro buff, because you're bound to come away with a prize: It's on the inland side of Kuhio Highway just south of the Coconut Marketplace, behind the green storefront across from Kintaro Restaurant. Watch for the multicolored sign just past the Wailua intersection (where Sizzler is). Little Bambulei is home to a charmingly displayed collection of vintage Hawaii collectibles, from salt-and-pepper shakers and '50s fiberglass-shade lamps to aloha shirts and vintage bamboo furniture, plus a small but quality selection of new aloha wear. It's a real joy to browse. Next door is Caffe Coco, an equally appealing spot for a light snack or a full meal (see Chapter 21).

On the north shore

The north shore is the Garden Island's premier shopping destination. The venues may be fewer and far between, but what's here is top quality all the way.

The simple town of Kilauea is home to the north shore's premier shopping stop: **Kong Lung Company,** housed in a historic stone building on Kilauea Road and Keneke Street, a few blocks from Kuhio Highway (☎ 808-828-1822; Internet: www.konglung.com). This roomy and gorgeous Asian-accented gallery of design brims with beautiful homewares and gifts from Hawaii and around the world, all artfully displayed. The collections of women's wear and aloha shirts in back are the height of casual island fashion. The shop is expensive, but not overpriced; this is beautiful stuff.

Behind Kong Lung Co. is **Island Soap & Candle Works** (☎ 808-828-1955; Internet: www.handmade-soap.com), a charming stop for fragrant island-made soaps and candles. You can even watch the craftspeople at work, fashioning sweet-smelling candles out of freeform wax. Next door is the **Lotus Gallery of Fine Art** (☎ 808-828-9898; Internet: www.jewelofthelotus.com), a pan-Asian gallery (with an emphasis on works from India, Nepal, and Tibet) that's something of an oddball but nonetheless boasts some incredible gold and talismanic jewelry as well as antique artifacts and carpets.

Relatively new to Kilauea is **Jungle Girl,** 2488 Kolo Rd. (☎ 808-828-1370), which specializes in affordable island-style imports from around the globe: sarongs, casual dresses, jewelry, and the like.

To reach Kilauea from Kuhio Highway (Highway 56), turn right at the sign for Kilauea Lighthouse (at the Menehune Mart and gas station, 23 miles north of Lihue); a few blocks down on your right is Keneke Street and Kong Lung. To reach Jungle Girl, take the first right off Kilauea Road. (Kilauea is tiny, so it's virtually impossible to get lost.)

Kilauea also boasts some great restaurants, my favorite of which is **Roadrunner Cafe** for nouvelle Mexican with Hawaiian accents; there's also **Lighthouse Bistro** if you're not in the mood for island-style Mexican. See Chapter 21 for details. If you're looking for a quick bite, stop into **Pau Hana Pizza/Kilauea Bakery,** just behind the Lighthouse Bistro at Kong Lung Center (☎ 808-828-2020; Internet: www.islandbreadsticks.com), which bakes up killer fresh pastry and innovative pizzas.

Hanalei boasts more great shopping. Two of the town's finest shops are at the entrance to Hanalei town, on the ocean side of Kuhio Highway just after the bridge and Kayak Kauai Outbound: **Ola's** (☎ 808-826-6937), a top stop for high-quality island crafts, including a gorgeous collection of jewelry and koa pieces; and **Kai Kane's** (☎ 808-826-5594), which is great for hip aloha and surf wear (their groovy collection of surfboards alone is worth a peek).

In the heart of Hanalei on the ocean side of the street, **Ching Young Village** covers the basics, from supermarket to pizza joint. Unrepentant shoppers should instead head across the street to **Hanalei Center,** which boasts a small but satisfying collection of boutiques. The stand-out is the **Yellowfish Trading Company** (☎ 808-826-1227), which features an eye-popping assemblage of vintage and contemporary Hawaiiana and gifts with wide-ranging appeal (read: you don't have to be a retro nut to love this place), plus vintage bark-cloth fabrics, in case you want to give your home that tropical touch. The **Hanalei Surf Company,** in the old school building at the Hanalei Center (☎ 808-826-9000), is the place to go for surf gear and beach goodies.

In the Poipu Beach Area

Poipu has few notable shopping opportunities. On your way to Poipu Beach you'll pass **Old Koloa Town,** a block-long collection of less-than-exciting storefronts; highlights include Kauai-made **Lappert's Ice**

Cream; a branch of the more-pleasing-than-you'd-expect local T-shirt chain **Crazy Shirts;** and another branch of **Jungle Girl** (see "On the north shore" earlier in this chapter).

Boutique lovers will find a good mix of sportswear, sandals, and the like at **Poipu Shopping Village,** 2360 Kiahuna Plantation Dr. (at Poipu Road). The standouts are **Honolua Surf Co.** (☎ 808-742-9152; Internet: www.honoluasurf.com), a Maui-based company that makes terrific quality casual wear whose appeal reaches well beyond the surf crowd; and **Hale Mana** (☎ 808-742-1027), a gorgeous boutique with a beautiful mix of vintage Orientalia, smartly designed jewelry, and new Asian-themed clothing and gifts.

My favorite stop for Hawaii-made crafts — even more so than the Kauai Museum Shop — is the Visitor Center at the **Allerton Garden,** on Lawai Road across the street from Spouting Horn (☎ 808-742-2623), where the simply displayed collection is small but high-quality. The emphasis is on smallish, affordable items such as koa accessories, lauhala hatboxes, botanical prints, and Hawaii-made paper goods, although a few excellent examples of koa calabashes and jewelry boxes are always on display.

Living It Up After the Sun Goes Down

Things really couldn't get much quieter than they already are on Kauai. This is an island made for daytime fun — so my advice is to make sunset the highlight, enjoy a leisurely dinner, and call it a night.

If you want a bit more action, Poipu Beach is your best bet. At the Hyatt Regency Kauai Resort & Spa, 1571 Poipu Rd. (☎ 808-742-1234), the **Seaview Terrace** makes a lovely spot for sunset cocktails and live Hawaiian entertainment. Once the sun goes down, head indoors to **Stevenson's Library**, a cozy librarylike lounge offering live soft jazz and a noteworthy menu of after-dinner drinks, including respectable single-malt and vintage port lists.

Even if you don't dine there, you can still stop at the lounge at the **Beach House Restaurant,** 5022 Lawai Rd. (off Poipu Road, toward Spouting Horn), Poipu Beach (☎ 808-742-1424; Internet: www.the-beach-house.com), for tropical cocktails and a glorious view of the sun setting over the Poipu surf.

At the Poipu Shopping Village, at Poipu Road and Kiahuna Plantation Drive, **Keoki's Paradise** (☎ 808-742-7534) features a lengthy tropical drinks menu in the relaxing tiki-style bar, plus live music (usually a trio performing a mix of Hawaiian standards and contemporary hits) Thursday and Friday nights. For a similar scene in Lihue, head to Keoki's sister restaurant, **Duke's Canoe Club,** on the beach at the Kauai Marriott and Beach Club, 3610 Rice St. (near Nawiliwili Harbor; ☎ 808-246-9599), which also features live Hawaiian music on Thursday and Friday.

On the north shore, my favorite hangout is **Sushi, Blues & Grill,** in Ching Young Village, 5-8420 Kuhio Hwy., Hanalei (☎ **808-826-9701**). This cavernous and casual-chic sushi bar and restaurant features great food (see Chapter 21), a big bar with extensive vodka, gin, martini, sake, and beer lists, and live jazz and blues or dance music three or four nights a week. When the music's on, this is one of the liveliest scenes on the island.

Just a stone's throw down the block is **Zelo's Beach House,** at Kuhio Highway and Aku Road in the heart of Hanalei (☎ **808-826-9700**), a hip, happy spot that brims with friendly energy and beachy charm. The welcoming tropical-style bar boasts a lengthy menu of tropical cocktails, martinis, and microbrews.

Another fine way to celebrate the end of another day in paradise is to set sail on a sunset cruise. **Bluewater Sailing, Capt. Andy's Sailing Adventures,** and **Captain Sundown** — all recommended earlier in this chapter, under "Cruising the Na Pali Coast and other on-deck adventures)" — offer regularly scheduled sunset sails, both with *pupus* (appetizers) and drinks (only Captain Andy serves booze, but you're welcome to BYOB on Bluewater's and Captain Sundown's cruise).

It's a good idea to book your sunset cruise up to a week in advance during high season.

Of course, for the most animated after-dark entertainment, head to — you guessed it — a luau. Kauai has some good options that increase the appeal of just-okay food with an open bar and surprisingly good island-style entertainment; for my recommendations on the island's best, see Chapter 21.

Part VII
The Part of Tens

The 5th Wave   By Rich Tennant

"Pssst - Philip! It's not too late to fly back
to a more civilized island."

In this part . . .

*I*t wouldn't be a ...*For Dummies* book without a couple of these lists of ten! In the first of the two chapters, I give you insider tips on how to ditch the tourist trappings and fit in like a local. In the second chapter, I give you the low-down on island dining and traditional Hawaiian eats and tell you how to decipher the local culinary lingo.

Chapter 23

Ten Ways to Lose the Tourist Trappings and Look Like a Local

● ●

In This Chapter

▶ Fitting in on the Islands

▶ Making yourself at home in paradise

● ●

*H*awaii may be the 50th state, but it's an ocean — and a world — apart from its 49 mainland brethren. In fact, since it didn't join the star-spangled party until 1959, Hawaii came into the Union as an adopted adult, complete with its own unique personality, fully formed (indeed, ancient) culture, and distinct world view.

That Honolulu sits closer to Tokyo than it does to Washington, D.C. — or even Chicago, for that matter — also affects matters, creating a further divide between the islands and the Eurocentric perspective that many Americans have of the world.

Even the population is dramatically different. Unlike in the rest of the U.S., no one ethnic group forms a majority in Hawaii. While Caucasian and Japanese are the two largest ethnic groups (each account for roughly 22 percent of the population), nearly 35 percent of islanders consider themselves of mixed ethnicity. Hawaii's residents, as a group, don't consider race a factor in marriage; they're just as likely to marry someone from a different race as not.

The fact that Hawaii is both exotic and familiar is one of its greatest appeals. It's also one of the biggest pitfalls for visitors, however: Since Hawaii is part of the good ol' U.S. of A., many first-time visitors think they have it all figured out. What could there be to know?

A few things, it turns out. If you'd rather come across as a *akamai* (smart) traveler instead of advertising your status as a *malihini* (newcomer), read on.

Mastering the Two Most Important Words in the Hawaiian Language

Everyone in Hawaii speaks English, of course. A few Hawaiian words and phrases have made their way into the common vernacular, though, and regularly pop up in everyday conversation.

You probably already know the Hawaiian word *aloha* (a-LO-ha), which serves as an all-purpose greeting — hello, welcome, or goodbye. It's a warm and wonderful word full of grace and compassion and good feeling, so use it liberally; there's no better way to get caught up in the true spirit of Hawaii.

A second word that every visitor should learn is *mahalo* (ma-HA-low), which means "thank you" and is used extensively throughout Hawaii. If you want to say "Thanks very much!" or "Thank you *so* much," say *mahalo nui loa* (ma-HA-low NOO-ee LOW-ah). Not only will the locals be impressed with your efforts to learn, but they'll be flattered by your graciousness, too.

Learning a Few More Hawaiian Words and Phrases

If you only learn *aloha* and *mahalo,* you'll do just fine. But if you consider yourself ahead of the curve and would like to know a few more useful words, take a few minutes to study the following list. That way, when you're in a restaurant and the waiter offers your little ones a *keiki* menu, describes today's lunch special as particularly *ono,* or asks you if you're *pau* when he comes to clear your plate, you'll feel like a regular *kamaaina:*

- **alii** (ah-LEE-ee): Hawaiian royalty
- **halau** (ha-LAU): School
- **hale** (HA-lay): House
- **haole** (HOW-lee): Foreigner or Caucasian (literally "out of breath" — pale, or paleface); a common reference, not an insult (usually)
- **heiau** (heh-EE-ow): Hawaiian temple
- **hui** (HOO-ee): A club, collective, or assembly (for example, an artists' collective is an artists' hui)
- **hula** (HOO-lah): Native dance
- **imu** (EE-moo): Underground oven lined with hot rocks that's used for cooking the luau pig
- **kahuna** (ka-HOO-nah): Priest or expert

✔ **kamaaina** (ka-ma-EYE-nah): Local person

✔ **kapu** (KA-poo): Anything that's taboo, forbidden

✔ **keiki** (KEH-kee): Child

✔ **kupuna** (koo-POO-nah): An elder, leader, grandparent, or anyone who commands great respect

✔ **lanai** (LAH-nigh): Porch or veranda

✔ **lei** (lay): Garland (usually of flowers, leaves, or shells)

✔ **luau** (LOO-ow): A celebratory feast

✔ **malihini** (ma-li-HEE-nee): Stranger or newcomer

✔ **mana** (MA-na): Spirit, divine power

✔ **muumuu** (moo-oo-MOO-oo): A loose-fitting dress, usually in a tropical print

✔ **ono** (OH-no): Delicious

✔ **pau** (pow): Finished or done

✔ **pali** (PAH-lee): Cliff

Pronouncing Those Pesky Hawaiian Words and Place Names

Since the Hawaiian language has only 12 characters to work with — the five vowels (*a, e, i, o,* and *u*), plus seven consonants (*h, k, l, m, n, p,* and *w*) — Hawaiian words and names tend to be long and difficult, with lots of repetitive syllables that can really get your vocal chords into a twist. Master just a few basic rules of thumb, however, and "Honoapiilani Highway" and "Haliimaile" will be rolling of your tongue like "Main Street" and "Anytown, USA" in no time.

Half of the letters in the Hawaiian language — h, k, l, m, n, and p — sound out just like they do in English. The one consonant that sounds different in Hawaiian is **w**. W usually carries the "v" sound when it follows "i" or "e"; for example, the Oahu town of Haleiwa is "Ha-lay-EE-vah." At the beginning of words and after "a," "u," and "o," though, it's usually your standard "w" — hence Wailea (why-LAY-ah) and Makawao (mah-KAH-wow), two Maui destinations.

The vowels are pronounced like this:

a	*ah* (as in father) or *uh* (as in above)
e	*eh* (as in bed) or *ay* (as in they)
i	*ee* (as in police)
o	*oh* (as in vote)
u	*oo* (as in too)

Almost all vowels are sounded separately, although some are pronounced together, as in the name of Waikiki's main thoroughfare, Kalakaua Avenue, which is pronounced "Kah-lah-COW-ah".

Here's the most important tip to remember when trying to pronounce a Hawaiian word or name: Get into the habit of seeing long words or names as a collection of short syllables, and you'll find them much easier to say. (Accents almost always fall on the second-to-last syllable.)

The trick is knowing where to put on the breaks. That leads me to important tip number two: All syllables end with vowels, so a consonant will always indicate the start of a new syllable. One of the best examples of this is the tongue-twisting Kealakekua Bay (the famous marine preserve off the Big Island's Kona coast), which throws nearly everyone for a loop. Break the syllables down by reading the consonants as red flags, though, and see how easy it becomes: "Kay-ah-lah-keh-KOO-ah".

The Hawaiian language actually has a 13th character: the glottal stop, which looks exactly like a single opening quotation mark (‘) and is meant to indicate a pause. I've chosen not to use the glottal stop throughout this book; it's often left out in printed Hawaiian and on things like store and street signs. While serious Hawaiian-language students would learn volumes about the glottal stop and its equal importance to its fellow consonants and vowels, you don't need to worry about it for your purposes; you can basically ignore it when you see it.

I've laid out these basics so that you can understand how the language works, but don't expect to become an expert at pronouncing Hawaiian words anytime soon. Whenever I return to Hawaii, I always feel as if it takes me a day or two to get my tongue back in working order — and I *know* this stuff. Still, it's fun to practice — and with these basic tools under your belt, you'll quickly get the hang of it. Practice with the first two examples at the start of this chapter and you'll really impress the locals when you get to Maui: Honoapiilani Highway (ho-no-ah-pee-ee-LA-nee) and Haliimaile (ha-lee-EE-MY-lee).

Knowing How to Give and Take Directions

Leave your compass at home, because islanders have a different sense of direction than mainlanders do. While locals do think of the islands as having north shores and south shores, west coasts and east coasts, seldom will anybody direct you using the most common directional terms.

Instead, they'll send you either **makai** (ma-KAI), a directional meaning toward the sea, or **mauka** (MOW-kah), meaning toward the mountains. Since each island is basically a volcano with a single coastal road circling it, those two terms are often enough to do the trick.

If you'd like to learn more

If the vocabulary list and pronunciation key in this chapter whet your appetite for the Hawaiian language, a few Web sites can help you learn more. Probably most comprehensive is the Hawaiian Language Web site (www.geocities. com/TheTropics/Shores/6794), but it may be too much for all but the most curious among you. Ernie's Learn to Speak a Little Hawaiian site (www.mhpcc.edu/~erobello) is a great resource for beginners; it boasts a more detailed pronunciation key and an excellent list of expressions, as well as some fun Hawaii links.

If you'd like to translate specific words or terms, use the searchable online dictionaries at the Coconut Boyz' Internet Island (www.hisurf.com) or the Mamaka Kaiao dictionary (www.olelo.hawaii.edu/OP/dictionary).

If you'd prefer a hard-copy Hawaiian-language reference or dictionary, a number are available at the online bookstores, including Arthur Schultz's *All About Hawaiian,* and the *New Pocket Hawaiian Dictionary,* published by the University of Hawaii and generally considered the standard.

When they don't, locals are likely to invoke relative terms rather than "north," "south," "east," or "west." If you're standing in Kapaa on Kauai's east shore, for instance, they'll tell you to head toward Lihue if they want you to go south. In Honolulu, people use **Diamond Head** when they mean to the east (in the direction of the world-famous crater called Diamond Head), and **Ewa** (EE-va) when they mean to the west (in the direction of the town called Ewa, beyond Pearl Harbor).

So if you ask an islander for directions on Oahu, you're likely to hear something like this: "Turn left and go two miles Diamond Head (east), turn at the light and go two blocks *makai* (toward the sea), then turn at the stop light. Go two more blocks, and turn Ewa (west); the address you want is on the *mauka* (mountain) side of the street." If you're on the Big Island at a luxury Kohala Coast resort and you're heading out to catch a snorkel cruise, for example, it's more likely to sound like this: "Go eight miles past Kailua-Kona (south) to mile marker 109. Turn *makai* (toward the ocean) on King Kam Road, then left at the bottom of the hill."

Remembering that You're in the United States

Don't say "back home in the U.S." when you're talking to folks in Hawaii. This seems like a real no-brainer, but that long flight across the Pacific and the one-of-a-kind Hawaii ambience and culture can really play tricks with your mind. Islanders are, by and large, a patriotic bunch, so they don't take kindly to being left off the national map. Refer to the continental United States as the mainland, which is what they do.

Another very important point in the same vein: Locals are always called "islanders," *never* Hawaiians, unless they have native blood, which very few islanders do. (Hawaiian is an ethnic label.)

Red Isn't Your Color: Wearing Sunscreen

You don't need a trained eye to spot the newest arrivals a mile away — they're the ones with the excruciating sunburns. *Way* too many newcomers fry themselves on day one of their vacations in a overzealous quest to tan, putting a major damper on their trip — and, sometimes, their long-term health — in the process.

Hawaii's sun-loving population has achieved the dubious distinction of having the highest incidence of skin cancer in the United States, and as a result has developed quite an attachment to sunscreen. The deep-tanning Coppertone days are a thing of the past, even among the most zealous sun worshippers — so people will merely look on in horror rather than admiration if you whip out a bottle of SPF 8 to spread on your just-flown-in virgin skin.

Most locals I know use SPF 25 or 30 sunscreen on a daily basis; you should, too. Never go out in the sun, not even for 10 minutes, wearing anything less than SPF 15; those of you with light complexions should stick with SPF 30.

Your best bet is to apply sunscreen — liberally — first thing in the morning, before you get dressed (to avoid missing those inch-below-the-cuff spots, which can result in nasty burns). Apply more sunscreen before you head to the beach, and do regular reapplications (every hour or two) as you sit on the sand. Don't throw on a T-shirt and consider yourself covered; the average white T-shirt only offers coverage equal to SPF 6 sunscreen. And ignore all claims of "waterproof" — always give yourself a fresh coat immediately after swimming.

 Always make sure you apply sunscreen under bathing suit straps, on the tops of your feet, on the back of your neck, and on your ears and lips — all spots that are the easiest to forget but the most sensitive to painful burns. To prevent sunscreen from dripping into your eyes, use a waxy sunscreen stick around your eyes and a high-SPF lip balm; both are available at just about any Hawaii convenience store.

Additionally, always wear sunglasses and a hat while you're in the sun. Throw away those $5 shades and splurge on a decent pair with UV filters to protect your corneas from sunburn and to prevent cataracts. Wear a hat with a wide brim that goes all the way around, as baseball caps leave some of your most vulnerable areas — your ears and neck — exposed to the sun's harsh rays.

Attention, mom and dad: Infants under six months should not be directly exposed to the harsh Hawaiian sun. Older babies need zinc oxide to protect their fragile skin, and kids should be slathered with high-SPF sunscreen every hour. They also need shades, hats, and other protective gear.

If you start to turn red, get out of the sun immediately. If your skin is red, it's burned, and that's serious; what's more, since sunburns often don't achieve their full redness until 8 to 24 hours later, it could be worse than you think. If you see even a hint of red, head to the shade.

If you do get a burn, the best remedy is to stay out of the sun until the redness is gone. Aloe vera (either straight from the plant or from a commercial preparation), cool compresses and baths, and over-the-counter anesthetic benzocaine may help to alleviate the pain in the meantime.

Dressing the Part

There's nothing more tacky-touristy than a bold tropical-patterned aloha shirt, right? Wrong!

Invented by an enterprising Honolulu tailor looking for a new way to drum up business in 1936, the aloha shirt has since spawned a whole style of bright, tropical-print wearables for men, women, and children, collectively known as aloha wear — and, in the process, it has developed into a way of life in the Hawaiian islands. Spirited, beautiful, easy to wear, and comfortable, aloha wear is the embodiment of the Hawaii lifestyle.

Aloha wear is acceptable just about anywhere in Hawaii, from the beach to the boardroom to the best table at a four-star restaurant. Of course, the key to wearing aloha wear well is understanding the line that separates sublime from goofy — or, in plainer terms, how to tell good aloha wear from bad aloha wear.

It's not hard. Aloha wear can come in any shape, from traditional aloha shirts (wearable by men and women alike) to generous women's muumuus or sexy minidresses. Basically, the key is quality. Silk is top of the line, and great for evening, but skip it for daywear on warm days (when you might perspire). Quality rayon and cotton are terrific alternates for day and evening.

Look for beautiful, well-designed prints with strong colors and no bleeding. Look for quality buttons (coconut or wood are best, but not a must) and pattern matching at the seams and pockets. Excellent brands that offer consistently top-quality aloha wear include Kahala Sportswear, Kamehameha Garment Co., and the Paradise Found and Diamond Head labels, all of which have revived vintage designs; Reyn's, which boasts beautiful patterns in a range of flattering styles, especially for women; and Tori Richard, which employs some of Hawaii's finest artists to design their patterns. If you visit Maui or the

Big Island, Sig Zane's all-cotton aloha wear is the height of subdued sophistication and nature-inspired beauty, while on Oahu, Mamo Howell has elevated the muumuu to haute couture status. Hilo Hattie is the largest manufacturer and distributor of aloha wear (producing more than 300,000 shirts annually); while their stuff isn't the height of aloha fashion, it has increased substantially in quality in recent years while remaining very affordable.

The cardinal rule of wearing aloha wear like a local rather than a tourist? No matching. No themed husband-and-wife shirts, no mom-and-daughter muumuus, no two garments on one person in the same pattern. Period.

Attention baseball fans: If you just don't want to wear an aloha shirt but you'd still like to impress the locals with your Hawaii savvy, get yourself a New York Mets T-shirt touting team slugger and Honolulu hometown boy Benny Agbayani. One of Hawaii's very few achievers in the major leagues, Benny is *very* popular in these parts.

At some of the high-end resorts or fancier restaurants — the big-money places, the kind that would require a jacket and tie if you were on the mainland — you'll be requested to wear "resort attire." For women, resort attire generally means a long or short dress or coordinating pants and top — more dressy-casual than full-on dressy, if you know what I mean. For men, it generally translates to pants (not shorts) and a collared shirt. Neatly presented aloha wear always does the trick, of course.

(A tiny handful of Hawaii's most expensive resort restaurants do require men to wear a jacket, but I don't recommend those. Go to Europe if you want to pack a blazer.)

Don't let a flower lei outstay its welcome. Fresh-flower leis are meant to be a short-term treat, enjoyed at the height of their fragrance and beauty and disposed of once the moment has passed. So don't wear old, dying leis; nothing will peg you as a tourist with a capital T quite so blatantly. Most leis only last a day — which provides you with the perfect excuse to find a fresh one tomorrow!

Remembering Your Island-Style Manners

As in many Eastern cultures, it's common practice to remove your shoes when you enter a private home in Hawaii — which is one reason why flip-flops and other slip-on-style shoes are so common in the island. You'll find that this practice is almost always upheld in bed-and-breakfasts, and even condos may request that you leave your shoes at the door. No one is policing you, of course, but be sure to honor the request.

Islanders pride themselves on their laidback manner and friendliness, and they really show it in their driving habits — so leave your need for speed at home. Take it easy. Don't be in a hurry. And don't honk your horn to chastise other drivers, which is considered the height of rudeness. If the car in front of you isn't moving quickly enough, say, or someone cuts you off, just let it slide. Car horns are used to greet friends in Hawaii.

Leaving Your Laptop at Home and Turning Your Cellphone Off

Even the Silicon Valley types who are buying up Hawaii real estate left and right with their dot-com millions understand the meaning of Hawaii. Don't cart your business worries halfway around the world; an island vacation is far too precious for that. Conveniently forget to give your boss your itinerary. This is the place to leave work behind and *relax.*

And don't just leave the work behind — dump the rat-race attitude, too. The quickest way to label yourself a "tourist" in Hawaii is to be pushy, aggressive, or demanding.

Islanders tend to take things nice and easy. They're not ruled by the clock and don't like to rush. It's called "island time." Buy into it — lock, stock, and barrel — while you're here. Do as the locals do: Take things as they come, don't stress if things don't happen with the utmost timeliness, and leave plenty of space in your day to do nothing but appreciate the beauty that surrounds you.

Smiling a Lot and Saying "Aloha" to Strangers

Who knows? You may even get yourself mistaken for a local.

Chapter 24

Ten Easy Steps to Island Dining

. . . .

In This Chapter

▶ Knowing what you're eating and how to eat it

▶ Maximizing your dining experiences

. . . .

A friend of mine once came back from a vacation in Italy and told me, "The food was good, but it was better in Hawaii."

Eating well in the islands is not a problem. Hawaii has lured a number of the world's finest chefs to its kitchens and managed to cultivate some stars of its own in the process. Anyone who loves quality seafood, fresh-grown veggies, and sweet tropical fruits will think they've died and gone to heaven.

But that's far from the end of the bounty, for Hawaii's melting-pot society sets a global table. While Asian flavors and cooking styles are most prevalent, island menus travel the globe, from old-world European culinary classics to good ol' ranch-raised, fire-grilled steaks. Hawaii's cooks have even managed to put their own spin on some of the world's most revered foods — pizzas, burgers, and burritos — with rousing success.

There are, however, a few things you might like to know about island dining before you sit down to a meal — the first being that Hawaii has two brands of homegrown cuisine. Local food is the traditional everyday eats of the locals, while Hawaii Regional Cuisine is the gourmet version. If you guessed that local food is down-home, casual cuisine and Hawaii Regional is the province of Hawaii's high-end restaurants, you'd be right. But each are hybrid cuisines, informed by both European and Asian influences. For more on island cuisine — and what else to expect on the culinary front — keep reading.

Fresh-Caught, Fresh-Grown, and Island-Raised: These Bounteous Islands

If you love seafood, I encourage you to make the most of your time in the Islands. It's no stretch to say that Hawaii's seafood may be the best in the world — in fact, some of the world's finest chefs think so — and the selection is generally much more diverse than what you'll find in your average supermarket. And if there's one thing that Hawaii's chefs know how to do best, it's selecting, preparing, and serving the fruits of the sea. (For details on the variations you might find on island menus, see "A Translation List for Seafood Lovers" later in this chapter.)

But Hawaii's bounty isn't limited to the sea. A wealth of fresh-grown vegetables, including leafy lettuces and vine-ripened tomatoes, thrives in the lava-rich soil. But fruits are Hawaii's real forte. All you need to do is head to the local supermarket to discover a whole new world of citrus, more varieties of banana than you ever knew existed, and other colorful tropical treats; see "The Joys and Sorrows of the Supermarket" later in this chapter for further details.

Tropical fruit comes as no surprise, of course, but who knew that Hawaii offered so much island-raised meat? While the state isn't exactly over-run with grazing lands, the Big Island offers plenty of room to spread out. In fact, the island called Hawaii is home to the largest privately owned cattle ranch in the United States: Parker Ranch, covering 225,000 acres, including more than 50,000 cattle, and serving as the heart of Hawaii's *paniolo* (cowboy) country. (Who knew, right?) Ranch-raised beef and lamb is served on many of Hawaii's fine-dining menus, but it's especially prevalent on the Big Island (surprise, surprise); **Merriman's** is a great choice to sample the local Angus (see Chapter 17).

Traditional Island Eats

Local food is a casual, catch-all cuisine, mirroring Hawaii's melting-pot soul. As evidenced by the list of food terms that appears later in this chapter (see "More Everyday Hawaiian Food Terms" below), outsider influences on the local cuisine arrived in Hawaii from all over the map, from Portugal to Japan and just about everywhere in between. Lomilomi salmon is the perfect example of local food as a hybrid cuisine: Islanders didn't have natural access to the cold-water fish, but they accepted it in trade from globe-trotting explorers and traders. Learning to prepare it ceviche-style for short-term preservation, they quickly became accustomed to accepting it in trade and incorporated it into their diet as a staple.

Local food is generally starch-heavy and high in calories, so don't expect it to have a positive impact on your waistline. It's most commonly served as a plate lunch, which usually consists of a main dish (anything from fried fish to teriyaki beef), "two scoops rice," an ice-cream-scoop serving of macaroni salad, and brown gravy, all served on a paper plate. Plate lunches are cheap and available at casual restaurants and beachside stands throughout the islands. Excellent places to indulge in the local traditions include **Sam Choy's Breakfast, Lunch & Crab** on Oahu (see Chapter 9) and Maui's **Aloha Mixed Plate** (Chapter 13).

Another great place to try local food is at a luau, a traditional feast that's not a tourist trap but a genuine part of island culture, thrown to celebrate everything from a baby's birth to a college graduation. For more on luaus, see "What to Expect at a Luau" at the end of this chapter.

The Gourmet Side of the Island Stove: Hawaii Regional Cuisine

About a dozen or so years ago, Hawaii's kitchens underwent a culinary revolution that went with its cultural renaissance: the birth of Hawaii Regional Cuisine. Island chefs were tired of living up to a continental standard that was unsuited to Hawaii living, so they created a new standard gourmet cuisine using fresh local ingredients in creative combinations and preparations.

It's often disguised under other names — Euro-Asian, Pacific Rim, Indo-Pacific, Pacific Edge, Euro-Pacific, Island Fusion, and so on — but it all falls under the jurisdiction of Hawaii Regional Cuisine. While there are variations, you can expect the following keynotes: lots of fresh island fish; Asian flavorings (ginger, soy, wasabi, seaweed, and so on) and cooking styles (searing, grilling, panko crust, wok preparations) galore; and fresh tropical fruit sauces (mango, papaya, and the like).

Hawaii Regional Cuisine has really matured and come into its own in recent years, with the finest HRC chefs putting clever multicultural spins on the established canon based on their training and heritage. You may already know of Roy Yamaguchi, who has installed outposts of his **Roy's Restaurant** chain not only on each island but around the world, from New York to Guam; and Sam Choy, who makes occasional appearances on the Discovery Channel. Other stars of the show include Jean-Marie Josselin (of **A Pacific Cafe** on Oahu, Maui, and Kauai), Beverly Gannon (of **Haliimaile General Store** and **Joe's Bar & Grill** on Maui), Peter Merriman (of **Merriman's** on the Big Island and **Hula Grill** on Maui), and James MacDonald, who works his magic at Maui's **I'o** and **Pacific'o.** But my favorite Hawaii chef is Alan Wong (of **Alan Wong's Restaurant** and the **Pineapple Room** in Honolulu), who serves as the standard-bearer by which all others should be measured. One of the only others who measures up is George Mavrothalassitis, who adds a delicate Mediterranean flair to the island style at **Chef Mavro,** also in Honolulu.

It may be a splurge — Hawaii Regional is almost exclusively prepared in Hawaii's priciest restaurants — but I encourage you to treat yourself to an HRC meal at least once during your trip. If you're going to be spending time on Oahu and you only want to indulge once, make it at either Alan Wong's or Chef Mavro; both offer stellar food and all-around world-class dining experiences (see Chapter 9).

A Translation List for Seafood Lovers

Even savvy seafood eaters can become confused when confronted with a Hawaiian menu. Although the mainland terms are sometimes included, many menus only use the Hawaiian names to tout their daily catches. What's more, some types of seafood that make regular appearances in Hawaii's kitchens simply don't show up on mainland menus at all.

You're likely to encounter many of the following types of seafood while you're in Hawaii:

- **ahi:** This dense, ruby-red bigeye or yellowfin tuna is a Hawaiian favorite — and it may be one of yours too, as popular as it has become on the mainland. Ahi is regularly served raw, as sushi and sashimi, or panko-crusted and seared in Hawaii Regional Cuisine. Yellowfin is the beefier of the two.

- **aku:** This meaty, robust skipjack tuna is also known as bonito (which might be familiar to you sushi fans out there). Aku is best as raw sushi, as it can get too dry if not expertly cooked.

- **au** (ow): This firm-fleshed marlin or broadbill swordfish some-times stands in for ahi in local dishes. Pacific blue marlin is some-times called kajiki, while striped marlin often shows up as nairagi.

- **hebi** (HEH-bee): This mildly flavored, almost lemony, spearfish is sometimes the day's catch in upscale restaurants.

- **mahimahi:** Like ahi, this white, sweet, moderately dense fish is likely to also be familiar to you; it's Hawaii's most popular fish, and shows up regularly on mainland menus.

- **monchong** (MON-chong): This exotic fish boasts a flaky, tender texture and a simple flavor. It's best served broiled, sauteed, or steamed.

- **onaga** (o-NA-ga): This mild, moist, and tender ruby-red snapper is served in many fine restaurants; be sure to sample it if it's available.

- **ono** (OH-no): "Ono" means "good to eat" in Hawaiian, and this mackerel-like fish sure is. Also called wahoo, it's similar to snap-per, but firmer and drier. You should have multiple opportunities to try this popular, distinctly flavored fish; it's often served grilled and in sandwiches.

- **opah** (OH-pa): This rich, almost creamy moonfish is good served just about any way, from sashimi to baked.

- **opakapaka** (oh-pa-ka-PA-ka): Either pink or crimson snapper, this light, flaky, elegant fish is very popular on fine-dining menus.

- **shutome** (shuh-TOE-me): This is what mainlanders call swordfish. It's a sweet and tender steaklike fish that is great grilled or broiled.

- **tombo:** This is albacore tuna — but this firm, flavorful whitefish surpasses the canned stuff by miles when prepared appropriately.

✔ **uku** (OO-koo): This gray — pale pink, really — snapper is flaky, moist, and delicate.

✔ **ulua** (oo-LOO-ah): Ulua is large jack trevally, a firm-fleshed, flavorful fish also known as pompano.

More Everyday Hawaiian Food Terms

All of the following foods are common in plate lunches and at luaus. A number of them will also pop up on gourmet Hawaii Regional Cuisine menus — usually with expensive ingredients and prepared with a twist, of course:

✔ **bento:** A Japanese box lunch.

✔ **haupia** (how-PEE-ah): Creamy coconut pudding, usually served in squares.

✔ **kalua pork:** Pork slow-cooked in an *imu*, or underground oven.

✔ **kiawe** (kee-AH-vay): An aromatic mesquite wood often used to fire the wood-burning ovens.

✔ **laulau:** Pork, chicken, or fish wrapped in ti leaves and steamed.

✔ **lilikoi** (lil-EE-koy): Passion fruit.

✔ **lomilomi** (low-mee-LOW-mee) **salmon:** Salted salmon marinated, ceviche-like, with tomatoes and green onions.

✔ **lumpia** (lum-PEE-ah): The Portuguese version of a spring roll, but spicier, doughier, and deep-fried (and usually stuffed with pork and veggies).

✔ **malassada** (mah-lah-SAH-da): The Portuguese version of a donut, usually round, deep-fried, and generously sprinkled with powdered sugar.

✔ **manapua** (man-ah-POO-ah): A bready, doughy bun with sweetened pork or sweet beans inside, like Chinese bao.

✔ **ohelo** (oh-HAY-low): A berry very similar to a cranberry that commonly appears in Hawaii Regional sauces.

✔ **panko:** Japanese bread crumbs, most commonly used to prepare *katsu* (deep-fried pork or chicken cutlet). Hawaii Regional Cuisine chefs often use it for other purposes, most commonly as a tempura-like crust on sushi-grade ahi rolls.

✔ **poi:** The root of the taro pounded into a purple, starchy paste; a staple of the island diet, but generally tasteless to most outsiders.

✔ **poke** (PO-kay): Cubed raw fish — usually ahi or marlin — seasoned with onions, soy, and seaweed.

✔ **ponzu:** A soy-and-citrus dipping sauce popular with Hawaii Regional Cuisine chefs.

✔ **pupus:** Appetizers or hors d'oeuvres.

✔ **saimin** (SAI-min): A brothy soup with ramen-like noodles, topped with bits of fish, chicken, pork, and/or vegetables. Saimin is served almost everywhere in Hawaii, from plate-lunch stands to museum cafes to McDonald's.

✔ **shave ice:** The island version of a snow cone, best enjoyed with ice cream and sweet *azuki* (red) beans at the bottom.

✔ **taro:** A green leafy vegetable grown in Hawaii; the root is used to make poi (see above), while the leafy part of the vegetable is often steamed like spinach.

Other Local Favorites

Lest all this unfamiliar food talk makes you think otherwise, remember that the majority of Hawaii islanders are red-blooded, flag-waving Americans — and they love a good burger just as much as your average mainlander.

My favorite burgers in Hawaii are the creations of an unassuming burger stand on the way to Kauai's north shore: **Duane's Ono Char Burger,** where the Local Girl — teriyaki, swiss, pineapple, mayo, lettuce, and beef on a bun — makes a perfect packet of juicy goodness. Kauai, in fact, excels on the burger front, with **Bubba Burgers** setting an equally high standard; see Chapter 21. On Oahu, **Kua Aina Sandwich** draws crowds both in Honolulu and on the north shore with its standout fare and excellent fries, while **Cheeseburger in Paradise** does the trick in Waikiki; see Chapter 9. Maui has its own branches of Cheeseburger in Paradise and Bubba's to satisfy the burger craving; see Chapter 13.

Hawaii has also co-opted Mexican cuisine and made the burrito its own, most successfully at **Maui Tacos,** where island-grown ingredients and fresh-caught fish provide top-quality surf-style filling; see Chapters 13 and 17.

Ethnic Eats

Thanks to Hawaii's proximity to the Eastern Hemisphere and its large, multifaceted Asian population, the Islands boast a wealth of fabulous Asian restaurants — Chinese, Thai, Vietnamese, Japanese, and so on. With the exception of Japanese (of course), most Asian restaurants tend to be very affordable. What's more, since island palates are much more used to dining Asian style, you'll find that dishes aren't gringo-ized for a mainland population; flavors are bold and strong, ingredients fresh and crisp. Dining out in Hawaii, you may just find yourself enjoying the finest ethnic food you've ever eaten.

I always seek out these spots while I'm in the islands:

✔ Chinese food doesn't get finer than the delectable dishes at **Hawaii Seafood Paradise;** I often fantasize about the head-on shrimp, doused in Hawaii salt and fried to delicate perfection. **Singha Thai Cuisine** is another excellent Waikiki choice. See Chapter 9.

- Maui's ethnic standout is **A Saigon Cafe,** whose piquant flavors and friendly service make it well worth seeking out in off-the-tourist-track Wailuku; see Chapter 13.

- The Big Island is an Asian-dining bonanza. Sushi lovers should make a point of visiting the simple but stellar **Ocean Sushi Deli** in Hilo. Each coast has its own Thai standout; Volcano village offers **Thai Thai,** which boasts simple but flavorful cooking, while **Thai Rin** is a bastion of authentic cooking in a tourist-catering town. For tasty satays and other Indonesian dishes at bargain-basement prices, visit **Sibu Cafe** in Kailua-Kona. See Chapter 17.

- Kauai excels at both Thai and Chinese at **Mema Thai Chinese Cafe.** Mema's is centrally located on the Coconut Coast, as is **Norberto's El Cafe,** a notable stop for authentic Mexican. On the north shore, a master sushi chef works his magic at **Sushi, Blues & Grill,** where fans will find lots of Pacific-water variations on the ahi-yellowtail mainland standard. See Chapter 21.

The Joys and Sorrows of the Supermarket

Whenever I'm in a foreign country, I always make it a policy to visit the local supermarket. While Hawaii is no foreign country, it's far enough removed from the mainland that you'll find a trip to the market to be an entertaining culinary adventure. Even if you're not staying in a condo, where you might want to stock the pantry, I highly recommend an excursion to your local Safeway, KTA, Star Market, or Foodland.

Hawaii supermarkets offer a number of treats that you won't find at your average mainland supermarket. Poi, for instance, comes in instant, premade, and make-your-own forms; I defy you to find poi in *any* form in your hometown supermarket. You'll find that the bounty in the seafood case is much more diverse than what you see at home; Hawaii refrigerator cases regularly contain such taste treats as sushi-grade tuna, fresh Pacific octopus, and whole squid (insert "yum!" or "yuck!" here, depending on your taste buds).

Just about any Hawaii supermarket will have multiple aisles devoted to Asian foods, from noodles to bizarre candies. The juice refrigerator case is also a treat, so don't be afraid to try something new; my husband never misses an opportunity to chug POG (passion fruit-orange-guava juice) when he's in the islands.

Java lovers, rejoice — because every Hawaiian island except Lanai has a coffee plantation, and the local brew is available in just about any average market. All Hawaii-grown coffees are delicious, but the world-famous Kona coffee, grown on the Big Island, is the top of the heap.

The greatest bounty can be found among the fresh fruits, where you'll find such fresh tropical treats as mangoes, guava, star fruit, lychee, lilikoi (passion fruit), and much more. Whenever I go to Hawaii, I eat as much papaya as I can, because the mainland imports just don't equal the island-grown fruits; cut your papaya in half, dig out the seeds, and serve with a squirt of lime — island breakfast doesn't get any better. Pineapples are another Hawaii taste treat; the small white pineapples are sweetest, and you'll usually find them clearly labeled at the market. The Big Island's lava-rich soil produces extra-flavorful citrus fruits; Kau oranges, for instance, are legendary for their sweetness. Even watermelon is an extra-special treat; Molokai-grown watermelons are the best in the world — full of seeds, but fabulous.

Among Hawaii-grown vegetables, Maui onions are the ultimate treat. They're very sweet, like Vidalias, but with a distinctive flavor all their own. Slice 'em thick and you'll find that you can throw them right on the barbecue grill. Dense, purple Molokai-grown sweet potatoes are another of my favorites.

Don't shy away from tropical fruits or other foods just because you're unfamiliar with them. Islanders are friendly and talkative folks. Supermarket attendants — or even your fellow shoppers — will be happy to advise you on how to cut or clean island fruits. Just ask, and you're likely to find yourself on the receiving end of some friendly conversation.

There is, however, a downside to shopping in Hawaii — namely, high prices. While you will save quite a few bucks over three-meals-a-day restaurant dining by stocking up and cooking for yourself back at the condo, be prepared to pay more for staples than you will back home. The rule of thumb is this: Expect anything that has to wing its way across the Pacific to be more than you usually pay.

Unfortunately, in Hawaii, supermarket prices are high all across the board. Fish is about the same price as on the mainland, and the quality is generally better — but pick up some ground beef for burgers, and expect to pay $2 or $2.50 a pound. Your average breakfast cereal goes for about $5 a box. At first glance, you might think the prices of the staffs of life, milk and bread, are a joke: Expect to pay about $5 a gallon ($2.71 per half-gallon at this writing) for milk, while a standard loaf of bread is around $4.50.

Another Island Tradition: Tropical Cocktails

While California entrepreneur Vic Bergeron — more popularly known as Trader Vic — is responsible for the birth of the mai tai, in Hawaii it's practically the official state cocktail. The classic mai tai is a magical sweet-tart concoction of Jamaican rum, fresh lime juice, and chunky ice, generally served in a tumbler and topped with a fresh sprig of mint.

It's a simple blend, and any bar worth its salt in Hawaii can mix you a well-balanced mai tai; score an out-of-sorts bartender on the wrong night, however, and you'll end up with either a sickly sweet syrup that couldn't do justice to a stack of flapjacks, or a thick, face-distorting blend strong enough to power up a Ford Explorer.

Why take your chances? Instead, head to one of the following first-rate bars, which offer the perfect blend of ideal mai tai–making and only-in-Hawaii ambience:

✔ On Oahu, the Halekulani's **House Without a Key** sets the standard, with the near-perfect mai tai served beachfront at Waikiki, usually accompanied by authentic hula and sounds by some of Hawaii's finest musicians; if you're going to have just one mai tai, this is the place to go. Other excellent versions are served overlooking the sand at the **Hau Tree Lanai** and **Duke's Canoe Club;** on the north shore, **Jameson's By the Sea**'s mai tai packs the perfect sunset wallop. For details, see Chapter 10.

✔ On Maui, the bar at any of the big resorts should be able to satisfy your sunset cravings. In Lahaina, **Cheeseburger in Paradise** is the place to go for the top concoction. See Chapter 14.

✔ The Big Island isn't big on nightlife, but it knows how to serve up a killer cocktail. Ultra-romantic **Edward's at Kanaloa** does an amazing job on the South Kona coast, while **Kilauea Lodge** in Volcano has a veritable secret weapon tucked away behind the bar, preparing a stellar version of the classic. Again, any of the big resort bars should be able to prepare a terrific mai tai as well. See Chapter 15.

✔ On Kauai, my top choices for a satisfying mai tai are the **Beach House** or **Keoki's Paradise** on the south shore, **Zelo's** on the north shore; see Chapter 22.

Of course, mai tais may not be your thing. If that's the case, don't worry — you'll find plenty of other ways to toast your time in paradise. Personally, I'm a big fan of the piña colada — not a Hawaii cocktail, sure, but it never fails to put me in the tropical mood, especially when a colorful paper umbrella and a generous slice of pineapple are included in the picture.

Hawaii is no Portland, but microbrews are serious business here. The finest wear the **Kona Brewing Company** label. You can go straight to the source in Kailua-Kona on the Big Island; see the restaurant listing in Chapter 17.

What to Expect at a Luau

A luau is the ideal place to experience island traditions — but only to a degree, of course. Any commercial luau (read: any luau you're likely to attend) will be tainted by its commercialism. But a few luaus do a great job of bringing genuine island culture into the mix.

The best luaus — offering the best mix of good food, amenities, setting, and authentic culture — are found on Maui. The **Old Lahaina Luau** and the **Feast at Lele** are the best luaus Hawaii has to offer, hands down. If you're going to be on the Valley Isle, be sure to book your spots now; see Chapter 13.

But if you're not visiting Maui, don't despair. Each island offers its own versions of the luau feast, with the Big Island garnering second-runner-up awards for its very respectable feasts at Kona Village and the Aston Keauhou Beach Resort (see Chapter 17).

What should you plan for when attending a luau? Luckily, most luau feasts are self-sufficient, idiot-proof ventures, so once you have your reservations in place, all you need to bring is your appetite and aloha spirit. Dress for the festivities in bright, bold colors, even if you don't own any aloha wear — bright colors really suit the mood. Other than that, just wear what's comfortable to you, and bring a sweater if the weather is expected to cool down after dark (all luaus take place out-of-doors, and most in breezy oceanfront settings).

When you make your reservations, you'll usually be told when the gates open and when you should plan to arrive. Come in plenty of time to wander the grounds, as the best luaus feature authentic craft-making, games, and the like in the hour before the festivities formally begin. The luau pig, which has been baking all day in its underground oven, is also unearthed early in the program, and unless you're squeamish about such things, you won't want to miss it.

Upon arrival, you're likely to be greeted with a lei, made of either fresh flowers or shells, and a cocktail, often a mai tai (or fruit juice, if you're too young or a teetotaler). You'll be led to your assigned seat, usually at a communal table with chairs (although the Old Lahaina Luau now features some traditional seating, on cushions facing low-slung tables).

Cocktails are usually included in the pay-one-price admission fee to a luau. Open bars are common, but some luaus limit you to a certain number or kind of drink. If it matters to you, be sure to ask when booking.

Once the luau pig is unearthed from the imu, everyone is usually asked to take their seats. You'll be invited to fill your plate from the buffet luau spread; the best luaus clearly mark the dishes so that you know what you're sampling. In addition to the kalua pork (shredded from the bone after the luau pig is unearthed), you can expect such traditional dishes as poi, the tasteless purple paste that's the staple starch of Hawaii. Poi is worth trying for its iconic status, but you're unlikely to become a fan. It's not usually eaten alone, but with other starches; ask an attendant what's best in the night's feast for poi-dipping. You're likely to prefer such dishes as lomilomi salmon, poke, and haupia (see "More Everyday Hawaiian Food Terms" earlier in this chapter). If you're a less-than-adventurous diner, don't worry — you'll find plenty of familiar dishes on hand, including chicken teriyaki, long rice, and salad. You'll be allowed to refill your plate as often as you like. After dinner comes the evening's entertainment, usually a hula show that lasts an hour or so before the evening winds down.

Most luau food is satisfactory at best, so don't expect a gourmet feast (the exception being the Feast at Lele, which eschews the standard setting for intimate seating, food prepared by one of Hawaii's best chefs, and full table service). Top-notch luaus like the Old Lahaina Luau and the Kona Village Luau serve the best-prepared fare, but remember that they're still cooking in bulk for hundreds. Come for the party, and plan to have a first-rate dinner at a standard restaurant on another night.

What kind of luau is right for you is entirely up to you; some luaus are more suited to couples, for instance, while others are great for families with kids. Some luaus feature wholly authentic Hawaiian entertainment (primarily chanting and dancing), while others blow the wad on glitzy Vegas-style extravaganzas with glittering costumes. (Note that any luau that calls itself authentically Hawaiian shouldn't have fire-knife dancers, which is a Samoan tradition.)

Luaus are pricey — usually $50 to $100 a head, depending on the fete — so it's important that you choose carefully. Before you commit, spend a few minutes flipping through this book (recommended luaus are listed at the end of each dining chapter) and ask questions of the reservations agent to make sure you'll end up at the party that's right for you.

Appendix

Quick Concierge

●●●

Fast Facts

*I*n addition to the list given here, note that each major island has a dedicated "Quick Concierge" section earlier in this book. For additional local facts and contacts, see Chapter 8 (Oahu); Chapter 12 (Maui); Chapter 16 (the Big Island); and Chapter 20 (Kauai).

American Automobile Association (AAA)

The only local AAA office is in Honolulu, on the island of Oahu, at 1270 Ala Moana Blvd., between Piikoi Street and Ward Centre (☎ 800-736-2886 or 808-593-2221; Internet: www.aaa-hawaii.com). The office is open Monday through Wednesday and Friday from 9 a.m. to 5 p.m., Thursday from 9 a.m. to 7 p.m., and Saturday from 9 a.m. to 2 p.m. For road-side assistance or information on becoming a member, call ☎ 800-AAA-HELP or point your Web browser to www.aaa.com, where you'll be linked to your regional club's home page once you enter your home zip code. See the sidebar "The AAA Advantage" in Chapter 3 for details on the many benefits of AAA membership.

American Express

American Express has branch offices on **Oahu** at Commerce Tower, 1440 Kapiolani Blvd., Suite 104, Honolulu (☎ 808-946-7741; open Mon–Fri 8 a.m.–5 p.m.); in the Tapa Tower at **Hilton Hawaiian Village,** 2005 Kalia Rd., at Ala Moana Boulevard, Waikiki (☎ 808-951-0644; open daily 7 a.m.–11 p.m.); and at the **Hyatt Regency Waikiki,** 2424 Kalakaua Ave. (☎ 808-926-5441; open daily 8 a.m.–9 p.m., financial services to 8 p.m.).

There are two AmEx offices on **Maui:** One in Kaanapali at the Westin Maui, 2365 Kaanapali Pkwy. (☎ 808-661-7155; open daily 8 a.m.–6 p.m.); and in South Maui at the Grand Wailea Resort & Spa, 3850 Wailea Alanui Dr., Wailea (☎ 808-875-4526; open daily 7 a.m.–6 p.m.).

AmEx has one office on the **Big Island:** on the Kohala Coast at the Hilton Waikoloa Village, 425 Waikoloa Beach Dr., off Hwy. 19 in the Waikoloa Resort (☎ 808-886-7958; open daily 7 a.m.–5 p.m.).

There's no AmEx office on **Kauai** at this time.

Cardholders and traveler's check holders should call ☎ 800-221-7282 for all money emergencies. To make inquiries or to locate other branch offices, call ☎ 800-AXP-TRIP or visit www.americanexpress.com.

Area Code

All of the Hawaiian Islands are in the **808** area code. When dialing, you can leave the area code off if you're calling someone on the same island that you're on. If you're call-ing someone on a different island, though — you're on Oahu, say, and you're calling to confirm a reservation on Kauai — you must dial **1-808** before the seven-digit phone number.

If you're calling from one island to another island, the call will be billed as a long-distance call, which can be more expensive than calling the mainland from Hawaii. So be sure to use your long-distance calling card when calling between islands to avoid adding inflated phone charges to your hotel bill.

ATMs

All of the islands, except Molokai and Lanai, have plenty of ATMs at hand in the major resort areas. Branches of Hawaii's most popular banks are plentiful , and all are connected to all the global ATM networks. Most supermarkets also have ATMS inside. Do yourself a favor, though, and don't head to a remote area — the north shore of Kauai, say, or the Big Island's North Kohala peninsula or Volcano area — without stocking up on cash first. These areas do have ATMs, but there's no sense wasting precious vacation time tracking them down and risking that they won't be on your network.

One of Hawaii's most popular banks, with branches throughout the state, is **Bank of Hawaii**, which is linked with all the major worldwide networks. To find the one nearest you, call them at ☎ 808-643-3888 or point your Web browser to www.boh.com/locations/atmdir.asp. You can also find ATMs on the **Cirrus** network by dialing ☎ 800-424-7787 or going online to www.mastercard.com; to find a **Plus** ATM, call ☎ 800-843-7587 or visit www.visa.com.

Credit Cards

If your **Visa** card is lost or stolen, call ☎ 800-645-6556. **MasterCard** holders should call ☎ 800-307-7309. **American Express** cardholders should call ☎ 800-221-7282 for all money emergencies.

Emergencies

No matter where you are in Hawaii, dial **911** from any phone, just like back home. To locate doctors and hospital emergency rooms on the specific islands, see the "Quick Concierge" sections in Chapter 8

(Oahu), Chapter 12 (Maui), Chapter 16 (the Big Island), and Chapter 20 (Kauai).

Liquor Laws

The legal drinking age in Hawaii is 21. Bars are allowed to stay open daily until 2 a.m.; places with cabaret licenses are able to keep the booze flowing until 4 a.m. Grocery and convenience stores are allowed to sell beer, wine, and liquor seven days a week.

Mail

To find the U.S. Postal Service branch nearest you, call ☎ 800-275-8777 and be prepared to give the operator the local zip code. This also serves as an all-purpose national info line, so call them if you have any questions about postage, zip codes, or shipping back home. You can also locate post office branches by going online to new.usps.com and clicking on Locate. To locate convenient local branches, see the "Quick Concierge" sections in Chapter 8 (Oahu), Chapter 12 (Maui), Chapter 16 (the Big Island), and Chapter 20 (Kauai).

Maps

Here's yet another reason to join AAA: They supply excellent maps of Hawaii to members only, and they're absolutely free if you're a card-carrier. For more information on becoming a member or locating Hawaii's only office, on Oahu, see the American Automobile Association listing at the beginning of this appendix.

All of the rental-car companies hand out very good free map booklets on each island, which will be all you need to navigate your way around.

If you want more complete topographic maps of each island, the best are printed by the **University of Hawaii Press**. They're available from just about any bookstore in the islands. If you'd like to order them before you leave home, contact **Basically Books,** 160 Kamehameha Ave., Hilo, HI 96720 (☎ 800-903 MAPS or 808-961-0144; Internet: www.basicallybooks.com).

Newspapers & Magazines

The *Honolulu Advertiser* and the *Honolulu Star Bulletin* are the statewide papers, although the *Advertiser* seems to be winning the paper wars; the *Bulletin* was for sale at press time. The main weekly entertainment rag is Oahu's *Honolulu Weekly* (www. honoluluweekly.com). Daily neighbor island newspapers include the *Maui News* (www.mauinews.com), the Big Island's *West Hawaii Today* (www.westhawaiitoday. com), the *Hawaii Tribune Herald* (www. hilohawaiitribune.com), and Kauai's *The Garden Island* (www.kauaiworld.com).

Hawaii magazine is a glossy monthly that's targeted to visitors; it offers a good introduction to the islands. You can usually find the current issue in the travel magazine sections at your local branch of the big chain bookstores, such as Borders and Barnes & Noble. Subscriptions are available by calling ☎ 800-365-4421 or 949-855-8822.

Pharmacies

Long's Drugs, Hawaii's biggest drugstore chain, has convenient locations on all of the major islands. To locate the nearest branch, point your Web browser to www.longs. com and click on Locate a Store. To locate convenient branches on each island, see the "Quick Concierge" sections in Chapter 8 (Oahu), Chapter 12 (Maui), Chapter 16 (the Big Island), and Chapter 20 (Kauai).

Smoking

In Hawaii, it's against the law to smoke in just about all public buildings. Hotels have non-smoking rooms available, restaurants have nonsmoking sections, and car rental agencies have nonsmoking cars. Most bed-and-breakfasts prohibit smoking inside their buildings.

Taxes

Hawaii's sales tax is 4 percent. Expect taxes of about 11.42 percent to be added to your final hotel bill.

Time

Hawaii Standard Time is in effect year-round. Hawaii is two hours behind Pacific standard time and five hours behind eastern standard time — so when it's noon in Hawaii, it's 2 p.m. in California and 5 p.m. in New York.

Hawaii doesn't observe daylight saving time, however, so when daylight saving time is in effect on the mainland — April through October — Hawaii is three hours behind the West Coast and six hours behind the East Coast (making it noon in Hawaii when it's 3 p.m. in California and 6 p.m. in New York).

For the exact local time, call ☎ 808-245-0212.

Weather & Surf Reports

For statewide conditions, call ☎ 808-935-5055. For statewide marine reports, call ☎ 808-973-4382. For statewide coastal wind reports, call ☎ 808-973-6114.

For local conditions and forecasts, call the following:

Oahu: ☎ 808-973-4380

Maui: ☎ 808-877-5111

Big Island: ☎ 808-961-5582

Kauai: ☎ 808-245-6001

Molokai: ☎ 808-877-5111

Lanai: ☎ 808-877-5111

To check the weather forecasts online, log onto www.hawaiiweathertoday.com. I like to compare, so you might also check www.weather.com or www.cnn.com/weather, both of which offer four- or five-day forecasts for hundreds of destinations around the globe.

Toll-Free Numbers and Web Sites

Airlines

Air Canada
☎ 800-776-3000
www.aircanada.ca

Air New Zealand
☎ 800-262-2468 in the U.S.
☎ 800-663-5494 in Canada
☎ 0800-737-767 in New Zealand

Alaska Airlines
☎ 800-426-0333
www.alaskaair.com

Aloha Airlines
☎ 800-367-5250 or 877-879-2564
www.alohaair.com

American Airlines
☎ 800-433-7300
www.americanair.com

American Trans Air
☎ 800-225-2995
www.ata.com

Canadian Airlines International
☎ 800-426-7000
www.cdnair.ca

Continental Airlines
☎ 800-525-0280
www.continental.com

Delta Air Lines
☎ 800-221-1212
www.delta.com

Hawaiian Airlines
☎ 800-367-5320
www.hawaiianair.com

Island Air
☎ 800-323-3345 from North America
☎ 800-652-6541 from Hawaii
www.alohaair.com

Northwest Airlines
☎ 800-225-2525
www.nwa.com

Pacific Wings Airlines
☎ 888-575-4546
www.pacificwings.com

Qantas
☎ 800-474-7424 in the U.S.
☎ 612-9691-3636 in Australia
www.qantas.com

Trans World Airlines (TWA)
☎ 800-221-2000
www.twa.com

United Airlines
☎ 800-241-6522
www.ual.com

Major Hotel and Motel Chains

Aston Hotels & Resorts
☎ 800-922-7866
www.aston-hotels.com

Best Western International
☎ 800-528-1234
www.bestwestern.com

Clarion Hotels
☎ 800-CLARION
www.hotelchoice.com

Comfort Inns
☎ 800-228-5150
www.hotelchoice.com

Doubletree Hotels
☎ 800-222-TREE
www.doubletreehotels.com

Four Seasons Hotels & Resorts
☎ 800-819-5053
www.fshr.com

Hilton Hotels
☎ 800-HILTONS
www.hilton.com

Holiday Inn
☎ 800-HOLIDAY
www.basshotels.com

Hyatt Hotels & Resorts
☎ 800-228-9000
www.hyatt.com

Marc Resorts Hawaii
☎ 800-535-0085
www.marcresorts.com

Marriott Hotels
☎ 800-228-9290
www.marriott.com

Ohana Hotels
☎ 800-462-6262
www.ohanahotels.com

Outrigger Hotels & Resorts
☎ 800-688-7444
www.outrigger.com

Premier Resorts
☎ 800-367-7052
www.premier-resorts.com

Quality Inns & Resorts
☎ 800-228-5151
www.hotelchoice.com

Radisson Hotels International
☎ 800-333-3333
www.radisson.com

Renaissance Hotels & Resorts
☎ 800-932-2198
www.renaissancehotels.com

Sheraton Hotels & Resorts
☎ 800-325-3535
www.sheraton.com

Starwood's Luxury Collection
☎ 800-343-6320
www.luxurycollection.com

W Hotels
☎ 877-946-8357
www.whotels.com

Westin Hotels
☎ 888-625-5144
www.westin.com

Wyndham Hotels & Resorts
☎ 800-822-4200
www.wyndham.com

Car-Rental Agencies

Alamo
☎ 800-327-9633
www.goalamo.com

Avis
☎ 800-331-1212 in Continental U.S.
☎ 800-TRY-AVIS in Canada
www.avis.com

Budget
☎ 800-527-0700
www.budgetrentacar.com

Dollar
☎ 800-800-4000
www.dollarcar.com

Enterprise
☎ 800-325-8007
www.enterprise.com

Hertz
☎ 800-654-3131
www.hertz.com

National
☎ 800-CAR-RENT
www.nationalcar.com

Thrifty
☎ 800-367-2277
www.thrifty.com

Where to Get More Information

Hawaii Visitors and Convention Bureau (HVCB)
Royal Hawaiian Shopping Center
2201 Kalakaua Ave., Suite A401A
Honolulu, HI 96815
☎ 800-GO-HAWAII or 808-924-0266
www.gohawaii.com

Planet Hawaii
www.planet-hawaii.com

Oahu

Oahu Visitors Bureau
733 Bishop St., Makai Tower, Suite 1872
Honolulu, HI 96813
☎ 877-525-OAHU or 808-524-0722
www.visit-oahu.com

Maui, Molokai & Lanai

Maui Visitors Bureau (also issues information on Molokai and Lanai)
1727 Wili Pa Loop
Wailuku, Maui, HI 96793
☎ 800-525-6284 or 808-244-3530
www.visitmaui.com

Kaanapali Beach Resort Association
2530 Kekaa Dr., Suite 1-B
Kaanapali-Lahaina, HI 96761
☎ 800-245-9229 or 808-661-3271
www.maui.net/~kbra

Kapalua Resort
800 Kapalua Dr.
Kapalua, HI 96761
☎ 800-KAPALUA or 808-669-0244
www.kapaluamaui.com

Maui.net
www.maui.net**Molokai Visitors Association**

P.O. Box 960
Kaunakakai, HI 96748
☎ 800-800-6367, 800-553-0404, or 808-553-3876
www.molokai-hawaii.com

Molokai Ranch
P.O. Box 259
Maunaloa, Hawaii 96770
☎ 877-726-4656 or 808-660-2817
www.molokai-ranch.com

Destination Lanai
730 Lanai Ave., Suite 102
P.O. Box 630700
Lanai City, HI 96763
☎ 800-947-4774 or 808-565-7600

The Big Island

Big Island Visitors Bureau
In the Kings' Shops
250 Waikoloa Beach Dr., Suite B-15
Waikoloa, HI 96738
☎ 808-886-1655
www.bigisland.org
Also at:
250 Keawe St.
Hilo, HI 96720
☎ 808-961-5797

Kohala Coast Resort Association
69-275 Waikoloa Beach Dr.
Kohala Coast, HI 96743
☎ 800-318-3637 or 808-886-4915
www.kkra.org

Kauai

Kauai Visitors Bureau
4334 Rice St., Suite 101
Lihue, HI 96766
☎ 800-262-1400 or 808-245-3971
www.kauaivisitorsbureau.org
www.kauai-hawaii.com

Poipu Beach Resort Association
P.O. Box 730
Koloa, HI 96756
☎ 888-744-0888 or 808-742-7444
www.poipu-beach.org

Fare Game: Choosing an Airline

Travel Agency: _____ Phone: _____

Agent's Name: _____ Quoted Fare: _____

Departure Schedule & Flight Information

Airline: _____ Airport: _____

Flight #: _____ Date: _____ Time: _____ a.m./p.m.

Arrives in: _____ Time: _____ a.m./p.m.

Connecting Flight (if any)

Amount of time between flights: _____ hours/mins

Airline: _____ Airport: _____

Flight #: _____ Date: _____ Time: _____ a.m./p.m.

Arrives in: _____ Time: _____ a.m./p.m.

Return Trip Schedule & Flight Information

Airline: _____ Airport: _____

Flight #: _____ Date: _____ Time: _____ a.m./p.m.

Arrives in: _____ Time: _____ a.m./p.m.

Connecting Flight (if any)

Amount of time between flights: _____ hours/mins

Airline: _____ Airport: _____

Flight #: _____ Date: _____ Time: _____ a.m./p.m.

Arrives in: _____ Time: _____ a.m./p.m.

Notes

Making Dollars and Sense of It

Expense	Amount
Airfare	
Car Rental	
Lodging	
Parking	
Breakfast	
Lunch	
Dinner	
Baby-sitting	
Attractions	
Transportation	
Souvenirs	
Tips	
Grand Total	

Notes

Sweet Dreams: Choosing Your Hotel

Enter the hotels where you'd prefer to stay based on location and price. Then use the worksheet below to plan your itinerary.

Hotel	Location	Price per night

Places to Go, People to See, Things to Do

Enter the attractions you would most like to see and decide how they'll fit into your schedule. Then use the worksheet below to plan your itinerary.

Attraction	Amount of time you expect to spend there	Best day and time to go

Going "My" Way

Itinerary #1

- ☐ _____
- ☐ _____
- ☐ _____
- ☐ _____

Itinerary #2

- ☐ _____
- ☐ _____
- ☐ _____
- ☐ _____

Itinerary #3

- ☐ _____
- ☐ _____
- ☐ _____
- ☐ _____

Itinerary #4

- ☐ _____
- ☐ _____
- ☐ _____
- ☐ _____

Itinerary #5

- ☐ _____
- ☐ _____
- ☐ _____
- ☐ _____

Itinerary #6

- ☐ _____
- ☐ _____
- ☐ _____
- ☐ _____

Itinerary #7

- ☐ _____
- ☐ _____
- ☐ _____
- ☐ _____

Itinerary #8

- ☐ _____
- ☐ _____
- ☐ _____
- ☐ _____

Itinerary #9

- ☐ _____
- ☐ _____
- ☐ _____
- ☐ _____

Itinerary #10

- ☐ _____
- ☐ _____
- ☐ _____
- ☐ _____

Menus & Venues

Enter the restaurants where you'd most like to dine. Then use the worksheet below to plan your itinerary.

Name	Address/Phone	Cuisine/Price

Notes

Index

• Dining •